Introduction to Sociology

Mavis Hiltunen Biesanz and John Biesanz

Prentice-Hall, Inc., Englewood Cliffs, New Jersey 07632

third edition

Introduction to Sociology

Library of Congress Cataloging in Publication Data

BIESANZ, MAVIS HILTUNEN.
    Introduction to sociology.
    Bibliography:
    Includes index.
    1.–Sociology.   I.–Biesanz, John Berry,
joint author.   II.–Title.
HM51.B483-1978   301   77-13600
ISBN 0-13-497412-3

Introduction to Sociology
third edition
Mavis Hiltunen Biesanz and John Biesanz

10   9   8   7   6   5   4   3   2   1

COVER ILLUSTRATION:
Original Watercolor by Glenn Heller,
© 1974.

PRENTICE-HALL INTERNATIONAL, INC., *London*
PRENTICE-HALL OF AUSTRALIA PTY. LIMITED, *Sydney*
PRENTICE-HALL OF CANADA, LTD., *Toronto*
PRENTICE-HALL OF INDIA PRIVATE LIMITED, *New Delhi*
PRENTICE-HALL OF JAPAN, INC., *Tokyo*
PRENTICE-HALL OF SOUTHEAST ASIA PTE. LTD., *Singapore*
WHITEHALL BOOKS LIMITED, *Wellington, New Zealand*

To Mother,
Hilja Lempia Hiltunen
with admiration, respect, gratitude, and deepest love

Outline

Contents

part three

Social Structure

6

Deviance and Social Control   105

7

Social Interaction and Social Structure   135

part four

Population and the Urban Trend

11

Sex Roles 235

12

Population and Ecology 267

part five

Social Institutions

13

Urban Life 289

14

The Family   319

Preface

The task of an introductory text in sociology is to present a clear understanding of social interaction, social structure, and social change. How do societies work? How do societies hang together? How do they change? How do they meet—and fail to meet—human needs?

We believe that sociology is one means for understanding, preserving, and improving human life. Sociologists increasingly recognize that complexity, conflict, and strain are inevitable in socio-cultural systems. They are also increasingly recognizing the urgency of social problems and the need to apply the knowledge that comes from careful research and analysis. This third edition of INTRODUCTION TO SOCIOLOGY reflects a greater concern with social problems and social policies, as well as a constant concern with the quality and meaning of life. Throughout the book, we try to make our own values explicit and to encourage valuing in the student.

Several themes attempt to unify the book in both content and point of view. The delicate balance of individual freedom and social cohesion is a concern throughout the book. The tension between social order and social change in a complex and changing world is also a recurring issue. And we continually draw attention to the transformation of societies around the world through the interrelated changes that are part of "modernization."

Two other themes give evidence to our essentially humanist orientation: the unity of the human race, and the right of each individual to live with a sense of freedom, dignity, and autonomy.

ORGANIZATION We have organized the material into six parts. Part One places sociology in the general context of the social sciences. It then shows what sociological research is and how it is done.

Part Two looks at culture and socialization. We believe that the concept of culture is essential to an understanding of the nature and functions of society. Chapters Three and Four explain the importance of the culture concept. Socialization is then discussed, and since socialization is never perfect, we go on to consider deviance and social control.

Part Three analyzes social structure and how it emerges from, and shapes, social interaction. We then look at three main aspects of social structure: stratification, minority relations, and sex roles.

In Part Four, we discuss population and urbanization. Measuring changes in a society's population can help sociologists predict where pressures on the social structure will occur. Since most societies are undergoing urbanization, we are concerned with its consequences for both society and personality.

The major social institutions are our concern in Part Five. The family is now a separate chapter, and thoroughly revised and expanded. Religion and education are analyzed in Chapter Fifteen. A new chapter on political and economic institutions concludes Part Five.

Part Six looks at social change. Chapter

Seventeen deals with collective behavior and social movements. Then the final chapter discusses social change and modernization. There we consider the directions and patterns of change, it sources and causes, and the possibilities for guiding it.

CHANGES IN THE THIRD EDITION We have benefited greatly from the comments and suggestions of users of our previous edition. The changes in this edition reflect their help as well as changes in the field of sociology.

Two major additions have been made. First, we have written an entirely new chapter dealing with sex roles and society. The study of sex roles has become increasingly important in recent years. Our awareness of sex roles and our knowledge of the extent to which they determine behavior patterns has increased considerably. We feel that the topic needs and deserves a separate chapter. The topic fits most conveniently in one of two places: it can be discussed as a major aspect of social structure (which is where we have placed it—Chapter Eleven), or it can follow Chapter Five on socialization, since much of the discussion of sex roles deals with socialization.

The second main addition is the expanded coverage of social institutions. In the second edition, the family, religion, and education were all dealt with in one chapter. In this revision, the family has become a separate chapter, with expanded and updated treatment, including such topics as violence in the family. Religion and education are combined in one chapter, and a new chapter on political and economic institutions has been added.

To make room for the expanded coverage, other material has been reduced and reorganized. The four chapters on culture in the second edition have been combined into two. We consider culture a very important concept and still devote more than the usual attention to it.

Chapters Eleven and Twelve from the second edition ("The Process of Becoming Human" and "Factors in Personality Development") have been combined and now appear earlier in the book as Chapter Five, Socialization. The deviance chapter has been entirely rewritten and now follows socialization.

Chapters Fourteen and Fifteen in the last edition ("Processes of Social and Cultural Change" and "The Great Transformation: Modernization") have been combined and now appear as the final chapter.

Overall, we feel that the third edition of INTRODUCTION TO SOCIOLOGY has broader coverage and better balance.

The third edition retains the feature of the previous editions and adds something new: a glossary.

KEY TERMS Teaching the "language of sociology" is a fundamental goal of the introductory course, and the text must help accomplish that task.

When a sociological concept is first presented, it is highlighted in color and boldface type. The term is then clearly defined and explained. Throughout the book, we use these concepts in various contexts and reiterate their definitions so students get repeated exposure to these key terms.

GLOSSARIES The third edition includes a glossary for the first time, and in *two* places.

First, a glossary appears at the end of each chapter and includes the terms introduced in that chapter.

We also have included a "master glossary" at the end of the book. Here all terms are listed alphabetically and the page reference (where they were first defined) is shown with each term.

SUMMARIES Each chapter concludes with a summary in color type to set it off from the regular text. The summary is intended as a guide for students to the important ideas and concepts in each chapter. And it should aid students in reviewing the text.

ILLUSTRATIONS   Various types of illustrations are used to visually reinforce and enhance the material in the text. Many times data can be more easily understood if properly presented in a graph or chart. Relationships sometimes become clearer if represented in a line drawing. Concepts can be illustrated with photographs that repeat the idea and usually make it more immediate. Cartoons are often good counterpoint to the text in addition to their obvious humor. We have tried to use all these visual devices to increase the effectiveness of the text.

SUPPLEMENTAL AIDS   A study guide/workbook is available for students. The study guide reviews the outline of each chapter and lists learning objectives. Key terms are tested in a matching question. Each chapter then has a pre-test (multiple-choice), a fill-in review outline and a post-test (also multiple-choice). Five essay questions or "questions for further thought" appear at the end of each chapter. All answers to the short answer questions are included in the workbook, along with the page number referring the

student to the discussion in the text. A thousand-item test file is also available for instructors. It includes mostly multiple-choice questions with answers and text page references. Essay questions are also included.

ACKNOWLEDGMENTS   In the end, an introductory text is the result of the energies and skills of a number of people. While final responsibility for the content must rest with the authors, we want to thank all those people who have helped us.

We have had comments from many users of the previous editions. We especially want to thank Paul Brezina, Thomas Carroll, Harold Cooper, John Klein, Linda Lindsey, Alvin Short, and Kenn Sinclair for their general reviews of the second edition. A number of sociologists read individual chapters. We appreciated their help and advice. We also want to thank Richard Biesanz for his careful reading of portions of the manuscript.

At Prentice-Hall, we had the help of a team of specialists, most importantly our development editor, Sandra Bloomfield. We also want to thank Walter Behnke, Patricia Cantlin, Irene Fraga, Penelope Linskey, Nancy Myers, Mira Schachne, Edward Stanford, Marvin Warshaw and Irwin Wint. It has been a pleasure to work with them.

M. H. B.

J. B.

part

1

introduction

chapter

1

The Study of Society

We all like to think of ourselves as intelligent, competent individuals with the free choice to plan our lives in whatever fashion we choose. But, to some extent, this may be an illusion. Unlike the Star-Child at the end of *2001: A Space Odyssey,* we are not born into the vacuum of space. We are members of society from the minute we are born, and thereafter much of what happens to us, and even who we are, is determined by the nature of that society.

For this reason, **sociology,** the systematic study of human relationships, has a lot to teach us about ourselves and the world. This book is designed to help you understand the basic knowledge we have acquired so far. It will not answer all your questions, but hopefully it will provide you with the tools to proceed on your own.

In this first chapter, we consider the nature of sociology, its goals, and how it differs from the other social sciences. We discuss the three main orientations developed by early social scientists: social philosophy, social observation and criticism, and empiricism. After a brief look at the present state of sociology, we discuss its various uses.

Sociology and the Other Social Sciences

Sociology is one of the social sciences. As such it is distinguished from the natural sciences (such as biology, physics, and chem-

istry) on the one hand and from the arts and humanities (such as literature, music, and art) on the other. All social scientists deal with human behavior—with the relationships and interactions of people in groups. Social scientists emphasize that we cannot understand human relationships by studying individuals any more than we can understand water by studying hydrogen and oxygen. Just as something new happens when hydrogen and oxygen are combined, so new things happen when people come together. Their behavior is not the action of A plus the action of B; it is the *interaction* of A and B, which is difficult or impossible to predict from their separate personalities.

In their common concern with group behavior, social scientists assume that people are part of the natural order and that, like all of nature, their behavior can be observed and understood by disciplined methods. Social scientists also assume that, because social order exists, the actions of people are largely rational and purposeful. Like all scientists, social scientists seek to generalize, to make broader sense out of accumulated facts. They believe it is worthwhile to work toward such generalizations, even though the delicate nuances of human behavior may disappear in careful abstractions and cold statistics. The arts and humanities have their insights to contribute; the social sciences also have theirs.

The social sciences—psychology, anthropology, sociology, history, economics, and political science—are the academic disci-

Social interaction: New things happen when people come together in groups. *Peter Vandermark for Stock, Boston.*

plines that deal with people in their social context. (Geography is also in some respects a social science.) These divisions developed through a historical process rather than through logic. The field of "political economy," for example, became "economics" when capitalist societies, under the influence of Adam Smith and laissez-faire philosophy, came to treat the economy as something quite independent of government and politics. Today, however, it is often impossible to determine whether a problem in economic policy is a problem in economics or political science.

Although they all study human social behavior and their concerns often overlap, the various social sciences do have different emphases and perspectives on group life. **Anthropology** is the study of biological and behavioral similarities and differences among the various peoples of the world. Physical anthropologists concentrate on the biological aspect, while cultural or social anthropologists concentrate on the behavioral aspects. Traditionally, cultural anthropologists have investigated groups distinguished "only by their lack of alphabet and breeches,"[1] but they have also carried out field work in more complex urban societies, as in the classic studies of Muncie, Indiana, made by Robert and Helen Lynd, which served as the basis for their books *Middletown* and *Middletown in Transition.* The invaluable contribution of anthropologists to human knowledge is the concept of *culture.*

Economics emphasizes people's activities as they use their environment to produce goods and services, and as they distribute and consume them. **Political science** is the study of political life and government and of the distribution of power in a society. It is concerned with the maintenance of social order and the achievement of social change by planning, reform, or revolution.

[1] Scott Greer, *The Logic of Social Inquiry* (Chicago: Aldine, 1969), p. 150.

5

History is the study of the human past. It is as much an art as a social science, for historians have to select and arrange the available data according to the way they perceive their relationships and significance. Historians may specialize by geographical areas, by time periods, or by approach to selected bodies of facts, such as political or economic history or the history of ideas or art forms. Increasingly they draw on the data and theories of the other social sciences for better understanding of their problems. Other social scientists, in turn, use historical data.

Psychology is the study of individual behavior. Social psychologists study large and small groups to find out how group membership influences individual behavior and how individual behavior influences the nature of groups.

Sociology is the systematic study of human relationships. The sociologist focuses on people in groups and on their relationships to one another, as well as on the relationships of groups to other groups, including the large, inclusive group called a society. The sociologist asks how these relationships arise, why they persist or dissolve, how they change, and what consequences they have for the people involved and for other individuals and groups.

The Development of Sociology

All human interaction—the normal as well as the abnormal, the everyday as well as the exciting—is grist for the sociologist's mill. Sociologists are interested in bums as well as beauty queens, whores and holy men, rioters and "respectable" people.

With the world and all its human relationships as his or her beat, a sociologist cannot hope to master all the theories, concepts,

All human interaction is grist for the sociologist's mill. *Jan Lukas from Rapho Guillumette.*

data, methods, and procedures of the discipline. Sociologists may choose to concentrate on theory, on a specific social institution such as religion or the law, on some concrete group such as a juvenile gang, on group relationships such as those of majority-minority groups, or on some area such as the city or Latin America. Whatever their specialty, they study it not only for the sake of knowledge about that specialty, but also in the hope of contributing to basic theories of social organization and social psychology.

Early Social Scientists

Just as the origins of physical science can be traced to the need of explorers and navigators for exact observations, the development of social science can be seen as a response to the need for knowledge about new phenomena that appeared with the economic and political revolutions of the eighteenth and early nineteenth centuries. Tradition furnished no guide to the new social realities of urbanization, industrial working classes, and the physical and social mobility that broke up families and long-established communities and challenged old values and patterns of human relationships.

SOCIAL PHILOSOPHERS Among early students of society, we may distinguish three main approaches to the problems of investigating these conditions. One is that of the grand theorist concerned with historical trends and human destiny, who works out a social philosophy that he claims will explain a broad range of phenomena and often constructs a model of a future "good society." Among the most influential of the early social philosophers were Karl Marx and Auguste Comte.

Karl Marx (1818–1883) was a prophet and a revolutionary who sought to change rather than simply interpret the world. Marx imagined a perfect, classless society, which he was convinced could come about only through class struggle. The misery of the workers in the new industrial societies and the failure of the political revolutions of 1848 led him to believe that economic factors determined social structure and culture, and that just as capitalism had superseded the even worse system of feudalism, so its evils would give way to "scientific socialism." Not only have his doctrines shaken the world, but his influence is reflected in studies of class systems and power relationships even among those social scientists who find his theory in general untenable.[2]

Like Marx, Auguste Comte (1798–1857) believed in progress toward a perfect society. He insisted, however, that it would come about not by political revolution but by the proper application of a new moral science, the study of society. Comte is thus generally recognized as being the "father of sociology." The highest of all sciences, it would use the "positivist" scientific method of observation, experimentation, and comparison to understand order and promote progress.[3] Thus, said Comte, a scientifically designed commonwealth could be built. Social control would be entrusted to the religion of humanity—with sociologists as its priests.

SOCIAL OBSERVERS Two Frenchmen illustrate another approach to the study of society—the observation and description of what *is* rather than speculation about what ought to be. *L'Esprit des Lois* by Baron Montesquieu (1689–1755), published in 1748, has been called "the first great de-

[2] Alvin W. Gouldner sees Marxism as the official social science of the Soviet Union, and American "Academic Sociology" as the other side of the fission of early sociology. Each increasingly displays the influence of the other. *The Coming Crisis of Western Sociology* (New York: Avon, 1970), pp. 20–24.

[3] Howard Becker and Harry Elmer Barnes, *Social Thought from Lore to Science,* 2nd ed. (Washington, D.C.: Harren Press, 1952), pp. 564–594.

scriptive treatise in sociology."[4] Montesquieu was the greatest advocate of the method of observation and comparison (rather than bookish scholarship and speculation) who had appeared up to that time.

Another shrewd observer, Alexis de Tocqueville (1805–1859), studied the new nation of the United States to examine trends that he believed would later appear elsewhere. In *Democracy in America,* he predicted such developments as the mass society sociologists perceive today and even foresaw that an autocratic Russia and a freedom-based America would one day divide the lion's share of world power between them.

SOCIAL EMPIRICISTS Among today's social scientists, social philosophy and grand theory are rare. Social description and criticism are much more common. But the main direction of modern social science is **empiricism,** the systematic collection and analysis of social facts. Empiricism goes back to early investigators in France and England who asked factual questions of ordinary people, especially in the new urban working class.

In the 1820s Adolphe Quetelet, a Belgian mathematician and astronomer, began to collect good census figures and to extract laws or generalizations directly from the facts he had gathered rather than from the "facts" in history books and those gleaned from unsystematic observations. He was influential in establishing the Statistical Society of London, whose members were concerned with the condition of the new urban masses. They collected facts and figures based on direct observation and interviews, even going down into the mines to investigate conditions at first hand.[5]

Frederic LePlay collected, classified, and analyzed first-hand data on the income and expenditures of over 300 working-class families. In his reports LePlay related data he collected to the policy problems and ideologies of the time. One of the first major empirical studies of society was his six-volume report published in 1855.

Émile Durkheim (1858–1917) was the first sociologist to systematically use statistical methods to analyze social behavior. One of his important contributions to sociological literature was his book *Suicide* (1894), which was the first large-scale empirical study of a social phenomenon. Durkheim was a major force in changing sociology from a social *philosophy* to a social *science.*

Max Weber (1864–1920) was interested in cultural values and institutions—economy, law, religion—and the parts they played in social life, particularly in capitalist societies. For example, Weber found a strong relationship based on common values between the rise of capitalism and the growth of the Protestant religion. He also wrote a massive and very influential study, based on empirical data, of bureaucracy, authority, and social stratification.

In recent years, sociology has flourished in a number of directions. It has become more empirical in its methods. There now exists a large body of factual information for sociologists to draw from. Three theoretical perspectives have dominated sociology during the twentieth century: structural-functionalism, symbolic interactionism, and conflict theory. As you will see, each of these theoretical perspectives has a unique influence on the way sociologists analyze social phenomena. For example, a structural functionalist assumes that a social structure exists because it serves some societal goal. A symbolic interactionist sees people's agreement on the meaning of symbols as the basis for their interaction and for the cohesion of society as a whole. And a conflict theorist describes society in terms of conflicts of interest between social groups.

[4] *Ibid.,* p. 560.

[5] Nathan Glazer, "The Rise of Social Research in Europe," in Daniel Lerner (ed.), *The Human Meaning of the Social Sciences* (Cleveland: World, 1959), p. 47.

The Uses of Sociology

What are the uses—actual and potential—of sociology? What can it do for the person and for society? In this section we consider these questions from several points of view: sociology as a career, the value of the sociological perspective in one's personal life, and sociology's contribution to the society as a whole. We conclude the chapter with a brief consideration of an issue that flares up periodically and has burned hotter than ever in recent years—what should be the sociologist's role in bringing about (or impeding) social change?

Sociology as a Career

Perhaps four out of five American sociologists are affiliated with colleges and universities and are engaged in teaching and independent research. Almost without exception they have advanced degrees (M.A.'s or Ph.D's) or are working toward them. Graduate programs for the doctorate begin with a year or two of courses in research, theory, and various fields, followed by a year or two of seminars devoted to more intensive study of particular areas of interest, ending with an independent research project, which becomes the doctoral dissertation.

Other sociologists are professionals rather than scholars, employed by public and private agencies to do research or to serve as advisers and consultants. They work in independent research institutes, such as the Social Science Research Council and the Russell Sage Foundation; for governments at various levels; and in corporations, political parties, churches, newspapers, hospitals, school systems, and social agencies. Some sociologists combine academic and professional roles, or shift back and forth between them, as consultants on specific problems,

urban planners, United Nations advisers on community development in foreign countries, advisers to the president, even mayors or city councilmen. Many feel they enrich their mastery of the academic discipline by applying their knowledge and methods in social action.

Personal Uses of Sociology

You may never look through a microscope again after you finish a biology course, or speak French after passing the exam, but you will probably live with people, vote, hold a job, pay taxes, and discuss social problems. To the extent that sociology contributes to a new way of looking at the person, the group, and the culture, it may help you make sense out of the world and handle your relationships with others in a more satisfying way. No matter what occupation you choose and what role you play in community life, the knowledge and awareness that come with the study of sociology may help you participate more successfully than you might otherwise. Whatever occupation you choose and whatever your position in a family and a community, you will find greater satisfaction in performing your role if you can relate it to a broader view of how society works. You can make judgments and decisions, both personal and professional, in a broader context.

Sociology may also help you understand yourself. New concepts such as culture, status, role, reference group, institution, class, mobility, and the self-conception may help you order the events of your life, reinterpreting the past and giving direction to the future. You may become aware of yourself as a participant in the social order, helping to make group decisions. You will learn that institutions have not always been as we know them here and now. Instead, they are products of time, culture, and human actions—and as such they are subject to change. This knowledge of alternatives may lead to a sense of patience and perspective toward the process of change—or perhaps to increased impatience about some long-standing problems that seem open to solution.

Sociology and Society

Each of the various sociological approaches contributes to information and direction within a society. Social philosophers open up new alternative visions of the future. Social critics and observers interpret trends and changes, predicting the possible consequences of alternative actions or policies. Empirical research adds to a growing body of solidly based knowledge upon which to base decisions.

GOVERNMENT USES OF SOCIOLOGICAL KNOWLEDGE AND METHODS From the founding of our country, government leaders have recognized that social science information is basic to democratic government. The Constitution provides for a census to be taken every ten years. Its primary purpose is to ensure fair representation in Congress, but it has lent itself to many other uses as well. In September 1929 President Hoover, often thought of as a staunch conservative, appointed a Research Committee on Social Trends—directed by sociologist William Fielding Ogburn—to anticipate the consequences of technological change and provide a basis for planning. President Franklin Roosevelt's Secretary of Agriculture, Henry Wallace, asked psychologist Rensis Likert to find out how much government regulation farmers would accept during the Depression. Public opinion polling has been very much a part of politics and policy ever since. After World War II, the Carnegie Corporation and the Ford Foundation asked the Social Science Research Council to support studies

of the Soviet Union as a prelude to better understanding, and in 1959 the Ford Foundation and other philanthropic agencies asked the Council to do the same regarding China.

In recent years some social scientists have become identified with a new role, that of "social accountant." Work toward a system of social accounting—that is, measuring the welfare of citizens through such "social indicators" as infant mortality—has been done by private foundations as well as government agencies. Sociologists urge that a Board of Social Advisers be established and charged with delivering to America's citizens an annual social report comparable to the annual economic report, thus fulfilling the Constitutional duty of the president to keep the people advised on "the state of the union."

SOCIOLOGY AND SOCIAL CHANGE Insofar as they question conventional wisdom, destroy old myths, suggest alternative ways of patterning social relationships, and provide new perspectives on human nature, sociology and the other social sciences threaten comfortable habits and vested interests. Sociologists can hardly avoid touching on controversial subjects when they deal with group conflicts and social problems and with such private and intimate subjects as religion and sex relations.

Because sociology views any given social arrangement as only one of a number of alternatives, it is inherently radical in the word's original sense of getting at the "root" of things. It can, however, just as truly be conservative in the sense of conserving what is worthwhile. By analyzing the possible consequences of various alternatives, sociologists can contribute to orderly change and prevent needless conflict and violence.

By testing propositions about man and society, then, social scientists provide us not only with a multitude of social facts, but also with knowledge of trends and of possible courses of action and their probable consequences, justifying the definition of social science as "man's working tool for continually rebuilding his culture."[6]

The Sociologist and Public Policy: Involvement or Neutrality?

But who is going to use this tool? And how is it to be used? Sociologists disagree sharply on their proper role. Is it enough to use the classroom to teach students ways of understanding social problems? Is the sociologist's job only to conduct careful investigations and make the findings public for whatever use others might make of them? Or should sociologists actively involve themselves in the political process through which goals and policies are decided?

This issue is often stated in terms of values. Many people say that sociology should have no value except truth. A true scientist is objective, value-free, and ethically neutral. At the opposite extreme are radical sociologists who believe all their work should be action-oriented. These sociologists are concerned with values and goals, with policies or the means to those goals, and with the political process in which goals are chosen and means worked out.[7]

The third position is more complex, and even those who take it do not agree on all its premises. They insist that sociology can never be completely value-free. To do one thing instead of another means making a choice, and values guide choices. Thus, the very choice of a problem to study reveals a value orientation. If we limit our concerns to what is rather than studying what might

be or ought to be, then, by default, we support the status quo. And if the status quo includes war, crime, discrimination, injustice, and repression, we are exhibiting moral indifference—we're copping out.

The position we take in this book is based on our belief that a social scientist who ignores the urgent issues of the day is "lecturing on navigation while the ship is going down," in W. H. Auden's phrase. Applications of social science knowledge to problems and policies cannot wait until some distant and unlikely day when grand theories and immutable laws of human behavior are established. Effective social science must combine moral vision with a devotion to careful research.

Plan of the Book

The second chapter of this introduction is devoted to sociological research, what it is and how it is done. Then, in the rest of the book, we look at the actual subject matter of sociology.

In our view a firm grasp of the concept of culture is essential to understanding the nature and functions of society. Thus, in Part Two, we look first at culture—what it is, how it develops, and how it works to shape our personalities. Then we consider socialization, the process of becoming a human being and a functioning member of a social group that teaches us its culture. Since this teaching never produces perfect conformity we also examine deviance and social control.

In the third part of the book, our general topic is social structure, the web of organized relationships among individuals and groups that defines their mutual rights and responsibilities. We see how it emerges from, and shapes, social interaction. And we examine the central concepts of status and role. After considering the various types and dimen-

---

[6] Robert Lynd, *Knowledge for What? The Place of Social Science in American Culture* (Princeton, N.J.: Princeton University Press, 1948), p. 200.

[7] A similar debate is going on in the other social sciences and in the natural sciences as well. Biologists, chemists, and physicists increasingly question the potential applications of their research to warfare, repression, and "human engineering."

sions of social groups, we turn to three other aspects of social structure: The ranking of people in systems of stratification, the relations of minorities and minority groups, and the roles and relationships of males and females.

In Part Four, we look at demography and urban life. Demography, the measurement of changes in a society's population, can help sociologists to predict where pressures on the social structure will occur. Most societies are currently undergoing urbanization, and we look at the city and its consequences for society and personality.

In Part Five, we examine social institutions—the family, religion and education, and politics and economics—what they are, the social functions they serve, and how they are changing.

In Part Six, we discuss social change. First we look at the forms of collective behavior and social movements that are often produced by and in turn produce change. We conclude the book with a discussion of social and cultural change and the effects of modernization.

The book is bound together by several themes. One theme is the problem of main-

taining a delicate balance between individual freedom and social control as the world becomes more complex and various groups come into conflict with one another and threaten social cohesion. Closely allied with this theme is the paradox that although we are more interdependent than ever before, many of us feel increasingly lonely and alienated. Some people argue that our institutions have failed to meet our needs and must be reformed. Others say that if we would only give those institutions the respect they are due things would get better. Some people are afraid that technology—with its promises and its dangers—has gotten out of hand. The tension between social order and social change is another recurrent theme.

Underlying all these themes, however, is our belief in the intrinsic worth of every human being. We believe in the possibility of achieving a society in which everyone has the opportunity to decide how they can best fulfill their potential and live with a sense of freedom, dignity, and autonomy. And we believe in the usefulness of social science as a means to understand, preserve, and improve human life.

Summary

Although all the social sciences deal with the interactions of people in groups, the various disciplines have developed somewhat different perspectives and emphases. Anthropologists are concerned primarily with culture; psychologists with individual behavior; sociologists with patterned group relationships; economists with the production, distribution, and consumption of goods and services (wealth); and political scientists with the use of power in keeping social order and effecting social change. Historians con-

tribute perspectives on social order and social change that can be gained only through studying the past.

Sociology takes all human interaction and human relationships as its field, but individual sociologists typically concentrate on some aspect of that field. Increasingly, social science research tends to be quantitative, conducted by teams working in major intellectual centers.

The systematic study of human society began in the nineteenth century as a response to the change and turmoil of the industrialization process. Three main approaches are exemplified by early social scientists: Karl Marx and Auguste Comte were grand theorists or social philosophers; Montesquieu and de Tocqueville were careful observers who described whole societies; Quetelet, Durkheim, and Weber were empiricists who used survey and statistical methods. Three dominant theoretical perspectives adopted by modern sociologists are structural-functionalism, symbolic interactionism, and conflict theory.

Sociologists may adopt an academic or professional role. Nonsociologists may find their personal, professional, and community life enriched by an understanding of the field.

Sociologists and other social scientists contribute to society by testing propositions about people and society, providing a multitude of social facts, identifying trends, and pointing out alternative policies and their likely consequences. Sociologists disagree, however, on the proper role of the sociologist in the arena of social and political action.

The position taken by this book is that the choice of a problem is guided by values; the process of investigation should be as objective and dispassionate as possible; but once the conclusions are reached, social scientists have a moral obligation to make clear their implications for the future course of events and even to recommend alternatives.

Glossary

Anthropology The study of biological and behavioral similarities and differences among the various peoples of the world.

Economics The study of people's activities as they use their environment to produce goods and services, and as they distribute and consume them.

Empiricism The systematic collection and analysis of social facts.

History The study of the human past.

Political Science The study of political life and government and of the distribution of power in a society.

Psychology The study of individual behavior.

Sociology The systematic study of human relationships.

chapter

2

The Conduct of Social Inquiry

The programs of sociology conventions make interesting reading for anyone who wants to know what sociologists think about. At a recent convention of the American Sociological Association, for example, a very random sampling of over 200 sessions (at each of which three or four papers were read and discussed) included "Problems of Getting Sociological Data in and out of a Computer," "Relative Deprivation as a Force in Ghetto Riots," "Television in the Lives of Disadvantaged Children," "Rethinking Role Theory to Include Women," and "Public Beliefs about the Beliefs of the Public." How do sociologists go about investigating such topics? Is sociology a science? What do studies of race relations, the effect of television on children, Indian and American self-conceptions, hippies, and riots have in common with studies of planetary movements, chemical reactions, and biological mutations? How are they different?

In this chapter we consider the main philosophies that guide social scientists, the ways in which knowledge is organized in a social science such as sociology, and the methods and techniques of research.

Approaches to Social Inquiry

Social science uses a variety of approaches. Some sociologists may carefully investigate the interaction of three or four people. One may try to imitate the precise measurements of the physicist; another may try to describe group life in all its complexity. Each approach—and those that fall somewhere in between—may be fruitful if properly applied.

Some sociologists take a broad view, examining such things as total societies, worldwide trends (modernization), historical phenomena, or the relationship between personality types and cultural differences. Thus, Max Weber related the rise of capitalism to the Protestant Reformation; David Riesman associated different character types with social trends; Robert MacIver focused on the competing claims of social order and individual conscience; and Robin M. Williams, Jr., analyzed American society.[1] Studies of such large-scale *macroscopic* phenomena are called **macrosociology.**

Other sociologists have typically concentrated on smaller, *miscrospic* problems: family relationships, juvenile delinquency, the social roles of waitresses and doctors, the self-conceptions of executives and convicts, the relationship between patterns of child-rearing and class status, and so on. These

[1] Weber, *The Protestant Ethic and the Spirit of Capitalism,* trans. Talcott Parsons (New York: Charles Scribner's Sons, 1948); Riesman, with Nathan Glazer and Reuel Denney, *The Lonely Crowd: A Study of the Changing American Character* (Garden City, N.Y.: Doubleday, 1955); MacIver, *The Web of Government,* rev. ed. (New York: Macmillan, 1965); Williams, *American Society: A Sociological Interpretation,* 3rd ed. (New York: Alfred A. Knopf, 1970).

These three people are interacting in the roles of waitress and customers. *Frank Siteman for Stock, Boston.*

kinds of small-scale studies are generally called **microsociology.** Sometimes these studies may be related to broader themes and theories. Robert Merton has suggested that the most profitable course for some time to come is to attempt to combine low-level empirical generalizations with "theories of the middle range," rather than trying to construct "grand theory." But, in recent years, many younger sociologists have objected to small-scale studies because they do not come to grips with the great problems of modern society.

Positivism and Humanism

For centuries Western thought has tended toward one or the other of two main approaches: *humanism,* which stresses individuality and freedom; and *positivism,* which stresses control over nature by means of objective observation and experimental analysis. Many sociologists try to fuse the two; others argue passionately for one or the other. A **positivist** stresses the need for

exact measurement, verifiable propositions rather than speculations, and hard data, the things you can see, hear, taste, or feel—and measure. Consciously or unconsciously, the positivist often looks to the natural sciences for his methods, and tries to be a "no-nonsense, brass-instrument, experimental scientist."[2]

In contrast, **humanistic** sociologists make the most of the fact that they are studying their own kind and thus have an inside track to knowledge that is unavailable to the physicist or chemist. They can feel empathy for those they study, take their roles, adopt their point of view, and thus arrive at a subjective understanding of their lives. Champions of this approach argue that the use of sympathetic understanding compensates for the fact that human studies can never achieve the formal precision of physics. Without empathy, they insist, we cannot understand

[2] George C. Homans, *The Nature of Social Science* (New York: Harcourt Brace Jovanovich, 1967), p. 4.

17

the meaning, value, and purpose of human behavior.

The positivist and humanistic approaches are both valuable. Indeed, they are complementary. "Certainly we need logical thinking and scientific techniques if we are to be effective social scientists; but we also need insight, imagination, an ability to respond to our feelings as well as to understand our observations, a recognition that art and science are components of the same reality."[3] Studies of some social phenomena (population, ecology, formal organization) seem to profit from positivist, scientific techniques. Others (personality, socialization, institutions, culture, social processes) seem more amenable to the humanistic approach.

Even the strictest positivist—and even in the more "exact" sciences—may make discoveries or connections and arrive at explanations by means other than painful and plodding calculation. He may have an illuminating flash of insight or a sudden inspiration or hunch. This often comes after he has been fruitlessly pondering a puzzling phenomenon and feels frustrated with the poor results of the more standard means of investigation. Archimedes' leaping out of his bathtub yelling "Eureka!" when the implications of the displacement of water struck him has had many echoes in "Aha!" moments of scientific inspiration.

Furthermore, while predictability and precision are greater in physical than in social science, they are not perfect. Propositions are stated with such qualifiers as: under certain circumstances, so far as we know, other things being equal, at sea level. They are also stated in terms of probabilities:

[3] Norman MacKenzie, ed., *A Guide to the Social Sciences* (New York: New American Library, 1966), p. 32.

Given A, the probability is from 90 to 95 percent that B will occur.

The Content of Social Science

Data

Each social science is based on a body of social facts or findings, which are called *data*. In sociology, **data** are (datum is the singular form) empirically verified (and reverifiable) descriptions of phenomena. Some social science data are "benchmark information," which allows us to interpret other data. For example, data about the distribution of the three major religious groups in the United States serve as benchmark information against which to measure their distribution in New York City. Other social facts useful to sociologists include data on income distribution, years of schooling, birth and death rates, marriage and divorce rates, the distribution of population, and the composition of the population by age, sex, and racial and ethnic groups.

Facts by themselves are of little use. Facts become significant when they have been evaluated, interpreted, defined, and classified. Researchers do not seek to collect *all* the facts, but choose relevant and useful ones, trying not to miss any. They have some notions, however, about how the facts fit together, and these lead them to perceive some phenomena and ignore others. If researchers are more concerned with finding truth than with proving their assumptions, they will modify their assumptions on the basis of new facts.

But a science is more than a collection of facts. In a science, data are organized by means of concepts, propositions, theories, models, and typologies.

Concepts

A **concept** is a word or phrase that represents a class of phenomena. For example, the concept "chair" represents a wide variety of objects constructed to hold one person with his back supported and his feet (usually) on the floor. Concepts help us to understand what we perceive. For example, before Galileo's time, motion was thought of as being a part of particular objects, just like their size and shape. Galileo and his contemporaries abstracted the idea of motion from the objects themselves. Once the concept of motion had been isolated from the concept of object, it could be studied in its own right. This led eventually to Newton's developing a law of gravity. Similarly, until Pasteur developed the concept of infinitely small living things—in this case, bacteria—anthrax in cattle was an unexplainable disease.

Concepts such as culture, social class, reference groups, and values help sociologists to perceive and explain the workings of the social order. (It is fascinating to hear a person who has acquired "the sociological imagination" discuss a commonplace event—say, a party you both attended—using concepts that describe the party in terms of processes of interaction, interpersonal relationships, and human motives.) Without concepts, sociology would be merely a catalogue of isolated phenomena.

Many sociological concepts are taken from everyday usage. They are, however, refined by careful definition, so that they can serve as tools for precise analysis. Such ordinary words as class, society, status, role, and race all have special, precise meanings in sociological thinking, and to present them and their relations to one another is one of the chief tasks of an introductory sociology course.

Although these basic concepts are simple enough, the feeling remains that it is somehow wrong to define them in simple terms and to describe their interrelationships in straightforward language. In every science there are some who resemble Gladstone, who, according to Disraeli, was "inebriated with the exuberance of his own verbosity." Like the young man in the operetta *Patience* (1881), the person who writes obscurely perhaps wants people to think,

If this young man expresses himself in terms too deep for me, Why, what a very singularly deep young man this deep young man must be!

There is also the possibility that he cannot express himself clearly because he cannot think clearly. A good idea can usually survive being said in simple words.

Propositions

A **proposition** is a statement of a relationship between two or more facts or concepts. To be scientific, a proposition must be open to proof or disproof. The proposition that an Indian rain dance when properly performed will produce rain is unscientific because it isn't susceptible to proof. If it doesn't rain, it may simply mean that the dance wasn't done properly.

There are several kinds of propositions. One is a hypothesis that has not yet been tested but is testable. For example, if A is true, then B will happen (perhaps because of C). Having constructed this hypothesis, a researcher might do a study to see if B really does have a relationship to A. Another is an empirically verified generalization. For example, the rate of social mobility between generations is currently about the same in all industrialized nations. This is the most common usage.

A proposition referring to unvarying associations is a **law.** A law is universally agreed upon within a science and is accepted with confidence. The most common example is Boyle's law: The volume of gas in an enclosed space is inversely proportional to the pressure on it. There are as yet few laws in the social sciences, but this does not necessarily mean that human behavior is unpredictable.

Theory

Data, then, are verified statements about phenomena. Concepts allow us to perceive or think about phenomena and to communicate about them. Propositions are statements of relationships among concepts and/or facts. None of them, however, *explains* the phenomena and their relationships. What do the facts *mean?* Answering this question—explaining or making sense of facts—is the main function of theory.

A **theory** is a set of systematically related propositions. A theory may be empirically grounded, interpretative, or philosophical. An *empirically grounded theory* is based on verifiable, observable data. Thus, "theory, inquiry, and empirical fact are interwoven in a texture of operation with theory guiding inquiry, inquiry seeking and isolating facts, and facts affecting theory. The fruitfulness of their interplay is the means by which an empirical science develops."[4]

Interpretative theory may or may not be firmly related to empirical findings. Typically it is less rigorous, but it is also legitimate and useful. Its aim is "to outline and define life situations so that people may have a clearer understanding of their world, its possibilities of development, and the directions along which it may move. In every

society, particularly a changing society, there is a need for meaningful clarification of basic social values, social institutions, modes of living, and social relations. This need cannot be met by empirical science, even though some help may be gained from analysis made by empirical science."[5]

Social philosophy is not generally considered social theory, for it typically deals not with what is but with ideas of what *ought to be,* of the ideal society. Marxism and Comte's positive philosophy are examples. But such theories do play a useful role in stimulating thinking about social goals.

Whether empirically grounded or interpretative, a good theory does more than give meaning to facts and direction and purpose to research. It also helps us see what is similar about different things, and what is different about things that look alike. Émile Durkheim built a theory of suicide by relating it to the degree of social cohesion in different groups such as Catholics and Protestants, married and unmarried people, and other categories.[6] Erving Goffman showed us similarities in such different institutions as convents, marine boot camps, mental hospitals, and prisons by applying a set of propositions about resocialization and self-identity.[7] Theory also promotes the growth of the body of knowledge in a science by serving as a framework into which new bits of knowledge are fitted. It serves as a pattern that gives structure. If bricks are piled up haphazardly, you wind up with a pile of

---

[4] Herbert Blumer, *Symbolic Interactionism* (Englewood Cliffs, N.J.: Prentice-Hall, 1969), p. 141.

[5] *Ibid.,* p. 140. Blumer also mentions policy theory, concerned with analyzing a given situation, structure, or action as a basis for policy or action. It is related to concrete situations, such as racial integration in a certain city.

[6] *Suicide,* trans. George Simpson (New York: The Free Press, 1951).

[7] *Asylums: Essays on the Social Situation of Mental Patients and Other Inmates* (Garden City, N.Y.: Doubleday, 1961).

Sociologists study the process of socialization in many settings. Here military training socializes recruits to a new institution and changes their self-identities. *Hirojo Kubota for Magnum.*

bricks; if you fit them into a pattern, you can build a house.

Models

A **model** is a guiding metaphor or analogy that serves as the skeleton of a theory. It is applied to some complex phenomenon and compared to it in *form* but not in content. The most common metaphors applied to society are the organic model, patterned after biology, and the machine model, patterned after physics. The *organic model* of society suggests that social groups and institutions are like organs of the body. They have specialized functions that contribute to the health and survival of the society as a whole and are in turn nourished by it. In the *machine model,* individuals are thought of as a part in a machine. They are placed by their social positions, moved by the specifications of their roles, and controlled by interaction with other parts. Society as a whole is seen as a machine moving through cycles that can be fixed by tinkering. A third model is the *cybernetic model,* based on

computer technology, which stresses the processing of information and feedback as important elements in interaction. Other models use other analogies for social interaction such as drama, ritual, and games.

Models generate ideas and guide the forming of concepts and research. The danger is that the analogy may be overworked and carried too far. Society, for example, should not be thought of as really *being* an organism or a machine.

Typologies

Another way of bringing order and meaning to facts is to classify them according to some typology. A **typology** is a way of grouping data and ideas, giving reference points that provide orientation for research and understanding.

Typologies may be logically constructed, or they may emerge naturally out of empirical observation. One kind of *logical typology,* which can be neatly fitted into a fourfold table, covers all the possible relationships between two variables. For example, by constructing a table showing the relationship between sex and income we create four types: males with incomes under $9,000 a year, females with incomes under $9,000 a year, males with incomes over $9,000, and females with incomes over $9,000. (These figures are not "social facts," but are purely illustrative.)

Percentage of Labor Force Earning Above and Below the Median Income, According to Sex		
	Income	
	Below $9,000 a Year	$9,000 a Year or Above
Male	45%	55%
Female	85%	15%

This typology suggests a number of questions. Clearly, males earn more money than females. What does this phenomenon mean? To what extent is it explained by sex discrimination? What are the "census characteristics" other than sex of the people in each of the four cells—that is, their age, education, ethnic background? What further refinements of the table would be necessary to test hypotheses about comparative incomes for men and women who do the same work?

Ideal types are another kind of logical typology. They may be based on reality, but they need not correspond to any one instance and may not fit any single empirical observation. Ideal types may also be consciously constructed or deduced from ideas rather than empirically induced from reality.

An ideal type may stand alone: for example, the "economic man" of classical economics—a person with perfect informa-

tion, rationality, freedom, mobility, and communication with others (a deduction from ideas). Or two ideal types may be thought of as *polar types,* with opposite and contrasting characteristics, standing at the extreme ends of a line or continuum, for example, extroverted and introverted personalities and folk and urban societies. While idealizations such as economic men have no actual counterparts—economic men "exist only in the pages of certain books and journals, and in the professional conversation of economists"[8]—polar types may exist, and all concrete instances may be placed somewhere along the continuum between them. The folk-urban continuum, for example, provides a framework for the comparative analysis of societies and is useful in the study of social change in a modernizing society.

Natural typologies emerge from observation of a situation. The observer may group people or events as he sees likenesses and differences, or he may find that the group itself has already distinguished its own natural types. For example, in *The Ghetto,* Louis Wirth reported on various social types already labeled as such in the Jewish culture: the *Mensch,* who has proudly kept his identity as a Jew while achieving superior economic status. The "allrightnik" is an opportunist who has thrown overboard the cultural baggage of the group. The helpless, shiftless *schlemiel* fails in everything he undertakes. The *Luftmensch* moves easily from one unsuccessful project to another, apparently living on air. There is the elderly Orthodox Jew whose conduct is above reproach, and so on.[9] Wirth saw this natural typology as a complete index of the cultural traits and patterns of the group and as a direct expres-

[8] Robert Brown, *Explanation in Social Science* (Chicago: Aldine, 1963), p. 181.
[9] *The Ghetto* (Chicago: University of Chicago Press, 1928).

sion of group values. Natural typologies are richly suggestive and broad-ranging. Logical typologies, in comparison, must leave out a great deal in order to serve as reference points for very specific problems in research.

Methods and Techniques of Social Research

The words "method" and "technique" are often used interchangeably. Generally, however, *method* refers to a broad approach, such as the quantitative or qualitative method, or to a general study design such as the case study or survey method. The word *technique* refers to a more specific procedure such as administration of a Rorschach test, the statistical technique called factor analysis, or a technique for administering a mass survey of public opinion.

The research process is often described as if it were clearly divided into a series of steps that follow, logically and chronologically, one after another. In actual practice—in any science—the process is not so neat. The phases are intertwined, and there may be backtracking as fresh insights are achieved and more interesting problems arise. The following discussion, therefore, is not of a series but of various aspects of the process, which *tend* to take place in the order given.

Exploratory Research

In all social inquiry, the first step should be to become as familiar as possible with the area of social life under study. Whether sociologists are studying the social world of ghetto dwellers, corporation managers, adolescent drug users, religious cultists, soldiers, professional politicians, revolutionaries, or any other category of people, they should get close to them, see how they meet a variety of situations, note their problems and how they handle them, join their conversations, watch their life as it flows along.

Such exploratory study is indicated even when an experimental or mathematical method is planned for the actual collection of data. Immersion in the social world allows the investigator to choose problems and select and analyze data on the basis of what is actually taking place and what it means to the people involved, rather than on the basis of preconceived notions and ideas. An investigator will be less likely to overlook something important or to impose personal meanings on the data. Sometimes such a naturalistic inquiry will by itself answer the problems that come up, but often it is a preliminary to more formalized inquiry.

Choice of a Problem

Investigators usually choose a problem that they consider important and that they feel they can get involved in. The choice, then, arises out of their own particular interests or values. Throughout the study, a core problem or set of problems guides and focuses the work and helps the researcher avoid wasteful and aimless data gathering.

Somehow investigators must justify their choices. Is there a shortage of data for some theory or a shortage of important knowledge about some area or social world? An investigator searches books and journals to see what has already been done to avoid duplication of research and to find new leads. In some cases a policy-making agency or a professional group may have a particular problem for the researcher to study. A researcher also may wish to test the validity of some generalization (whether common-sense or scientific) or to try out a new technique.[10]

[10] Much of this section draws on a course in Methods of Social Research taught by Dr. Louis Ferman at Wayne State University in 1960.

Formulation of Hypotheses

Many nonsociologists explore other social worlds and think about the same problems as sociologists do. What, then, distinguishes the sociologist from other observers of human behavior? James A. Davis puts it this way.

Some students find it hard to think like a sociologist, not because a sociologist's thought is so eccentric, but because at first glance it appears so similar. By and large, sociologists think about the same things everybody does: friends, family, personal opinions, groups, organizations, money, and sex. What is different is the intellectual framework: The professional sociologist tends to think in terms of a *structure of probabilistic relationships among operationally interpreted variables.*[11]

A **variable** is an action or attribute that can be measured (say, degree of urbanism) or categorized (sex, for example). A **hypothesis** is a statement of a probable or expected relationship between two or more variables: for example, if A, then B. Variable A may be the attribute of education, B the act of voting. The hypothesis may be stated as a cause-and-effect relationship—A causes B—or as a statistical correlation—A is associated with B. It may also be stated as a *null* hypothesis: A and B are *not* associated; the degree of education makes no difference in voting.

When two variables are being tested, one is termed the *dependent* variable, the other the *independent* one. Thus, in the preceding hypothesis, voting behavior, the dependent variable, is assumed to be related (or not related) to education, the independent variable. But it might also be related to sex, rural or urban residence, age, income, or occupation. Sociologists try to control the

variables, making sure they screen out the effects of all other independent variables on voting behavior so that they come close to the truth about its relation to education. Scholarship in the field and scrutiny of the empirical social world are especially important in helping scientists to realize what possible variables might be associated with the variable they are trying to understand. And knowledge of statistical techniques helps them to unscramble the effects of these variables.

The hypothesis may also include an intervening variable: If A, then B, because of C. We may find that Catholics tend to vote Democratic more often than Protestants do. But is this a direct correlation between religion and politics, or is there an intervening variable? Perhaps, we hypothesize, the foreign-born tend to vote Democratic more than the native-born, and the foreign-born are also more likely to be Catholic. Ethnicity, then, may be an intervening variable, the explanatory connection in the reformulated hypothesis.

It is necessary, especially with quantitative studies, to state the variables in terms of indices or operational definitions that are measurable and testable. Ideally, an *index* is perfectly correlated with what it signifies and is more easily seen than the variable for which it stands. Suppose we make this hypothesis: The higher a person's social class, the greater will be his intelligence (or vice versa). We may operationally define social class in terms of income and intelligence in terms of score on IQ tests. Although both are controversial and crude measures, they are frequently used as indices because they are numerical and easily measured. Thus, the rate of absenteeism may be taken as an index of morale in a work group, and the number of new houses that are built as an index of economic prosperity. In surveys concerned with such abstract variables as prejudice, happiness, or modernism, the

[11] *Elementary Survey Analysis* (Englewood Cliffs, N.J.: Prentice-Hall, 1971), pp. 1–2.

measures may need to be indirect.[12] By the same token, a doctor does not ask a patient if he has heart disease. He asks a series of questions about shortness of breath, pain in the chest, and other indicators that are part of his operational definition of heart disease.

A good hypothesis is simple, tight, and

[12] See Joseph A. Kahl, *The Measurement of Modernism: A Study of Values in Brazil and Mexico* (Austin: The University of Texas Press, 1968), for lucid explanations of the research process, including the use of operational definitions of values.

Knowing "census data" about this voter, a sociologist might feel fairly confident about predicting her choice. *Daniel S. Brody for Editorial Photocolor Archives, Inc.*

concise. It is capable of disproof as well as of proof. It is a plausible, educated guess, but should not be ridiculously self-evident or obvious. In the early stages of research, investigators may brainstorm a dozen or more hypotheses, choose several working hypotheses, and refine and narrow them down to one or two research hypotheses as they go along. As they begin their work, theory helps them formulate hypotheses; as they analyze their data, theory helps them explain why research has confirmed or negated their hypotheses.

Data Collection: Research Design

While exploring the social world and choosing problems for study, social scientists must also choose a research design. They may decide that their hypotheses can best be tested by means of a sample survey, a field study, an experiment, or a combination of two or all three methods.

SAMPLE SURVEY The **sample survey** is very popular among sociologists, social psychologists studying attitudes, political scientists, and economists in certain fields, such as market research. The *sample* is a statistical term for a number of people chosen from a *population* such as freshman college students, voters, farmers, adult females, and so on. Trained statisticians select the sample so that they can, with very little error, draw conclusions about the whole population from a small portion of it. The *survey* is the collection of data on the relevant variables—the career ambitions of freshmen, the probable presidential choice of voters, the income of farmers, the number of children born to females of a certain age. The questionnaire must be very carefully drawn up, however, so that it is *valid*—so that it measures what it is designed to measure. There are also problems of *reliability:* Is it measuring accurately? If some people will not or cannot answer correctly or at all, the results will be thrown off.

The questions asked in a sample survey—which is essentially a mass interview—are usually simple and direct. Their aim is to discover objective facts or indices of attitudes and opinions. Usually census data are sought, so that whatever the dependent variables of the study, they may be correlated with some or all of the following independent variables: sex, age, race, rural or urban residence, education, income, occupation, religion, marital status, and so on. The questions relevant to the dependent variables must be carefully phrased in ways that have been shown to yield valid and reliable responses.

Sample surveys are especially useful in measuring changes over time. Repeating them provides information about social change. Surveys also supply information about the correlation of variables, such as income and political affiliation. They measure large numbers of people on a few characteristics. The most familiar example is the public opinion poll.

CASE STUDIES   A **case study,** in contrast, is an in-depth examination of a person, a social group or a culture, usually over a long period of time. Community studies such as *Middletown* are essentially case studies, as are studies of changing neighborhoods, street corner gangs, or the life histories of psychotics. Because they are based on a sample of one person, group, or area, case studies rarely *prove* anything, but they are rich sources of ideas and provide insights that come only with intensive probing.

In some kinds of case studies, data are collected primarily by **participant observation,** which is *the* method of social anthropology. The social scientist immerses himself in the situation and, so far as possible, becomes part of it, living with an Australian tribe, joining funeral processions and fiestas in a Panamanian village, becoming a precinct delegate, standing on the street corner with a gang, merging into the drug subculture. This method is especially valuable for discovering meanings, values, and patterns of personal relationships. Unlike the survey method, it focuses on behavior as it is occurring rather than as it is recalled and thus reveals the continuity of events. Participant observation has drawbacks, however. The group may behave differently because outsiders are present, although chances are that they will soon be taken for granted. Successful participant observers may even learn to think as the group thinks, but if they become too involved they may lose their objectivity. Also, they must decide whether to be straightforward about the fact that they are investigating the group, or whether to adopt a "cover" at the risk of being exposed and accused of bad faith. They must also decide when to participate actively and when to observe passively.

Nonparticipant observation is more easily structured. In some cases, as in indirect observation of nursery-school children through a one-way window, the observed are unaware of the observer. The observer carefully notes the time, the people involved, regularities in interaction and deviations from these regularities, indices of group cohesiveness, and many other factors. Categories have been constructed into which observations of small-group interaction, for example, may be fitted. Behavior in disasters, riots, classrooms, and playgrounds has been observed by similar methods.[13]

EXPERIMENTS   In an **experiment** the investigator intervenes in a situation (or creates

---

[13] See John Madge, *The Tools of Social Science* (London: Longmans, Green, 1953), Chap. 3, "Observation," pp. 117–143, for an excellent discussion.

one) to control or manipulate a variable and observe or measure the result. Usually experimenters seek to keep all other variables constant. For example, they often introduce the variable into one group but not into a control group. Thus, a student of nutrition might give two groups of rats the same diet, except that one group is deprived of Vitamin B-12. A social psychologist may attempt to determine the effect of propaganda by measuring the attitudes of two groups with matched characteristics, then exposing the experimental group to some propaganda, and remeasuring their attitudes.

The experiment is a highly efficient method of research, especially in untangling cause-and-effect relationships. Experimental intervention in the social sciences, however, is limited by moral and humanitarian considerations. We can hardly bring up one group of children one way and another quite differently under laboratory conditions. But experimental situations may occur naturally. Psychologists have compared the health and intelligence of babies brought up by their own mothers in prison and babies brought up by nurses in a foundling home. Two Paraguayan villages may be much alike, but when one becomes the site of a cotton mill, we can measure the effects of industrialization by comparing the two.

Intervention, even when morally acceptable, may alter the situation being studied in such a way that one must ask whether the change occurred because of the variable being manipulated or because of the investigator's presence. In the famous Hawthorne experiment, a group of women who worked together in a factory for a long period constantly increased their output regardless of whether they had more light or less, more rest periods or fewer, piecework or straight wages. The causal variable, as it turned out, was the feeling that the experimenter was interested in them, which raised their morale

noticeably.[14] Despite its precision, then, the experimental method is best used in combination with other methods.

Whether one is studying a group or a whole society, the art of watching and listening—and taking systematic notes—is essential to fruitful investigation. For example, when one of Ernest Burgess's students complained to him about the talkative landlady in the roominghouse where he was living while collecting data about homeless men, Burgess pointed out that instead of being bored when she told her life story, the student should see it as an invaluable opportunity to find out what kind of person becomes a roominghouse keeper and why, what her problems are, and how she keeps her house orderly in a slum area.[15]

In addition to observing, listening, asking questions, and recording observations and the answers to questions, the sociologist may turn to documentary sources—public records such as census statistics, economic data systematically gathered by special agencies, minutes of meetings, organizational records, election records, historical archives, books, periodicals, newspapers, and manuscripts. In community studies, maps, telephone books, and city directories are also useful.

To grasp a situation of any depth and complexity, the investigator usually finds that using a combination of research designs and techniques is the best way to reach valid conclusions. The camera and tape recorder (figurative or literal) of exploratory research

[14] Elton Mayo, *The Human Problems of an Industrial Civilization* (New York: Macmillan, 1933).

[15] Ernest W. Burgess and Donald J. Bogue, eds., *Urban Sociology* (Chicago: University of Chicago Press, 1967), p. 9. Other sources of data for an intensive case study of a person might include interviews with people who know him, personality tests, diaries, and letters. In their study, *The Polish Peasant in Europe and America*, Vols. 1 and 2 (New York: Dover, 1971), W. I. Thomas and Florian Znaniecki paid special attention to the subjective factor, finding their data in "human documents," especially life histories.

Handelsman in the *Saturday Review.*

"I'm doing a survey of lower-middle-class life. May I come in and unobtrusively plug in my tape recorder?"

may well be supplemented by the telescope of a sample survey, the microscope of a case study, and the test tube of an experiment. It is tempting to use survey methods alone, simply because they provide numerical data that are easily fed into a computer. But there is a danger that the conclusions, though precise, will be trivial or meaningless or both. "Not everything that can be counted counts, and not everything that counts can be counted."[16]

Evaluation Research

All that we have discussed so far in this chapter is generally referred to as basic or pure research. But basic research, involving theories, hypotheses, and the like, is not the only type of research done by sociologists. A second type is called *applied research,* which deals more directly with social problems. In recent years, there has been an increasing need for a type of applied research called evaluation research.

Evaluation research is used to determine if current social programs set up to help people are doing what they were designed to do. Sociologists performing evaluation research are, in effect, "quality-control inspectors."[17] Programs that deal with such social needs as community health, legal services, housing, and welfare are expensive to run, and good intentions do not always guarantee effective delivery of services. Evaluation research can tell which programs work and which don't. Because a society has limited resources, it is important that we learn to use them effectively.

The primary difference between evaluation and basic research is in their ultimate goals, not in their methods. Evaluation researchers use any or all of the standard methods we have been discussing. But while basic research is used to develop theory, evaluation research is concerned with specific practical objectives. Out of evaluation research come decisions with direct social impact.

Analysis, Interpretation, and Publication

The process of analysis and interpretation is continuous. It does not begin when all the data are in. *Analysis* is the means of finding the relationships of variables, the connections between the data. They may be established by judicious reflection or by statistical correlation. The formulation of hypotheses anticipates the analysis. The

[16]William Bruce Cameron, *Informal Sociology: A Casual Introduction to Sociological Thinking* (New York: Random House, 1963), p. 13.

[17]H. W. Smith, *Strategies of Social Research: The Methodological Imagination* (Englewood Cliffs, N.J.: Prentice-Hall, 1975), p. 294.

more precise the hypotheses are and the better the operational definitions, the easier the analysis.

Interpretation relates the findings to theory. It suggests why the connections between data exist. Here most of the work goes on above the eyebrows. "Why?" is not automatically answered. The data must be interpreted if they are to add to the fund of social science knowledge and lead to further hypotheses and research.

Finally, the data and interpretations, complete with an account of procedures, must be made *public*. Research findings are often presented at professional meetings, published as books or as articles in scholarly journals, or filed as graduate theses. In each case they are available for scrutiny and criticism. The growth of science depends less on the cool objectivity of individual scientists than on the fact that their work is open to appraisal and use by others.

Summary

Some sociologists study world-wide phenomena, such as modernization. Others concentrate on smaller problems, such as juvenile delinquency. Most research is either positivist and modeled after research in the physical sciences, or humanistic, a qualitative approach stressing empathy and insight. Both approaches are useful; they may be complementary.

A science is more than a collection of facts. In sociology as in the natural sciences, data are organized by means of concepts, propositions, theories, models, and typologies. The functions of social science theory are to explain facts, guide research, sharpen our perception of reality, and serve as a conceptual framework for the systematic accumulation of knowledge.

The research process consists of several steps that tend to take place serially. Through open-minded exploratory research the sociologist becomes familiar with the area of his or her concerns and thus is more likely to choose a significant problem. The

investigator states this problem in terms of one or more hypotheses, which are tested by means of a sample survey, a case study, an experiment, or a combination of methods. The investigator collects data by various means, above all by asking questions, both formally and informally; by observing, as either a participant or a nonparticipant; and by taking notes and keeping records. All this is generally referred to as basic or "pure" research because it is designed to answer theoretical questions. Applied research, on the other hand, deals with specific social problems. One fairly new and potentially important form of applied research is evaluation research, which is designed to determine whether or not current social programs are really effective. Throughout this process the researcher analyzes and interprets data. The final account, with the researcher's conclusions, is made public so that other sociologists may criticize it and profit from it.

Glossary

Case study An in-depth examination of a person, group, or society.

Concept A word or phrase that represents a class of phenomena.

Data (singular *datum*) Empirically verified descriptions of phenomena; facts or findings.

Evaluation research Applied research used to measure the results of specific social programs.

Experiment Intervention in, or creation of, a situation in order to control or manipulate a variable and observe or measure the result.

Humanism The approach stressing empathy, role-taking and understanding the meaning, value, and purpose of human behavior.

Hypothesis A statement of a probable relationship between two or more variables.

Law A proposition referring to unvarying associations, universally agreed upon within a science.

Macrosociology The study of large-scale social phenomena such as total societies or worldwide trends.

Microsociology The study of small-scale social phenomena such as social roles and relationships among individuals.

Model An analogy that serves as the skeleton of a theory.

Nonparticipant observation Observation of a situation without personal involvement in it.

Participant observation The method by which the researcher both participates in and observes a situation.

Positivism The approach stressing use of objective information, experiments, and measurable data.

Proposition A statement of a relationship between two or more facts or concepts.

Sample survey A mass interview of a sample drawn from a certain population, measuring large numbers of people on a few characteristics.

Theory A set of systematically related propositions aimed at explaining phenomena.

Typology A way of grouping or classifying data and ideas.

Variable An action or attribute that can be measured or categorized.

part

2

Social Interaction

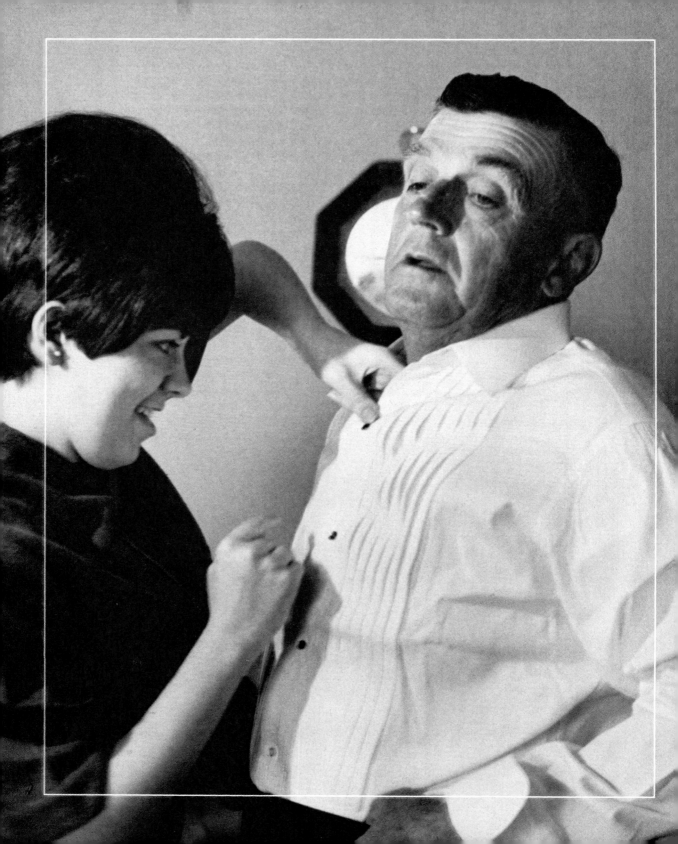

chapter

3

Culture

What is culture? In the general sense, **culture** is the learned portion of human behavior, the patterned ways of thinking, feeling, and doing that we ourselves have developed and made part of our environment. Culture adapts us to our physical environment, our biological nature, and our group life. In the specific sense, **a culture** is the distinctive way of life of a society, that combination of behavior and beliefs that makes one society different from another. Culture is learned and shared by members of the group, and it is presented to the growing child as the social heritage of past generations. Although highly stable, a culture changes through time, and elements of culture spread from group to group.[1]

In this chapter, we stress the learning and sharing of culture, which are made possible by our biological nature and group life. We pay particular attention to language as the basis of learning and sharing. We consider the major elements of culture: norms; knowledge, beliefs, and values; material objects; and social structure. Then we see how the major elements of culture are organized into systems and consider the relationship of culture integration to stability and change in society.

[1] Note that society, personality, and culture are all bound together in the human situation, and we can pull them apart only in the abstract, for analysis and study.

Culture as Learned Behavior

In our general definition of culture we stated that it is the learned portion of human behavior. All animals learn to some extent, but it is the human being's superlative learning abilities that make us the only animals able to acquire and build culture.

Human Learning Capacity

Our species, *Homo sapiens,* is different from all the other members of the animal kingdom in the capacity for learning, for communicating, and for manipulating physical objects. We have this capacity because we lack some biological traits that other animals have and because we have some traits that other animals lack.

For example, we are highly flexible and adaptable because we *lack* the fixed, inborn patterns of behavior and the specific biological adaptations to environment that other animals have. We are born with only a few reflexes or automatic responses, and each is attached to a specific stimulus. For example, our pupils contract in strong light, and our muscles contract when we feel pain. But aside from our few reflexes, we inherit no fixed response patterns.

On the other hand, much animal behavior is governed by *instincts*—inherited modes of

Drawing by Ton Smits; © 1968 The New Yorker Magazine, Inc.

"Me Homo Sapiens."

behavior that have a physiological basis, clearly determine behavior, and are universal in expression in the species.[2] Human behavior is not governed by instincts. Even the so-called maternal instinct is learned. Little girls and childless women may act maternally. The childbearing organs may stop working as a result of surgery or old age without changing a mother's love for her children, as would be expected if that love depended only on physiology. Moreover, some mothers reject their children, and infanticide (killing of unwanted babies) is practiced in some societies.

Few animals are fitted for more than one kind of climate, food supply, or life situation. These animals' remarkable adaptation to one set of surroundings makes them unable to live in many others. Our *lack* of specific biological adaptations, on the other hand, allows us to be highly flexible. We are free to create our own adaptations, in the form of culture, to different conditions.

On the positive side, what biological characteristics do we possess that help us to build and acquire culture, the human means of adapting to the environment? For one thing, we have a *prehensile* (grasping) *hand,* and a *thumb* that we can oppose to each of our fingers. Thus, we can manipulate and create with our hands. Our hands, moreover, are freed for doing work by our *upright posture.* We can stand on our two long legs because our *curved spine* and *arched foot* cushion the shock of walking and prevent injury to the brain. We also have *binocular vision* and can focus our eyes for different distances.

The great apes and monkeys, our distant cousins, share these attributes with us to some degree, and trained observers and experimental psychologists have seen them make and use simple tools to reach food. The use of tools is one of the *necessary* bases for society and culture—in fact, for the evolution of *Homo sapiens* from the prehuman forms of man. But it is not a *sufficient* basis for culture. Culture is based primarily on language, and only humans, it seems clear, have the biological traits that make it possible to speak and write and think abstractly. Thus, the essential biological differences between humans and the rest of the animal kingdom are those differences that make language possible.

Language and Culture

Language ability is the "real, incomparably important, and absolute distinction" between humans and other living organisms.[3] The very limited success of experiments in teaching chimpanzees to communicate in gestures

---

[2] We may note here that even in the lower animals much behavior is the result of early and rapid learning—but always in the presence of the object.

[3] George Gaylord Simpson, "The Biological Nature of Man," in S. L. Washburn and Phyllis C. Jay, eds., *Perspectives on Human Evolution* (New York: Holt, Rinehart & Winston, 1968).

or to recognize words and even create sentences with plastic tokens representing words only points up the enormous gap between human and nonhuman communication.[4]

THE NATURE OF LANGUAGE　Every culture has a "silent language" of meanings conveyed by gestures, postures, facial expressions, tones of voice, uses of time and space, and even smells.[5] But "language" usually means *words*. To define language more precisely, we must distinguish between natural and conventional signs.

Natural signs derive their meaning from concrete situations—the red glow of burning

[4] For an account of two such experiments, see John E. Pfeiffer, *The Emergence of Man* (New York: Harper & Row, 1969), pp. 396–401.

[5] Edward Hall, *The Silent Language* (Garden City, N.Y.: Doubleday, 1959), and *The Hidden Dimension* (Garden City, N.Y.: Doubleday Anchor Books, 1969).

This man's gesture and facial expression convey so much meaning that we can easily imagine his words. *Arthur Grace for Stock, Boston.*

wood, the falling barometer, the click of a Geiger counter in the presence of radioactive materials, a child's fever at the onset of an illness. Animal cries to warn of danger or to express anger, however, are somewhat different kinds of signs, for they communicate meanings to other animals and thus approach the nature of conventional signs, which are the building blocks of human language.

Conventional signs, or **symbols,** derive meaning from usage and mutual agreement. They are not naturally linked to the things they stand for. There is nothing about the nature of a carrot, for example, that demands it be called a "carrot." It can just as well be called a potato or a proverb if everyone in the group agrees. Moreover, different cultures can assign different meanings to the same words or gestures. For example, the gesture that Americans interpret as "Come here" is understood by Guatemalans as "Goodbye."

All words, then, are symbols. **Languages,** whether spoken or written, are systems of symbols that are voluntarily produced and have specific and arbitrary meanings in a given society. *Every* human society has a well-developed language. Anthropologists report no tribe with a vocabulary of fewer than 5,000 to 10,000 words, and many "primitive" languages have a grammatical structure far more complicated than that of "civilized" societies. How does language help to make culture possible?

FUNCTIONS OF LANGUAGE　Language is, first of all, a means of communication, of sharing thoughts and feelings. It is not the only one, nor is it perfect, but it is a remarkable instrument. It is also the main vehicle of thought or problem solving. We think in words, the significant symbols of our culture.

Language extends and enlarges experience in time. It allows us to remember the past and to imagine the future. These abilities are essential to morality and ethics. Similarly, language lets us go beyond the world of concrete sense experience. Words may stand for something as tangible as one's own hand; they may also stand for abstract ideas such as souls, culture, and honesty. Words enable us to visualize atoms, voodoo rituals, Napoleon's retreat from Moscow, and Hobbits. Without language we would have little art, and even less science.

A language guides, even "programs," perception and action. We tend to perceive only those things we have concepts for. A language names and classifies things and people in terms of their significance for behavior. A child learns that the persons called father, friend, enemy, priest, teacher, and customer are each to be treated differently, and that food is to be eaten and poison to be avoided. Eskimo children learn numerous words for different states of what we consider one substance—snow. The Hanunóo of the Philippine Islands have 92 words for rice, their staple food.

Often a language itself is emotionally charged. In bilingual Paraguay, Spanish is the neutral, necessary language of government, commerce, and schooling. But the old Indian language, Guaraní, is the language of home and friendship. Thus, a common language binds a social group together. To "speak the same language" is to have a strong bond, whether this language is professional jargon, a criminal's slang, or merely a set of attitudes toward the world.

Finally, language enables us to preserve and transmit culture, to build a cumulative tradition and pass it on.

The Necessity of the Human Group

We have said that culture is learned. To this we must add the essential words "from others." For culture is shared and is socially transmitted. It exists only in a human group. In spite of our biological potentialities and even our unique capacity to use language, none of us would acquire culture if we were not nurtured by a functioning social group. We would never use our hands to hit a home run or weave a basket, or our brain and vocal apparatus to learn a language. In the social scientist's sense of the word, we would not even be human.

The first years of our long childhood are especially crucial for our acquisition of culture and personality—in short, of human nature. Our slow maturation and extreme dependence on others[6] would be disadvantages for other animals, but they become advantages for us. During the long period of dependence, the human child is flexible, adaptable, and highly capable of learning. In addition, this helplessness compels the child to be in close and continued contact with those who can pass on the culture—parents, siblings, and the neighborhood play group.

Cases of people who lived in extreme isolation from social contacts help to prove that human nature is a product of social life. The case of Isabelle is an example.[7]

Isabelle was an illegitimate child, kept in seclusion for over six years. She spent most of her time in a dark room with her deaf-mute mother, with whom she communicated by means of gestures. When she was found, she exhibited the behavior traits of a 6-month-old child. Lack of sunshine and proper diet had left her with rickets, and she was thought to be deaf and feeble-minded.

Nonetheless, those in charge of her began a systematic program of training. After she finally began to respond, she went through the usual stages of socialization that a child experiences from ages 1 to 6 in proper

---

[6] Primates generally have a proportionately longer infancy than other mammals, mammals longer than reptiles, and so on.

[7] Kingsley Davis, *Human Society* (New York: Macmillan, 1949), pp. 204–220.

succession and far more rapidly than normal, learning in 2 years what ordinarily takes a child 6 years to learn. Only about 2 months after she first began to speak, she was putting sentences together, and by the eleventh month she was reading, writing, counting, and retelling stories. When she entered school, she took a normal part in all activities.

Her case shows how little purely biological resources contribute to personality, and how essential communication with other people is to the process of becoming human. Isabelle's rapid acquisition of culture invites speculation. Just how long could a person be kept in seclusion before losing the capacity to acquire culture? Davis speculates that it might be only 10 years, and certainly no more than 15.

The Elements of Culture

Suppose a member of a New Guinea tribe, trained as an anthropologist, is doing field work in a suburb of Minneapolis. Sitting in a large building with windows of many bright colors, he observes women in shiny gowns being escorted up the aisle by young men. Other men, mostly in dark suits, accompany them and sit on the long benches. Up in front a man in a long robe and two young men in dark suits and white shirts appear and stand looking down the aisle toward the entrance. Soft music has been playing; suddenly it is louder. Heads turn to watch several young women wearing long pastel gowns and carrying flowers move slowly up the aisle. The music changes. Everyone rises and there are whispers and rustles as a young woman in a long white gown, her head covered with a sheer white veil, comes slowly along the aisle on the arm of an older man. A complicated procedure ensues, with much bowing of heads and kneeling, and repeated incantations. One of the young men places

a gold ring on the third finger of the left hand of the woman in white. They kiss. There is another burst of music, and they come down the aisle smiling. As they enter a shiny black automobile, waving and smiling, some of the guests throw handfuls of rice at them. Others wipe away tears and blow their noses.

What does all this mean? Why are there tears as well as smiles? Why are old shoes and tin cans tied to the back of the automobile? What are the roles and relationships of the various actors? To answer such questions, the anthropologist from New Guinea may consult some of those present, attend similar affairs, and arrive at some generalizations.

In similar fashion, we must settle on some way of isolating and classifying the component elements of a total situation. While there are any number of ways to do it, we begin our explanation in terms of the following: norms or behavior patterns; understandings, including knowledge, beliefs, and values; material things and their meanings and functions; and social structure. Let us consider each of these elements of culture.

Normative Behavior

NORMS   Rules or patterns for behavior are called **norms.** Norms define what is expected, customary, right, or proper in a given situation. They are guides to what a person must, may, or should think, do, and feel. They are enforced by **sanctions,** rewards for correct behavior and punishments for behavior that is incorrect.

Norms are ideal patterns, carried in the minds of the participants in a culture as expectations of one's own and others' behavior. They are sometimes explicitly formulated as laws or regulations. Real behavior may deviate considerably from the norms. Consider American weddings. The wedding observed by our hypothetical New Guinea

MISS PEACH by Mell Lazarus

Courtesy of Mell Lazarus and Field Newspaper Syndicate.

anthropologist conformed to the ideal pattern, but many others do not. Our culture permits many variations—shotgun weddings, elopements, simple ceremonies before a justice of the peace, even weddings on horseback, on TV, in the woods, or at home before the fireplace.[8] For ease in discussion, norms are broken down into folkways, mores, technicways, fashions, fads, and laws.

FOLKWAYS Usages that govern most of our daily routine and ordinary contacts with other people are called **folkways.** They define what is socially correct and are enforced informally and nondeliberately (but nonetheless effectively). Violations of folkways, however, are not considered a threat to the group at large.

[8] In addition to the gap, great or small, between ideal and real behavior, there may be a gap between both of these and what people *think* others do—that is, *presumed behavior.* (Cara E. Richards, "Presumed Behavior: Modification of the Ideal-Real Dichotomy," *American Anthropologist* 71, No. 6 [Dec. 1969]: 1115–1116.) This distinction would seem to apply especially to actions, thoughts, and feelings that might be kept secret, such as stealing, violating sexual norms, doubting a religious doctrine, or hating one's mother.

Folkways may be purely arbitrary conveniences, like weights, measures, and monetary systems. The proper way to greet friends is a folkway, whether it be very casual (the "Hi!" Americans so often use) or very elaborate (the smiling, handshaking, shoulder-patting routine, accompanied by inquiries after one's health and that of one's entire family, typical of encounters between middle-class Latin Americans), or anything in between. Such greeting patterns are special rituals for behavior that we call *convention* and *etiquette.* Although they have no deep meaning, these sets of mutual expectations are convenient in social relations.

Other folkways define proper behavior in various roles. They distinguish "men's work" from "women's work," for example, and set up ideals for ladylike and gentlemanly conduct. Folkways also govern our general style of housing, dress, recreation, childrearing, courtship, and so on, and they also define what is beautiful and pleasant. They compose the large underlying body of custom that is strongly rooted in tradition. Folkways are often charged with considerable emotional fervor. Let a woman try to

Some weddings mix traditional rituals and non-traditional elements. *Frank Siteman for Stock, Boston.*

do a "man's work" in most societies; or worse, let a man be found doing a woman's! Most young women who don't wear a bra know how strong an emotional reaction this arouses in some of their elders.

Nonetheless, folkways change. Women now do many things that were once "men's work." They are doctors, professors, lawyers, ambassadors, and cab drivers. Britain has changed its ancient and unwieldy system of weights and measures to the metric system. (Americans, who pride themselves on being progressive, have fewer women in the professions than most other Western countries and are only now beginning to adopt the metric system.)

Folkways are effectively enforced by such rewards as praise, approval, and acceptance in a group, and by such punishments as ridicule, gossip, and nonacceptance. Most people do not want to be considered rude, queer, ignorant, or uncouth by the standards of their group. They want to belong, to be accepted. Therefore they conform, usually

without even thinking about alternative ways of behaving.

MORES Behavior patterns that are considered vital to the welfare of the group are called **mores.** They are not simply proper, like folkways; they are *obligatory.* Mores define right and wrong—morality and immorality. They may be expressed in terms of "must-behavior" ("Thou shalt"), or they may be negative ("Thou shalt not"). Negative mores are called *taboos.*

It is often said that mores can make anything right. Behavior that is sternly prohibited in one culture may be permitted or even encouraged in another. In some cultures it is moral to have several wives, to kill unwanted baby girls or helpless old people, to wear only a string of beads, or to take whatever has been left unguarded. Cannibalism has been considered moral in some cultures. In our culture, long-standing mores include wearing a certain amount of clothing, having only one husband or wife

40

at a time, and being loyal to our country. Bigamy, murder, theft, treason, and incest are among our taboos.

The sanctions that enforce the mores are invested with greater emotional content than are those that enforce the folkways. These emotions vary from one society to another. Those who violate the mores may feel shame if they are discovered and guilt whether or not they are discovered. They may be ostracized by their peers; they may be demoted, whipped, pilloried, excommunicated, stoned, imprisoned, exiled, or killed. Wrongdoing is punished not so much to teach the guilty person as to remind others that the mores must be obeyed. Unless individuals are held accountable for their behavior, the web of mutual expectations crumbles, and with it the social order.

Mores, like folkways, do change, but somewhat more painfully and slowly. Slavery, once considered moral, is now considered highly immoral in most cultures. But bitter conflict tore American society apart while the change in attitude was taking place. Periods of strictness regarding sexual relations have alternated with periods of permissiveness over the centuries of Western history.

TECHNICWAYS Some behavior patterns are so new and are so closely associated with

technological developments that they have none of the "right and proper" connotation of folkways. **Technicways,** as they are called, are simply the skills or habits associated with some material, utilitarian object. Most job skills in modern industrial society are technicways. There is, of course, a "right and proper" way to drive a car, type a manuscript, use a dishwasher, and land an airplane, but it is a matter of technique, rather than of cultural custom. In simple societies, the cultivation of crops is governed by custom and often imbued with sacred meanings. In modern societies, it is simply considered a matter of technical know-how.

The sanctions for the technicways are simple. Getting and keeping most jobs depends on mastery of technical skills. Modern life is full of delay, awkwardness, inconvenience—and yes, even ridicule—for those who cannot drive a car or tune a TV set.

FASHIONS A **fashion** is "any relatively short-lived folkway in a given society with which there is widespread, conscious, and voluntary conformity because of the status value associated with such conformity."[9] We usually think of fashions in women's clothing and may consider changes in style rather

[9]Thomas Ford Hoult, *Dictionary of Modern Sociology* (Totowa, N.J.: Littlefield, Adams, 1969), p. 131.

Technicways predominate over other norms in flying a plane. *Tyrone J. Hall for Stock, Boston.*

Streaking was an early 1970's fad. Students at a midwestern university got exposure to their fellow students, the news media, and the cold. *Daniel S. Brody for Stock, Boston.*

irrational and superficial. Herbert Blumer points out, however, that fashion operates in many areas of modern life. Fashion influences the content of the pure and applied arts, entertainment and amusement, child-raising, medicine, business management, literature, philosophy, political doctrine, and even science, including social science as well as the physical sciences. Those who fail to abide by fashion may be labeled oddballs, misfits, or out of date.

FADS Fashions that come and go very quickly are called **fads.** They are usually associated with amusement or adornment and have an irrational and intense fascination. Some hit songs become "golden oldies," but most go the way of "Mairzy Doats" and "Open the Door, Richard." Some slang phrases win a permanent spot in the dictionary, but what was "groovy" yesterday and is "far out" today will probably be something else tomorrow. During the 1930s college boys swallowed goldfish and sat on flagpoles. In the early 1960s they crowded into telephone booths and pushed beds along highways. In spite of their transitory nature, fads, like fashions, are part of culture, for they are learned and shared patterns of behavior.

LAWS In a small and unified society, informal sanctions are enough to keep most behavior in line with the norms. But in a complex society more formal norms and sanctions are necessary to coordinate the behavior of the society's members so that it can continue to function in an orderly fashion.

Laws are deliberately formulated rules of behavior enforced by a special authority. The sanctions that enforce them are specific and formal such as fines, damage penalties, imprisonment, and execution. These sanctions are carried out by designated personnel such as police, court and prison officials.

Laws serve several purposes. They enforce the mores accepted by the dominant cultural group in the society. They regulate new situations not covered by custom. They fill the gap when old ways fail in meeting a crisis. And they bring real cultural patterns more into line with the ideal patterns and dominant values.

For example, mores enforced by law in our society are monogamy, a man's responsibility for his wife and children, and the taboos against murder, theft, and rape. New situations not defined by custom arose with the invention of automobiles, airplanes, radio, and TV. The government had to pass laws to control the use of these new inventions—regulating traffic, licensing radio and television stations, and so on—to prevent chaos. Governments also enacted laws dur-

42

ing the Great Depression of the 1930s, when many people were hungry and ill-clothed, and old ways of regulating business and labor proved inadequate.

The fourth function—bringing real patterns more closely into line with ideal patterns—is served by any law aimed at social reform. For example, Americans believe in equality of opportunity, but in reality the white majority practices discrimination in housing, education, employment, and other fields. Fair employment acts and Supreme Court decisions against state-upheld discriminatory practices have been intended to bring real behavior closer to ideal patterns.

Laws are most effective when they are firmly grounded in the mores. Drinking, for example, was not considered immoral by a majority of Americans, so the prohibition law was a failure. Widespread use of marijuana is leading to a relaxation of laws against it.

Knowledge, Beliefs, and Values

Norms are based upon and justified by what people know, believe, and value. Each culture contains a body of **knowledge,** lore, or science that involves intellectual awareness and technical control of matter, time, space, and events. People in every culture also "know" a great many things that they seldom if ever formulate in so many words. "Thus one group unconsciously assumes that every chain of actions has a goal and that when this goal is reached tension will be reduced or disappear. To another group, thinking based upon this assumption is meaningless: they see life not as a series of purposive sequences but as made up of experiences which are satisfying in and of themselves, rather than as means to ends."[10]

Every culture provides some answers to the mysteries of human existence—our place in the universe, the meaning and purpose of life, the why of misfortune and death. These answers are expressed in religious doctrines, myths, legends, superstitions, philosophy, folklore, and proverbs. They are **beliefs** about what is not known, and—even in a highly sophisticated culture—*cannot* ultimately be known. They provide some relief from uncertainty and anxiety, and although regarded as just as real and true as science or lore, they are matters of faith and emotion rather than intellectual or scientific truths and realities.

Values, on the other hand, may be explicit or implicit. **Values** are the underlying standards or principles by which social and personal goals are chosen and the criteria by which ends and means are judged. Values determine what is considered desirable, important, and worthwhile; they explain and justify behavior.

But not all values are equally important. Cultural values are arranged in a scale on which several core values dominate and others are subsidiary. The core values determine the chief goals of the society or group, or at least justify and give meaning to them. All other values and goals tend to be measured in terms of these basic values and goals and to be directed toward their fulfillment. Harmonious values (such as work and material success) reinforce and complement one another. Contradictory values (humanitarianism and rugged individualism) check and limit one another.[11]

Members of a society are expected to accept its dominant values without question, and the values tend to endure because they are grounded in emotion. Indeed, a society may regard a verbal attack on its dominant

[10] Clyde Kluckhohn and William H. Kelly, "The Concept of Culture," in Ralph Linton, ed., *The Science of Man in the World Crisis* (New York: Columbia University Press, 1945).

[11] Robin M. Williams, Jr., *American Society: A Sociological Interpretation,* 3rd ed. (New York: Alfred A. Knopf, 1970), p. 463.

values as a greater threat than actual deviation from the norms they support.

Many of the most important values in a culture are implicit. They have an "of course" quality; they are taken for granted. Only philosophers, artists, and bohemians (or beatniks or hippies) put basic values into words, question them, defend or attack them, seek their sources, or urge their abandonment in favor of other values. Most people feel disturbed when their basic values are challenged, even though they can rarely express them articulately. To understand any society, nonetheless, we must determine what its members value most highly. How can we discover the values of a society or group?

There are a number of clues to the values implicit in a culture and to their importance. One is choice. What do members of the society choose to do, to say, and to buy? Do they carefully preserve old buildings because they value tradition, or do they tear them down because they value modernity and progress? What words recur in such rituals as national anthems, pledges of allegiance, and holiday speeches? Do these words glorify war, conquest, national superiority, faith, work, peace, progress, or ancestors? Do they stress past, present, or future? Do people spend their money on land, stocks, jewelry, charity, pilgrimages, or fun? But the yardstick of choice is tricky, mainly because people may say one thing and do another. Americans say they value education highly, but they spend more money each year on tobacco and liquor than they do on schools.

The folklore, history, religion, and literature of a culture are useful sources of information about values. How might each of these help a foreign anthropologist understand American culture? The legend of Paul Bunyan would suggest to him we admire things done on a big scale. Our elevation of Abraham Lincoln to the status of a culture hero is a clue to our values of honesty and compassion, traits most Americans believe Lincoln to have had. The Jewish and Christian religions offer the Ten Commandments as a set of norms expressing the values of worship of one god, love for our parents, chastity, honesty, respect for human life and personal property, and so forth. But, having absorbed all this, the foreigner would probably be bewildered by "sexploitation" movies, books, and magazines.

The system of rewards and punishments may be examined for further clues to values. What actions result in feelings of guilt, shame, or loss of self-respect? What infractions are most severely punished? In one society, a mother will spank a child for stealing but not for "sassing" her. In another, stealing is not considered immoral, but lack of respect for elders is unthinkable. As for rewards, professors are much more deferentially treated and saluted with titles in Europe and Latin America than in the United States. We can also ask who makes the most money in a society: statesmen? poets? movie stars? scientists? writers? doctors? business executives?

But it is one thing to examine a foreign culture and quite another to analyze our own. Even a trained anthropologist would find it almost impossible to discover all the values of his own culture. "If one could bring to the American scene a Bushman who had been socialized in his own culture and trained in anthropology, he would perceive all sorts of patterned regularities of which our anthropologists are completely unaware."[12]

Material Things and Their Meanings

Culture developed as people learned to use symbols and make things. We live surrounded by **material culture**—man-made things

[12]Clyde Kluckhohn, *Mirror for Man* (New York: Fawcett World Library, 1964), p. 36.

(artifacts) and man-made alterations in the natural environment. We can hardly do much more than contemplate our navels without their aid. As you read this, you may be using glasses to correct for nearsightedness, a lamp to enable you to see the paper, a desk to hold other necessary items, a chair to hold you in a comfortable position, a house to keep you warm and dry and give you privacy, clothing to keep you warm and respectable. Whether for protection, work, play, sustenance, beauty, or pleasure, our material culture has meaning for us. But the meanings of some aspects of it might be hard for the New Guinea anthropologist to arrive at.

Like actions, things are part of *overt* (visible) culture, but have no cultural meaning aside from the *covert* (not readily observable) ideas people share about their proper forms, uses, and purposes. Every culture has a concept of property that includes norms regarding ownership of things, how one gets and gives. Cultural norms and knowledge, including skills or technicways, dictate the

way things are to be made and used, while cultural beliefs and values give things meaning. For example, consider chairs. A chair may be seen as having a strictly utilitarian meaning. "A chair is to sit," in a child's pragmatic definition. It may have a purely aesthetic value, affording pleasure to the senses. Thus, a Louis XV chair may be preserved in a museum only to be looked at, never sat on. Chairs may have symbolic meaning or value, whether sacred (a papal throne), sentimental-emotional (Grandmother's rocker), or status-indicative (the chair at the head of the table). Things are so intimately interwoven with thought, feeling, and action that—much as we may abstract and analyze—we cannot imagine a specific culture without its distinctive material elements.

Many anthropologists, particularly those interested in cultural evolution and culture as adaptation, see technology as central to

The animal-drawn plow indicates that this society is at the agricultural level of technology. *Franklin Wing for Stock, Boston.*

the total pattern of a culture. The **technology** of a society is the body of knowledge and skills and tools and machines involved in producing goods (such as food and clothing) and services (such as transportation). So many other aspects of culture are related to technology that societies are often classified by levels of technology. One common classification distinguishes five levels: hunting and gathering societies, which depend mostly on muscular energy; horticultural societies, in which the digging stick and the hoe supplement muscle power; pastoral societies, which herd animals for food and clothing; agricultural societies, which turn over the soil with animal-drawn plows and irrigate and terrace land; and industrial societies, which apply scientific knowledge to production and thus harness such sources of energy as steam, electricity, and the atom.

Social Structure and Institutions

An important aspect of every culture is its **social structure,** the web of organized relationships among individuals and groups that defines their mutual rights and responsibilities. This structure is based on differentiation—at the very least on the basis of age and sex, and usually according to other criteria as well. Differentiation is expressed in the system of stratification and in the major social institutions of a society.

The system of **stratification** cuts across all the groups in a society, ranking relative positions in terms of prestige, power, and privilege. While these social levels are not organized into groups or units as are institutions, the consequences of stratification are very real and very important in all but the simplest communities and societies.

Most of the social structure of a society is found in its major institutions. **Institutions** are clusters of norms organized and established for the pursuit of some need or activity

of a social group, supported by the group's knowledge, beliefs, and values, as well as by meaningful aspects of the material culture. The pivotal institutions that are found in all cultures are the economic system, the government (or other agencies of group decision making and social control), religion, the family, education, and the expressionistic and aesthetic institutions, including recreation and the arts. Each of these institutions is an established way of meeting a central and universal need that arises out of our biological, psychological, and social nature.

Let us look at the cultural pattern of the family as a pivotal institution—as a cluster of folkways, mores, and laws that fulfills basic biological, psychological, and social needs. The functions of mating, reproduction, and childrearing are essential to the perpetuation of society, as are orderly gratification of our sexual drives and of our need for security and affection. The norms of courtship, marriage, and parenthood are designed to meet those needs in socially acceptable ways. In our culture, dates, weddings, and homes apart from the in-laws are among the folkways associated with marriage. Long-standing mores include monogamy, postmarital fidelity, and the rights and duties of husband and wife with regard to each other and to their children. A legal framework has grown up to support the mores: licenses, legal ceremonies, laws against bigamy and nonsupport, laws providing for divorce under certain conditions, laws against marriage of close relatives, and laws against marriage under a certain age without parental consent. The meaningful things associated with the institution range from rings worn on the third finger of the left hand through all the paraphernalia of housekeeping and childrearing, licenses, documents, insurance policies, keepsakes, photographs, and gifts.

The noun "institution" can be turned into a verb, "institutionalize." To institutionalize an activity is to formalize and stabilize it, thus recognizing it as the established way of doing something. A casual love affair is not institutionalized; a marriage is. A dip in the old swimming hole is not institutionalized; a swimming meet at the "Y" is. A friend's newsy phone call is not institutionalized; the evening paper is. If many segments of human behavior were not institutionalized, there would be very little order in modern society.

The Organization and Integration of Culture

Having looked at what culture is and what elements compose culture, we still have more to learn about this distinctly human aspect of our lives. How are cultural elements organized into a system? How do various members of a society share in its culture? What aspects of culture promote integration and harmony? These are the questions we now consider.

Traits, Complexes, and Patterns

A culture is more than the sum of the norms, understandings, and artifacts shared by a group. These elements of culture can be interrelated and organized in various ways, which give new meaning to the parts. One concept often used to indicate an interrelated group of culture elements, as we saw, is "institution." Another is a scheme based on traits, complexes, and patterns.

A **trait** is the smallest unit of culture—one item of behavior, one idea, or one object. Some traits tend to stand alone and are not deeply integrated with the central culture. Fads are an example. But most traits are related to others and fit into larger meaningful wholes called trait complexes. A number of complexes in turn come together to form a culture pattern.

A **complex,** then, is a system of interrelated traits that functions together as a unit. A **pattern** is a specific and enduring system of trait complexes. To return to the example of a wedding: The act of slipping a gold ring on the third finger of the left hand of a woman in a long white gown involves two culture traits—a norm of behavior and a meaningful object. These in turn are part of a trait complex called a wedding, which in turn forms part of the culture pattern we call "marriage and the family," an institution that includes such other complexes as courtship and childrearing.

Trait complexes are systematically organized and tend to persist and cohere as units. Each complex is limited to some one aspect of the culture. For example, weddings are linked to the family, monotheism to religion, plow agriculture to subsistence. Some complexes, such as marriage and the family, have a great deal of coherence. We can trace such complexes through history and compare them across cultures, because their basic plan has remained relatively unchanged over long periods.

It is not only differences in traits, but differences in the organization of traits that makes one culture different from another.

A culture consists of elements or single traits, but the significance of a culture is less in its inventory of traits than the manner of integration of the traits. . . . By simple analogy, a mason may take two identical piles of bricks and equal quantities of mortar. Yet according to the manner in which he lays his bricks, he may produce a fireplace or a garden wall.[13]

Cultural Systems

Because traits are interrelated and organized into complexes and patterns, we may think

[13] Harry L. Shapiro, ed., *Man, Culture, and Society* (New York: Oxford University Press, 1956), p. 177.

of culture in terms of systems. At one extreme, the systems approach sees every culture trait as ultimately related to every other, so that one could begin an analysis of a culture with any trait in any sector and find threads leading to all the rest of the culture. This extremely "holistic" approach is typical of some *functionalists,* who insist that every item of culture contributes in some way to fulfilling the needs of society, and that no trait can be understood outside of its full context.

A more realistic approach recognizes that there is indeed a "strain to consistency" among cultural traits, but that "a single culture may comprise a very large number of deeply contradictory, contrasting, discrepant themes."[14] Traits are best understood in context. A doll is one thing if it is a child's toy, quite another if it is a tool for witchcraft, a fertility symbol, or an item in a collection of historical interest. But traits may also be conveniently abstracted from their context and compared to similar traits from other cultures for various purposes. Furthermore, the interrelatedness of various aspects of culture may be rather loose and distant, and some spheres of activity may be relatively independent. In modern society particularly, people tend to regard religion, art, and economic activity, for example, as very separate things.

Cultural Integration

The term **cultural integration** refers to the extent to which various people share common norms, understandings, and material cultures. One way of considering the extent of sharing is by measuring the scope of a cultural system.

Thus, we may speak of the "great tradi-

[14] Margaret Mead, *Anthropology: A Human Science* (Princeton, N.J.: D. Van Nostrand Company, 1964), p. 135.

tions," such as Western civilization. By "Western civilization" we mean the ways of life common to Europe, the modern sector of the Western hemisphere, and Australia, which are rooted in the Greco-Roman and Judeo-Christian traditions. Western civilization obviously embraces a number of societies with different national traditions and languages. We may also speak of "culture areas," in which a number of neighboring societies have certain elements in common. This is a useful way of classifying various American Indian cultures, for example.

When we speak of a culture, however, we ordinarily refer neither to the great cultural traditions of the world nor to geographic areas, but rather to the way of life of a **society,** a group with one dominant language that lives within clear territorial boundaries. This may be as small as a hunting-gathering band or as large as a modern nation-state. Modern societies are characterized by *heterogeneity*—that is, they include many different groups that have their own feelings of identity and unity, their own distinctive norms, and often a distinctive material culture as well. These groups may be called **subsocieties,** and their ways of life **subcultures.** In American society, class status, ethnic background, rural or urban residence, religious affiliation, and geographic region are major subcultural influences that shape the ways of life of various Americans. Thus, we might speak of the urban middle-class Jewish subculture or of the rural Southern black subculture as being distinct forms of American culture.

Subcultures may also be cross-cultural. Similar groups in several societies may feel a sense of identity and have similar norms and understandings. The international "jet set" and the youth counterculture are current examples. Further, a person may belong to more than one subculture—in fact, as many as any one sociologist cares to distinguish. One may, for example, be urban,

When discovered in the Philippines a few years ago, the Tasaday tribe was completely isolated from the rest of the world. It included only 24 members, but constituted a society, nonetheless. *Magnum.*

wealthy, intellectual, and of Puerto Rican ancestry. The concept of subculture has proved useful to sociologists studying various groups and associations such as juvenile gangs, hippies, hospitals, and convents.

Within both the society and the subcultural group, different members share the culture in varying degrees. Theoretically, all of the culture is there for us to learn, but we will not learn all of it by any means. Variations in innate capacity and motivation to learn limit participation in a culture, particularly when the culture is literate and complex and when cultural definitions of status limit the opportunity to learn. Even in a simple, primitive society people's age and sex limit their participation in the culture. Ralph Linton classified the customs and understandings of a culture into three categories—universals, specialties, and alternatives—according to how widely they are shared among the members of a society.

Universals are the customs and understandings shared by all normal adult members of the society. There are many universals in a simple and unified society, fewer in a larger and complex one. They include the basic ideas of how people are to behave toward one another and toward property. Language is also a universal in every group with a distinct culture or subculture. The most important universals are the core values of a culture.

Specialties are understandings and patterns of behavior shared by particular kinds of people. They are born with or grow into some of these patterns. Others are chosen voluntarily. In most societies, sex is the clearest basis of specialization and differentiation, not only in biological roles such as childbearing, but also in culturally determined personality differences and in the division of labor. In many societies, age groups are clearly distinguished, with "rites of passage" occurring at the various stages to signify new privileges and obligations. In some, such as the traditional caste system of India, each status group has its specialties.

More clearly voluntary, in most societies, are occupational specialties and particular recreational, scientific, artistic, or academic interests. Although many of these specialties require such a high degree of knowledge and skill that others cannot share them without long training, nonspecialists have the culturally defined right to expect certain definite results from specialists—such as doctors and cooks. Like universals, most specialties are accepted by the members of the society, for they allow the development of skills that produce greater satisfactions in the forms of goods and services than would be possible without specialization.

Alternatives, like specialties, are not common to all members of a society. They differ from specialties in that they are not even common to any special categories such as occupations. Rather they are acceptable ways of thinking, believing, and doing from which the members of the society may choose more or less freely. A couple may develop its own patterns for sex relations and childrearing, for example, from within the broad limits set by modern society. Choices between or among mutually exclusive alternatives are more limiting. A person cannot be both a Roman Catholic priest and a husband.

But what about the ideas and behavior patterns a person develops for himself, without learning them from some group or category of which he is a member? *Individual peculiarities,* although frequently learned, are not shared and thus are not a part of the culture. For example, you may have learned an abnormal fear of thunder because of some harrowing experience, but almost everyone else in the society considers thunder harmless. In general, the cultures of complex societies are less uniform and predictable than the cultures of simple societies, which embrace a larger proportion of universals.

Sources of Cultural Integration

Margaret Mead, in speaking of the discrepancies and contradictions in every culture, says they do not matter "provided some over-all recognition of commonality or community makes each individual member feel that all these behaviors, in spite of their diversity, are parts of the same over-all culture to which he gives his allegiance."[15] We may look, then, for the sources of cultural integration in those things that produce feelings of belonging, unity, security, and allegiance to a system.

Integration is fostered by consensus regarding certain basic and dominant ideas, beliefs, and values concerning the nature of things, the purpose of existence, and the comparative desirability of various actions or states of being. These dominant understandings cluster in integrative principles or themes and in cultural myths and are expressed in symbols, rituals, and ceremonies that appeal to the emotions.

INTEGRATIVE THEMES OR PRINCIPLES   Cultural patterns tend to be integrated around *central themes* or principles—the fundamental attitudes, perceptions, or preoccupations of a society. While many themes are expressed in such overt patterns as folklore, others are implicit and operate largely on the unconscious level. They are the taken-for-granted premises of each culture.

According to Ruth Benedict, in some societies all patterns express one central principle. Thus, Pueblo Indians tended to orient all their cultural patterns around the value of moderation, an "Apollonian" view of life. In their search for a relationship with a supernatural power, they learned to practice their rites in mild and orderly fashion, faithfully rendering traditional prayers. In contrast, the Pacific Northwest Indians and many other North American tribes valued excess carried to the point of frenzy, the "Dionysian" view. The Kwakiutl of the Pacific Northwest, for example, sought visions through fasting, self-torture, and violent dancing.[16]

But few cultures are so dominated by one integrative principle. In most, several principal themes limit and balance one another. Morris Opler mentions three themes of Chiricahua Apache culture: "Men are physically, mentally, and morally superior to women"; "Long life and old age are important goals"; and the principle of "validation by participation." Each is expressed in many patterns, but where two conflict one must give way somewhat to the other. Thus, alth-

[15] *Ibid.*

[16] *Patterns of Culture* (Boston: Houghton Mifflin, 1934), pp. 78–87, 175–182.

ough the old are respected, the principle of "validation through participation" demands that leaders must be physically fit and active as well as wise and experienced. Most leaders, therefore, are middle-aged men.[17]

MYTHS, SYMBOLS, RITUALS, AND CEREMONY
Another way of looking at the integrative principles or values of a culture is to examine their embodiment in myth and their expression in symbols, rituals, and ceremonies. A cultural **myth** embodies a society's values, hopes, and fears. It is more or less sacred, being grounded in emotion and taken on faith. We may identify three levels of myth: (1) stories or legends; (2) myths of the origins and place of humankind in the universe, and of the events of each life and of the society as a whole. And, (3), there are the more abstract beliefs and values that are true central myths, the taken-for-granted assumptions, of a culture.

The simplest kind of myth is a story, with or without a factual basis, that expresses some one cultural value in terms of a folk hero or god, who represents some virtue or flaw. Such myths are built not only around history book heroes but also about those who embody the dominant values of a period, whether they are business titans, kings, movie stars or other popular idols, or religious figures. The myth of George Washington and the cherry tree brings the value of honesty down to a child's level of understanding, provides a model, and appeals to emotion as well as reason. Similarly, Nathan Hale stands for patriotism; Andrew Carnegie for thrift, hard work, and material success; Thomas Edison for technological progress. Minerva represented wisdom;

Diana, chastity. Benedict Arnold means treason, Cain murder, Narcissus vanity.

Myths also evolve around the origins of a people, the great events in their history, and the recurrent crises of the life cycle. These myths are often expressed in symbols, dramatized in rituals and ceremonies, and celebrated in festivals. The British regard their queen as a symbol of their highest values and dearest traditions. To Soviet citizens the embalmed body of Lenin symbolizes the Communist Revolution. The hammer and sickle, the Stars and Stripes, the Union Jack, the tri-color—each flag has a profound and emotion-packed meaning for the citizens of the country it represents. An American child internalizes our nationalist myth during the ritual and ceremony of raising the flag, reciting the Pledge of Allegiance, and singing "The Star-Spangled Banner."

Ritual and ceremony are powerful means of sustaining the social order, for they dramatize traditional beliefs and values and invest them with emotional content. A **ceremony** is a formal, dignified procedure that impresses observers and participants with the importance of an occasion. A wedding, a funeral, a church service, even a Boy Scout Awards Night are lifted above ordinary events by ceremony. Ceremony, being out of the ordinary, satisfies what seems to be a basic human need—escape from boredom.

The most distinctive element of ceremony is usually **ritual**—a formal, rhythmic series of symbolic acts that are repeated on appropriate occasions. The wedding procession, the exchange of vows, the giving of rings, the smashing of the wine glass, or the nuptial blessing and the pronouncement that the two are now husband and wife—whatever the religion, its wedding ceremony is as stylized as classical ballet. Like rituals surrounding birth, initiation or confirmation, and death, the marriage ceremony restates a culture's definition of the people's relationship to nature, society, and the super-

---

[17] Morris E. Opler, "Themes as Dynamic Forces in Culture," *American Journal of Sociology* 51, No. 3 (Nov., 1945): 192–206.

natural. Each of these rituals dramatizes the meaning of a major crisis in the life cycle. Participants in such rituals may experience awe, gratitude, and rapture, and a renewed sense of personal identity and of group belonging.

Festivals—times or days of joyous feasting and celebration—also contribute to cultural integration. Christmas, Thanksgiving, and Easter, secularized and commercialized as they are, still provide common bonds, annually reinforced. The female puberty rites of the San Blas Cuna of Panama involve feasting, drinking, and dancing, as well as chants recounting the myths about tribal origins and the life cycle.

CENTRAL CULTURAL MYTHS It is on a third, and probably the most important, level that the concept of myth is most elusive. The great *central myths* of a culture are pervasive complexes of values and beliefs that are generally so deep that they are rarely if ever verbalized, but are experienced unconsciously and taken for granted. It is often difficult to perceive the prevailing myths

until they have disintegrated and are being replaced by new ones.

What are some central cultural myths? Psychoanalyst Rollo May sees the main myths of modern, Western societies as rationalism and individualism, along with nationalism, competition, and the faith that problems can be solved by amassing and analyzing technical data. These replaced the Christian myth that prevailed through the Middle Ages, and they in turn are being questioned as people seek new values: a myth of one world, collectivism, cooperation, and the value of inner or subjective experience.[18]

May sees myth as essential to social integration and mental health. Myths give meaning and value to experience by answering the questions: Who are we? Where did we come from? Where are we going, and why?—for the society as a whole as well as for individual members. People choose their goals by the myths in which they place their

[18] Rollo May, "Reality beyond Rationalism," presented at Concurrent General Session of the 24th National Conference on Higher Education, Chicago, March 3, 1969.

Even the ritual of "graduation" from kindergarten develops a sense of personal identity and group belonging. *J. Berndt for Stock, Boston.*

faith. The myth system interprets reality and gives people a sense of identity in relation to others and to the world. Myths help a person to handle anxiety, face death, deal with guilt, and find an identity and a purpose. Through its expression in rituals, myth helps people negotiate the crises of life.[19]

Integration and Adaptability

Is a highly integrated culture a good thing for a society? On one hand, a harmonious culture tends to produce a sense of security and satisfaction among its members (unless the culture itself, like that of the Dobuans of New Guinea, contains elements that make them feel hostile and insecure).[20] But, on the other hand, thorough integration may mean that change, even if it begins in only one aspect of culture, may cause the whole culture to disintegrate like a house of cards. When the British abolished headhunting in Melanesia, for example, the results were disastrous. Why? Headhunting was the center of social and religious institutions. It pervaded the whole life of the people. They

needed to go on headhunting expeditions because they needed heads to propitiate the ghosts of their ancestors on many occasions, such as making a new canoe, building a house for a chief, or making a sacrifice at the funeral of a chief. Although their expeditions lasted only a few weeks, and fighting itself only a few hours, preparations lasted for years. With the integrating pattern of their lives denied them, the Melanesians lost interest in living.[21]

Apparently a culture with a lower degree of integration, in which the various themes and patterns are less perfectly coordinated, adapts more easily to circumstances that bring about change. In a society in which there is very little harmony and integration of cultural norms and understandings, however, there will be much conflict, confusion, waste, insecurity, and social unrest. When the prevailing myths lose their power, many people become disoriented, alienated, and unsure of their identities and goals. The disintegration of the myth system is a sign (but not a cause) of disunity and trouble. But people can create new myths and symbols to meet new needs.

Summary

Lacking the instincts and specific biological adaptations of other species, the human being is flexible and adaptable. The crucial difference between us and other creatures is our capacity for speech and thought.

Every society has a silent language of natural signs, which are linked to concrete situations, as well as conventional signs, which derive their meaning from usage. Language, a system of conventional signs, is a means of communication and a vehicle

for thought. Language allows us to extend our experience in time and foresee consequences. It affects the way people perceive the world, binds groups together, and allows them to transmit culture.

Culture is learned. Despite our biological capacities, we cannot acquire human nature unless we are nurtured by a functioning social group. The first years of life are especially crucial in the acquisition of culture.

The four basic elements of culture are

---

[19] The *New York Times* (Nov. 25, 1968): C 49.
[20] Ruth Benedict, *Patterns of Culture*, pp. 78–87.

[21] W. H. R. Rivers, ed., *Essays on the Depopulation of Melanesia* (New York: Macmillan, 1923), pp. 101–102.

norms; knowledge, beliefs, and values; material things; and social structure. Every society has a system of norms or patterns for behavior and rewards and punishments to enforce them. These norms include folkways defining right and proper ways of doing things, and mores defining right and wrong, moral and immoral behavior. Especially important in modern industrial society are technicways, or skills and habits associated with the use of things; laws, or formal rules enforced by a special authority; fashions, relatively temporary folkways operating in areas of behavior where various possibilities are not subject to objective testing; and fads, superficial and transitory patterns typical of amusement and adornment. Knowledge defines reality; beliefs provide answers to the mysteries of human existence; values, or guiding principles establish the relative desirability and worth of various goals.

Both observable actions and material things may be regarded as overt expressions of the covert ideas, beliefs, and habits of a society's members. Neither actions nor things have meaning apart from the covert aspects of culture.

Societies may be classified according to the level of technology—the body of knowledge, skills, and material things involved in producing goods and services.

Social structure is the web of organized relationships among individuals and groups that defines their mutual rights and responsibilities. Its main features are a system of stratification, or ranking, and a set of institutions.

An institution is a cluster of norms, organized and established for the pursuit of some need or activity of a social group, and supported by the group's knowledge, beliefs, and values, as well as by meaningful aspects of its material culture. The chief means of organizing social relationships in any society are found in six pivotal institutions: marriage and the family, the economic system, the political system, education, religion, and the expressive institutions of play and the arts.

Culture traits are organized into interrelated complexes, which in turn are part of larger cultural patterns. In general, the more completely integrated a culture, the less adaptable it is, although no culture is ever totally static.

The scope of cultural systems varies depending on whether we are concerned with traditions, such as Western civilization, geographic areas in which several societies share a number of cultural patterns, societies as large as nation-states and as small as hunting-gathering bands, or the subcultures of groups within a society. Participation in culture and the degree to which items are shared may be analyzed in terms of universals, specialties, alternatives, and individual peculiarities.

A society must have a certain minimum of fit and harmony among its elements: sufficient agreement on overt behavior patterns and procedures to permit functioning, and sufficient consensus regarding beliefs and values to promote a feeling of unity and belonging. The integrative values and beliefs of a culture are embodied in myth, expressed in symbols, rituals, and ceremonies, and celebrated in festivals. Myth has a sacred quality, being grounded in emotion and taken on faith. A myth may embody one value in a folk hero or god. It may give a society a sense of its origins and its mission and provide individuals with answers to questions of identity, especially at crises in the life cycle, or it may consist of a deep, underlying complex of values and beliefs that are taken for granted.

Glossary

Beliefs Answers to the mysteries of human existence, based on faith and emotion rather than reason and science.

Ceremony A formal, dignified procedure that impresses participants and observers with the importance of an occasion.

Complex A system of interrelated culture traits that functions together as a unit

Conventional signs or symbols Those signs that derive meaning from usage and mutual agreement and are not naturally linked to the things they stand for (e.g. words and gestures).

Cultural integration The sharing of common norms, understandings, social structures, and material traits; a matter of scope and degree of sharing

Culture The learned portion of human behavior

A culture The distinctive way of life of a society.

Fads Fashions that come and go very quickly.

Fashions Shortlived folkways with status value that motivates widespread conformity.

Festivals Times of joyous feasting and celebration.

Folkways Norms of proper behavior that govern most of our daily routine and ordinary contacts with others and are informally enforced.

Institutions Clusters of norms organized and established for the pursuit of some need or activity of a social group.

Knowledge Lore or science that involves intellectual awareness and technical control of matter, time, space, and events as well as unconscious assumptions underlying behavior.

Language A system of symbols that are voluntarily produced in speech and possibly in writing and have specific and arbitrary meanings in a given society.

Laws Deliberately formulated norms enforced by a special authority.

Material culture Man-made things (artifacts) and man-made alterations in the environment.

Mores Norms of obligatory behavior considered vital to the welfare of the group, including taboos on prohibited behavior; heavily charged with emotional meaning.

Myth The embodiment of a society's values, hopes and fears in stories and legends; in conceptions of the origins and place of human beings in the universe and of the events of each life and society; and the underlying taken-for-granted assumptions central to a culture.

Natural signs Those signs that derive their meaning from concrete situations, e.g. the red glow of burning wood.

Norms Rules or patterns for behavior.

Pattern A specific and enduring system of trait complexes.

Ritual A formal, rhythmic series of symbolic acts repeated on ceremonial-occasions.

Sanctions Rewards for observing the norms and punishments for violating them.

Social Structure The web of organized relationships among individuals and groups that defines their mutual rights and responsibilities.

Society A group with one dominant language that lives within clear territorial boundaries.

Stratification The system that ranks individuals and groups in various levels according to prestige, power, and privilege.

Subculture The way of life of a subsociety.

Subsociety A distinctive cultural group within a society.

Technicways The skills or habits associated with material utilitarian objects.

Technology The body of skills and knowledge, and tools and machines, involved in producing goods and services.

Trait The smallest unit of culture—one item of behavior, one idea, or one object.

Values The underlying standards or principles by which social and personal goals are chosen and the criteria by which means and ends are judged.

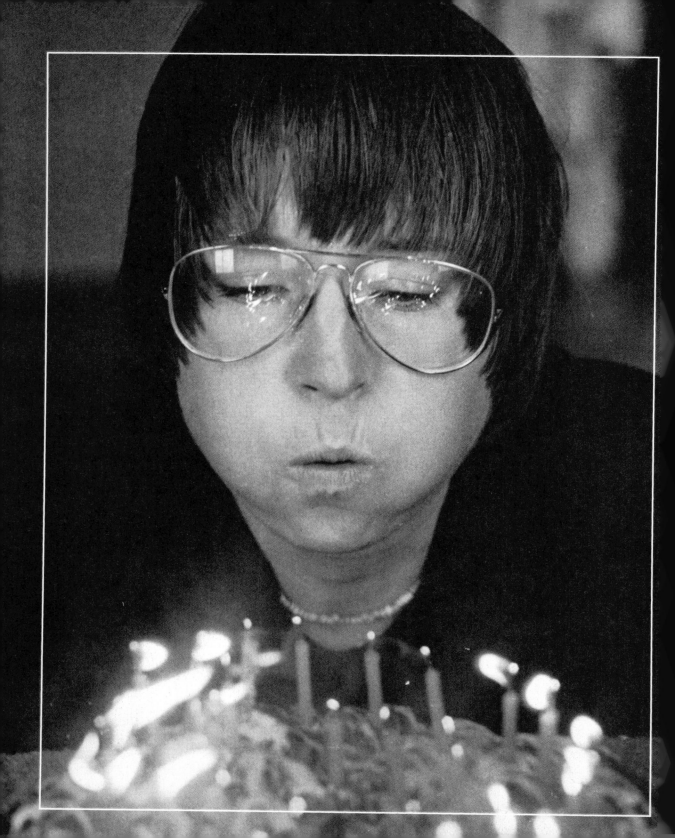

chapter

4

The Importance of Culture

Habit has been called "the shackles of the free." Almost all our minor actions are patterned so that we are barely conscious of them, and major decisions, like the choice of a mate, are more patterned than most of us realize. If we think about the impact of culture on our lives, we can hardly avoid wondering at its power and pervasiveness.

In this chapter we ask: How does culture adapt people to their physical environment? Does it ever work against survival and adaptation? How does culture foster group cohesion and survival? How is culture related to individuals? Does it free us or control us, or both? How does it encourage and impede understanding of other cultures?

The Functions of Culture

No list of needs and of culture elements that satisfy them is more than a device. There is no one-to-one correspondence between a culture element and the purpose it serves. Culture is a complex and interrelated whole, and any one aspect may have many meanings for the complex human beings who interact in a society. To take a simple example, a birthday cake is food in the strictest sense, but to classify it as serving the need for nutrition is obviously ridiculous. It also gives pleasure to children and perhaps ego gratification to the person who baked it and is part of a ritual celebration marking what Americans (but not all peoples) see as a special day in life.

Furthermore, when we say "culture does this and that," we do not mean that culture is an entity in itself, something superhuman that pushes people around. It is always *people* who behave according to cultural patterns and understandings, deviate from them, enforce them by means of sanctions, and pass them on to their children. Even so, culture is a useful abstraction for the regularities in the behavior of members of a group. In a more general way, we think of it as the way we adapt to our physical environment, the imperatives of our group life, and our biological and psychological nature.

Culture as Adaptation to the Environment

Culture is mankind's survival kit. The human being is born with only very generalized capacities and tendencies to action. "Between what our body tells us and what we have to know in order to function, there is a vacuum we must fill ourselves, and we fill it with information (or misinformation) provided by our culture."[1]

Culture extends our powers and senses. Stone hammers and bulldozers are extensions of our hands, tamed horses and 747s of our feet, spectacles and television of our

[1] Clifford Geertz, "The Impact of the Concept of Culture on The Concept of Man," in Yehudi A. Cohen, ed., *Man in Adaptation: The Cultural Present* (Chicago: Aldine, 1968), pp. 16–29.

58

eyes, telephones and radio of our ears, books and newspapers of our speech, abacuses and computers of our brain. But none of these extensions is specifically linked to biological features; all can be changed as conditions change. The slow processes of biological evolution have been almost entirely replaced by swift and cumulative cultural adaptation.

People can find food, clothing, and shelter in even the harshest environment. Our clever hands, fertile brain, and capacity for speech combine to enable us to make tools and weapons, discover fire and metals, invent machines and containers, domesticate plants and animals. Language enables us to accumulate information, generation after generation, in an ever-growing storehouse of knowledge from which our descendants can draw.

This versatility more than makes up for the fact that human beings are weak, slow-moving animals. It has allowed us to dominate and use the strength and speed of the horse and then to invent the jet plane and space capsule. Our capacities make up for our thin skin and the exposure of our highly vulnerable internal organs when we stand upright. We learn to utilize skins, fibers, bark, wood, stone, sod, leaves, reeds, sand, mud, and metals for housing and clothing and eventually to live in gas-heated skyscrapers and wear Dacron suits. Perhaps some day we will use this same versatility to adapt ourselves to life on another planet—unless we choke on poisoned air or find ourselves back in a cave hiding from a radioactive cloud, victims of our own inability to control the forces leading to war. Cultures or, more strictly speaking, culture-bearing animals not only solve problems, they create them. Not everything in our survival kit serves the purpose.

Culture and Society

If culture in the general sense is the means of adaptation for the species as a whole,

what consequences does each specific culture have for the society? Ralph Linton warned that we cannot speak of societies as having needs of their own apart from the needs of their individual members.[2] Yet many cultural patterns are oriented toward the maintenance of society rather than the satisfaction of individual needs. If a society is to function successfully and endure through time, certain conditions must be fulfilled. What are they?

First, individual psychological and biological needs must be met, and pivotal institutions (the family, religion, education, and so on) emerge to do so. Second, new members, usually newborn babies, must be socialized, indoctrinated with the social values, and trained to occupy positions in the social structure. Third, behavior must be guided toward what is socially desirable, through norms and sanctions. Every society must have a system of control to regulate the expression of aggression, sexual behavior, and property distribution. There is no known society where people are allowed to rape, rob, or kill.

Fourth, for individuals to function in a society, interaction must be largely regular and predictable. There is always an element of uncertainty in interaction, but it is minimized insofar as the participants accept established norms or arrive at a consensus on new ones.

Fifth, the members of society must feel they belong to the group and are motivated to act according to its rules. The constellation of beliefs and values we call myth tends to meet this imperative. It sets social and individual goals, gives a sense of origin and purpose, and invests experience with meaning and value.

All these conditions—the institutionalized meeting of individualized needs, indoctrina-

---

[2] *The Cultural Background of Personality* (New York: Appleton-Century-Crofts, 1945), pp. 23–24.

tion of new recruits, social control of behavior, predictability of interaction, and the sense of belonging and purpose—enable a society to function and endure. Even this generalization, however, has exceptions. People continue to fight, kill, get sick, and go mad. Some cultures have actually led to the extermination of the society. The Kaingang of Brazil, for example, had a cult of force and blood revenge that led to their progressive annihilation, and the Shakers, who prohibited sexual relations, failed to recruit enough new members to keep their group going.

Culture and the Individual

The newborn baby enters a social group that already has a culture. He learns it almost as naturally as he breathes, for his parents, siblings, and playmates transmit its patterns to him as if there were no others. Partly through deliberate instruction, but largely through unconscious imitation and absorption of value orientations and even of ways of walking and standing, he adopts the

The baby enters a social group that already has a culture. *Raimondo Borea for Editorial Photocolor Archives, Inc.*

society's ways. For most of us the main form and content of our personalities reflect that early experience. Let us consider what culture does for a person.

The culture provides an established pattern for satisfying biological needs. We do not need to work out our own ways to keep warm, to satisfy our hunger and thirst, to fulfill our sexual desires, to get our rest. Patterns that regulate and channel these elemental functions are present in the culture and guide us from infancy on. We are taught how, when, where, and with whom we may satisfy these needs. We learn the diet pattern of our culture and the modesty and hygiene of elimination. A person

. . . takes the bait of immediate personal satisfaction, and is caught upon the hook of socialization. He would learn to eat in response to his own hunger drive, but his elders teach him to "eat like a gentleman." Thus, in later years, his hunger drive elicits a response which will not only satisfy it but do so in a way acceptable to his society and compatible with its other culture patterns.[3]

Besides providing patterns for satisfying our elemental needs, each culture sets goals and creates desires that come to be regarded as needs. Group living appears to create a need to belong, to feel accepted, and this is an effective basis for socialization to the norms of the group. Some desires are not biologically beneficial, even though a person's need—for cigarettes and alcohol, for instance—may seem just as strong to him as his requirements for food or sleep. In a culture where aesthetic satisfaction, success, spiritual commitment, or wealth is highly valued, the desire of some people for these things is often stronger than their sexual drives. Even physical survival itself may seem less important than honor or freedom or country.

[3] Linton, *The Cultural Background of Personality*, p. 25.

The language of each culture is a distinctive way of forming a person's perception of reality. As language is learned the child comes to perceive and interpret the world largely from its perspective and within its limitations. The language guides one not only to observe the world in a certain way, but also to express oneself and react to it in a certain way. Various societies perceive reality differently. Dorothy Lee compared the concepts of the Trobriand Islanders concerning the relationships of events to our own.[4] The Trobrianders have no tenses—no linguistic distinction between past and present—nor do they arrange activities and events according to causes, or means and ends. In contrast, we are extremely conscious of time and use many tenses to express various time relationships. We are also conditioned to think of each event as followed by another in a series of stages leading to some goal or climax. To the Trobrianders, each stage has its own meaning. For example, they have a different name for a yam at each of its stages. When it is ripe and round it is no longer considered the same yam as when it was small and green.

Cultural patterns guide and channel our interactions with others. Culture defines situations and outlines expectations for whatever role we play. Children learn how good sons and daughters act—and a good father, a good friend, a good teacher, a good warrior. At a wedding we are expected to behave in one way; at a funeral, in another. We greet friends, discipline our children, and meet strangers with actions prescribed by the culture. The rules of social interaction help us adapt to the group.

In a more general way, we may say that institutions channel human actions into patterned grooves, much as instincts channel the actions of insects. They present a limited number of alternatives and bar other options so effectively that to the members of any one society the available patterns seem to be the only right and proper ones. In our society, for example, a young man attracted to a woman does not think of making her one of a harem, or of rejecting her because his parents have chosen another mate for him. Our system of norms lays out a path for him.

As we said in discussing myths, culture gives meaning and value to experience. It defines what the child should regard as normal and abnormal, good and bad, pleasant and unpleasant, beautiful and ugly, interesting and uninteresting. It even defines the emotions a person should feel in different situations. People must *learn* to love flags, worship stones, and feel sexual jealousy. In some Moslem societies, for example, a person is grievously insulted if someone touches him with a shoe or with his left hand. Cultural patterns also guide the expression of emotions. In one society loud voices and violent motions express anger. In another the only visible sign of anger may be a cold stare through narrowed eyelids. In some societies it is proper for men to weep. In others only women may weep.

Finally, culture and group living combine to make human beings of infants, to give them personality. As Clifford Geertz says, a person without culture would not be a mindless ape, but a mental basket case, an unworkable monstrosity. Having a culture makes us human—and not just human in a general sense, but human by the specific definitions of our own society.

When seen as a set of symbolic devices for controlling behavior . . . culture provides the link between what men are intrinsically capable of becoming and what they actually, one by one, in fact become. Becoming human is becoming individual, and we become individual under the guidance of cultural patterns, historically created

---

[4]Dorothy Lee, *Freedom and Culture* (Englewood Cliffs, N.J.: Prentice-Hall, 1959), pp. 105–120.

systems of meaning in terms of which we give form, order, point, and direction to our lives. . . . One of the most significant facts about us may finally be that we all begin with the natural equipment to live a thousand kinds of life but end in the end having lived only one.[5]

Culture and Personal Freedom

The processes of socialization and continuing social control operate largely below our level of awareness. According to Edward Hall,

. . . most of culture lies hidden and is outside voluntary control. . . . Even when small fragments of culture are elevated to awareness, they are difficult to change, not only because they are so personally experienced but *because people cannot act or interact at all in any meaningful way except through the medium of culture.*[6]

Are we, then, prisoners of culture? If we recognize the great power of culture, do we deny free will and individual initiative? That is an enormously controversial question, debated over the centuries.

The romantic philosophers of the Enlightenment saw the human being as a "noble savage," innately pure and good until corrupted by society. The ideal human being was to be looked for "behind," "under," or "beyond" the customs of society. Then anthropologists came along who sought to discover a universal human nature by classifying and comparing the content of different cultures. Still others divorced humanity from culture, denying that people had anything to do with the course of cultural evolution once they had given it the original push by starting to make tools and use language. These cultural evolutionists or determinists see that beginning as "the last creative act in which man ever engaged" and

regard culture as having a dynamism of its own quite apart from people. Culture proceeds automatically by laws of its own.[7]

In contrast Morris Opler and other humanist anthropologists insist that "culture is the work of humanity; we have the impression that it is autonomous only because it is anonymous. It is the story, not of impersonal forces or prime movers and shakers, but of countless millions, each of whom has left a trace."[8]

Quite aside from the debate over whether people are simply the creatures of culture or its creators, what about individual freedom? We have seen already that an individual growing up alone and provided in some fantastic fashion with food and warmth would not really be free. Because of the lack of instincts and biological adaptations, such an individual would not even be free in the sense that an animal is free; he would be the prisoner of his own helplessness. Robinson Crusoe survived alone on his island because he was an adult who remembered a store of culture that he ingeniously applied to the problems of survival and comfort. But a lone infant, like Isabelle, would not be free to develop her potentialities as a human being.

Culture and society provide that freedom. Paradoxically, culture does so precisely because it is a set of ready-made patterns for behavior. We learn the accepted ways of satisfying our needs. Habits free our minds and energies for more creative thought and action and for enjoyment of life. Furthermore, by patterning the behavior of many individuals and groups within a society, culture makes it possible for any one of us to predict the behavior of others with varying degrees of accuracy. When we know what

[5] Geertz, "The Impact of the Concept of Culture."
[6] Edward Hall, *The Hidden Dimension* (Garden City, N.Y.: Doubleday Anchor Books, 1969), p. 188.

[7] Morris E. Opler, "The Human Being in Culture Theory," *The American Anthropologist* 66, No. 3 (June 1964): 507–528.
[8] *Ibid.*

to expect of others, we eliminate much wasted effort and many possible sources of conflict. Conformity has its very real uses, and one of these is furthering personal freedom.

But the degree to which specific cultures allow personal autonomy and provide freedom to the individual varies greatly. "In some societies, we find what amounts to a dictatorship; in others, the group may demand such sacrifice of individual uniqueness as to make for totalitarianism. On the other hand, in some societies we encounter a conception of individual autonomy and democratic procedures which far outstrip anything we have practiced or even have conceived of as democracy."[9]

Some American Indians show the individual absolute respect from birth and value the child "as sheer being for his own uniqueness." No adult would presume to make choices for him. A mother in the Sikh tribe of British Columbia, for example, took excellent care of her 18-month-old baby, but did not cut the hair that fell over his eyes. Her reason? He had not asked her to. The language of the Wintu of California expresses this respect for others: Instead of saying, "I took the baby," they say, "I went with the baby"; instead of "The chief ruled the people," they say, "The chief stood with the people."

There is a margin of free play, experiment, and innovation in every culture. Some people make more use of it than others. They know that culture is carried in the minds of people, not engraved in stone.

Education is a pivotal institution in Paraguay, as in every other society. *Peter Menzel for Stock, Boston.*

Similarities in Culture

Although culture serves the same general functions in most societies, it is obvious that all societies do not arrange their culture in the same way. Human identical twins exist, but "cultural twins" do not. In spite of this, a remarkable degree of similarity can be seen among the world's cultures.

There seems to be a single fundamental plan, which anthropologists call the "universal culture pattern," along which all cultures are constructed. The major aspects of this pattern are language; materials; knowledge, beliefs and values; ways of handling time, space, quantity, and sequence; and the six pivotal social institutions we discussed earlier (the economic system, government, religion,

[9] Lee, *Freedom and Culture*, p. 6.

family, education, and expressive and aesthetic institutions).[10]

Besides these broad general similarities, a number of more specific elements are found in most cultures. Among them are age-grading, athletic sports, bodily adornment, calendars, cleanliness training, courtship, dancing, division of labor, dream interpretation, ethics, feasting, folklore, funeral rites, games, gift giving, greetings, joking, luck superstitions, modesty concerning natural functions, obstetrics, personal names, propitiation of supernatural beings, soul concepts, surgery, visiting, and weather control.[11] What is the explanation for this "psychic unity of mankind"?

First of all, we are all members of the same species. All people have the same basic needs and drives, although there is no general agreement on a list of them. But certainly all human beings must eat, drink, breathe, urinate, and defecate. All are helpless infants for a long time. All have sexuality, and all reproduce and give birth in essentially the same way. All feel anger, frustration, anxiety, love, and fear. Yet there are so many different norms associated with all these functions and emotions that they are not sufficient to account for universal patterns, and many institutions, such as the family, provide for more than one need.

A further explanation may be sought in the universal conditions of human existence. These provide similar stimuli the world over. One is the physical environment, the facts of the earth, sky, water, sun, moon, and stars. Another is the anatomy and physiology of the human species, aside from its needs and drives. People everywhere have beliefs about blood, hair, the genitals, menstruation, childbirth, sickness, and death. Furthermore, people everywhere live in groups of people of two sexes and varying ages.

The range of responses to these stimuli is wide, to be sure, but there are limits to the likely, and even the possible, responses. Nature puts limits on such things as the ways pottery can be made, cows milked, diseases cured. There are only a few satisfactory ways to dispose of the dead, and only three possible ways of affiliating a child with relatives through a rule of descent (by father, mother, or both). For these reasons, there are cultural similarities among people who have had no contact with one another.

A further reason for similarities, according to George Murdock, is the human tendency to generalize, identifying one situation with another. For example, supernatural beings are typically conceived of in human terms, political organization often follows the model of the family, and menstruation is frequently identified with the moon because of its similarity to the lunar cycle.[12]

Cultural Diversity

Cultures vary greatly in specific details, in the size and complexity of their cultural inventory, and in the emphasis placed on one aspect or another of the culture. Although food is a universal need, eating habits differ greatly. Thus, some people loathe milk and canned foods, but will eat fried snails or decayed wood or head lice with gusto. There are many ways of giving directions. Americans name and number streets and number houses by location. The Japanese name intersections rather than streets and number the houses in each neighborhood according to when they were built.

---

[10] But, as Ralph Linton points out, this "universal culture pattern" is essentially a matter of convenience for comparison, like any system of classification based on recognized resemblances. It is inadequate for any deep penetration into the nature of culture. [*The Study of Man* (New York: Appleton-Century-Crofts, 1964), p. 394.]

[11] George Murdock, "The Common Denominator of Cultures," in Linton, *The Science of Man,* p. 123.

[12] Murdock, "The Common Denominator."

Every society has a ritualized means of dealing with crises such as death. In New Guinea whitened faces signify mourning. *From Language and Faith—Wychliffe Bible Translators.*

Cultural emphases also vary. One culture may stress acquisition of material goods, and another may concentrate on the supernatural. The whole life of the Todas of India centers around their buffalo herds and on the ritual of perpetuating and renewing the soured buffalo milk. The dairymen are the priests, the holy of holies is the sacred cow bell, and most of the taboos have to do with the sacredness of milk.

Cultures also vary in the size and complexity of the cultural inventory. An Australian aborigine may own nothing but a couple of spears and a boomerang, but he may have a rich oral lore of poetry and myth. A modern industrial society has an immense material culture, a tremendous store of scientific knowledge, and numerous patterns of beliefs and styles of living. An Oriental society may have a small and simple material culture in comparison, but a large and varied pantheon of gods and a variety of rituals throughout the year.

Why this immense variety in culture? Two answers frequently given—and refuted by social scientists—are, first, that each group inherits its culture as part of its biological heritage from the race to which it belongs, and, second, that habitat, or geographic setting, determines human behavior, that is, culture. These fallacies are so commonly believed that they deserve some attention.

Racial Determinism

If it were true that culture is biologically transmitted along racial lines, then each culture would belong to a different race. But anthropologists now distinguish about a thousand cultures—and no one claims that there are a thousand races. True, we can distinguish any number of races we care to make classifications for, by differences in such things as skin color, hair texture, and eyelid formation. But these racial types have no proven differences (such as "superiority" and "inferiority") in mental or physical capacity or in organic drives. They are, moreover, so intermingled that only a minority of each group conforms to the group's "ideal" physical type, and there are greater differences among individuals within a race than among races. The notion of any inherent connection between physical type and culture is also disproved by the fact that people of any racial background can learn any culture into which they are born. Furthermore, over the centuries no one group has displayed a greater capacity for culture building than any other. While the Europeans were still wearing bearskins, the Chinese were building palaces and producing highly sophisticated art and literature, and the Egyptians were enjoying bronze plumbing. Finally, the racial determinist would have to explain cultural change—which constantly occurs in all societies—by genetic change, which we know to be far slower.

Geographic Determinism

The second fallacy, that geographic environment—the natural setting or habitat—determines culture, appears on the face of it to be a more reasonable explanation for the diversity of cultures. It seems obvious, for example, that Eskimo culture could not exist anywhere but in the Arctic, that rainfall, temperature, and soil affect crops, that topography is related to trade routes and settlements. Some observers have gone so far as to say that habitat *determines* the culture. These "environmental determinists" are easily proved wrong by two complementary observations. First, different cultures are found in similar settings. The Eskimos hunt animals and build igloos. The Siberians, in a similar habitat, herd reindeer and build huts of wood and skins. The Pueblo Indians are cultivators. The Navajo,

in the same desert setting, are sheepherders. Second, similar cultures are found in different settings. Essentially similar Polynesian cultures are spread over such different habitats as the Hawaiian Islands and New Zealand.

What, then, is the relationship of habitat to culture? Habitat is but one of a number of forces that shape culture. Its impact is greater on some aspects of culture than on others. Technology and economics are more closely related to natural resources, for example, than are art, religion, and the family system. The habitat thus exercises a *selective limitation* on behavior. People cannot make pottery if there is no clay or weave baskets if there are no reeds, rushes, or young willow trees. The influence of habitat is greatest where primitive people cope with a harsh environment, as in the Arctic or the desert. As their technology becomes more efficient, however, people become less dependent on the physical environment. They can even alter the habitat to a great degree.

We may say, in short, that culture and habitat stand in a reciprocal relationship. Habitat exercises a selective limitation, but culture is not passive. It acts upon the very environment that serves as its physical setting, and this action intensifies as technology becomes more efficient.[13]

Origins of Cultural Diversity

If neither our physical makeup nor the physical environment explains the great variety in cultures, what does? The answer appears to be a combination of the effects of adaptability, creative energy and intelligence, and the accidents of original choices and their further elaboration.

---

[13] This discussion is based on Melville J. Herskovits, *Man and His Works* (New York: Alfred A. Knopf, 1948), pp. 153–165.

Human beings, as we have seen, are highly flexible and adaptable. Our basic needs can be satisfied in any number of ways. Our digestive system, for example, will tolerate an enormous variety of foods, and our need for clothing can be met by grass, bark, animal or vegetable fibers, furs, skins, and synthetics, in a limitless array of styles. Housing need not even conform to our image of four walls and a roof. It may be a lean-to, a sampan, a round hut, or a cave. We build strikingly different social arrangements around the needs for reproduction and protection of the group. And once people have solved their basic problems, they have a great deal of creative energy and intelligence left over, for they are restless animals and find pleasure in experiment and play.

Human beings select from the "great arc of potential human purposes and motivations" (to use anthropologist Ruth Benedict's phrase) and elaborate certain aspects of their culture at the expense of others. They may elaborate technology and science, as Americans have, or religious ceremonials, as do certain Australian tribes, or art and architecture, as did the Mayans of Central America. Once they have selected an area of special interest and elaboration, they continue to develop it. Thus differences pile upon differences.

These influences account, then, for variation in general, and for the different emphases in different cultures. But what explains the variation from simple cultures to highly complex ones? Contacts with other cultures are important sources of cultural change through **diffusion** of cultural traits. The stronger the links with the past, the greater the cumulative tradition that is preserved, passed on, and built upon. The number of people in a society is also related to complexity. The more people, the more likely that there will be specialists and innovators. And finally, the greater the quantity of food available, the more some

The harsh Arctic environment forces such cultural adaptions as snowshoes. Yet, the eyeglasses indicate the diffusion of elements from other cultures. *Ward W. Wells for Design Photographers International, Inc.*

members of the society can specialize in various nonagricultural occupations.[14]

Differences in culture are fascinating, but in the long run the basic similarity of human behavior all over the world is more impressive. It is human nature everywhere not only to eat, sleep, seek shelter, and have sexual intercourse—like many other creatures—but also to think about one's behavior, judge it, set up rules and institutions, communicate with others in many ways, and create languages, art, religion, and philosophy. Only human beings can conceive of themselves

[14] John J. Honigmann, *Understanding Culture* (New York: Harper & Row, 1963), pp. 309–310.

as rational and moral creatures, with minds and souls.

Cultural Relativity

The concept of culture is as important to understanding human behavior as are the concepts of evolution to biology, of gravity to physics, and of disease to medicine.[15] But to use the concept fruitfully, people must be aware of the tendency to believe that their "own usages far surpass those of all others"—a tendency noted by Herodotus, the much-traveled historian of ancient Greece. One must try to acquire an attitude of respect for cultural differences. In this final section, we concern ourselves with these conflicting attitudes (ethnocentrism and cultural relativity), their sources, and their significance for human behavior and society.

[15] Clyde Kluckhohn, *Mirror for Man* (New York: Fawcett World Library, 1964) p. 18.

In addition, we sum up the implications of the concept of culture in order to anticipate its uses in the rest of the book and in the broader context of group life.

Ethnocentrism

As people are socialized, they come to feel that "the axis of the earth runs right through their home town." The tendency to judge other groups and cultures by the norms and values of one's own, and to regard them as inherently inferior, is called **ethnocentrism** (from the Greek word *ethnos* or "nation").

Ethnocentrism is a universal phenomenon. Every group sets "us" off from "them." The ancient Greeks thought that people who spoke no Greek "babbled" and called them "barbarians." Finnish immigrants in Minnesota and Michigan refer to people who do not speak Finnish as *toiskielinen,* meaning "other-tongued."

A team of researchers studied this attitude in five neighboring communities in Rimrock,

Societies once dependent on animals for transportation have adopted motorized vehicles from other cultures. *Ira Kirschenbaum for Stock, Boston.*

an area of western New Mexico.[16] A different ethnic group lives in each community: Navajo and Zuñi Indians, Mormons, Texan homesteaders, and Spanish-Americans. Members of each community were asked to suppose that a 10-year drought had driven everyone away, and that the rains then returned and God allowed one group to come back to build a good new community. Which one should it be? Each thought his own group would be by far the most desirable for the area.[17]

Nationalism is the most prominent form of ethnocentrism today. People's belief in the superiority of their group may also include pride in and loyalty to the community or home town, their school, fraternity, or state. And this same belief may take such socially disruptive forms as racism, sexism, religious bigotry, and the overzealous and belligerent patriotism called jingoism.

The assumption that one's own group is superior and the tendency to judge others by one's own standards are practically inevitable. A social group *teaches* its members to be ethnocentric, both through the informal process of socialization and social control and through deliberate instruction by school, church, and government. The ways of our own group seem natural and right, because our own morals and values are the only standards we have for judging behavior. As we become aware that there are other groups with other ways, we may be willing to think in terms of their cultural values, but we are able to do so only to a limited extent. For example, the practice of bride-purchase among the cattle-raising Guajiro Indians of her country disturbed a Colombian anthropologist, who "felt terribly sad that a Colombian woman could be sold like a cow." But her Indian informant lost all respect for her when she learned that the anthropologist's husband had not given even a single cow for her: "You must not be worth anything."[18] Our thinking stems from certain premises. Members of other societies think according to different premises. So with equal logic we and they arrive at different conclusions.

Ethnocentrism is not altogether objectionable. It has certain definite advantages for the "we group" and its individual members. It makes for social integration, reduces conflicts within the group (by deflecting many frustrations outward), and promotes cultural stability and uniformity (if what we do is right and natural and human, why change?). In a nation at war ethnocentrism is obviously an asset and is encouraged by various means.

Besides holding the group together, ethnocentrism is psychologically satisfying. People can participate vicariously in all sorts of wonderful things that other members of the group have or do. The third-string quarterback's ego is enhanced if he is a member of a championship team, however little he may personally have had to do with the team's success. A nationality gives people an identity, a sense of belonging.

But in the modern world the harmful effects of ethnocentrism outweigh its advantages. First, ethnocentrism, especially in its more extreme manifestations, tends to be accompanied by a sense of satisfaction with the status quo—with things as they are—and by a resentment of anyone who questions conditions or suggests ways to improve the cultural and social order. Social changes, when they come, are thus far more disruptive and violent than a gradual process of intelligently guided change would have been.

---

[16] Evon Z. Vogt and Ethel M. Albert, eds., *People of Rimrock: A Study of Values in Five Cultures* (Cambridge, Mass.: Harvard University Press, 1966).

[17] *Ibid.*, pp. 27–28.

[18] Virginia Gutierrez de Pineda, quoted in George M. Foster, *Traditional Cultures and the Impact of Technological Change* (New York: Harper & Row, 1962), p. 69.

Second, modern societies such as ours are highly complex. Extreme ethnocentrism in subcultural groups in our society incites conflict among these groups, or at best prevents them from working together as effectively as they might for the good of the whole society. Intolerance and misunderstanding among racial, religious, and nationality groups stem largely from each group's conviction of its own "rightness."

Most important of all, ethnocentrism hinders nations from solving mutual problems and settling their disagreements. Narrow nationalism is the chief stumbling block to a really effective world organization. Ethnocentrism breeds ill will whenever members of one society display it in their dealings with members of another. Only a deep belief in the superiority of English culture over native cultures enabled the British to rationalize their imperialism in terms of "the White Man's Burden." In their contacts with so-called underdeveloped areas, Europeans and Americans have been especially prone to tread roughshod over the cultures of other peoples and, as a consequence, to produce confusion, disorganization, and distrust in many societies. Disdain and contempt for the ways of others breed resentment and in time often provoke aggression.

Although everyone is ethnocentric to some degree, extreme ethnocentrism in our society has been found to correlate with a person's general orientation toward authoritarian rather than democratic values. T. W. Adorno and his associates constructed an opinion-attitude scale for measuring ethnocentrism. Respondents were asked to rate their agreement or disagreement with such statements as the following on a scale of six degrees:

1. To end prejudice against Jews, the first step is for the Jews to try sincerely to get rid of their harmful and irritating faults.

2. Negroes have their rights, but it is best to keep them in their own districts and schools and to prevent too much contact with whites.
3. The worst danger to real Americanism during the last 50 years has come from foreign ideas and agitators.
4. America may not be perfect, but the American Way has brought us about as close as human beings can get to a perfect society.[19]

Adorno found that a person who is ethnocentric in one of these areas (say, a white racist) is very likely to be ethnocentric in the others as well. He is likely to be hostile to each outgroup, although he dislikes some more than others, and he tends to idealize the ingroup as superior in morality, ability, and general development and to give it blind obedience and loyalty. The irrationality of extreme ethnocentrism, especially in the United States, is apparent.

Culture Shock

No matter how willing a person may be to understand the ways of another group, he is bound to experience some **culture shock**—to feel like "a fish out of water"—when he first visits a strange country or even a subcultural group. Peace Corps volunteers experience culture shock in spite of intensive training, and after their two years in the field they suffer a "reentry crisis." A volunteer home from Pakistan and wearing the national dress was recognized in an elevator as the heroine of a Peace Corps recruiting film. When everyone in the car turned to look at her, she was so embarrassed that she became dizzy and nearly fainted. Why? Women do not get that kind of attention in Pakistan, and she was reacting like a Pakistani. Typical returnees see their own country differently: as "a crowded, car-jammed, commercialized mess—surfeit and

---

[19] T. W. Adorno et al., *The Authoritarian Personality* (New York: Harper & Row, 1950), p. 142.

superabundance everywhere. . . . Friends and relatives seem none too clear on where he had been or what he did there or why it was important. They don't appear much interested in the rest of the world."[20] Perhaps the chief difference between him and them is that he has acquired an attitude of cultural relativity.

Cultural Relativity

The concept of **cultural relativity** refers to an attitude of respect for cultural differences. The concept includes several ideas. Every culture must be seen intact, with its values inseparably interwoven into the whole. Each body of custom has an inherent dignity and meaning as the way of life that one group has worked out for adapting to its environment, answering the biological needs of its members, and ordering group relationships. And our own culture is but one among many, one that most of us happen to prefer primarily because we grew up in it.

Although cultural relativity means respect for other ways, it does not necessarily mean loss of respect for our own. People may decide, after rational reflection, that their ways are *the* best, or the best for their group, or the best for them (because they want to adjust to their group). As Clyde Kluckhohn said, anthropology does not destroy the need for standards, "the useful tyranny of the normal."[21] It does teach us, Ruth Benedict points out, to recognize that other cultures are as significant to their members as ours is to us.[22] It may also suggest ways we might change our own culture or life style.

In any case, culture has such a hold on us that most of us never escape our own established patterns to more than a limited extent—and relatively few of us try to do so. Even anthropologists are rooted in their own cultures. Besides, one "who was truly and utterly free from his own culture would be no more competent to study other ways of life than an individual who has lost his memory is able to grasp what is going on around him."[23]

Evaluating Cultures

Judging cultures is a risky business, but people do it constantly. We often hear cultures called high or low, barbaric or civilized, decadent and imitative, or active and innovative. Usually such judgments reflect the observer's own culture. Americans tend to judge other nations by their attainment of the things in which we take most pride—bigness, speed, material abundance, comfort, and efficiency. Latin Americans are more likely to judge in terms of art, literature, music, courtesy, and enjoyment of life.

Often we comment on special aspects of culture, admiring something about this one, something else about that. We may admire the Plains Indians for devising special norms for men who did not fit the masculine warrior role. An expert on preliterate art and myth admires the magnificent songs of the Navajo, while noting that the Pueblo have few songs but elaborate ceremonials, and that Australian aborigines have a high order of myths. Similarly, England has always had an abundance of great writers, but fewer painters proportionately than the Flemish, and fewer composers than the Germans. The Polynesian account of the Crea-

[20]Richard B. Stolley, "The Re-Entry Crisis," *Life*, pp. 98 ff.

[21]*Mirror for Man*, p. 41.

[22]*Patterns of Culture* (Baltimore: Penguin, 1946), p. 37.

[23]Clyde Kluckhohn, "Common Humanity and Diverse Cultures," in Daniel Lerner, ed., *The Human Meaning of the Social Sciences* (Cleveland, Ohio: World Publishing, 1959) pp. 245–284.

tion "makes Genesis read like the comic strip *Tales from the Great Book*."[24]

Some cultures, insists Morris Freilich, *are* inferior—Nazi Germany, for instance. Although it is not easy to devise measuring rods for evaluating cultures, he argues, the attempt should be made.[25] What might we tentatively suggest as guidelines for such an attempt?

First, we might ask how well a society fulfills the basic functions of protecting the individual and preserving the social group. How well does it cope with the environment? How well does it adapt to change? How well does it reconcile conflicts? Does it provide for health and safety? Is it on a self-destructive path, like the Kaingang of Brazil and the nuclear powers? In today's interdependent world, we cannot be content to judge a culture strictly in terms of its inner functioning. It must adapt not only to geography and climate but also to other societies.

Adaptability and successful functioning may be measured by such social indicators as economic distribution, infant mortality, life expectancy, political stability, and mental health. Attempts to measure the quality of life—what makes one society happier than another—include these and more elusive indicators, such as availability of outdoor recreation, opportunities for participation in creative arts, and freedom from anxiety about illness, violence, and crime.

The social order is based on trust. We venture out on the road trusting hundreds of other drivers. We trust that stores will be open, that the mail will be delivered, that we can safely go about our business. Does the culture support or erode this trust? Swiftness of communication, ever increasing

with the development of communications satellites, is usually held to be a good thing, uniting more and more people. But some fear that the mass media tend rather to *divide* people and destroy their sense of community and communion. "As we hear and read much about the acts of violence and injury men perpetrate upon one another, year after year, with so little emphasis placed on the loving, caring, and humanitarian acts of man, we begin to trust our fellow men less, and we thereby diminish ourselves."[26]

Second, we might ask how well a society lives up to its own cultural values and goals. Does it provide opportunities to satisfy the desires it creates and achieve the goals it sets for its members? Social problems are indications that something is out of gear: racism and inequality of educational opportunity in a democracy, poverty in an affluent society, militarism on the rise in a nation that prides itself on being peace-loving.

Third, we might ask what kind of people result from the sociocultural patterning. The Alorese of Indonesia, for example, bring up children in a way that produces unhappy and spiteful adults. Children are teased, frightened, tolerated, half-abused, and neglected by their mothers. As adults they are suspicious, mistrustful, fearful, and anxious. They lack in confidence and self-esteem and are nonaggressive (preying on their neighbors with lies, deception, and chicanery). They are unable to sustain a love relationship or friendship based on voluntary interest. They are chronically unhappy, frustrated, and confused, convinced that they can expect only the worst from life. They have a limited capacity to master or enjoy their social world.[27]

[24] John Greenway, "Conversations with the Stone Age," *Saturday Review* (Feb. 16, 1964).

[25] Morris Freilich, ed., *Marginal Natives: Anthropologists at Work* (New York: Harper & Row, 1970), p. 582.

[26] Herbert A. Otto, "New Light on the Human Potential," *Saturday Review* (Dec. 20, 1969), 14–17.

[27] Cora DuBois, *The People of Alor* (Minneapolis: University of Minnesota Press, 1944).

Finally, we might ask to what degree does the culture realize human potential—innate intelligence, length of life, and the capacity for love and joy, for spiritual and aesthetic experience? Does the process of socialization stifle or develop a sense of awareness, empathy, imagination, and creativity?

Uses of the Culture Concept

An attitude of cultural relativity and an understanding of the concept of culture and its implications can be of value to the student and to society in a number of ways. To be very practical, you will need both to study the rest of this book as well as further courses in the social sciences. In a broader and less immediate sense, cultural relativity is essential to a liberal education. An understanding

of the culture concept can make us more at home in a world where intergroup contacts steadily increase. A thorough grasp of the culture concept also makes us more objective toward our own culture. "The last thing a dweller in the deep sea would be likely to discover would be water. He would become conscious of its existence only if some accident brought him to the surface and introduced him to air. . . . Those who know no culture other than their own cannot know their own."[28] Comparing our own culture with others in an open-minded way, we may find that things we regard as fundamental seem minor to others, and we see alternative ways of doing things—alternatives an ethno-

[28] Ralph Linton, *The Cultural Background of Personality,* p. 125.

Drawing by W. Miller; © 1968 The New Yorker Magazine, Inc.

"I see your people putting down roots. I see them becoming renowned for cheeses, buffet-style dinners, sexy blondes and modern furniture."

centric attitude would prevent us from considering. Britain, for example, does not treat drug addicts as criminals, but as sick people whose habit need not lead to crime.[29] Where an ethnocentric person is rigid in his judgments of others even in his own society, a culturally aware person is more tolerant of harmless deviations from cultural patterns.

As we come to recognize the oneness of humanity, to feel more at home in the world, to regard our own culture more objectively, and to tolerate differences and harmless deviations, we may also come to understand ourselves better. An awareness of alternative norms and values gives us an opportunity to choose, to guide our own lives. We gain greater control of our own behavior.

Once we understand the role of culture in human behavior, we become more optimistic about the eventual solution of social problems. If the people of a warlike nation were "born that way," little could be done to change them. But such people are aggressive because their culture has shaped them that way, and culture does change. The ancestors of today's neutral, peace-loving Swedes were the warlike Vikings. Under different circumstances many criminals might have been law-abiding citizens.

Summary

Because people are born with generalized and diffuse capacities and tendencies, they could not survive without culture, which is the uniquely human form of adaptation to the environment. Cultural evolution is far swifter than the biological evolution by which all animals adapt.

If societies are to endure, cohere, and function successfully, they must satisfy individual biological and psychological needs, socialize new recruits to fill their positions in the social structure, guide behavior to what is socially desirable, provide for regularity and predictability in interaction, and instill a feeling of belonging and a desire to work toward group goals. The system of norms, sanctions, beliefs, knowledge, and values fulfills these social imperatives, especially through institutions.

A society's culture provides patterns by which the individual can fulfill both elemen-

tal needs and culturally created desires; presents a codification of reality, primarily through language, which shapes his thoughts and perceptions; guides and channels his interaction with others; gives meaning and value to his experience; and makes a human being out of a helpless biological organism. Individuals absorb the culture of their group largely through subtle processes of which they are unaware.

Cultural determinists insist that culture is governed by its own laws and develops independently of human initiative. Humanist anthropologists stress the active, innovative role of individuals. There is a great difference among cultures in the degree to which individual autonomy and personal freedom are valued and encouraged.

The universal culture pattern includes language, materials, knowledge, beliefs and values, and ways of handling time, space, quantity, and sequence, in addition to the six pivotal cultural institutions (economics, government, religion, the family, education, and the arts). Similarities in culture the world over are attributed to the fact that human-

---

[29] Amitai Etzioni and Fredric L. Dubow, *Comparative Perspectives: Theories and Methods* (Boston: Little, Brown, 1970).

kind is one species, to the universal conditions (social, geographic, and physiological) of human existence, to the limits of possible responses to these conditions, and to the psychological tendency to generalize.

Cultures vary not only in detail, but in emphasis, and in the size and complexity of the cultural inventory. Neither physical differences usually considered racial, nor geographic differences—except for the limitations imposed by habitat—account for cultural variety. Instead, anthropologists find the answers in our great adaptability, our creative energy and intelligence, the accidents of original choice and their further elaboration, the possibilities for new ideas afforded by contacts with other groups, the accumulation of ideas made possible by links with the past, and the opportunities for specialization and innovation encouraged by sheer numbers of people and by an adequate food supply.

A mastery of the culture concept is essential to understanding human behavior. Ethnocentrism, the tendency to regard one's own group as superior and to judge all others by its norms and values, blocks such understanding. To some extent it is inevitable, and it makes for group cohesion. But extreme ethnocentrism bars intelligently guided change and fosters misunderstanding and conflict. A classic study by Adorno and

associates found that authoritarian personalities are more likely to be ethnocentric than democratic ones, and that their ethnocentrism extends to numerous outgroups.

An attitude of cultural relativity, in contrast, includes a respect for cultural differences and a belief that each culture is valid as a more or less satisfactory way of adapting to environmental, biological, and social needs. It does not preclude evaluating cultures—if one is aware of one's criteria. Among guidelines for judging cultures are adaptability, success in preserving the group and meeting biological and psychological needs, provision of opportunity to satisfy the desires and reach the goals set by the culture itself, the kind of personality produced by the culture, and the extent to which a culture promotes the human potential for learning, health, and happiness.

The study of culture is essential not only to fruitful study of human behavior in all the social sciences, but also to a liberal education. It makes people more at home in a world where intergroup contacts steadily increase, more objective toward their own culture, more aware of the oneness of humanity, and more conscious of their own identities. It also is useful in guiding attempts to solve social problems, especially those arising from ignorance and misunderstanding.

Glossary

Cultural relativity An attitude of respect for cultural differences.

Culture shock The difficulty felt in adapting to the ways of a strange society or subcultural group.

Diffusion The spread of culture traits from one society to another.

Ethnocentrism The tendency to judge other groups and cultures by the norms of one's own and to regard them as inherently inferior.

chapter

5

Socialization

How does the red, damp, squally, squirmy newborn baby grow up to be a participating member of society? In this chapter we discuss **socialization**—the process by which a member of the species *homo-sapiens* becomes a functioning member of the human race and is incorporated into a social group. Through socialization each of us learns the cultural values, norms, and beliefs of our social group, our place in it, and how we are expected to behave. We also acquire a personality, the individual version of human nature.

Personality refers to the (more or less) organized ways of behaving that characterize given individuals, including their patterns of thought, feeling, and action. It embraces all their modes of adjusting to and attempting to master the environment—habits and skills, perspectives or frames of reference, style of interaction in interpersonal relationships, the things they "know" as matters of fact and believe on faith.

When we think of personality, we are generally thinking of its unique aspects, those that distinguish each of us from the other billions in the world. But in many respects each of us is also like some other people and all other people. This likeness results from similarities in the three main factors that shape personality: our biological organisms, our nurturing as infants, and the society and culture into which we are socialized. The many possible variations in each of these factors, and their dynamic interplay, plus the accidents and circumstances of life,

all contribute to the uniqueness of the personality. Each personality is not a result of passive reactions to these influences but rather an effortful, striving, seeking unity.

In this chapter we look at several answers to the question of how the human organism acquires human nature and personality. Then we examine variations in human nature in different societies and subcultures.

The Process of Becoming Human

There are several theories about how the personality is formed. Before we look at the most complex—those that emphasize individual factors in personality development— let's consider the simpler ones—those that claim to have the "master key" to the mystery of human nature and personality.

Biological Determinism

Human nature and personality depend on the baggage babies bring with them into the world. That is the basic premise of theories of **biological determinism.** According to these theories, human behavior is simply an expression or unfolding of inborn drives or tendencies such as instincts, needs, constitutional makeup, or preprogrammed action patterns.

While the recognition that the human being is a biological organism helped to open the subject of human behavior to scientific study, the more extreme forms of biological determinism no longer command attention among social scientists and psychologists. The absurdities of classical instinct theory, for example, became apparent when one psychologist proposed two instincts as the keys to behavior, while others have compiled lists of 13, or 250, or even 1,500. New versions of biological determinism, nonetheless, appear at intervals. A popular one these days is suggested by ethologists, who attribute such behavior as aggression to preprogramming in the genes (a new way of phrasing "instinct"), laid down thousands of years ago when early men and their ancestors lived much as ground apes do today. The main contribution of such studies, when they are not summarily rejected, is to remind social scientists that "in the beginning is the body."[1]

Cultural Determinism

Human nature and personality depend on the society into which a baby happens to be born. That is the basic premise of theories of **cultural determinism.** Leslie White sees the individual as a helpless slave of culture, a sort of puppet whose wishes, hopes, and fears have nothing to do with creating culture. At some point in the distant past, people did start the cultural ball rolling, but it has been out of our control ever since. White admits that "Man must *be* there, of course, to make the existence of the culture process possible," but the human being is "merely the instrument through which cultures express themselves. . . . Culture makes man what he is and at the same time makes itself."[2]

[1] Dennis Wrong, "The Oversocialized Conception of Man in Modern Sociology," in Robert Endleman, ed., *Personality and Social Life* (New York: Random House, 1967), pp. 39–50.
[2] Leslie White, *The Science of Culture* (New York: Grove Press, 1949), pp. 340, 353.

Such a scheme does not explain the uniqueness of personality and denies the capacity of persons to discover, interpret, and select other types of behavior. It perpetuates the view that the individual and society are completely separate entities and fails to explain how the person acquires culture.

Karl Marx was, in effect, a cultural determinist, although he emphasized the influence of social structure rather than the culture in general. He regarded the occupation and social class into which a person is born as the basis for motivation. Under capitalism, both worker and capitalist are enslaved by circumstances not of their own making. Industrial capitalism thus turns people into things and the slaves of things. It destroys their individuality. According to Marx, only under full communism will people realize self-fulfillment.

Marxism is a classic example of those one-sided or "single-factor" theories that contribute a much-needed emphasis on a neglected factor—in this case by counteracting the assumption that human motivations are purely individual in origin and showing that people could be commonly motivated by shared circumstances.

Behaviorism

In sharp contrast to biological and cultural determinists, behaviorists focus on the individual organism and its capacity to learn. Although there are different schools of behaviorism, in general it may be said that they agree on the following principles.

1. Psychology is essentially the study of animal behavior, and experiments with lower animals can furnish knowledge directly applicable to human behavior.
2. Only overt behavior is a proper subject of scientific study. Subjective experience that can be studied only by introspection is to be ignored.
3. Behavior can be understood in terms of stimulus and response. The process of learn-

ing consists of *conditioning*—attaching the proper responses to various stimuli through a system of reward and punishment, or *positive and negative reinforcement,* which works because in general the organism seeks to avoid pain and to experience pleasure.

4. Aside from narrow physiological needs such as those for food, water, and sex (which provide the energy for all psychological processes), the newborn infant is infinitely plastic and can learn anything.

This last belief was stated in extreme form by John B. Watson, the founder of behaviorism.

Give me a dozen healthy infants, well-formed, and my own specified world to bring them up in and I'll guarantee to take any one at random and train him to become any type of specialist I might select—doctor, lawyer, artist, merchant-chief and, yes, even beggar-man and thief, regardless of his talents, penchants, tendencies, abilities, vocations, and race of his ancestors.[3]

Behaviorism thus is the belief that personality is nothing more than learned behavior, that behavior can be predicted on the basis of past conditioning and can be changed or corrected by reconditioning in the present.

B. F. Skinner, a leading behaviorist, insists that societies must make desirable behavior pay off. His arguments are based largely on years of experimenting with laboratory animals, which he taught to perform complex operations by rewarding correct movements with food. Skinner believes that human (like other animal) behavior is determined and that it represents the consequences of past conditioning. He has no patience with such concepts as consciousness, mind, imagination, and purpose. According to Skinner, even when people invent something or write a poem or establish a business, they are simply expressing the determining effects of their past history.

Skinner even argues that freedom, in which the individual is subjected to arbitrary, unguided, and often contradictory experiences, is dangerous. In his Utopian novel, *Walden Two,* Skinner suggests that people would be much happier in a society where all behavior is controlled through "social engineering" (positive reinforcement for desirable actions).[4]

Critics of Skinner's Utopia ask, Who will be in charge of conditioning? Who will control the controllers? Such a society, they say, must be authoritarian or even totalitarian. Critics of behaviorism in general believe that our mastery of language sets us so far apart from rats and pigeons that any knowledge gained from laboratory experiments with them is extremely limited in application. They also quarrel with the behaviorists' dismissal of subjective and emotional phenomena as something to be ignored because they cannot be measured. Learning, those critics insist, is far more complex and dynamic a process than stimulus and response can explain. Society cannot be understood as a maze in which organisms are taught the rules of the game by judicious administration of rewards and punishments. Finally, while infants are capable of learning, they are not infinitely plastic. There are innate differences in drives, temperament, and intelligence that affect the response patterns of the growing child.

But whatever its shortcomings, behaviorism did contribute to a deemphasis on heredity, even among those who do not accept extreme environmental determinism. It encouraged sociologists as well as psychologists to develop theories derived from overt behavior, to formulate operational definitions, and to test their hypotheses in such

---

[3] *Behaviorism,* rev. ed. (Chicago: University of Chicago Press, 1930), p. 104.

[4] B. F. Skinner, *Walden Two* (New York: Macmillan, 1948). A nonfictional exposition of the same ideas is found in *Beyond Freedom and Dignity* (New York: Alfred A. Knopf, 1971).

a way that another scientist could repeat the experiment. It also focused the psychologists' attention on the learning process.

Psychoanalytic Theory

Sigmund Freud (1856–1939), one of the giants of personality theory, has influenced scientific and popular thinking tremendously. Whenever we accuse a friend of a "Freudian slip" of the tongue, label a person "an anal character," tell someone he should see a shrink, or worry about how to toilet train our children, we are reflecting the Freudian revolution in the human image.

Freud was concerned with the unconscious, irrational, covert, and emotional aspects of human nature and with their roots in early childhood experiences. Where behaviorists stress the effect of environment or biological capacities, Freud stressed biological imperatives. Where behaviorists stress external stimuli and reward, Freud stressed inner motivations and emotional attitudes. He also believed that "anatomy is destiny." Women not only *feel* inferior because they lack a penis, they *are* inferior. (Freud always viewed women as mysterious and problematic creatures.)

Where the cultural determinists see personality as reflecting culture, **psychoanalytic theory** sees culture as merely a reflection of individual psychology. All our prescriptions for living, Freud believed, are based on our eternal effort to handle the problems of sex and aggression. The social roles people play are crystallizations of mechanisms they have collectively decided are acceptable for harnessing their antisocial impulses. But living in society is costly for the individual. The price of having civilization is discontent. We are victims of pressures that frustrate our natural impulses and distort our personalities. The frustration of our sexual impulses forces us to find new channels to express them. Thus we build culture.

Social cohesion, according to Freudian theory, is explained by the concept of *identification.* This concept implies not only shaping oneself after an admired model but also reacting to the status and characteristics, the possessions and achievements, of another person or group as if they were one's own. This gives a sense of belonging and security.

A second group of psychologists who have been heavily influenced by Freud call themselves neo-Freudians (*neo* means "new"). Neo-Freudian psychologists accept much of Freud's theory, but not all of it. For example, they recognize cultural influences, the importance of language, and the possibility that experiences during adolescence and adulthood may have significance in themselves rather than simply as reproductions or recapitulations of childhood experience.

Erik Erikson, a prominent neo-Freudian psychotherapist, studied with Freud in Vienna, but later came to realize the importance of sociocultural influences. He studied anthropology and worked with people in different cultures, including the Sioux and Yurok Indians. Erikson insists that "personality (not anatomy) is destiny," that we live in a social order and a personal order as well as a somatic (biological) order. It is the interaction of these three that shapes personality.

All through the various stages of the life cycle, says Erickson, a person seeks **identity,** which is a sense of personal awareness continuing through time. Erikson described the life cycle as a series of stages, each of which involves new dimensions of social interaction. In each, especially in adolescence and young adulthood, a person has an identity crisis. To the extent the crisis is resolved, one can probably handle the next stage satisfactorily.

Humanistic Psychology

Dissatisfied with both experimental-behavioristic psychology and Freudian theory, a number of present-day psychologists stress subjective experience and the search for meaning and value in existence. Abraham Maslow called this "third force" (which includes neo-Freudian, existential, Gestalt, and ego or personality psychologists, among other schools) **humanistic psychology.** Maslow equates the humanistic revolution in psychology, which is just beginning, with the Freudian. "It is as if Freud supplied to us the sick half of psychology and we must now fill it out with the Healthy half."[5]

On the basis of pilot research, bits of evidence, personal observation, theoretical deduction, and sheer hunch, Maslow developed a hierarchy of "instinctoid" needs. The evidence that we need each of these—love, for example—is exactly the same, in Maslow's view, as the evidence that we need Vitamin C. We can tell if needs are inborn, he said, if their absence breeds illness, their presence prevents illness, their restoration cures illness, and healthy persons do not demonstrate a deficiency of those things that gratify these needs. The five basic needs, as he saw it, are life, safety or security, belongingness and affection, respect and self-respect, and self-actualization. Life takes precedence over the others. Only when the first three needs are gratified does a person seek the other two.

Maslow and other humanist psychologists make use of everyday words that are often ignored or taken for granted in psychological inquiry. We should, he said, regard as miracles such things as decision, choice, responsibility, self-creation, autonomy, and identity itself. Maslow saw humanness as a matter of degree, self-actualization being the achievement of full humanness.

Modern Social Psychology

Social psychologists believe that an adequate and valid theory of personality development must take into account all those things pointed to by the theories we have been examining—the biological organism, born with needs, drives, and a capacity to learn, especially through language; the socially structured groups that nurture and teach him, interacting with him as he plays various roles; and the cultural beliefs, values, and norms that pattern this interaction. Many social psychologists find the basic framework of such a theory in **symbolic interactionism.** Like humanists and neo-Freudians, symbolic interactionists consider a person's concept of self or identity crucial to his actions. And they see the emergence of the self as the process by which the newborn baby becomes a human being.

Mind, Self, and Society: The Theory of Symbolic Interactionism

Every socialized person is aware of being a "self," as being distinct from others, as a being having unity and continuity. We can almost always distinguish between what happens to us and what we ourselves do. It is the self that makes sense of the confusion of the world "out there." The self serves as a sort of reference center for planning and orientation, for sorting and assessing the issues of life in terms of their relative importance. The **self,** then, is the core of personality, which accounts for its unity and structure.[6]

---

[5] Abraham Maslow, *Toward a Psychology of Being,* 2nd ed. (New York: Van Nostrand Reinhold, 1968), p. 5.

[6] Gordon W. Allport, *Becoming: Basic Considerations for a Psychology of Personality* (New Haven, Conn.: Yale University Press, 1955), p. 43.

But this self is not something in the organism at birth, waiting to be drawn out or developed. It emerges, rather, in the course of socialization, the general process by which a baby becomes a human being, and the process by which a member of a group is fitted into its social structure through interaction with family, peers, teachers, and others. How do these agencies "get inside" a person and socialize him? How do they contribute to the emergence of a self?

Philosopher George Herbert Mead (1863–1931) tried to answer these questions and, in so doing, developed the framework of symbolic interactionism. Demonstrating the intricate interrelationship of culture, society, and personality, his theory outlines the process by which newborn specimens of *Homo sapiens* become human beings, playing their culturally defined roles in the social structure of their group.

"Human society as we know it," said Mead, "could not exist without minds and selves."[7] He also insisted that rational minds and conscious selves arise only in society. They are products of social interaction and especially of symbolic communication through language. Mead emphasized meanings rather than stimuli and saw the person as an acting and thinking agent rather than simply a reacting or responding organism. He recognized the presence of irrational impulses, but he stressed the rational and creative aspects of personality.

Mead saw self-control and empathy[8] as the psychological bases of social order. The process of socialization ideally produces ma-

ture social beings who are self-critical and reflective and therefore capable of controlling their own behavior, and who have insight into the feelings and expectations of others and therefore can participate successfully in social interaction and interpersonal relationships.

Mead's theory of symbolic interactionism involves a number of interrelated concepts woven into a coherent theory by a process of philosophical reasoning so subtle and complex that a brief account can only suggest the bare outline. The key to the emergence of the self, in Mead's view, is the capacity of people to think of themselves reflexively, to be objects to themselves. An *object* is not simply something that exists. It is something that can be referred to—a concept with meaning. In this sense, things existing in the natural environment are not objects until they are discovered and named. Things that do *not* exist in the natural environment can be objects. Thus to the nonliterate tribesman with influenza, the influenza virus, of which he has no concept, is not an object (although he is just as sick as the modern doctor who has a word for it). But the angry god he blames for his illness *is* an object. The tribesman does not orient his actions toward destroying the virus, but toward appeasing the god.

The culture of each group consists of its world of meaningful objects. The mind of each of us consists of our world of meaningful objects. These meanings serve to orient behavior. They are not simply stimuli, because one of the objects that a person acquires in the process of socialization is a self. As we come to see ourselves as an object—a unique, separate object with unity and continuity—we can think about ourselves, love ourselves, hate ourselves, be ashamed of ourselves, be proud of ourselves. But above all, as compared to the monster that is an unsocialized toddler, we can *control* ourselves. This is because we can think—interact

---

[7] *Mind, Self, and Society,* Charles W. Morris, ed. (Chicago: University of Chicago Press, 1934), p. 227. Reprinted from *Mind, Self, and Society* by permission of the University of Chicago Press.

[8] *Empathy:* Psychol. The intellectual identification with or vicarious experiencing of the feelings, thoughts, or attitudes of another. *Random House Dictionary of the English Language.*

with ourselves and communicate with ourselves. We construct our own action or conduct. Our behavior is not simply reaction to stimuli. We cope with things, consider them, take them into account, then act or decide not to act (which is in itself an act).

The Conversation of Gestures

Social interaction, said Mead, may be viewed as a conversation of gestures. This can occur on a nonverbal level, among humans as well as animals. A *conversation of gestures* consists of the mutual adjustment of behavior, in which each participant uses the initial gesture of another's action as a cue for his or her own action, and that response becomes a stimulus to the other, encouraging either a shift in attitude or completion of the originally intended action. Mead used the dogfight as an example of a conversation of gestures on the rudimentary level. "One dog is attacking the other, and is ready to spring at the other dog's throat; the reply on the part of the second dog is to change its position, perhaps to spring at the throat of the first dog. There is a conversation of gestures, a reciprocal shifting of the dogs' positions and attitudes."[9]

The Symbolic Nature of Interaction

Some human action occurs on somewhat the same rudimentary level as the dogfight, as when two people going in opposite directions on the street shift positions to get by one another, or when one person responds to another person's tone of voice or facial expression. This is an unconscious or nonsignificant conversation of gestures, consisting of simple stimulus and response. But most human interaction—increasingly so as a person becomes socialized—is symbolic,

that is, it depends on *shared understandings about the meanings of gestures.*

For the purposes of Mead's theory, a *significant symbol* is a gesture that arouses the same response or attitude (tendency to respond) in the self that it arouses in the other. It conveys an idea and arouses the same idea in the mind of the other. This sharing is essential to communication. Vocal gestures or words (as well as written or sign language) are the most satisfactory kinds of significant symbols—the most reliable and versatile. When language is used, the conversation of gestures is conscious. As we speak, we are aware of what we are doing and of the response we hope to arouse. Thus symbolic interaction is not only conscious, it is *self-conscious.*

Only human beings are capable of symbolic interaction through language. With it we build the set of significant symbols called a culture and the system of social relationships based on this culture called a society.

The Emergence of the Self

As infants, we have no conception of ourselves as individuals, no notion that we are set apart from other individuals. Only as we interact with our mothers and others, bump up against things, find we have a name, are clothed and bathed, and feel the boundaries of our bodies, do we begin to be aware of a separate identity. Roughly at the age of two, we begin to use the pronouns "I," "me," and "you," indicating that we are beginning to be conscious of ourselves and of other persons as separate individuals. This awareness grows as we acquire language and can participate in symbolic interaction.

We learn to perceive roles and their relationships. As we observe and respond to others, they become meaningful objects that can bring us pleasure, pain, security, and so on. In order to win the responses we want, we must learn to anticipate their ac-

---

[9] Mead, *Mind, Self, and Society,* p. 63.

tions by putting ourselves in their places—by *taking the role of the other*. In doing so we become objects to ourselves, able eventually to look at ourselves from outside ourselves, so to speak. Thus, we become aware of our moods and wishes and ideas as objects. We can act toward and guide ourselves.

Mead saw two main stages in the child's process of acquiring a self—the play stage and the game stage. In the early years, the *play stage* of development, the process of role-taking is learned by "playing at" different roles. Anyone who has watched small children at play knows that they "try on" various roles, switching from one to another with ease. Children will address themselves as storekeeper and answer themselves as shopper, or they may take turns being parent and child. A conversation of gestures is going on, and they are stimulating and responding to themselves. At this stage, however, the self is not yet a unity, an organized whole. It is made up of the particular attitudes of specific others to the child and toward one another as they participate in specific social acts.

It is in the *game stage* that an organized personality develops, and people become capable of functioning in society. In their early school years, children learn to participate in games with rules. Playing baseball, for example, children of eight or so find they must carry in their minds a knowledge of the roles that all the others play in the game and the relationships of these roles to one another. In order to do what they should do, they must know what behavior to expect of the others, and what is expected of themselves. *The child must take the role of all the others on the team as an organized unit.*

Like the ball game, society is an organized system of interrelated roles. In the game stage, and in continuing socialization, knowledge of the roles and attitudes of others becomes more generalized—more abstract, less dependent on specific persons. In childhood, we are made to feel that we *must* do or not do things in order to avoid negative sanctions or enjoy positive sanctions from specific persons. As we grow older, a larger, more inclusive "other" comes to

An organized personality develops during the game stage of childhood. *Bohdan Hrynewych for Stock, Boston.*

control our actions. We feel we *ought* or *ought not* to do things in order to avoid self-blame or to keep and enhance self-esteem. We have become aware of the moral voice of the community as a whole and have internalized its mores and values as a conscience or character. In short, we have acquired what Mead calls a *generalized other.* Through the generalized other (expressed in self-control) the community exerts control on the person and ensures the cohesion of society.

Structure of the Self

Mead recognized that the self is neither completely rational and responsible nor a mirror image of social structure. It also has an innovative, impulsive, unpredictable aspect. To account for both the stability and the unpredictability of personality, as well as its relationship to culture and society, Mead developed the concepts of three components of the self—the "I," the "me," and the "generalized other."

The "I" is the impulsive, nonreflective, expressive portion of human nature. It is the acting self, which may be creative and innovative. The "me" is composed of the significant symbols internalized from the culture. It is conventional and habitual. It exists in remembered experience and thus can anticipate the consequences of various kinds of behavior, including impulsive actions. It can halt responses, evaluate, and select the appropriate way to behave. Nonetheless, the acting "I" at any given moment is always a bit unpredictable and may surprise even the individual. A common remark may illustrate the distinction: "I don't know why I did that; it was not at all like me." The "me" is the organized core of personality; the "I" is the sometimes errant actor that gives a sense of freedom and spontaneity. The self is different in different situations and relationships. But the generalized other—the conscience—gives it unity.

Mind and Thought

Like the self, mind emerges in the process of social interaction, and by virtue of language communication. It is "an internalization of the conversation of significant gestures, as made possible by the individual's taking the attitudes of other individuals toward himself and toward what is being thought about."[10] It appears, then, through the apparatus of taking the role of the other and using it to control one's own conduct. Mind is social. Even in the "inner forum" of the mind, thought is "a conversation carried on by the individual between himself and the generalized other,"[11] and it always implies expression of this inner conversation to an audience.

The essential characteristic of intelligent behavior is delayed response—a halt in behavior while thinking is going on. It is possible for us to delay response and to think about what to do because of the nature of our central nervous system and our command of language. Using the ideas or significant symbols of their culture, people can foresee some possible consequences of various courses of action and guide their behavior accordingly.

Implications of Symbolic Interactionism

In symbolic interactionist theory, culture is seen not only as a set of significant symbols, but also as shared perspectives arrived at through interaction and communication. These perspectives define situations and constitute agreed-upon conceptions of reality. To quote W. I. Thomas, "If men define situations as real, they *are* real in their consequences." Santa Claus, ghosts, and in-

[10] *Ibid.*, p. 192.
[11] *Ibid.*, p. 254n.

herent racial differences are real to many people because they define them as real, and they act accordingly.

People develop conceptions of reality in social interaction. As they participate in groups, they come to perceive reality as it is defined in the culture of the group. They check and test these views of reality as they communicate with others, and they feel confident of their validity so long as others support and reinforce them and act according to them. This support of one's conception of reality by others may be called *consensual validation*. A member of a sect that believes the world is flat or that it will end next July 27 at two o'clock feels secure in his belief because it is shared by his reference group. Consensus makes it appear valid.

To the extent that the members of a group share the same perspectives, there is cultural unity. The effort of a society's members to arrive at a common definition of a situation, at least long enough to agree on a common course of action, is the effort to achieve consensus. Where perspectives are in sharp conflict, consensus is extremely difficult to achieve, and the society's course of action wavers. In any multigroup society, people interact—perhaps often and closely—with others who define situations very differently, and as a result there is tension and conflict. But learning and adjustment do go on. A drugstore clerk said to two black males in their early twenties, "What can I do for you boys?" Seeing their reaction as they laughed a bit and looked at each other, she hastily amended her words: "What can I do for you gentlemen?" She had succeeded in taking the role of the other and revising her own conduct accordingly.

To the extent that there is reciprocal role-taking, there is sharing of the definition of the situation and thus consensus—and there is regularity, stability, repetitiveness, and predictability in joint action. But if the members cannot communicate and understand, their definitions of the situation continue to differ, and the attempt to arrive at workable relations suffers accordingly. This is why, in our discussion of culture, we stressed its nature as a set of shared understandings.

Drawing by Frascino; © 1968 The New Yorker Magazine, Inc.

We try to enhance our bodies to fit our ideal selves. *Gilles Peress for Magnum.*

The Self-Conception

As we said, our image of ourselves is an essential part of our concept of reality. The **self-conception** has two chief elements: a sense of *identity,* which is the answer to the questions "Who am I?" and "What am I?"; and a sense of *self-esteem,* which is the answer to the question "What am I worth?" We may measure both elements against an *ideal self,* which incorporates our aspirations or long-range goals as guided by the generalized other. The ideal self answers the question "What would I like to be worth?" The self-conception is the core around which personality is organized. Much of our behavior is designed to arrive at, live up to, defend, and enhance our self-conception.

The Organic Basis of the Self-Conception

Each of us has a name, which seems an integral part of us. Each of us also has a body to which this name is attached. Our body has quite definite limits (if one does not get too technical about air and food and so on), and its sensations are peculiarly our own. We have an image of and an evaluation of its shape, size, strength, coloring, proportions, stamina, and skill. We try to enhance it to fit our ideal selves.

Our bodily sense is "a lifelong anchor for our self-awareness." Gordon Allport drives home the "warmth and importance" of our own bodies by asking us first to imagine swallowing our own saliva which has collected in the mouth, and then to imagine spitting it into a glass and swallowing it from the glass. "What I perceive as belonging intimately to my body is warm and welcome; what I perceive as separate from my body becomes, in the twinkling of an eye, cold and foreign."[12]

But the self-image also includes our estimates of our characters and personality traits and of our intelligence and learning. It is extended into the possessions, causes, ideals, and groups we call our own, and into the people with whom we identify—people whose actions can cause us to feel pride or shame in much the same way we feel it for our own accomplishments and failures. It extends backward in time to our ancestors and forward to our descendants.

The Self-Conception as a Social Product

The self-conception is a social product. It arises in social interaction and is continually

[12] Allport, *Becoming,* p. 43.

88

tested, and confirmed or changed, in social interaction. Our sense of identity arises as we learn our statuses and roles. Our self-esteem (whether high or low) is established as we perceive the reactions of others to us. Later, when we have become objects to ourselves, self-esteem also depends on our own evaluations as we interact with ourselves and compare ourselves to others and to our ideal selves.

Status and Role

Statuses and roles are central to the self-conception. Some statuses can easily be dropped, but others are learned early and appear to be of great importance to self-identity. Among them are those ascribed by the groups and classes to which we belong—sex, ethnic group, religious affiliation, and position in the family. In one study, a group of 288 college students was asked to write 20 answers to the question "Who am I?" (an operational definition of the concept of "self"). The respondents tended to describe themselves in terms of their group and class memberships before listing any evaluations of themselves as individuals. That is, the first answers included such terms as girl, student, Catholic, and Negro, and only later in the list did they include such evaluative terms as happy, fat, and intelligent. [13]

Each culture has its own definition of masculine and feminine roles. Cases of mistaken sexual identity demonstrate that sex roles are learned long before a child is aware of primary sex differences. At the age of five Frankie, who had been raised as a boy because of uncertain genital structure, was discovered to be female. Nurses and interns in the hospital found it difficult to treat Frankie as a girl because she considered girls'

toys and activities to be "sissy," refused to wear a dress, and became extremely belligerent when anyone tried to treat her as a girl. [14] The socialization process had effectively organized her behavior along masculine lines quite independently of her feminine anatomy.

Some achieved statuses, such as marriage and certain occupations, are also crucial to the self-conception. A bride may feel strange with her new status and title, as often as she may have written her new name secretly. But the ritual and ceremony of a wedding, the support of the community, the use of her new name by tradesmen and correspondents, help her identify it with herself. Social recognition helps her to sustain her new status until it is firmly a part of her. Similarly, the rites of ordination, the garb and new title of a priest or minister, are reinforced by the deference he is accorded. The role shapes people's actions, and increasingly we become what we play at being.

"THE LOOKING-GLASS SELF" In the beginning, and to a great extent all through our lives, the perceived reactions of others influence our self-esteem. This aspect of the self-conception has been called the "looking-glass self" and is associated with Charles Horton Cooley.

A self-idea of this sort seems to have three principal elements: the imagination of our appearance to the other person; the imagination of his judgment of that appearance; and some sort of self-feeling, such as pride or mortification. The comparison with a looking-glass hardly suggests the second element, the imagined judgment, which is quite essential. The thing that moves us to pride or shame is not the mere mechanical reflection of ourselves, but an imputed sentiment, the imagined effect of this reflection upon an-

---

[13] M. H. Kahn and T. S. McPartland, "An Empirical Investigation of Self-Attitudes," *American Sociological Review* 19 (1954), 68–76.

[14] Alfred R. Lindesmith and Anselm L. Strauss, *Social Psychology,* 3rd ed. (New York: Holt, Rinehart & Winston, 1968), pp. 338–339.

other's mind. This is evident from the fact that the character and weight of that other, in whose mind we see ourselves, makes all the difference with our feeling. We are ashamed to seem evasive in the presence of a straightforward man, cowardly in the presence of a brave one, gross in the eyes of a refined one, and so on. We always imagine, and in imagining share, the judgments of the other mind. A man will boast to one person of an action—say, some sharp transaction in trade—which he would be ashamed to own to another. [15]

SIGNIFICANT OTHERS Not all others, of course, are of equal importance to the self-conception. Each of us has some "significant others" whose judgments of us concern us far more than do the judgments of the rest of those with whom we come in contact. For a student trying to earn a good grade, his teacher is a significant other. Experts or colleagues within one's special field of interest—whether in work, sports, or hobbies—are significant others. The members of any reference group are our significant others.

Most important to our self-esteem, however, is the disinterested love, approval, and acceptance of family and intimate friends. Being valued by the people we know intimately is essential to our emotional wellbeing. In such groups we have "personal status" as ourselves, not simply as occupants of statuses. Positive evaluation and disinterested love are especially important in infancy and early childhood, setting a level of self-esteem that is difficult to change for better or worse in later life, regardless of success or failure in conventional roles.

Self-Esteem

Social psychologists have conducted a number of studies of self-esteem and interpersonal relationships. [16] Stanley Coop-

[15] Charles Horton Cooley, *Human Nature and the Social Order* (New York: Charles Scribner's Sons, 1903), pp. 151–153.

[16] A number of instruments for measuring attitudes may be found in John P. Robinson and Phillip R. Shaver, *Measurements of Social Psychological Attitudes* (Survey Research Center, Institute for Social Research, University of Michigan, Ann Arbor, 1969).

Drawing by Lorenz; © 1971 The New Yorker Magazine, Inc.

"I need reassurance, Miss Kimball. Send someone in on his hands and knees."

ersmith, for example, set out to answer the question "What are the conditions that lead an individual to value himself and to regard himself as an object of worth?" He administered a self-esteem inventory of fifty items to a sample of 8- to 10-year old school children, a questionnaire regarding their behavior patterns to their teacher, and a questionnaire about their upbringing to their mothers. He also interviewed the mothers at length and tested the children's behavior in tasks that indicated level of aspiration, selectivity and perception and memory, constancy and independence of judgment, and ability to tolerate stress and adversity.

High self-esteem, he concluded, is related to the following factors: total or near-total acceptance of the child by his parents, clearly defined and enforced limits of behavior, and respect and latitude for individual action within these limits. Parents who seem permissive because they are vague about rules for their children, but punish them severely when, in the parents' judgment, they misbehave, produce low self-esteem in their children.[17]

We have seen that we become who we are by interacting with our environment. Let us now go on and look at the biological and environmental factors that determine personality in more detail.

Factors in Personality Development

As we noted before, people everywhere are born with the same involuntary reflexes—automatic responses, each attached to a given stimulus, which can be altered only slightly. They are also equipped with primary defense reactions. The simplest are the startled

crying and withdrawal of infants who are afraid of being dropped or of a sudden loud noise. Many psychologists believe emotions such as rage, disgust, shame, and grief, as well as fear, are based on such reactions. At any rate, emotions appear to be closely linked with the physiology of the organism, for under emotional stress there are measurable and often striking changes in body functioning. Emotions are subject to considerable conditioning through experience, however, as are such more distinctly primary or innate drives as sex and hunger. It also appears that people vary in the strength of innate urges and their capacities for emotion.

Biological Variables

The way the genes happen to combine into a nuclear cell at the moment of conception determines all the "hereditary" aspects of an individual. *Sex* is fixed at this moment by the presence of an X or Y chromosome in the sperm cell. The particular combination of genes also determines our probable *appearance*—our eye and hair colors, stature, and other physical features (although prenatal and subsequent environmental factors—nutrition in particular—affect our actual stature, weight, muscular development, and the like). Heredity also determines the limits of our *intelligence* and probably has much to do with our *temperament* or prevailing mood. Closely related to growth, temperament, and behavior is our *glandular balance,* which affects many bodily functions. Studies of infants show that they are different from birth. Alexander Thomas and associates conducted intensive studies of eighty infants from birth to age 2. They found a "primary reaction pattern" characteristic of each child, which led him or her to react selectively to stimuli.[18] Thus the

[17] Stanley Coopersmith, *The Antecedents of Self-esteem* (San Francisco: W. H. Freeman, 1967).

[18] *Behavioral Individuality in Early Childhood* (New York: New York University Press, 1963).

biological heredity of the individual apparently predisposes personality in certain directions and sets limits to possible development.

Some of the potential traits and capacities of the organism appear only with *maturation,* that is, with physical growth to a given level of development. Until the eye is capable of discerning letters, for example, the child cannot learn to read. Although the rate of maturation varies from one individual to another, it always follows the same developmental sequence—children sit before they stand, walk before they run. They are never ready for any stage of development until their organisms are ready.

The rate of maturation varies not only among members of a society at any given time, but also over long periods of time. Probably because of improved nutrition, sexual and physical development—and possibly mental development as well—come far earlier now than they did in previous generations. About 1900, European men did not stop growing until age 26. Now they reach their full growth by 17 or 18. The age of *menarche,* or first menstruation, has dropped 2 to 5 years since the seventeenth century, and even in recent decades in the United States.[19]

There is much debate about the degree to which intelligence is biologically determined. Intelligence may be defined in various ways—as the capacity of the organism to adjust to its environment, as "the ability to solve present problems on the basis of past experiences in terms of possible future consequences,"[20] as the capacity for thought and creativity.[21] As a potential of

mankind in general, intelligence is the basis of culture. As an attribute of individuals, intelligence varies greatly among members of any society. The variation is a result of both heredity and environment. The quality of the brain and nervous system is the inborn potential. It does not depend, however, entirely on genetic heritage, for the quality of the pregnant mother's diet has been shown to be highly correlated with her child's intelligence, as has the infant's diet during the first year of life.

Intelligence cannot be measured at all accurately. It can only be guessed at from the way the brain functions as a result of an individual's experience. Nor is it yet clearly understood whether intelligence is a general ability or a number of specific abilities. But it is clearly a biological potential that emerges only as a result of social experience.

Innate intelligence sets limits to a person's capacity to learn. However, people rarely use their intelligence to its limits. A meager culture, emotional blocks or anxieties, a narrow ideology, malnutrition, or simply illness or lack of time may prevent people from utilizing all their intellectual potential.

Our *biological equipment,* then, is one factor that makes us like all other people, like some other people, and like no other people.

Variations in Infant Nurturing

In recent decades scientists have come to believe that the very early care of infants has tremendous consequences for their personalities. We are speaking here of influences distinct from the potentials and urges of the biological organism and also distinct from the largely verbal socialization by which children learn the culture and their place in the social structure: the way a mother holds her child, the way she feeds and later weans him or her, diaper-changing, toilet-

[19] Walter Sullivan, "Boys and Girls Are Now Maturing Earlier," The *New York Times* (Jan. 24, 1971).

[20] Tamotsu Shibutani, *Society and Personality* (Englewood Cliffs, N.J.: Prentice-Hall, 1961), p. 78.

[21] Mary Ellen Goodman, *The Individual and Culture* (Homewood, Ill.: Richard D. Irwin, 1967), p. 4.

training, and other infant disciplines. These are infants' first experience of another organism, of the world around them.

Infant nurturing thus appears to be responsible for universal human nature, the basic orientation of the personality toward others, health and survival, and even the realization of potential intelligence. Cooley, who called primary groups (the family, friendship groups, the neighborhood) "the nursery of human nature," speculated that it is because infants in most societies experience fondling, petting, and frustration in the intimate interaction of the family group that we can feel empathy for those from very different cultures, put ourselves in their places, and understand their emotions and sentiments. That is also why folktales and literature from all over the world often have very similar themes and plots.

Studies show that the character of infant care—whether warm and loving or cold and mechanical—is directly related to an individual's ability to establish emotional relationships with others, to feel a sense of security and mastery, and to experience and understand such sentiments as love, sympathy, envy, and pity. Psychiatrists suggest, for example, that the psychopathic personality—completely self-centered, incapable of emotional ties with others, lacking both internalized standards of right and wrong and a sense of guilt—may be the result of inadequate primary-group relationships during infancy, especially the lack of a warm, nurturing mother.

As a result of his work with autistic children—children who have normal intelligence but who have shut themselves off from the world—psychologist Bruno Bettelheim is convinced that the way children's first "spontaneous moves toward the world" are met during the crucial period of their first six months either frustrates or encourages them in their natural tendency to be active, seeking agents.

A warm, nurturing mother is especially important to the process of acquiring "human nature." *Jerry Frank for Design Photographers International, Inc. and Jeane-Claude Lejeune for Stock, Boston.*

93

Tender loving care is as important as food to the health and survival of an infant. René Spitz compared the handling of infants in an excellent foundling home, where each nurse gave seven babies nutritionally perfect food in hygienic surroundings, with the care imprisoned women gave their own babies in inferior conditions. Of the prison children, all survived the first year, while 30 percent of the foundlings died. The prison-reared children were normal or superior in height, weight, ability to walk, and vocabulary. The foundlings were distinctly below normal.[22] In other studies, it has been found that middle-class mothers who stressed hygiene and schedules and "crying it out" had sicklier babies than did warm, nurturing lower-class mothers who were indifferent to strict rules of baby care.[23]

Even more dramatic evidence of the importance of intensive emotional relationships in early childhood comes from a study of two groups of mentally retarded children. At age 3, thirteen were placed in the care of women inmates in a state institution for the mentally retarded, one child to a ward, while a control group remained in an orphanage. In $1\frac{1}{2}$ years the experimental group had gained 28 IQ points, from 64 to 92. The average of the control group had dropped 26 points. It was then possible to place the experimental group for adoption. A follow-up study 30 years later found all thirteen self-supporting. All but two had completed high school and four had one or more years of college. Members of the control group were all either dead or still institutionalized.[24]

Culture and Personality

Common-sense knowledge holds that there are differences in personality from one society to another. These differences are expressed, for example, in stereotypes of Germans as authoritarian and phlegmatic, Italians as impulsive and emotional, Latin Americans as sensual and mercurial. Social scientists have explored this idea of a "modal" or *basic personality type* in various ways, ranging from pure speculation to rigorous empirical study, but as yet have arrived at few firm generalizations. Depending on their orientation, they attribute these differences to different patterns of infant nurturing and childrearing; to the world view, core values, and ethos of the culture; to definitions of sex roles; and to the handling of crises in the life cycle.

Sweeping generalizations about the relationship of sociocultural patterns of infant nurturing to personality have been characteristic of some psychoanalytically oriented anthropologists. They relate the "national character" of great modern nations to norms of swaddling, weaning, toilet training, and other infant disciplines, sometimes with such great emphasis on these experiences that they have been called "chamber-pot determinists" or "the nipple-and-diaper school." Weston LaBarre, for example, based a theory of Japanese modal personality on descriptions of their presumably severe early training in bowel habits. Trauma at the anal level of development, he declared, produced a neurotic personality characterized by se-

---

[22] "An Inquiry into the Genesis of Psychiatric Conditions in Early Childhood," *The Psychoanalytic Study of the Child* 1 (1945), 53–74. See also R. A. Spitz, "Hospitalism: A Follow-up Report," *The Psychoanalytic Study of the Child* 2 (1946), 113–117.

[23] Margaret Ribble, *The Rights of Infants* (New York: Columbia University Press, 1944).

[24] Harold M. Skeels, "Adult Status of Children with Contrasting Early Life Experiences," *Monographs of the*

Society for Research in Child Development 31 (1966), Serial No. 105. Experiments have shown that monkeys raised without maternal closeness were never able to form normal adult sexual relationships, and if females nonetheless became mothers they rebuffed their offspring and often displayed extreme cruelty. See Harry F. Harlow and Margaret K. Harlow, "The Effect of Rearing Conditions on Behavior," *Bulletin of the Menninger Clinic* 26 (1962): 213–224.

cretiveness, fanaticism, cleanliness, ceremoniousness, and other traits.[25]

A landmark study by Cora DuBois was more firmly grounded in evidence. She applied psychoanalytic techniques—the collection of life histories; the administration of Rorschach, Thematic Apperception, and word association tests; and the analysis of drawings and dreams—to the Alorese of Indonesia, and had her material independently analyzed by several experts. The Alorese tend to be spiteful, suspicious, frustrated, and confused. She attributed these traits to the inconsistent, neglectful, and even abusive treatment of children.[26]

Dissenting from the psychoanalytic approach to the study of modal personality, Francis L. K. Hsu points out that since psychiatry deals with the abnormal, there is a tendency to view the traits of other cultures in terms of neuroses—because their behavior would be so defined in American society. "Infant and childhood experiences," he insists, "are much less important (to the anthropologist) than the roles, structures, and cultures of the societies in question. At best the early training of the individual may be used as a symptom of some of the cultural emphases."[27] Cultural influences on personality continue throughout life.

Chief among these cultural influences, in Ruth Benedict's view, are the dominant world view and values of a society. Each society, she believed, has a different conception of the ideal personality, and most people come to approximate that type naturally and easily. The warrior and visionary were the ideals of the Plains Indians, who rewarded self-reliance, initiative, individualism, and ability to see visions. As a result, men cultivated frenzies and endured danger and discomfort in order to win approval and prestige. The Zuñi Indians of New Mexico, in contrast, discourage individualism, violence, and power. They value moderation and self-effacement and suspect that anyone who likes to wield power practices witchcraft. The Dobuans, who live on rocky volcanic islands off the New Guinea coast, make virtues of ill will and treachery. Existence appears to them an unending struggle for each of the goods of life against deadly antagonists. Suspicion, cruelty, animosity, and malignancy are common among Dobuans.[28]

One study of *subcultural personality differences* in the United States centers on differing reactions to a life crisis—an illness involving considerable pain. Among patients with similar problems in a veterans' hospital in New York City, both Jews and Italians were very emotional in their responses to pain. They were not ashamed to talk about their pain, groan, complain, and cry. The Italians, however, were concerned with the immediate situation, and once they got relief, they were happy and optimistic. Jewish patients, in contrast, were anxious about the source of the pain and about possible side effects of pain-relieving drugs, as well as about the meaning of the pain in relation to their general health and the future of their families. Where Jewish patients tried, semiconsciously or otherwise, to provoke worry and concern on the part of others, Italians tried to provoke sympathy.

Most of the doctors, being "old American" or WASP types, found it easier to understand the reaction of "old American" patients,

[25] "Some Observations on Character Structure in the Orient: The Japanese," *Psychiatry* 8:319–342. The article was written during World War II, when it was impossible to collect empirical data, and when even behavioral scientists might have been more affected by ethnocentrism than under other conditions.

[26] *The People of Alor.*

[27] "Anthropology or Psychiatry: A Definition of Objectives and Their Implications," *Southwest Journal of Anthropology* 8 (1952), 227–250.

[28] *Patterns of Culture* (New York: Penguin Books, 1946).

whose complaints were essentially reports defining the quality, location, and duration of pain, and who preferred to be left alone when they reacted emotionally. They appeared optimistic, confident that experts would tinker efficiently with the troublesome mechanism.

Inquiring into their childhoods, the investigators found that the parents of Jewish and Italian patients had been worried and overprotective, quick to respond sympathetically to crying and complaints, and reluctant to let their children take part in sports. Where the Jewish parents, however, were concerned with the symptomatic meaning of the child's aches and pains and looked on each deviation from normal behavior as a sign of illness, Italian parents expressed sympathy but not anxiety, and at the same time they often punished their children for not taking care of themselves. Parents of "old American" patients, in contrast, had exhorted them not to be sissies, encouraged games and sports in spite of the risk of injury, and taught them to take immediate care of an injury or illness rather than crying and getting emotionally upset.[29]

In all the studies we have discussed here, the emphasis is on intimate interaction between parent and child or on general world view, values, and personality traits. In modern industrial societies, however, socialization is institutionalized and is shared by clearly identifiable and even specialized agencies. The structure and functioning of these agencies, and the ways in which they work together or fail to do so, are reflected in personality, as we shall see from a comparison of childrearing patterns in the United States and the Soviet Union, with some data from other modern societies.

Socialization in Modern Societies: American and Soviet Styles

In the United States, raising children is regarded as a private matter and is left largely to the nuclear family and the informal pressures of the peer group. In the Soviet Union it is seen as a major responsibility of the society at large. In comparing these societies we ask two questions: What effect does a society's approach to upbringing have on individual personality? What are the consequences for that society? We base our discussion largely on an extensive empirical study by Urie Bronfenbrenner.

His observations in the USSR and several other countries alerted him "to the impressive power—and even greater potential—of models, peers, and group forces in influencing the behavior and development of children."[30] One criterion for judging the worth of a society, he suggests, is the concern of one generation for the next. He is disturbed by the fact that most Americans leave the socialization of children after a certain age almost entirely to peer groups and the mass media, while parents, other adults, and older youths are largely removed from active participation in their lives. This, he believes, will result in increased alienation, indifference, antagonism, and violence among children of the middle class as well as the disadvantaged. Sixth-graders were found to spend twice as much time with peers as with parents. Peer-oriented children held rather negative views of themselves and the group and of their own future. They rated their parents lower on affection and discipline

[29] Mark Zborowski, "Cultural Components in Responses to Pain," *Journal of Social Issues* 8(1953), 16–31.

[30] *Two Worlds of Childhood: U.S. and U.S.S.R.* (New York: Russell Sage Foundation, 1970), p. 1. With the assistance of John C. Condry, Jr.

than did adult-oriented children. Between ages 6 and 16, American children spend an average of 22 hours a week watching television as compared to 14 in Britain. By the time the average American child is 16 he has spent 12,000 to 15,000 hours in front

deCarlo in the Saturday Review.

of the TV set—15 to 20 solid months of 24 hours a day. Yet we know little about the effects of TV on personality.[31]

In sharp contrast to this laissez-faire approach, the Soviet Union makes proper socialization a duty of responsible citizens. A. S. Makarenko's *A Book for Parents* (the Soviet equivalent of Dr. Spock's book) declares that, "in handing over to you a certain measure of social authority, the Soviet state *demands* from you correct upbringing of future citizens," and that they *must* give their

children parental love.[32] Upbringing, says Bronfenbrenner, "is virtually a national hobby." Teenage boys—complete strangers—would swoop up his 4-year old son on the street, hug him, and swing him around. Strangers scold others for wearing their skirts too short or littering the street.

Emotional ties between parents and children are stronger in the Soviet Union and Germany than in the United States, as indicated by maternal protectiveness, overt display of physical affection, and the time adults spend in play and conversation with children. Obedience is stressed. Withdrawal of love is the most common sanction for misbehavior.

The most distinctive feature of Soviet upbringing is the "children's collective," which is by no means an autonomous peer group, but one firmly guided by adults (some of whom, in nursery school and kindergarten, are actually called "upbringers"). For about 5 percent of Soviet children, the first collective is an infant nursery, and one child out of five between ages three and six is in a preschool. In the nurseries six to eight babies live in each raised playpen. There is one upbringer for every four children. She is more than a babysitter, as she provides fondling and other sensory stimulation. The collectives encourage self-reliance. By 18 months they expect children to be completely toilet trained. Sharing, cooperation, and joint activities are encouraged from the start. Small children serve at the table, clean up, garden, and care for animals.

The first day of school is a gala occasion, a national holiday when family and friends accompany children to school and present the teachers with flowers. Each classroom is a unit of the Communist youth organization for the particular age level. The teacher does not correct or discipline the individual

[31] Social psychological experiments suggest, however, that people observing aggressive models, even on film, may act more aggressively, especially toward those they dislike. Albert Bandura, Dorothea Ross, and Sheila A. Ross, "Transmission of Aggression through Imitation of Aggressive Models," *Journal of Abnormal and Social Psychology* 62 (1961), 575–582.

[32] Bronfenbrenner, *Two Worlds of Childhood*, p. 3 (Emphasis added).

child, but calls on his peers for criticism. Competition is not among individuals, but groups: first the "links" or rows in a classroom, then classes, schools, cities, and regions—and not only in academic achievements and sports, but also in shop work, service projects, housekeeping, personal grooming, and moral conduct.

Criticism of others in the group is regarded as a duty, not tattling as it is in our society. Adult organizations are also involved in upbringing. A shop, factory, or city agency may "adopt" a school, and its members give the pupils much of their free time. Similarly, a fourth grade may adopt a first grade in the same school, escort the children to and from school, play with them in the schoolyard, teach them games, read to them, and help with their schoolwork.

One consequence of this pattern of socialization is that Soviet children are much less willing to engage in antisocial conduct than are children in the United States, England, and West Germany. An American child is *more* likely to engage in misconduct if his classmates know of it. The opposite is true in the Soviet Union. Asked what they would do if they knew of another's misbehavior, 20 percent of a sample of Swiss children said they would do nothing, while only 1 percent of Soviet children gave that reply.

Assessing the consequences of this system, Bronfenbrenner cites standards of behavior among sixth-graders in England, Switzerland, the United States, and the Soviet Union, concluding that "Soviet youngsters placed greater emphasis on overt propriety, such as being clean, orderly, and well-mannered, but gave less weight . . . to telling the truth and seeking intellectual understanding."[33] Another observer credits the

[33] *Ibid.*, p. 81.

"Upbringers" with their charges in a children's collective in the Soviet Union. *Eve Arnold for Magnum.*

system with providing "a sense of identification and purpose that is so often lacking among youth in modern societies" and playing "a significant part in creating an able, skilled, highly educated poulation." But, he says, "It has also contributed to the intellectual and moral paralysis that was and is the legacy of Stalinism," and he adds that a number of young people are indifferent or even rebellious simply because the youth program is imposed from above and there are no alternatives.[34]

Bronfenbrenner sums up what Americans might learn from the Soviet system:

The principles that we in the West have investigated in—and largely confined to—the laboratory, the Russians have discovered and applied in practice on a national scale. . . . If the Russians have gone too far in subjecting the child and his peer group to conformity to a single set of values imposed by the adult society, perhaps we have reached the point of diminishing returns in allowing excessive autonomy and in failing to utilize the constructive potential of the peer group in developing social responsibility and consideration for others.[35]

However you feel about Bronfenbrenner's conclusions, one thing is clear from all studies of culture and personality and of comparative patterns of socialization: The process of becoming human, which we described as the development of a self, is also inevitably the process of becoming a member of a specific society and learning its culture. The two aspects of socialization cannot be separated. As babies learn to be human, they learn to be a *particular kind* of human.

[34] Allen Kossof, *The Soviet Youth Program: Regimentation and Rebellion* (Cambridge, Mass.: Harvard University Press, 1965) pp. 1–2, 174.

[35] Bronfenbrenner, *Two Worlds of Childhood*, pp. 151, 165–166. For other studies of collective socialization, see discussions of Israeli *kibbutzim* in Bruno Bettelheim, *The Children of the Dream* (New York: Macmillan, 1969), and Melford Spiro, *Children of the Kibbutz* (New York: Schocken Books, 1965). For a critique of the former by Urie Bronfenbrenner, see 'The Dream of the Kibbutz," *Saturday Review* (Sept. 20, 1969).

Socialization Through the Life Cycle

In focusing on child development so far in this chapter, we do not mean to imply that socialization is complete when we reach a certain level of maturity. We may be considered socialized when our behavior enables us to fit into a group and interaction can proceed without serious hitches. But in a stricter sense, socialization is never finished. First, there is always some resistance to it: "Do I *have* to? Why?" Second, we enter new statuses as we go through the life cycle and join new groups and even new societies.

For several reasons the first five years are most important in forming personality. Growth and development are fastest during those years. The learning process is a sequential one, building on what has gone before—so it is much easier to learn something entirely new than to stamp out something and replace it. Basic values and motives are instilled in childhood. Later socialization is more concerned with overt performance. If the values and motivations for an adult role are lacking, and a person is extremely resistant to socialization in a new role—say that of soldier—he may be excluded from it, or jailed, or assigned some lowly status.

Assuming, then, that basic values and motivations have been learned in childhood, *adult socialization* includes learning new skills (mainly by combining old ones in new patterns, with perhaps some new material); getting to "know the score," to know what the real patterns are as compared to the ideals learned as a child; and resolving role conflicts, striking some sort of bargain, for example, between being a dedicated organization man and a good family man. Adult socialization is more specific than childhood learning, although in some instances socializing agencies must deal in general orientations as well. College fraternities, for example, may teach lower-middle class boys the norms and values of a higher social class. An adult has usually decided who his really significant others are and may virtually ignore people who do not matter, while an adolescent may try to please everyone. People also tend to initiate action more frequently as they get older.[36]

Continuities and Discontinuities

As we grow, mature, and age, we must learn new roles and relationships. In some societies this process is fairly smooth. In others it may be jerky and traumatic, with sharp discontinuities. Ruth Benedict compared the way a boy becomes a man in American society to the way this happens in several Indian societies. In ours, "the child is sexless, the adult estimates his virility by his sexual activities; the child must be protected from the ugly facts of life, the adult must meet them without psychic catastrophe; the child must obey, the adult must command this obedience."[37] While an American child is expected to play and an adult to work, in American Indian societies the child is gradually entrusted with responsibilities he can handle. An American child may be spanked if he disobeys his father. A Crow Indian takes spanking as a sign of lack of love and interprets his child's disobedience as a sign that he will become a man.

Other tribal societies minimize the strain of discontinuity in the life cycle by a system of age-grading, with rites of passage to different age groups. Socialization into a new age status is made easier by the support of peers, by ritual and ceremony, and by the prestige of the new status.

Each stage in the life cycle alters the self-conception and may even change personality traits. Measuring married and unmarried women according to the California Personality Inventory, a social psychologist found that married people changed in such traits as self-acceptance and dominance, the more so the earlier they married.[38]

Resocialization

A person may be socialized in one society and then through some turn of fate or choice move to another. This is the common case with immigrants, many of whom find themselves "marginal men," at home in neither culture. Dramatic instances of quite thorough resocialization are afforded by inmates of or recruits to *total institutions.*

An army recruit, a novice in a severely traditional order of nuns, a prisoner, or a mental patient sheds an old identity and, through a process that in all these cases is very much alike, takes on a new one. Erving Goffman has described the resocialization process in such total institutions as involving these elements: isolation from the outside (perhaps by virtue of barbed wire, high walls, or locked doors); spending all one's time in the same place with the same people at work, play, and sleep; shedding of individual identity by giving up old clothes and posses-

[36] Orville G. Brim, Jr., "Socialization in Later Life," in Orville G. Brim, Jr., and Stanton Wheeler, *Socialization after Childhood* (New York: John Wiley & Sons, 1966), pp. 18–33.
[37] "Continuities and Discontinuities in Cultural Conditioning," *Psychiatry* 1(1938): 161–167.

[38] Edgar F. Borgatta, ed., *Social Psychology: Readings and Perspective* (Chicago: Rand McNally, 1969), p. 247.

sions for uniforms or habits and standard equipment, and being called by first or last name, number, rank, or status ("sister" or "soldier"); a clean break with the past; and loss of freedom of action. A similar process accounts for the success of the Chinese Communists in "brainwashing" some American soldiers during the Korean War.[39]

Once a person has been thoroughly socia-lized into a very specific role, it is hard for him to reenter the society at large. Returning war veterans, for example, find it hard to tailor their language to their families and to experience empathy and compassion once they have been encouraged to regard people as dehumanized things. They feel like stran-gers among their old friends.

Summary

Personality is the individual version of human nature, the organized patterns of thought, feeling, and action that characterize a given individual. The process of becoming human, of acquiring a personality, is a com-plex one, and there are many theories of how it occurs.

Biological determinists find the master key to human behavior in inborn patterns or constitutional tendencies. Cultural deter-minists see individuals as mere reflections of their cultures or of the particular status into which they are born in the social struc-ture.

Behaviorists see newborn babies as infin-itely plastic and believe they can be condi-tioned to almost any conceivable kind of behavior, depending on the stimuli to which they are exposed and the rewards and pun-ishments they perceive to be consequences of their actions.

Freudian psychoanalysts see culture as a set of ways that the group has evolved for handling sex and agression. Society always

represses natural impulses. The price of civilization is discontent. Freud emphasized the irrational, emotional, and unconscious aspects of personality. While he made us aware of the complexity of human behavior, he neglected or underplayed the role of reason, language, and cultural variation. Neo-Freudians, in contrast, take these fac-tors into account. Erik Erikson sees the life cycle as a series of stages, each of which is successful to the extent that previous stages were successful, especially if the identity crisis is satisfactorily resolved.

Humanist psychologists stress subjective experience and the search for meaning and value in existence. Abraham Maslow, for example, has described a hierarchy of needs, the highest being self-actualization or achievement of full humanness.

Symbolic interactionist theory as devel-oped by George Herbert Mead demonstrates the intricate relationship of culture, society, and personality. Because people can become objects to themselves, they can control their own behavior through self-interaction. Be-cause we feel empathy, we can take the roles of others and know what to expect of them and what they expect of us. Minds and selves arise in the process of symbolic interaction.

[39] Erving Goffman, *Asylums: Essays on the Social Situation of Mental Patients and Other Inmates* (Garden City, N.Y.: Doubleday, 1961).

A culture is a set of significant symbols shared by a group. A person's mind is his or her set of significant symbols. Children acquire a self in two stages: the play stage, in which they take the roles of particular others toward themselves, and the game stage, where they acquire a generalized other, the moral voice of the community as a whole, which is their conscience or character.

The self-conception is crucial to behavior. It includes a sense of identity, a level of self-esteem, and an ideal self. Although it has an organic basis, it is a social product, resulting from one's statuses and roles, one's self-evaluation, and feedback from significant others.

So far we have dealt with socialization as the general process of becoming a functioning member of the human race. Now we turn to socialization as the process of incorporating each of us into a specific social group, and the factors that make for similarities and differences in personality.

Each of us is a unique personality, a dynamic, complex system whose growth is a process of creative becoming because we can interact with ourselves, reflecting on our perception and our chosen action.

But we are also like some other people and like all other people. All members of the human species are born with essentially the same biological attributes, but even so there is great variation in reaction patterns, strength of drives and reflexes, temperament as affected by glandular balance, and potential intelligence. The rate of maturation and the development of potential intelligence depend on many experiences, including psychic and organic nutrition. Among these is the kind of nurturing one gets in infancy and early childhood, which affects one's general orientation to life and to others, one's health and survival, and the degree to which one's potential intelligence is realized.

Studies of the ways in which culture shapes personality have related the most typical traits of members of a society to its general world view and core values, to its patterns of child rearing, and to its role definitions. A comparative study of American and Soviet patterns of socialization concludes that the Soviet system of children's collectives, with great interest shown by older youth and adults in the "upbringing" process, produces conformist personalities with a sense of purpose and belonging that is lacking in our own society. In the United States the autonomous age-segregated peer group and the mass media appear to produce people who are more likely to feel alienated and engage in antisocial behavior. At the same time, our system leaves more room for intellectual curiosity and innovation.

Socialization is a lifelong process, but in general basic values and norms are learned in childhood, and more specific skills in adulthood. In some societies the transition to various stages of the life cycle and to new roles is jerky and traumatic. In others it is either a continuous, gradual process or is eased by such devices as age-grading and rites of passage. Resocialization into a new society or a total institution may make one a marginal person, at home in neither, or may drastically change one's self-conception.

Glossary

Behaviorism The theory that personality is entirely learned and that behavior is the result of conditioning.

Biological determinism The theory that human nature is simply an expression or unfolding of inborn drives or tendencies.

Cultural determinism The theory that human nature and personality depend on the society into which a baby happens to be born and individuals have no control over its culture.

Humanistic psychology The school of thought that stresses subjective experience and the search for meaning and value in existence.

Identity A sense of personal sameness continuing through time, a concept central to neo-Freudian theory.

Personality The organized ways of behaving and feeling that characterize given individuals.

Psychoanalytic theory The Freudian theory that culture is merely a reflection of individual psychology and is based on the effort to handle the problems of sex and aggression, especially in childhood.

Self The core of personality, accounting for its unity and structure.

Self-conception Our image of ourselves, including a sense of identity, self-esteem, and an ideal self.

Socialization The process of becoming a functioning member of the human race and part of a social group.

Symbolic interactionism The theory of the emergence of the self as the process by which a newborn baby becomes a human being.

chapter

6

Deviance and Social Control

Ever since Eve ate the forbidden apple, people have violated the norms they were taught. The process of socialization does not turn out batches of perfect conformists. Most of us do conform to the rules most of the time. But all of us break some of the rules some of the time, consciously or unconsciously, with or without a sense of guilt. Some people deviate from some of the rules most of the time, and their behavior may or may not be regarded as a social problem. The power of internalized cultural norms and of social group sanctions, nonetheless, is so great that no one—except for a few extremely retarded or psychotic persons—violates most or all of the rules most or all of the time.

Today, in our rapidly changing society, laws and other norms are often violated. Especially in urban areas, crime rates have risen sharply. And to the older generation much contemporary behavior, illegal or not, appears shocking, sinful, and wrong. But neither their disapproval nor the growing body of formal laws and enforcement agencies appears to have curbed crime and other deviant behavior very much.

In this chapter we look at deviance and at society's efforts to control it. We first examine the nature and variety of both deviant and conforming behavior. Then we consider some theories about the causes of deviance. Next we discuss various ideas of how a person becomes "a deviant." We then ask whether deviance may have positive as well as negative functions. We close the

chapter with a discussion of crime and law enforcement.

Kinds of Deviance and Conformity

Deviance is behavior that is contrary to the norms of a group, exceeding its limits of tolerance for nonconformist behavior and subject to punishment if discovered. Some deviant behavior is simply *improper* and frowned upon, but is punished only informally. Laughing at a funeral is a deviant act, but there is no law against it. Yet it rarely occurs because the norms against it are thoroughly internalized, and the social pressure against it is great. Other kinds of deviant behavior may be seen as antisocial, self-destructive, or immoral according to the norms of any given group or society. *Antisocial behavior* such as assault and robbery endangers other people and their property. Drug addiction, alcoholism, suicide, and mental illness are seen as *self-destructive* to the deviant. Some behavior, such as prostitution, homosexuality, gambling and political corruption, is seen as *immoral* rather than really dangerous. It is tolerated or winked at in some communities and societies, regulated in others, and punished in still others. But some deviance is seen as *destructive to the society* itself, or at least to its rulers. Treason, incitement to riot, and conspiracy are the kinds of deviance most severely punished by those in power.

Some of these deviant acts are **crimes**—behavior prohibited by law and punishable by law-enforcement agencies. All criminal acts are considered deviant, but not all deviant acts are criminal. The degree of disapproval and punishment of deviant behavior depends on how vital the violated norm is to the cohesion and survival of the society as defined by its traditions and its leaders. Parking violations, although they are punishable by law, are "not too bad." Murder and terrorism are dangerous and outrageous. The public attitude and the formal norms also vary from one time to another. The use of certain drugs such as marijuana, for example, was not defined as a serious social problem until many middle-class people became involved.

No act is inherently deviant. Whether or not it is judged to be deviant depends on the context in which it is performed, whether that context is a specific situation or a specific culture. In wartime, killing is a duty. It is not defined as the crime of murder. In the United States, suicide is illegal; in Japan it is considered an honorable act.

Deviance is a collective action. Like love, it takes two: the person and the rest of society who judge that person. Individuals are aware of those other people and adjust their behavior accordingly. "The adjustment may consist of deciding that since the police will probably look *here,* I will plant the bomb *there,* as well as deciding that since the police are going to look, I guess I won't make any bombs at all or even think about it anymore."[1]

Most people seem to be comfortable with a certain amount of deviance. Only when deviance gets out of hand, when it makes significant numbers of people feel threatened, does it become a social problem. For example, we have a norm that says it is wrong to steal other people's property. But stealing pencils and paper from an employer, though

[1] Howard S. Becker, *Outsiders: Studies in the Sociology of Deviance* (New York: Free Press, 1963), p.182.

This man's eccentric appearance is deviant in one sense, but does not exceed the limits of tolerance for nonconformist behavior. *George Malave/Stock, Boston.*

very common, is not a social problem. Neither is bank robbery, because it does not happen very often. But mugging—stopping people on the street and taking their money under a threat of violence—is a social problem in some cities.

But most of us conform most of the time. Conformity makes it easier for the individual, in most situations, to adjust and get along with others. It avoids much uncertainty and anxiety. Yet, like deviance, conformity can be overdone. Two main kinds of conformity draw the fire of social critics. The first kind is unthinking or even compulsive adherence to conventional beliefs and behavior patterns. The second type is characterized by yielding to group pressures against one's better judgment. The first form may simply be the "useful tyranny of the normal," the habitual acceptance of the language, food patterns, and other folkways of a culture. But it may also include the belief that only one religion, one economic system, or one political arrangement is moral. Conformity of this type depends largely on past influences. The second type depends on present pressures. Both are to some extent the inevitable results of socialization. But carried to extremes, they stifle the constructive innovation that produces necessary social changes. "Where everyone thinks alike, no one thinks very much."[2]

Conformists may be so thoroughly socialized that it never occurs to them to question the norms. They may repress contrary impulses, or may sublimate them into approved kinds of activity. On the other hand, conformists may be aware of impulses to deviant behavior, but may not give in to them for any of the following reasons.

1. Through the process of self-interaction, they exercise self-control, knowing that the cost of deviant behavior would be guilt, shame, and loss of self-esteem.

2. They want to keep the approval of their significant others.

3. They may fear punishment, ostracism, loss of their jobs, citizenship, freedom, or life.

4. They may see no point in deviating from the straight and narrow if the rewards of deviance do not seem glamorous.

5. They may simply have no opportunity for deviant behavior despite fantasies and impulses toward it.

If one or more of these five blocks to deviant behavior is lifted, and motives are strong enough, such behavior may occur. In a riot, for example, deviant behavior is rewarded by acquiring things and by the release of frustrations. There is opportunity on all sides. People who have weakly internalized norms may well join in. And yet a large majority of people in riot areas do not engage in such behavior, possibly because it does not fit with their self-conceptions, norms, and values, or because they identify with a reference group such as a

Farris in The Saturday Review

"Do you suppose they know something we don't?"

[2] Norman Tallent, *Psychological Perspectives on the Person* (Princeton: D. Van Nostrand, 1967), p. 212.

church or family that would not condone such deviance.

All of us have probably found ourselves in situations where we had the opportunity to deviate from norms. Some of us may have done so. Others may not. Why do some people deviate when others do not?

Causes of Deviance

Social scientists have been occupied for years trying to find out where deviance comes from. The majority of them have viewed deviance as illness or pathology. If they could isolate the factors that lead people to become deviant, perhaps they could find a "cure" for it. Their attempts to discover the causes can be classified as biological, psychological, or sociological.

Biological Theories

In the last century, before the advent of psychoanalysis, deviant behavior was assumed to be physiological in origin. Criminal tendencies were thought to be inherited. A person had "good blood" or "bad blood." A basic belief was that some people were "born criminals."

One scientist who subscribed to this belief was Cesare Lombroso, an Italian doctor. He measured the inmates of several Italian prisons and came to the conclusion that convicts' physiques were more "primitive" than those of noncriminals.[3] This belief, that one could tell a book by its cover, received enthusiastic support, and Lombroso's theory dominated criminology for 35 years. Then Charles Goring, a prison medical officer in England, also compared prisoners and noncriminals.[4] But he did not find the primitivism and degeneracy reported by Lombroso. His study convinced the majority of researchers that the sources of deviant behavior lay elsewhere.

Like Lombroso, William Sheldon believed that the body revealed the character of the person.[5] He classified people according to the degree that they conformed to each of three general body types (see Figure 6-1). Each body type had a distinct physical appearance and reflected specific personality

[3] Cesare Lombroso, "Introduction" to Gina Lombroso Ferrero, *Criminal Man According to the Classification of Cesare Lombroso* (New York and London, Putman, 1911).

[4] Charles Goring, *The English Convict* (London: His Majesty's Stationery Office, 1913).

[5] William H. Sheldon, with the collaboration of Emil M. Hartl and Eugene McDermott, *Varieties of Delinquent Youth* (New York: Harper, 1949).

Figure 6-1 Sheldon's three basic somatotypes. The person on left ranks high in endomorphy, the person in the center is high in mesomorphy, and the person on the right is high in ectomorphy. *After W. H. Sheldon, The Varieties of Temperament. New York: Harper & Row, 1942.*

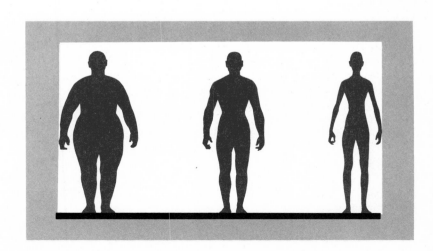

traits. The *endomorph* is sociable, relaxed, and self-indulgent and has a round, rather soft body. At the other extreme is the *ectomorph,* who is very thin, nervous, and rather introverted. In the middle is the *mesomorph,* the typical athlete—well-muscled, physically active, restless, and relatively insensitive. Sheldon stated that, while no body type could be said to cause deviance, mesomorphs were the most common type found in a group of over 200 delinquent boys. He concluded that selective breeding was the answer to the problem of deviant behavior.

Sheldon Glueck and Eleanor Glueck confirmed Sheldon's findings but drew different conclusions.[6] They agreed that mesomorphs, because of their strength and vitality, had the potential to be what Sheldon called "predatory people," who do what they want without much regard for the rights or needs of others. However, Glueck and Glueck stressed that some ectomorphs and endomorphs also turn to deviance. They might be seeking from other deviants the social acceptance and gratification that most other people deny them because of their less-than-ideal physique.

Lombroso's and Sheldon's theories have gone out of favor today. But the search for biological bases of deviant behavior continues. A recent discovery that has captured some attention involves sex-chromosome abnormalities in males. Normal males have two sex chromosomes, an X and a Y, in every body cell. Some men, however, have an extra Y chromosome. These XYY men are typically taller than average and may have somewhat lower IQs. A number of men in prison have been found to be XYY males. This discovery at first appeared to be the long-sought biological factor. But later researchers have found XYY males who lead normal, law-abiding lives. Thus, simply having an extra Y chromosome is no guarantee

that the man will display deviant behavior. Some researchers have suggested that such men are simply more impulsive than most people. Some may eat impulsively; others may steal impulsively. But contrary to what was first thought, they are not more aggressive and violent than the average man.[7]

Others have examined the brain as a possible source for deviant behavior. In the last century, a form of personality analysis called *phrenology* was popular. Different brain structures were thought to control various traits and abilities. Phrenologists would feel the bumps on people's heads and would analyze their clients' characters on the basis of the relative sizes of their bumps.

Some investigators today do feel that certain basic drives such as aggression, sex, and pain/pleasure may be localized in specific areas of the brain. Studies that involve placing electrodes into people's brains and watching their behavior have lent some support to this theory. But even if we could "map" the brain, it is doubtful that we could find one single "deviance center." And even if such a center existed, ethical considerations would limit what we could do about it.

This is not to say that the physiology of the brain does not affect behavior. It does. Some mental problems, schizophrenia for example, have been found to be related to chemical imbalances in the brain. Some people who have had brain injuries act in deviant ways. The most famous such case is that of Charles Whitman. For no apparent reason, he killed his wife and mother and then terrorized the city of Austin by sniping at people from a tower on the University of Texas campus. He was later found to have a brain tumor. But such cases are uncom-

---

[6] *Physique and Delinquency* (New York: Harper, 1956).

[7] John Money, "Prenatal Hormones and Postnatal Socialization in Gender Identity Differentiation," *Nebraska Symposium on Motivation* (Lincoln: University of Nebraska, 1973), pp. 221–295.

mon. Most people feel that it is more fruitful to look to psychological and social factors for the causes of deviant behavior.

Psychological Perspectives on Deviance

Both biological and psychological theories may be called "kinds of people" theories. They suggest that only certain kinds of people become deviant. If we can find out which kinds, perhaps we can isolate the factors that predispose them to deviance and thus correct the problem. Psychologists have taken several different approaches.

According to classical psychoanalytic theory, we all have the same basic drives or instincts. Satisfaction of such needs as hunger, thirst, and sex results in pleasure. However, if these needs are not satisfied, we feel pain. Since it is natural for all organisms to seek pleasure and avoid pain, our initial impulse is to satisfy our needs immediately in any way we can. But living in society means that we must learn to control ourselves. We must learn to postpone the satisfaction of our needs until we can find a socially acceptable way to do so.

Deviant behavior occurs when people are not able to control themselves satisfactorily. Psychologists believe this is generally a result of poor socialization in childhood. Inconsistent, undependable, or morally weak parents may not provide their children with the support and good example they need to develop a strong conscience. The result of extremely poor socialization is the so-called psychopath. Such people may be intelligent, charming, and pleasant to be around, or they may be clods and dullards. What distinguishes them from the rest of us is their lack of "guilt, compassion, and humane regard for others."[8] They are the wolves among the sheep. Fortunately, cases of true psychopathy are rare. They are so rare, in fact, that some scholars think the category should be discarded. But to the degree that people lack strong internal controls, they do seem to be predisposed to deviance.

An outgrowth of classical psychoanalytic theory is the frustration-aggression hypothesis. Simply stated, frustration results in aggression.[9] Moreover, the stronger our need is, the more frustration we feel when we are blocked from satisfying that need. And the greater the frustration, the stronger the feelings of aggression that result. This highly popular theory has more general application than the self-control theories. People may or may not have had the childhood experiences necessary to form a well-developed conscience, but all of us daily find ourselves in the kinds of situations that result in frustration.

Whether or not we express that aggression may still depend on self-control. Obviously, not all frustration results in overt aggression. While the theory may help explain why a specific individual committed a specific act of deviance, it does not explain deviance in general.

This criticism may be applied to all the "kinds of people" theories. They may seem adequate when dealing with specific cases, but they cannot be generalized.

Sociological Theories of Deviance

Most people still feel that deviance is sickness, that only certain kinds of people become deviant because there is something wrong with them. The sociological approach does not deny that people are ultimately responsible for their behavior. But sociologists look

[8] Albert K. Cohen, *Deviance and Control* (Englewood Cliffs, N.J.: Prentice-Hall, 1966), p. 56.

[9] John Dollard, Leonard W. Doob, Neal E. Miller, O. H. Mowrer, and Robert R. Sears, *Frustration and Aggression* (New Haven, Conn.: Yale University Press, 1939).

for external circumstances that make deviant behavior more likely. Sociological theories deal with people not as unique personalities but as occupiers of various positions in the community or society.

In the 1920s, sociologists at the University of Chicago found that the highest concentration of delinquency occurred in the "transition zone" surrounding the central business district. Successive groups of poor people moved in and out of this zone. The researchers believed that these neighborhoods were socially disorganized and that this, combined with poverty, explained their high rates of deviant behavior.[10] Although this idea has been greatly modified, it generated a lot of interest in the social view of deviance.

ALIENATION Some theorists believe that people commit deviant acts because they feel alienated from the larger society. **Alienation** is defined as a feeling that one is an alien, a stranger—to others, to one's environment, and even to oneself. Alienation is measured against the ideal of personality integration. Integrated people feel at home in the world and at ease with others. They know who they are and where they belong. They have an adequate level of self-esteem. They feel they have some control over the course of their own lives. They feel committed to the values and goals of their group and they play their roles responsibly.

In modern urban society, however, millions of people are alienated. First, they are cut off from the natural world as a source of wonder and pleasure. (A teacher asked her class to be sure to watch a lunar eclipse that night. "What channel?" one youngster asked.) The alienated feel cut off from others. Perhaps they do not know the norms and therefore lack guidance for behavior.

Or else they reject the norms and values of the larger society. Or they distrust the motives of others and feel that others regard them as things to be used for their own ends. Alienation may also involve a sense of meaninglessness, a loss of goals and values, a feeling that one is alone and that no one cares or understands. It may mean a feeling of helplessness, or even hopelessness, stemming from anxiety in a world that is too complex to be controlled.

Those who feel alienated do not necessarily deviate from cultural norms. They may, in fact, ward off anxiety by conforming compulsively. But most alienated people reject or feel rejected by the larger society and do not abide by some of its norms. Whole groups, such as oppressed minorities, may feel alienated and not bound by the rules. Self-defeating forms of deviance, such as alcoholism and drug addiction, are also an escape from anxiety. Those who suffer from mental and emotional disturbances are also more or less deeply alienated from themselves and others.

ANOMIE Related to alienation is a feeling of anomie, or normlessness. **Anomie** results when there is a scarcity of socially acceptable institutionalized means to satisfy people's legitimate needs.[11] People learn to value certain things—money, prestige, education—only to find that they have limited access to them if they conform. Thus they may come to feel that conformity is foolish because they have little to gain. This situation results in a feeling of tension or strain. If it goes on long enough, it can weaken people's commitment to the society as a whole.

People can cope with social strain in several ways. One way is simply to ignore the strain and continue to conform. Merton

[10] Clifford R. Shaw, *Delinquency Areas* (Chicago; University of Chicago Press, 1929).

[11] Robert K. Merton, "Social Structure and Anomie," *American Sociological Review,* Vol. 3 (October, 1938), pp. 672–682.

described four other ways of coping, all of which could be considered deviant.[12] *Innovators* retain the accepted cultural goals, but reject the legitimate means for achieving them. Students who cheat on exams rather than studying for them may thus be thought of as innovators. *Ritualists,* on the other hand, do follow the rules. But they have lost sight of the goals the rules were designed to achieve. An example is a bureaucrat who does things only "by the book." *Retreatists,* as the name implies, reject both goals and means. They cope with strain by dropping out entirely, like drug addicts and alcoholics. *Rebels* also reject both goals and means. But rather than dropping out, they seek to replace cultural goals and means with others they feel are more fair and workable.

Thus, according to anomie theory, deviance is not necessarily sick. It is an attempt to resolve problems that arise when institutionalized means to achieve culturally approved goals become scarce, inadequate, or ineffective. Anomie theory is an important contribution to sociological literature on deviance. But it is not wholly adequate as a general theory. It is most obviously applicable to the poor, and thus it appears to support the idea that crime is strictly a lower-class phenomenon.

CONFLICT THEORY Another approach sees deviance as the result of conflict between social groups. According to this perspective, conflict is inevitable in any society that includes diverse elements—ethnic groups, groups with different norms and values, different socioeconomic levels, and so on. Conflict is not necessarily disruptive. It can encourage cooperation, identity, and unity within a group. It can also lead to needed social change. But when conflict results from a differential distribution of power among various social groups, social cohesion may be threatened. The groups that have power are likely to use it for social control. These powerful groups attempt to influence public policy. If they succeed, they are able to control the lives of the less powerful groups. The moral attitudes of those at the top are reflected in public attitudes toward deviance, which are embodied in laws. The laws will express the powerful groups' versions of morality. Their avowed standards of behavior are thus imposed on the less powerful groups.

A theory of how deviance develops has grown out of this perspective.[13] Behavior is defined as deviant when it conflicts with the interests and values of the powerful groups that shape public policy. Because crimes are defined as such by these groups through their influence on law enforcement authorities, deviance is seen by conflict theorists as externally imposed. Although the standards for all groups will be set by the powerful segments of society, the behavior of the least powerful groups is most likely to be judged as deviant. This damages the self-image of members of such groups and may lead to criminal behavior as a self–fulfilling prophecy.

Like anomie theory, conflict theory is descriptive rather than explanatory. But it was designed that way. According to Richard Quinney, criminologists have been mistaken in channeling most of their energy into looking for causes of deviance. Quinney feels that deviance can be understood and explained without knowing why such behavior occurs in specific individuals. Because conflict is inevitable, deviance is also inevitable. The reasons for specific acts of deviance are likely to be unique for each individual and

---

[12] Robert K. Merton, *Social Theory and Social Structure,* revised and enlarged ed. (New York: Free Press, 1957).

[13] Richard Quinney, *The Social Reality of Crime* (Boston: Little, Brown, 1970).

thus are probably not open to explanation by some as-yet-undiscovered general theory.

Most sociologists do not accept Quinney's dismal view of causation theories. Their focus on causes is related to the idea that deviance—especially crime—is a blight that must be eliminated. But experience of deviance itself, what it means to the individuals involved in it, is also important. Let us now look at what sociologists have learned about how people become deviant.

The Process of Becoming Deviant

Consider the following stories:

Elizabeth was a bright, attractive 15 year old who had grown up in a house crowded with in-laws, brothers, sisters, nieces and nephews. Her parents both worked and were rarely at home. Her older brothers and sisters also worked, leaving their youngsters to manage for themselves. No one particularly cared whether Elizabeth, or any of the other children, got to school, needed anything, or were happy. They were just there to grow up as best they could.

As a result of these conditions, Elizabeth became pregnant.

Liz was a bright, attractive 15 year old whose family was forced to move to a new neighborhood. Before moving there, Liz was innocent with regard to sexual matters. She became friendly with a 16 year old, Jane, who lived next door. Subsequently, Liz became a popular member of Jane's high school crowd. Liz sensed that Jane's crowd was a bit fast but so enjoyed the popularity she had gained that she was loath to risk it by appearing puritanical. Through Jane and her friends, Liz met Jim.

As a result of these conditions, Liz became pregnant.

Betty was a bright, attractive 15 year old whose parents were affectionate but rather traditional in outlook. They felt, on both educational and moral grounds, that Betty's development would be best served by attending a parochial school.

By and large, Betty enjoyed going to parochial school. However, there was one Sister who constantly dwelled on the importance of chastity, and who displayed her views in an inquisitorial manner. Betty rather resented the accusations of the Sister, but being of basically sound personality managed to take them in stride. She frequently dated boys, but aside from an occasional kiss kept her virginity intact.

One evening, Betty and her new steady boy friend were sitting in his car just talking. Her boy friend, Dick, decided at 10:30 to take his nightly allotment of one deep kiss. At precisely that moment, Officer Larkin, who was the Sister's brother, threw open the car door. He proceeded to derogate Betty and Dick, calling Betty a slut and threatening Dick with a statutory rape charge. His tantrum spent, Officer Larkin's manner turned fatherly and in the end he smiled and said, "You look like good kids so I'm gonna give you a break this time. But don't let me catch you up here again." Betty and Dick, who remained speechless throughout, did not say a word for another 3 minutes. At 10:43, they simultaneously uttered the words, "what the hell!"

As a result of these conditions, Betty became pregnant.[14]

These anecdotes illustrate three perspectives on how people become deviant. Elizabeth illustrates situational drift. Liz's deviance can be explained by differential association. And Betty's story is an example of the negative effects of labeling.

Situational Drift

Situational drift, one important sociological theory of deviance, attributes deviant behavior to circumstances. People rarely become deviant deliberately. Many simply drift into deviance because of the circumstances that surround them in everyday life. Certain personal, social, economic, or cultural conditions may predispose people toward de-

---

[14] David Matza, *Becoming Deviant* (Englewood Cliffs, N.J.: Prentice-Hall, 1969), pp. 88–89.

viance. The most common circumstance reported by researchers is poverty.[15]

The first deviant act, called *primary deviance* by Lemert, is likely to be an experimental step taken by the individual. At this point, the person is aware that the act is deviant and that it is risky. The values it represents are foreign to the person, and there is great fear of punishment. But if pressures from peers or circumstances are great enough, he or she will decide to take the risk.

Secondary deviance is the change in a person's self-conception to include the idea of *being* a "deviant." It may come about simply through repeatedly committing deviant acts. As a person drifts farther and farther away from conformity, deviant behavior seems increasingly acceptable and finally becomes part of the self-image. Secondary deviance may also be forced on the individual by the strength and character of society's reactions to his or her deviance.[16]

Differential Association

Another influential sociological theory is **differential association.** This theory, developed by Edwin Sutherland,[17] may be briefly summarized as follows.

1. Just like any other behavior, deviant behavior has to be learned.
2. It is learned through communicating or interacting with other people, particularly in intimate or primary groups.
3. In addition to learning techniques, the individual also learns attitudes that are favorable to deviance.

4. A person who has more information favorable to deviance than to conformity will be more likely to violate norms, given the opportunity.
5. The "frequency, duration, priority, and intensity" of people's differential associations will vary. But the skills needed to learn anything will be assets in learning deviance.
6. Deviants share basically the same needs and values as nondeviants. Thus needs and values alone will not explain deviant behavior.

In order to become deviant, then, a person must be exposed to others who are deviant and must decide to adopt their behavior patterns. These patterns will be new to the individual, but are well developed in the others. A person learns from the experiences of others that deviance can have negative consequences, but will choose to commit deviant acts if presented with enough information favoring them. This theory discredited the idea that one is doomed to deviance by prior circumstances. Exposure may make one willing, but one is not forced to become deviant.

Differential association theory has been criticized as being too general to be testable. It probably does describe *how* many deviants get that way. But it does not explain why, and it gives no clues for prevention. However, by showing how deviance can be related to learning and culture rather than to some personal defect or one's social class, it made an important contribution.

Labeling

Labeling theory is a third perspective on deviance. This approach emphasizes the processes rather than the causes of deviance. A person may commit a deviant act because of deviant interests, willingness to try new things, or involvement with other deviants. But society and the deviant come into conflict only if and when the deviant (or suspected deviant) is "caught." Being caught is "one of the most crucial steps in the process of

[15] Matza, *Becoming Deviant,* p. 94.

[16] Edwin M. Lemert, *Human Deviance, Social Problems, and Social Control* (Englewood Cliffs, N.J.: Prentice-Hall, 1972), pp. 62–92.

[17] Edwin H. Sutherland and Donald R. Cressey, *Principles of Criminology* (New York: Lippincott, 1974).

building a stable pattern of deviant behavior."[18]

Simply put, one of society's reactions when it catches someone acting deviant is to say: "What you have done is bad. *You* are bad. You are now, and always will be, a deviant." Society thus not only punishes deviant people through formal means such as imprisonment, but it puts labels on them. This has several implications. First, it allows the society at large to recognize which people are deviant. "To name is to know." Second, it increases the punishment suffered by deviants by making their deviance public. Public knowledge of their deviance has the effect of making it harder for them to function in the "normal" world. Third, after repeated instances of being caught and labeled, deviant individuals are likely to accept the label as part of their self-concept. As more and more legitimate avenues become closed to them, they must increasingly turn toward deviance. Because society labels them as deviant, they eventually do adopt a deviant life style and self-conception.

In addition, although punishment, such as a prison term, is finite, the label lingers on. When the punishment is over, new labels are invented. The "thief" becomes an "ex-con" rather than an "ex-thief." The person released from a mental hospital is not spoken of as a "healthy individual" but as an "ex-mental patient."

After the deviant is caught, labeling may or may not occur. One's chances of being labeled deviant depend on one's social class, income, and educational level. They also depend on where the law enforcement officials are concentrating their energies, and on the status of the victims of any deviance that may have been committed.

Though it is such a destructive process, labeling is rather haphazard and even whimsical. It depends in part on whether the particular rule that the deviant broke is going to be enforced or not. It also depends on the attitudes law enforcement officials form toward the deviant. According to one study, aside from having a record of prior deviance, the most important factor in police disposition of juvenile suspects was their demeanor. The more middle-class they seemed in appearance and values (measured by respectfulness and repentance), the more likely they were to be treated leniently.[19] Those who looked "tough" and behaved disrespectfully were usually prosecuted and thereby labeled.

According to Edwin Schur, labeling involves several key processes.[20] The first is *stereotyping*—judging a person by category, such as race or class. Law enforcement officials have a good deal of leeway in handling deviants, particularly juveniles. Their biases may influence their judgment one way or another. Sending a lower-class juvenile to a training school while recommending probation for a middle-class youth may be the result of stereotyping rather than the actual facts of the case.

After being called a deviant, the person is seen in a "new light." Schur calls this *retrospective interpretation.* All relevant past information about the person is collected into a file to help officials determine the proper treatment. The kind of material collected and its interpretation may both be influenced by the person's having been labeled a deviant. Some previous behavior, unremarkable when it occurred, may now be given labels such as "predelinquent" after the fact. As Erving Goffman said, writing about mental patients:

---

[18] Becker, *Outsiders,* p. 31.

[19] Irving Piliavin and Scott Briar, "Police Encounters with Juveniles," in William J. Chambliss, ed., *Criminal Law in Action* (Santa Barbara, Calif.: Hamilton, 1975), pp. 214–221.

[20] *Radical Nonintervention: Rethinking the Delinquency Problem* (Englewood Cliffs, N.J.: Prentice-Hall, 1973), p. 120.

This file is apparently not regularly used to record occasions when the patient showed capacity to cope honorably and effectively with difficult life situations. Nor is the case record typically used to provide a rough average or sampling of his past conduct. One of its purposes is to show the ways in which the patient is "sick" and the reasons why it was right to commit him and is right to currently keep him committed; and this is done by extracting from his whole life course a list of those incidents that have or might have had "symptomatic" significance.[21]

Thus, not only are deviants seen as different from other people, but those who judge them insist on seeing them as consistently different. It is still a case of "that kind of people." Most authorities may be sincerely anxious not to accuse innocent people of crimes or declare healthy people mentally unhealthy. But collecting data on a person that indicate a long history of questionable behavior gives them confidence in their conclusions.

It is at this point that the third process, *negotiation,* begins. An arrested deviant and a judge, for example, discuss which label to give the deviant. "Plea bargaining," in which the offender agrees to plead guilty to a lesser charge, is a common example of negotiation. Obviously, the results of negotiation reflect the relative power of the parties involved, and the deviant is not in a strong bargaining position. But social and economic factors can influence officials. Middle- and upper-class people are able to negotiate more successfully than lower-class people.

How do deviants themselves react to labeling? Joseph Rogers and M. D. Buffalo found several different responses.[22] Some

deviants accept the label passively. They incorporate society's negative judgments into their own self-concept. Others may protest the label. They may claim, for example, that they were framed or that they are innocent. Some, whose protests received effective support, have been able to force society to remove the label or to treat them normally in spite of it. Others may try to run away from the label. They may move to another part of the country and try to establish a new identity. Or they may withdraw into drugs, alcohol, mental illness, or suicide. Some may seek to evade responsibility for their deviance and its label by rationalizing their actions. They may try to blame other people or external circumstances for their behavior. Or they may rephrase the label so it doesn't sound so bad, like calling themselves "social drinkers" instead of "alcoholics."

In any case, once labeled, the individual has acquired a new "master identity" that overshadows all others. A doctor is always a doctor first, before being a wife, husband, father, mother, black, or white. The deviant also becomes a deviant first. Having broken one rule, deviants are treated as though they are likely to break all the rules. A deviant is denied access to "the ordinary means of carrying on the routines of everyday life open to most people."[23] The deviant thus becomes increasingly caught up in illegitimate means and in rule breaking.

Group Membership and Deviance

A significant step in deviant careers is joining a more or less established deviant group. Membership in such a group reinforces the individual's self-concept as a deviant. The

---

[21] *Asylums: Essays on the Social Situation of Mental Patients and Other Inmates* (Garden City, N.Y.: Doubleday/Anchor, 1961), pp. 155–156.

[22] Joseph W. Rogers and M. D. Buffalo, "Fighting Back: Nine Modes of Adaptation to a Deviant Label," *Social Problems* (October 1974), pp. 101–118.

[23] Becker, *Outsiders,* p. 35.

Belonging to a deviant group or subculture reinforces one's deviant behavior. *Ellis Herwig/Stock, Boston.*

group also gives deviants a new community to belong to and thus makes them feel less anxious about their deviance. It also supports them by justifying and rationalizing their deviant behavior. The homosexual subculture is a good example. Homosexuals publish articles in praise of homosexuality, have demonstrations for equal rights, do political lobbying, and arrange legal services on behalf of their group. Such tactics may or may not be effective in changing public opinion, but they do help the deviant silence remaining internal doubts and rationalize continuing in the deviant pattern. Belonging to a deviant group makes it easier to be successful in a deviant career. The group provides a network of contacts who help one another avoid trouble with the rest of society.

A deviant subculture has several charac-

teristics. Its members are socialized into patterns of deviance by those who already know the tricks of the trade and the use of facilities. They are subject to sanctions for refusing to obey the norms of the deviant group. They feel a stronger sense of belonging to the deviant group than to the larger society. They turn to it for sympathy, understanding, and protection and confine most of their meaningful interaction to it. In short, they share its values and norms and feel a sense of belonging.

Criminologists Marvin E. Wolfgang and Franco Ferracuti have studied "subcultures of violence" scattered throughout the world. These subcultural groups account for a very high proportion of assaultive crimes such as murder. (Only about 5 percent of all murders are premeditated, and a few more are committed by psychotics. But by far the largest share, according to Wolfgang and

Ferracuti, arises out of a style of life geared to violent aggression.)

They found similar subcultures of violence in Colombia, Sardinia, a lower-class black district in Philadelphia, and in Albanova, an Italian district of 30,000 people near Naples with the highest rate of assaultive crime in Europe. All have similar values and norms and a life style that takes the form of "a culturally transmitted and shared willingness to express disdain, disgruntlement, and other hostile feelings in personal interaction by using physical force."[24] Because violence is the norm in these subcultures, its use arouses no feelings of guilt.

The people of Albanova, for example, accept a code of honor that demands that they kill to redeem an offense and carry on ruthless vendettas. They ostracize the nonviolent person, whom they consider not quite a man (deviant by their own norms), and place such a ritualistic value on weapons that a godfather commonly gives his godson a gun at his christening. The Philadelphia study found that many acts that middle-class norms define as trivial—a jostle, for example, or a slur on one's race or mother or masculinity—are interpreted by lower-class males as insults calling for violent retaliation. Where knives and guns are common and people are socialized to be ready to use them in attack or defense, crimes of violence will obviously be numerous.

Such established subcultures may be distinguished from *emergent* subcultures. Interacting in an anomic or normless setting, a group of boys, seeking satisfactions of various needs and sharing similar problems and feelings of alienation, tentatively explore and test one another's reactions to various possible actions. They may, as a result, settle on theft as a norm for action. This is not the same as being socialized into a subculture that already includes theft as an established way of reaching goals. If a norm of theft persists and is transmitted to new recruits by a socialization process, then it becomes a subcultural source of deviant behavior. A number of studies show that of every ten offenses committed by juveniles, at least six, and possibly as many as nine, occur in groups—usually small groups of two to four members, who in turn may belong to larger gangs.[25] "Popular thinking about delinquency and crime is quite correct in its emphasis on the role of 'evil companions' in this behavior."[26]

Deviant subcultures obviously exist and thus present the individual with an alternative to conformity. But the individual decides which alternative to follow. Most researchers see deviant subcultures as supportive of deviance but not as responsible for it. One study of juvenile gangs, for example, reported that violence is not necessarily the most important characteristic of lower-class gang life.[27] Moreover, leaders have only a limited ability to force gang members to obey. In fact, membership in such gangs changes so rapidly and so often that gangs are not the stable social organizations that the subculture of violence thesis would lead us to expect.

Another study compared the attitudes of men who had "little," "moderate," or "high" experience with violence. According to the subcultural thesis, attitudes favoring violence should increase with level of exposure to it. But regardless of income or educational

---

[24] *The Subculture of Violence: Towards an Integrated Theory in Criminology* (London: Social Science Paperbacks, 1967), p. 152.

[25] James F. Short, Jr., ed., *Gang Delinquency and Delinquent Subcultures* (New York: Harper & Row, 1968), p. 297.

[26] Marshall B. Clinard, *Sociology of Deviant Behavior* (New York: Holt, Rinehart and Winston, 1968), p. 229.

[27] Howard S. Erlanger, "The Empirical Status of the Subculture of Violence Thesis," *Social Problems*, (December 1974), pp. 280–292.

level, the values of all the men questioned in this study were very similar.[28]

The subcultural thesis sees violence as normal in the context of the group. Thus, people who are violent should be more highly respected by other group members and should also have a higher level of satisfaction and well-being. More blacks fight than whites, and the poor are more likely to fight than the nonpoor. The disadvantaged groups do value violence but not to the degree suggested by the subculture of violence thesis. Moreover, members of all groups—white, black, poor, nonpoor—reported feeling more unhappy the more violent they were.[29]

The Social Functions of Deviance

We have mostly been discussing the negative aspects of deviance. However, deviance can serve positive social functions.

[28] Sandra J. Ball-Rokeach, "Values and Violence: A Test of the Subculture of Violence Thesis" *American Sociological Review*, Vol. 38, No. 6 (December 1973), pp. 736–749.

[29] Erlanger, "The Empirical Status of the Subculture of Violence Thesis," p. 289.

Positive Functions of Deviance

At certain times and under certain circumstances, deviance may make positive contributions to the success of a social system.[30] In emergency situations, deviance may become necessary when red tape hinders fast action. Deviance can also be a safety valve. Constant conformity can be a strain. Breaking small rules may help people relieve their frustration and thus prevent them from breaking bigger rules.

Because there are rules, people can interact with each other with less anxiety and uncertainty. Our own deviant acts and those of others can help us learn those rules. Cases of "borderline" deviance—an unmarried man and woman living together, for example—are especially useful because they force society to redefine and clarify ambiguous rules.

Deviance can also contribute to social cohesion by uniting people against it. "The deviant may . . . contribute to the integration of the group in much the same way as do witches, devils, and hostile foreign powers."[31] Deviance can also unite the group

[30] Cohen, *Deviance and Control*, pp. 7–10.
[31] *Ibid.*, pp. 8–9.

Juvenile gangs may or may not behave in deviant or violent ways. *J. Berndt/Stock, Boston.*

in support of the deviant, as in India when the populace united in support of Mahatma Gandhi.

Deviance can make people feel better about themselves when they conform. This "contrast effect" can make conformity seem special and particularly worthy. Comparing themselves to deviants increases people's sense of community and can make life more satisfying.

Deviance, like physical pain, can be a warning signal that something is going wrong in the social system. The deviant can highlight areas that need reform. Deviance thus may help the majority "who may be subject to the same strains, but prefer to suffer them rather than break the rules."[32]

Negative Functions of Deviance

However, in spite of these positive functions, deviance is still regarded as a negative, potentially destructive phenomenon by most people. Smooth functioning of the system depends on everyone's behaving as expected, that is, according to the social norms. Thus, to the extent that it interferes with this smooth functioning, deviance has a negative effect on society. But most social systems can tolerate a certain amount of deviance. The severity of the interference depends on whether or not the deviant behavior affects a vital point. These points vary from society to society. What is vital to one may be unimportant for another.

Deviance can undermine people's commitment to conformity. Not all deviance is observed, and not all observed deviance is punished. Crime, for example, can indeed pay. When people feel that crime is paying better than conformity, their satisfaction in law-abiding behavior may decrease.

"The most destructive impact of deviance on organization is probably through its impact on trust, on confidence that others will, by and large, play by the rules."[33] Each member of a group, whether respectable or deviant, has made a commitment. His or her efforts will seem worthwhile only if others also fulfill their commitments. Distrust of others weakens one's own commitment and confidence in the future.

Crime and Public Policy

Rising Crime Rates

Crime is a fact of life in our society. Compared to the 1930s (when figures on crime rates were first collected), violent crimes, particularly assault and forcible rape, have gone up. Burglary and grand larceny have increased substantially, although there has been a slight decrease in robbery (see Figure 6-2). Several reasons have been cited for this striking increase in crime.[34]

First, the age composition of our population has changed. There are greater numbers of 18- to 24-year-olds now than formerly. This is the age group that is most likely to be involved in crime. Another factor is urbanization. More and more of our people live in or near a metropolitan area, and crime rates have traditionally been higher in cities than in rural areas. Third, there are more things to steal and they are less well-guarded than in the past. Fourth, members of minority groups are more likely to be the victims of crime. In the past, many were disillusioned with the response they received from law enforcement agencies and would not report crimes. But now, they feel more free to demand their right to police

---

[32] *Ibid.*, p. 10.

[33] *Ibid.*, p. 5.
[34] Edwin M. Schur, *Our Criminal Society: The Social and Legal Sources of Crime in America* (Englewood Cliffs, N.J.: Prentice-Hall, 1969).

protection. Finally, some of the increase in crime rates may simply be due to better official records.

None of these factors alone can account for the rising crime rate. For example, if urbanization were the answer, we would expect all cities to have the same sorts of crime rates. But this is not the case. A city such as Los Angeles may rank 1st for rape and 4th for aggravated assault but only 20th for murder.[35]

Sociologists are very cautious when citing statistics about crime because such figures are notoriously unreliable. Agencies that release such statistics may have reasons to inflate or deflate the incidence of crime. The police, for instance, to show that they are doing a good job, may slant their data to reflect a decrease in crime. On the other hand, to get approval for additional officers

[35] President's Commission on Law Enforcement and Administration of Justice, *Task Force Report: Crime and Its Impact—An Assessment* (Washington, D.C.: U.S. Government Printing Office, 1967).

and equipment, it may be necessary to statistically create a crime wave. In addition, many crimes still go unreported. People may be pessimistic about the police's ability to apprehend the offender. Or they may not be able to take time off from work to appear in court. Or they may be intimidated by the police. For example, although there have been great improvements in the police handling of rape cases, many victims still do not report attacks.

But the main reason that crime statistics are unreliable is that many people who commit crimes are never caught, and some who are caught are innocent.

The Criminal Offender

It is difficult to develop a profile of the typical offender. However, it is possible to make some generalizations about which people are most likely to become involved with law enforcement agencies.

First of all, women are far less likely to commit crimes than men. This is almost

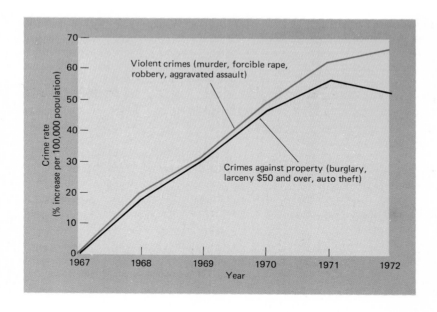

Figure 6-2 Increase in crime rates, 1967–1972. *Federal Bureau of Investigation, Uniform Crime Reports, (Washington, D.C.: U.S. Government Printing Office, 1972), pp. 3, 4.*

certainly due to differential socialization in childhood. Women are trained to fulfill domestic functions and to be taken care of by men. Men, on the other hand, are trained to succeed in occupational functions. The qualities we train our sons to have fit them equally well for success in normal careers or in crime. As women become more able to enter legitimate, traditionally male occupations, their share of illegitimate activity can be expected to increase.

In general, crimes that go unrecorded are more likely to be committed by upper- or middle-class people. Thus, lower-class people are disproportionately represented in official statistics. In America, because of the Protestant ethic, it is somehow assumed that the poor must be less moral, while the rich must be very moral because they are so successful. Thus, it is proper to treat the poor harshly and to be lenient to the rich.[36] The example of the Nixon administration scandals may remind us how simplistic and unrealistic this notion is. But it still has considerable impact on our criminal justice system.

In addition to believing that crime is generally a lower-class phenomenon, many people believe that most crimes are committed by minority groups. It may seem racist to say that this assumption is correct. But, in fact racial minorities do commit a disproportionate number of crimes. But they are not inherently criminal. Any poor or lower-class person who lives in a city and who is denied access to legitimate means of social mobility is a high risk for deviance. A distinction must be made, therefore, between the mobile poor and the nonmobile poor. Among blacks, for example, level of income does not appear to be as important as educational level in predicting criminal behavior.

The typical offender, then, is a male, under 25 years old, belongs to a racial minority, has a low level of education, and lives in a lower-class or poor neighborhood in a city.

Any person, from any social class, could theoretically commit any type of crime—with one exception. There is one type of crime that lower-class people are exempt from: white-collar crime. This is strictly a middle- and upper-class phenomenon, committed by people ordinarily considered respectable. Typical white-collar crimes are fraud, embezzlement, price-fixing, and other illegal business practices. To commit such crime one must have a well-paying, fairly high-level job. Because of their class status, white-collar criminals may not be prosecuted. If they are, they may be more leniently treated than lower-class law breakers. Thus it is possible for them to avoid being labeled. The economic cost of white-collar crime probably greatly exceeds the cost of "regular" crime. Moreover, it creates distrust, which is destructive to the social order.[37]

Most people are generally law-abiding. They feel threatened by deviance and want it prevented or controlled. Society has two general means of controlling deviance: informal control and formal control.

Informal Control

Informal control involves people's internalization of the norms of the society through socialization. Thus the majority of informal social control is self-control. As we have seen, however, poor socialization in childhood can lead to weakly internalized norms. A poorly socialized person is more likely to behave in a deviant way if provided with an opportunity. Another indicator of potential deviance is the strength of one's attachment

[36] Jack D. Douglas, *Deviance and Respectability,* (New York: Basic Books, 1970), p. 17.

[37] Edwin H. Sutherland, *White-Collar Crime* (New York: Holt, Rinehart and Winston, 1949, 1961).

The criminal justice system is designed for deterrence, punishment, and rehabilitation, but the effectiveness of formal control is questionable. *David Strickler/Monkmeyer Press Photo Service.*

to one's family, church, or school. As these institutions are the primary agents of socialization in our society, a lack of commitment to them will indicate a lack of commitment to the norms they represent.

Informal control also involves peer group pressure. Most of us are anxious for the approval of our friends and associates. Peer group pressure may propel us toward deviance, as in the case of youth gangs. But it may also strengthen our willingness to conform, if we sense that those around us disapprove of deviance.

Formal Control

Obviously, informal social controls are only partially effective. Therefore, modern societies have created systems of formal control to deal with deviant behavior. **Formal control** involves the police and the justice system, including courts, prisons, mental hospitals, reformatories, probation and parole, and the law.

The rising concern about crime in the United States has been accompanied by a critical examination of the system of formal control. Our system is designed to do three things: deter people from committing crimes, punish those who are not deterred, and rehabilitate those who are punished. The idea of deterrence is that the potential criminal will not commit crimes because of fear of penalty, such as arrest and imprisonment. Effective punishment therefore must be "severe enough to outweigh the potential pleasures the crime might bring, administered with certainty, administered promptly, administered publicly, and applied with the proper judicial attitude."[38] If the system functioned well, there should be only a limited number of repeated acts of deviance.

Does our system effectively deter and rehabilitate criminals? Apparently not. In a study conducted by the FBI, it was found

[38] William C. Bailey, "Murder and Capital Punishment," in Chambliss, *Criminal Law in Action*, p. 411.

124

that 65 percent of offenders arrested from 1970 to 1972 had been arrested before (see Figure 6-3).[39]

This high rate of **recidivism**—return to criminal acts after arrest and punishment— can be explained, in part at least, by labeling theory. With each successive contact with police and the courts, the deviant becomes more identified with and more committed to deviance. For example, juveniles who were arrested but referred to community treatment centers rather than jail had higher recidivism rates than juveniles who were released after arrest.[40] Deterrence theorists,

on the other hand, would explain this by saying that being sent to a community treatment center was not a severe enough punishment to deter people from further deviance.

Our law enforcement system also fails to deter criminals because it cannot catch every single deviant. Committing deviant acts without being caught makes continued deviance seem less risky. Even though having been caught significantly increased people's belief that they would be caught again, the average shoplifter, for example, stole over five times after the first arrest.[41] Apparently criminals still figure that the odds are in their favor, particularly for less serious crimes, because there is such a degree of uncertainty that they will be caught and punished.

[39] Federal Bureau of Investigation, *Crime in the United States: Uniform Crime Report, 1972* (Washington, D.C.: U.S. Government Printing Office, 1973), p. 36.

[40] Suzanne B. Lincoln, "Juvenile Diversion, Referral, and Recidivism." Paper presented to the annual meetings of the Society for the Study of Social Problems, 1973. See also Malcolm W. Klein, "Labeling, Deterrence, and Recidivism: A Study of Police Dispositions of Juvenile Offenders," *Social Problems* (December 1974), pp. 292–303.

[41] Robert E. Kraut, "Deterrence and Definitional Influences on Shoplifting," *Social Problems* (February 1976), pp. 349–368.

Figure 6-3 Rates for repeating criminal acts. *Federal Bureau of Investigation, Crime in the United States: Uniform Crime Reports, 1972, (Washington, D.C.: U.S. Government Printing Office, 1973), p. 37.*

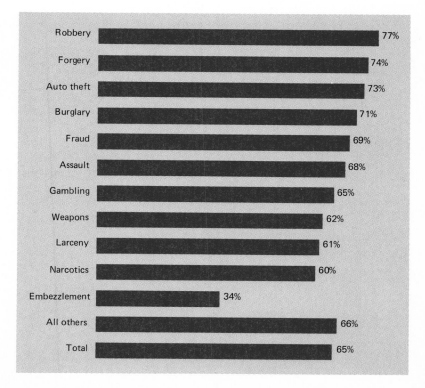

Category	Rate
Robbery	77%
Forgery	74%
Auto theft	73%
Burglary	71%
Fraud	69%
Assault	68%
Gambling	65%
Weapons	62%
Larceny	61%
Narcotics	60%
Embezzlement	34%
All others	66%
Total	65%

Most research on deterrence has centered on the effectiveness of capital punishment as a deterrent. Because of its extreme severity and the very limited number of crimes related to it, conclusions about capital punishment cannot be applied to punishment in general. However, the bulk of the research indicates that capital punishment is not an effective deterrent. States that abolished the death penalty saw no increase in murder. Those that reinstated it after a period of abolition saw no significant decrease in murder.[42] One reason for this may be that

[42] Bailey, "Murder and Capital Punishment," p. 409.

Even after being arrested for shoplifting, an offender is very likely to repeat the deviant act. *Mimi Forsyth/Monkmeyer Press Photo Service.*

most murders are committed in "hot blood," that is, on the spur of the moment. People angry or desperate enough to kill will not take time beforehand to weigh their actions against the risks involved.

Thus it appears that our system of formal control is not deterring would-be lawbreakers, rehabilitating criminals, nor even handing out punishment fairly. Various aspects of police work, the courts, correctional institutions, and the law itself may account for this fact.

THE POLICE The police have wide latitude in deciding whether or not to arrest someone and whether or not that person will be prosecuted, referred to some other agency, or simply released. Where the evidence is weak or a rarely enforced rule has been broken, the attitude of the police officer toward the offender is often the deciding factor.

Police officers' attitudes are shaped by the nature of their work. Regardless of background, police officers show a high similarity of attitudes after a few months on the job.[43] These attitudes are shaped primarily by two inescapable aspects of police work: danger and authority. The danger they face makes police officers suspicious. The need to maintain authority can make them brutal. "The most serious crime in the books is contempt of cop."[44] Regardless of the situation or their attitudes toward the suspected offender, anyone who challenges a police officer is very likely to be arrested. Police officers generally respond more aggressively when they are challenged by a minority group member or lower-class person.[45]

[43] Jerome H. Skolnick and Elliott Currie, eds., *Crisis in American Institutions* (Boston: Little, Brown, 1970), p. 389.
[44] *Ibid.*, p. 390.
[45] Paul Chevigny, "Force, Arrest, and Cover Charges," in Skolnick and Currie, *Crisis in American Institutions*, p. 393.

One researcher has noted that very often minor situations such as traffic violations or domestic disputes become much more serious after the police become involved.[46] This is believed to be due to strong agreement among police officers that they are most effective when people are scared of them. Faced with even a minor incident, the first thing the police do is establish their authority. Some people, particularly minority groups, may respond to this with resentment. If the police interpret this resentment as a challenge, they may arrest people who might otherwise have avoided any further involvement with law enforcement.

THE COURTS The increase in deviance can be seen in our overcrowded courtrooms. In the lower courts, where cases are first tried, judges may hear 200 to 400 cases a day.[47] For this reason most offenders are encouraged to plead guilty. Those who demand their right to a jury trial are often given stiffer sentences, perhaps as punishment for having "wasted" the court's time. The sentence given is generally up to the judge. In court, as with the police, the race and socioeconomic status of the offender can make quite a difference.[48] Another factor is whether the individual was able to raise bail after arrest or had to spend the pretrial period in jail. Offenders who could not raise bail were more likely to receive heavier sentences. Thus, the poor, who are more

likely to be arrested in the first place, are more likely to receive longer prison terms.

A special branch of the court system designed to deal with youthful offenders is the juvenile court. It is a civil rather than a criminal court and has different procedures and rules. It was set up to allow law enforcement officials to deal with juveniles without involving them with hardened, adult criminals. Unique aspects of the juvenile court include sentences phrased as help rather than punishment, no criminal stigma because the court's records are kept confidential, and indeterminate sentences. The proceedings are structured as informal fact-finding sessions rather than formal guilt-or-innocence trials. The focus is not on the offense but on the conditions that led the juvenile to commit the offense. It appears that simply being brought into court is a sign that the juvenile needs treatment or help of some kind. The hearing is designed to determine the sort of help needed, not the individual's guilt or innocence.

The juvenile court system, however, seems to be failing to deal with juvenile delinquency. Because the focus of the court is treatment rather than punishment, even a juvenile murderer will still be treated as a youngster in need of help. It is small wonder that the system is not taken seriously. People under 18 years of age commit 44 percent of all serious crimes. Almost 20 percent are committed by youths under 15 years of age.[49] In New York City, "70 percent of all the violent juvenile crime in the city is committed by fourteen- and fifteen-year-olds."[50] At the age of 16, when they are old enough to be dealt with in the adult criminal court, many of these youngsters are

[46] John H. McNamara, "Uncertainties in Police Work: The Relevance of Police Recruits' Background and Training," in David J. Bordua, ed., *The Police: Six Sociological Essays* (New York: John Wiley & Sons, 1967), p. 168.

[47] Edward J. Barrett, Jr., "Mass Production," in Gresham Sykes and Thomas Drabek, eds., *Law and the Lawless* (New York: Random House, 1969), p. 341.

[48] Whitney North Seymour, Jr., "Social and Ethical Considerations in Assessing White Collar Crime," *American Criminal Law Review*, Vol. 11, No. 4 (Summer 1973), pp. 821–834.

[49] Federal Bureau of Investigation, *Crime in the United States,* p. 126.

[50] Nicholas Pileggi, "Inside the Juvenile Justice System: How Fifteen-Year-Olds Get Away with Murder," *New York* (June 13, 1977), p. 39.

stunned when they first discover the concept of punishment.

CORRECTIONS Offenders found guilty in court are generally sentenced to a term in a correctional institution. The primary goal of our correctional institutions—prisons, reformatories and training schools, as well as mental hospitals—is rehabilitation. Here again, there is quite a gap between the ideal and reality.

Correctional institutions, along with monasteries, convents, and the armed services, have been described as *total institutions.*[51] They differ primarily in the view we have of the inmates. We may admire monks, nuns, and soldiers, but prisoners and mental patients are thought of as dangerous to the society or to themselves. Moreover, their commitment is generally involuntary.

In a total institution all activities that generally are carried out in different localities on the outside take place within the institution. Thus, all the inmates eat, work, sleep, and play together. Where, when, and how they work, sleep, eat, and play are dictated by the staff of the institution rather than by individual preferences.

Another central feature is the transformation of the person from a being with a certain internalized self-concept into an inmate. This process requires that each person be stripped of any self-identifying features such as personal possessions, unique clothing, and grooming style. The individual's self is gradually worn down through humiliating and debasing treatment until the character of inmate emerges. Expressions of anger against such treatment backfire. The staff labels protest as troublemaking and becomes more convinced that such people need institutionalization.

The psychological effects of such treatment can be damaging to the point that an individual may not be able to readjust suc-

cessfully after release. "Release is likely to come just when the inmate has finally learned the ropes on the inside and won privileges that he has painfully learned are very important. In brief, he may find that release means moving from the top of a small world to the bottom of a large one."[52] Moreover, the skills required for success in the institution—obedience, acceptance, and passivity—are handicaps in the larger society where initiative, aggressiveness, and self-assertion are valued.

In one study, two dozen college students were randomly assigned to be guards and inmates in a simulated prison. The experiment was designed to last several weeks, but was stopped after one week because the experimenter became alarmed at the increasingly sadistic behavior of the guards and the effect this was having on the prisoners. "In less than a week, the experience of imprisonment undid (temporarily) a lifetime of learning; human values were suspended, self-concepts were challenged and the ugliest, most base, pathological side of human nature surfaced. . . . [Several of the guards] became quite inventive in their techniques of breaking the spirit of the prisoners and making them feel they were worthless."[53]

There may be some individuals who are so dangerous that they cannot be helped. In these cases confinement may be the only way to protect society. But for the majority of people, confinement appears to do more harm than good.

Criminal Law and Overcriminalization

Behavior may be strange, unusual, or peculiar, but only when it breaks a law is it labeled criminal. The criminal label leaves the indi-

---

[51] Goffman, *Asylums*, p. xiii.

[52] *Ibid.*, p. 73.
[53] Philip G. Zimbardo, "Pathology of Imprisonment," *Society*, Vol. 9 (April 1972), pp. 4–8.

Prisoners are inmates in a total institution which tends to strip them of self-identifying features. Here, however, in a more innovative program, administrators allow inmates to decorate their cells. *Wide World Photos.*

vidual open to formal means of interference and control.

It is obvious that the more laws a society has, the more likely it is that any person's actions will be labeled criminal. Many sociologists today believe that the best way to relieve the burden on the police, the courts, and the prisons is to change the laws.

The laws that most need reform are those that concern private morality. The crimes covered by these laws, such as prostitution and gambling, are referred to as *victimless crimes* because the act could not take place without the mutual consent of the parties involved. "It is quite possible that the attempt to suppress gambling, drinking, prostitution, and narcotics has produced more crime than it has suppressed."[54] The main reason for removing these laws is that they do not work. They are by and large unenforceable. They take up too large a share of law enforcement resources, court time, and prison space. In addition, their existence results in labeling people who would otherwise have no contact with law enforcement.

[54] Skolnick and Currie, *Crisis in American Institutions,* p. 442.

The gap between the letter of the law and actual enforcement practices has several negative effects. First, it diminishes the credibility of the law and thus has an unhealthy effect on people's respect for the law in general. Second, because these laws are difficult to enforce, "good" police work may require the use of questionable methods such as harassment and entrapment, which may damage the image of law enforcement. Other negative effects may include official corruption and discrimination against poor, less skillful, or more desperate offenders. Thus, attempts to control "sin" through law backfire and have negative social consequences.

Necessary as laws and formal enforcement agencies are in modern society, they are by no means the most important method of social control. Social order still rests primarily on shared values, norms, and beliefs, and on the effective socialization of newcomers to society. While deviance adds some spontaneity and creativeness to group life, it also shows us the importance of a certain degree of conformity—"the useful tyranny of the normal."

Summary

Deviance is behavior that violates the norms of a social group. Deviant acts that violate laws are crimes. Deviance may be dangerous to persons and property, destructive for the individual, or simply immoral or improper. No act is inherently deviant. All actions must be judged in their context, which may be a specific situation or a specific culture.

Most of us conform to the norms most of the time. Conformists may be aware of impulses to deviant behavior but may not give in to them for several reasons. They may exercise self-control in order to avoid guilt, or to keep the approval of their significant others. They may fear punishment, or they may not value the rewards of deviance enough to risk punishment. Finally, they may simply have no opportunity.

Biological, psychological, and sociological causes of deviance have been suggested by various theorists. Biological theories include the idea that criminals have more primitive physiques than noncriminals. One theory classified people into three body types: endomorph, ectomorph, and mesomorph. While no body type could be said to cause deviance, mesomorphs were believed to be most likely to become deviant. Other biological theories involve sex-chromosome abnormalities in males and the localization of functions in the brain.

Both biological and psychological theories may be called "kinds of people" theories. According to classical psychoanalytic theory, deviance occurs because of poor socialization in childhood, which results in the formation of an inadequate conscience. The extreme form of this is the psychopath. An outgrowth of classical psychoanalytic theory is the frustration-aggression hypothesis. This theory states that aggression is the result of frustration.

Sociological theories also deal with people but as occupiers of various positions in the social structure rather than as individuals. This approach to deviance began in the 1920s when sociologists analyzed settlement patterns in Chicago and concluded that the transition zone, just outside the central business district, had the highest rate of deviance because of its social disorganization and poverty.

Some sociologists believe that people commit deviant acts because they feel alienated from the larger society. Alienation is a feeling of not belonging. Related to alienation is a feeling of anomie, or normlessness. Anomie results when there is a scarcity of socially acceptable means to satisfy people's legitimate needs. Accordinging to Merton, people cope with the resulting strain in five ways, four of which are more or less deviant. They may conform or become innovative ritualists. They may retreat from the conflict altogether by dropping out of the society. Or they may become rebels.

Another approach sees deviance as arising out of the inevitable conflict between social groups. The more powerful groups influence public policy, including law and law enforcement. Anyone who behaves in ways that conflict with the interests of the more powerful groups can be labeled deviant and punished.

Several theories try to explain the process of becoming deviant. Situational drift suggests that people rarely become deviant deliberately. They simply drift into it because of the circumstances that surround them in everyday life. The first deviant act, called primary deviance, is likely to be an experiment. Secondary deviance, on the other hand, represents a new way of life and new self-conception. It comes about as a result of contact with society's reactions to primary deviance.

Differential association theory sees becoming deviant as a conscious process of learning. Information favoring deviance and teaching new techniques is received from people who are already accustomed to deviance.

A third approach looks at the process of labeling and its effect on the individual. In addition to being caught and punished, the individual is further punished by being publicly labeled as deviant. The label may force individuals to continue a deviant life style because legitimate avenues are closed to them. Labeling is a rather indiscriminate process. It can depend on one's social class, income, demeanor, or on the attitudes of law enforcement officials.

Deviant groups provide the deviant with emotional support and a way to rationalize continued deviance. Deviant subcultures have their own values and norms, and a life style centering around their type of deviance. Most researchers see deviant subcultures as supportive of deviance, not as responsible for it.

Although deviance can have positive effects on society, its negative consequences, especially in the destructive erosion of trust, receive far more attention.

Crime rates have risen steadily since the 1930s. Changing age composition of the population, urbanization, greater affluence, increased willingness to report crime, and better record keeping are factors in this increase. However, crime statistics are notoriously unreliable.

The typical offender is under 25 years old, of a racial minority, male, with little education, and lives in an urban lower-class or poor neighborhood. White-collar crime is the one type of deviant behavior that is committed only by otherwise respectable people in the course of their work. Because they are middle- or upper-class, white-collar criminals may escape prosecution or may only be punished lightly.

Society has two main ways of controlling deviance: informal control and formal control. Informal control involves people's internalization of the norms of the society.

Formal control involves the police, courts, prisons, mental hospitals, probation and parole, and the law. The system is supposed to deter people from committing crimes, punish those who are not deterred, and rehabilitate those who are punished. But it is unsuccessful in both deterrence and rehabilitation.

Institutions such as prisons, reformatories, training schools, and mental hospitals are referred to as total institutions because all of the inmates' activities take place within them. Life in such a total institution usually does not prepare people for successful readjustment on the outside. Rather, it trains them to be good inmates.

Many sociologists today are coming to the view that the best way to control deviance is to change the laws, particularly those concerning victimless crimes that are matters of private morality.

Despite the emphasis on formal control in modern society, the most effective social control still rests on effective socialization.

Glossary

Alienation A feeling that one is a stranger to one's environment, to others, and even to oneself.

Anomie A condition of normlessness; results when there is a scarcity of institutionalized means to satisfy people's legitimate needs.

Crimes Deviant acts prohibited by

law and punishable by law enforcement agencies.

Deviance　Behavior contrary to the norms of a social group, exceeding its limits of tolerance for noncomformist behavior and subject to punishment if discovered.

Differential association　Exposure to deviants as an essential part of learning some kinds of deviant behavior.

Formal control　Institutionalized means for preventing or punishing deviant behavior; involves laws, police, courts, and correctional institutions.

Informal control　Social control through socialization and peer group pressure.

Labeling　The process of reinforcing deviant behavior by attaching a label to the person who commits it.

Recidivism　Return to criminal acts after arrest and imprisonment.

Situation drift　Nondeliberate commission of deviant acts attributable to circumstances.

part

3

Social Structure

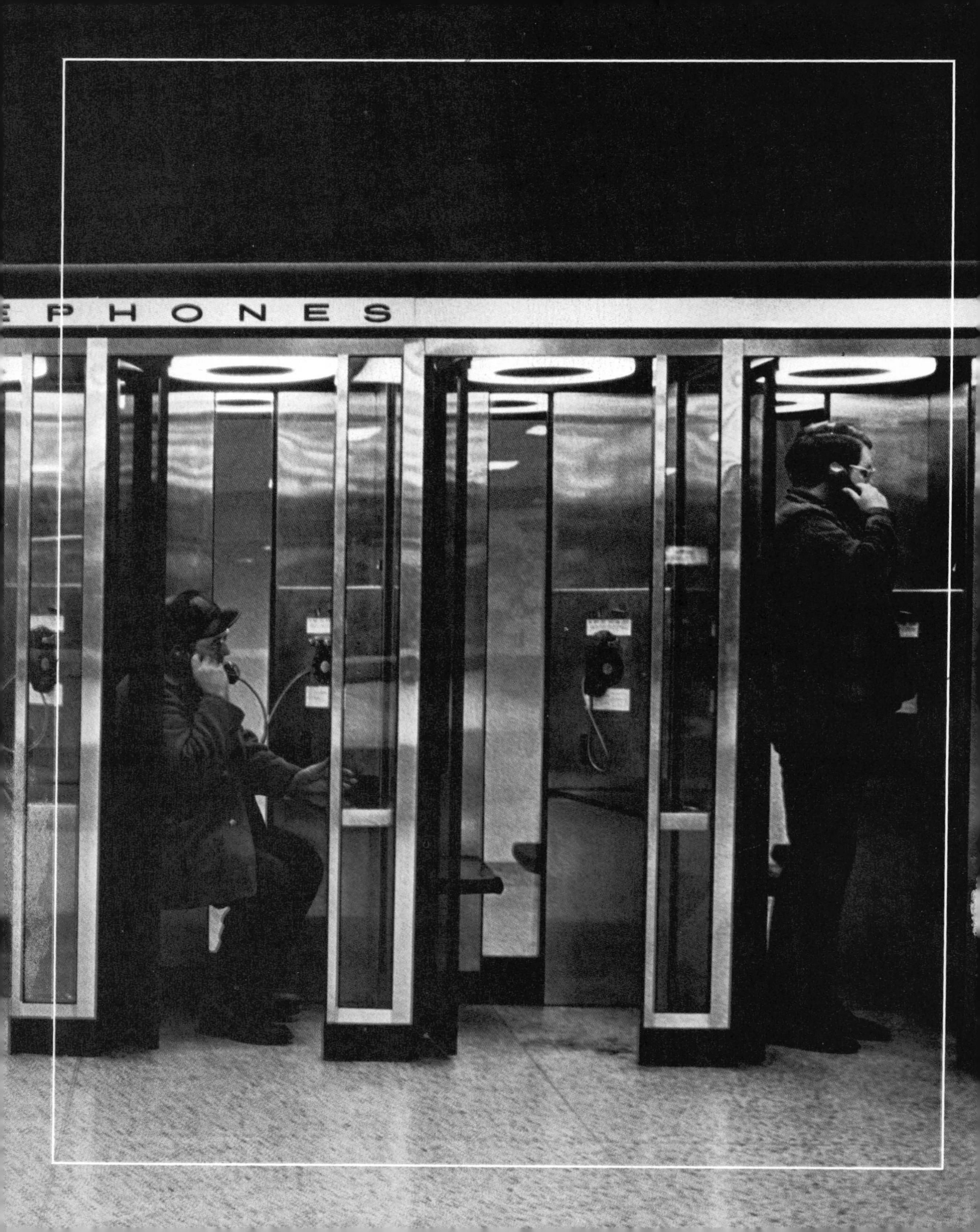
EPHONES

chapter

7

Social Interaction and Social Structure

We members of the human species are constantly acting, thinking, and feeling—and interacting with others. We send and receive signals with shrugs, smiles, frowns, movements toward or away from another person. But most often we use language signals to tell others how we feel, to ask them what to do, to soothe, hurt, inform, deceive, amuse, persuade. This *symbolic* interaction is the social process most basic to human society.

The cultural norms that a society has developed serve as guidelines for interaction. These norms help people to define the situation, to guess what others intend to do and what they expect us to do. Much of the time there is no problem. We know we are expected to act happy at a wedding, subdued at a funeral, or relaxed at home.

We usually know what norms to apply because we recognize the statuses of the people involved. Family relationships, for example, are defined by the status labels of father, mother, husband, wife, son, daughter, brother, sister. We have learned the corresponding roles. "Shame on you for hitting your little brother." "You don't speak to your mother like that, young lady." "How was your day, dear?"

Interaction in most situations is cooperative, but we also compete—for prizes, jobs, grades, mates, prestige, and other scarce values. Sometimes, too, we feel hostile and we fight, seeking to destroy or hurt the others involved. Later we may accommodate our differences and resume peaceful interaction.

We find ourselves in groupings and in categories. Often, as in clusters of shoppers or pedestrians, we do not feel we belong to these groupings. Nor do we always feel we belong to such categories as those based on age, race, nationality, education, or the fact that we are diabetic or overweight or color blind.

The largest group to which most of us feel we belong is a society. It may be a small folk society or a huge modern society. Or it may fall somewhere in between. But most of you who read this book have spent all your lives in large complex modern societies. In such societies, much of our interaction occurs in formal organizations or is greatly influenced by them. From birth through old age, our lives are largely ordered by schools, churches, corporations, retail stores, the mass media, the government, and other large-scale formal organizations to which we may feel little or no allegiance.

What Is Society?

Society unlike culture, is not limited to humankind. In the general sense, **society** refers only to an association of living creatures functioning in organized relationships of mutual dependence. Specifically, however, **a society** is a group that is organized into a more or less permanent division of labor, lives in a certain territory, and shares common goals.

136

By this definition, almost all animals and insects show some degree of **social structure,** a web of interdependent relationships among individuals and groups. But, as we have already seen, the human group is very different from other animal groups because of our capacity for building culture. Culture enables us to live in societies based not only on division of labor and interdependence but also on shared values and beliefs. It enables us to have many different kinds of social relationships and to interact with our fellows in many different ways. As language and the use of tools developed, society became more efficient in its basic functions of protection, nutrition, and control of reproduction. It thereby enabled humans to live in larger and more complex groups and to make their cultures more elaborate.

Starting with our broad definition of society and adding the effect of culture, we can now define **human society** as a complex system of relationships among individuals and groups, based on shared symbolic values and common beliefs and norms. In other words, human society is based on culture. Society, a system of relationships, and culture, a system of common understandings, together form a *social order* or a *social system* that has structure, pattern, stability, and adaptability.

Any specific human society—from a nonliterate jungle tribe to a modern nation-state—will have these distinguishing characteristics.

1. It is not a subgroup of any other group. It has a definite territory, within which its members have a common life. Their needs are provided for by a system of interdependence based on division of labor.
2. It has a distinctive culture. Most or all of its members accept and abide by the universal or core values and norms of the culture.
3. Its members have a sense of belonging to it, a "we-feeling" that sets them off from nonmembers. It is the largest group within which most or all of them have this feeling of common identity.
4. Most or all of its recruitment of new members occurs through biological reproduction and the socialization of the newborn. Thus it is selfperpetuating. Both sexes and all ages live out their lives within it.
5. Its organization as a functioning whole encompasses all the social groups and individuals within its bounds.

Processes of Social Interaction

Social structure emerges from social interaction and, in turn, guides further interaction. **Social interaction** is the reciprocal influencing of behavior through symbolic communication between people. Thus, as people come into contact with one another, and as they become aware of one another as more than mere physical objects, their behavior both modifies and is modified by the behavior of others. Each defines the situation partly in the light of cultural norms and past experience. And each has an idea of what the situation means to the others involved, what they intend to do, and what they expect in return.

Social interaction always involves communication by means of gestures or language, although we are not always conscious of sending or receiving signals. It does not necessarily involve face-to-face contact. It can take place through phone calls, letters, books, paintings, and even a piece of music, although here the reciprocity of influence is less evident. The processes of social interaction have been categorized in various ways. Here we focus on behavior—who does what to (or with) whom?—and its consequences. Is the process *associative,* bringing people together, or *dissociative,* dividing them?

Cooperation

Cooperation is the combined effort of two or more social actors to reach a shared goal. Clearly an associative process, it pervades all forms of group life and is indispensable to its existence. It is an element in all situations except overt personal conflict. Cooperation may take several forms. It may be shoulder-to-shoulder effort in a common task, such as harvesting a crop. It may be direct exchange for the benefit of both ("You scratch my back and I'll scratch yours"). Or it may be conformity to the norms of behavior that make it possible for a society to function.[1] Most interaction in the routine of daily life is cooperative simply because of the interdependence of persons that results from the division of labor.

In small nonliterate societies, cooperation is often a leading cultural value. It is consciously used to regulate the interaction of members in farming, fishing, hunting, and house building. In a highly complex society, division of labor is carried to such extremes that cooperation may be less apparent. But it is just as necessary as in a simple society. Members of the society may not often be aware of cooperating as they go about their daily routine. But all the traffic of a city, the schedule of a university, the buying and selling in stores depend on cooperation. When you stop for a red light, when you appear in class at the same hour as your

---

[1]A special form of cooperative interaction is more asymmetrical and episodic: giving (charity) or helping behavior (the Good Samaritan). Here the emphasis is more on the social relationship between giver and taker than on a common goal. Deviant behavior may be defined as noncooperation, and its forms are as varied as are the forms of cooperation.

Traffic signals command cooperation in modern society. *Mimi Forsyth/Monkmeyer Press Photo Service.*

instructor and classmates, when you answer the telephone, you are cooperating.

Competition

Competition is the striving of two or more social actors for the same goal which is limited in quantity. Each wants the whole pie or the lion's share of it, whether the pie consists of money, power, prestige, safety, public office, a certain man or woman, or some other scarce value. Whatever the prize, their primary aim is to get it for themselves, not to injure or destroy their competitors. Competition is carried on within an accepted system of rules that limit the acceptable means of trying to gain the prize. It is often impersonal. When competitors *are* aware of one another—as in the case of candidates for the presidency or for someone's hand in marriage—we call their relationship *rivalry*. In such situations, as in games and contests, the group has laid down certain cultural rules of fair play. Losers are supposed to bow to the decision with good grace—to congratulate the president-elect or to dance at the wedding.

Like cooperation, competition is present in all cultures. In any society, people will compete for status according to the cultural values. In a monastery where austerity and piety are the chief values, status may be won by the monks who are most zealous in denying themselves physical comforts or who spend the most time in devotions. In a middle-class suburb, status may depend on visible signs of wealth, the husband's occupation, and the colleges attended by the children.

Competition is a conspicuous element in much interaction occurring in a society where many statuses can be achieved, whether in jobs, politics, business, school and college, sports, and even in the family ("Mommy, do you love me best?"). Our

culture is distinguished for making competition a positive value, a "good thing." Americans are convinced that, although cooperation gets things done, competition assures that they will be done *well*.

Conflict

"Social **conflict** consists of interaction in which one party intends to deprive, control, injure, or eliminate another, against the will of that other."[2] Conflict may be regulated by cultural norms, and its goals may be limited. For example, in games, the parties are primarily bent on winning, but they play by the rules. Pure conflict, however, is a fight. Its goal is "to immobilize, neutralize, destroy, or otherwise harm an opponent."[3] Unlike cooperation, conflict must by nature be intermittent. Unlike competition, it always involves awareness of the other parties in interaction.

The scope of conflict ranges from marital discord to total war. However, when we refer to *social conflict* we usually think of intergroup conflict within a society. Such collectivities as racial and religious groups, students, workers, and revolutionaries fight against other groups and against the control system of the political establishment. They engage in riots, strikes, lynchings, gang fights, guerrilla warfare, confrontations, and violent demonstrations met with violent countermeasures. For obvious reasons, sociologists are currently very much concerned with the study of conflict.

What are the sources of conflict? There are many different theories. Ethologists say

[2] Robin M. Williams, Jr., "Social Order and Social Conflict," *Proceedings of the American Philosophical Society*, 114, No. 3 (June 1970): 217–225. This section on interaction draws in part on a seminar on social conflict conducted by Dr. Williams at Wayne State University, Fall Quarter, 1970.
[3] *Ibid.*

aggression is programmed into us in our genetic makeup. Like other animals, we will fight to defend our territory against intruders. Some sociologists suggest that ethnocentrism—not merely hostility to others, but loyalty, even blind devotion, to one's own group—is the main cause of conflict, and that it is learned in the socialization process. Psychoanalytically oriented theorists believe the inevitable frustrations of living in society lead to feelings of aggression, which may or may not be overtly expressed. Adorno associated aggressiveness with authoritarian personality traits. Marx believed conflict is built into society in the class system, which in turn depends on economic structure.

Robin Williams sees three classes of opposition as the main sources of conflict: incompatible claims to scarce things of value, such as money; incompatible beliefs, values, and norms, including loyalties and obligations to different groups and individuals; and emotional dispositions and impulses that are expressed in anger toward some vague antagonist, such as "the establishment."[4] A society *guarantees* conflict, he suggests, if rewards for work are unpredictable and if work is unsatisfying and central aspirations are blocked.

Conflict may have positive results. When babies come into conflict with their mothers, they are developing their sense of self and learning cultural norms. The group fighting another group is strengthened in its "wefeeling." If it is confined to issues, conflict (between husband and wife, for instance) may clear the air of tension. During a period of rapid social change, conflict serves to define the status of persons and groups, as did the labor-management conflict of recent decades. It may force awareness of injustice. And it may (like recent wars) spur technological innovation and scientific research.

[4] *Ibid.*

Much conflict, however, is destructive and dissociative. It breeds more problems than it solves. Riots may deepen differences between collectivities and increase alienation of one group from another. Strikes and lockouts result in loss of income, production, and profits. War "is unhealthy for children and other living things."

ACCOMMODATION AND ASSIMILATION Conflict may result in annihilation of one of the parties or in subjugation, slavery, or some other form of dominance or repression. But it may be resolved or even avoided through

Striking nurses are in conflict with hospital management. *Sybil Shelton/Monkmeyer Press Photo Service.*

the social process called accommodation. **Accommodation** is the reduction of conflict and the restoration of peaceful interaction. It is achieved through such measures as compromise, arbitration, mediation, truce, toleration, contract, or the judicial process. Examples are labor-management agreements and the peaceful coexistence of essentially hostile nation-states. Similarly, incompatible beliefs and values may be reconciled through debate, persuasion, a mutual agreement to live and let live, or mutual withdrawal from interaction. Or the party against whom aggression is directed may define the other's behavior as neurotic, psychotic, mistaken, or accidental, thus denying any valid attempt to injure and refusing to respond in kind.[5]

None of these measures really eliminates potential sources of conflict, but they do enable persons and groups to go about their business without overt conflict. In one sense, accommodation is the basis of all formal social structure. Government, for example, is designed to harmonize the interests of different groups sufficiently so the society can function effectively. Because the incompatible values and goals still exist, accommodation has been called "antagonistic cooperation."

An experiment run by Muzafer Sherif studied various processes of interaction. Using groups of boys in summer camps, Sherif and his associates were able to produce two integrated and cooperative groups. They then created hostility and conflict between them, and finally brought about a friendly and cooperative relationship. During the period of competitive games, hostilities erupted, but the solidarity of each group increased. The hostile groups were then brought into close association under pleasant circumstances. Instead of reducing conflict, the close contact provided opportunities for further name calling and fighting. Then the experimenters created a series of urgent natural situations to challenge the boys. Water came to the "Robbers Cave" camp in pipes from a tank about a mile away. The flow was interrupted, and both groups worked together to locate the break. A truck that was to bring food to an outing broke down ("accidentally on purpose"). The groups helped start it by pulling it with a rope. Further cooperative acts gradually reduced friction and conflict until finally the groups actively sought opportunities to mingle, entertain, and "treat" each other. "In short, hostility gives way when groups pull together to achieve overriding goals which are real and compelling to all concerned."[6]

Assimilation is the social process whereby individuals and groups come to share the same sentiments, values, and goals. It commonly refers to the absorption of immigrants into the social order of a large modern society such as the United States. It can with equal accuracy be used to describe the process of adjustment in a successful marriage or even the socialization of the growing child. The cultural assimilation of new members of a society may or may not be accompanied by a process of biological *amalgamation* in which the physical difference of the incoming groups also disappear through intermarriage with members of the receiving group.

Cultural assimilation and biological amalgamation occur most frequently in multigroup societies such as ours. Cooperation, competition, conflict, and accommodation occur in every society, but they are found in varying proportions depending on the complexity of the society and the value placed on any one process. For example, in the United States competition is believed to promote efficiency. In the Soviet Union

---

[5] *Ibid.*

[6] "Experiments in Group Conflict," *Scientific American* 195, No. 5 (Nov. 1956): 54–58.

the idea of class conflict on a world-wide scale has long justified and motivated public policy.[7]

Similarly, we find varying blends of the different social processes in the interaction of groups and orgainzations within a society. Cooperation and assimilation are essential to family life. Yet the very intimacy of family relationships intensifies competition and conflict when these occur. Accommodation in parent-child and husband-wife relationships permits peaceful interaction in spite of conflicting interests and values.

Social Relationships and Social Groups

Social relationships are patterns of more or less recurrent, regular, and expected interaction between two or more social actors, which may be persons or groups. These patterns are based on the participants' mutual expectations regarding one another's behavior. The more often social interaction of whatever type is repeated, the more fixed and predictable the behavior of the actors becomes. Such social relationships as father and son, policeman and speeder, employer and employee, and even unfriendly neighbors are meaningful only in terms of the reciprocal expectations that shape the interaction.

Unorganized Behavior

Not all human behavior is social, and not all social behavior is organized. Organization may be entirely or almost entirely lacking when people are thrown together in new

---

[7] For a comparative anthropological study, see Margaret Mead, ed., *Cooperation and Competition among Primitive Peoples* (Boston: Beacon Press, 1961).

and undefined situations. In such situations, existing cultural norms that might guide interaction do not apply. This is the case with some crowds and mobs, which engage in what sociologists call *collective behavior.*

Organization is also lacking in behavior that is not coordinated by a system of social relationships but shows a certain regularity simply because it occurs in response to common stimuli. If a water engineer observes a heavy drain on water supplies during a television commercial, it is due to individual behavior that happens to coincide. It is not due to organized behavior. Other regularities within a social system are the result of many uncoordinated decisions rather than of organization. Birth rates are one example. While they fluctuate over the years, extreme changes are usually explained by social influences that affect many potential parents.

Nongroups: Aggregates and Categories

We often find ourselves in *physical aggregates,* collections of people who happen to be in physical proximity. Examples are clusters of people waiting for a bus or walking along Main Street, or people who happen to live as neighbors on a block. While aggregates are not social groups, they may have sociological meaning, for the spatial distribution of people affects social relationships in various ways.

Statistical aggregates or categories are logical classifications of people based on the existence of one or more common characteristics: the same age, sex, race, religion, marital status, hair color, hobbies. The list can be expanded almost indefinitely. People in a category may or may not have a "consciousness of kind" with other members. Ordinarily they do not interact on the basis of their categorical similarity. Some social groups, however, are consciously formed on just such a basis. Overweight men and women, for example, may join Weight Watchers. And categories such as class and race are recruiting grounds for the formation of interacting groups. When a statistical category is based on one or more statuses in the social structure (such as class, race, or parenthood), we may refer to it as a *social category.*

Quite aside from any interaction among the people who compose them, social categories may be highly significant for sociology because they enable researchers to see patterns that might not be visible in individual cases. For example, Durkheim related suicide rates to various social categories and found that the suicide rate is higher among Protestants than among Catholics. It was also higher among single than among married people, and among army officers than among enlisted men. (Of course, he did not stop there. He also related his findings to other factors affecting the categories, such as the degree of group integration within them.)[8]

What Are Social Groups?

Significant as many aggregates and categories are, they are not social groups. A **social group** is made up of two or more people who interact, feel a sense of identity that sets them off from others, and have social relationships consisting of interrelated and reciprocal statuses. Their interaction may be short or long-lasting. They may relate to one another with varying emotions. What they have in common may be some task, territory, interest, belief, or value. But to form a genuine group, they must believe that it makes a difference. The group boundary takes in all those the members refer to as "we" or "us" ("You and I, darling,"

---

[8]Émile Durkheim, *Suicide,* trans. George Simpson (New York: The Free Press, 1951).

or "My fellow Americans"). Their relationship may be as direct, close, and equal as that of two friends. Or it may be as indirect, distant, and unequal as that of the president of General Motors and a janitor in his office building.

The Structure of Groups: Status and Role

The network of interrelated statuses, the pattern of relationships that is sufficiently regular and lasting to be perceived, is the *social structure* of a group. Thus, a political scientist sees patterns in party politics as well as in the more formal structure of government. And thus a friendship group of two or three, or even a pair of lovers, behaves in fairly predictable ways as its members establish lasting relationships.

Status

A teacher named M. B. Smith will serve to illustrate the various concepts we use to analyze social structure. The word "teacher" is a label that identifies a **status,** a position in a social structure. As the basic element in social structure, status is a key concept in sociology and therefore merits our detailed consideration.

A status is independent of any one person. The status of teacher does not depend on Smith's occupying the position. The status exists even though the school board may have had trouble filling the position and may not have employed Smith until school had been in session for a week.

A status is always *relational* or *reciprocal;* that is, it only has meaning in terms of at least one other status. Thus the status "teacher" is meaningless without students.

A person's statuses are *multiple.* We may now identify our teacher as an adult, a

A status is always relational or reciprocal. The status "teacher" is meaningless without students. *Hugh Rogers/Monkmeyer Press Photo Service.*

woman, Mary B. Smith, as a wife, Mrs. John Smith, as a mother, a daughter, a daughter-in-law, and a homemaker. She also is a member of the American Association of University Women, secretary of the local chapter of Phi Beta Kappa, a Democrat, and a member of the First Congregational Church. On occasion she occupies still other statuses. She is a tennis player, a patient of a certain doctor, a customer at a local supermarket, a taxpayer, a voter, and a tourist.

But all people have a *key status,* a position by which they are chiefly identified. In modern society, nearly all men are identified first in most situations by their occupations. The key status of most women has long been that of wife–and–mother.

Some of a person's many statuses are *compounded* or clustered. That is, they go with other statuses. Mrs. Smith's statuses as mother, wife, and homemaker are compounded with her status as adult female. Although males or children can be tennis players, tourists, and customers, only an adult female (by our cultural norms) is a mother, wife, or homemaker. And if she is one, she is likely to be all three.

Some statuses are *sequential* in that we fill them in a fixed order. Thus, Mrs. Smith was a student before she was a teacher, a high school graduate before she was a college graduate.

Statuses may be classified as communal or associational. A *communal* status is defined by the general culture. Everyone in our society has a general idea of what it means to be a woman, an adult, or a member of a general occupational category such as teacher, plumber, or writer. However, within

144

a special group—an association—status is more precisely defined. To others in the school system, Mrs. Smith has not only the communal status of teacher, but also the *associational* status of fourth-grade home-room teacher at Oakland Elementary School.

Statuses are *ranked* within a group. Each carries with it a certain freight of prestige, privilege, and power in relation to the other statuses in the group. In most formally organized groups there is an explicit pattern or hierarchy that indicates who has authority over whom and to whom each person in turn owes obedience and deference. Thus, the principal has authority over Mrs. Smith but in turn owes obedience to legitimate instructions from the school board and the superintendent.

Role

Every status in a social structure implies a minimum pattern of behavior that is expected (and perhaps demanded) of anyone occupying the status. This pattern is a **role,** a bundle of norms that defines the rights, obligations, and privileges of a person who occupies a particular status. However, the role is not identified with the occupier of the status. It is attached to the status itself. Note that a role ideally gives a person rights and/or privileges as well as obligations. Doctors are obligated by oath to treat sick people whether or not they like them personally. They are usually rewarded with a high income and the respect of society. Roles are elements of culture, just as statuses are elements of one aspect of culture, social structure. To understand the distinction more clearly, imagine the status of teacher as part of the social structures of the United States and of the People's Republic of China. Then think about the concept of role. You will realize that in the two societies the norms attached to the status of teacher are very different. The beliefs, values, goals, and degree of modernization are very different,

and the teachers are expected to teach different things.[9]

As we noted earlier, we all occupy more than one status and thus have multiple roles to play because each status has its own role. Robert Merton has taken this analysis one step further.[10] According to Merton, each social status has more than one role. Thus, our teacher, M. B. Smith, plays one role with her students, one with their parents, another with her colleagues, another with the principal, and so on. These roles—and the people she interacts with while playing them—are called by Merton a *role-set,* because they are all dependent upon her occupation of a single status—that of teacher.

Looked at this way, the number of roles

[9] J. Milton Yinger, *Toward a Field Theory of Behavior* (New York: McGraw-Hill, 1965), includes lucid discussions of social structure.

[10] Robert K. Merton, *On Theoretical Sociology: Five Essays Old and New* (New York: Free Press, 1957).

Drawing by Chon Day (reprinted from *Look*)

Of course I love you. I'm your husband. That's my job

we have to play is dramatically increased. But, paradoxically, the task of organizing other people's expectations and our own behavior is made easier. Becoming aware of the many roles we have to play makes us more aware of—and thus more willing to respond to—other people's expectations. This increased awareness should reduce conflict caused by inappropriate behavior and should encourage smoother social interaction according to Merton. But he admits this is not always the case. When members of a role-set are of different social statuses and thus have different values, expectations, and beliefs, there is always a potential for conflict.

INSTITUTIONALIZATION OF ROLES Although the roles of friend and lover are largely culturally defined, these roles are subject only to the judgment of the other person involved. But some roles are *institutionalized*. They are subject to explicit rules laid down by authorities or by customs that have the force of law. Institutionalization is a matter of degree. The roles of clergyman and teacher are highly institutionalized. They are subject to a great deal of formal and informal control by others. But the role of parent is subject to little outside control. Only flagrant neglect of the parental role—lack of support, refusal to send a child to school, unmerciful beating—brings on formal actions by officials.

We sometimes assume roles that are institutionalized for others but not for ourselves. Mrs. Smith may play nurse to a sick child, but she does not have the status of nurse, and there are no formal sanctions for the way she goes about it. A stranger on a plane may play the role of confidant, and often does, because the person who unburdens himself feels sure he will not see the stranger again. He is not, however, an institutionalized confidant, as are family doctors, lawyers, clergymen, and psychiatrists. In

many social structures a person playing a deviant sex role has no corresponding status; in others the role is institutionalized. For example, among the Plains Indians a male transvestite assumed the status of *berdache* and was allowed to dress as a woman after going through a ceremony similar to marriage.[11]

Institutionalized roles are firmly attached to statuses and are applied to certain situations. Just as the mores can make anything right in a culture, so a certain status can make behavior right that would be improper or even illegal for someone occupying another status. When a man is functioning in his status as a doctor and is playing the accompanying role, it is perfectly all right for him to ask a woman to undress. He might also be tempted to do so at a party when another guest pesters him for free medical advice, but the norms do not permit it.

COMMUNAL AND ASSOCIATIONAL NORMS Just as there are communal and associational statuses, so there are communal and associational norms defining roles. Communal norms are present in the general culture. Sex, age, and kinship roles are typically communal. Associational norms, though, are peculiar to a group smaller than the society as a whole. They may arise in the course of interaction, as in a group of friends or a gang of criminals. Or they may be specified when a group is formally organized, as in the constitution of a club or the rules and regulations of a business.

Members of any formally organized group bring to it certain norms to guide their behavior, but there are also associational norms they must learn. Our teacher, Mrs. Smith, knows in a general way what American society expects of her as a wife

[11] Michael Banton, *Roles: An Introduction to the Study of Social Relationships* (New York: Basic Books, 1965), p. 8.

and mother, and she knows somewhat more specifically what it expects of her as a teacher. In the course of interaction with her husband and children, more specific associational norms arise concerning mutual rights and obligations, such as mealtimes, chores, allowances, errands, and the like. These are not spelled out as clearly, however, as the associational norms of her school. There a series of memos and meetings keeps her informed about her hours and duties. Some norms are never verbalized. Without ever being told, Mrs. Smith learns that the principal expects teachers to laugh at her jokes.

Assignment of Status and Role: Ascription and Achievement

The statuses into which a person is born and those which are automatically assigned with the passage of time—those over which we have no control—are **ascribed statuses.** Those we attain by our own efforts or by a stroke of good fortune are **achieved statuses.**

ASCRIBED STATUSES   The accidental chromosome combinations that occur at the moment

of conception determine many things about one's life in any society. *Sex* distinctions almost always provide a clear-cut basis for cultural norms that prescribe much of a person's behavior.

In societies with less advanced technologies, and to some extent everywhere, sex differences call for a division of labor that keeps the woman close to home and engaged in fairly routine tasks such as cooking, cleaning, foraging for food, gardening, and sewing, and perhaps weaving and pottery making, which do not interfere very much with pregnancy and child rearing. The man is typically assigned duties that demand physical strength and long periods away from home; he is the hunter, fisherman, warrior, and herder of cattle.

But aside from these general distinctions, each society uses sex as an arbitrary peg on which to hang many other assignments of status and role that have little or nothing to do with physical capacities. The definitions of men's and women's roles include not only division of labor but also many other norms regarding appropriate behavior.

Age serves as another universal basis for ascription of status and role. Most societies identify infancy, childhood, adulthood, and

The bar mitzvah ceremony impresses the thirteen-year-old boy with his new status of manhood in Jewish society. *Cary Wolinsky/Stock, Boston.*

old age as distinct statuses, but the lines of demarcation vary noticeably. The transition from childhood to adulthood may be easy and gradual in one society. In another it may be marked with impressive rituals, ceremonies, and ordeals. And it may be ambiguous and difficult in a third society. Among the Masai of Africa, for instance, every male passes through three clear-cut stages: boy, warrior, and elder. In the United States, in contrast, there is no clear definition of status by age. The age of legal maturity is an arbitrary one unmarked by rites of passage or tests of civic judgment or legal responsibility. Puberty is a private affair. Sexual maturity comes long before economic independence. Schooling is extended longer and longer. Much of the strain of adolescence in American culture is thought to be a result of the ambiguity that keeps the "teenager" a child in one situation and an adult in another.

Kinship also universally ascribes a number of statuses and roles. The child learns a series of rights and obligations in relation to his parents and siblings. In a number of societies the kinship structure includes many other relatives. It also defines a person's status in relation to the whole clan or tribe and governs behavior toward them throughout life. In such a system, marriage rules are tied to the kinship structure. They may state that a man may marry only his mother's brother's daughter, for example, or provide for marriage only outside the clan in order not to blur kinship lines. Royal or aristocratic status is also assigned at birth, and the order of birth frequently determines the right of succession to a title.

Several statuses may be assigned the newborn infant simply because they are those of the parents. In a *caste* system children keep their parents' caste status for life. It usually determines occupation as well as many other aspects of life. In a *class* system, a person's initial position is that of the parents. Although individuals may go up or down the social ladder, whether they have a head start or a handicap in life depends on where they start. *Citizenship* and *religion* are also those of the parents, but these are sometimes changed. And the newborn infant is assigned its parents' *racial* or *ethnic* status where such distinctions are made.

ACHIEVED STATUSES An increasing number of statuses open themselves to achievement as a society industrializes, largely because there are so many new occupations in the specialized system of production and distribution. How does one achieve a status? Typically, one learns the role (the communal and associational norms of the status) through education, training, and experience. Then one convinces others—voters, perhaps, or audiences or employers—that one deserves the status and can perform the role satisfactorily. Achieved statuses require some decision and action, such as a marriage proposal and ceremony to achieve the statuses of husband and wife.

Few statuses are gained or held entirely by ascription or entirely by achievement. Although occupational status in modern society is largely achieved, a doctor's child has an initial advantage in a medical career. A farmer's son is much more likely to be a farmer than is a lawyer's son. Aspirants to the position of President of the United States are limited by Constitutional provision to those occupying the ascribed statuses of native-born citizen over 35 years of age.

Role Performance

Once we know the social structure of a group—its network of statuses and their attached roles or norms—we can outline the general pattern of interaction within the group without reference to any specific people and their particular personalities. But it is **role performance** that makes up the

A farmer's son is much more likely to be a farmer than is a doctor's son. *Peter Menzel/Stock, Boston.*

ongoing social interaction of any group. In the performance of roles we see the dynamic interplay of culture, society, and personality. We do not usually go to see just any movie. We go to see Woody Allen performing a role. Our interest in what goes on around us—fun, novels, movies, and social change—all have their roots in the great variety of role performances that can occur within the same statuses. No role can be more than a *guide* to the behavior of a performer because it can never describe the subtle variations in a specific person's role behavior.

Several variables affect role performance. One is the latitude of its interpretation. Another is the degree of compatibility or conflict with other roles. Role performances are also affected by the performer's degree of internalization of norms and by the degree of enforcement of sanctions by others.

LATITUDE OF INTERPRETATION Certain kinds of roles permit a wider range of interpreta-

tion than others. Among these are *diffuse* roles, which apply to many situations, as compared to the *specific* roles of a special occupation. The interaction of friends and family in most societies is governed by very diffuse norms, as opposed to the narrow and rigid role requirements of an occupation. For example, the half-humorous reference to a "Jewish mother" indicates a particular interpretation of the role of mother fairly common within a subcultural group. But given the more precisely defined role of plumber, we find that a Jewish plumber plays the role just about like any other plumber. New and undefined roles—such as television producer—that arise as a society changes and becomes more complex are defined by the persons who first performed that role. There is also great latitude in the performance of roles in which interaction with others is infrequent, and reciprocal expectations are few. A painter or a novelist is much more free to experiment than a physician or teacher.

149

ROLE CONFLICTS Performance of a role is reinforced if a person's other roles are compatible with it. When a person has assumed incompatible or conflicting roles, performance is often weakened. The working mother may experience role conflict. Mrs. Smith, for example, may have chosen to be a teacher in part because her schedule would conform pretty well to that of her school-age children. But if one of them is sick at home, she suffers from a feeling that if she goes to work she is not being a good mother. Yet if she stays home she is not being a good professional. Then she may not perform well in either role. Black policemen may feel they are trapped in the middle and "get it from both sides." Some statuses are defined by legal or other norms as incompatible. Thus a Secretary of Defense should not be a large stockholder in any industry that might have military contracts.

Even where role conflicts are not clearly evident, a person may experience *role strain* simply because, in modern society, the total role obligations demand too much. There just isn't enough time, money, or energy to meet all the demands of all the roles. One has to seek a *role bargain*—a balance among roles that permits fulfillment of the major ones satisfactorily and some of the others passably. In the process a person may have to abandon one or two roles entirely. A writer who is also a wife and mother experiences considerable role strain, and occasionally something has to "give."

INTERNALIZATION OF ROLES The internalization of a role occurs as part of the process of socialization. This process is most intense

Table 7-1 The Polar Concepts of Traditional and Modern Societies

Variable	Traditional Society	Modern Society
Size	Small; maximum of about 2,000	Large
Composition	Homogeneous	Heterogeneous
Relation to other societies	Isolated; self-sufficient	Interdependent
Degree of division of labor	Low; simple	Extensive
Group memberships	Few; ascribed	Many; voluntary
Character of social organizations	Small; informal	Large-scale; formal
Dominant form of social structure	Kinship group	Citizenship in nation-state
Dominant type of social relationships	Primary; personal	Secondary; impersonal
Nature of institutions	Interrelated	Formal and distinct
Assignment of status	Ascription	Achievement
Scope of roles	Diffuse; clustered	Specific; fragmented
Nature of norms	Constraining; prohibitive	Permissive in primary relations, prescriptive in secondary ones
Type of sanctions	Informal	Formal
Orientation to change	Resistant; values tradition; static	Innovative; dynamic; oriented to the future
Predominant values	Sacred; traditional	Secular; scientific
Basis of cohesion	Consensus	Symbiosis; interdependent
Functions of social structure	Expressive	Instrumental
Degree of cohesion	High; cultural unity	Low; tends to anomie

in childhood but continues throughout life as learning, punishment, and reward continue. As a role is internalized, the person comes to accept its norms as right and to feel emotionally committed to the values underlying them.

We may say that a role is thoroughly internalized when a person feels guilty or uncomfortable about not conforming to its norms. This emotional commitment tends to ensure adequate role performance. But even when a role is less thoroughly internalized, people may still conform so long as they want to avoid the consequences of nonconformity. On the other hand, they may not conform at all because they care about neither the values nor the sanctions.

MUTUAL REINFORCEMENT OF ROLE PERFORMANCE Because roles are reciprocal, they tend to reinforce each other. An actor who fails to perform adequately makes it difficult for others in the play to do so. Often roles are so interrelated that failure or success in one role imposes similar results on another. A student who fails displeases parents as well as teachers.

A person's role performance is also affected by the degree to which others in a role-set enforce sanctions. If Mrs. Smith does not care how well or badly her students perform on tests, she will exert no influence toward good performance. On the other hand, even if she does not really care how much they learn, yet she wants to be considered a good teacher by her superiors and gain tenure, she will encourage them to do well. This pressure from "third parties" acts as a powerful social control. What will people say? What will the neighbors think? What will the principal say if my pupils do badly on the Stanford Achievement Tests? The more specific and closer the third party in a situation, the more effectively that person or group reinforces role performance.

Traditional and Modern Societies

We began this chapter by attempting to define society. We looked in general terms at the processes that characterize human social interaction regardless of type of culture or structure of society. By looking at the two extreme ends of the spectrum of social structure, we may gain a clearer understanding of how these processes operate (see Table 7-1).

The polar concepts of traditional and modern societies represent ideal types. These types have also been called folk and urban, preindustrial and industrial, *Gemeinschaft* and *Gesellschaft,* status and contract, primary and secondary, communal and associational. Perhaps a few isolated tribal societies and peasant communities are near the traditional pole, but most societies are moving ever closer to the modern type.

The Folk or Traditional Society

The **folk society** is small.[12] It may consist of a few families, or as many as 2,000 people. At any rate, all its members can have face-to-face interaction. It is isolated from other societies and therefore must be economically self-sufficient. Because it is small and isolated, its members are biologically similar, relatively speaking (there are still individual differences, of course). It has a highly integrated culture that imparts great meaning

[12] The discussion of the folk society is based on the model developed by Robert Redfield (*The Folk Culture of Yucatan* (Chicago: University of Chicago Press, 1941). For a critique arguing that this model is too idyllic and overlooks elements of strain, change, secularity, and conflict, see Oscar Lewis, "Tepoztlan Revisited," in Alex Inkeles, ed., *Readings in Modern Sociology* (Englewood Cliffs, N.J.: Prentice-Hall, 1966), pp. 51–64.

The folk society is small and isolated, like this Taos village. *Paul S. Conklin/Monkmeyer Press Photo Service.*

to action and makes people feel that what they are moved to do is well worth doing. Its institutions are so interrelated that religion, for example, is inseparable from making a living. Robert Redfield, who wrote the classic description of the folk society said that for its members, life "is not one activity and then another and different one; it is one large activity out of which one part may not be separated without affecting the rest."[13]

The folk society is characterized by a strong sense of community—identification with the group, belonging. That is why we refer to it as *communal*. It is a *familial* society, based on the extended family. Even when its members are not all relatives, kinship terms are ceremonially extended to them

by means of blood brotherhood, godparenthood, and so on.

In such a society, the family or the group rather than the individual is thought of as the basic unit. The group structure is composed of ascribed statuses with clearly defined roles. These outline all rights and obligations. No special arrangements or contracts are necessary. Nor is there any need for legislation. The folkways and mores govern all relationships, and informal controls keep members in line. The norms are (in the ideal type, but never in reality) unchanging. Tradition rules. There is no written language. The elders are the respected storehouses of folk wisdom.

There is little or no division of labor in folk society, except on the basis of sex and age. Although the technology may be admirably adapted to its purpose, as is the case with Eskimo tools, it is simple. No machines are used to make tools or other machines, and natural power is untapped. Every adult male or female does just about the same

[13]Robert Redfield, "The Folk Society," *American Journal of Sociology*, 52 (1947): 293–308.

152

things as others of the same sex and shares essentially the same life experiences.

The members of a traditional society do not question, criticize, or analyze its culture and social structure. There is no institutionalized science. Consensus is (again ideally) so complete that cultural values and goals need never be formulated in words. Behavior is traditional, spontaneous, and uncritical. Behavior is also personal. No one is ever treated as a "thing" to be used, as is often the case in the impersonal contacts prevailing in modern societies. Personalization extends to the natural environment. Trees, rocks, winds, waters, sun, moon, and stars are given human attributes.

The folk society is a sacred society. Ritual acts are not empty conventions. They are loaded with meaning. Sacred objects are regarded with awe and protected from profanation. Just as nature is personalized, it is also sacred. A Navajo Indian regards a cornfield as a holy place, a stray kernel of corn as a lost and starving child. In a folk society, such activities as planting and harvesting are not simply practical and instrumental. They are holy acts, expressing the ultimate values of the society.

The Urban or Modern Society

At the other extreme is the **modern society,** based on an advanced technology and a highly developed store of knowledge. It is large and heterogeneous, with a far weaker sense of community and less consensus than the folk society. Highly urbanized and industrialized, it depends on other societies for raw materials and markets. It is never self-sufficient, nor is any one of its members. An extensive division of labor makes everyone dependent upon many others for most needs, and the various specialties are coordinated in a complicated system of production and distribution. Being highly specialized, statuses and roles are specific and narrow

rather than clustered and diffuse. Being based on training and experience, most statuses are achieved rather than ascribed.

The diversity of occupations is accompanied by diversity of interests, expressed in a great variety of voluntary associations. In actual fact, though not essential to the model of an associational society, modern industrial societies tend also to be multigroup societies. They are made up of peoples of diverse cultural, racial, and religious backgrounds. This diversity results in a variety of values and norms, and widely different patterns of behavior are tolerated.

The culture is secular. Few objects are regarded as meaningful in themselves, few activities as more than means to ends. Each institution is allotted its special function. Religion is set apart from everyday affairs. Sacredness is confined to religion and to a few values such as patriotism, the flag, the king, the constitution. Science and progress are highly valued, and change is regarded as good.

The size, diversity, secular values, and rapid change of a modern society mean that tradition and informal controls are insufficient to maintain order. Legislation and formal sanctions are needed. The nation-state is the social structure that exercises ultimate power and controls all other associations and institutions.

Other large-scale formal organizations dominate in business and industry, and, to a smaller extent, in education, religion, medicine, and other areas. Bureaucratic administration characterizes business and government. Impersonality, rationality, and efficiency are positive values in such organizations. People are evaluated on the basis of effective performance of their roles. Secondary relationships in fragmented roles are the basis of much social interaction.

The transition from traditional to modern society is part of the great transformation that is occurring throughout the world. This transformation is easily seen in many ways—in scientific and technological changes and their effects, in changes in the numbers and distribution of population, in the class structure, in relations among various groups, in personality types and problems, and in changes in the institutions of the family, education, religion, economy, and government.

Summary

Social structure is the network of relationships among persons and groups. A society is the largest unit of organization, the largest group in which people interact and feel a sense of belonging. Both nonhuman and human societies are organized into a continuing division of labor, live in a certain territory, and share common goals, such as protection, nutrition, and reproduction of members. Culture enables human societies to become increasingly large and complex.

Social interaction is the reciprocal influencing of behavior through symbolic communication between persons. The main processes of interaction are cooperation, competition, conflict, accommodation, and assimilation.

A social relationship is a pattern of interaction between two or more social actors—persons or groups—based on their mutual expectations of behavior. Not all human behavior is social, and not all social behavior is organized. That is, some social behavior is not coordinated by a system of social relationships. Neither are all groups genuine social groups. They may be physical or statistical aggregates or social categories.

Genuine social groups consist of people who feel they belong together because of something significant they have in common. They interact according to mutually accepted norms, and have interrelated and reciprocal statuses.

Social structure refers to a pattern of social relationships, a network of reciprocal statuses with their accompanying roles. A status is a position in a social structure. A role is the pattern of expected behavior accompanying a status. A person has one key status among multiple statuses, which tend to be clustered or compounded. Some statuses are sequential. Some are communal; others are associational. Statuses are often ranked within a group. Some are ascribed (age, sex, kinship, caste, nationality, race). Others are achieved (occupations and public offices in modern society).

Performance of a role varies according to the personality of the performer; the permissible scope of its interpretation, its compatibility or conflict with the person's other roles, the degree to which one has internalized its norms and feels committed to their underlying values, and the degree of enforcement of norms by others in the role-set as well as their performances.

Statuses, then, are the positions that can be mapped, as in the organizational chart of a corporation or bureau, according to the lines of authority and influence flowing down a hierarchy or horizontally from one person or subgroup to another. Roles are the "job descriptions" attached to these positions, the bundles of norms that outline the behavior expected of each status occupant and the rewards and rights that person can in turn expect. Role performance is the "play-by-play account" of actual behavior in the role, of actual interaction in a given situation.

Much of the world is undergoing a transformation from a social structure that fits rather closely the folk type of society toward an increasingly modern society. The folk society is small, isolated, and homogeneous. It has a highly integrated culture in which sacred values predominate. Although its technology is simple, it is self-sufficient. Folk societies are ruled by tradition. There is complete consensus on core values among its members, who feel a strong sense of community. Primary or personal relationships predominate.

Modern societies, in contrast, are large, heterogeneous, and highly interdependent. Their cultures are secular. Change is regarded as good. Formal organization and secondary or impersonal relationships predominate.

Glossary

Accommodation The reduction of conflict and the restoration of peaceful interaction.

Achieved status A status attained by one's own efforts or a stroke of good fortune.

Ascribed status A status into which a person is born or one which is automatically assigned with the passage of time.

Assimilation The social process whereby individuals and groups come to share the same sentiments, values, and goals.

Competition The striving of two or more social actors for the same limited goal.

Conflict Interaction in which one social actor tries to deprive, control, injure, or eliminate another against the other's will.

Cooperation The combined effort of two or more social actors to reach a shared goal.

Folk society A small traditional society; an ideal type contrasted to a modern society.

Human society A complex system of relationships among individuals and groups, based on culture.

Modern society A large urbanized society based on advanced technology and a highly developed store of knowledge; an ideal type contrasted to a folk society.

Role A bundle of norms that defines the rights, obligations, and privileges of a person who occupies a particular status.

Role performance The way a specific person plays the role corresponding to a status.

Social group Two or more people who interact, feel a sense of identity that sets them off from others, and have social relationships consisting of interrelated and reciprocal statuses.

Social interaction The reciprocal influencing of behavior through symbolic communication between people.

Social relationships Patterns of more or less recurrent, regular and expected interaction between two or more social actors, which may be persons or groups.

Social structure The network of interrelated statuses in a group; its persisting pattern of relationships.

Society An association of living creatures functioning in organized relationships of mutual dependence.

A society A group that is organized into a more or less permanent division of labor, lives in a certain territory, and shares common goals.

Status A position in a social structure.

chapter

8

Social Groups

An army has a clear-cut organization indicating lines of authority from the Commander in Chief and the Chief of Staff down to the rawest new recruit. Rules are numerous and strictly sanctioned. Salutes and prescribed forms of address indicate deference to the rank rather than the person. Within the army, though, each enlisted man finds sympathy and companionship in a few buddies who feel they are a separate group from the others in their platoon. They use first names or nicknames, joke, argue, and go out on the town together.

The contrast between the army as a whole and the small groups within it illustrates the three closely related aspects of social structure that we shall consider in this chapter: the size of the group, the nature of the social relationships within it, and the degree to which its structure is formalized. In general, the smaller the group, the more likely it is to be informally organized and characterized by personal relationships. The larger the group, the more likely it is to be formal and impersonal. We shall also consider the cohesion or unity of groups—the ties that bind them, more or less effectively.

Small Groups

A **small group** consists of two or more people who repeatedly interact face-to-face. The man who boards the same bus every morning and the driver who wishes him "Good morn-

ing" do not constitute a small group in spite of recurrent contact, but two auditors who share an office do. No more than fifteen or twenty members fit the definition, for even before a group reaches that size, it tends to break down into subgroups, cliques, and factions. If each person in the world belongs to five or six groups on the average, and we allow for overlap, it is estimated that there may be 4 or 5 billion small groups in existence at this moment. *Most* social groups consist of seven persons or less. In fact, nine out of ten social groups consist of only two or three people.[1]

Small groups interest social scientists because of what they mean to the individual and society. They are a primary source of social order, mediating between society and individuals, socializing and motivating them. Because of their psychological hold over members, they are a powerful means of social control. A person is likely to conform to small-group pressures because he or she wants the emotional satisfactions, the sense of belonging, identity, and self-esteem they can provide. Cohesiveness (unity) and morale tend to be higher in small groups than in large ones.

Even within the limits of two to twenty, variation in size is significant. The smaller the group, the more intense the interaction tends to be. *Dyads,* or groups of two, and

[1]John James, "A Preliminary Study of the Size Determinant in Small Group Interaction," *American Sociological Review,* 16 (Aug. 1951): 474–477.

Most social groups consist of only two or three people who repeatedly interact face to face. *Richard Kalvar/Magnum Photos, Inc.*

triads, groups of three, have characteristics that are not only different from those of larger groups but also different from each other. Dyads are conscious of their mortality If one member of a dyad withdraws the group no longer exists. Group opinion must be unanimous for action to occur. Dyads such as husband and wife are "characterized by high tension and emotion, a high tendency to avoid disagreement, a tendency for one to be the active initiator and the other the passive controller with veto—all because of the delicate balance involved in the situation where there is no other support within the group for either participant in case of disagreement and where getting along is necessary for survival."[2]

A dramatic change in a husband-wife relationship occurs when the first child is born. Unlike a dyad, a triad is potentially immortal. It can persist by replacing one member at a time (like The Supremes). Its most significant property is the tendency to break into a coalition of two against one,

as all parents who have watched their children with playmates know. Each member serves to unite and to separate the other two. The third member may act as an intruder (even though, like a baby, he or she may be welcome), as a mediator, as an "enjoying third" who exploits and benefits from the dissension of the other two, or as an oppressor who instigates conflict for his or her own purposes.

Much of the world's work is done by hierarchical triads, such as leader-lieutenant-follower and manager-foreman-worker. The concept of triads may also be applied to social systems of three interacting groups: "two triads of the same type may behave very similarly, although one consists of three small boys and the other of three large bureaucracies."[3]

Social psychologists who have conducted experiments in group size suggest that, for maximum efficiency and interpersonal commitment, the optimum size of a group is five or seven people (note the uneven numbers). Perhaps no more than seven peo-

[2] Bernard Berelson and Gary A. Steiner, *Human Behavior,* shorter ed. (New York: Harcourt Brace Jovanovich, 1967), pp. 63–65. Based on the research of Robert F. Bales and Edgar F. Borgatta.

[3] Theodore Caplow, *Two against One: Coalitions in Triads* (Englewood Cliffs, N.J.: Prentice-Hall, 1968), p. 1.

ple can really take account of one another as individuals, and members of a group of five find more personal satisfaction than they would in smaller or larger groups. Why? Because "there is ease of movement within the group, a two-to-three division provides support for the minority members, and personal recognition."[4] When a group divides into equal numbers on opposite sides of a question, compromise is hindered.

Small groups also serve some instrumental purposes better than do larger ones. John James found that action-taking committees in a large bank averaged six or seven members, while committees that did not take action but discussed questions and served as sounding boards averaged fourteen members.[5] Subcommittees of the House of Representatives average about eight members.

Large Groups

If a small group consists of no more than twenty people, then a **large group** must consist of more than twenty people and could be as large as a nation-state. What happens as a group grows larger?

First of all, as we noted earlier, groups larger than six or seven people tend to *split into subgroups.* Second, as the number of possible channels of interaction increases geometrically with the addition of new members, interaction becomes chaotic and unwieldy. If the group is to persist and function, a *structure of authority* that blocks off some of the channels of interaction and

[4]Berelson and Steiner, *Human Behavior,* p. 63.

[5]"A Preliminary Study of the Size Determinant."

The optimum size of a group is five or seven members. Having an uneven number is important. *Peter Southwick/Stock, Boston.*

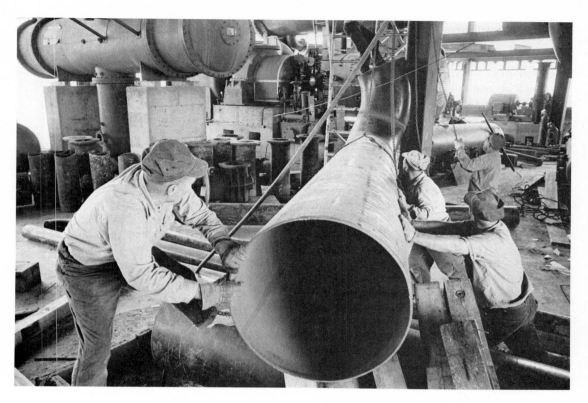

Specialization and coordination of activities are necessary in a factory. *J. Alex Langley/Design Photographers International, Inc.*

facilitates the use of others must emerge. The ideal educational group may be a student on one end of a log and a teacher on the other, but most schooling goes on in classrooms with twenty, thirty, or more students. If all the possible channels of interaction were open, the lesson plan would be neglected and any learning that occurred would be unplanned and incidental. To accomplish the group's purpose, the teacher must have authority to block or regulate interaction among the students and to direct their attention. The situation becomes "structured"—that is, statuses become differentiated and explicit, their accompanying roles are clearly defined, and an order of authority by rank emerges.

As a group comes to include two or more subgroups, this authority structure may become a hierarchy, more or less pyramid-shaped. It usually has one person or a small committee at the top and several distinct levels of authority down the line. Thus, all the teachers in a school system would be the leaders of subgroups at the same level. All the principals would be a level above them, each with a staff as a subgroup below, and so on, up to the superintendent.

Third, *roles tend to become more specialized.* The functions of people and subgroups become more differentiated and more interdependent. In a small restaurant, for example, the same person might take your order, cook it, serve it, and accept payment. In a large one, there are many specialized roles such as cook, waitress, pantry worker, kitchen helper, dishwasher, bartender, hostess, and cashier, all under the authority of a manager.

Fourth, as the group becomes more fragmented, specialized, and interdependent, the need for *coordination of interrelated parts* arises. A change in any subgroup may affect many or all of the others. A deprived group in a community or society, for example may have accepted their status for years. But if they grow rebellious, all other groups are affected, and some new form of accommodation must be arrived at if the society is to function and achieve its goals.

Fifth, the larger and more complex the group becomes, and the greater its need for coordination, the more essential *communication* among the parts becomes. At the same time, more possibilities arise for this communication to be blocked. For example, subgroups may be separated by physical distance. Then, too, people in the same subgroup or category tend to interact mostly with one another and thus to share the same values and norms. In effect they develop subcultures whose understandings and behavior patterns may differ from those of other subgroups to such an extent that they act as barriers to communication. (This principle will be evident in our discussions of class and race in the next two chapters.) Subgroups may also seek different and conflicting goals within the larger group. A labor force may seek only job security, higher wages, and fringe benefits, while management expects employees to share concern for production and profits.

Two more things occur as a group gets larger: Personal relationships tend to become less intimate, and organization becomes more formal. We shall consider these dimensions of social organization at some length.

Primary and Secondary Relationships

Sociologists often analyze complex social phenomena by means of polar types, pairs of opposites regarded as the extremes of a straight line or continuum. Because they are ideal or abstract, polar types seldom describe any one situation perfectly, but they permit the investigator to analyze a situation by placing its various elements in positions along the continuum.

Primary and secondary relationships are such polar types. Human groups, including whole societies, may be characterized as primary or secondary groups according to which relationships predominate.

Primary relationships are "personal, spontaneous, sentimental, and inclusive."[6] The groups in which they predominate are typically small and homogeneous, the result of intimate association over a long period of time. Primary group interaction is expressive rather than instrumental. In other words, it is not a means to some specific goal, but is valued for itself, for the feelings of companionship, affection, and security that arise from it. Each person cares what happens to the other or others. Primary relationships involve deep, but not necessarily positive, emotions (both "I love you, darling" and "Shut up, you make me sick" indicate a primary relationship). If primary relationships are unsatisfactory, people feel tense, unhappy, and frustrated. They may feel trapped and smothered by a relationship that is too close, and lonely and isolated if they have no close ones at all.

Membership in a primary group is nontransferable. Each person is valued for him-

[6] Kingsley Davis, *Human Society* (New York: Macmillan, 1949), p. 294.

Drawing by Scott Val Taber. Copyright 1969
Saturday Review, Inc.

Drawing by Scott Val Taber.

close friends, and the neighborhood are the primary groups that are fundamental to every society. Every person starts life in them. They transmit the culture and shape personality when the child is young and impressionable. Throughout life they serve as the principal sources of motivation and social control.

Secondary relationships, on the other hand, are impersonal, superficial, transitory, and segmental. Even though secondary contacts may involve face-to-face interaction, this interaction is not intimate. It involves only the particular segment of the personality—the status and role—relevant to the situation. Unique personal attributes are not ordinarily taken into account.

Secondary relationships are instrumental. The license clerk is there only to serve us (and to earn money); we are there only as clients who want to be served. The relationship between license clerk and applicant would be changed very little if another person were to perform the role. The applicant interacts with the clerk, not with Susan Anderson, the woman known to family and friends as affectionate, warm-hearted, idealistic, hard-working, thrifty, and subject to blue moods on rainy days.

self or herself. The quality of the interaction would necessarily be different with a different person in the group. A person is not seen in terms of race, class, or occupation, but as a person with a personal meaning to *me:* my friend Jean, my brother Bob.

The family, the play group or circle of

This primary group interacts on a personal level while paying bills incurred in secondary relationships. *Sybil Shelton/Monkmeyer Press Photo Service.*

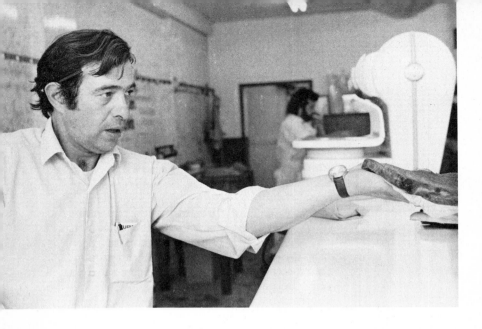

This man is acting in his secondary role as butcher serving a customer. *Owen Franken/Stock, Boston.*

Secondary relationships are especially prevalent in large groups and in modern societies. We could not possibly know all the people with whom we come into contact in city living. When we go out to work or shop, most of our contacts are fleeting and impersonal. We may engage in minor transactions or brief conversation with dozens of people. Yet we don't know their names, their family backgrounds, or anything at all about them except their function in relation to us and what they look like. Often we don't even notice that.

As a rank-and-file member of a secondary group such as a political party, student body, or audience, an individual acts not as a "whole person" but in a segmental or partial role based on the particular status as voter, student, or spectator. Membership is transferable. When one person leaves the scene, the people who remain will experience no sense of loss or loneliness. The group will simply be smaller by one. Anyone else can fill the gap and make up the loss to the party's registration rolls or the theater's profits. Instead of the intimate sharing of common values that characterizes the primary group, the secondary group involves

a rational pursuit of common interests. Secondary groups are typically larger than primary groups, and as we saw, large groups manifest a far greater differentiation of roles and clearer social structure than do small ones. Sanctions are formal and explicit.

Formal and Informal Organization

All social groups are organized in the sense that they have a structure consisting of coordinated social relationships. In long-standing social units such as the family and the tribe, this structure is defined by traditional folkways and mores. In other units, where people are thrown together by circumstance, a structure emerges in the course of social interaction. We see such informal organization when children who happen to be growing up in the same neighborhood form play groups and street gangs. In contrast to groups that "just happen," formal organizations are deliberately created for a specific purpose, and their structures are clearly outlined.

164

Informal Organization

In informal organizations, social structure emerges in the course of social interaction in a small group and is non-institutionalized. The Hawthorne experiments at the Western Electric Company in Chicago provide classic examples of the emergence of informal organization within large formal organizations. The experiment in the Relay Assembly Room, conducted by Elton Mayo of Harvard, was based on three assumptions. First, the workers must be studied as isolated units. Second, workers resemble machines whose efficiency can be measured scientifically. Finally, workers' efficiency depends on their emotions, fatigue, and the physical environment—light, heat, humidity, seating, and so on. But the results of the experiment upset every assumption.

The investigators set out to study the effects of illumination on productivity. In both the control group, in which lighting was unchanged, and the experimental group, in which various kinds of changes in lighting were made, output went up. Why? A second series of experiments was necessary. Two women were asked to choose four more women to join them in a workshop where they would assemble telephone relays, small mechanisms of about forty separate parts. For five years an experimenter sat with the team in the workshop. He observed them, kept them informed about the experiment, listened to their talk and complaints, and asked them for advice and information.

Productivity was recorded at the outset. Then one condition after another was changed, each for a period of 4 to 12 weeks. The women were put on piecework and then returned to straight wages. They were given longer and shorter rest pauses or more frequent ones, dismissed half an hour earlier, given a free hot meal. Output went up with each change. Output did not go up,

however, when numerous rest pauses were introduced (the women complained that their work rhythms were broken) and when the group was dismissed early. Then during the final 12 weeks the women were returned to their original hours and working conditions—a 45-hour, 6-day week, at straight wages, with no piecework, no rest pauses, and no free meal. Output was the highest ever recorded![7] The investigators concluded that their own interest was one factor in high morale. The other was the emergence of a cohesive group whose members felt a sense of purpose and belonging.

The phenomenon of informal organization is universal. Although its rules and roles are not institutionalized, they are real. Group pressure enforces norms; force or other coercion is seldom necessary. A subculture of patterned behavior emerges, "a subtle blend of overt activity, speech, gestures, feelings and ideas which comes to serve as an identifying badge for the 'insider' as against the 'outsider.' "[8] The Soviet term for this phenomenon, "familyness," conveys this feeling of the "we-group."

Formal Organization

In **formal organization,** the means by which a social group hopes to reach an explicit goal are systematically planned by those in authority. Such a group does not, like families or friendships or tribes, "just happen." It is organized at a given time. It is given a name or title, such as General Motors, the San Francisco Athletic Club, or the Red Cross. Its goals are outlined, perhaps in a constitution, and means for reaching them, including a division of labor, are planned. A set of rules and regulations is spelled out,

---

[7] *The Human Problems of an Industrial Civilization* (New York: Macmillan, 1933).

[8] Michael Olmsted, *The Small Group* (New York: Random House, 1959), p. 30.

with explicit sanctions for good or bad role performance (increased wages or loss of a job, honorable or dishonorable discharge, and so on). Property is acquired in the name of the group. This may be as simple as a notebook for records or as complex as a worldwide chain of offices.

The existence of a formal organization does not hinge on particular members. This, in fact, is the infallible test of a formal organization: Can it substitute personnel, and even survive a complete turnover in membership? Because its purpose is instrumental rather than expressive, members are typically not emotionally involved in the interaction needed to carry out group goals. They interact in segmental roles.

In small societies dominated by tradition, the formally organized group is rare. But as societies grow and become more complex, formal organization increases. Without it there could have been no Roman Empire, no Catholic Church, and no conquering armies. However, domination of social life by formally organized groups, both large and small, is something quite new.

We can get an idea of the dominant role of formal organizations by thinking for a moment of how many needs in modern complex society are met through different **voluntary associations**—groups organized by individuals who share some common interest or enjoy the same spare-time activity. Such groups as sports or country clubs, bridge clubs, civic luncheon groups, and alumni associations not only serve their explicit purposes, but also are substitutes for declining primary group relationships. Many formal organizations with specifically commercial goals also allow face-to-face association. The small businessman knows all his employees, and interaction among them proceeds on a basis of primary as well as secondary relationships.

A formal organization may be called large-scale when most of its members are not in face-to-face contact with one another. The large-scale formal organization dominates so much of modern life that its rise has been called "the most striking development in social structure in the twentieth century."[9] In the United States the trend began after the Civil War with the emergence of a few giant producers in such heavy industries as oil, steel, and railroad transportation. Before long, most industrial manufacturing was similarly consolidated and conducted by a few huge financial organizations. Advertising the products of large-scale

[9] Don Martindale, *Institutions, Organizations, and Mass Society* (Boston: Houghton Mifflin, 1966), p. *xiii.*

Voluntary associations help fill the gap left by declining primary relationships. *Daniel S. Brody/Editorial Photocolor Archives.*

industry called for mass media. Chains of newspapers appeared, and the number of independent papers in each city dwindled. The growth of radio and TV was followed by their coordination into large networks. To regulate all these organizations, government had to grow correspondingly. Labor, professions, and farmers organized to defend their special interests. Formal education, too, became increasingly a function of large organizations. Even charity has become a matter for coordinated "community chest" drives.

Bureaucracy and Large-Scale Organization

Because large-scale organizations are oriented toward specific goals and must coordinate the actions of many different people, their paramount values are efficiency, rationality, expertise, and discipline. To realize these values, they create a clear social structure, which is typically *bureaucratic*. In a **bureaucracy,** there is an explicit division of labor in which each status has a name or "job title." Each accompanying role is spelled out in a "job description" that includes clearly assigned tasks, responsibilities, and privileges. Each status is analyzed in terms of rationality and efficiency—the contribution it makes toward reaching the goal of the organization. Statuses are coordinated in a *hierarchy,* a chain of command that indicates who has authority over whom. An ambitious junior executive knows which rungs of the ladder to climb in order to achieve a desired status.

We usually think of bureaucracy in connection with government. There bureaucracy is established to meet a demand for order and protection of rights without regard to political party, social class, or heredity. Once established, it is enduring. It is one of the hardest social structures to destroy. Parties and rulers come and go, but the officials in a typical bureaucracy stay on and work much the same way with one regime as with another. No new set of rulers can afford to replace all the bureaucratic officials. Their expertise is necessary to the functioning of a modern nation, just as it is to a modern corporation or army.

The German sociologist Max Weber described the model type of government bureaucracy as an administrative structure under legal authority, made up entirely of appointed officials, except perhaps for the supreme chief, who may be designated by election or succession.[10] The bureaucracy, and each official within it, has a clear-cut area of jurisdiction, both geographically and as a sphere of competence. It has a set of files and records. It also has a set of rules and regulations that are supposed to cover all problems arising in the course of administration, and that are to be applied impersonally and equally to all.

In bureaucracies, whether found in government or corporations, a clearly defined hierarchy of offices with a graded system of centralized authority exercises strict and systematic discipline and control over each official's conduct. Office holding becomes a career with definite steps upward. It demands the entire work capacity of the office holder for a long period of time. Officials are not selected on the basis of personal relationships, but on the basis of examination scores or certificates of technical training. Officials become expert by concentrating on one small area, and the hierarchy coordinates their expertise with that of others.

Bureaucratic officials normally have life tenure, with guarantees against arbitrary dismissal. They are paid a fixed salary at each level of the hierarchy. Their official life is supposed to be entirely divorced from

[10] *The Theory of Social and Economic Organization,* trans. A. M. Henderson and Talcott Parsons (New York: The Free Press, 1957).

The Board of Directors is at the top of a bureaucratic organization. *Owen Franken/Stock, Boston.*

their personal life. Any violations of this rule are considered graft or corruption. In other words, primary relationships and self-interest should not influence behavior in the secondary group.

Bureaucracy may have negative consequences. Its stability may be seen as rigidity and its regard for rules and proper procedure as red tape. Its impersonality is seen as lack of concern for human problems. Changing conditions and unusual cases are typically not allowed for, and initiative is stifled. Bureaucrats may not see the forest of organizational goals for the trees of its minor regulations. Spoofing the negative side of the bureaucratic personality, the National Association of Professional Bureaucrats adopted as their seal a rampant duck snarled in red tape. They came out in favor of the status quo and buck passing and using executive pencils with erasers at both ends. They urged due recognition of

"the inarticulate fingertappers of the world who, by their steadfast dedication to the principle of dynamic inactivism, have kept things from happening, and thereby have prevented mistakes from being made."[11]

Robert Merton observed that the "bureaucratic personality" is highly conformist and suggested that graded careers encourage conformity and even timidity. Bureaucracy's need for "methodical, prudent, disciplined employees" may lead officials to consider obeying the rules as an end in itself. And professional bureaucrats may band together to defend their own interests rather than those of clients, sometimes making things difficult for elected officials whom they dislike.[12] An extreme example of

[11]Al Blanchard, *Detroit Free Press* (Oct. 16, 1970).
[12]Robert Merton, *Social Theory and Social Structure* enlarged ed. (New York: The Free Press, 1968), Chap. 8, "Bureaucratic Structure and Personality," pp. 249–260.

Merton's view has been challenged. Melvin L. Kohn argues that the bureaucrat is more likely to be flexible, open, and self-directed than the nonbureaucrat, per-the bureaucratic personality man is the so-called Eichmann phenomenon, "the individual who can be a major cog in a machinery designed to exterminate people and yet maintain his innocence since he 'only obeyed orders.'"[13]

But the technical advantages of bureaucracy are similar to the advantages of machinery as compared to manual labor: precision, speed, economy, efficiency, and reduction of friction. In addition, the bureaucratic official is ideally discreet (as well as impersonal) and familiar with the files and the rules. This very impersonality tends to ensure that the rules will be applied equally to all, a democratic tendency that levels social differences. For these reasons, Max Weber called it "the most rational known means of carrying out imperative control over human beings. . . . For the needs of mass administration today, it is completely indispensable."[14]

Cohesion and Control in Social Groups

Why do groups—societies in particular—endure? **Group cohesion,** the unity that enables groups to endure as identifiable units, is one of the central concerns of sociology? In this section we discuss sources of group cohesion: consensus, coordination, control, and individual commitment.

---

haps because he is better educated, better paid, and more secure, and his work is more complex. ("Bureaucratic Man: A Portrait and an Interpretation," *American Sociological Review* 36 (June 1971): 461–474.

[13] Steven E. Deutsch and John Howard, *Where It's At: Radical Perspectives in Sociology* (New York: Harper & Row, 1970), p. 482.

[14] *The Theory of Social and Economic Organization,* p. 337.

Consensus

Consensus, or agreement on norms, values, and goals, is essential to cohesion. It depends first of all on what the members of the group have in common, and on their belief that what they have in common is important. But they must also agree on a certain amount of overt conformity to behavior patterns if they are to interact smoothly and know what to expect of others. Even in the most complex society, they must agree on certain core values. For such agreement to arise and endure, there must be a flow of communication among members.

Coordination

Although groups must have something important that all members hold in common, they also require role differences among members, and these differences must be **coordinated** so that each role contributes to achievement of the group goal. Leaders emerge or are appointed to assign functions and power to the occupants of various statuses. To mobilize skills, there must be a chain of command that integrates specialized roles. The chief task of leaders and managers is that of delegating responsibilities. When this delegation is formal and institutionalized (that is, firmly attached to statuses rather than to persons), the formal group is highly rational and subject to manipulation. Occupants of statuses are judged by performance and can be replaced. Coordination is especially vital to the cohesion and productivity of formal organizations.

Control

Groups **control** the behavior of members through positive and negative sanctions or through coercion. Sanctions may be emotional satisfactions or material rewards. When a primary group distributes affection, approval, and esteem, it is using positive sanctions. Withholding these rewards is a negative sanction. A formal group exerts control through prestige rewards, ritual and ceremony, persuasion, and manipulation of the mass media. In the primary group, a mother denies dessert if a child misbehaves, or gives a new bicycle if grades improve. Formal organizations, on the other hand, allocate different amounts of salaries and wages, fringe benefits, and so on. The emotional cost of leaving a family and the financial cost of leaving a firm may keep a member within the group.

But many groups are held together by the possibility or actuality of coercion or force. Prisons and armies obviously depend on such power. The state relies ultimately on the fact that a citizen who disobeys the law may be subject to pain, death, imprisonment, discomfort, and denial of access to many satisfactions such as sex and good food. Most groups employ a combination of controls in the same way that parents use the carrot and the stick, the promise of candy and the threat of spankings.

Commitment

The cohesion of a group rests ultimately on **commitment**—the willingness of its members to remain within it and contribute to it. The more members feel they have something important in common with others (a sense of belonging), and the more satisfied they are with the rewards of participation as compared to the costs of leaving, the more highly committed they will be.

Even without a firm sense of belonging and identification, people may participate in a group for instrumental (utilitarian) rewards. But if they do not feel involved or identified with the group and are only nominally members of it, they are *isolated*. Those who once felt the power of group ties, but then feel cast adrift and turn against the group or resent its coercive power, are said to be *alienated*. Those denied admission to a group to which they feel they have a right to belong (especially if the core values of the culture agree with their own), are said to be *segregated* or discriminated against. Feelings of isolation, alienation, and segregation are obviously disruptive to the cohesion of a group or society.

Summary

Three closely interrelated aspects of social organization are the size of groups, the kinds of relationships within them, and the degree of formality of organization.

Most interaction occurs in small face-to-face groups, which are important because of their psychological hold over members, their effectiveness in producing decisions and action, and their role in mediating between individuals and the larger society. They are also interesting sociologically because, like larger groups, they evolve cultural

codes and social structures, and social processes can be easily observed in such groups. There are striking differences in interaction in dyads, triads, and larger groups.

As a group becomes larger, it tends to split into subgroups. A structure of authority emerges, roles become more specialized, and interrelated parts of the system must be coordinated. The proportion of secondary (segmental, impersonal, and instrumental) relationships to primary (personal, expressive, spontaneous) ones rises. Organization also becomes more formalized. However, informal organizations often emerge within large-scale formal organizations.

The test of a formal organization is that it can survive a turnover of personnel. Bureaucracy is typical of the administration of large formal organizations. It is an impersonal means of exerting social control and of achieving group goals in modern society.

The cohesion of a group depends on consensus on norms and values, coordination of interdependent functions, effective control of members and a sense of commitment and involvement that keeps members participating.

Glossary

Bureaucracy A hierarchical social structure for administering large scale organizations rationally, efficiently, and impersonally.

Commitment The willingness of members to remain with and contribute to a group.

Consensus Agreement within a social group on norms, values, and goals.

Control Power over the behavior of group members employed through positive and negative sanctions or through coercion.

Coordination The systematic meshing of roles by leaders so that group goals may be achieved.

Formal organization A clearly outlined social structure deliberately created for a specific purpose and not dependent on specific group members; characteristic mainly of large groups.

Group cohesion The unity that enables groups to endure as identifiable units.

Informal organization Non-institutionalized social structure that emerges in the course of social interaction in a small group.

Large group A group consisting of more than twenty people; it may be as large as a nation-state; generally has smaller sub-groups.

Primary relationships Personal, spontaneous, sentimental, and inclusive social relationships characterized by expressive interaction.

Secondary relationships Impersonal, superficial, transitory and segmental relationships characterized by instrumental interaction.

Small group From two to twenty people who repeatedly interact face to face.

Voluntary associations Groups organized by individuals who share some common interest or activity.

chapter

9

Social Stratification

Suppose you were stuck in an elevator with a strange man for half an hour. You would note his sex and probable "racial" identity immediately, and perhaps make a guess about his age. But you would probably also compare him to others you know in terms of his grammar and diction, his clothes, his manners, and perhaps, if you talked enough, his occupation, education, and income. You might mentally label him as belonging to a certain social class that is inferior, superior, or equal to your own. If you found out where he lives, what schools he attended, what church and clubs, if any, he belongs to, you would feel more sure of your conclusions.

Even though one of the core values stated in the Declaration of Independence is that "All men are created equal," Americans rank people according to various measures of status.[1] They use a number of terms that indicate awareness of class differences: rich and poor; the country-club set and people from the other side of the tracks; "old money" and social climbers. Perhaps we feel ill at ease when we are around people who use different grammar or less soap than we do. As much as we may believe in equality of opportunity, we recognize the reality of inequality of many kinds.

In this chapter we ask, first, if social stratification is universal, and how it arises.

Second, we consider variations in systems of social stratification. Next we look at the consequences of stratification for life chances, group interaction, ways of life, and personality. We then ask how wealth, prestige, and power are distributed and how we can measure them. After considering these general questions, we sketch the class structure of the United States as sociologists see it at the level of the local community, the large city, and the nation. Finally we look at social mobility—the ways in which the status of individuals and groups can change.

The Meaning of Social Stratification

Sociologists define **social stratification** as an institutionalized system of social inequality that ranks individuals and groups according to their share of scarce and desirable resources such as wealth, prestige, and power. These groups may be families, racial or ethnic groups, religious groups, occupational groups, neighborhoods, towns, or even nations.

People in different age and sex categories tend to have different amounts of wealth, prestige and power in each society. But because everyone goes through similar stages of the life cycle and because families are made up of both sexes, they are not stratified in the sense we are using in this chapter. Race, ethnic background, and religion,

---

[1] For many purposes, such as the census, the units for classification are "families and unrelated individuals," the latter including people who live alone. When we refer to families in connection with class, we also mean such individuals.

Reprinted by permission of Cartoon Features Syndicate.

"Don't bother to get up—I'm just passing through."

however, often do lend themselves to stratification. In fact, some sociologists see American society as divided by *two* systems of social stratification. One is based on class criteria, the other on racial, religious and ethnic criteria. In this chapter, we shall concentrate on the first type. (The second is the subject of the next chapter.)

A **social stratum** (or *layer*) may be defined as a category of people with similar amounts of wealth, prestige, and power, and similar life chances and ways of life. People within a stratum tend to recognize one another as social equals and those in other categories as being either inferior or superior.

We refer to social stratification as *institutionalized* because it is part of the social structure, given stability and relative permanence by support from cultural beliefs, values, and norms, and by the fact that individuals are initially (and in some systems permanently) assigned to the stratum of their parents. Members of the society tend to perceive the different levels or strata as real. Their relative positions within the system have important consequences for their life chances, their behavior, their values and attitudes, and their personalities.

Is Social Stratification Universal?

Like the pecking order of chickens, a ranking order is found in all known societies. But not all are stratified in the sense of hereditary ranking of families. In many simple societies, chieftains or elders may hold office only temporarily and not be permitted to pass it on to their children. The Kwakiutl society of the Pacific Northwest included many different ranks and titles. But each was passed on from person to person, and during a lifetime one man might be anything from a commoner to a chief at any given time.[2] Using the files of the Cross-Cultural Survey at Yale University, George Murdock found no system of stratification (except by age and sex) in 74 of 250 societies.[3]

As a society becomes larger it also becomes more complex and breaks into subgroups. According to Robin Williams all large-scale or long-continued social groupings have differential ranking of people as individuals and as members of social categories.[4] As statuses and roles become more specialized,

[2] Helen Codere, "Kwakiutl Society: Rank Without Class," *American Anthropologist* 59 (June 1957), pp. 473–586.
[3] George Murdock, *Social Structure* (New York: The Macmillan Company, 1949), pp. 87–88.
[4] Robin M. Williams, Jr., *American Society: A Sociological Interpretation*, 3rd. ed. (New York: Alfred A. Knopf, 1970), p. 100.

An expensive car may represent "class," but to sociologists, the matter of social class is far more complex. *Ema / Design Photographers International, Inc.*

rewards tend to become more unequally distributed. A structure of authority emerges to direct and coordinate the action of the various groups and subgroups. Some have power to direct and command. Others must follow and obey. In every complex society—thus far, at least—there has been an unequal distribution of wealth, prestige, and power. If those at the top were overthrown, a new system of stratification, not a classless society, emerged. And it always resulted in the hereditary ranking of families. An infant was always assigned its parents' status even in systems where it could later achieve higher status, or lose status. Many sociologists are watching with interest attempts to achieve equality in Cuba and China.

How Does Stratification Occur?

Few if any modern thinkers agree with Aristotle that there are by nature freemen and slaves, and that both find their condition just and agreeable. One explanation of the rise of stratification systems is psychological. All human beings tend to *differentiate* among objects, including people and groups, to assign labels to them, and to *evaluate* them according to these perceived differences. It is theoretically possible for us to see each person as unique and valuable without making comparisons. We could see persons and groups as different but equal. But almost always differentiation and evaluation lead to ranking in terms of superiority, equality, and inferiority. Students are ranked by grades, warriors by bravery, athletes by skill. But these are individual rankings and do not lend themselves to a system of stratification. The stability of a system depends in large part on *inheritance* of status—the fact that infants are assigned their parents' position.

Karl Marx believed that the class system is related to the ownership of the means of production. He believed that there will always be a class system as long as there is private property. Under slavery, feudalism, and capitalism, society is divided into distinct and hostile classes. As each stage nears its end a class struggle occurs that leads each society one step closer to the classless society of communism. We are all prisoners of the system. None of us can help belonging to a certain class and sharing its motivations. Even the capitalist exploiter is simply acting out his historical role. Only when the proletariat, tired of oppression, overthrows the upper class or *bourgeoisie* and eliminates private property will inequality and exploitation vanish, according to Marx.

Functionalist sociologists also see social inequality as inevitable, but they see it as essential and functional. It is an efficient way of getting all of a society's necessary jobs done. Those that demand the most talent and sacrifice are the most highly rewarded.

Historically, systems of stratification have arisen through force and conquest as well as evolution toward greater complexity. However they arise, they tend to persist because, as Max Weber pointed out, systems of stratification are multi-dimensional, and their various dimensions are closely interwoven. Those with wealth also tend to have prestige and power. Whichever of these resources people or groups acquire first, it helps them get the other two. And the combination of the three tends to endure, for power protects wealth and prestige, wealth helps perpetuate power, and so on.

Variations in Systems of Stratification

Three ideal types of stratification systems are caste, estate, and class. At one extreme is the **caste system,** in which the strata are hereditary, endogamous (mates must be chosen from within the group), and permanent. A person is born into one caste, marries in it, and dies in it. At the other extreme is the **open-class system,** in which only individual achievement matters. One rises or falls in social class according to one's own merits. But even here, an infant is assigned its family's status at birth and thus has an initial advantage or disadvantage in life. In the **estate system,** classes are defined by law and are relatively rigid and permanent, but there is some opportunity to shift one's status. The best-known caste system is that of traditional India. The United States is considered by many of its citizens to have the most open and mobile class system in the world. Feudal Europe is the most notable example of an estate system. Both the ideal types and the actual systems vary in many ways. (See Table 9-1.)

NUMBER OF STRATA Only two broad categories, such as slaves and freemen, or the elite and the masses, may be distinguished in some societies. More commonly, however, there are three or more broad categories. Ancient tradition classified all Hindus into four chief castes: priests and teachers of the sacred lore (Brahmins); warriors (Kshatriyas); peasants, craftsmen, and merchants (Vaisyas); and manual laborers and servants (Sudras). Outcastes or untouchables were considered to be outside the Hindu spiritual community. In medieval Europe, the various estates included the secular feudal aristocracy, the clergy, and the serfs or peasants who worked the land and labored for the manor. Some sociologists find from three to six major classes in modern industrial societies. Others insist that any such number is arbitrary because of variations in criteria and their application.

CRITERIA OF RANK Mark Twain once said, "In Boston, they ask, How much does he know? In New York, How much is he worth? In Philadelphia, Who were his parents?" Learning, property, "blue blood," authority, prestigious occupations—whatever the community or society values most, the upper strata have (or are believed to have) more of it than those below. In estate systems, relation to the land was the criterion for the secular classes, position in the church hierarchy for the clergy. In traditional India the higher castes were presumed to be closer to perfect purity according to their religion.

In South Africa the caste system is based on belief in the superiority of whites to blacks, with "coloreds" in between. In some societies, such as the Soviet Union and the People's Republic of China, status in the political hierarchy is extremely important and may replace property as the criterion of rank. In many developing countries and new nations, bureaucrats occupy a commanding position.

So many criteria are used to judge class in the United States that Gerhard Lenski sees not one class system but a number of class hierarchies based on different criteria. He believes all members of American society can be rated by their position in occupational, property, racial-ethnic, educational, age, and sexual class systems. Social movements aiming to raise the status of certain groups—to increase the importance of criteria such as

Table 9-1 Caste, Estate, and Open-Class Systems of Social Stratification

	Caste	*Estate*	*Open-Class*
Example	Traditional India; South Africa	Feudal Europe; Pre-revolutionary Russia	U.S.A.; Japan
Number of Strata	Four, plus the untouchables; Numerous subcastes	Three	Three to six
Criteria of Ranking	Ascribed status (permanent)	Ascribed status (some mobility possible)	Achieved status (limited by ascription)
Sharpness of Stratum Boundaries	Clear	Clear	Vague; gradual
Social Distance	Formal	Formal	Informal
Degree of Mobility	Very low	Low	Fairly high
Degree of Complexity	High	Low	Very high
Institutionalization	Religion; tradition	Hereditary relationships to land; church	Belief in equality of opportunity

educational and occupational accomplishments, for example, and diminish the importance of birth or sex or race—are all, in this sense, class struggles.[5] A more commonly held view of the American class system is that although one's status is initially that of one's parents, things that can supposedly be achieved by anyone with the necessary talent and drive are the main criteria.

SHARPNESS OF STRATUM BOUNDARIES Castes and estates are discrete strata, clearly marked off from one another. Everyone knew exactly where they and others belonged in the traditional caste system. Each Indian subcaste, for example once had its own religious cult, distinctive dress, food customs, and linguistic usages. Each was identified, in its community, with an exclusive hereditary occupation. The estate system, too, was a clear hierarchy in which each lord's standing was symbolized by knightly trappings and by acts of deference to those above and from those below. In modern class systems, however, differences in dress, manners, diction, and possessions are more subtle. There are no sharp breaks in the distribution of property, prestige, and power. Class lines are blurred. Even when categories are marked off more clearly, there are many marginal cases not easily assigned to one stratum or another. That is why some sociologists conceive of the American class system as a continous gradation of social statuses rather than as a set of separate categories or strata. On the local level, however, personal knowledge of others permits categorical placement of most people, and intimate interaction promotes the formation of distinct status groups. Both locally and nationally, boundaries appear to be sharpest at the highest and lowest levels of the system.

SOCIAL DISTANCE AND CONFLICT Social distance is "a feeling of separation or actual social separation between individuals or groups. The greater the social distance between two groups of different status or culture, the less sympathy, understanding, intimacy, and interaction there is between them."[6] Eating together, visiting one another, and intermarrying indicate the absence of social distance. In India, a complicated set of rules governed interaction among persons of different castes. A person of high rank avoided inferiors because he believed their touch (or even their shadow) would pollute him and make it necessary to take a long ritual bath. Endogamy was so strong that each subcaste was in effect an extended family or kin group. In open-class systems, even in the absence of such rules, intimate interaction and intermarriage are most frequent among social equals.

In many modern societies, there is sharp awareness of one's own status as compared to that of others. This is especially true where feudal systems once prevailed and have left some cultural legacies, as in Europe and Latin America. It is less true in societies with a strong cultural belief in equality. Class awareness may or may not be accompanied by a feeling of solidarity with those in one's own class and of hostility to others. Class conflict, however, is common to all stratified societies. Though it may rarely break out in overt violence or revolution, it may occur through established channels such as political parties and pressure groups.

DEGREE OF MOBILITY "The sons of mandarins," runs a Vietnamese proverb, "will one day be mandarins. The sons of the poor will spend their days lighting coals." In completely closed systems of stratification,

---

[5] *Power and Privilege: A Theory of Social Stratification* (New York: McGraw-Hill, 1966), p. 81.

[6] George A. Theodorson and Achilles G. Theodorson, *A Modern Dictionary of Sociology*, (New York: Thomas A. Crowell, 1969), p. 388.

there is no legitimate way for a person to rise to a higher stratum. All an Indian traditionally could do was accept his lot in life and hope to be born into a higher caste in the next incarnation. But as India modernizes, it is increasingly common, especially in the larger cities, to marry across caste lines and otherwise deemphasize ritual status. For example, more emphasis is put on economic and political status. The medieval clergy, being sworn to celibacy, recruited its upper orders from the nobility and its lower orders from promising members of the lower estates, thus providing a measure of mobility. In modern class systems, movement up and down the social ladder is frequent because industrialization demands a skilled labor force that is not bound by traditional occupations. Formal education in the necessary skills often becomes the main avenue to social advancement.

The first black Supreme Court Justice, Thurgood Marshall represents status inconsistency. He also represents significant gains for Black Americans since World War II. *Wide World Photos.*

COMPLEXITY The complexity of a system depends on the combination of all the factors we have mentioned: the number of strata, the number of criteria, sharpness of stratum boundaries, social distance, and degree of mobility. Even the caste system is complex. There are actually about 3,000 castes in India, most of which are further divided into subcastes. Any one village may contain 20 or 30 caste groups. And in large cities a class system cuts across caste lines. In the estate system, too, there were various degrees of aristocracy and of freedom and servitude.

Stratification systems in heterogeneous modern societies, notably that of the United States, are especially complex. Ascribed statuses assigned at birth coexist with achieved statuses—those acquired through individual merit or effort, collective movements, and changes in other aspects of the social structure such as industrialization, business cycles, or social reforms. As a result, a person's or group's status depends on a number of variables at any given time, and it changes over time. This results in considerable blurring of class lines and a number of cases of status inconsistency—of high standing by one or more important criteria and low standing by others. For example, if one rates blacks low and Supreme Court justices high, then how does one rank Thurgood Marshall? Where does a wealthy racketeer or an impoverished member of the "First Families of Virginia" stand?

The differentiation and evaluation that we said appear natural to human beings goes only so far. To economize on thinking, people also tend to simplify and categorize. Therefore, complex as the American system is, people actually tend to think and act in terms of a single system with several broad levels of stratification.

INSTITUTIONALIZATION Though some systems of stratification originate in conquest or slavery, force alone is not enough in the long run. Those who have power in a society seek to ensure that power by institutionalizing the system of structured inequality that allows them to exploit the lower, less powerful classes. Religion, law, cultural myths, the inertia of established folkways and mores—any or all of these help preserve the status quo by making it seem somehow right and fair. This defuses the resentment of the lower classes enough to allow the system to keep functioning. In medieval Europe the estate system was institutionalized by hereditary relationships to land, sanctioned by law and private contract in which an oath of loyalty to one's lord was a holy vow. The custom of the manor fixed individual rights and duties and protected serfs from unusual exploitation. The preachings of the Church also justified the system. "Some fight, some work, some pray." Religion and tradition as well as a system of economic interdependence provide the basic justifications for the Indian caste system. They also justify racist doctrines (with less success, except in the minds of whites) for apartheid in South Africa.

In modern class systems social inequality is usually rationalized—especially by the upper classes—as based on achievement and reward. Both the United States and the Soviet Union proclaim goals of equality or classlessness. Both also proclaim a cultural myth of equality of opportunity, which reconciles the myth of equality to the reality of inequality. Each person is believed to be in the position he or she deserves, because every one supposedly has an equal chance. This encourages people who have not achieved a high position to blame themselves (or other groups, or bad luck) rather than the system as a whole. As long as most people are convinced that the system is fair, inequality poses no serious threat to social cohesion.

Consequences of Stratification

Rigid systems of stratification such as caste and estate change as a society modernizes. An industrial society requires an educated, skilled labor force, not bound by occupational inheritance and free to move from job to job. Therefore, as we have already suggested, modern class systems tend to be open, to stress achievement rather than ascription, and to allow mobility, especially through education. Class boundaries tend to blur, and the proportion of those in the middle range grows. During the modernization process, says Alex Inkeles, the social pyramid changes from a broad base of peasantry to a trapezoid or even a diamond shape as more and more people become middle class.[7]

Nonetheless, people have unequal chances to compete for wealth, power, and prestige. These valuable resources are not evenly distributed. What consequences does this inequality have for an individual member of a modern class society?

Life Chances

Chances for "life, liberty, and the pursuit of happiness" are closely related to social class status. The farther down the scale one goes, the more limited are opportunities, the more restricted are choices, the greater are the risks of illness, deprivation, and broken homes, and the less is one's freedom or capacity to take a hand in one's own development.

The most basic life chance is the chance to stay alive. In the early nineteenth century,

[7] "Social Stratification in the Modernization of Russia," in Cyril Black, ed., *The Transformation of Russian Society* (Cambridge, Mass.: Harvard University Press, 1960), pp. 338–339.

life expectancy was low for everyone, largely because babies died like flies. The most well-to-do people in one mill town had only a 28-year life expectancy. Yet this was over twenty times that of the children of simple weavers, which was a year and four months![8] Average life expectancy in modern industrial societies is many times higher, and the gap between classes much narrower. Yet the gap is still there.

Because of class differences in life chances in the United States, the higher we go on the social scale, the taller, healthier, and heavier are the members of each class, and the higher they score on IQ tests. The poor have less dental care, more heart trouble, a higher incidence of illness and disability— both mental and physical—and poorer care in the home and hospital when they are sick. Infant mortality among the poor is twice the national average. The poor pay more for less in housing, groceries, and furnishings (for which they pay a high rate of interest on loans or installments). The poorer a person, the greater the risk of being a victim of crime and of being charged with and convicted of crime.[9] The poor are more likely to suffer the stigma of public welfare, to be alienated from the mainstream of American life, and to feel hopelessness and despair.

Because formal education is the main avenue to advancement in modern industrial society, chances for schooling are among the most crucial life chances. The farther one goes up the social ladder, the more years of schooling children are likely to receive, the better the schools, the greater the chance of professional graduate training. (One exception: The upper middle class is more highly educated than the upper class.) Only 17 percent of the heads of poor families have graduated from high school, but the gap promises to be narrowed. It is estimated that by 1980 community colleges will be enrolling about 40 percent of the college-age population. This share will come largely from the lowest economic level.[10] Quite aside from the intrinsic value of education to personal fulfillment, lifetime earnings are correlated with amount of schooling. And *which* college one attends may become more important as mass education increases.

Where political loyalty is a determinant of status, it also necessarily affects life chances. In the Soviet Union people branded as politically unreliable may lose their job, be transferred to a distant region, lose good housing, and be denied higher education or promotion. In addition, just as in the United States, a child's chances of getting a "good" education are affected not only by native ability and the availability of schools, but depend largely on "the income, motivations, and values of his family and on the region where one was born. . . . A child born in a family of kolhoz [collective farm] peasants, for example, in Kazahkstan, has a poorer chance to attend . . . any university than the child of a high civil servant, engineer, or scientist living in some of the urban areas of European Russia. The chances of such a child may not be quite as bad as those of an illegitimate child of a Negro mother living on welfare in Mississippi, but they are still rather dim."[11]

Life Styles

When F. Scott Fitzgerald said that the very rich are different from you and me, Ernest Hemingway snapped, "Yes, they have more

[8] J. Fourastie, *The Causes of Wealth* (Glencoe, Ill.: The Free Press, 1960).

[9] See A. B. Hollingshead, *Elmtown's Youth* (New York: Wiley, 1949), pp. 102, 110, and 119–120, for a comparison of the public record of criminal charges and convictions by class status.

[10] *The Center Magazine* (March 1970).

[11] Paul Hollander, ed., *American and Soviet Society: A Reader in Comparative Sociology and Perception* (Englewood Cliffs, N.J.: Prentice-Hall, 1968), p. 125.

money." But most sociologists would agree with Fitzgerald. The people in various social classes *are* different. They have different styles of life, patterns of social participation, beliefs, values, and attitudes. This differentiation is not a direct consequence of variations in wealth, prestige, and power (except to some extent for those lowest on the scale, who have the fewest options). Rather it arises from the tendency of those in each class to associate more often and more intimately with those they perceive to be similarly situated. The more they limit their interaction to such people, the more they come to form "status groups" with similar styles of life, norms, and values—in short, subcultures. The more stable a society, the more marked are subcultural differences. But even in our rapidly changing society, members of the various classes participate differently in social groups and carry out their institutional roles as family members, students, church-goers, voters, producers, and consumers in different ways. Inevitably such differences are correlated with variations in personality, in manners, speech, and traits, including modes of interpersonal relationships.

All over the world political affiliation is correlated with social class, with the "right" generally associated with upper classes, the "left" with lower classes, and the "center" with middle classes. A 1960 study showed that in every election in the United States since 1936, when such studies were first begun, "the proportion voting Democratic increases sharply as one moves down the occupational or income ladder."[12] Religious affiliation has also been shown to be class-linked, as have patterns of childrearing and husband-wife relationships.

Although we have referred to differences in life chances and life styles as consequences

[12]Seymour Martin Lipset, *Political Man: The Social Bases of Politics* (Garden City, N.Y.: Doubleday, 1960), Chap. 7.

of stratification, they also have consequences *for* stratification. They reinforce and perpetuate systems of stratification by reducing social mobility and by motivating people to limit their intimate interaction to those of similar status.

The Distribution of Wealth, Power, and Prestige

As we noted, the three general types of resources that people value and compete for are wealth, power, and prestige. Let us now look at the way these are distributed and measured.

The Distribution of Wealth in the U.S.

Residents of the United States received a median income of $13,720 per family in 1975.[13] By this index, Americans are the

[13]U.S. Bureau of the Census, *Current Population Reports*, Series P-60, No. 103 (September 1976), "Money Income and Poverty Status of Families and Persons in the United States."

Table 9-2 U.S. Family Income (March 1976)

Number of Families	Percentage of Population	Income
(millions)		
7.9	14.1	$25,000 +
17.1	30.3	15,000 – 25,000
12.6	22.3	10,000 – 15,000
11.9	21.1	5,000 – 10,000
6.8	12.0	below 5,000

Source: U.S. Bureau of the Census, *Current Population Reports*, Series P-60, No. 103 (September 1976), "Money Income and Poverty Status of Families and Persons in the United States."

richest people in the world. But other figures reveal great inequalities in the distribution of wealth and income.[14]

There is a rather steeply rising curve of income by different economic classes. (See Figure 9-1.) When the population is divided into five equal parts by family income, the poorest fifth received 5.5 percent of aggregate income. The second fifth received 11.9

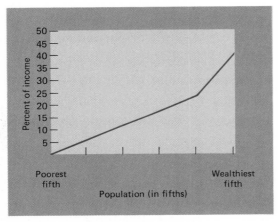

Figure 9-1 Percent of income received by each fifth of the population.

percent; the third, 17.4 percent; the fourth, 23.7 percent; and the top fifth, 41 percent. The top 5 percent of families received 16.0

[14] Being numerical, wealth and income appear easy to measure and compare. But there are many pitfalls in the process and much disagreement on how figures should be interpreted. One scholar can use them to prove that inequality is decreasing, and more income than formerly goes to the lower income groups; another could draw the opposite conclusion. See Herman P. Miller, *Rich Man, Poor Man*, 2nd ed. (New York: Thomas Y. Crowell, 1971); Gabriel Kolko, *Wealth and Power in America: An Analysis of Social Class and Income Distribution* (New York: Praeger, 1962); Robert J. Lampman, *The Share of Top Wealth-Holders in National Wealth, 1922–1956* (Princeton, N.J.: Princeton University Press, 1962); and Ferdinand Lundberg, *The Rich and the Super-Rich: A Study in the Power of Money Today* (New York. Bantam, 1968).

percent of income.[15] Measured in terms of wealth rather than income, concentration is even greater. A tiny fraction—0.2 to 0.3 percent—of the population owns 22 percent of all privately held wealth and 60 to 70 percent of all privately held corporate wealth.[16] Few of these fortunes are accounted for by the "rags to riches" stories of the nineteenth-century classics. Almost every holder of wealth in the upper 0.5 percent of the population inherited it.

American Myths Regarding Economic Distribution

Many Americans believe that "we are all becoming middle class" because our general level of living has improved. True, median income in constant dollars has doubled since World War II. But the share of each fifth of the population has changed little since then.

Another myth is that our system of taxation and of such benefits as social security redistributes the wealth and makes up for income inequalities. Census Bureau expert Herman P. Miller says that although federal income taxes are progressive (taking a higher percentage of their incomes from the rich), state and local taxes (such as the sales tax, property tax, and fixed-percentage income tax) do just the reverse. Such taxes are regressive, taking a higher percentage of their income from the poorer classes. In a typical year (1965), people at all income levels between $2,000 and $15,000 paid about 27 percent of their income in taxes. 7 out of 10 dollars paid for personal income taxes came from people earning less than $20,000. Those with incomes less than $2,000, ac-

[15] U.S. Bureau of the Census, *Current Population Reports*, Series P-60, No. 85 (December 1972), "Money Income in 1971 of Families and Persons in the United States."

[16] G. William Domhoff, "The Power Elite," *The Center Magazine* 3, No. 2 (March 1970).

cording to the Council of Economic Advisers, paid 44 percent in taxes, and those with incomes over $15,000, 38 percent. There are many tax loopholes for the rich. Capital gains are taxed at a low rate. There are depletion allowances on oil and depreciation on real estate. Expense accounts and some other kinds of income are not taxed.[17]

A third myth, thoroughly exploded in recent years, is that no one goes hungry in America.

Poverty in the United States

In any system of inequality, some people are bound to be at the bottom of the heap. Can all of these people be thought of as poor? To answer, we must distinguish between absolute and relative poverty. **Absolute poverty** refers to extreme inadequacy in the essentials of food, clothing, and shelter. It means malnutrition or starvation, chronic ill health, low life expectancy, rags, and hovels and slums. **Relative poverty,** on the other hand, is comparative. It is measured against the greater plenty of others. Because it is rooted in inequality, it may persist even when the standard of living of all groups improves.

Depending on the yardstick used, 10 to 20 percent of Americans are living below the poverty line. Using an income of $5,500 for a nonfarm family of four as the poverty threshold, there were 25.9 million poor Americans in 1975. And some of these know absolute poverty. About 10 million are chronically malnourished; 13.5 million were on welfare in 1971, a rise of 70 percent in 5 years.

Poverty hits the old and young especially hard. One of every three Americans over 65 is poor—almost one-fourth of elderly whites and one-half of elderly blacks. One child in five (and according to some esti-

[17] *Rich Man, Poor Man.*

mates, one in three or four) is growing up in poverty, and nearly half of these live in families of five or more children. But of all population groups, households with dependent children headed by a woman have the highest likelihood of being poor— among whites, 26.3 percent in 1974, among nonwhites, 53.8.

Why does poverty still exist in the United States? Three related factors appear to explain much of it: the rapidly changing requirements of our technological society, the nature of today's poverty as compared to that of half a century ago, and the failure

Poverty hits the elderly in America especially hard. Many must live on fixed incomes. *Vicki Lawrence/Stock, Boston.*

of government policies to deal with the swift transition from rural to urban living, from subsistence to commercial farming.

An advanced industrial society has little or no room for unskilled labor, and less and less for semiskilled labor. Automation creates unemployment that may be offset by greater opportunities in the long run, but only for those who are technically trained. Cotton-picking machines are symbols of the agricultural revolution that has displaced millions of tenant farmers and sharecroppers.

Today's poverty is not like that of immigrants who worked themselves out of the slums in a generation or two, or the "all-in-the-same-boat" poverty of the Depression. It is largely self-perpetuating. Seven out of ten poor families have four or more children, and many of the mothers bring them up alone. They have such low chances for schooling, health care, and jobs that when they grow up they repeat the pattern. Some poverty, as has always been the case, is due to personal misfortunes and handicaps. Some is aggravated by discrimination against certain categories of people.

American poverty is not so different from poverty in developing nations where an agricultural revolution pushes people off the land into city slums. Although we have produced a surplus and have paid farmers not to grow crops (the bulk of these payments going to the wealthiest farmers), we find hunger and malnutrition in rural slums and urban ghettos. Thinking in terms of tractors, chemicals, and "efficiency," agricultural policy-makers have failed to modernize or rehabilitate farm families left behind by the new technology.[18] And in comparison to

most other industrialized nations, including those with largely capitalist or free-market economies, our government provisions for public assistance are inadequate. We do not really have a "welfare state."[19]

The Distribution of Power

Americans find the idea of a "ruling class" distasteful, Marxist, and un-American. We prefer to think of our equality at the ballot box and of decisions being made by formal systems of government. But sociologists and political scientists are taking an increasing interest in the nature and distribution of power, and a number have concluded that it tends to be more concentrated than wealth and prestige.

What is **power?** It is control over the decisions that affect the way people live and over the allocation of scarce and desirable resources. Power is exercised through economic and social institutions as well as through government structures.

How is power distributed in American society? Some see it *pyramidal,* with a power elite at the top. Others see it as *pluralistic,* with many groups struggling for advantage and checking and balancing one another. Theoretically, there could also be *equal distribution* of power throughout society, a sort of "mass democracy" of one-person-one-vote regarding all important decisions and policies affecting freedom of choice and allocation of resources. If the first pattern were true in any one community or society, the same leaders at the top of the pyramid would

---

[18] See Sidney Baldwin, *Poverty and Politics* (Chapel Hill: University of North Carolina Press, 1969), for an account of what went wrong in America's transformation from handcraft-and-labor farming to modern capital-intensive agriculture. Subtitled "The Rise and Fall of the Farm Security Administration," it relates the story of a short-lived effort to aid families as well

as production by providing counseling and guidance to poor farm families and communities during the Depression of the 1930s.

[19] Hyman Lumer, "Why People Are Poor," in *Poverty: Its Roots and Future* (New York: International Publishers, 1965), pp. 13–32.

make all or nearly all the significant decisions, would agree on them, and would not be responsible to an electorate. If the pluralistic pattern prevailed, the leaders would vary from issue to issue, and any concentration of decision making would be in the hands of duly chosen public officials. If there were a mass democracy, the community would be ruled by the people, with a majority influential in almost all cases.[20]

Community Power Studies

Social scientists studying community power have generally ignored formal positions in government and used one of two approaches: the *reputational approach,* in which informants are asked who the leaders are; and the *participational* or *decision-making approach,* in which an attempt is made to find out who actually decides important issues.

Floyd Hunter studied "Regional City" (Atlanta, Georgia) using the reputational approach. He identified forty top leaders, interviewed them, and observed them in action. All of them, he concluded, were economically powerful and known to one another. Few wished to be singled out as leaders. They relied instead on government officials to carry out their wishes. "They [were] able to enforce their decisions by persuasion, intimidation, coercion, and, if necessary, force."[21] The mayor, the county treasurer, and the heads of various government departments consulted the economic leaders before making major decisions. Some made frequent trips to Washington and foreign countries and were part of a broader network of power and influence.[22]

The reputational approach apparently leads to a conclusion favoring the theory of a power elite. But the decisional approach leads to the conclusion that power (at least at the local level) is pluralistic. Robert Dahl studied New Haven, Connecticut, and concluded that middle-class leaders take over decision-making roles, that different people are influential in different areas, and that the top leaders are not a united and hidden elite but "a coalition of public officials and private individuals who reflect the interests and concerns of different segments of the community. [And] it would be unwise to underestimate the extent to which voters may exert *indirect* influence on the decisions of leaders by means of elections. . . . If the leaders lead, they are also led."[23]

But power involves much more than political decision-making. It involves social control through the mass media, through manipulation of credit, hiring and firing, and social approval or ostracism.[24] Robert Presthus found that the eighty leaders (0.005 percent of the population) in two communities were divided into two different decision-

---

[20]Aaron B. Wildavsky, "Leadership in a Small Town," in Willis D. Hawley and Frederick M. Wirt, eds., *The Search for Community Power* (Englewood Cliffs, N.J.: Prentice-Hall, 1968), pp. 115–124.

[21]*Community Power Structure: A Study of Decision Makers* (Chapel Hill: University of North Carolina Press, 1953), p. 24.

[22]Of these 40 top influentials, 11 direct or administer large commercial enterprises, 7 direct and supervise banking and investment operations, and 5 have major industrial responsibilities. The other leaders include 5 lawyers, 1 dentist, 2 labor leaders, and 5 social or civic leaders who have no business offices. Only 4 are in government positions. Coleman and Neugarten found the leaders of Kansas City more heterogeneous and more visible. Delbert Miller found businessmen dominate "Pacific City," but in a comparable English city the "key influentials" came from a broad representation of various sectors of community life. He suggested businessmen have less prestige in English than in American culture. ("Industry and Community Power Structure: A Comparative Study of an American and an English City," *American Journal of Sociology* [1958]).

[23] *Who Governs?* (New Haven: Yale University Press, 1961).

[24]Thomas J. Anton, "Power, Pluralism, and Local Politics," *Administrative Science Quarterly* 7 (March 1963): 448–457.

making systems, political and economic. The economic leaders, not being subject to the electoral process, enjoyed greater continuity in the power structure, and their bases of power were "more extensive, constant, and durable."[25] Some decisions were arrived at through cooperation and competition between the two elites. A third elite, "the specialists," participated in some decisions, but were rarely nominated as "influentials" when the reputational method was used. They were highly educated, had professional statuses, and played active, highly visible roles in community affairs, and thought in terms of community welfare. Presthus also found that community power seemed to be declining. Where resources were of local origin (schools, hospitals, and new industry), local power still operated. But, in other spheres, more and more decisions are made at higher levels of government and industry.

Power at the National Level

Empirical studies of power at the national level have been few, but theory, speculation, and debate have been lively, centering around the opposing views of a power elite and pluralism. Our formal power system, as outlined in the Constitution and as supposedly practiced through the two-party system is pluralistic. Pluralists hold that power is widely diffused among "veto groups" that balance one another. Some think that this discourages effective decision making and leadership,[26] others that this ensures a democratic consensus.

The leading advocate of the "power elite" school of thought was sociologist C. Wright Mills. He argued that American society is dominated by a power elite that is quite different from other ruling classes in history because our society is very different. Its members have not seized power by design. They occupy the positions of power in large-scale formal organizations that have grown ever stronger. They make or influence decisions about "the size and shape of the national economy, the level of employment, the purchasing power of the consumer, the prices that are advertised, the investments that are channeled."[27] There is an "interlocking directorate" of top-ranking military, political, governmental, and business leaders. Like the changing inner circles of Soviet Russia, the American power elite exerts influence undreamed of by the Caesars because economic corporations are so huge, the nation-state controls such giant armies and lethal weaponry, and the masses are so powerless.

Mills believed that the interest group and political party conflicts emphasized by pluralists do not occur at the top level of power, but at the middle levels. Here professional politicians, members of Congress, pressure groups, and "the new and old upper classes of town and city and region" bargain over lesser decisions. The power elite dominates the careers of middle-class members of large formal organizations. These white-collar people, though ever more numerous and indispensable, are neither politically aware nor politically organized. At the bottom of the power structure is a "masslike society," fragmented and impotent.[28]

Floyd Hunter tested Mills' much-debated thesis by empirical methods. He concluded that Mills was essentially correct. Using a reputational method similar to that he employed in Atlanta, he developed a list of 100 leaders who are reputedly highly influ-

[25] *Men at the Top: A Study in Community Power* (New York: Oxford University Press, 1964).

[26] See James MacGregor Burns, *The Deadlock of Democracy* (Englewood Cliffs, N.J.: Prentice-Hall, 1963).

[27] *The Power Elite* (New York: Oxford University Press, 1956), p. 125.

[28] *White Collar* (New York: Oxford University Press, 1951).

Enormous wealth is concentrated in the hands of a very small number of people. Here the "home" of the late J. Paul Getty is literally a tourist attraction. *Wide World Photos.*

ential in national affairs. He then documented the network of relationships among them and found that politicians, the very rich, and the top military brass do tend to know one another personally and to have close social, political, and business connections.[29]

G. William Domhoff agrees that there is a power elite. He also believes that there is a governing class based on wealth. They partly overlap. Some members of the governing class occupy positions of power, but many members of the power elite do not belong to this class. Neither group is all-powerful. There are opposing interest groups and classes—workers, farmers, small businessmen, and consumers. And there are restraints on power in cultural values manifested in the Constitution and laws, as well as in our mores. "Most of all, there is the

right to vote, which means that the leaders are accountable to all the people."[30]

Prestige and Social Interaction

Though wealth, prestige, and power tend to go together and reinforce one another, they do not always coincide. The town's richest person is not necessarily the most respected.

Empirical studies of prestige have relied largely on the evaluations of chosen "prestige

[29] *Top Leadership, U.S.A.* (Chapel Hill: University of North Carolina Press, 1959).

[30] *Who Rules America?* (Englewood Cliffs, N.J.: Prentice-Hall, 1967), p. 151.

189

judges" and on observation of social interaction. Numerous studies have been made in fairly small towns for decades. More recently, studies of subjective evaluations of status have also been made in large cities and the nation as a whole. This approach to stratification harmonizes with American beliefs and values, for it is based on the idea that classes are what people say they are. We tend to reject ideas of economic class and power as either Marxist or medieval.

Community Studies

Among the most notable studies of prestige in local communities are those conducted by William Lloyd Warner and his associates in "Yankee City" (Newburyport, Massachusetts, a town of 17,000) in the 1930s, and by A. B. Hollingshead in "Elmtown," a Midwestern city of 10,000 in the 1940s.[31] In long interviews, informants were asked how many classes they perceived, what characterized each class, and what standards they used to measure status. Researchers observed who associated with whom and then compared the styles of life of the different status groups. Informants agreed closely on ratings of individuals and families, and on the criteria for these ratings. Both Warner and Hollingshead concluded that even those who denied the reality of classes acted as if they existed. Hollingshead outlined five classes and Warner, six: in the New England town a self-conscious old aristocracy still existed and formed an "upper-upper class."[32]

---

[31] W. Lloyd Warner and Paul S. Lunt, *The Social Life of a Modern Community* (New Haven: Yale University Press, 1941), and A. B. Hollingshead, *Elmtown's Youth* (New York: John Wiley and Sons, 1949).

[32] Warner's class structure: Upper-upper class, 1.4%; lower-upper class, 1.6%; upper-middle class, 10%; lower-middle class, 28%; upper-lower class, 33%; lower-lower class, 25%. Hollingshead: Class I, only a few families; Class II (corresponding to Warner's upper-middle class) 6 to 8%; Class III, 35 to 40%; VI, 40%; and V, 12 to 15%.

The use of subjective evaluations by prestige judges is limited to fairly small communities. There most people have personal knowledge of others, of the class meaning of street names and neighborhoods, and of the class significance of cliques, clubs, and associations.[33] The test of social status in communities like Elmtown and Yankee City is "What is the highest status group in which I am accepted as a social equal, an intimate friend?" Other studies have demonstrated that even in larger communities, intimate interaction—eating together, visiting, intermarriage—is closely bounded by the lines of local prestige classes. The smallest class unit is the friendship group or clique. Most people are far more interested in local prestige than in broader systems. They can perceive their own prestige in the judgments of others, and they feel more comfortable when they stick with their own kind.[34]

Prestige in Large Cities

Richard P. Coleman and Bernice L. Neugarten believed that prestige could be judged in large urban communities by using both the evaluated participation techniques of Warner and Hollingshead and more objective socioeconomic indices. They first interviewed a sample of 200 residents of Kansas City for the relative rankings of residential address, occupational titles, club membership, and so on, regarding this approach as the urban equivalent of asking small-town people to rate one another directly.[35] They found high agreement on ranking of neighborhoods, and even streets and blocks. Churches, clubs, schools, houses, clothing,

---

[33] Leonard Reissman, *Class in American Society* (New York: The Free Press, 1959), p. 388.

[34] For a summary of findings and citations of various studies, see Williams, *American Society*, pp. 140–142.

[35] *Social Status in the City* (San Francisco: Jossey-Bass, 1971), p. 8.

the stores one patronized, and the car one drove also served as clues to social status. After interviewing 462 people aged 40 to 69, they composed an Index of Urban Status that combined occupation, income, housing, neighborhood, club memberships, community participation, ethnic identity, educational background (including that of a man's wife), and church affiliation. They concluded that face-to-face contacts are not necessary to judge social prestige. "In a metropolis, social class is evaluated in terms of the observable social characteristics of hypothetical equals, rather than by reference to specific individuals. As a consequence, status in a city can be assessed in almost the same way that residents themselves assess it."[36]

Prestige at the National Level

Coleman and Neugarten then compared Kansas City with seven other communities studied by anthropologists and sociologists and concluded that "people of similar characteristics are perceived, both by their fellow citizens and by the social scientist, as equal to each other in status from community to community. Thus we can speak meaningfully of a nationwide status system."[37] Average Americans, however, do not think in terms of a status system. They recognize people as equal or superior or inferior, whether they are specific people in their own community or people in abstract categories identified by various clues and criteria.

Some generalizations about prestige at the national level are fairly well-established. The most important distinction is still, as it was in the Lynds' "Middletown" in the 1920s and 1930s, between those who work with their hands and those who do not. Another touchstone is the attitude toward a college education. Talcott Parsons distinguishes the upper-middle from the lower-middle class by this criterion: if a family takes it for granted that its children will go to college, it is upper-middle class. Finally, the occupation of the head of the family serves as the best single indicator of class status. It is the one most often used to delineate a national class system. In industrial societies, a person's occupation is his or her major role, governing the rewards received and the power held. Americans are especially likely to consider work their most important activity. The first question after an introduction is likely to be, "What do you do?" or "What business are you in?" It has been demonstrated repeatedly that occupation correlates very highly with income and education, which in turn are correlated with a style of life. Thus occupation is a valuable clue to social class status.

The National Opinion Research Center conducted two studies, in 1947 and 1963, to measure the comparative prestige of ninety occupations. The highest were Supreme Court Justice, physician, nuclear physicist, scientist, and college professor. Farther down and rating about the same were novelist, electrician, and farm owner and operator. Policeman, carpenter, plumber, and barber were about equal; coal miner and shoe shiner were at the bottom. The findings were substantially the same in both years, and studies in twenty-three other countries, including several underdeveloped ones, had very similar results.[38]

Ranking occupations by income produces somewhat different results than ranking

---

[36] *Ibid.*, p. 83. The authors saw Kansas City as divided into thirteen levels, with two levels in the upper class, three each in the upper-middle class, the lower-middle class, and the working class, and two in the lower class.

[37] *Ibid.*, p. 26.

[38] Hodge, Siegel, and Rossi, "Occupational Prestige in the United States: 1925–1963," and Robert W. Hodge, Donald J. Treiman, and Peter H. Rossi, "A Comparative Study of Occupational Prestige," in Bendix and Lipset, *Class, Status, and Power*, pp. 309–321.

them according to prestige. For example, an electrician may make more money than an accountant, but the accountant would be accorded greater prestige. But this is only an apparent inconsistency. Analyzing occupations solely in terms of money income neglects such aspects of the job as job security, opportunities for advancement, and other intangible advantages that make the accountant better off in the long run.[39]

The American Class Structure

As noted in our discussion of "Prestige at the National Level," comparative studies indicate that the class systems of American communities are basically similar. Warner suggests that "a good test of this statement is that people who move from one region to another recognize their own and other levels in the new community and know how to adjust themselves."[40] But the national class system is not a conglomeration of local systems, which vary somewhat and are based on fairly precise personal knowledge. It has a much larger range of inequality than most local systems, more anonymity, and, in the middle class, a greater tendency toward equality.

Robin Williams finds evidence that a nationwide class system exists in several facts. By objective indices, differences in income, wealth, and power endure. There is a high level of agreement about the prestige of different occupations. Members of the upper class all over the country know one another and interact intimately. And there is a web of communication and mobility that links

together people of similar class position in different parts of the country.[41]

Using the criteria of occupation, income, and education, Coleman and Neugarten made a rough estimate of the national class structure. They see an upper class of about 1 percent; an upper-middle class of 10 percent; a lower-middle class of 32 percent; a working class of 39 percent; and a lower class of 18 percent.[42]

The Upper Class

The upper class is a clearly identifiable group, a truly national class that freely mixes and intermarries within its rather definite boundaries which are "guarded by social secretaries, private schools, social clubs, and similar exclusive institutions."[43] Its core is the "business aristocracy" of corporate fortunes, most of which originated after the Civil War. It is unlike the upper class of any other country. "Only the American upper class is made up exclusively of the descendants of successful businessmen or corporation lawyers—whatever their pretensions, few families are 'old' enough or rich enough to forget this overriding fact."[44] The older families are largely Protestant, generally Episcopalian or Presbyterian.[45]

Attendance at exclusive private schools and elite universities, membership in exclu-

---

[39] Frank Parkin, *Class Inequality and Political Order: Social Stratification in Capitalist and Communist Societies* (New York: Praeger, 1975).

[40] *American Life*, p. 53.

[41] *American Society*, p. 104.

[42] *Social Status in the City*, p. 273. By similar criteria, one student concluded that the Soviet class structure has an upper stratum of 3.8%; upper-middle 6.6%; lower-middle, 15.7%; upper-lower, 27.5%; and lower-lower, 46.4%. Boris Meissner, *Sowjetgesellschaft im Wandel* (Stuttgart: Kohlhammer, 1966). Although the elite have many special privileges, there is less conspicuous inequality and no affluent idleness. (Hollander, *American and Soviet Society*, p. 126.)

[43] Domhoff, *Who Rules America?*, p. 33.

[44] *Ibid.*, p. 12.

[45] E. Digby Baltzell, *The Protestant Establishment* (New York: Random House, 1964), and *An American Business Aristocracy* (New York: The Free Press, 1958).

sive clubs, and listing in the various urban Social Registers are reliable indices of upperclass status. Its members are active in business, law, and finance. A number are also physicians, professors, and architects. Most of them, says Domhoff, do not fit the stereotype of the jet set or cafe society or the "functionless genteel." They are hardworking and competent, by no means a "leisure class." Many own farms or ranches. Their distinctive—and expensive—sports include horseback riding, fox hunting, polo, yachting, and sailing.

The national upper class, then, is more than a category. It is an interacting group whose members either know one another or know of one another. It is according to Domhoff, a governing class—an "establishment." But it is not entirely unified. The "staunchly Protestant, Anglo-Saxon industrialists and bankers" clearly dominate the Republican party. Old-time aristocrats, the "ethnic rich," and smaller big businessmen dominate the Democratic party. According to Domhoff, many of the power elite come from the upper class, and others are dominated by the upper class. Thus, the upper class, though neither monolithic nor omnipotent, is a governing class.

The Middle Classes

Below the clearly defined upper class and above those engaged in manual labor is a large amorphous middle class, nearly half the population. Its core beliefs and values are those generally identified with "the American Way of Life." But within it sociologists (and ordinary citizens as well) distinguish at least two subclasses.

THE UPPER-MIDDLE CLASS Perhaps one American in ten is a member of the upper-middle class, the proportion being larger in big cities. Its core are college-educated business managers and successful profes-

sionals in large cities. In smaller communities, especially among the older generation, the independent businessperson is more typical of this class.[46]

Members of the upper-middle class look at the world in a rational, purposeful, manipulative way. They feel personally responsible for what happens to them, emphasize doing and achieving, and look to the future. They tend to practice self-control and to be impersonal in social interaction. Career advancement is a central value. They are socially and geographically mobile, always willing to move to greener pastures. They are extremely active in voluntary associations and community activities. They train their children to delay gratifications and work for future benefits. They emphasize individual competitiveness and disciplined effort. Often they try to emulate the life style of the upper class and associate with them in formal organizations. In many American cities, this class, like the upper class, has long been made up largely of white, Anglo-Saxon Protestants.

THE LOWER-MIDDLE CLASS Historically the class of clerks, salesmen, and small businessmen, the lower-middle class now has as its core the white-collar workers "who will never reach full-fledged managerial status in their respective corporate or governmental bureaucracies. It also is coming to include both the blue-collar technician and the well-educated, well-housed gray-collar service worker."[47] A generation ago a high school education distinguished the lower-middle class from the working class, but this index is no longer reliable. Its members value respectability, thrift, hard work, and honesty. They are also strongly family-oriented. Hollingshead found that in Elmtown

---

[46] Coleman and Neugarten, *Social Status in the City*, p. 262.
[47] *Ibid.*, pp. 262–263.

members of this class were more active, although less influential, in political and church affairs than their superiors, and that they supported lodges and women's auxiliaries.

The Working Class

Some sociologists believe the lower-middle class and the upper-lower class manual workers have the same values, life styles,

When the upper class shops, cost is of relatively little concern. The process of selecting a dress is quite different for this woman compared to the middle class women buying clothes off a rack. *Harvey Barad/Monkmeyer Press Photo Service.*

Middle and working class consumers are much more concerned about the cost and usefulness of a product than they are in the style in which they purchase it. *Sybil Shelton/Monkmeyer Press Photo Service.*

and income. Numbering half the population, they make up the "white majority," or the "average" people. Others believe that even when manual workers own things long considered symbolic of middle-class status, they remain working-class in values, attitudes, and actions.

Roughly two Americans out of five are "working class." They work in skilled or semiskilled manual jobs and form the stable element of the blue-collar labor force. They believe such work is *real* work, and that white-collar jobs and supervisory jobs are not. They prefer working with things to working with people. Although many have a hard time making ends meet, they "get by."

Many are of recent foreign background. Louise Kapp Howe reminds us that the "average man" in the United States is not the blond, blue-eyed Robert Redford–type but what sociologists call a "white ethnic" of "any one of the still amazing number of national origins represented in this country."[48] Many belong to Catholic or salvationist-cult churches as well as to an array of Protestant denominations.

Possessions, especially houses, are working-class symbols of success. Bennett M. Berger, in a study of a new working-class suburb, found its residents exhilarated at being "homeowners in a bright new world of lawns, patios, electrical appliances, and pastel bathroom fixtures."[49] But despite our myth of suburbia, they are not middle class. Both before and after moving to the suburbs about half identified themselves as working class, and those who think of themselves as middle class do so because Americans often

use this term for a decent, comfortable standard of living that includes home ownership. Nor is their style of life middle class. It does not automatically change with a move to suburbia.

Working-class patterns of social participation are different from middle-class patterns. Berger found that 70 percent do not belong to any voluntary organization, and only 8 percent belong to more than one. Few have really close friends. Some did not know the occupations of those they called closest friends. Almost half the sample spends more than 16 hours a week watching TV. Their social interaction centers around relatives, neighbors, and the informal work group.

What are the consequences of this limited social participation? There is less of a generation gap in the working class because young people are less exposed to the currents of contemporary thought. Working-class women have a more simple view of their role as compared to the complexities and uncertanties of college-educated women. Avoidance of voluntary orgazinations, and limiting participation mostly to primary groups protect members of the working class from the impersonality and demanding role requirements of modern society but limit their ability to cope with the complex modern world.[50]

Not only life styles, but the personality traits, values, and attitudes differentiate the working class from the middle and lower classes. Mirra Komarovsky found the most surprising aspect of the blue-collar world not in the manners and morals reminiscent of the past. Rather she found that its members focus on sensory, concrete details and use a low level of abstraction. Women

[48] Louise Kapp Howe, ed., *The White Majority: Between Poverty and Affluence* (New York: Random House, Vintage Books, 1970), p. 4.

[49] *Working-Class Suburb: A Study of Auto Workers in Suburbia* (Berkeley and Los Angeles: University of California Press), p. 80.

[50] Jack L. Roach, Llewelyn Gross, and Orville Gursslin, eds., *Social Stratification in the United States* (Englewood Cliffs, N.J.: Prentice-Hall, 1969), p. 180.

were asked, for example, if their mothers could help them when they were feeling depressed. A standard answer was, "No, she doesn't have any cash to spare."[51]

Many working-class young people do not expect much out of life. They want to do well and to be well-liked. They hope to live in simple comfort, marry and raise families, and retire on small pensions plus social security. They do not think in terms of sacrificing present pleasures to work toward future careers. But they do take pride in working and supporting themselves; in home ownership and possessions; and in courage, loyalty, and endurance. Most are afraid of slipping into the lower class.

There are some signs of a growing feeling of alienation among white members of the working class. Many feel trapped and insecure, unable to control their own lives. They feel ignored or treated with disdain by those who look on them as bigoted "hardhats." They resent the feeling that they are neglected while other groups get their demands. Unemployment and inflation contribute to this feeling, and income statistics disprove the myth that they are middle class and sitting pretty. Between 1965 and 1970 the real incomes of blue-collar workers declined.[52]

The Lower Classes

So many different kinds of people make up the 16 to 20 percent in the "lower class"

that we might say there are any number of lower classes. Unskilled workers (including domestic and migrant workers) who are often unemployed, who work part time, are paid little and often have to resort to public assistance; mothers on Aid to Families of Dependent Children; the disreputable poor such as petty thieves and skid row bums; the most disadvantaged members of minority groups; the unfortunates who are poor because of age, sickness, or accident—are they a "class" or a heterogeneous mass, outcasts who are not part of the American class hierarchy at all?

Regardless of our answer, most of us would call lower class those people who live in urban and rural slums; have little money, prestige, or power; and are discriminated against. Most live all their lives at or below subsistence level.

They live with danger as well as poverty. People around them are out to hurt or exploit them in many ways. They learn that in their neighborhoods "they can expect only poor and inferior service and protection from such institutions as the police, the courts, the schools, the sanitation department, the landlords, and the merchants."[53] Under these circumstances there seems no point in adopting the goals of the good life and career success that guide most Americans. They seek strategies for sheer survival. One is an expressive life style, whether through benign forms such as fun, singing, dancing, and lively slang, or more destructive forms such as drug addiction, drunkenness, and dropping out. When expressive strategies fail, some of the more desperate turn to violence. Older people are more likely to adopt depressive strategies for coping with

---

[51] Komarovsky, "Blue-Collar Marriages and Families."

[52] The average industrial worker with a wife and two children got $96.78 a week in 1965, $116.58 in 1970. But with inflation his real annual income declined by $209.56. The Labor Department reported that the financial needs of a family with growing children rose by 61% in the 1960s, while the average earnings of skilled workers increased only 41%, as compared with 64% for blacks as a group and 61% for executives. (*Christian Science Monitor* [Feb. 6, 1971].)

[53] Lee Rainwater, "A World of Trouble: The Pruitt-Igoe Housing Progect," in Victor B. Ficker and Herbert S. Graves, *Deprivation in America* (Beverly Hills: Glencoe Press, 1971), pp. 102–111.

life, retreating into isolation and constricting their goals to surviving as a simple organism rather than as a human being.[54]

Lee Rainwater, who has studied the lower class extensively, does not believe they reject middle-class values. Lower-class people simply know that, given their conditions and opportunities, they cannot gain a sense of self-esteem in terms of middle-class values. They have an even lower level of social participation and fewer informal contacts than members of the working class. Physical distance limits their choice of friends. They are not only almost completely isolated from formal community organizations but also from friendship cliques, except in their youth. They "interact minimally and lack identification even with those of their own kind."[55]

A profile of more or less typical lower-class people (outside of criminals and other outcasts) might include these traits and attitudes. They live from day to day; they do not plan; they act on impulse and seek immediate gratification; they are not concerned with status advancement but with subsistence. They are fatalistic, seeing themselves as trapped in a cruel, unyielding system. They profoundly distrust the world and are full of fears and worries.[56] They are poor not only in goods but also in interests, ambition, self-confidence, and self-esteem. They have a low level of aspiration and a low degree of confidence in their ability to control their own life. If they belong to any religious group it is likely to be a fundamentalist sect or a magical cult.

Is there a "culture of poverty" that characterizes the lower class? This has been much debated. Oscar Lewis studied poor families in many countries and wrote richly detailed accounts of their lives and personalities based on numerous taped interviews. He believed there is a culture (or more strictly speaking, a subculture) of poverty, with similar traits in many nations. It is cross-national because it results from "common adaptations to common problems." In London, Glasgow, Paris, New York, San Juan, and Mexico City, Lewis found "remarkable similarities in family structure, interpersonal relationships, time orientations, value systems, spending patterns, and the sense of community" among the poor.[57] In all these places, the poor did not participate effectively in the major institutions of the larger society. They hated the police, distrusted the government, and were cynical about the church. They evolved informal institutions to take their place. Informal credit without interest, for example, was a substitute for banks and usurious moneylenders; herb cures and midwives for mistrusted hospitals; a saint's shrine at home for priests. Families tended to be mother-centered.

This culture of poverty, according to Lewis, is not found among peasants, primitives, or the working class. It flourishes under colonialism and in the early stages of industrial capitalism. It does not include all the poor, but only those whose poverty is persistent. In the United States it might include, Lewis thought perhaps 20 percent of the poor.[58]

---

[54] *Ibid.*

[55] Roach, Gross, and Gursslin, *Social Stratification in the United States,* p. 200.

[56] Jack L. Roach, "The Crawfords: Life at the Bottom," in *Ibid.*, pp. 213–218, for a report of taped interviews with a lower-class family.

[57] *La Vida: A Puerto Rican Family in the Culture of Poverty—San Juan and New York* (New York: Random House, 1965), pp. xlii–xlviii.

[58] For a clear critique of the concept of a culture of poverty, see Jack L. Roach and Orville R. Gursslin, "An Evaluation of the Concept 'Culture of Poverty,'" in Roach, Gross, and Gursslin, *Social Stratification in the United States,* pp. 203–13. Roach warns against concluding in effect that "the traits of the poor are the cause of the traits of the poor."

Social Mobility

Social mobility is the movement of persons or groups up or down the ranking order of a social stratification system. It is the dynamic aspect of stratification and may be seen as a source, a consequence, and an index of social change. A person who achieves complete social mobility (up or down) changes his or her degree of prestige and style of life as well as the more objectively measurable occupational and economic rankings.

Attitudes toward social mobility vary. A Corsican villager, for example, can rise to a prominent position (perhaps elsewhere). But if his grandfather was a goatherder, old-timers still regard him as a goatherder, and he cannot sit in the same cafe as the landowners.[59] As Weber noted, status groups try to limit power and privilege to themselves. In a stable society they may be quite successful. An aristocracy develops and effectively controls wealth, power, and prestige. If someone gains an entering wedge through wealth, he or she is looked down on as a social climber. In most industrial societies, however, the self-made person is a hero, and "getting ahead" is a core value.

Structural Sources of Mobility

Changes in social structure that open up opportunities for mobility may arise from violent revolution. Or they may have their source in large-scale but peaceful changes such as demographic trends, changes in technology and deliberate attempts to change the system of inequality through collective action or government policy.

For example, before 1917, Russia was an estate society. The rights and duties of the clergy, the hereditary nobility, urban merchants and workers, and peasants were all defined by law. The Bolshevik Revolution destroyed this system, and there was a great deal of sudden mobility, both upward and downward, as properties were taken over by the new government and members of the aristocracy and intelligentsia killed or exiled. The country was changed into a vast bureaucracy under central planning with a new type of hierarchy.

Modernization usually produces more openness and mobility in any system of stratification. As a country industrializes, the occupational skills it demands keep changing. In the early stages, peasants become members of an urban proletariat, working in factories, and a middle class emerges to guide and administer the process. There is considerable mobility. Ambitious sons of low status families, not tied to traditional notions of prestige, may take over important positions, while the old middle or upper class may cling to traditional ways and lose status.[60] Education and training become the keys to advancement. In fifteen Latin American countries, Germani found that the relative size of the middle class was closely related to the degree of industrialization, urbanization, and literacy.[61]

This process continues in developed countries. In the United States, for example, the shift from lower-class and working class occupations to middle-class occupations in the past century was especially marked from 1950 to 1970. The rise in the percentage of professional and technical jobs in those

---

[59] John L. Hess, "Lo, the Poor Corsican Landowner," *The New York Times* (Aug. 23, 1969).

[60] Neil J. Smelser and Seymour Martin Lipset, eds., *Social Structure and Mobility in Economic Development* (Chicago: Aldine, 1966), p. 48.

[61] Glaucio Ary Dillon Soares, "Economic Development and Class Structure," in Hodge, Siegel, and Rossi, *Class, Status, and Power*, p. 196.

Table 9-3 Changes in the Distribution of the U.S. Labor Force

	Percentage of the Working Force			
	1870	*1910*	*1950*	*1970*
Professionals	3.0%	4.4%	8.5%	14.8%
Propietors, managers, and officials:				
Farmers	24.0	16.5	7.3	1.9
Others	6.0	6.5	8.6	8.3
Clerks, salespeople, etc.	4.0	10.2	18.9	25.1
Skilled workers and foremen	9.0	11.7	13.8	13.9
Semiskilled workers	10.0	14.7	21.7	28.8
Unskilled workers:				
Farm workers	29.0	14.5	4.3	1.2
Others	9.0	14.7	8.3	4.5
Domestic servants	6.0	6.8	6.3	1.5

Source: adapted from Judah Matras, *Social Inequality, Stratification, and Mobility* (Englewood Cliffs, N.J.: Prentice Hall, 1975), Table 4.1, p. 98.

two decades and the drop in the number of farmers and farm workers are particularly striking. (See Table 9-3.)

Urbanization also contributes to the degree of mobility. Freed from local knowledge of family background, the new urban dweller finds it easier to achieve more prestige. In the anonymity of the city, old ascriptions tend to lose their power. According to Peter Blau and Otis Dudley Duncan,[62] a person's chances of success are most heavily influenced by the sort of place in which he or she was raised, and the more urbanized it was the better. Urban migrants, whether they go to other cities or smaller towns, and city dwellers, whether migrant or native, do better than rural migrants and nonmigrants.

Blau and Duncan also found that family stability can affect occupational success. In broken families the children and their father often do not do as well as their peers from more stable families. Family size and children's position among their siblings, exert

an even more important affect on their chances for success. In general, according to Blau and Duncan, the more siblings, the less chance one has for occupational success, probably because parents of smaller families are able to provide better educations for their children. Superior educational opportunities may also explain why oldest and youngest children do better than middle children. Older children in general are more handicapped by larger family size than younger children are.

But the success picture for people in these circumstances is not as bleak as it appears to be. According to Blau and Duncan, "men who successfully have overcome obstacles to their advancement are more likely to progress to still higher levels of attainment than those who never had to confront such problems."[63]

Differential reproduction has also opened up opportunities. In general, the higher one goes in the social scale, the smaller the

[62] *The American Occupational Structure* (New York: Wiley, 1967).

[63] *Ibid.*, p. 411.

number of children per family. Even if every rich man's son stepped into his father's shoes, there was room at the top as population grew and the society became industrialized. These new statuses had to be filled from below.

Groups may organize and struggle for a collective gain in status, as workers do through labor unions. Reformers may gain enough political power to initiate policies that improve conditions and opportunities. Schooling and the vote have been extended to more and more citizens of modern societies. Governments improve the condition of the lowest classes through legislation providing social security, tax reforms, family allowances, medical care, unemployment insurance. Such measures reduce both inequality and resentment of inequality. Some sociologists are studying not only the facts of mobility, but alternative policies for promoting it. These sociologists feel that stratification keeps many people with badly needed talents from achieving the positions they merit, and that political institutions should be used to create greater equality of opportunity and greater motivation for achievement.[64]

Collective Mobility

Changes in the wealth, power, and prestige of entire strata or of substantial groups within them may occur through such structural changes as revolution, modernization, and reform, as well as through the "class struggle" of unionization. Or a whole group may decide to change its way of life and thus rise in status according to cultural values. Some disadvantaged Indian subcastes take on the customs, rituals, and symbols of higher castes, becoming "Sanskritized." They stop eating pork or beef and change to fish or mutton, which are considered less degrading, and substitute fruit and flowers for blood offerings to their gods. Thus the Brahmin way of life spreads through the society.[65]

Individual Mobility

When opportunities for individuals to rise in social class status open up in the society, who takes advantage of them? Who has the ability and the motivation? How do they go about the climb? How do we measure the amount of mobility?

Individual mobility may be seen as *inter*generational or *intra*generational. The first measures a son's advance or fall relative to his father's class. The second considers only his own lifetime. He may climb or skid dramatically, going from "rags to riches" or vice versa. The more normal pattern is a slight shift or a steady climb up a career hierarchy.

Numerous empirical studies of intergenerational mobility based on occupation have established a number of generalizations. There is considerable mobility in the United States, and more of it is upward than downward. Between one-half and three-quarters of the men in professional, business, clerical, or skilled jobs have climbed relative to their fathers.[66] There is also considerable mobility in other industralized urbanized nations. In France, Germany, Switzerland, Sweden, and Japan, as in the United States, roughly a third of the sons of men in the industrial

[64] John Porter, *The Vertical Mosaic: An Analysis of Social Class and Power in Canada* (Toronto: University of Toronto Press, 1965). See also S. M. Miller and Pamela Roby, "Strategies for Social Mobility: A Policy Framework," *The American Sociologist 6,* Supplementary Issue on Sociological Research and Public Policy (June 1971): 18–22.

[65] M. N. Srinivas, "A Note on Sanskritization and Westernization," in Hodge, Siegel, and Rossi, *Class, Status, and Power,* pp. 552–560.

[66] Joseph A. Kahl, *The American Class Structure* (New York: Holt, Rinehart and Winston, 1965), p. 272.

labor force achieve nonmanual positions.[67] Most upward mobility, however, occurs within the middle range of the stratification system. At the extremes of upper and lower class, it is much more likely that the son will stay at the same level as his father. Most mobility is limited in extent—for example, from the working class to the lower-middle class. An unskilled worker's son rarely becomes a professional man. In an industrial society, advances in occupational status typically occur step by step through the clearly defined bureaucratic hierarchies of large formal organizations. Most upwardly mobile women, being largely dependent on their husbands for their social status, try to "marry well" and may choose careers as nurses or white-collar workers with one eye on opportunities for meeting desirable men. Studies reveal that daughters of manual workers who marry upward have already achieved education or white-collar jobs on their own.

[67] Bendix and Lipset, *Class, Status, and Power*, p. 17.

While changes in occupations are the primary measure of mobility, people also measure their success by such things as home ownership. Upwardly mobile people tend to adopt the life style of the class to which they aspire. *Fredrick D. Bodin/Stock, Boston.*

The best predictor of mobility or lack of it is one's initial class status, for this affects not only opportunities but motivations. Only as children do we have trouble choosing between becoming an astronaut or the president. By adolescence, most of us have adjusted our sights more realistically. But in a society committed to equality of opportunity, the most serious defect of the system of social stratification is that lower-class and working-class youth lack motivation and awareness of opportunities that may actually be open to people with ability. Their aspirations are low. They seek jobs not for the satisfactions of the work itself but for quick material rewards and measure their success by job security, home ownership, and money. The middle classes, in contrast, take material rewards more or less for granted and seek education, friends, and prestige.[68] This low level of aspiration, learned in the family and peer group, may help explain the fact that even where educational opportunities have been greatly expanded, the lower classes fail to take advantage of them, as shown in studies in Great Britain and the United States.[69]

While the lower classes aspire not at all or only a step higher, the middle classes live in a milieu of continuous striving. Their goals beckon them ever onward, but seldom is there any assurance that they have arrived. And if they do not arrive, achieve, accomplish, the burden of failure is their own, for they believe that they live in a land of opportunity.[70]

How do the upwardly mobile individuals go about climbing? First of all, they seek education and a prestigious occupation with a high income. But the economic dimension alone does not give prestige. They must win it through changing their life style. This is easier to achieve in our swiftly changing society than in older, more stable societies. Physical mobility may facilitate social mobility, especially in the anonymity of large cities. "City air makes one free," goes an old saying. In smaller places, on the other hand, newcomers undergo a thorough grilling designed to place them socially. Strivers often move to better neighborhoods as they achieve economic success, cultivate a new group of friends, join new clubs, and perhaps switch religious and political affiliations as well. They may even change their names to play down ethnic backgrounds. A spouse may be an asset or a liability, depending on how well he or she manages their style of life. Coleman and Neugarten, for example, found "education of wife" highly correlated with social status and upward mobility. Corporation executives often judge the acceptability of a prospective junior executive's spouse before promotions.

An aspirant to upper-class status, perhaps newly rich, first joins charitable and cultural organizations. Then he perhaps hires a social secretary who is usually a member of the upper class. He knows he has made it when he is nominated for membership in an exclusive club and his wife makes the Junior League. Their parents may have sent them to private schools and elite universities. In any case they consolidate their status by sending their own children to such schools. Newcomers to higher classes abandon their old values and attitudes as well as their old styles of life. In fact, strivers use the class to which they aspire as a reference group, adopting their values and attitudes and insofar as possible emulating their life styles even before they have quite been accepted.[71]

The social escalator moves down as well

[68] Ephraim Mizruchi, *Success and Opportunity: A Study of Anomie* (New York: The Free Press, 1964), pp. 61–90.

[69] Miller and Roby, "Strategies for Social Mobility."

[70] *Ibid.*

[71] Domhoff, *Who Rules America?*, pp. 22, 140.

as up. Low intelligence and motivation, addiction to alcohol and other drugs, and ill health, especially on the part of workers such as carpenters, electricians, and painters who work by the job or the hour, largely account for downward mobility. Structural factors such as unemployment and occupational obsolescence also contribute.

Summary

Social stratification is an institutionalized system of social inequality in a community or society that ranks individuals and groups in categories or strata according to their share of scarce and desirable resources such as wealth, prestige, and power. It arises from the psychological processes of differentiation and evaluation from force and conquest, and from a society's evolution toward greater complexity. A social stratum is a category of people with similar amounts of wealth, prestige, and power, and similar life chances and ways of life. They tend to recognize one another as equals and those in other categories as superior or inferior.

In caste systems, strata are hereditary, endogamous, and permanent. They are sanctioned by religion and mores, and upheld by economic interdependence. Estate systems depend on hereditary relationships to land defined by law. Ascription of status is nearly as permanent as in caste systems. Open-class systems stress individual achievement. They have considerable mobility and blurring of stratum boundaries and are justified by belief in equality of opportunity. Modernization generally breaks up estate and caste systems and moves a society toward an open-class system.

One's life chances—opportunities for long life, health, education, safety, self-determination, and dignity—are directly correlated with social status. Different subcultural patterns—consumption styles, patterns of social participation, values, and attitudes—characterize different classes. Religious and political affiliations, recreational patterns, and family relationships also vary according to class status.

Economic inequality, and especially poverty and the concentration of wealth, has received considerable attention in recent years. It appears that economic distribution in the United States has stayed about the same since the end of World War II.

According to many scholars, power over social and economic arrangements and political decisions tends to be concentrated at the upper levels, especially in national economic and political affairs, and to be more pluralistic at state and local levels. But the majority of people have little power and take little interest in decision making or policy.

Studies of prestige find that people do think in terms of social classes and use them as a map of social reality. In small communities status judgments are personal and subjective, but in large cities very similar rankings are arrived at through more impersonal clues. On the national level, occupation is the best index of prestige.

In the class structure of the United States, boundaries are clearest for the 1 percent in the upper class and the 16 to 20 percent in the lower class. The upper class is mainly a business aristocracy, freely intermarrying and interacting across the nation. A power elite includes many of the upper class and others who have high positions in institutions controlled by the upper class.

About 10 percent of Americans are upper-middle class. Their central value is career advancement. The lower-middle class of about 32 percent is concerned with hard work, respectability, thrift, honor, and decency. Middle-class values are the core American values.

The working class includes the 40 percent of Americans who work at skilled or semi-skilled manual jobs. They participate less than the higher classes in voluntary organizations and formal and informal groups, limiting their social interaction largely to peer groups and kin. They tend to think in terms of concrete and practical details, to limit their aspirations, and to feel increasing resentment and alienation because they believe they are losing ground in comparison to other groups.

The lower class, the remaining 17 percent, includes many different kinds of people who have not made it into the industrial working class or have skidded down for various reasons. They tend to distrust the world and to be full of fears and worries. They do not plan ahead but live from day to day. Some exhibit the traits of a culture of poverty transmitted from generation to generation, manifesting itself in many countries through similar responses to similar conditions.

Social mobility is movement up and down the system of social stratification. It may arise through structural changes brought about by industrialization with its demand for an educated, skilled labor force. It may be fostered by struggles for collective gains through such organizations as labor unions, and by political reforms or revolution. People also rise or fall in the scale according to their level of aspiration and opportunities for education, both of which depend largely on initial class status. Most industrial societies have about the same amount of intergenerational mobility. Upward individual mobility is complete when one has acquired the education, occupational prestige, and income of a higher class, as well as its values and life style.

Glossary

Absolute poverty Extreme inadequacy of food, clothing and shelter.

Caste system A system of stratification into hereditary, endogamous, and permanent strata called castes.

Estate system A system of stratification in which strata are defined by law and are relatively rigid and permanent, with some mobility.

Open-class system A system of stratification in which, although

one's initial status is that of one's parents, there is opportunity to rise or fall according to merit.

Power Control over the decisions that affect the way people live, and over the allocation of scarce and desirable resources.

Relative poverty Comparative inadequacy of resources when measured against the advantages of others.

Social mobility The movement of persons up or down the ranking order of a system of social stratification.

Social stratification An institutionalized system of social inequality that ranks individuals and groups according to their share of scarce and desirable resources such as wealth, prestige, and power.

Social stratum A category of people with similar amounts of wealth, prestige, and power, and similar life chances and ways of life.

chapter

10

Minorities and Intergroup Relations

In most modern societies, people are far more conscious of racial, religious, nationality, and cultural differences than of class differences. They are aware that they belong to such groups and are hostile to members of other groups. This *ethnocentrism* sets "us" off from "them." Religious differences divide the Hindus and Moslems of northern India, who are alike racially and culturally. Canadians are divided according to Anglo-Saxon or French backgrounds. Language divides the Flemings and Walloons of Belgium. Race is the major line of cleavage in Rhodesia and South Africa as well as in the United States.

Some of these differences are the heritage of colonialism, some of immigration and of slavery. Many others arise as the establishment of new nation-states brings different tribes, language groups, religions, and races under one flag and as modernization brings them into contact.

Such differences do not always lead to tension and conflict. Switzerland, with its three national divisions, and Hawaii, with its many "races," demonstrate that people of diverse backgrounds can live together peacefully. Despite some intergroup conflict in the United States, many Americans are increasingly aware that group differences enrich our own culture in many ways.

In many societies, however, racial, national, and religious differences are expressed in prejudice and hatred; in discrimination and oppression; in riots and civil war. The problem of intergroup conflict, furthermore, is international in scope. Many of the two-thirds of the world's people who are not white define the present situation as a huge conflict with the whites, who for centuries have ruled their countries and treated them as "natives."

In this chapter, we first look at the core of the problem: prejudice and discrimination. We discuss how prejudice starts, how it spawns discrimination, and how both may be institutionalized by society. Next, we examine several general patterns of intergroup relations that are typical of modern societies. Then we sketch the structure of intergroup relations in the United States. In the remainder of the chapter, we look at possible goals in interracial relations and discuss various ways of achieving those goals.

You should remember as you read this chapter that, in spite of the title, we are not talking only about minority group problems. There are two sides to the coin. What this chapter is really about is majority-minority group relations. We do focus on the minority half of the equation, but most of this book has been devoted to describing the majority. Most people, sociologists included, tend to concentrate on the minority group when seeking solutions to problems and conflicts. As we shall see, this may not be the most effective way to improve intergroup relations.

Discrimination and Prejudice

A **minority** is a category of people who are subordinate in power to the majority (even though, like the Bantu of South Africa, they may far outnumber them). This subordination rests on three conditions. Minority groups can be distinguished on the basis of physical or cultural characteristics. They are collectively regarded and treated as different

Reprinted by permission of Cartoon Features Syndicate.

and inferior on the basis of those characteristics. And they are excluded from full participation in the society and therefore have poorer life chances, fewer rights, and fewer privileges than the majority.

Prejudice

When we speak of intergroup relations, we usually use the term **prejudiced** to mean a *negative* prejudgment of some group on the basis of its race, religion, or national background. **Intergroup prejudice** may be defined as an attitude of hostility or rejection based on faulty and inflexible generalizations about a group or category of people. These generalized beliefs are called **stereotypes.** We presume that all members of a category share the group's objectionable qualities. This kind of prejudice produces fear, suspicion, revulsion, and hate.

When we believe that all members of a category are "like that," we carry a picture in our heads, a stereotype, whether or not we know any members of the category. "Do not obtain your slaves from Britain," Cicero warned Atticus in the first century B.C., "because they are so stupid and so utterly incapable of being taught that they are not fit to form a part of the household of Athens." The ideas that all redheads are trigger-tempered, all fat men jolly, and all professors absent-minded are stereotypes. So is the upper-middle-class liberal's idea that all white members of the working class are racist bigots. Like other generalizations, stereotypes simplify our thought processes. In intergroup relations, they also serve to justify and explain our behavior (favorable or otherwise) toward a group.

Discrimination

While prejudice refers to how we think of the members of certain groups or categories, **discrimination** refers to overt behavior, to the way we actually act toward them. It usually implies *unfavorable* conduct based on prejudice against some ascribed status group: women, youth, blacks, Moslems, untouchables.

Discrimination may involve political and legal barriers. It always involves social and economic barriers. Among forms of discrimination *officially* practiced in various societies, the United Nations lists inequalities in legal rights, political participation, and personal security; housing, recreation, and health services; freedom of movement, residence, thought, religion, communication, and peaceful association; and, finally, choice of employment, enjoyment of the right to marry and found a family, and opportunity for education and cultural participation. In addition, the U.N. points to official approval of such indignities as forced labor, special taxes, sumptuary laws (forbidding the wearing of certain clothing, for example), public libel, and the forced wearing of distinguishing marks.

Even when officially outlawed, discrimination often continues unofficially. A white personnel manager may tell a black applicant that he would not want him to be embarrassed by prejudiced employees. Or he may say that the requirements of the job have changed since the ad was placed—and yet the ad continues to run unchanged. A realtor may be reluctant to sell houses in white neighborhoods to blacks.

Segregation—isolation of one group from another—sets up barriers to interaction. If extreme, this form of discrimination makes other forms unnecessary, so to speak, for there are no opportunities for unwanted contacts. Such segregation characterizes colonialism. Parks and residential areas in Canton, China, for example, once bore signs, "Dogs and Chinese not allowed." Even when less extreme, segregation in housing, schools, churches, and clubs isolates groups and thus increases chances for the formation of unfavorable stereotypes.

Like this Berlin couple, all Jews in Nazi Germany in the 1930s were required to wear identifying badges. *Wide World Photos.*

The Relationship between Prejudice and Discrimination

There may be prejudice without discrimination, and there may be discrimination without personal prejudice. For example, real or imagined pressures from other people can influence a person's behavior. A family may wish to sell their house to blacks but may hesitate because their neighbors would be angry with them. Thus they may discriminate although they have little or no prejudice. On the other hand, prejudiced people may decide they cannot afford to discriminate. One woman admitted that she did not like the idea of black neighbors, but said that her husband's work required that he get along with blacks. Moving away could stigmatize him as prejudiced. She later became good friends with her black neighbors, and her prejudice declined.

The looseness of the relation between prejudice and discrimination is illustrated by a classic experiment by a white American social psychologist, Richard LaPiere. In the 1930s he traveled widely in the United States with a Chinese couple, stopping at 66 sleeping places and 184 eating places. They were refused service only once. Yet when these same places were asked by letter if they would take members of the Chinese race as customers, more than 9 out of 10 said they would not. A control group of places LaPiere and his friends had not visited gave similar replies.[1]

Other experiments have also shown that verbal expressions of discrimination may not result in actual discrimination. Most prejudiced people, when challenged with a face-to-face situation, prefer not to create a scene, especially where they do not have the support of a powerful group.

Racism and Discrimination

The words "racist" and "racism" have been rather commonly and loosely used in recent years, especially to account for the problems of American blacks. "White racism" is said to permeate all institutions and to be at the root of discrimination, conflict, and violent protest. The Kerner Report (the report of the President's National Advisory Commission on Civil Disorders, appointed after the destructive riots of the summer of 1967) used the term in this way. But there is danger of its becoming a catch-all term and being regarded as the one cause of all the problems in the complex race-relations scene. It therefore bears analysis.

Michael Banton defines **racism** as "the doctrine that a man's behavior is determined

by stable inherited characteristics deriving from separate racial stocks having distinctive attributes and usually considered to stand to one another in relations of superiority and inferiority."[2] The doctrine originated as a serious scientific theory in the 1800s, even though on present evidence it seems naïve. It was seized upon as a convenient and conscience-easing justification for colonial exploitation and discrimination as well as slavery. It assured the dominant nations that people of dark skin were naturally inferior to white people, who were destined to rule and lead by inborn right of superior endowments. It convinced them that biological crossing leads to degeneration and that it is therefore safest to forbid social contact between the races.

There *are* obvious physical differences among the earth's people—in the chemical composition that colors their skins, in hair texture and curl, in stature, in the shape of the eyelid fold, and so on. But there are no "pure" races. There are only arbitrary categories or pigeonholes people have constructed. There is, furthermore, no proven relationship between race and innate intelligence, as diligently as some people have sought such proof. Cultural achievements are not related to inborn differences. When the now-dominant Europeans were living in a comparatively primitive fashion, Africans were using iron, and Chinese civilization astounded Marco Polo and other adventurers. Changes over time provide further proof. The warlike Vikings and the pacifist Swedes come from the same gene pool, perhaps slightly altered over the centuries by intermarriage. People are, then, all one species with a few minor biological differences that have no correlation with intelligence or culture.

Why, then, do we treat these minor dif-

[1] "Attitudes versus Action," *Social Forces* 13 (1934): 230–237.

[2] *Race and Racialism* (London: Tavistock, 1970), p. 18.

ferences in a sociology text? Because people *think* they are important and use them as cues to guide their interaction. The American definition of "Negro" is a prime example of the fact that racist fallacies can be sociologically important. Over the centuries, black women were subject to the sexual whims of men of the dominant caste. As a result, many people now classed as black have more "white blood" than black. Yet if they have one known black ancestor, they are said to be black. "In no other area of biology would we reason similarly. Imagine a dog breeder saying, 'Most of this pup's forebears were cocker spaniels, but he's really a Doberman Pinscher'—meaning that one of his great-grandparents was."[3]

Biological nonsense this may be, but as W. I. Thomas, a pioneer American sociologist, said, "If men define situations as real, they are real in their consequences." The social definition of a black, in the United States, for example, puts all people with "Negro blood" in a category that is marked off different and—in the minds of white racists—inferior, and hence to be discriminated against. For the purposes of social interaction and social relationships, people are white or black *if others in the society think they are.*

Sources of Prejudice and Discrimination

Where does prejudice come from? Why does it persist? Why is discrimination practiced and perpetuated?

STATUS DIFFERENCES Prejudice and discrimination do help to preserve the wealth, prestige, and power of a dominant group. Economic gains are obvious enough in the case of colonial exploitation and slave labor, and

[3] Raymond W. Mack, *Race, Class, and Power*, 2nd ed. (New York: American Book, 1968), p. 104.

the high rents and low wages of a caste system. The dominant group also escapes such drudgery as cotton picking and housework. The men of a dominant majority often enjoy sexual gains as well. They have access to low-status women, but shield women of their own class. Finally all members of the dominant caste experience a prestige gain. The poorest white coal miner may feel superior to the best-educated black.

Prejudice may persist because certain people or groups want it to persist. The British in India, for example, encouraged Hindu-Moslem hatreds, following the principle of "divide and rule." They established separate waiting rooms and drinking fountains for each group in public places.

Thus, prejudice can serve the interests of the dominant group in a society, and in the short term, it may appear to be to their benefit to encourage it. But we have still not answered our first question: Where does prejudice come from? Several different sources have been suggested.

ETHNOCENTRISM In our discussion of culture, we pointed out that ethnocentrism—judging different cultures on the basis of one's own and generally finding them inferior—was in large part responsible for mistrust and hostility between nations. Ethnocentrism can exist within nations as well as between them. Ethnic jokes, insulting nicknames, and prejudice express ethnocentric attitudes. Ethnocentrism, whether intra- or international, arises out of a natural human tendency to differentiate, generalize, and categorize our environment. Judging another group to be different is simply easier/for most people than trying to find similarities. But there is that second component of ethnocentrism: labeling the out-group as inferior simply because it is different. This second component is the essence of prejudice.

Menial laborers in majority-dominated societies come largely from minority groups.
Nicholas Sapieha/Stock, Boston.

SOCIALIZATION Prejudice must be learned. We must be taught to label people or groups as inferior. Thus, prejudice cannot be considered innate or natural. A prejudice is learned in an informal way, along with other items of culture, as part of the process of socialization.

The power of culture to shape prejudices and stereotypes was vividly demonstrated in the 1920s by the "social distance" tests devised by Emory Bogardus. Respondents were asked to indicate which of seven degrees of social intimacy they would accept for various groups. Would they admit them "to close kinship by marriage"; "to my club as personal chums"; "to my street as neighbors"; "to employment in my occupation"; "to citizenship in my country"; "as visitors only to my country"; and finally, would they "exclude them from my country"?

All groups across the United States, regardless of such variables as region, income, occupation, and education, indicated about the same pattern of preference. True, each minority rated itself high on the list, but it rated all *other* groups just about the same way that white Gentiles rated them. That is, native white Americans of Anglo-Saxon ancestry, Englishmen, and Canadians were considered most acceptable, followed by French, Germans, Norwegians, Swedes, and other North Europeans; then Spaniards, Italians, South and East Europeans, and Jews; and finally, Negroes, Japanese, Chinese, Hindus, and Turks. Negroes rated Jews just about the same as did white Gentiles. Thus, even for minorities, the standards of the dominant majority served as a frame of reference.[4]

INTERGROUP CONFLICT AND COMPETITION
Prejudice and discrimination are also rooted in intergroup conflict.[5] As we have seen, people may be predisposed to judge other

[4] E. S. Bogardus, *Immigration and Race Attitudes* (Boston: D. C. Heath, 1928), pp. 13–29. Later studies by Bogardus and others have had substantially the same results.

[5] William Newman, *American Pluralism: A Study of Minority Groups and Social Theory* (New York: Harper & Row, 1973), p. 224.

people and groups. But if there is no conflict, there is likely to be less judgment of inferiority. Group size and proximity help determine whether a minority group will arouse fear of competition within the majority group. If the minority is small or, even if large, has a territory of its own distant from that of the majority, prejudice is less likely to occur.

A sense of threat is often associated with intensified prejudice. A group may come to feel entitled to its advantages and fearful when another group competes for them. Panamanians, for example, have long felt a racist prejudice against West Indian black immigrants and their descendants—although Panama itself has a large percentage of native-born, Spanish-speaking blacks—largely because the West Indians speak English and thus have had an economic advantage with the Canal Zone Americans.

Institutional Discrimination

The focus of investigations into majority-minority group relations has changed several times during the past twenty-odd years. Before 1960, prejudice was considered to be the cause of the problem, and thus most of the research dealt with how *attitudes* are formed and changed. During the active phase of the civil rights movement, in the early 1960s, the problem was analyzed in terms of discrimination, and social scientists and lawmakers concentrated on changing people's *behavior*. Investigators concluded that the attitudinal and behavioral dimensions of prejudice and discrimination were personal and were therefore controlled by psychological factors. The person may be really prejudiced, or may prefer not to make waves and therefore bows to the prejudices of neighbors and colleagues.

The failure of civil rights legislation to dramatically improve the lives of minority

group members has led to another change of focus. Recently sociologists have turned to institutional discrimination as the key issue in majority-minority group relations. The term **institutional discrimination** is used to describe inequities that emerge from the total social system. Such policies and practices theoretically affect all citizens and are thus not obviously discriminatory. But even if all personal prejudice disappeared, these policies, woven into the fabric of the social structure, would remain, and thus discrimination would still exist.

Note that, unlike personal prejudice and discrimination, institutional discrimination is impersonal. For example, the killing of three civil rights workers in Mississippi by members of the Ku Klux Klan is an illustration of discriminatory behavior based on personal prejudice. An example of institutional discrimination is Mississippi's failure to prosecute the killers.[6] Another, more typical example is the use of IQ tests and other procedures to screen job applicants. Blacks and several other minority groups typically score lower on such standardized tests because they are based on a knowledge of white, middle-class culture. Perhaps employers using such tests, unlike the government of Mississippi, do not mean to be discriminatory. After all, they give the same tests to everyone. But it is the result that matters, not the intention. Many of our social structures result in discrimination.

From childhood on, we are taught to take pride in the American system of justice, representative democracy, public education, and our economic system. This pride may make it hard for many of us to realize how these institutions themselves contribute to discrimination.

Even the Kerner Report, while admitting

[6]Louis L. Knowles and Kenneth Prewitt, *Institutional Racism in America* (Englewood Cliffs, N.J.: Prentice-Hall, 1969).

that "white institutions created [the ghetto], white institutions maintain it, and white society condones it,"[7] still phrases its recommendations in terms of black problems. For instance, the report states that the improvement of communications between the ghetto and city hall would help relieve the tension in the black community. But if politics were not a discriminatory institution, blacks would not need better communication. They would have equal and effective *representation.*

Even if we can see the faults in our social system, analyzing and correcting institutional discrimination is difficult. Institutional discrimination is impersonal, and thus it is hard to spot. It is subtle and may be well masked. It is often impossible to isolate the persons or regulations responsible for it. In spite of the difficulty of the task, our racial problems cannot be solved without a long, hard look at our institutions.

Patterns of Intergroup Relations

Thus far in this chapter, we have concentrated on the negative aspects of majority-minority group relations. It is true that most

[7] *Report of the National Advisory Commission on Civil Disorders* (New York: Bantam, 1968).

patterns of intergroup relationships are destructive to the minority group. But other more positive patterns are theoretically possible. According to Norman Yetman and C. Hoy Steele, there are five possible patterns: separation, pluralism, melting pot, transmuting pot, and genocide or exclusion. (See Figure 10-1).[8] In modern societies, various mixtures of these patterns exist both as ideal goals and as actualities.

The Melting Pot

Around the turn of the century, the "American dream" was that a new man would be forged in the crucible of a new nation through cultural assimilation, intimate interaction, and biological amalgamation. In 1908 Israel Zangwill wrote a drama, *The Melting Pot,* in which he portrayed the various poor and oppressed peoples of Europe come to the "fires of God" to be made into "the American." All distinctions were to be erased, and a homogeneous type would emerge through "Americanization." This myth was echoed recently in the Kerner

[8] *Majority and Minority* (Boston: Allyn & Bacon, 1975).

Figure 10-1 Patterns of intergroup relations.

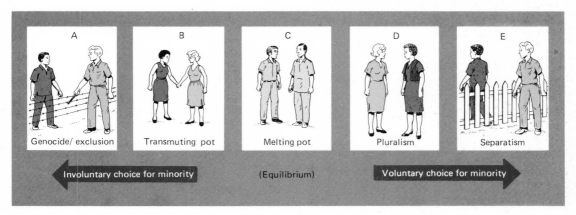

A Genocide/ exclusion
B Transmuting pot
C Melting pot
D Pluralism
E Separatism

Involuntary choice for minority   (Equilibrium)   Voluntary choice for minority

Report, which stated as the American goal "the creation of a true union—a single society and a single American identity." To some extent Mexico has been a melting pot in which Spanish and Indian people and cultures have produced a new blend called "mestizo." The melting pot, then, is the center on the scale of possible social patterns. It would be the situation of perfect equilibrium. There would be no majority and no minority, only one people. It remains only an ideal form, because few of the world's people favor the complete assimilation of a "melting pot."

Majority-Dominance Situations

Various patterns involving a dominant majority and a subordinate minority (or minorities), which were typical of colonialism, prevail today, regardless of lip service to other ideals. According to Yetman and Steele, the dominant majority may adopt any of the four following policies.

GENOCIDE/EXCLUSION At the extreme negative end of the scale, the dominant majority may try to annihilate the minority, to drive them out, or to isolate them in reservations or camps. Thus the Nazis put the Jews in concentration camps and attempted to answer the "Jewish question" by genocide. Similarly, in nineteenth-century America, "good Indians" were either on reservations or dead.

TRANSMUTING POT Yetman and Steele use this term to describe a situation in which, in order to get along in the society, the minority group must surrender most of its unique culture and adopt that of the majority. Other names for this pattern are *assimilation* and *integration*. This situation is distinct from the melting pot. In a melting pot, the various minorities intermarry until the population is homogeneous. With the exception

of intermarriage, however, the transmuting pot is much like the melting pot. In both types, the minority group members must sacrifice their cultural identity to get along with the majority and to gain access to full participation in the society.

PLURALISM Pluralism, the third pattern of intergroup relations, arises from the interaction within a society of a number of ethnic groups. *All* social groups that are based on the categories of race, religion, or nationality, says Milton Gordon, may be called **ethnic groups,** because the members of such groups share "a sense of peoplehood." (*Ethnos,* from which both *ethnic* and *ethnocentrism* are derived, is the Greek word for "people.") This *sense of group identity and belonging* is one of the three major characteristics of the ethnic group. Second, an ethnic group is a *subsociety* within the larger society. Within it members find most or all of their primary relationships and perhaps many of their secondary relationships as well. Third, an ethnic group has a distinctive *subculture.*[9]

Except where a whole minority group forms a distinct lower caste, the vertical walls of subsocieties are also crisscrossed by the horizontal class lines of the larger society. Members of the same class share a similar style of life. But members of the same ethnic group also share a sense of belonging. People interact most intensely, relax, and participate most easily with those who are in *both* the same class and the same ethnic group. In this sense, even the dominant majority form an ethnic group, in spite of their lack of a feeling of separateness from the larger society.

Ethnic groups of this kind may arise within the caste division of a majority-mi-

[9] Milton Gordon, *Assimilation in American Life: The Role of Race, Religion, and National Origins* (New York: Oxford University Press, 1964), pp. 29, 58–59. The term "ethnic" is more commonly used to refer to nationality background.

In majority-dominance situations, minority groups often surrender much (but not all) of their unique culture. *Henry Monroe/Design Photographers International, Inc.*

nority situation. More commonly we think of them as making up a **pluralist** society, in which various ethnic groups are considered as different but equal, or as different and ranked in a loose hierarchy in which ethnic background serves as one determinant of social class. In either case, under a pluralist system, the majority allows ethnic groups to maintain their own identities as long as they are loyal to the larger society. They can retain much of their traditional culture and communal life as long as they participate as citizens in the political and economic systems of the society. Note, however, that maintaining their culture does often imply certain limitations on the minority group's full participation in the society.

The history of most ethnic groups in America underscores the basically pluralistic nature of our society. New immigrants sought out earlier arrivals from their own lands. Banding together for protection and comfort in an indifferent and even hostile environment, they established "Little Polands," "Little Italies," and so on, thus creating a condition of cultural pluralism. During the time of heaviest immigration, from the late nineteenth century to before World War II, the dominant majority was strongly asserting the need for assimilation. In spite of this, the immigrants clung to their ethnic groupings.

After World War II, undoubtedly stunned by Hitler's extreme version of majority dominance, American public opinion became somewhat more tolerant of cultural pluralism. As opportunities opened up after the war, many second-generation Americans felt more comfortable. They began coming out of their ethnic closets and assimilating as much as they could of the dominant culture. Recently, however, a significant number of people have begun to reassert their ethnic identities. Israel Rubin suggests that this may represent a longing for a sense of community that has been weakened by increasing urbanization and social mobility.[10] Thus, rather than turning a society into a clump of hyphenated factions, a true ethnic community may be a source of social cohesion.

SEPARATISM At the other end of the scale from involuntary exclusion is separatism. If the majority will permit, minority groups

[10] Ethnicity and Cultural Pluralism," *Phylon,* 36:2 (June 1975), pp. 140–148.

Many ethnic groups have asserted pride in their identity in recent years. *Owen Franken/Stock, Boston.*

may voluntarily separate themselves wholly or in part from the dominant society. Again, this involves major limitations on the minority's ability to share equally in the resources of the society. The classic example of separatism in America is the Amish. Other groups who voluntarily segregate themselves, at least as far as their primary relationships are concerned, are Orthodox Jews and many middle-class blacks. In the early part of this century, a separatist movement started by Marcus Garvey, promising blacks a home in Africa, received widespread support. The enterprise failed, however, apparently because Garvey's subordinates were dishonest.[11]

A Blend of Integration and Pluralism

While complete unity is impossible in a multigroup society, we have seen that pluralism *is* possible. It has allowed our religious and nationality subsocieties to remain distinct while sharing a strong undergirding of cultural unity on core values, a sense of belonging, and a sense of loyalty to the larger society. But interracial relations have been characterized neither by unity nor by pluralism. Rather, there is what J. Milton Yinger calls "subcultural anomie," with a threatened drift to full anomie. That is, there is so great a lack of agreement in the mutual expectations for interaction that it threatens social cohesion. Whites and nonwhites disagree on or simply fail to communicate the nature of their goals. To the extent that they do agree in a general way on goals, they disagree on means for reaching them.

On the one hand, many nonwhites see the various ethnic divisions as having been designed not to keep members in but to keep them out. And whites in turn are bewildered and sometimes frightened by the more extremist, militant, and separatist fac-

[11] Franklin, *From Slavery to Freedom,* pp. 489–492.

tions of minority protest. Do they want to secede from American society? Do they want to destroy it? Is pluralism compatible with racial desegregation and integration? Would not one or more of the groups always be singled out as a minority and discriminated against?

Yinger looks to Hawaii for clues. Our fiftieth state, he says, has preserved distinctive groups with visibly different subcultures, among which there is some hostility but relatively little stereotyping and discrimination. On the basis of the Hawaiian situation Yinger has developed four principles to help us distinguish between "arbitrary and discriminatory segregation" and "legitimate pluralism."[12]

First, segregation is undesirable when it is related in hidden ways to other lines of separation. For example, the principle that a man has a right to pick his friends may justify exclusion of some people from a men's club. That he has a right to pick his neighbors may be used to justify neighborhood segregation. But if the men's club also has lines into political and economic power and not merely friendship, it is discriminatory. And if the neighborhood separates the excluded children from opportunities for schooling and other kinds of cultural participation, this, too, is discriminatory.

Another principle is that "when separation is systematic or total it is undesirable segregation." Thus a city may have a few snobbish, exclusive, and lily-white neighborhoods (as does Honolulu). But if it does not also have massive ghettos and provides its minorities with many "escape hatches" from the slums, it is perhaps providing freedom both to be snobbish and to buy wherever one can afford to buy. Third, when segregation is exclusive rather than inclusive—de-

signed to keep certain groups *out* rather than certain groups *in*—it is unjust. Finally, the criteria of membership should have some cultural or functional significance. Jewish neighbors will not feel offended at not being invited to join the Methodist Mission Circle, nor sociologists to the Engineering Society. But if black Methodists are barred from the church or Chinese-American engineers from the society, that is discrimination rather than legitimate separation based on functional or cultural criteria.

To Yinger's four principles, Gordon would add a fifth—that a proper blend of integration and pluralism means that any person may freely choose to stay within his ethnic subsociety or may with equal freedom cross its lines and make friends with, and even marry, members of other subsocieties. In Hawaii, most lines of separation are legitimate by these five tests; on the mainland they fail.

Racial Divisions in the United States

Historically, Americans have used national background, religious affiliation, and racial heritage as bases for differential treatment. The antagonisms and conflicts between people of different nationalities and religions have given way to a pattern of accommodation, assimilation, and even varying degrees of integration within a context of pluralism. The same cannot be said for several other minority groups, who are characterized by racial rather than ethnic or religious differences. Let us look at some of the smaller racial minorities before we consider black Americans.

Indians and Eskimos

Only Indians and Eskimos are truly native Americans. When Columbus discovered the

---

[12]*A Minority Group in American Society* (New York: McGraw-Hill, 1965). See also Yinger, *Toward a Field Theory of Behavior* (New York: McGraw-Hill, 1965), pp. 188–197.

Navajo women are given driver training on an Arizona reservation. American Indians have been largely dependent on government paternalism. *Paul Conklin/Monkmeyer Press Photo Service.*

New World, there were probably between 1 and 3 million Indians in what is now the United States. Dispossession and genocide by the invading whites reduced them to about 340,000 by 1860 and an all-time low of 220,000 in 1910. The 1970 census, however, records 792,730 Indians, an increase of more than 100 percent in 20 years.

The first of 284 reservations was established in 1853. In 1871 Indians were made wards of the federal government and assured of the protection of the president. Under a system of treaties with various tribes, they were to retain land and water rights and have the protection and help of their own bureaucracy, the Bureau of Indian Affairs (BIA). Thus they became the only territorially distinct minority, formally dependent on government paternalism. In 1924 Indians were granted citizenship. In the 1930s they were allowed to set up economic corporations and self-governing agencies. By the 1950s they were allowed and even encouraged to leave reservations for industrial cities, thus forfeiting their rights to tribal lands. Their lands had been dwindling as treaty after treaty was broken and the reservations could no longer support growing numbers of Indians. In 1887 Indians held 138 million acres; now they hold about 55 million.

When the "Americanization" movement was strongest in the late nineteenth century, the BIA often took children from their families and placed them in boarding homes, forcing them to abandon Indian ways. This kind of treatment, plus the dubious paternalism of an unwieldy and generally slow-moving bureaucracy, has resulted in much personal and social disorganization, both on and off the reservations. Division into some 300 tribes has impeded awareness of common problems. The average income of families on reservations is $1,500, less than half the minimum that marks the poverty line. The birth rate is about 2.2 times that of whites. The average age at death is 64.0 years as compared to 70.5 for all races in the United States.[13] Indians average 5.5 years of schooling. Unemployment is about 20 percent on the more affluent reservations, 80 percent on the poorest. Rates of alcoholism and suicide (even among teenagers) are high. But the dramatic increase in Indian population since 1950 reflects improved health: tuberculosis has declined, and infant mortality dropped from 63 per 1,000 live

[13]Average age at death for all races in the United States is 70.5. Data from "Facts on Indian Affairs," mimeographed bulletin from U.S. Department of the Interior; Bureau of Indian Affairs, July 1971.

births to 31 (as compared to 22 for whites) in 1968.

Another reason for the increase in numbers of Indians is increased pride in their identity. In former censuses, 26 percent Indian blood was the criterion. In 1970, self-identification was relied on. Many Indians are seeking a way to retain this identity and at the same time improve their life chances. Closing down reservations does not appear to be the answer. The incidence of suicide, crime, alcoholism, and registration for welfare is high among the 200,000 who have moved to cities. "Integrity, Not Integration" is a popular slogan. Among values the Indians stress are pride and dignity (which have impeded protest), their tradition of communal ownership, and closeness to nature. Their leaders seek more control over their own affairs—lands, schools, resources, businesses—and more efficient assistance from the BIA.[14]

Eskimo life chances are also meager. Native Alaskans have a life expectancy of only about 35 years, and a per capita income less than one-fourth that of white Alaskans. Unlike the American Indians, they were never conquered by Russia or the United States and never signed away their rights to land. Therefore they stand to gain economically from the use of Alaskan territory by oil and mineral interests.

Asian Minority Groups

Asians on the United States mainland numbered about 600,000 in 1960. Of these, 207,000 were Japanese-Americans, 200,000 Chinese-Americans, and 107,000 of Filipino ancestry. The differing stories of the Chinese and Japanese illustrate the play of such

factors as the class of people that migrated, when they came, and under what circumstances.

Chinese contract laborers began to come to the West Coast in large numbers in the 1850s. Mostly poor villagers, they were highly visible because of their appearance, dress, language and writing, and their willingness to do domestic labor. Most came as "sojourners," planning to stay only a while and to go back after earning some money. In the lawless setting of the frontier, especially in hard times, they were often subject to violence, to which they usually reacted with passivity and withdrawal. Immigration was highest in the 1870s. But in 1882 an exclusion act was passed, under which Asians were declared "unassimilable." Because of this exclusion (which ended in 1943), and because so many came as sojourners, Chinese-Americans now number only half the total of 400,000 that came. Although the China-towns of the large cities are in some respects slums, many Chinese-Americans protest the mysterious and exotic aura with which white stereotypes surround them. Many members of the group have achieved middle- and upper-middle-class status, and many of these are Christian. Prejudice has declined, and acculturation is so nearly complete that young people complain of identity problems.

Although the Japanese also suffered from the exclusion act and were singled out for unreasonable treatment in World War II, they have, on the whole, become a "model minority." They are often compared with the Jews because of their occupational and educational achievement; low rates of crime, delinquency, and mental illness; stable family life; community cohesion; and acculturation to American middle-class values. They began to emigrate later than the Chinese, when Japan was already modernizing. Though highly respectful of authority, they were less passive, and they accommodated to technological and economic demands more easily.

---

[14]Based in part on Charles F. Marden and Gladys Meyer, *Minorities in American Society*, 3rd ed. (New York: American Book, 1968), Chap. 16, "Indians in the United States," pp. 356–377.

At first laborers and domestics, the Japanese found more opportunity and less discrimination in farming. Having learned intensive agriculture in Japan, they were very successful with fruit and vegetable farms.

But suddenly in 1942 all West Coast Japanese were herded into ten hastily built concentration or "relocation" camps. Their property was sold at about 10 cents on the dollar. This rash and ill-considered action followed our declaration of war against Japan and was intended to prevent sabotage. Although the government has never officially renounced this policy or made restitution, Japanese-Americans have adjusted successfully since then. Prejudice and discrimination have declined greatly. The third generation has largely discarded the old language and become quite thoroughly acculturated. Many have achieved success in such prestigious occupations as architecture, the arts, and medicine.[15]

Mexican-Americans

In the 1970 census, 9.2 million Americans, almost 5 percent, identified themselves as of Spanish-speaking origin. (Other estimates are as high as 12 million.) Eight out of ten were born in the United States or Puerto Rico, and half still speak Spanish at home.

The 5 million Mexican-Americans (or Chicanos) are different from other minorities in many ways. We discuss them here as a racial minority, primarily because much prejudice and discrimination against them

Following Japan's attack on Pearl Harbor in 1941, Japanese-Americans were hastily taken from their homes and placed in concentration camps. *Wide World Photos.*

[15] Harry H. L. Kitano, *Japanese Americans: The Evolution of a Subculture* (Englewood Cliffs, N. J.: Prentice-Hall, 1969).

is racist in nature, even though it is directed largely at their cultural differences. Mexican-Americans themselves "have no very clear consensus on whether they are a racial group, a cultural group, or even if they are white or nonwhite," yet most of them have a strong feeling of ethnic identity.[16] Most do not like to refer to themselves as members of a minority group.

Mexicans settled in New Mexico a generation before the Pilgrims landed. Their descendants were incorporated into the United States through conquest and annexation. Thus they are one of the oldest minorities. But only recently have they come in huge numbers, and in a stream that still continues. Eight out of ten live in the five Southwestern states of California, Arizona, New Mexico, Colorado, and Texas, but many are migrating to Northern cities. Most came, legally or illegally, as agricultural laborers. They were ambivalent about the new land and were ready to return across the border after earning some money. Their culture was extremely different from that of the almost entirely Protestant whites of the area. They were stereotyped as innately lazy, cowardly, and cruel, and at the same time (especially from contacts with "Spanish" white Mexicans of the upper class) as warm, charming people who know how to enjoy life.

Being territorially concentrated in a region with a long Spanish tradition and constantly reinforced by new immigration, Mexican-Americans have retained many aspects of their cultural tradition. They celebrate "La Raza" (their ethnic identity), the Spanish language, and the Catholic religion as embellished by Mexican customs. Their world view is one of acceptance and appreciation of things as they are. The core values of La Raza are honor, dignity, manliness (*machismo*), courtesy, and fulfillment of obligations to family and friends.[17]

This very cultural cohesion, and especially the emphasis on language, places Chicanos at a disadvantage in schooling and employment. One in four has less than 5 years of schooling, the definition of functional illiteracy. One in five speaks no English. Those in the Southwest have a median of 6.2 grades of schooling as compared to 8.7 for blacks and 10.7 for whites in the area, and their dropout rate is twice the national average. In Houston, only 2 percent of those entering first grade complete high school.

The language barrier is thus the Chicano's major problem in achieving full participation in society. Joan Moore and Alfredo Cuellar suggest that many Chicanos do not value the learning of English very highly because they do not intend to take up permanent residence in this country. The lack of commitment to America is also shown by the low number of Mexicans who seek to become naturalized citizens.[18]

Families of Spanish-speaking origin had a median family income of $7,330 in 1970 as compared with $6,280 for blacks and $10,240 for whites. Their families are larger. The median age of their population is under 20 as compared to 28.6 for Anglos (as they call whites). Over a third of the poor in the Southwest are Mexican-Americans. As you can see by Table 10-1, Mexican-Americans are somewhat worse off than other Spanish-speaking Americans.

Where they are concentrated—as in Texas, where 2 million Mexican-Americans live—they are increasingly conscious of "brown power" and are politically organized

---

[16] *Mexican Americans*, 2nd ed. (Englewood Cliffs, N.J.: Prentice-Hall, 1976), p. 160. Only in the 1930 census were their racial backgrounds tabulated, showing less than 5% as "white" and the rest as "colored." The population of Mexico has been described as 10% white, 30% Indian, and 60% mestizo (mixed). The U.S. Census classes them as white.

[17] Marden and Meyer, *Minorities in American Society*, pp. 134–135.

[18] *Mexican-Americans*, p. 60.

Table 10-1 Comparison of Families of Mexican Origin and Other Spanish-Speaking Groups (1975)

| Characteristic | All Income Levels | | Below Poverty Line | | | |
| | Other Spanish-speaking | Mexican | Other Spanish-speaking | | Mexican | |
			Total	Percent	Total	Percent
Families	2,499,000	1,442,000	627,000	25.1	381,000	26.5
Mean Family Size	4.19	4.34	4.39	n/a	4.61	n/a
Head 65 years or more	165,000	94,000	52,000	31.8	33,000	35.5
With dependent children under 18 years	1,891,000	1,116,000	550,000	29.1	341,000	30.6
Mean number of children	2.59	2.65	2.94	n/a	3.04	n/a
Head over 25 years & non high school graduate	1,391,000	863,000	440,000	31.6	272,000	31.5
Head worked 1974	1,941,000	1,172,000	305,000	15.7	230,000	19.6
Worked all year full-time	1,327,000	784,000	119,000	9.0	92,000	11.7
Families headed by female	522,000	245,000	279,000	53.6	141,000	57.8

SOURCE: U.S. Bureau of the Census, *Current Population Reports*, Series P-60, No. 106.

in such parties as La Raza Unida. The Chicano movement, which backed the grape strike to improve conditions for migrant workers, also indicates growing cohesion and awareness among this minority.

Black Americans

Twenty-three million Americans of African ancestry, 11 percent of the population, form the largest and most visible minority group in the nation. Only 24 of the more than 130 nation-states and self-governing territories in the world have populations outnumbering Afro-Americans.

The history of the involuntary African immigrants and their descendants is not simply one of an era of slavery suddenly followed by an era of freedom. Black Ameri-

cans have experienced ups and downs that were related not only to shifting patterns of prejudice but also to economic conditions, political decisions, social movements, and broad social changes that affected the whole society. The institution of slavery, however, does make the black experience unique among the other racial groups in America.

The decades since 1940 have witnessed the transformation of black Americans from an agricultural peasantry concentrated in the South into an increasingly urban minority, half of whom live in the North. Only traces of the old paternalistic pattern of interracial relations, which is characteristic of traditional societies, remain. Accommodation has given way to the tension and conflict of the competitive pattern. Caste barriers are no longer legal, and depriving a person of civil rights is now a federal offense.

CHANGES IN ECONOMIC STATUS Many blacks have achieved middle-class status. Black families with husband and wife both present earned 57 percent of average white income in 1960, and 72 percent in 1969. Most of this gain occurred among 532,000 Northern black families with husband and wife under age 35, who now average about $9,000 annual income, 91 percent of that of their white counterparts. This is a significant gain over the 62 percent figure in 1960 for similar families. In 1970, 61 percent of blacks between 20 and 29 had completed at least a high school education as compared to 40 percent 10 years earlier. Proportionately more Northern blacks voted in the elections of 1966 and 1968 than did Southern whites. Nearly 1,500 blacks held elective public offices in 1970. Among them were Congressmen, state legislators, and mayors of cities as large as Cleveland and Gary.[19] A black man sits on the Supreme Court of the United States. The percentage of blacks who are professional and technical workers, teachers, and medical and health workers has risen steadily, and the percentage who are farm workers, domestic workers, and nonfarm laborers has declined.

How did these postwar gains come about? Not because prejudice declined and white Americans decided not to discriminate. They are due largely to impersonal social forces, some of which affected all Americans. They are also due to a shift in government policy toward active support for civil rights and to pressures from blacks themselves.

Industrialization and urbanization led to the migration of rural Southern blacks to large Northern cities. In 1940, 77 percent of the nation's blacks lived in the South; by 1970, only slightly more than half. In the first decade after 1940, 2 million blacks moved North; in the next, 1.7 million; in the 1960s, 1.4 million. Better job opportunities, especially in wartime, and better schools attracted them, while mechanization of agriculture pushed them off the land in the South. In addition, federal measures such as social security, minimum wages, unemployment insurance, and aid to dependent children gave all citizens a new measure of security.

Meanwhile, America's role, assumed during and after World War II, as the champion of freedom in the world, put a spotlight on our treatment of minorities. Gunnar Myrdal, hired to lead a group studying the race problem, set forth his analysis in 1944 in *An American Dilemma*.[20] Its central thesis was that there is a tension between our ideals and reality—between our core values of moral concern, rationalism, liberalism, equality of opportunity, and freedom, and the discrimination and inequality that exist.

GAINS IN LEGAL STATUS Taking the lead in resolving this moral dilemma, the Supreme Court in 1948 declared that restrictive covenants intended to keep neighborhoods white or Gentile or both were unconstitutional. Then, on May 17, 1954, it handed down an epoch-making decision in the case of *Brown v. Board of Education of Topeka, Kansas* (and in several other cases involving other states). Reversing an 1896 decision, the Court declared that separate school facilities were *inherently* unequal, and that to separate children "from others of similar age and qualifications solely because of their race generates a feeling of inferiority as to their status in the community that may affect their hearts and minds in a way unlikely ever to be undone." Other postwar government measures included an executive order desegregating the armed forces, laws to en-

---

[19] *The New York Times* (Feb. 12, 1971); *Current Population Reports*, Series P-20, No. 204 (1970); *Saturday Review* (April 4, 1970).

[20] *An American Dilemma: The Negro Problem and American Democracy* (New York: Harper & Row, 1944).

courage registration of black voters, and a Court decision outlawing state laws against racial intermarriage. Black ambitions were also heightened by the newly independent black African states.

THE BLACK PROTEST MOVEMENT The most striking result of these changes in economic class and legal status is an increase in black power, expressed not only in the vote but also in other forms of pressure. As blacks become a majority in the central city limits of many metropolitan areas, their votes are ever more eagerly sought. Led by such integrationists as Martin Luther King, blacks discovered the power of nonviolent demonstrations—boycotts, passive resistance, sit-ins, freedom rides. Many whites joined their attempt to enter the mainstream of American life, to achieve civil rights. Other leaders rejected the idea of integration. They formed such separatist movements as the Black Muslims, and militant ones such as the Black Panthers, spurning white help, white values, and even white society. Such a trend toward militancy and extremism occurs in every revolution.

The turning point in the black protest movement came when blacks began a series of violent and illegal protests, primarily riots and armed sit-ins. The white majority in this country reacted to what it saw as a major threat to its safety with loud cries for "law and order." The late sixties saw a decrease in white tolerance of violence, which in turn led to a decrease in black violence.

Since then, blacks have begun to explore legitimate political means of achieving their goals. Their gains have therefore been somewhat less dramatic. Lewis Killian has referred to Nixon's election in 1968 as the "end of the second Reconstruction."[21] He sees the black revolution as being in a state

of dormancy, while its leaders wait for the new bureaucracy created by civil rights legislation to have an effect, and take the pulse of the black population before deciding where to move next.

RELATIVE DEPRIVATION Revolutions do not typically occur when a group is still in the depths of oppression, but rather when an advancing group is blocked and frustrated in its desire to advance faster and farther. The group measures its advances not against its former status, but against the status of other groups. Schools, magazines, newspapers, movies—and especially TV—show how middle-class whites live. Aspirations rise, and the feeling of relative deprivation increases. Even though blacks have gained on many fronts, there is still a considerable gap between their life chances and those of white Americans. This gap is likely to remain for some time to come. Black progress has generally depended on strong economic growth. Such a strong economy characterized the period during and immediately following World War II, when many blacks achieved middle-class status for the first time.

Blacks are frequently compared to immigrant groups like the Jews and the Irish who, without governmental support and assistance, had to overcome tremendous obstacles to achieve full participation in our society.[22] This may be unfair and unrealistic. Despite similarities with European immigrant groups, the history and visibility of blacks make their subsociety very different from other ethnic subsocieties. Blacks cannot shed their blackness as Europeans could shed their accents. Even those blacks who are middle-class Americans in every sense are

---

[21] *The Impossible Revolution,* (New York: Random House, 1968), p. 160.

[22] The "immigrant analogy" was proposed by Nathan Glazer in "Blacks and Ethnic Groups: The Difference and the Political Difference It Makes," *Social Problems* 18 (Spring 1971), pp. 444–461.

Many blacks achieved middle-class status for the first time in the economic boom that followed World War II. *Suva/Design Photographers International, Inc.*

still visible. And they immigrated late. They came to the Northern cities, not when everyone else was poor, but when affluence surrounded them. They immigrated, moreover, into an economy that no longer needed untrained workers. The Kerner Report concluded that while earlier immigrant groups could find places for themselves in a growing economy, blacks do not have the same opportunities and something else must be done.[23] That "something else" includes some changes in our social structure to eliminate institutional discrimination.

EFFECTS OF DISCRIMINATION: LIFE CHANCES
Although the income gap is closing, it is still considerable. In 1965 the median income of black families was 54 percent that of whites. By 1969 it had risen to 61 percent. This discrepancy is often attributed to lack of education. But after differences in education, class, and family size are all allowed for, there still remains a gap of about $1,400 a year in the incomes of black and white men that can be accounted for only by discrimination.[24]

Unemployment and poverty are high among blacks, especially recent migrants from the rural South, teenagers, and those who stay behind on farms where machines have taken their traditional jobs. One of three blacks lives in poverty, as do half of all elderly blacks. About one-half of all poor black families are headed by females. This situation is due in part to the disintegration of many black families during the slavery era. But it is also due to welfare policies that punish families for staying together. An unemployed man may leave his wife and children so that they can qualify for welfare. "The United States is the only major industrialized nation that provides public welfare *after* the family has broken up rather than before to keep it together."[25]

All figures on health and mortality throw the gap in life chances into startling relief. There is still a gap of about 7 years in the life expectancy of blacks and whites (although this is an improvement from the 15-year gap in 1900). Black babies are about twice as likely to die in infancy as whites. The incidence of deaths from tuberculosis and syphilis is three times as high. Maternal mortality is six times greater.[26]

[23] *Report of the National Advisory Commission on Civil Disorders* (New York: Bantam, 1968), p. 282.
[24] *Toward a Social Report*, p. 26. Rapid social mobility has been found to be associated with *increased* prejudice.

[25] Robert A. Liston, *The American Poor* (New York: Dell, 1970), pp. 102–103.
[26] Alphonso Pinkney, *Black Americans* (Englewood Cliffs, N.J.: Prentice-Hall, 1969), p. 43.

227

Blacks are much more likely than whites to be victims of crime. When suspected of crime, they are more likely than whites to be arrested, more likely to be convicted, and more likely to be penalized. Rates of drug addiction are also high, but appear to be declining even though white rates are rising.[27]

Housing discrimination makes it difficult for blacks to find a decent place to live. Fair housing measures and federal mortgaging are often nullified by attitudes of brokers and officials. When blacks do move into a neighborhood, many whites leave. They believe the neighborhood will soon be all black, and, in a classic example of a self-fulfilling prophecy, they flee to the suburbs.

[27] *Ibid.*, p. 136. Pinkney warns that data on crime are inadequate and often contradictory.

While fair housing laws have brought progress, minorities still have a difficulty obtaining better housing. *Phoebe Danz/Design Photographers International, Inc.*

Slum rents are high. Urban renewal projects have been branded as "black removal," for slum clearance often makes room either for freeways or for housing that the poor cannot afford. As a result, three out of ten blacks live in substandard housing.

Residential segregation produces *de facto* school segregation, which is just as real as the *de jure* segregation outlawed by the Supreme Court—except that, as writer James Baldwin puts it, "nobody did it." Most blacks attend predominantly black schools (except in Northern high schools), and these facilities are just as unequal as black schools in the South. Busing to achieve school integration has met resistance in all parts of the country. Schools in urban slums are usually physically inadequate and also difficult to staff. Teachers prefer well-behaved middle-class youngsters, and where there is choice of assignments slum schools must often make do with "permanent substitutes." Teachers also tend to share the race prejudice of the American community in general, or, if they are black,

to have class prejudices against slum children.

SOCIAL COSTS The social costs of discrimination are conspicuous in the higher incidence of poverty, disease, and crime in minority groups and in the drain on public funds. An untrained, unemployed, or underemployed group represents an untapped and wasted natural resource, one that, unlike oil reserves, cannot be stored for later use.

But the problem of social costs goes much deeper. The final cost may be the cohesion of our society. The Kerner Report warns that unless the trend is reversed the United States will come to consist of two separate and unequal societies, a poor black one concentrated in the central cities and an affluent white one in the surrounding metropolitan areas.

By playing together, young children become immunized to some extent against prejudice. *Dan O'Neill/Editorial Photocolor Archives, Inc.*

Goals and Means in Intergroup Relations

Let us assume that a blend or balance of pluralism and integration would bring about the greatest improvement in life chances for minority Americans and serve as the best guarantee of social cohesion. How can this balance be achieved?

The formula of the vicious circle or self-fulfilling prophecy—in which prejudice justifies discrimination, discrimination results in low status, and low status reinforces prejudice—suggests three angles of attack. These are reduction of prejudice, reduction of discrimination, and improvement of status.

REDUCTION OF PREJUDICE A direct attack on prejudice requires that parents, teachers, churches, the mass media, and other agencies attempt to educate people on the facts of racial, religious, and nationality dif-
ferences, and on the causes of tension and conflict. One aspect is preventive—a sort of immunization against the poison of prejudice, which, like smallpox vaccine, is best administered early in childhood and regularly thereafter. Although prejudice is not innate, it is learned very early and very easily. Frances Ilg advocates a program that begins with children at age 3, when they should begin to play with children of other racial groups.[28]

But none of these attempts will be effective unless they are reinforced by reference groups. This means that the problem cannot wait until a new and unprejudiced generation grows up. Adult attitudes need to be

[28] Judith D. R. Porter, *Black Child, White Child: The Development of Racial Attitudes* (Cambridge. Mass.: Harvard University Press, 1971); reports that actual interaction patterns of preschool children do not reflect the prejudices they express. Playmates are chosen on the basis of sex, personality, and play style.

229

changed, mostly through *equal-status contacts in pursuit of a common goal.* These do more to teach people their essential similarity than all the scientific research and formal teaching in the world. The factory worker who stands next to a black day after day soon sees him as an individual. The college student whose class is mixed is more likely to judge members of minority groups on the basis of individual traits and abilities than one whose school excludes minorities, no matter how many books both may read on race relations. A black who saw combat in Vietnam says, "At first the white guys in our unit were ashamed that they had to associate with you, but after our first combat, we were real buddies."[29] Another said that for the first time he found out that not all white people are geniuses and not all blacks are idiots.[30]

REDUCTION OF DISCRIMINATION   The attack on prejudice is primarily educational. The attack on discrimination depends largely on the power of government. It was long believed that legislation could do nothing to solve the problem of interracial relations because it could not "change people's hearts." But this belief did not take into account the formula of the vicious circle. Let us consider the effect of the court rulings, executive orders, and laws that have outlawed discrimination.

Frequently, the results have demonstrated that where discrimination is prohibited, prejudice actually declines. Legislation helps create a changed social climate and thus helps change attitudes. When people are asked, for example, what they think of fair employment practices, of having minority group mayors, doctors, teachers, nurses, or neighbors, they often object vehemently, predicting dire results and destructive conflicts. But if the policy is put into effect firmly and without fanfare, the results are almost always contrary to these predictions. Fair employment practices legislation and nonsegregated housing projects have been highly successful where they have been tried.

The great majority of Americans, according to James Vander Zanden, fall into two categories. There are those who are not prejudiced but stand silently by or give discrimination passive support because it is expedient or profitable to do so. And there are others who are prejudiced but will not discriminate if it is made difficult to do so—who prefer to conform. Laws that punish discriminatory practices are highly effective with both kinds of people, and thus they can give people a chance to be accepted—or rejected—on their own merits.[31]

IMPROVED STATUS FOR MINORITIES   The third angle of attack on the vicious circle is aimed at improving the status of minority groups. In the framework of Weber's analysis of social stratification, this in turn involves three dimensions. *Economic position* at present causes the life chances of most minorities to lag behind those of whites. *Status* or prestige, in their own eyes and those of others, diminishes self-hatred and aggressive tendencies on both sides. The third dimension is *power* to influence others and to determine the course of their own lives. Like other approaches to the problem, these are intricately interrelated. Success in one dimension promotes and reinforces success in the other dimensions. A steady job for an unemployed father, for example, increases his self-respect, improves family stability, provides his children with a model for

---

[29] *Newsweek* (Nov. 20, 1967).
[30] Whitney M. Young, Jr., "When the Negros in Vietnam Come Home," *Harper's Magazine* (June 1967), pp. 63ff.

[31] *American Minority Relations: The Sociology of Race and Ethnic Groups,* 2nd ed. (New York: Ronald Press, 1966), p. 512.

achievement, with better food and medical care, and frees the family from dependence on public welfare funds.

The means to these ends are subjects of controversy. Quite aside from the "let-them-pull–themselves–up–by–their–bootstraps" school of thought, there are those who would prefer to attack the problem of poverty in general without any special reference to race. Others say the minority groups are like an underdeveloped nation within our borders, victims of *internal colonialism*. It lags so far behind that it needs huge injections of "foreign aid" for schools, job training, housing, health, and welfare in order to break the self-perpetuating cycle of poverty. Economic improvement helps. Reduction of prejudice and discrimination helps. But the growing strength of minority group subcultures may help even more.

Summary

Most modern societies are divided along the lines of race, religion, and nationality. In many cases, these divisions breed bitter conflict. Negative intergroup prejudices are based on faulty and inflexible generalizations or stereotypes of what all the people in an outgroup are like. Prejudice refers to a negative prejudgment of others on the basis of these stereotypes. Discrimination refers to how we actually do behave toward them, depriving them of the advantages of the dominant group according to their category and not on the basis of individual qualities. Segregation, by setting up barriers to interaction, increases the likelihood of unfavorable stereotypes. Although discrimination is usually based on or justified by prejudices and stereotypes, prejudice does not invariably lead to discrimination.

A particularly virulent form of prejudice is racism, the belief in inborn and ineradicable differences among categories of people, which places all members of one category in a position of inferiority or superiority in relation to others. Although no correlation between intelligence or cultural achievement and the inherited physical differences by which men are categorized into races has ever been proved, such differences are important because people *think* they are.

Discrimination and prejudice may persist because they bring one group gains in wealth, power, and prestige; because that group fears competition; and because cultural beliefs persist through inertia and through the operation of the vicious circle or self-fulfilling prophecy. Individuals acquire prejudice from the groups in which they are socialized and to which they aspire. Social distance tests indicate that, even for minorities, the standards of the dominant majority serve as a frame of reference.

Institutional discrimination refers to inequities that arise out of the everyday operation of a society's institutions, particularly government and the economy. Although in the past, most people analyzed minority group problems in terms of prejudice and discrimination, lately attention has focused on how our institutions can undermine efforts to secure equality for minority groups.

There are five general patterns of majority-minority group relations. In the melting pot, all differences would be discarded and blended into something new. The most prevalent pattern, however, is that of a dominant majority and a subordinate minority or minorities. At one extreme, the minority group may voluntarily choose to separate themselves from the majority altogether. At the other extreme, the majority may resort to genocide or exclusion. Or they may insist on a transmuting pot, in which the minority must give up its own culture and adopt that of the majority.

In a pluralistic pattern, ethnic groups based on ascribed differences form subsocieties with subcultures that give their members a sense of peoplehood. As long as they are loyal to the political and economic institutions of the larger society, they are allowed to maintain their own identities. Most people find their primary relationships within an ethnic group and among members of the same social class.

Racial minorities continue to suffer discrimination, with its consequences of inferior life chances and costs to society and personality. Indians form a unique minority, almost annihilated under early settlers and the U.S. Army, then placed on reservations under the paternalistic administration of a special federal bureau. For complex reasons, especially a disparity in cultural values, communal living appears to offer them more promise of improved life chances than does assimilation. Japanese- and Chinese-Americans were long subjected to discrimination and even oppression and violence, but have become so thoroughly acculturated that many Chinese fear a loss of identity and the Japanese are seen as a "model minority" comparable to Jewish Americans. Mexican-Americans are a cultural and especially a linguistic minority, subject to racist prejudice and discrimination reflected in their life chances.

But the largest minority, Americans of African descent, presents the most serious challenge to social cohesion and implementation of core values. Although remarkable gains have occurred, they have resulted mostly from general economic growth and the great migration of blacks to Northern cities since World War II. There is perhaps more consciousness of relative deprivation now than formerly.

Despite some extremist advocates of separatism and revolution, most minorities appear to want to work within the social system. They seek a blend of pluralism and integration that would improve their life chances and self-esteem, as well as their freedom to participate in many aspects of American life. No one approach appears adequate. Prejudice will not decline unless discrimination, both personal and institutional, is also attacked. And both are interrelated with improvements in material comforts, educational opportunities, and self-esteem.

Glossary

Discrimination Unfavorable behavior based on prejudice against an ascribed status group.

Ethnic groups All social grou based on the categories of rac religion, or nationality, forming subsocieties with subcultures.

Institutional discrimination Impersonal discriminatory policies and practices woven into the social structure through such institutions as the economy, government, and education.

Intergroup prejudice An attitude of hostility or rejection based on stereotypes.

Minority A category of people who are subordinate in power to the majority, though they may outnumber the latter.

Pluralism The pattern of intergroup relations in which various ethnic groups are considered as different but equal, or as different and ranked in a loose hierarchy in which ethnic background is one criterion of social class status.

Prejudice A negative prejudgment of a person or group on the basis of ascribed status.

Racism The doctrine that behavior is based on stable traits which characterize separate racial groups as superior and inferior.

Segregation Isolation of one group from another; a form of discrimination.

Stereotypes Faulty and inflexible generalizations about a group or category of people.

chapter

11

Sex Roles

The moment you were born and wrapped in a blue or pink blanket, you were started down a path marked "male" or "female." Except for the presence of male or female genitals, you did not seem very different from any other baby. Your glands, however, produced a blend of hormones more male or more female, which predisposed you toward certain traits rather than others. Even more important from the sociological point of view, society labeled you by sex. This ascribed status—like age or race—helped determine a great deal about your personality. Your awareness of being male or female is at the very core of your self-conception. It also has a lot to do with what you might expect out of life and what others would expect of you.

In most societies **sex roles**—the definitions of what it means to be male or female—are very clear. They program behavior and guide interaction all through life. However, traditional sex roles are being questioned in many societies. There have always been "feminists" even among males. The feminists of the turn of the century, smashing shop windows and mail boxes to dramatize their demand for the vote, have their somewhat less militant but equally angry counterparts in today's Women's Liberation movement. They constitute a rising, though somewhat divided, social movement and have made many people—men as well as women—aware of the restrictions that traditional stereotypes have placed on both sexes.

The very fact that the sex role is so central to one's identity makes these changes and protests disturbing to many people. Social and behavioral scientists are trying to get at the roots of sex differences, both inborn and acquired. They are also examining the nature and causes of sexism, which is seen as parallel to racism. **Sexism** refers to "the entire range of attitudes, beliefs, practices, policies, laws, and behaviors discriminating against women (or men) on the basis of their gender." [1] Because its negative consequences for women are far more apparent at first glance than those for men, it has been called another form of "internal colonialism," an even more pervasive one than racism because its victims live in the same houses and sleep in the same beds as their "oppressors."

In this chapter we shall ask first, trying to disentangle fact from myth, What are the differences between males and females? To what extent are they biological and inborn? To what extent are they culturally imposed? To the extent that ideas about sex differences are myths, why do they persist?

Then we shall consider how children learn their gender identities and acquire the appropriate sex roles, and how these are expressed in adolescence and young adulthood and reinforced by schools, peer groups, and the mass media. Next we consider the consequences of sex role stereotypes. Like racism,

[1] Constantina Safilios-Rothschild, *Love, Sex, and Sex Roles* (Englewood Cliffs, N.J.; Prentice-Hall, 1977), p. 1.

sexism has important consequences for life chances, personality, and society, and many of these are negative.

In the final section of the chapter, we look at the changing perceptions of sex roles. We ask what factors bring about these changes. What social policies might ease the problems of the transition to new roles and relationships? And we consider how both males and females might achieve greater self-actualization through wider options and richer relationships.

Sex Differences: Fact and Myth

A member of the French parliament once said in debate that there was only one small difference between the sexes. *"Vive la différence!"* a colleague shouted. Most people, however, think there are many differences and that they are inborn. On this basis, different statuses and roles have been assigned to the two sexes. Almost always an inferior one is assigned to the female. Members of both sexes have supported the social structure of superiority and inferiority, dominance and submission, with stereotyped beliefs about biological and inborn psychological differences.

Geneticists, psychologists, and social scientists have tried to unscramble fact from myth. What dominant tendencies make a newborn boy different from a newborn girl? What traits and tendencies may be due to social structure and its underlying cultural beliefs? Which traits and tendencies, either in a given society or in all societies, are a result of genetic inheritance? In what ways may socialization affect these tendencies?

Stereotypes encourage men to see women as sex objects and women to use sex manipulatively. *Jan Lukas/Editorial Photocolor Archives.*

Biological Differences

Geneticists are close to being able to consistently predict the sex of a baby before it is born. They are also working on ways to ensure the conception of either a boy or girl according to parental preference. Usually, however, the moment of birth is greeted with a ritual cry, "It's a girl!" or "It's a boy!" With very few exceptions that label "M" or "F" follows the person throughout life.

This clarity of identification is due, first of all, to the winner of the race among millions of sperm swimming madly toward a mature egg. Eggs and sperm each contain 23 pairs of chromosomes. All forty-six are carried in every cell of a human body from the moment egg and sperm unite until the organism dies. In twenty-two pairs are genes that determine such things as the color of eyes, skin, and hair, the shape of features. The twenty-third pair are the sex chromosomes. The egg has an X chromosome, and the sperm has either an X or a Y. If the fertilizing sperm carries the X chromosome, the baby will be a girl. If a Y, the baby will be a boy.

Before the baby is born, however, there are several forks in the road toward clear sexual differentiation. For six weeks the embryo appears sexually neutral. Then somehow the Y chromosome—if one is present—sends a message to the gonads, which as yet have been sexless, to start becoming testicles. However, if the sex chromosome in the father's sperm was X, six weeks more go by with no change. Then a message reaches the undifferentiated gonads to develop into ovaries full of enough egg cells to last a lifetime. The developing testicles or ovaries then begin to send out a mixture of hormones to all parts of the embryo. Androgen is the masculinizing hormone, and estrogen the feminizing hormone. Both are present in each one of us, but the level of each varies. Testicles produce enough androgen to dominate the estrogen in males, and ovaries produce enough estrogen to dominate the androgen in females. Almost always, however, one hormone is so dominant that one set of the reproductive organs present in the embryo begins to develop while the other shrinks away and usually disappears entirely. Finally comes the molding of the external genitals, which got you the M or F on your birth certificate.

What does that M or F really mean? Basically there are just four biological imperatives laid down for all males and all females. Only men can impregnate; only women can menstruate, give birth, and secrete milk. But societies also distinguish—sometimes sharply, sometimes not—between "men's work" and "women's work" and the proper traits and behavior of each sex. And they usually assume or insist that these differences are inborn. Males, being taller, bigger, stronger, and more aggressive, on the average, than females, are meant to dominate. Women are meant to submit, and to care for men and children.

Researchers have studied males and females, especially during infancy and early childhood, in an attempt to find which traits and behaviors are biologically determined and which are learned. Psychologist Corinne Hutt believes that males and females are predisposed toward different traits by their different "physiological wiring-up." She cites evidence from studies of primates as well as preschool children. Certain inborn sex differences among primates, including humans, have prevailed over time and also are present in widely different cultures. She concludes that "it seems highly improbable that they are entirely culturally ordained."[2] Hutt notes, however, that most studies show

[2] *Males and Females* (Middlesex, England: Penguin Books, 1972), p. 131.

an overlap of traits and behavior—a greater tendency for one sex to exhibit certain behaviors which are also present in some members of the opposite sex. She attributes these to inborn differences due to particular hormone mixes. A girl with a higher androgen level than normal for females, for example, is likely to be more aggressive than most other girls.

Psychological Traits and Social Behavior

Unlike biologists and ethologists, anthropologists stress the cultural differences in sex roles—the great variation, rather than the similarity, in the norms that define sex-appropriate traits and behavior. In a study of three New Guinea tribes, Margaret Mead found two that make no personality distinctions between men and women. Among the mountain-dwelling Arapesh, the chief cultural goals are growing yams and raising children. Both men and women act in a fashion Americans would call "feminine." Both are cherishing, gentle, maternal, mild. Not far away live the fierce, cannibalistic Mundugumor. Both men and women of this tribe act in ways we would call predominantly "masculine." Both "are expected to be violent, competitive, aggressively sexed, jealous and ready to see and avenge insult, delighting in display, action, and fighting."[3] Every man is against every other, including his father and his brothers. The things that give him greatest satisfaction are fighting and the competitive acquisition of women. Children are unwanted. The world is charged with hostility and conflict.

Instead of ignoring sexual differences in personality, the third tribe, the Tchambuli, define male and female roles in a way that is the reverse of ours. Women manage and dominate. Men gossip, wear curls, and go shopping. They are emotionally dependent upon women and less responsible.

Psychologists Eleanor Maccoby and Carol Jacklin compiled, reviewed and interpreted over 2,000 books and articles about sex differences in motivation, social behavior, and intellectual ability. They concluded that "there is a great deal of myth in the popular views about male-female differences. There is also some substance."[4] It is a myth that girls are more "social" than boys, although it appears true that boys interact in larger groups and are highly oriented toward peer groups, while girls prefer to gather in small groups. It is a myth that girls are more suggestible than boys and are more likely to imitate other people spontaneously. Boys, in fact, often change their own values if these conflict with those of the peer group. Girls do not have lower self-esteem than boys either in childhood or adolescence. But girls are more self-confident about their social competence, while boys more often see themselves as strong and dominant.

A fourth myth is that girls lack motivation to achieve. They may be even more strongly motivated. Boys, it was found, need an appeal to ego or competition to reach the same level of motivation as girls. Some studies have found that girls excel at rote learning and boys at reasoning. But Maccoby and Jacklin concluded that this, too, is false. Boys are not better at analyzing, that is, responding to a particular aspect of a situation without being influenced by the larger context. Both sexes, contrary to the myth of superior male intelligence, learn with equal facility. While some studies have found that girls respond better to sounds and boys to sights, there is no solid basis for these findings.

---

[3] *Sex and Temperament in Three Primitive Societies* (New York: Dell, 1935), p. 213.

[4] *The Psychology of Sex Differences* (Stanford: Stanford University Press, 1974).

Contrary to one of the many myths about sex differences in childhood, girls do not lack motivation to achieve. In fact, they may be even more strongly motivated than boys. *Grete Mannheim/Design Photographers International, Inc.*

There are several sex-related differences, however. Males *are* more aggressive than females, physically and verbally. This difference shows up from the time they begin to play with others at about age two. Their primary victims are other males. Second, girls have better verbal ability. During preschool and up to about age eleven, there is no sex difference in verbal ability. From then on, however, girls score higher on all levels of tasks that involve understanding and producing language. A third difference is that adolescent and adult males excel in perceiving figures or objects in space and their relations to one another. Finally, although boys and girls do equally well in grade-school arithmetic, about age 11 or 12 boys' mathematical skills begin to increase faster than do girls'.

Other differences have also been researched, but the findings neither refute nor support many common beliefs. It cannot be established scientifically that girls are more timid or anxious, that boys are more active; that males are more dominant, that females are more compliant. It cannot be established that females are more altruistic and helpful, nor even that females are more passive. Maccoby and Jacklin are inclined, nonetheless, to think that females *are* more compli-

ant. "The traditional assignment of certain jobs to men and others to women has come about not so much because men are in jobs that call for aggressiveness as because women, being slower to anger, are less likely to protest onerous assignments. . . . Girls are more likely than boys to comply with demands that adults make upon them. Although it has not been demonstrated, it appears likely that in adulthood as well they will 'take orders' from authority figures with less coercion. To put the matter bluntly, they are easier to exploit." [5]

Although greater male aggressiveness has been clearly established, there is plenty of evidence that the way aggression is expressed is learned. The fact that parents and other adults punish boys for aggression rather than encouraging it suggests that an inborn predisposition is also at work—that boys are more biologically prepared than girls to learn aggressive behavior. [6]

Origins of Cultural Stereotypes

Heavy social reinforcement of inborn differences—basic or slight—began in prehis-

[5] *Ibid.*, p. 371.
[6] *Ibid.*, p. 361.

tory. The struggle to survive dictated that breast-feeding mothers had to stay close to their young, while adult males left them to hunt and fight. "These conditions no longer govern our survival, but their influence is perpetuated in average differences between men and women collectively in size and muscular strength, in the prenatal sex hormone effect on brain pathways, and in cultural traditions including language."[7] The need for a division of labor still explains sex roles to a great extent in many small tribal societies. In large modern societies,

[7] John Money and Patricia Tucker, *Sexual Signatures* (Boston: Little, Brown, 1975), p. 79.

John Wayne most often plays the "strong silent type"—the stereotype of the American male sex role. *World Wide Photos.*

however, most differentiation in roles, aside from the reproductive ones, rests on *beliefs* about innate differences. Many of these are firmly grounded in religious beliefs. Others rest on theories such as Freud's that women are incomplete men, doomed by their sex to neuroses and a sense of inferiority and penis envy. "Anatomy is destiny" according to Freud.

American Sex Stereotypes

There are, then, undeniable differences between males and females. There are also innate psychological or behavioral tendencies determined by such factors as the hormone mix predominant in each sex, and reinforced—or perhaps squelched—by socialization. Even those that are clearly proven to predominate in one sex or the other overlap, however. Some members of each sex are capable of the skills and exhibit the traits ascribed to the other.

But stereotypes die hard. Most Americans are likely to agree with these descriptions of what it means to be the ideal male or female:

An American adult male is ambitious for material success and leadership. He strives to get ahead. He is the provider for the family. Except in an emergency, he is not responsible for housework or child care. The job comes first. He is tough and independent, knows all the answers, does not seek help. He controls his emotions; he does not cry or embrace other men. He is more intelligent than women. He initiates and dominates sexual relations from the first advance to bed. He may seduce women to prove his manliness, but his bride must be a virgin. He is interested in sports. His ideal is the strong silent cool type—John Wayne or the Marlboro man. He is "masculine."

An American adult female is primarily a wife and mother, caring for husband, children, and home. She is self-sacrificing, sweet, and gentle. She is fragile and fearful and needs to be protected.

She is passive, dependent, and submissive. She looks up to men. If she dominates her husband, it is through devious womanly wiles, being attractive, coy, and helpless, and of course his intellectual inferior. She is scatterbrained and illogical and cannot balance a checkbook. She is sexually attractive but modest, a virgin before marriage and a faithful wife thereafter, but she does not enjoy sex. She is tender and affectionate, and is free to express her emotions, which in any case she cannot control. She is "feminine."

You may quarrel with some of these statements, because many stereotyped notions of sex roles have changed and are changing. But many others persist, especially among traditionally oriented groups. And the general stress on masculinity and femininity as desirable and important patterns of behavior exert a continuing influence on behavior and personality.

Why do these stereotypes persist in the face of many exceptions and much evidence to the contrary for many of the traits listed? They are advantageous for the dominant sex. Like racism, sexism based on these stereotypes is a pattern of discrimination that keeps women, the lower caste, "in their place." This of course frees men from scrubbing floors and changing diapers, jobs for which the possession of a uterus apparently qualifies any woman. Sex stereotypes are also reinforced by, and even built into, most languages. In English, "mankind" technically omits half the human race. "He" is seldom qualified by adding "or she" or changing "he" to "person." English grammar is awkward for those who would erase sexism from language.

All stereotypes and other unfounded beliefs persist because people ignore evidence that does not fit their preconceptions and notice things that reinforce them ("Isn't that just like a man!"). And sex stereotypes persist because women as well as men believe that men are superior. Psychologist Philip Goldberg asked college women to evaluate a series of professional articles. Each evaluator had the same set of articles, except that an article was supposedly written by John Smith, for example, in one set, and by Jane Smith in another. The same paper got a higher ranking if a man's name appeared so often that Goldberg concluded, "Women seem to think that men are better at everything—including elementary school teaching and dietetics!"[8]

The belief in male superiority is acquired gradually. Children are socialized to think according to sex stereotypes. By adulthood both sexes consider men more worthy.

Inge Broverman and her co-workers tested a number of clinically trained psychologists, psychiatrists, and social workers, divided into three groups including both men and women, to see what kind of person they would consider healthy, mature, and socially competent. One group chose from a long list the traits that would characterize such a person. The second group picked from the same list the traits that would characterize such a man, and the third, such a woman. "The three profiles that emerged showed that the group's concept of an ideal person was almost identical with the concept of an ideal man but not very much like the concept of an ideal woman. In other words, the better the woman you are in our society, the less of a person you are, even in the eyes of people with the training and experience in working with people as individuals these subjects had."[9]

Gender Identity, Sex Roles, and Behavior

Your **gender identity** is your sense of yourself as male or female. "Your gender identity puts its mark on everything you think and

[8] "Are Women Prejudiced against Other Women?" *Trans-Action* S(5): 28–30.

[9] "Sex-Role Stereotypes and Clinical Judgments of Mental Health," *Journal of Consulting and Clinical Psychology* 34 (1970): 1–7.

feel, do and say. Your understanding of yourself and others is limited by your understanding of what it means—to you and to them—to be a man or a women." [10]

Gender identity is usually in agreement with the M or F on one's birth certificate. John Money describes the case of twin brothers who at seven months of age were taken to be circumcised. Through a most unusual accident, one boy's penis shriveled to almost nothing during the electrical cauterization. Learning of the Johns Hopkins Hospital program for working with transsexuals (people who have the sex characteristics of one sex but feel themselves to be the other, and are in some cases helped to assume a new gender identity through surgery and counseling) the parents went there for help. The doctor described the alternatives, stressing that there would be no turning back once gender identity had been established. They decided to reassign the child's sex as a girl and to bring her up as one. She conformed so well to the feminine sex role that her only "masculine" traits are now interpreted as tomboyish. Although she is not yet an adult, "her record to date offers convincing evidence that the gender identity gate is open at birth for a normal child no less than for one born with unfinished sex organs or one who was prenatally over- or under-exposed to androgen, and that it stays open at least for something over a year after birth." [11]

Acquiring Gender Identity in Childhood

How do children come to behave in sex-typical or sex-appropriate ways? For some types of behavior, an innate tendency or biological predisposition exists. For others it does not.

In either case, sex-typed behavior is acquired through social learning.

We have been speaking of sex as either male or female, with totally heterosexual females at one extreme and totally heterosexual males at the other. But people are infinitely varied in their expression of their sexuality. In most cases, nonetheless, by the age of three or so, a boy firmly believes he is a boy and a girl is equally sure she is a girl. Once they learn that, they try to find out what it means to be a boy or girl. What kinds of things do girls or boys do?

Because of the importance of *learning* gender identity and sex roles, Money calls the brain "the most potent of the human sex organs." [12] Very early in life signals come to the child that help him or her decide which gender identity is appropriate. The critical period for learning gender identity coincides with learning to speak and understand language. By the time a boy can say with certainty that he is a boy, he has also been subject to three interacting processes that help him learn boylike behavior, or the masculine sex role. These are identification with and imitation of admired models, formal and informal socialization by others, and self-socialization.

IMITATION OF MODELS Whether or not the young child learns sex roles by imitating models of the same sex is still an open question. Maccoby and Jacklin found no evidence that young children closely resemble the same-sex parent in their behavior. The modeling process, they conclude, "is crucial in the acquisition of a wide repertoire of potential behaviors, but this repertoire is not sex-typed to any important degree." [13] They tell of a 4-year-old girl who insisted that only boys could become doctors and girls could become nurses. She did not iden-

---

[10] Money and Tucker, *Sexual Signatures*, p. 9.
[11] *Ibid.*, p. 98.

[12] *Ibid.*, p. 140.
[13] *The Psychology of Sex Differences*, p. 363.

tify with her closest real-life model, her mother, who was a doctor!

Later in childhood and adolescence, however, modeling does play an important role. This is especially significant for boys, whose fathers are often absent from the home. They must choose their models from their peer groups and somewhat older youths. Two psychologists who studied men and masculinity believe this choice—along with the fact that relations between fathers and sons tend to be somewhat less close than those between mothers and daughters—helps explain why "boys, as a group, tend to resemble their fathers in personality and attitudes much less than girls resemble their mothers." [14]

Children learn sex roles from books and television as well as from people. An experiment tested the influence of storybook characters as models. Three groups of preschool children were each read a story. One depicted achievement-oriented behavior (working hard to solve a problem) by a male, another depicted the same type of behavior by a female, and the third was a neutral or control story with no such behavior. Then the children's own achievement-oriented behavior was assessed. Like other studies, this one showed a strong tendency for children to imitate the behavior of members of their own sex. [15]

The educational system, churches, and mass media, as well as peer groups, strongly reinforce a child's self-conception as a boy or girl and its expectations of adult sex roles.

Children's books have been notoriously sexist in favoring the masculine role. Boys' and girls' roles were clearly differentiated in most of the 2,760 stories in 134 books studied by the National Organization for Women. In 65 of the stories in 134 books, boys demeaned girls; in only two did the opposite occur. Girls are often pictured as demeaning themselves with comments like, "It's easy. Even I can do it. And you know how stupid I am." Readers for later grades picture men in 166 occupations, women in only 25. Not one girl in all the stories "becomes a doctor, lawyer, professor, astronaut, engineer, or even a computer operator or a salesperson. Among the 25 options for girls, however, are witch, cleaning lady, baby-sitter, queen and fat lady in the circus." [16] It is no wonder such negative models make boys avoid anything feminine, even such positive qualities as helping and nurturing.

Even in the Scandinavian countries, where a long tradition of equal educational opportunity exists, analysis of school textbooks in the 1960s showed they were permeated with sexism. Swedish arithmetic books showed only men buying land, negotiating loans, building houses, and drawing up budgets. History books often omitted any discussion of the status and accomplishments of women. Women were usually portrayed in domestic roles and girls were doing household chores. Studies in Michigan and Canada had similar results. Only men follow diversified occupational pursuits, occupy high positions, and play active roles. Women are housewives and mothers above all, although they occasionally are shown in such "feminine" occupational roles as saleladies, maids, waitresses, and nurses. "Men are shown as making important decisions and bringing about significant social changes while women follow and obey

[14] Ruth E. Hartley, "Sex-Role Pressures and the Socialization of the Male Child," *Psychological Reports,* 5 (1959): 457–468.

[15] Leslie Zebrowitz McArthur and Susan V. Eisen, "Achievements of Male and Female Storybook Characters as Determinants of Achievement Behavior by Boys and Girls," *Journal of Personality and Social Psychology* 33 (April 1976): 467–473.

[16] Warren Farrell, *The Liberated Man* (New York: Bantam, 1974), pp. 33–35.

At early ages, children begin to learn sex roles through identification with and imitation of admired models.

J. Berndt / Stock, Boston.

Henri Cartier-Bresson / Magnum.

these decisions and prepare the men's meals."[17]

Teachers and administrators also perpetuate sex role stereotypes by discouraging girls (often through ridicule) from taking "masculine" courses, by assigning boys and girls to sex-appropriate activities, games, and sports, by expecting higher achievement of boys, and by punishing, praising, and helping them more than girls.[18]

Among the mass media, TV has been especially singled out as strongly reinforcing sexist stereotypes. About 20 percent of TV time goes to commercials, and by age 17, the average viewer has seen about 350,000 commercials. A sample study of weekday broadcasts showed that 57 percent of the central figures in commercials were male, and that 70 percent of these were portrayed as authorities, even on products used primarily by females. Female central figures were usually portrayed in roles that defined them in relation to others—as wives, girlfriends, mothers, or housewives. Males were more often shown in roles defined as independent of others—workers, professionals, celebrities, or narrator-interviewers. Females were more often depicted at home, men in occupational settings. And "females were more likely than males to obtain the approval of family and the opposite sex as reward for using a given product, while males more frequently obtained the approval of their friends, social advancement, and career advancement."[19]

SOCIALIZATION There is surprising similarity in the rearing of boys and girls. According to studies of the first five years of life, boys and girls are treated with equal affection, equally allowed and encouraged to be independent, and equally discouraged from aggression.[20] Parents and other agents of direct socialization nonetheless steer behavior along "masculine" or "feminine" paths in a thousand ways, formal and informal, harsh and gentle. They give boys toy cars and guns, while girls are given dolls and frilly dresses. They reward sex-appropriate behavior with sanctions as subtle as smiles or frowns or as explicit as presents and spankings. Statements such as "Boys don't do that; you don't want to be a sissy," or "Act like a nice girl, sweetie" also teach children sex-appropriate behavior. Parents put especially intense pressure on boys against engaging in "girlish" behavior. A girl may be a "tomboy" but heaven help the boy labeled a "sissy"!

A study of fifth graders showed that they spent about half of their non-school time in play and games. Janet Lever observed six clear sex differences: (1) Boys play outdoors far more than girls. (2) Though both boys and girls play alone about 20 per cent of the time, when they are in social play, boys play in larger groups, whether indoors or out. (3) Although children between 8 and 12 more often play in groups of the same sex and similar age, when boys' games need more players, they allow younger ones to join; they are more likely, then, to play in age-mixed groups than girls are. (4) Girls play in predominantly male games more often than boys play in girls' games. When they do play in mixed groups, girls are expected to play the boys' game seriously, but if boys enter girls' play, they guard against the "sissy" label by teasing or acting

[17] Constantina Safilios-Rothschild, *Women and Social Policy* (Englewood Cliffs, N.J.: Prentice-Hall, 1974), pp. 26–28.

[18] *Ibid.*, p. 29.

[19] Leslie Zebrowitz McArthur and Beth Gabrielle Resko, "The Portrayal of Men and Women in American Television Commercials," *The Journal of Social Psychology*, 97 (December 1975): 209–220.

[20] Maccoby and Jacklin, *The Psychology of Sex Differences*, p. 362.

the clown, often to annoy the girls. (5) Boys play competitive, formal games with goals and rules more often than girls do. (6) Finally, Lever observed that boys' games last longer than girls' games. She suggests that games like baseball demand a higher level of skill that can go on developing for years, while jumping rope and playing hopscotch do not, and soon become boring. She also noted that boys solve disputes during a game more effectively than girls. Though they often quarrel, they go on playing after the dispute is over. Thus they gain more consciousness of rules and more experience in applying them. She suggests that

Boys' games may help prepare their players for successful performance in a wide range of work settings in modern society. In contrast, girls' games may help prepare their players for the private sphere of the home and their future roles as wives and mothers.[21]

More specifically, boys' games give training in independence, organizational skills, and settlement of disputes, as well as in dealing

[21]"Sex Differences in the Games Children Play," *Social Problems* 23 (April 1976): 478–487.

(left) Boys' play tends to be more competitive and formal, requiring both physical and organizational skills that can be developed over a period of years. *Blair Seitz/Seitz Photographers.* (right) Girls' play tends to be more cooperative and informal, requiring a lower level of physical skill and developing empathy rather than organizational skills. *Hugh Rogers/Monkmeyer Press Photo Service.*

with impersonal competition and in cooperating in situations where people are interdependent. Girls' play, on the other hand, "may provide a training ground for the development of delicate socio-emotional skills." It usually occurs in small intimate groups (often groups of two) in private places. It mimics primary group relationships such as the family rather than participation in formal games. When girls play with younger children, they practice nurturant skills such as care and affection. Their play tends to be less structured and more spontaneous and cooperative than that of boys. Their frequent "Let's pretend" may help them take the role of the other in a different way from the "Let's play ball" of boys, developing empathy rather than organizational skills.

247

SELF-SOCIALIZATION Not all socialization in sex roles is "done to" children. They first develop a concept of what it means to be male or female and of which sex they are. Then they try to fit their behavior to their gender identity. This begins even before gender identity is fully fixed. Lawrence Kohlberg considers self-socialization even more important than modeling or direct parental reinforcement.[22] The child induces a set of rules from what he or she observes and is told. These rules often distort reality, being cartoon like—"oversimplified, exaggerated, and stereotyped." They emphasize features that are obvious and easily described, such as hair styles and dress. They are generalizations of information gathered from many sources. These generalizations become more accurate as the child grows. At first a girl knows in a general way that she is a girl, then that other children are either girls or boys. Later that the general category of grown-ups also is divided into male and female categories that include boys and girls. Once the child understands sex groupings, he or she can identify sex-appropriate behavior by observing what kinds of things males do as distinct from what females do, and, knowing her or his own gender identity, can develop a sex role that fits.

Gender Identity in Adolescence and Young Adulthood

The body changes that occur in adolescence initiate a period of changes in self-concept. Being an adolescent boy or girl is different from being a child-boy or girl. New behaviors and responsibilities must be learned.

Adolescence is not a stormy period in many societies, nor with all teenagers in American society. It is not even defined as a stage of life in every culture. Historically, it was a brief transition between childhood and adulthood. When an American boy a half-century ago put on long pants he became a man and soon went to work. A girl's putting up her hair meant she was ready to look for a husband.

Today adolescence is a much longer stage of life, because two things have happened in recent decades. The age of social maturity and economic independence is reached much later than before. Complex industrial technology has created a host of new occupations, many of which demand long years of formal education. At the other extreme, puberty is reached earlier. In Europe and the United States, the age of onset of menstruation declined progressively from age 17 in 1833 to less than 13 in 1962. This trend appears to be worldwide. Puberty is not, however, a single event such as first menstruation. It is, rather, a progression which lasts about four years. "Psychologically and behaviorally, it is a time of revelation, not a turning point. Puberty guns the motors of growth, sex differentiation, and sex drive, but it does not change the course set in childhood."[23]

Anxiety may accompany the onset of adolescence. One source is fear of homosexuality. A few exposures to homosexual experience in adolescence do not, insists Money, create "adult obligatory homosexuals." Any erotic preference was established in childhood as gender identity was fixed. There are, in fact, societies in which a period of homosexuality is part of the normal process of growing up for adolescent boys. The cultures of the Batak people in northern Sumatra and the Marind Amin people of

---

[22] "A Cognitive-Developmental Analysis of Children's Sex-Role Concepts and Attitudes," in Eleanor E. Maccoby, ed., *The Development of Sex Differences* (Stanford: Stanford University Press, 1966), pp. 82–172.

[23] Money and Tucker, *Sexual Signatures*, pp. 153–158.

New Guinea have endured successfully for centuries. In each adolescent boys invariably follow a homosexual period with stable heterosexual marriages, and researchers have found no obligative homosexuals in either society.[24]

A central failing of our own society is the attitude toward knowledge about the male and female genitals and reproductive behavior. Children get the idea that sex is dirty because adults squirm when they ask about it. They are hushed or told that they are too young to understand. Simply reciting the facts of reproduction is not enough. It gives children an inadequate concept of sex because the emotional component is left out. To leave out that part of the explanation is to separate love from lust. Before puberty, children accept those explanations matter-of-factly and in easy installments. Those who are told too little too late and too poorly turn to other sources of information, which may color it obscene.

Early and accurate knowledge gives people a firm basis for their self-conception as male or female. This strengthens their self-confidence in their sex roles and leaves them more flexibility in conforming to or deviating from definitions of "masculinity" and "femininity" found in clichés and stereotypes. A person who is overly concerned about conforming to the stereotype restricts the range of possible behaviors.

The Power of Gender Identity over Behavior

Much "masculine" or "feminine" behavior in a person whose gender identity has been long and firmly established is taken for granted. "Naturally" a man goes out to work and comes home to drink beer and watch a football game on TV. "Naturally" a woman stays home or, even if she has a job outside,

does the cleaning and shopping and cooking and laundry. But much gender-related behavior is also unnoticed and comes to light only on occasion. The way we sit, stand, walk, talk, hold our heads, approach or touch others, use our hands—all these apparently trifling behaviors are consistently sex-typed.

Jan Morris, who underwent a sex change operation, notes in her autobiography that every aspect of existence is different for men and women, including subtle responses such as the posture and tone of voice others now use when addressing her. The more she was treated like a woman, the more of a woman she became—even finding herself unable to open bottles or lift heavy objects as she had once done so easily.[25]

Mirra Kamarovsky has shown in her studies of blue-collar families that traditional sex roles prevail more strongly in the working class than in other classes. There is little communication and interaction between the sexes. A man goes out with "the boys" while his wife is "limited to a small circle of parents, relatives, and two or three friends who set her standards in life—from food and house furnishings to politics, sex, and religion—and the normal universe seems to have the unity of the simple society of the past."[26]

Much behavior that appears related to sex differences is specific to the situation. Females are usually thought of as more conforming and less intelligent than males. This becomes a self-fulfilling prophecy, say two psychologists, in situations where a person wants to please someone of the opposite sex who is thought to believe the stereotype. The "problem" of female inferiority, they suggest, "resides not so much within women, but rather within the social situations and normative expectations with which they are

---

[24] *Ibid.*, p. 165.

[25] *Conundrum* (New York: Harcourt Brace Jovanovich, 1974).

[26] "Blue-Collar Marriages and Families," in Louise Kapp Howe, ed., *The White Majority* (New York: Random House, 1970), p. 40.

typically faced." Men, too, when they very much want to impress another person, will behave in ways they believe conform to that person's expectations and desires. For example, a male who very much wants to impress a female who he knows holds untraditional views of the masculine role would probably portray himself as less aggressive and career-oriented, and more dependent and sentimental than the traditional stereotype.[27]

Another experiment studied leadership situations involving 48 three-person groups of two men and one woman or two women and one man. Leadership was assigned randomly in each group, but some were led to believe that the leader was appointed, some that leadership was achieved. The results were completely consistent with sex-role stereotypes. Male leaders concentrated significantly more than female leaders on recognizable leadership behavior. Female leaders acted in such a way as to play down their role and soften their image and thus make their leadership more acceptable. And female leaders were less likely to choose themselves as future leaders than were males. Even more significant, however, was the fact that female leaders presumably chosen by chance showed little involvement and minimal performance. Those whose status was presumably achieved showed intense involvement in attaining the goal (solving a puzzle). At the same time, they also engaged in "the expected encouraging and tension-relieving behavior. Like some working wives, they took on two jobs." Male leadership, in contrast, did not differ in achieved and randomly assigned statuses.[28]

[27] Mark P. Zanna and Susan J. Pack, "On the Self-Fulfilling Nature of Apparent Sex Differences in Behavior," *Journal of Experimental Social Psychology* 11 (November 1975): 583–591.

[28] Arlene Eskilson and Mary Glenn Wiley, "Sex Composition and Leadership in Small Groups," *Sociometry* 39 (September 1976): 183–194.

Consequences of Sex Role Stereotypes

Sex role expectations simplify the problems of a society in some ways. They assign functions according to a masculine-feminine division of labor, and generally promote cooperation by meshing complementary roles. On the other hand, especially in modern complex societies, sexism has many negative consequences. Sex discrimination affects life chances, especially for women, limits the personality development and self-actualization of both men and women, and—like discrimination on the basis of class, race, religion, and nationality—results in various costs to the society as a whole.

Patterns of Discrimination

Although we stress American patterns here, sex discrimination is worldwide. It is often said that women have achieved equality in Scandinavia and in the People's Republic of China as well as the Soviet Union. In China, great strides have been made toward emancipation of women from their centuries-old subjugation in a patriarchal system. Both husband and wife are equally free to work and engage in social activities outside the home and are equals in management of property and income. However, women still do all the housework. Sons are preferred because it is still considered important to carry on the family line. There is also discrimination in pay and in obtaining important jobs. Though women participate in politics at the grassroots level, they are conspicuously underrepresented at the national level.[29]

[29] Lawrence Hong, "The Role of Women in the People's Republic of China: Legacy and Change," *Social Problems* 23 (June 1976): 545–557.

Male superiority, then, is an almost universal pattern, even where ideology proclaims the equality of the sexes. It is to some extent a self-fulfilling myth. Women, for example, are stereotyped as the weaker sex even where they carry huge bundles on their heads and work in the fields all day. In our society they are kept weaker by discriminatory patterns of participation in sports and games. In crises, however, they suddenly become strong enough to drive trucks and handle big machines. "Rosie the Riveter" was a wartime phenomenon, but postwar America returned to traditionalism so wholeheartedly that the baby boom and the suburban house were symbols of the American dream of the late 1940s and the 1950s.

As in other types of discrimination, sexism results in different life chances for men and women—most, but not all, negative for women. Women have fewer opportunities for the high educational, occupational, and political achievement that help one win wealth, power, and prestige. Most women take on the status of, first, their fathers and then their husbands. The picture regarding mental and physical health is less one-sided.

Physical Health, Mental Health, and Survival

While more male babies are spontaneously aborted, so many more are conceived—140 to 100—that 105 boys are born to every 100 girls. But females have a longer life expectancy, and greater stamina under stresses such as starvation, fatigue, shock, and illness. They are the weaker sex only in physical strength for such strenuous acts as lifting and carrying, and even here many women are stronger than many men.

Although they have a longer life expectancy, American females are sick oftener than males from all acute conditions except injuries and are in bed or restricted to the house for longer periods. They are also more likely to have multiple chronic conditions, but they have less severe ones or report feeling less limited by them. Since the National Health Interview Survey is based on self-reports rather than clinical data, however, it is suggested that females may have been socialized to be more sensitive to ailments, or more willing to report them, or both, while males learn to ignore symptoms. Females may also be socialized to take care of themselves and may have less time constraints to prevent them from doing so. (Employed females report less illness and disability than nonemployed ones.) Their life styles subject them to less risk, although it appears to be a moot question whether males or females are generally under more stress. Women's greater attention to symptoms may be one explanation of their longevity. But most middle-aged Americans rank "good health" as the variable most closely related to satisfaction with life, and the mere fact that females simply do not feel well as often as males "generates large costs to individuals, families, and the population's productivity."[30]

A study of Swiss couples shows that wives are most likely to have psychosomatic symptoms if they hold traditional norms for their sex roles and the family relationships also fit traditional norms. Because the norms coincide with social reality, the wife could not perceive this reality as problematic. Instead of openly protesting or trying to change the reality, she reacted to stress with such illness. In families with less traditional norms, she was more likely to cope with stress by seeking friendships and joining voluntary associations.[31]

[30] Lois M. Verbrugge, "Females and Illness: Recent Trends in Sex Differences in the United States," *Journal of Health and Social Behavior* 17 (December 1976): 387–403.
[31] Rene Levey, "Psychosomatic Symptoms and Women's Protest: Two Types of Reaction to Structural Strain in the Family," *Journal of Health and Social Behavior* 17 (June 1976): 122–134.

Acceptance of one's socially defined sex role as an indicator of mental health has dominated psychotherapy for decades. But many studies in the 1960s and 1970s showed that, like the Swiss housewives, American women who showed symptoms of unhappiness and mental illness were those who were trying to adhere to sex-stereotyped roles. Other studies show that when both spouses try to adhere to sex stereotypes the wife often feels frustrated and unhappy. Middle-aged women who had devoted their lives to motherhood and housekeeping and then were deprived of those roles were found to have a high rate of depression, especially as compared to those who worked outside the home.[32]

If women try to play an active, dominant, or aggressive role, they may be punished by being diagnosed as mentally ill. Or the obstacles, stresses, and conflicts they encounter may actually produce so much stress that the diagnosis of mental illness is correct by professional standards. Mental illness statistics in the United States from 1950 to 1969 show that women are more likely than men to be psychiatric patients. These are "women who are having 'nervous breakdowns,' crying fits, temper tantrums, paranoid delusions; women who attempt suicide, who take unknown quantities of drugs to smother their anxieties, their hostilities, their ambitions, their panics, their sexual unhappiness—and their visions," in the angry language of Phyllis Chesler, a psychologist who wrote *Women and Madness*.[33] In 1968, women comprised 62 percent of those in private hospitals, and 60 percent of those in general psychiatric wards. Most therapists are male.

Chesler believes that many men are also severely disturbed but the male role allows a much wider range of behavior within which they can "act out" their drives. Typically "female" and "male" symptoms of emotional disturbance appear in childhood. Boys are most often referred to child guidance clinics for aggressive, destructive, and competitive behavior. Girls are referred (if they are referred at all) for personality problems, such as excessive fears and worries, shyness, timidity, lack of self-confidence, and feelings of inferiority.[34]

Male mental hospital patients tend to be destructively hostile and aggressive. They are prone to assault, robbery, rape, and alcoholism and are likely to indulge their impulses in socially deviant ways. Typically female symptoms often show a "dread of happiness" in Thomas Szasz's phrase—features of "slave psychology" such as chronic fatigue and a feeling of lifelessness. They are on strike against their masters, indulging in covert but unsuccessful rebellion. Frigidity, anxiety, and depression, and generally a "harsh, self-critical, self-depriving and often self-destructive set of symptoms" characterize female patients.[35]

Suicide is the ultimate protest against unhappiness, and it is often sex role related. A study of suicide in London, Ontario, between 1969 and 1971 found that females and young persons are more likely to attempt suicide, while males and older persons are more likely to complete it.[36] In the United States, too, women are more likely to attempt suicide, men to commit it. The attempt is often a cry for help. Of all attempted suicides in the United States, 69 percent in recent years have been by females; of all successful suicides, 70 percent by males. When both attempted and completed suicides are lumped together, housewives comprise the largest single category, and about five times

[32] Safilios-Rothschild, *Women and Social Policy,* p. 126–129.

[33] *Women and Madness* (New York: Avon, 1972), p. *xxii.*

[34] *Ibid.,* p. 39.

[35] *Ibid.,* p. 337.

[36] George K. Jarvis et al., "Sex and Age Patterns in Self-Injury," *Journal of Health and Social Behavior* 17 (June 1976): 146–155.

as many widows commit suicide as attempt it, while twice as many widowers commit it as attempt it.[37]

Just as sex roles traditionally have dictated a double standard of sexual behavior in the narrow sense, so there is a double standard of mental illness. The standard of mental health in American culture is masculine. Females are punished (by incarceration in psychiatric facilities) for acting out too completely the negative elements of the female role such as passivity and fearfulness, or by acting in masculine ways. But the stress of the masculine role as a producer of mental and physical illness must not be understated, as the 70 percent rate of completed suicides shows. Up to the end of adolescence, mental illness seems to be more frequent among boys than girls. And the shorter life expectancy of males may be related to the stress on achievement as well as traditional limitations on expression of emotion.

Education, Occupation, and Income

"Women's work" brings them little in the way of power, prestige, and pay. In America, most occupations—at least 70 percent—are largely sex-segregated. That is, a large majority of workers in an occupation are of one sex and, according to cultural norms, that is as it should be. High-ranking occupations have typically been male ones. Within an occupation, a "sexual pyramid" according to relative amounts of pay, power, and prestige has most of the women at the base, declining proportions in higher positions, and few if any at the top.

Comparing labor force participation, status, and income in various countries, Marjorie Galenson found that conditions affecting women are basically the same all over the West and in Eastern Europe.[38]

[37] Chesler, *Women and Madness*, pp. 48–49.
[38] Marjorie Galenson, *Women and Work* (Ithaca: N.Y. State School of Industrial and Labor Relations, Cornell University, 1973), p. 6.

In the Soviet Union, women often work in the same manual jobs as men but still have limited access to higher positions. *Editorial Photocolor Archives.*

Though women in the Soviet Union build apartment houses and sweep streets, they also constitute three-fourths of doctors. But they are paid two-thirds of the wage of a skilled factory worker, and medicine is a low-prestige occupation. In Russian academies over half the research workers are women, but less than one-fifth of the professors. Men administer collective farms and women do the heavy manual work. Women are concentrated at the lower grades of political and bureaucratic hierarchies. In both the Soviet Union and the United States, aspiring women complain that their advancement is blocked by an "old boy network"—an informal organization of men operating along lines learned since they were socialized in adolescent peer groups. Just as there are very few female plant directors in the West, there are few in the state-owned industries of the East. And women workers still must do the shopping and housework after they leave the workplace. This appears

253

to be the case in virtually all industrialized nations.

In recent decades (except for an upsurge in the 1970s) American women lost rather than gained ground in higher education. They earned a smaller proportion of advanced degrees in the early 1960s than during the 1930s and early 1940s and the proportion on college and university faculties also declined. One explanation is the GI Bill, which favored men by giving thousands of veterans who might otherwise never have gone to college a chance to do so.

Law schools and medical schools categorically excluded women for many years, even though women not only have better academic records than men but also tend to do better on tests for admission given by medical and law schools.[39] Explicit or subtle discrimination against women in college takes many forms. Typically, even at the undergraduate level, but much more so at the graduate level, department chairmen, advisors, and other professors (including some of the few women who are at high levels in faculty and administration) discourage women from applying to their departments. When pressed for reasons, they say that women are usually not serious about careers. They will waste their training if they marry and have children. And they will add no luster to the department because even the few women who work almost never achieve outstanding successes. College women often encounter pressure to transfer to "feminine" fields with less prestige (education, liberal arts, nursing, for example) even if they are interested in a traditionally masculine field and show they are capable of mastering it. Women who do make it in masculine fields, it is generally agreed, must be conspicuously brighter and work a great deal harder than their male counterparts.

Comparatively few women, until recent years, have aspired to careers in "masculine" fields. They have been socialized to the roles of wife and mother, and this socialization is reflected in their decisions in college. Shirley Angrist and Elizabeth Almquist studied 87 women born in 1948 and socialized to the traditional feminine role during their early years. They followed the women's definitions of work and family roles as they progressed through four years of college. They found that 35 percent consistently saw themselves as housewives, while only 16 percent repeatedly pictured themselves as career women. Most were work-oriented but not career-centered. "These women try to be flexible and open to fit the unknown spouse and with him an unknown life style. . . . This struggle to complete the puzzle while the big pieces are still missing haunts all the women."[40] They stall for time and make their career choices late, usually settling for traditional women's fields such as teaching, nursing, and secretarial work, which can be practiced no matter where a husband's job may take him. While some develop career interests, others relinquish them even though they are work-oriented and would enjoy interesting and stimulating jobs at a time in life that will permit or require them to work—such as when they are first married and have homes to furnish and later when children need college tuition and no young children remain at home. They are more concerned with life styles than careers. For them the *timing* of jobs and not the choice of a career is the crucial factor. Young men can think in terms of careers without considering the total life styles involved. But "all the plans young women make are contingent upon the kind of marriages they will have." Now that work is a realistic option even for wives and mothers, they try to anticipate and juggle their several roles and

---

[39] Safilios-Rothschild, *Women and Social Policy*, p. 37.

[40] *Careers and Contingencies* (New York: Dunellen, 1975), pp. 80–81.

to stay flexible so that they can somehow "mesh marriage, parenthood, personal interests and career aspirations."[41]

Many women, of course, must settle for a job with no future, for something far less than a professional career. Women were 20 percent of the U.S. labor force in 1920, 25 percent in 1940. World War II lifted the ban on employment of married women, and by 1944, married women constituted almost half the female labor force. By 1960, women were a third of the entire labor force, and 41 percent in 1976.

While employment rose, sex segregation in jobs remained and the income gap between men and women actually widened. In 1960, elementary school teachers and registered nurses accounted for almost 54 percent of all female professional employment; in 1976 for just over 46 percent. There are, in a sense, two labor markets, one for each sex.

The composition of the female labor force has changed. In 1920, the typical working woman was single, under 30, and from the working class. Today, most are married, more than half are 40 and older, and they come from the entire socio-economic spectrum. Of married women living with their husbands, 43 percent now work outside the home. Since the mid-1960s, the greatest increase in labor force participation has been among those in the 25–34 age range, when women are most involved in raising children. Only 36 percent in this age group were employed in 1960 as compared to 50 percent in 1973. Of married women with pre-school children, only 12 percent were in the labor force in 1950; over a third in 1974.[42]

Greater opportunities for employment and changed attitudes toward working women are only part of the reason for these changes. Many women not only can work and want to work, but *must* work. Many women in the labor force are single, widowed, divorced, or separated. To a greater or lesser extent, they are economically on their own.

Of all full-time year-round workers, nearly two-thirds of females earned less than $7000 in 1972, while over three-quarters of males earned more than that amount.[43] The income differential persists even when level of education and number of hours worked are accounted for. "If women had the same occupational status as men, had worked all their lives, had the same education and year-round full-time employment in 1966, their income would be . . . 62 percent of that received by men."[44] According to a 1976 study by the Department of Labor, this pay gap is wider now than it was 20 years ago. The average female college graduate earns less than the average male high school dropout. Even for those in traditionally male professions, there is a gap. Women college professors earn 91 percent as much as their male colleagues, high school teachers 81 percent, scientists 76 percent, engineers 85 percent.

A similar income gap exists even in countries noted for female liberation and sexual equality, such as Finland and Sweden. In Sweden, with a widely accepted ideology and tradition of sex equality, as well as laws against discrimination, the gap was 34 percent in 1970. But when broken down by levels of income, it was 41 percent at the highest and 41 percent at the lowest. This shows how hard it is to break the vicious circle of *existing* inequality even when laws prohibit discrimination.[45]

Many women have no desire to enter the labor force. Being a housewife does not in

---

[41] *Ibid.*, p. 106.
[42] U.S. Department of Labor, 1975 report.

[43] 1975 Manpower Report of the President.
[44] L. E. Suter and H. P. Miller, "Components of Differences between Incomes of Men and Career Women," *American Journal of Sociology* 79 (1973): 962.
[45] Safilios-Rothschild, *Women and Social Policy*, p. 47.

itself make women happy or unhappy. One study compared employed American wives, housewives who did not want to work outside the home, and housewives who wanted jobs. The unhappiest group were those who wanted to work outside the home but did not. They were mainly working-class, had the least education among those studied, and were the lowest in self-esteem and satisfaction. They felt they were powerless pawns of fate, kept from getting jobs because of family responsibilities, illness, lack of anyone to care for their children, and a bad job market. Employed wives, though less happily married than the full-time housewives in the study, had higher feelings of competence and self-esteem. Housewives who did not want to work reportedly had happy marriages, felt in control of their lives, and had the best mental and physical health of the three groups.[46]

Consequences for Personality

Sex role stereotypes have been condemned because they narrow the options for both sexes in "being" as well as "doing." In general, the American man (especially the white middle-class male) is expected to "do" and the woman is discouraged from "doing." By the same token, the woman is expected to "be"—to be "feminine" above all—and the man is restricted in emotional expression and empathy.

ACHIEVEMENT AND SELF-ESTEEM Males are expected to prove themselves in traditionally masculine fields, especially sports and jobs. Little boys are asked, far more often than little girls, "What do you want to *do*?" The expected answer is a choice of occupation.

Boys are expected to prove themselves

first in team sports such as baseball. Then they must make it with girls. They must choose and prepare for a job that will bring them some measure of wealth, prestige, and power. The nonachiever as a boy—the loner, the nearsighted, shy, weak, or sickly youth—undergoes agonies. He may or may not compensate by brilliance in studies or creative arts, which brings him little respect or admiration until late in high school and in college. Even the "masculine" boy has a high level of anxiety. It is not as easy to be a boy as many girls think.

Even in a "man's world" it is not necessarily easy to be a man. Men are supposed to be strivers all the way. Rarely is there any stopping place on the road to success. Men suffer stress, anxiety, and fear of failure all along the route. The achiever must keep on achieving because it is so hard to know when he has "made it"—and there is always new competition. The executive ulcer and the feeling of being caught in a rat race are symptoms of the pressure on the middle- and upper-middle-class male to succeed. The working-class male may not suffer career and success pressures, but he may be subject to other pressures—getting and keeping a job, and resisting boredom. And the man of any social class level whose job is at the core of his self-conception finds little to keep up his sense of worth in a society that abruptly retires or fires him.

Both sexes enter high school more or less as equals in intellectual potential and motivation to achieve. But the pressures toward femininity create special anxieties in girls. White adolescent females, according to one study, are much more self-conscious and have less stable self-conceptions and somewhat lower self-esteem than white males and black females. These differences appear in early adolescence when the constant changes of puberty make them anxious about their physical appearance just when they most

[46] Linda Fidell and Jane Prather, "Women: Work Isn't Always the Answer," as reported by Carol Tavris, *Psychology Today* (September 1976), p. 78.

want to be attractive to boys. Their greater anxiety, according to the researchers, is due in part to the greater value they place on marriage as compared to black girls.[47]

Many women, it must not be overlooked, gain a sense of self-esteem and achievement in feminine roles, whether as housewives or as workers in traditionally feminine fields. But many others would like to enter traditionally masculine fields such as medicine and law, and business at the managerial and executive level, and they feel as bright and potentially capable as many men they see there. Yet they are often said to be afraid of trying and even more of succeeding, because they might be rejected by desirable males (potential husbands and lovers) as unfeminine, and by other women as well. In a famous experiment, Matina Horner

asked 90 women to write brief stories that began, "After first-term finals, Anne finds herself at the top of her medical school class," and asked 88 men to write about "John" in the same situation. Nine out of ten men were highly approving of John's success. Sixty-five percent of the women, in contrast, wrote stories depicting Anne as ugly, unhappy, rejected, or otherwise unpleasantly treated. One woman even wrote that Anne was killed by a car as she was leaving her graduation ceremony. Horner concluded that women are motivated to avoid success because they feel it is somehow inappropriate or unfeminine.[48] This fear of success appears

[48]"Feminity and Successful Achievement: A Basic Inconsistency," in J. M. Bardwick et al., eds., *Feminine Personality and Conflict* (Belmont, Calif.: Brooks-Cole, 1970).

[47]Roberta G. Simmons and Florence Rosenberg, "Sex, Sex Roles, and Self-Image," *Journal of Youth and Adolescence* 4 (September 1975): 229–257.

Many women are entering traditionally masculine fields. The military academies, for example, have recently begun to admit women. *Owen Franken/Stock, Boston.*

at first glance to have considerable popular support in clichés describing the woman who succeeds in masculine fields—pushy, mannish, hard, cold, perhaps a lesbian or a castrating bitch. It also appears to be reflected in the fact that both males and females have been found to attribute men's success to ability and effort; women's success to luck.

Many researchers, however, have since studied this so-called fear of success and found it in widely varying percentages of women—and equal numbers of men. Women may not fear success so much as anticipate the difficulties of juggling several roles. Studies have shown that high female achievers have several things in common. They had strong support from their parents, especially their fathers.[49] They had more liberal conceptions of sex roles than those who settled for traditional occupations.[50] And they had high self-esteem. Apparently, self-esteem is highest among both males and females who are highly motivated to achieve and who have a sex role identification closer to the masculine stereotype. But which comes first, achievement or self-esteem?

One study suggests that high self-esteem gives a woman freedom to deviate from the feminine role and creates a "salutary circle" (as opposed to a vicious circle). Her strong achievement motive and effort build up her self-esteem, which in turn creates confidence that allows her to achieve more.[51]

If there are highly motivated, bright women, where are the great creative female geniuses? Many potential ones may still be juggling roles. And many more have probably been frustrated because opportunities have been either closed to women or considerably less open to them.

SELF-ACTUALIZATION AND EMOTIONAL EXPRESSION Men are trained to be competent, cool, tough, dominant, and successful—in careers for the middle class, and in providing for the family through jobs for the working class. If bright and aspiring women feel their ambitions stifled by a patriarchal system, it is equally true that men's emotional expressiveness is discouraged and their emotional development is stunted.

American boys are taught early that "Men don't cry." They must be tough and not ask for help. If a man *does* cry, he is branded a weakling. Senator Muskie dropped out of the presidential primaries in 1972 after shedding tears in public, provoked by malicious attacks on his wife. If a man *does* admit that he was depressed and sought professional help, he may pay a high price, as did Senator Eagleton in 1972 when he was asked to resign his candidacy for vice president. But if you do neither, you are, in Warren Farrell's phrase, "emotionally constipated," with no outlet but ulcers.[52] In some societies, such as Italy, men are allowed to shed tears and to embrace one another. The upwardly striving American middle-class male generally, however, may use his inexpressiveness to help him win and maintain a position of power and privilege.

Women's freedom to express their emotions may to some extent act as a safety valve, although statistics on mental illness indicate it often fails. Many women use this freedom to get their way, manipulating others by acting helpless and turning on the tears. (If they used male tactics to get their way, they would be called pushy and aggressive.) Two hundred fifty college students revealed sex role patterns in essays on "How I get my

[49] Vaughn Crandall et al., "Parents' Attitudes and Behaviors and Grade-School Children's Academic Achievements, *"Journal of Genetic Psychology"* 104 (March 1964): 53–66.

[50] Letitia Anne Peplau, "Impact of Fear of Success and Self-Role Attitudes on Women's Competitive Achievement," *Journal of Personality and Social Psychology* 34, 4 (1976): 561–568.

[51] Anne B. Stericker and James E. Johnson, "Sex-Role Identification and Self-Esteem in College Students: Do Men and Women Differ?" *Sex Roles* 3 (February 1977): 19–26.

[52] *The Liberated Man,* p. 66.

way." Almost half the women, but only 27 percent of the men, said they deliberately showed emotion, and women mentioned 75 percent of the negative expressions of emotions listed—such as pouting, sulking, and crying. Half the men, but only a fifth of the women, mentioned anger. "Feminine wiles" are not necessarily more effective than nonfeminine strategies. When students were asked to rate the effectiveness of a woman who tried to get her way by acting helpless and that of one who claimed to be an expert, they at first judged the helpless woman to be slightly more effective. But after her second attempt they found her considerably less successful and no more likable than the more aggressive woman.[53]

Not only do men build up tension by keeping emotions bottled up, but the ban on self-disclosure also means that they fail to develop insight and empathy. Socialized to act impersonally, they come to *feel* impersonal and detached. This detachment and

lack of empathy affects all their relationships with others, including friends and family.

Stereotypes encourage men to see women as sexual objects, to be highly aware of a woman's figure, face, and clothes. This interferes with their ability to relate to her as a whole person. From the adolescent dating game onward, they feel they have to prove themselves dominant. They are expected to "perform" well. Women, on the other hand, learn to use sex manipulatively, to gain other ends. All these attitudes diminish sensitivity and awareness. The masculine lack of insight and empathy can make them incompetent at demonstrating affection and love. It can also make them difficult to love. "Some men," says a clinical psychologist, "are so skilled at dissembling, at 'seeming,' that even their wives will not know when they are lonely, bored, anxious, in pain, thwarted, hungering for affection. And the men, blocked by pride, dare not disclose their despair or their need."[54]

[53] Paula B. Johnson and Jacqueline D. Goodschilds, "How Women Get Their Way," *Psychology Today* (October 1976): 69–70.

[54] Sidney Jourard, *The Transparent Self* (New York: D. Van Nostrand, 1971).

The Women's Liberation Movement has protested beauty contests for perpetuating many of the traditional female stereotypes. *Steve Lacey/Design Photographers International, Inc.*

Even so, men are much more likely to turn to women than to male friends for comfort and reassurance. Most male friendships remain on a fairly superficial level. Only certain carefully prescribed kinds of intimate interaction are permitted between men, particularly in mainstream American culture. A man cannot enjoy "a purely friendly relationship with a woman since he, she, or society, and probably all three, will distort the relationship by assuming it is a sexual one." Similarly, the masculine stereotype "taints a man's friendships with other men with the fear of homosexuality. That fear makes men excessively wary of their friendly reactions to other men and sets narrow limits on the way they permit themselves to show whatever love the competitive spirit allows them to feel for other men."[55]

The stereotyped assumption that women stay home to keep house and look after the children while men work to bring home the bacon—along with the belief in a "maternal instinct"—has freed (or robbed?) many fathers of close relationships with their children. They are supposed to be good fathers, but the competitive race of middle-class strivers leaves them little time or energy for it. Doing things with the kids does not necessarily mean communicating with them.

While it takes a rugged physique to offset the disadvantage of a creative talent in boys, we have already noted obstacles to creativity in girls. This is especially true as they approach adulthood and begin to anticipate role strain. Creativity often springs from a certain spontaneity and playfulness that is stifled by the limits of sex roles. Boys and men rarely play for the pure joy of the game; they are out to win. And in the bureaucracy where so many American middle-class males find their careers, spontaneity is discouraged and conformity exacted.

Despite masculine dominance, the male ego is notoriously fragile. A man's identity and self-esteem rest on gainful employment or career success, sexual potency, and enviable social status. When age or other circumstances rob him of any or all of these, he no longer sees himself as manly and worthwhile. Sidney Jourard sees this as another lethal aspect of the male role. A man's loss of self-esteem may lead to suicide or to premature illness and death. Women, he hypothesizes, continue to find meaning in life longer than do men, and that is one reason they live longer.[56]

Changing Perceptions of Sex Roles

The "sexual revolution" and "women's liberation" indicate fundamental changes in sex roles and relationships. Many fear that they mean a reversal of roles, that it will become a "woman's world" instead of a "man's world." But most social scientists and psychologists believe that men, and society as a whole, have as much to gain as women. There is talk not only of women's liberation, but also of "men's liberation" and of "human liberation." Safilios-Rothschild says, "Liberation of men and women requires that they act according to their wishes, inclinations, potentials, abilities, and needs rather than according to the prevailing stereotypes about sex roles and sex-appropriate modes of thought and behavior. . . . The liberation of society . . . means that the different social institutions and the prevailing social-structural conditions will be such that they permit men and women to take options for which they are most inclined and best fit, rather than make choices as sex-stereotyped roles dictate."[57]

---

[55] Money and Tucker, *Sexual Signatures*, p. 200.

[56] *The Transparent Self.*
[57] *Women and Social Policy,* p. 7.

Sex role steretotypes are changing. Home economics classes are not necessarily all female. *Mimi Forsyth/Monkmeyer Press Photo Service.*

Factors Influencing Changes in Sex Roles and Relationships

While the women's liberation movement is often given most of the credit for change, it appears rather that education and employment operate to change attitudes. As attitudes change, further advances occur in occupation and employment which in turn increase attitudinal changes. Such changes have been rapid and pervasive in the present decade. A team of sociologists studying five surveys taken between 1964 and 1974 found, for example, that in the 1970s attitudes changed at approximately the same rate among women of all educational and socioeconomic levels. Only one teenage girl in four interviewed in 1976 wanted to be "just a housewife."[58] These attitudes in turn help explain the rise of the movement.

In recent years women have been entering masculine fields of study and work at a much faster rate than during past decades. Women are also entering traditionally blue-collar jobs. They drive cabs, deliver mail, pump gas, repair telephone lines, enter military academies and police departments, and even mine coal and work as carpenters.

Technology has made it easier for women to enter such occupations. Sheer physical strength is no longer necessary in many lines of work, and in any case, many women are stronger than many men. Labor-saving devices in the home, smaller families, and longer life expectancy, as well as the increasing need to support families, have all encouraged women to seek work outside the home.

Women's protests against discrimination, especially when accompanied by effective organization and lobbying and other pressures, have resulted in greater opportunities in the academic world. Publishers and educators are now extremely conscious of sexism in texts. Writers and illustrators are often given detailed guidelines to keep new books as free as possible of both racism and sexism. But the elimination of sexism from books is not enough. It must also be eliminated from curricula, vocational counseling, and sports. More honest sex education at home and in school may help provide the strong gender identity that is essential to a feeling

[58] Karen Oppenheim Mason et al., "Change in U.S. Women's Sex-Role Attitudes, 1964–74," *American Sociological Review* 41 (August 1976): 573–596.

of confidence that allows flexibility in sex roles and relationships.

Sex Roles and Social Policy

Laws and regulations may not be *sufficient* to change things very much. The early feminist movement and the granting of the vote to women have shown that legal steps make little difference unless attitudes change and people are ready for liberation. But often laws and regulations are *necessary* to break through discrimination patterns. Other social policies, not necessarily defined by law, are also needed to liberate social

While "Husband Liberation" may only be a reaction against the Women's Liberation Movement, the transition to more liberated sex roles is clearly important for both men and women. *Elinor S. Beckwith.*

structure, norms, and social institutions. Changes in attitudes, patterns of socialization, and family relationships are also necessary but not sufficient. They have to go hand in hand with changes in social policy.

As just one example of sexist policy, the handling of rape victims is such that many women are accused of provoking the attack, and their testimony is usually doubted. If the victim knew the rapist previously, or is known to have violated the double standard of sex behavior at any time, the attacker is almost always acquitted. Lack of evidence—especially of witnesses—is usually given as grounds for acquittal.

Because housework and child care are perceived as the main obstacles to women's jobs and especially to professional careers, social policies to allow part-time work, to give both mothers and fathers leave from work to care for children, and to provide adequate child-care centers would help relieve working mothers of their double burden. Sweden already has such laws, and some men have opted for the role of "househusband," preferring, at least for a time, to reverse roles, with the wife as provider.

"Affirmative action" laws are based on the premise that women, like blacks, have been discriminated against for so long that for a time they will need special help (reverse discrimination) to overcome their disadvantages. The Department of Health, Education, and Welfare, for example, requires public colleges and universities to plan affirmative action to employ a more equitable number of women at all levels and in all fields within a certain period, under penalty of withdrawal of federal funds.

The Transition to New Roles and Relationships

In her book, *Women and Social Policy,* Safilios-Rothschild emphasizes that the transition to more liberated roles is a slow and painful process. It is during the transition period that law and social policy are most important. She believes, for example, that attendance of both boys and girls in home economics, child care, industrial arts, and pre-vocational courses should be compulsory for a time. Once prevailing sex stereotypes about housework, child care, and outside occupations have been broken down to some extent, free choice of courses can be restored.

Both men and women resist changes. Some members of both sexes call "women's libbers" neurotic, angry, and, worst of all, "unfeminine." A survey of 890 men and 616 women found that "only a small proportion of men are truly threatened by the movement, but only a small proportion are truly in favor of it; most are caught in the easy middle ground, where attitudes are liberal and behavior is traditional." The most conservative women in the sample were housewives whose husbands did not want them to work. They were the most likely to believe that the children of working mothers are maladjusted and the least likely to support day-care centers and shared housekeeping. The researcher, Carol Tavris, found that attitudes and values are the best predictors of male support of or resistance to the women's movement. The more liberal men were in politics and religion and the more

strongly they believed that sex differences are learned and not innate, the more they supported it. For women, on the other hand, experience—"with discrimination, with work, with sexism, with the difficulties of combining work and marriage"—had the strongest influence on their support of the movement.[59]

Even men who are intellectually for liberation find it hard to overcome the effects of traditional patterns of socialization—to divide housework, child care, and economic responsibility, for example. This is much easier for those now in their teens and twenties to accept. Many men, however, support women's liberation not only on intellectual grounds but because they feel it can help free them. It can widen their own options as well as those of women.

It seems clear, then, that more flexibility in sex roles and greater freedom in relationships with others of the same sex as well as of the opposite sex is coming about. Many changes have fostered it—changes in attitudes, social structure, technology, family size, and the economy. In turn, new perceptions of sex roles promise to allow members of both sexes a greater latitude of options in work, play, parenthood, friendship, love, and self-actualization.

Summary

In most societies sex roles, definitions of what it means to be male or female, are very clear. They program behavior and guide interaction throughout life. And in most, sexism—discrimination against one sex, almost always women, with male dominance and female submissiveness—is practiced.

The basic biological differences are that only women can menstruate, get pregnant and give birth to children, and give milk, while only men can make them pregnant.

Other traits predominate in one sex or the other, but there is a great deal of overlap. Certain behavioral differences similarly overlap, though they appear more often in one sex, possibly due to different hormone levels.

Anthropologists stress the great variety rather than the uniformity in behavior and

[59]"Who Likes Women's Liberation—and Why: The Case of the Unliberated Liberals," *Journal of Social Issues* 29 (1973): 175–198.

traits seen as "masculine" or "feminine" in various societies. Society reinforces inborn predispositions, but most sex role stereotypes are based on groundless beliefs about innate differences. Although they are changing, they tend to persist even in the face of evidence that they are largely false.

Gender identity is your sense of yourself as male or female and is central to your self-conception. Although almost always in agreement with biological sex, both gender identity and sex roles are learned through identification with models, through formal and informal socialization by others, and through self-socialization. Boys feel more pressure than girls to behave according to the prescribed role. Peer groups, schools, churches, and the mass media all reinforce cultural sex role stereotypes.

Sexism has many negative consequences, especially for women. Women have more mental illness, possibly in part as a result of the constrictions of their role, but also because the definition of mental health is a masculine one. Women also have more physical illness, both chronic and acute, than men. On the other hand they have a longer life expectancy. Women are more likely to attempt suicide, men to commit it. Housewives lead all other categories in both attempted and completed suicides.

Women have fewer opportunities and less motivation for the high educational, occupational, and political achievement that bring wealth, power, and prestige. Occupations are largely segregated by sex, and within an occupation women have lower status and income than men. They are discriminated against for professional training in academic fields, law, and medicine. But comparatively few women aspire to high professional achievement. While this fact has been attributed to a fear of success, it appears that more often it is based on a realistic assessment of the difficulties of juggling the roles of wife, mother, homemaker, and career woman.

Women now make up 41 percent of the United States labor force. Most women employed outside the home are married and over 40 years old. They represent all social classes. Employed wives have greater feelings of competence and self-esteem than do full-time housewives. But the latter are more happily married. The unhappiest group, largely of the working class, are women who want jobs but cannot get or take them for various reasons.

Sex role stereotypes have important consequences for personality. They stress achievement and dominance in males; femininity and passivity in females. As a result, they put such pressure on males to succeed in sports, sex, and careers that many have a high level of anxiety. At the same time they stifle emotional expression, notably in the American middle-class male, and encourage women to use displays of emotion to manipulate men.

Sex roles and relationships are changing rapidly, and the change has accelerated since the early 1970s. Women are entering traditionally masculine professional fields as well as blue-collar occupations at an increasing rate. Such measures as elimination of sex discrimination in employment and of sexism from books and the mass media have made some progress. But transition to liberation of women, men, and society from oppressive and dehumanizing sex stereotypes is a slow and painful process.

Glossary

Gender identity   A person's sense of self as male or female.

Sex roles   Social definitions of what it means to be male or female.

Sexism   Prejudice and discrimination against people (usually women) on the basis of their sex.

part

4

Population and the Urban Trend

chapter

12

Population and Ecology

A recent television program on the energy crisis was called "We Will Freeze in the Dark." An overly dramatic title, to be sure, but the implications are real. The resources of this planet—space, soil, water, and minerals—are limited. The earth's atmosphere is fragile. We have exploited the natural wealth of our planet, and our population has grown too great to be supported comfortably on what remains.

The problems of population and environment are very complex. All five systems in which human social behavior takes place—culture, social organization, personality, the human organism, and the ecosystem—are involved. Our emphasis in this chapter is on the human organism in terms of population and on the ecosystem in relation to population pressures and other aspects of human social behavior. What do demographers and ecologists tell us about our future? What do sociologists and others offer in the way of possible solutions?

Demography

The word "demography" comes from the Greek words *demos* (people) and *grapho* (written descriptions; lists). **Demography** is the science concerned with describing human populations. *Formal demography* concentrates on the mathematical and statistical interrelationships of demographic variables. *Social demography,* on the other hand, focuses on how social and cultural factors are related to population structure and processes. When describing a population, demographers look at its size, composition, and distribution in a given area. They are also interested in how populations change. Rates of fertility, mortality, and migration, for example, are important demographic variables.

The *composition* of a population can have important social consequences. For example, demographers can determine a population's **sex ratio**—the number of males compared to the number of females. If there are fewer males about age 20–25 compared to females 15–20, there is a "marriage squeeze." Men generally marry women a few years younger than they are, and thus many women will be without husbands. Another important measure is the **dependency ratio,** which compares the number of people under 15 years and over 65 to the 15–64 age group of the population. High dependency ratios, where large numbers are too young or old to work, indicate that much of what is produced by those age 15–64 must go toward support of dependents rather than economic growth.

The composition of a population can be shown as an "age-sex pyramid" (see Figure 12-1). This pyramid can take many different shapes, reflecting different birth rates, death rates, and sex ratios. It is a graphic way of showing where the populations of different countries stand at any one time or how a single country's population has changed over time. For example, the pyra-

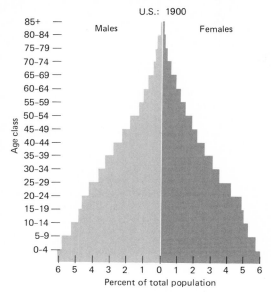

(A) U.S. POPULATION OF 1900 had the age composition shown in this pyramid. Its shape is characteristic of a fast-growing population with high birth and death rates where the average life expectancy is under 60. A third of Americans were under 15 years of age.

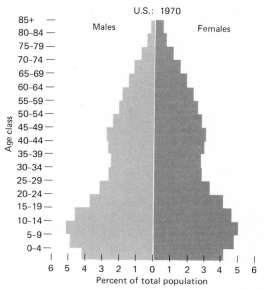

(B) U.S. POPULATION OF 1970 gave rise to a pyramid whose sides are pinched in because of low birth rates that prevailed during the years of the Great Depression. The bulge centered on the 10 to 14 year old age group is a consequence of the postwar baby boom.

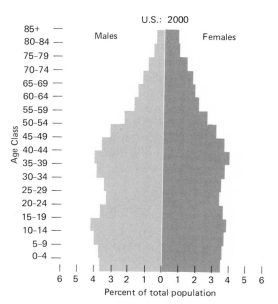

(C) U.S. POPULATION OF YEAR 2000 will form this age pyramid if fertility stabilizes at replacement levels from now until the end of the century. Five to 19 year olds of 1970, who will then be 30 years older, will have produced a second bulge of 5 to 19 year olds.

Figure 12-1 Age-sex pyramids for the United States, 1900, 1970, and 2000. *From Charles F. Westoff, "The Populations of the Developed Countries." Copyright © September, 1974 by Scientific American, Inc. All rights reserved.*

mid of U.S. population in 1900 is typical of countries that have rapidly growing populations with high rates of birth and death. The 1970 pyramid, on the other hand, shows several changes. The narrowed base indicates a decrease in the birth rate. The bulge just above that represents the postwar baby boom, while the "waist" of the pyramid indicates a decrease in the birthrate due to the Depression. If we have zero population growth from now until the year 2000, our population will look as it does in the last pyramid in Figure 12-1.

Another basic demographic concept is **fertility,** the amount of reproduction actually achieved (which is distinguished from *fecundity,* or reproductive capacity). The **fer-**

tility rate is the number of births per 1,000 women of reproductive age, usually limited to ages 15–45. Demographers also calculate specific fertility rates for age groups, such as 20–24 and 25–29. The birth rate, however, is indicated in terms of the population as a whole: so many live births per 1,000 population.[1] (This is often called the gross or *crude birth rate* because it includes people not exposed to the risk of childbearing.) Death rates may be similarly calculated for the population as a whole, for each sex, or for age, ethnic, and other groups.

The rate of natural increase of a population is the difference between the crude birth rate and the crude death rate. Thus the world's crude death rate of 12, subtracted from its crude birth rate of 30, gives us a natural increase of 18 per 1,000. This is usually converted into a percentage or annual *growth rate,* in this case 1.8 percent. The population of any one country may also fluctuate because of migration. Thus the rate of natural increase for the United States was 0.8 percent in 1976, but immigration brought total population increase to 1.0 percent.[2]

Demographic facts affect the market for wedding gowns, bedroom furniture, high chairs, and coffins, as well as the political orientation of a society. In this chapter, however, we are concerned primarily with the overwhelming demographic fact of the "population explosion" and its consequences for the human race.

---

[1] No known society has a birth rate that reaches the upper limits of human fecundity, estimated at about 70 per 1,000, or about twice the world's present crude birth rate. [Shirley Foster-Hartley, *Population: Quantity vs. Quality* (Englewood Cliffs, N.J.: Prentice-Hall, 1972), p. 40.]

[2] Bureau of the Census, *Current Population Reports,* 1 (Series P-20, No. 292, March 1976), "Population Profile of the United States," Table 2.

The Growth of the Human Population

"All that tread / the globe," said the poet, "are but a handful to the tribes / That slumber in its bosom."[3] If we date the appearance of *Homo sapiens* at 600,000 years ago, a reasonable guess is that 77 billion members of the species have walked the earth, only about 12 billion of them before 6000 B.C. If we accept a date a million years earlier, then there have been 96 billion humans, 32 billion of whom lived before 6000 B.C. Today's 4 billion inhabitants of the globe are probably no more than 4 percent of all who have ever lived.[4]

The Population Explosion

The human population grew very slowly for many thousands of years (see Figure 12-2). Perhaps 5 to 10 million people existed at the beginning of the agricultural era, and somewhere between 200 and 400 million at the time of Christ. Not until 1650 A.D. did the world's population reach half a billion. Even a very low rate of annual increase could have given us today's huge population, but there were numerous setbacks—wars, famines, and epidemics. During relatively stable periods, birth rates of at least 35 per 1,000 and probably as high as 40 to 50 soon replaced the losses.[5]

As long as death rates remained high, the growth rate of the population stayed

---

[3] William Cullen Bryant, "Thanatopsis."

[4] Robert C. Cook, ed., "How Many People Have Ever Lived on Earth?" *Population Bulletin,* Population Reference Bureau, 18, No. 1 (Feb. 1962).

[5] *The World Population Situation in 1970.* United Nations Department of Social and Economic Affairs, Population Studies, No. 49 (1971): 6.

low. Up to 1750, it probably averaged considerably less than 0.1 percent a year; from 1750 to 1900, about 0.5 percent; from 1900 to 1950, about 1 percent. At present, the growth rate is about 2 percent. This does not at first glance seem very high. But "if the human race had begun with a single couple at the time of Christ, and had grown steadily at 2 percent per year since then, there would now be 20 million people alive on the earth today! That would be the equivalent of 100 people per square foot of the earth's surface."[6]

Because of this accelerated growth rate, the doubling time of the world's population has become shorter and shorter (see Table 12-1). It took 200 years, from 1650 to 1850, to double from a half-billion to a billion.

[6] Hartley, *Population*, p. 4, citing calculations by the Population Council, 1965.

In only 75 years it had doubled again. "According to the best demographic estimates, the world's present population of 4 billion may reach nearly 7 billion by the end of the century, and may go as high as 12 billion before levelling off. It is doubling, at the present rate, every 37 years."[7] United Nations demographers predict that the 1970s may show the highest rate of growth in history.[8]

[7] Lester Brown et al., *Twenty-two Dimensions of the Population Problem* (Washington, D.C.: Worldwatch Institute Paper No. 5, 1976).

[8] *The World Population Situation in 1970*, p. 46.

Figure 12-2 The growth of the human population through history. *From B. Berelson, et al., "World Population: Status Report 1974. A Guide for the Concerned Citizen," Reports on Population/Family Planning, No. 15, January, 1974. By permission of the Population Council.*

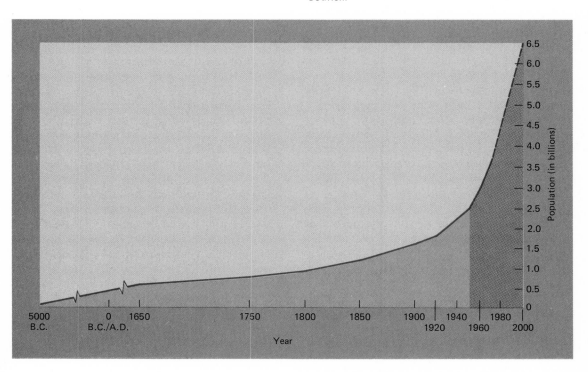

Table 12-1   Doubling Times at Various Rates of Increase

Annual Percent Increase	Doubling Time (Years)
0.001	70,000
0.01	7,000
0.05	1,400
0.1	700
0.3	240
0.7	100
1.0	70
2.0	35
3.0	24
5.0	14
7.0	10
10.0	7

SOURCE: Norman D. Levine, "Demography and Human Population Dynamics," in *Human Ecology* (North Scituate, Mass,: Duxbury Press, 1975), Table 11.1, p. 271.

"Demographic Transition"

Aside from immigration and emigration, when only enough people are born to replace those who die, the population is considered to be stable. The society is said to have **zero population growth (ZPG).** For many thousands of years death rates were so high that birth rates also had to be high if the population were to grow at all. When death rates decline, there is, for a time, a "demographic gap" between high birth rates and low death rates. At first the population grows rapidly. Then birth rates begin to follow death rates downward. The shift from a balance of high birth and death rates (through a period of growth as declining death rates create an imbalance between fertility and mortality) to a new balance of low birth and death rates, is called the **demographic transition.** Rapid population growth ends when this transition is complete. Such a demographic transition has been seen in some highly developed modern societies, but not in all.

Many other countries have never gone through the transition.

Historically, death rates have declined because of five factors.[9]

1. Increased production and an improved level of living
2. The emergence of a stable government over larger areas, with better distribution of goods and services
3. Environmental sanitation
4. Improved personal hygiene
5. Modern medicine and public health programs

In 1650, when the first dramatic rise in population began, the death rate was about 40 per 1,000 population per year. The first two factors caused the population to double during the following 200 years. These factors have accounted for perhaps a third of the population increase since 1650. All five factors have been responsible for growth since 1850. But the fifth—medicine and public health—is the chief cause of the population explosion since World War II.

The theorists who popularized the concept of the demographic transition emphasized that economic development, industrialization, and urbanization caused not only the initial decline in mortality but also a decline in fertility in the early twentieth century. And indeed at about the time of World War II, low birth rates in Western industrialized nations appeared to bear out the theory. But after the war, fertility rose sharply, especially in the United States, even though affluence, urbanization, and industrialization increased greatly (see Figure 12-3). Those who saw economic development as *the* solution to the population explosion were forced to reexamine their assumptions. The death rate in what UN experts

[9] Philip M. Hauser, ed., *The Population Dilemma,* for the American Assembly of Columbia University, 2nd ed. (Englewood Cliffs, N.J.: Prentice-Hall, 1969).

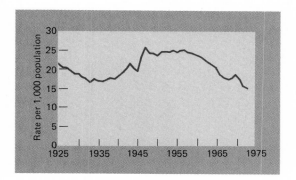

Figure 12-3 U.S. crude birth rate, 1925–1972. *From "Vital Statistics Rates: 1925–1973," Statistical Abstract of the United States, 1974, U.S. Bureau of the Census.*

call "the more developed nations" is now generally below 10, with a life expectancy at birth of about 70 years. But the birth rate is about 18. Thus even industrialized societies have not completed the demographic transition and will grow in population at an annual rate of at least 1 percent during the 1970s.[10] As Table 12-1 shows, 1 percent annual growth rate would result in a doubling time of 70 years.

Population Growth in Preindustrial Societies

The greatest growth in population, however, is occurring in less developed regions. Two out of three of the earth's inhabitants now live in underdeveloped areas. By the end of the century, at present growth rates, 77 percent will live in such areas. There will be at least 4 billion Asians, half a billion Africans, and 600 million Latin Americans.[11] The main reason for this is that since World

[10] *The World Population Situation in 1970,* p. 18.

[11] Georg Borgstrom, *Too Many: A Study of Earth's Biological Limitations* (London: Macmillan, 1969), p. 318.

War II the more developed nations have exported "death control" with great success. Although living standards have not generally risen, death rates have fallen dramatically because of such modern public health measures as vaccines, antibiotics, and insecticides. In the first postwar decade, for example, the World Health Organization helped cut the death rate in Ceylon from 20.3 to 11. The use of DDT cut the death rate from malaria alone by 70 percent. In just one year, 1946, the death rate fell 34 percent.[12]

But birth rates have not followed death rates downward.[13] They average about 40 in the less developed regions, and in some areas are as high as 50–54. At a 2 percent increase per year, population doubles in 35 years. Current growth rates in less developed regions are 2.7 percent. Countries with especially high rates include Kuwait with 5.9 percent, Libya with 3.7 percent, Mexico with 3.5 percent, and Kenya and Rhodesia with 3.4 percent. Such high growth rates may temporarily result in lower death rates than in industrialized nations because of the high proportion of young people. The young also provide the dynamite for further population explosions. The crucial effect of high birth rates combined with low death rates is that more female children survive to bear children of their own, and their daughters in turn live to child-bearing age.

[12] Although this drop in the death rate is the main cause of the population explosion, health measures have also increased fecundity (reproductive capacity) by reducing sterility due to venereal disease, improving general health, lengthening life spans, and lowering the age of puberty. The result has been a slight rise in fertility, or actual production of offspring. Hartley, *Population,* p. 41.

[13] U.N. experts report the world birth rate as 33.8 per year between 1965–1970. It was 18.6 in the more developed and 40.6 in the less developed regions. In North America, Europe, and Japan, it was between 17.5 and 19.4; in Africa, 46.8; in Central America, 45; in South Asia, 44.3; and in Latin America as a whole, 38.4. *The World Population Situation in 1970,* p. 18.

Predictions of Population Trends

One basis for *projections* into the future is assuming that present trends will continue. But this is not what demographers do. They make alternative assumptions about future rates. Then, on this basis, they give a range of projections within which they expect the actual situation to be. UN experts, for example, make high, medium, and low projections. But recent high projections have proved consistently low as the projected dates were reached. In 1958, for example, they predicted that by 1980 Africa would have 333 million people. That figure was reached in 1969—in half the time. Using the medium projection, based on the assumption that growth will continue at about 2 percent until about 1985 and gradually decline thereafter, they predict a world population of nearly 6.5 billion in the year 2000.[14] Many other demographers consider this also an underestimate.

Many projections of world population trends read like horror stories, predicting "standing room only" in a few generations. *At present growth rates* there would be nearly 14 billion people on earth by 2050 A.D., averaging 265 per square mile as compared to an estimated density of 74 in 1975. Some predict 30 billion 100 years from now. But, they add, if we do not intervene drastically to prevent this from becoming a reality, the death rate will climb again because of hunger, disease, and war.

Paul Ehrlich, author of *The Population Bomb* among other books, insists there is no reason for complacency in short-term indications of a decline in fertility. The future mothers of a far greater population are already born, which means that even at low growth rates stability would not be achieved for many decades. Even if it were reached

[14] *The World Population Situation in 1970*, p. 45.

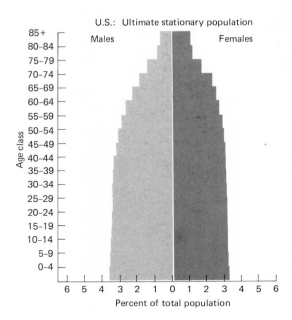

Figure 12-4 Zero population growth in the United States. *From Charles F. Westoff, "The Populations of the Developed Countries." Copyright © September, 1974 by Scientific American, Inc. All rights reserved.*

immediately, it would take until 2037 for the United States to complete the demographic transition.[15] Some people who are pessimistic about population trends admittedly *prefer* to sound the alarm, because awareness of the consequences of high rates may in itself help prevent them from continuing.

Others are more optimistic. Donald Bogue insists that fertility control programs are beginning to pay off, that the pace of population growth began to slacken in about 1965 and will continue to decline with each passing year as such programs take increasing effect. He expects zero or near zero population growth rates to be reached by

[15] *The New York Times* (Jan. 14, 1971), quoting Conrad Taueber, chief demographer of the Census Bureau.

the end of the century. "It is quite reasonable to assume," he insists, "that the world population crisis is a phenomenon of the 20th century, and will be largely if not entirely a matter of history when humanity moves into the 21st century."[16] He attributes this prospect to changed public attitudes, aroused political leadership, and accelerated professional and research activity. He also cites a slackening in death control as the more easily preventable diseases decline and solutions for other health problems remain difficult or unknown. Social-psychological motivation, communication about fertility control, and improved contraceptive methods are also important factors.

While few demographers share Bogue's optimism, there is some indication of a decline in fertility in the United States and elsewhere. Views on ideal family size have been found to be accurate predictors of long-term trends in the birth rate. Now Americans apparently want smaller families than formerly. If each woman had 2.1 children, ZPG would eventually be achieved.

Married women age 18 to 24 surveyed in 1967 expected to have 2.9 babies; in 1971, a similar group 2.4. In 1967, only 44 percent wanted 2 or less; in 1971, 62 percent. According to the Gallup poll, in 1945 nearly 50 percent of the American adults polled favored families of 4 or more children (and the following years saw the baby boom). It was 40 percent in 1967, and only 23 percent in 1971. The younger adults tend to be more strongly in favor of smaller families.[17] Having families of 2 children or less can make quite a difference. With an average 2-child family, our population would increase by about 350 million people in a hundred years. The simple addition of one extra child per family would give us a population increase of nearly a billion people by then.[18]

However, ZPG in the United States will not make a big dent in the world's population. High growth in the less developed countries produces the high growth rate in the world. A number of such countries, however, show a decline in birth rates in

---

[16] "The End of the Population Explosion," *The Public Interest* (Spring 1967). See also his *Principles of Demography* (New York: John Wiley & Sons, 1969).

[17] *The New York Times* (Feb. 17, 1972).
[18] *Population and the American Future: The Report of the Commission on Population Growth and the American Future* (New York: New American Library, 1972), pp. 19–20.

Young American adults tend to prefer small families. *Mimi Forsyth/Monkmeyer Press Photo Service.*

recent years, whether or not they permit abortion (which is the chief means, legal or illegal, of fertility control around the world). The change in Costa Rica, for example, may be particularly significant because of its traditionally high birth rate and its great pride in it. From 45 in 1938 and 49.2 in 1953, the rate declined to 43 in 1965 and 33.9 in 1969.[19] In 1976, it was 29.5.[20]

Even if we are inclined to accept the more optimistic projections, the size of the existing population and the fact that so many future mothers are already alive put a stable world population far in the future.

Consequences of Population Growth

The consequences of demographic trends are complex. Let us consider, first, what happens when mortality declines in a society. Then, let us look at the impact of the current population explosion on society, culture, and personality.

David M. Heer outlines several changes that appear to follow a drop in the death rate, warning that much of what he suggests is speculative and should be investigated. Pointing out how often American families were broken by death in the past, he notes that "contemporary citizens of developed nations rarely encounter death, except among the aged."[21] The institutions of mourning have consequently declined. Norms of behavior for the bereaved and their friends are no longer clear. Rituals are lacking, and people tend to act as if the death had not occurred. Religion has shifted from an other-worldly to a this-worldly emphasis, and general concern with immortality has declined. Families are smaller and more independent of relatives, more mobile, more isolated from the larger kin group.

In societies where mortality is high, on the other hand, arranged marriages are common. Possibly interpersonal ties such as those between parents and young children are less intense, as if parents feared becoming too attached. In low-mortality societies marriage is typically by free choice, and emotional ties are intense. Since it is likely that the couple have many years ahead of them, there is also pressure for easier divorce. Members of high-mortality societies may tend to discount the future and enjoy the present. They may be reluctant to make sacrifices for their children's education or to give up present enjoyment for other future goals, which death may prevent. Finally, when the death rate drops, people tend to have fewer children, partly because they realize that there is more likelihood that those they do have will grow to maturity.

Growth in sheer number of members in a society has historically been associated with power, success, and security. But for most societies, and certainly for the world as a whole, the current population explosion is a cause for great concern and alarm. Even an optimist like Bogue foresees some years of "acute crisis" immediately ahead for several nations, including India, China, the Philippines, Indonesia, Pakistan, Mexico, Brazil, and Egypt. Unless international emergency measures are taken, there will probably be severe famines in some areas. Others, notably Ehrlich, call the "population bomb" a threat to world peace and order, a barrier to economic development, a menace to the quality of life, and even a danger to the survival of all life on the planet.

The unequal distribution of the good things of life and the absolute deprivation of millions create misery and unrest. In spite of "the Green Revolution," which developed new and higher-yielding grains, "the limits of human capability to produce food by conventional means have very nearly been reached. Problems of supply and distribution

---

[19] *Information Please Almanac* (1972), p. 636.
[20] Census Bureau: San Jose, Costa Rica, July, 1977.
[21] *Society and Population* (Englewood Cliffs, N.J.: Prentice-Hall, 1968), p. 43.

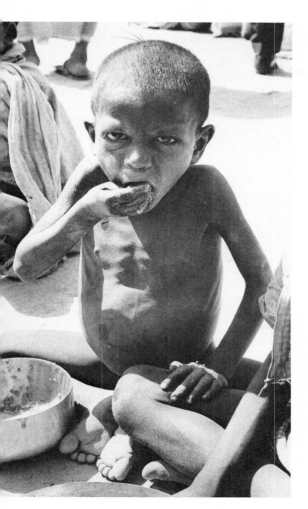

This starving child is one of many millions in the world. *Marilyn Silverstone/Magnum.*

already have resulted in roughly half of humanity being undernourished or malnourished. Some 10–20 million people are starving to death annually now. . . . There is reason to believe that population growth increases the probability of a lethal worldwide plague and of a thermonuclear war."[22]

[22] Paul R. Ehrlich and Anne H. Ehrlich, *Population, Resources, Environment: Issues in Human Ecology* (San Francisco: W. H. Freeman, 1970), pp. 321–322.

A growing population demands resources that might otherwise be invested in economic development and may consume any increase in production, making modernization impossible. In many underdeveloped countries, 40–45 percent of the people are under age 15, as compared to a maximum of 23–30 percent in industrialized nations. This means that people in the productive ages have many others to support. Typically they are peasants with a small patch of land. Where the economy is not expanding, food production may not keep pace with population growth. Then the level of living often falls. Rapid rates of growth occurred between 1960 and 1975 in such countries as India, Pakistan, Mexico, and Indonesia—countries that were already struggling with problems of economic development, and in 15 years added 40–60 percent more people. Not only food, but housing, schools, roads, medical facilities, and jobs must be provided for all these people if they are to participate in society and fulfill their potential in any measure.

Overpopulation is a menace to the quality of life in a number of ways. It is often accompanied by overcrowding, which puts pressure on facilities for housing, recreation, and medical care. Crime rates also appear to be related to high population density. Peace, privacy, dignity, aesthetic surroundings, and quiet are ever harder to come by. In a huge population it appears to be very hard to retain an emphasis on the value of each individual. Increasingly we see life becoming computerized, regulated, restricted, licensed, and dehumanized, and we hear people complaining that they are treated as mere numbers.

According to Philip Hauser, even if the population were stabilized, pollution could continue to rise through increased consumption per capita or the relaxation of efforts to cope with it. And conversely, even if population continued to increase, pollution might be decreased by reallocating re-

Overpopulation results in overcrowding and a lowered quality of life. *Douglas Corry/Design Photographers International, Inc.*

sources.[23] The President's Commission on Population Growth and the American Future sees the impact of overpopulation this way:

What are commonly referred to as population problems can be viewed more profitably as environmental, economic, political and social problems that are aggravated by population growth and density. The closest thing to a "population problem" in the pure sense is the speculation that increases in sheer density of numbers have undesirable effects on social behavior. We regard

[23] "On Population Problems and Population Policy," *Sociological Focus: On Population* 4, No. 1 (Fall 1970): 63–78.

278

population growth, however, as an intensifier or multiplier of many problems impairing the quality of life in the United States.[24]

Whatever the cause, it appears to be a lost one without some form of population control.

Ecology and Ecosystems

Ecology is the study of all forms of life and their natural settings, and of their interdependence. It raises fundamental questions about the universe and our role in it.

The *ecosphere* or environment is the thin shell around the globe on which life depends. In the *lithosphere* or earth's crust are rocks, which wear so slowly that it takes 500 years to build one inch of good topsoil. In it also lie the fossil fuels that we exploit for energy, and the minerals we use in other ways. The zone of living things is the *biosphere,* the thin, fragile, and exquisitely complex portion of the earth's crust and atmosphere that supports life. On land, it extends as deep underground as the roots of trees, as high (370 feet) as the top of the tallest redwood and as far up mountain slopes as life can exist. It includes the *hydrosphere,* the seven-tenths of earth's surface covered by oceans, where marine life teems in the upper 500 feet, and in some forms exists right down to the ocean floor. Ocean currents and evaporation are essential to life on land. The biosphere also includes the atmosphere, the blanket of gases essential to life. About two-thirds of its mass is the *troposphere,* extending about seven miles above earth, where weather is born, clouds move, and jets fly. Still higher is the *stratosphere,* extending about 25 miles above the earth. Then

[24] Interim Report (Mar. 16, 1971).

the atmosphere thins out further, and beyond it is the emptiness of space, shot through with cosmic rays from which the atmosphere protects us—empty except for a dead moon, a life-giving sun, and mysterious planets and faraway solar systems.

Within the biosphere exist any number of ecosystems. Each **ecosystem** is the sum total of living and nonliving elements that support a chain of life within a given area (and this may be as large as the global system or as small as a pond). The chain of life has four primary links.

1. Nonliving matter such as sunlight, water, oxygen, carbon dioxide, and the organic compounds and other nutrients necessary for the growth of plants

2. Plant organisms (as tiny as the microscopic phytoplankton in water, such as algae, and as huge as redwood trees) that use sunlight, carbon dioxide, and water to produce carbohydrates through the process of photosynthesis

3. Consumers, higher organisms that feed on plants, or on animals that have fed on plants, or on animals that have fed on other animals

4. Decomposers, including insects, bacteria, and fungi, that break down dead vegetable and animal matter and return their chemical compounds to the ecosystem so they can be used again by growing plants

Thus matter cycles through the ecosystem and is used again and again.

All living things, including people, depend on the cyclical processes in this chain of life. While green plants are converting carbon dioxide into food, fiber, and fuel, they are also producing oxygen (there is *no* other source) and converting inorganic nitrogen into the protein animals need. Animals in turn generate the chemicals plants need, and microorganisms break them down. Whether people are vegetarians or meateaters, "the human brain, so frail, so perishable, so full of inexhaustible dreams and hungers, burns by the power of the leaf."[25]

The global ecosystem is closed, finite, and complex. In a closed system "everything counts." Nothing is ever "consumed." If you put 20 gallons of gasoline weighing about 240 pounds into your car and drive about 300 miles you burn it up, and the tank is empty. But the gas is still in the ecosystem—now in the air, as 240 pounds of carbon dioxide, carbon monoxide, nitrogen oxide, carbon and other gases, and particles of solid matter.[26] Being finite, the ecosystem can take only so much. Being complex, it is subject to the interplay of a multitude of variables. And we have added to this complexity and interfered with its balance so drastically that many people consider the environmental problem the one overarching concern of humankind. It is a concern that cannot be divorced from many others—least of all from the population explosion.

Modernization and the Environment

Anthropologist Loren Eiseley compares the human population to a malignant fungus growth. People are aggressive "earth-eaters," out of balance with the natural world.[27] Our exploitation of our environment and the resulting pollution are two major ecological problems.

[25] Loren Eiseley, *The Unexpected Universe* (New York: Harcourt Brace Jovanovich, 1969).

[26] Harold W. Sim, Jr., "Can Man Overcome the Noah Complex?" *The Florida Naturalist* 44, No. 4A (Nov.–Dec. 1971): 1–2 ff.

[27] *The Invisible Pyramid* (New York: Scribner's, 1970).

Exploitation of Natural Resources

Our zeal to conquer nature rather than understand it and live in harmony with it is most apparent in the ruins of magnificent forests. Through carelessness, profiteering, ignorance, and the battle to provide for their families, people—especially American pioneers and robber barons—cut down the woods. We are still paying for it in loss of water reserves, erosion of soils, and ugliness, as well as in loss of the oxygen that only growing green things contribute to the biosphere.

Mineral resources are vanishing, and poorer grades of fossil fuels are now being exploited, often at great expense in pollution of the air, water, and landscape, as in strip mining. Europe is depleting its ground water reserves at three times the replacement rate; the United States at twice the rate. Tokyo is slowly sinking into the sea. Some parts have sunk 6 feet since World War II, mostly because industries pump water from underground reserves.

Latent Consequences of Modernization

The exploitation of natural resources is an obvious consequence of industrialization and has long been a subject of concern. Only recently, however, have such latent consequences as pollution, with its many ill effects, and the disturbances of the ecosystem created by dams, paving, and large-scale agriculture become alarmingly apparent. For example, on certain days in Los Angeles, smog alerts recommend that children not jump, run, or engage in athletics. DDT is found in mother's milk in higher concentration than in cow's milk. It is also found in Antarctic penguins, thousands of miles from

any place where it is sprayed. Automobiles spew 95 million tons of noxious gases and chemicals into the air of the United States each year, nearly half of all air pollution. Industrial wastes, sewage, and detergents kill organisms in lakes and rivers. Solid wastes pile up. Highways and buildings eat away at land that could be used to grow plants that would provide more oxygen and more beauty. Emphysema, a lung disease, is the fastest growing cause of death in the United States. The National Academy of Sciences has estimated that 15,000 Americans die every year because of air pollution. Noise pollution not only affects adult nerves but may even damage unborn babies. Dr. Paul Kotin, director of the National Institute of Environmental Health Sciences, estimates that a tenth of the nation's $70 billion a year for health services goes for treating illnesses resulting from environmental pollution. Americans lose another $28 billion through missed wages and the cost of compensation and rehabilitation resulting from such illnesses.[28]

The agricultural revolution, with its shift to large-scale farming with machinery, fertilizers, and insecticides, is responsible for much pollution. Nitrogen and DDT run off the land and into the waters. Species of birds become extinct. Some foods—for example, fish in Japan—become dangerous to eat. Exporting American agricultural know-how to underdeveloped countries has sometimes backfired by disturbing the ecological balance. In 1949, for example, American development interests promoted the widespread use of insecticides in the Canete Valley of Peru to raise cotton yields. "Seven years later, the cotton crop had gone down 50 percent and species of destructive insects had doubled. . . . [Later] the insecticide program

[28] *The New York Times* (Oct. 7, 1970).

was dropped in favor of biological control, which has been successful."[29]

Furthermore, above-ground nuclear testing has resulted in the presence of strontium-90 in the bones of every young person growing up since it began, and it "will be carried in the bodies of several future generations."[30]

Approaches to the Problems of Population and Pollution

The interrelated problems of population and pollution involve three major aspects. First, our exploitation of the earth's resources has become inadequate to support the world's increasing population. Second, there is unequal distribution and consumption of those resources. Third, pollution is becoming a worldwide problem. Any solution to these problems must take all three of these aspects into account.

It is generally agreed that these problems must be attacked from many angles, and on the international as well as national and local levels. But the specific means to these goals excite a great deal of controversy. Some condemn science and technology as the villains that brought about the current crisis. Others say they are the solution. Some insist that all corrective measures be strictly voluntary and based on education. Others urge governmental and institutional pressures of various kinds.

Population Control

Four solutions to the problem of population pressure are theoretically possible: an increase in the death rate, migration from overpopulated to underpopulated areas, a rise in food production sufficient to take care of the increase in population, and a decrease in the birth rate.

The first two solutions evade the problem. No one favors an increase in the death rate. Yet, as we have seen, such an increase may occur in spite of—and even because of—our scientific and technological knowledge. Migration merely shifts the problem in space and postpones the final reckoning in time. True, it did help to save Europe from starvation during its own population explosion in the eighteenth and nineteenth centuries. But there are no new Americas to populate, and even Australia is reconsidering its encouragement of immigration. Fantastic science-fiction schemes for transporting people (and garbage) to other planets are logistically ridiculous. We must settle for solving our problems where we are.

The most influential student of population the world has known was pessimistic. Thomas Malthus, an English clergyman, published his famous *Essay on Population* in 1798. Population, he said, depends on the means of subsistence but will always tend to outrun the means of subsistence. Malthus wrote that, because of the human being's strong sexual drive, population when unchecked has a tendency to double every 25 years, increasing in geometrical ratio—1, 2, 4, 8, 16, and so on. Food supplies, however, increase only in arithmetical progression, as 1, 2, 3, 4, 5, and so on.[31] Only vice, misery, poverty, famine, disease, and war keep population within bounds. In his later edition, Malthus added to these "positive checks" the idea of "preventive checks" and thus was able to "soften some of the harshest conclusions." Among these preventive checks were

[29]Robert Kahn, *The Christian Science Monitor* (Dec. 19, 1968).

[30]Barry Commoner, *Science and Survival* (New York: Viking, 1966).

[31]These ratios have not proved to be true.

late marriage, celibacy, sexual continence, and moral restraint. Although he did not have much faith in people's ability to exercise these controls, he disapproved of contraception (which "neo-Malthusians" advocate as the only ultimate solution). Thus in his view there was little to look forward to but growing populations ever subject to the evils of the positive checks. Even humanitarian efforts to help poor and starving people backfire, according to the *Malthusian dilemma.* They only result in increases in population and reduce them to a worse state of misery than before.

The only real solutions to the pressure of population growth are, then, an increase in food production—part of economic development—and a decline in the birth rate. Most demographers feel that one cannot work without the other.

How can a decline in the birth rate be achieved? Ireland offers a classic example of Malthusian principles, including the adoption of preventive checks. It also emphasizes the role of social institutions in controlling reproduction.

The Irish learned the Malthusian lesson the hard way. In 1700 they had a population of about two million. They were living in misery on small grains. Then someone introduced the potato, which was a great technical improvement, enabling a larger amount of food to be grown per acre, and indeed per man, than before. For a while the standard of life of the Irish improved, infant mortality declined, and there was a great increase in population. By 1846 there were eight million people living in misery on potatoes. Hardly any better example of the utterly dismal theorem can be found. Then came the failure in the potato crop and the great famine. Two million people died of starvation. Two million emigrated and the four million who remained had learned a lesson. The population of Ireland has increased very little in over a hundred years, partly as a result of emigration, but more as a result of limitation of births. In this case the limitation was achieved through late marriages and the imposition of a strongly puritan ethic upon the young people which seems to have the effect of strongly limiting the number of children born out of wedlock. It is striking that one of the most successful examples of population control should have taken place in a Roman Catholic country, one, however, in which Catholicism takes an unusually puritanical form.[32]

But in much of the world no such limitations are the rule. In the scale of human values, birth and death are at opposite poles. Death is feared, and death control accepted eagerly. Birth, on the other hand, has a positive value. It is a blessed event; increase and growth are good. Because high death rates long made it necessary to "be fruitful and multiply and replenish the earth," high fertility has been valued by most human societies and encouraged by religion, government, and other institutions. Children have also been a form of social security and of cheap labor. They have been proof of a man's virility and a woman's fertility, a fulfillment regarded as natural and desirable. Many couples keep trying until they have at least one child of each sex. Sons are especially valued in most societies. The ability to predetermine sex of children, therefore, may contribute to reducing fertility by increasing the number of males born. But informal group pressures persist: "What? You've been married two years and no sign of a child?" "Your daughter is three. Doesn't she need a little brother?"

How can these values be changed so that people want fewer children? Modernization seems to bring with it a desire for smaller families, even before industrialization and urbanization occur. Literacy and mass edu-

[32] Kenneth E. Boulding, *The Meaning of the 20th Century: The Great Transition* (New York: Harper & Row, 1964), pp. 129–130.

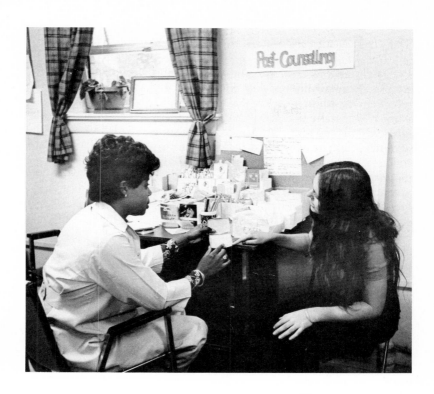

Family planning centers provide individual counseling on birth control. *Sybil Shelton/Monkmeyer Press Photo Service.*

cation in Finland and Hungary as well as England and Wales apparently contributed to a decline in fertility that began in the 1880s.[33] As infant mortality falls, as public agencies provide help, and as kinship ties decline in importance, many couples want fewer children and may take advantage of available means of preventing births. As the status of women rises, they find fulfillment in fields formerly closed to them. Often they postpone marriage and decide to have no children or only one or two.

But as the example of the United States demonstrates, modernization is not enough. A positive program aimed at reducing fertility is advocated in more and more countries. Generally, it takes the form of "family plan-

ning," of making it possible for couples to have no more children than they want. If this goal were achieved, births would decline somewhat more even in the United States. A national fertility study conducted in 1970 by the Office of Population Research at Princeton University found that 44 percent of all births to currently married women between 1966 and 1970 were unplanned. Only 1 percent of first births were unwanted, but nearly two-thirds of all sixth or higher-order births were. This implies that 2.65 million births would not have occurred during those years if the couples had had access to perfect fertility control. Many of these children, of course, were nurtured and cherished once they were on the scene. But according to the parents, 15 percent were *never* wanted.[34]

[33] Ronald Freedman, "Norms for Family Size in Underdeveloped Areas," *Proceedings of the Royal Society* 159 (1963): 220–245.

[34] *Population and the American Future*, pp. 163–164.

Unwanted births are most common among those with the least education and income. American women with no high school education reported that 31 percent of their children were unwanted at the time of conception, as compared to 7 percent for college graduates. The Commission on Population Growth declares that if minority groups, such as blacks, had access to various means of fertility control, as well as to the education and income so closely connected with that access, their birth rate would be about the same as that of the majority white population.[35] Some black leaders, however, suspect the programs of fertility control aimed at the poor are a pretext for "race genocide." Many Third World leaders have a similar attitude toward foreign aid programs that finance family planning projects.

The chief shortcoming of the "family planning" approach is that it is individualistic. People make decisions about having children in the light of their own needs, rather than those of the nation and the world. They continue to want more than the number necessary for ZPG to be attained. Family planning programs, says Kingsley Davis, sanctify the idea that every woman should have the number of children she wants, instead of asking why women desire so many children and how this desire can be influenced. Institutional and cultural changes must be added to medical and educational approaches. "Changes basic enough to affect motivation for having children would be changes in the structure of the family, in the position of women, and in the sexual mores."[36] There are some indications that such changes are taking place in the People's Republic of China.

Differential Consumption

The "first-class passengers" on Spaceship Earth account for most of its environmental problems and for consumption rates out of proportion to their numbers. Although Americans compose only 6 percent of the earth's people, they consume 40 percent or more of the natural resources and produce 50 percent of industrial pollution.

The average American uses more electric power than fifty-five Asians or Africans. The generation of electric power is a prime producer of pollution. A single American accounts for more detergents, pesticides, radioactive substances, fertilizers, fungicides, and defoliants in the rivers and oceans than are produced by a thousand people in Indonesia—a nation that is generally cited as a prime example of human overcrowding. One American is responsible for putting more carbon monoxide and benzopyrene in the air than 200 Pakistanis or Indians. One American consumes three times more food than the average person who comes from places that account for two-thirds of the world's population. The average American is responsible for 2,500 pounds of waste per year—many times the world average. If abandoned refrigerators, automobiles, and other bulky objects were included, the figure would be astronomically higher.

The United States . . . accounts for almost 30 percent of poisons being dumped into sky and the seas. The notion, therefore that Americans are less of a drain on the Earth than Chinese or Indians, because there are so many fewer of us, is an absurdity and a dangerous one.[37]

In some ways economic development as it has been promoted thus far has made the problem worse in the long run, both in advanced industrial societies and in those to whom these societies send foreign aid. The benefit of commercial agriculture must be weighed against the pollution of air and

---

[35] *Ibid.* Black women reported 61 percent unplanned pregnancies as compared to 42 percent for whites.

[36] "Population Policy: Will Current Programs Succeed?" *Science* (Nov. 10, 1967).

[37] Norman Cousins, "Affluence and Effluence," *Saturday Review* (May 2, 1970): 53.

water by machinery, fertilizers, and pesticides. And paying subsidies for *not* producing seems irrational in a hungry world.

Like our exportation of death control, our exports of food have kept many citizens of underdeveloped nations alive, in misery, to produce more children to live in misery. No humanitarian would deny people food. But agriculturist Georg Borgstrom believes that equal distribution of all available food would only make hunger universal.[38] He questions the morality of trade patterns in which affluent nations, high consumers of fat and protein, import these materials from starving nations. "Is it reasonable that tropical Africa, so critically short of both fat and protein, is parting with a quantity of protein in the form of peanuts, consisting of one-third of its production, to feed the dairy cattle and poultry of Western Europe and to bolster the fat intake of Europeans?"[39]

Saving the Environment

Like the problem of overpopulation, that of pollution can be solved only through a change in individual and collective goals and values, and in the system of rewards and punishments. Both are extremely urgent, and both must be based on sound research.

The Latin American shopper goes to market with her basket and fills it with unwrapped fruit and meat wrapped in banana leaves. The Asian farmer uses night soil to fertilize his land. These people are more in harmony with nature than the American housewife who loads her supermarket basket with processed and packaged foods raised on inorganically fertilized soil, sprayed with insecticides, and loaded with preservatives. Changes in life style—ways of using less electricity, gasoline, paper, water, fewer pollutants, fewer calories—will be required in order to preserve our environment.[40]

Collective goals and priorities must also be changed. Most ecologists question the long-sacred goal of economic growth in advanced countries. They insist that a "high standard of living" inevitably leads to a low quality of life.[41] They suggest that corporations should be given incentives through taxes and other legislation for preventing or cleaning up pollution. They feel that the system of rewarding those who use up resources like oil (through depletion allowances, for example) should be reversed. The social costs of production, such as pollution, should be charged to their source rather than to the public in general. Use of mass transit rather than private automobiles should be promoted. Consumers of large amounts of electricity should be charged at a higher rather than lower rate. Above all, no technological innovation should be allowed without prior assessment of its probable ecological consequences.

---

[38] *Too Many*, p. 323.

[39] *Ibid.*, p. 328

[40] See Garrett De Bell, ed., *The Environmental Handbook: Prepared for the First Environmental Teach-in* (New York: Ballantine/Friends of the Earth, 1970), section on "Eco-Tactics."

[41] William Murdoch and Joseph Connell, "All about Ecology," in Irving Horowitz, ed., *The Troubled Conscience: American Social Issues* (Santa Barbara: The Center for the Study of Democratic Institutions, 1971), p. 323.

Summary

In this chapter we have emphasized two of the five systems in which human social behavior occurs—the human organism (in terms of demography) and the environment (in terms of ecology).

Demography, the science of human populations, is concerned with their size, composition, and distribution, and their change through fertility, mortality, and migration. Our focus is on the population explosion that began in 1650, accelerated rapidly as modernization proceeded, and, through diffusion of "death control," has been most rapid since World War II in less developed societies. The drop in birth rates that occurred in industrialized nations before World War II led to the theory of a "demographic transition" to a stable population. But no country has yet completed this transition. The more developed countries grow at about 1 percent a year, the less developed at 2.7 percent. High birth rates combined with low death rates mean that increasing numbers of females survive to the childbearing years and in turn give birth to more potential mothers.

Demographers arrive at predictions of population growth largely through projection of current trends, taking other factors into account. Optimists like Donald Bogue believe fertility is declining so rapidly that zero population growth rates may be reached by the year 2000. Most demographers, however, take sharp issue with him, pointing out that enormous numbers of future mothers already exist, that they will probably have more children than needed for replacement, and that most population projections in the past have been too low.

Overpopulation also blocks economic development, erodes the quality of life, and threatens human survival. Even optimistic demographers foresee years of acute crises and famine.

Ecology is the study of all forms of life and their natural settings, and of their interdependence. The global ecosystem is finite, closed, fragile, and almost infinitely complex. All living things—including people—depend on the cycling of matter through a chain of life in a closed system.

The imbalance of human beings and the rest of nature has two chief aspects: the exploitation of natural resources and the latent consequences (such as pollution) of modernization.

The interrelated problems of population growth, differential consumption, and environmental deterioration are extremely pressing and closely interrelated. Both demand changes in values and goals, in collective priorities, in social structure, and in norms and sanctions.

Population control cannot be morally and ethically achieved through an increase in the death rate or the other Malthusian "positive checks." Migration is no longer a solution. Economic development is hampered by the problem itself. Therefore, prevention of births is the only answer. Thus far most policies have taken the "family planning" approach, making information about contraception available to those who want no more children. But individual values and social pressures, as well as current laws and tax systems, influence people to have more children than are needed for replacement of population. Kingsley Davis believes that only through changes in the social structure, the role of women, and the sexual mores will population growth be checked.

Saving the environment depends on changes in values and life styles. It also demands a system of rewards for acts that prevent or counteract pollution and punishments for those that increase it.

Glossary

Birth rate The number of live births per 1,000 population.

Demographic transition The shift from high birth and death rates through a period of high population growth to a new balance of low birth and death rates.

Demography The science concerned with human populations.

Dependency ratio The number of people under 15 and over 65 as compared to those considered productive, ages 15–64.

Ecology The study of all forms of life and their natural settings, and of their interdependence.

Ecosystem The sum total of living and nonliving elements that support a chain of life within a given area.

Fertility The amount of reproduction occurring in a group, category, or society.

Fertility rate The number of births per 1,000 women of reproductive age (usually 15–45).

Rate of natural increase The difference between the number of births and the number of deaths per 1,000 population.

Sex ratio The number of males compared to the number of females in a given group or category.

Zero population growth (ZPG) A balance of births and deaths that allows only for population replacement.

chapter

13

Urban Life

To some people, the word "city" means "civilization." To others, the word "urban" is always followed by "crisis" or "problems." Two hundred years ago, Samuel Johnson thought that only in cities could people be truly civilized. To be tired of London was to be tired of life. But Oliver Goldsmith, seeing the deserted villages and the smoky factory towns of the early Industrial Revolution, worried about the loss of a "bold peasantry, their country's pride," and damned cities as places "where wealth accumulates, and men decay." "God made the country and man made the town," wrote William Cowper in the nineteenth century. Oliver Wendell Holmes retorted, "God made the cavern, and man made the house."

Early urban sociologists reflected the American cultural bias which sees rural life as normal and moral, city life as corrupting and unnatural. During the decades when immigrants poured into city ghettos, factories mushroomed, and the Depression revealed many weaknesses in the social order, sociologists tended to emphasize urban disorganization. In recent years, however, they increasingly see the urban community as much more complex, including the simpler elements of rural society as well as some new forms that emerge in the new setting.

In this chapter we ask, first, what constitutes a city, and what is urbanization? We then trace the history of the urban revolution, emphasizing the speed and degree of recent changes and their different manifestations in cities, suburbs, metropolitan areas, and urban regions. We consider how this trend differs in various societies, and how it is related to industrialization and to modernization in general.

Next, we look at urbanism. Is it a distinct way of life, or are there many different ways of urban life? Is the city as such responsible for the life style or styles we find there? Then we study urban ecology, the ways in which cities assume their characteristic patterns.

We then consider the role of cities in newly developing societies and the place of rural life in today's world. Finally we ask, What alternative futures may we envision for cities, and how might these come about?

The City and Urbanization

What is a city? The most neutral definition is *demographic,* meaning that it concerns the distribution of people in space. In this sense, a **city** is a relatively dense concentration of people settled in a relatively small geographic area. Usually it is taken for granted that these people are engaged, for the most part, in nonagricultural pursuits.

The *social* definition of a city includes features of culture and social organization: heterogeneity (mixed as opposed to uniform populations), specialization, interdependence, mobility, and an "urban way of life" that is assumed to result from these factors and to have certain consequences for the

290

During the subway rush hour thousands of city dwellers are even more crowded together than at other times. *Donald C. Dietz/Stock, Boston.*

social relationships and personalities of city dwellers. This definition is usually associated with industrialization and other aspects of modernization. Culture and social structure are quite different in preindustrial cities, where home and work-place are less likely to be separated than in a modern city.

The definition of urbanization, like that of a city, may also be primarily demographic or primarily social. In the demographic sense, **urbanization** refers to *where* people live—to "the proportion of the total population concentrated in urban settlements, or else to a rise in this proportion."[1] It is not the same thing as the growth of cities as such, for if they grow at the same rate as the rural population, no change in rural-urban proportions would occur. Nor is it the same as the population density of a whole society. Argentina, for example, has a low density and a relatively high degree of urbanization, whereas India, a land of numerous peasant villages as well as huge cities, has a high density and a relatively low degree of urbanization.

In the social sense, *urbanization* refers to *how* people live, to their occupations, behav-

ior patterns, and social relationships. An enduring sociological concern is the extent to which these two aspects of urbanization are related—the consequences of *where* people live for *how* they live. Is there something inherent in the crowding together of large numbers of people in a relatively small space that makes their social life, their personalities, their beliefs and values, and their health and happiness different in significant ways from those of people who live on isolated farms, in peasant or tribal villages, and in small towns? Or are both the benefits and the problems of urban living due not to this crowding but to the other trends we associate with modernization, such as industrialization, secularization, and bureaucracy?

The Urban Revolution

We speak of urbanization as a revolution because it has proceeded so very rapidly since 1800, and because of its effects on culture, society, and personality. Although there can be cities without industry, and industrialization without great cities, the two tend to go together. The mechanization of agriculture pushes people off the land, and the

[1] Kingsley Davis, "The Urbanization of the Human Population," *Scientific American* (Sept. 1965): 41–53.

hope of jobs, schooling, freedom from primary group controls, and excitement pulls them to the city.

Early Cities

About 10,000 years ago, during the Neolithic era ("New Stone Age"), when people first learned to cultivate crops and began to store grain, they congregated in villages.[2] Urban centers, with administrative buildings, food storage systems, and written symbols for calculating and recording business transactions, emerged in the Fertile Crescent of Southwest Asia—in Mesopotamia, Iran, and the Indus Valley of Pakistan—as early as 3900 B.C., and there is no doubt that by 2300 B.C. true cities existed. The cities of Mexico discovered by the Spanish conquistadores in the 1500s had emerged as early as 100 B.C. In both regions, cities were integrated not on the basis of kinship or other ascriptive relationships, but on the basis of economic and political functions. At first cities were theocracies governed by priests. Later, cities became militaristic as the urge to expand their territories increased.[3]

As we said in our definition of a city, the majority of modern city dwellers are engaged in nonagricultural occupations. This was true in the early cities as well. Obtaining a steady supply of food is thus a major concern. Initially, cities got the food they needed from nearby peasants through force or taxation. Later, cities traded city-made goods and supplies from other regions

for food. Besides being warehouses for such wealth as grain, cities were centers of distribution, of exchange with other cities, and of crafts. They were linked to one another by transportation networks and to the rural areas by reciprocal needs.[4] The city was thus a means of accumulating and organizing capital and labor for such projects as large-scale irrigation, water conservation, and flood control, which made greater productivity possible.

But no society was really *urbanized* until modern times. At its height, the city of Rome may have had a million people, but nine out of ten citizens of the empire lived in peasant villages. After the decline and fall of the empire, social organization was structured around small communities such as feudal manors. Later in the Middle Ages, such European ports as Venice and Bremen grew into city-states through commerce. It was in cities like these that the urban revolution began.

World Urbanization

Not until the complex of trends we call modernization got under way, however, did urbanization gain momentum. Since 1800, when only about 3 percent of the world's people lived in settlements of 5,000 or more, the trend away from farm and village has accelerated with hardly any setbacks. About a third of the world's people now are urban. In 1970 more than a quarter of the world's people lived in cities of 20,000 or more. In what United Nations demographers call "the more developed regions," two out of three people live in cities. In the "less developed" regions, only one out of four lives in a city.[5]

[2] Recent excavations in Thailand indicate that the agricultural revolution may have begun 5,000 years earlier in Southeast Asia. [Wilhelm G. Solheim, II, "An Earlier Agricultural Revolution," *Scientific American* (April 1972): p. 34.]

[3] Robert McC. Adams, "The Evolution of Urban Society: Early Mesopotamia and Mexico," in Sylvia Fleis Fava, ed., *Urbanism in World Perspective: A Reader* (New York: Thomas Y. Crowell, 1968), pp. 98–115.

[4] Norton Ginsburg, "The City and Modernization," in Myron Weiner, ed., *Modernization: The Dynamics of Growth* (New York: Basic Books, 1966), pp. 122–137.

[5] *The World Population Situation in 1970.* United Nations, Department of Social and Economic Affairs, Population Studies, No. 49, 1971.

Moscow is one of the great "World Cities."
Design Photographers International, Inc.

While population has grown enormously during this period, urbanization has proceeded even faster. From 1800 to 1850 world population grew 29 percent, but the number living in large cities (over 100,000 people) grew 76 percent. From 1900 to 1950, population grew 49 percent, large cities 254 percent.

A striking feature of this trend is the emergence of really enormous cities. Twelve percent of humanity is clustered in 141 urban areas of a million or more people.[6] Among these are "the World Cities," which are not only great centers of population, but also dominant centers of national and international political power, trade, transportation, banking and finance, professional talent and learning, art and entertainment, libraries and museums, publishing and communication, riches and luxury. Prominent among them are London, Paris, New York, Tokyo, Moscow, the Rhine-Ruhr area of Germany, and the Randstand complex of the Netherlands.[7]

Noel Gist and Sylvia Fava distinguish three levels of urbanization according to the proportion of population living in large cities. First, countries with more than 20 percent of their population in large cities include three levels of modernization:

1. The established urban-industrial countries, including England and northwestern Europe and the countries that drew most of their colonists from these areas: the United States, New Zealand, and Australia. These tend to have the highest levels of urbanization.

2. The newly industrial countries that have achieved significant levels of modernization

[6] Jorge Arango, *The Urbanization of the Earth* (Boston: Beacon Press, 1970), p. 9.

[7] Peter Hall, *The World Cities* (New York: McGraw-Hill, 1966).

in the present century: Spain, Italy, Hungary, Poland, the Soviet Union, and Japan.

3. The "overurbanized" countries where industrialization lags far behind urbanization: Venezuela, Argentina, Uruguay, Mexico, Costa Rica, Cuba, Jamaica, Colombia, Egypt, Syria, Lebanon, and Korea.

Second, countries with between 10 and 20 percent of their population in large cities typically have low levels of industrialization. They include many countries of Latin America, the Near East, the rim of South and Southeast Asia, northern Africa, and a few European countries. Third, the least urbanized nations, with less than 10 percent in large cities, are also the least industrialized and Westernized. Asia, except for Japan, and Africa are most highly represented in this category. Albania and Yugoslavia in Europe and the Guianas in the Western Hemisphere are also minimally urbanized.[8]

---

[8] *Urban Society,* 5th ed. (New York: Thomas Y. Crowell, 1964), pp. 58–61.

Urbanization in the United States

Once a large expanse of farmland and wilderness punctuated here and there by cities, the United States today presents a picture of numerous sprawling urban areas linked by heavily settled corridors, and vast open stretches, especially in the Midwestern plains, where many small towns are almost deserted. But it also includes a number of thriving small towns and cities. Several trends have produced this pattern.

First of all, immigrants typically arrived in America at a city. Some moved on to farming regions, but the majority stayed on, starting their new life in this country as urban dwellers. Second, industrialization has drawn rural people to cities. The shift from farm to city, which is what we usually mean by demographic urbanization, was as great in volume—about 40 million people—as the flood of immigrants that came to the United States between 1820 and 1960. And it occurred in a much shorter period, from 1920

Table 13-1   Where Americans Live

Type of Residence	1970	1974 (estimate)	% Change 1970–1974
U.S., total	199,819,000	207,949,000	4.1
All metropolitan areas	137,058,000	142,043,000	3.6
Central cities	62,876,000	61,650,000	−1.9
Suburbs	74,182,000	80,394,000	8.4
Metropolitan areas (1 million plus)	79,489,000	81,059,000	2.0
Central cities	34,322,000	33,012,000	−3.8
Suburbs	45,166,000	48,047,000	6.4
Metropolitan areas (less than 1 million)	57,570,000	60,985,000	5.9
Central cities	28,554,000	28,638,000	0.3
Suburbs	29,016,000	32,347,000	11.5
Nonmetropolitan areas	62,761,000	65,905,000	5.0

SOURCE: Adapted from Bureau of the Census, *Current Population Reports,* Series P-23, No. 55 (Sept. 1975), Table E, p. 5.

to 1970. The sixties were especially dramatic. The number living on farms dropped from 15 million to 10 million. Half a century ago, the American population was almost evenly divided between city and farm. In 1970 three out of four Americans were urban, and most rural residents were "rural non-farm."

Urbanization embraces several other trends: metropolitanization, suburbanization, and the emergence of urban regions. Seven out of ten Americans now live in **metropolitan areas,** which include a number of cities and urban fringe areas that form a social and economic community (but seldom a political one). The influence of some metropolitan areas extends over the entire country. Others dominate a region. Some cities are satellites of the giant metropolises. Others are not integrated at all with their adjacent areas (see Table 13-2).

According to the official definition, a Standard Metropolitan Statistical Area (SMSA) includes at least one city of 50,000 or more people as well as adjacent counties whose populations are urban in character and economically integrated with the central city. There are now 243 such SMSAs in the United States. The number of SMSAs with over a million people rose from 24 in 1960 to 33 in 1970.

The metropolis is not simply a traditional city grown larger. It is a new and complex urban form. Most metropolitan areas consist of a "downtown" commercial business district and a ghettoized "inner city." Surrounding the city are satellite towns and suburbs, some predominantly residential, some largely commercial and industrial. Beyond these areas is unincorporated

San Francisco is the center of one of the largest metropolitan areas in the United States, but the city of San Francisco itself is relatively small. *Julie O'Neil/Stock, Boston.*

Table 13-2 Relative Importance of Some Larger American Cities

National Metropolis	Regional Metropolis		Average City		Unintegrated City
Atlanta	Cincinnati	Los Angeles	Akron	Milwaukee	Baltimore
Chicago	Columbia (S.C.)	Nashville	Columbus	Philadelphia	Baton Rouge
Dallas	Denver	Phoenix	El Paso	Rochester	Binghampton
New York	Detroit	St. Louis	Indianapolis	Spokane	Flint
	Kansas City	San Francisco	Jacksonville	Syracuse	San Diego
	Little Rock	Seattle	Louisville	Tulsa	Scranton

SOURCE: Adapted from Mark Abrahamson, *Urban Sociology* (Englewood Cliffs, N.J.: Prentice-Hall, 1976), p. 223, Table 10-4.

"urban sprawl" which spreads out along highways.

In recent decades, most central cities have lost population. Cities in the North and North Central part of the country especially have been affected. Cities elsewhere, primarily in the South and Southwest, have grown. In general, most cities of over one million people have declined in population since 1970. (Cities of less than a million people have remained more or less the same.) According to the U.S. Census Bureau, this loss is due almost entirely to the movement of white people out of the central cities.

About 7.7 million whites moved from the cities to the suburbs from 1970 to 1974. There was some reverse migration, and about 3.5 million whites moved to the cities from the suburbs. But that is still a loss of about 4.2 million people. Moreover, those who moved out of the cities generally were making more money than those who moved in.[9]

Suburbanization is thus inseparable from metropolitanization. During the 1960s, 14

[9]Bureau of the Census, *Current Population Reports*, Series P-23, No. 55 (Sept. 1975).

Table 13-3 Largest U.S. Metropolitan Areas: 1973

Rank	Metropolitan Area	1970 Population	1973 Estimate
1	New York, N.Y.–N.J.	9,973,716	9,739,066
2	Chicago, Ill.	6,977,611	7,002,458
3	Los Angeles–Long Beach, Calif.	7,041,980	6,923,813
4	Philadelphia, Pa.–N.J.	4,824,110	4,805,746
5	Detroit, Mich.	4,435,051	4,445,758
6	San Francisco–Oakland, Calif.	3,107,044	3,143,300
7	Washington, D.C.–Md.–Va.	2,910,111	3,029,233
8	Boston, Mass.	2,899,101	2,897,860
9	Nassau–Suffolk, N.Y.	2,555,868	2,630,044
10	Dallas–Ft. Worth, Tex.	2,378,353	2,464,090
11	St. Louis, Mo.–Ill.	2,410,602	2,391,384
12	Pittsburgh, Pa.	2,401,362	2,364,637

SOURCE: U.S. Bureau of the Census.

million whites and 800,000 blacks moved to the suburbs. In 1970, suburbanites became the largest sector of the population, more than 71 million, exceeding by far the 59 million in central cities and edging ahead of the 71 million in smaller cities and rural areas.

The suburbs were initially "bedroom communities." People lived in them but worked in the city. The availability of cars and superhighways connecting suburbs to cities made it easier for people to get to work. Eventually, easy motor transportation, as well as available building space and cheaper labor costs, made it easy for industry and commerce to come out to the people. Suburbs thus became more self-contained, full-service communities. Now many suburbanites never go into the city at all.

The farther one gets out of the city, the cheaper land is to acquire and build on. In addition, irritations associated with city living—noise, crowds, traffic, pollution, and crime—are less of a problem in the suburbs.

Like cities, suburbs are composed of people of various religions, ethnic groups, and social classes. There are blue-collar, white-collar, and upper-middle-class suburbs; Protestant, Catholic, and Jewish suburbs; Irish, German, and Italian suburbs. "In general, the differences among suburbs are greater than the average differences between cities and suburbs."[10]

The major difference between cities and suburbs is in racial composition. Blacks make up 27 percent of the population in cities of over 1,000,000 and 17 percent of the population of smaller cities. They account for only 5 percent of suburban population, in spite of the fact that 550,000 blacks have moved to suburbia since 1970.[11]

Social class is another difference. In general, suburban residents have more education and hold more prestigious jobs than city residents. Thus, as would be expected, they make more money. In 1974, the median income for a suburban family was $14,000, as compared to $11,300 for city-dwellers.[12]

This is an important new pattern. Most preindustrial cities, including those of mid-nineteenth-century America, cities in newly industrializing countries, and many contemporary cities in the Southern United States show the opposite pattern. The well-to-do reside in the city. The farther out one goes, the poorer the residents are. According to Claude Fischer, the modern American pattern of better-off suburbs surrounding a central city will become more typical as time goes by. "Most major metropolises not yet in that pattern are evolving toward it."[13]

In addition to the trends toward metropolitanization and suburbanization, there is also the trend toward urban regions. **Urban regions** are defined as "areas of one million people or more comprised of a continuous zone of metropolitan areas and intervening counties within which one is never far from a city."[14] It is estimated that by the year 2000, urban regions will occupy one-sixth of the continental United States land area and contain five-sixths of the population. Projections of national population distribution indicate that 54 percent of all Americans will be living in the two largest urban regions by the year 2000. The urban region stretching along the Atlantic seaboard and westward past Chicago would contain 41 percent of all Americans. Another 13 percent would be in California between San Diego and San Francisco. This trend means that some parts

[10] Claude Fischer, *The Urban Experience* (New York: Harcourt Brace Jovanovich, 1976), p. 211.

[11] Bureau of the Census, *Current Population Reports,* Series P-23, No. 55 (Sept. 1975).

[12] *Ibid.*

[13] *The Urban Experience,* p. 214.

[14] *Population and the American Future: The Report of the Commission on Population Growth and the American Future* (New York: New American Library, 1972), pp. 40–42.

of the country will be very densely populated while others will be sparsely settled. In the central cities of the United States, the average density is 8,000 people per square mile, yet a large number of Americans live in towns of less than 50,000. Seventeen states do not have a single county with a density of 500 per square mile, the accepted measure of suburbanization, much less 1,000 per square mile, the measure of an urban area. "In short, what is developing in the United States is the spread of a relatively low-density population engaged in urban economic pursuits."[15]

Urbanism as a Way of Life

Still concentrating mainly on cities in Western industrial countries and especially the United States, we turn now from where people live to how they live. Is there something about the settlement patterns of cities and their various areas that always produces a distinctive "urban way of life?"

The Impact of Size, Diversity, and Density

Louis Wirth was one of the first to analyze the effects of **urbanism,** the distinct way of life that characterizes cities.[16] He concluded that the simple fact of living in a city—because of its size, density, and heterogeneity—has direct and mostly destructive effects on people and on the quality of life.

From a psychological point of view, the essential feature of city living is *sensory overload.* City dwellers cannot possibly absorb and respond to all the sights, sounds, smells,

and people they are exposed to daily. They must try to protect themselves by controlling their emotional responses to their surroundings. This emotional control leads to a lack of involvement with others. Thus, city dwellers become impersonal, isolated, and independent. Wirth claimed that these attitudes weakened urban primary groups and made city dwellers more prone to irritation, personal frustration, and nervous tension because they lacked the emotional support of others.

Looking at urbanism from a sociological perspective, Wirth reached the same negative conclusion. *Community differentiation*—based on the many occupations found in cities and on the allotment of city spaces for various activities—compartmentalizes the city dweller's life. This causes social cohesion to become weak for two reasons. First, consensus in the community is more difficult to achieve because people's needs are so different. Second, cohesion in primary groups is also weakened, because people's activities (work, play, and so on) increasingly take place outside them.

This weakening of social bonds, Wirth said, leads to anomie and weakened support for the group's norms. To solve this problem, city dwellers call in agents of formal authority (police, courts, politicians) to maintain control. This in turn has the effect of further insulating the individual from involvement in the community.

For all these reasons, said Wirth, we can expect the incidence of "personal disorganization, mental breakdown, suicide, delinquency, crime, corruption, and disorder" to be higher in cities than in rural communities.

As Wirth himself recognized, his thinking was probably both time-bound and culturebound. The cities he saw in the 1930s were shaped by the task of assimilating immigrants, the recency of the shift from rural to urban living, and the Depression. Wirth saw that "the direction of the ongoing

---

[15] Daniel J. Elazar, "Are We a Nation of Cities?" *The Public Interest* (Summer 1966).

[16] "Urbanism as a Way of Life," *American Journal of Sociology* 44 (July 1938): 3–24.

changes in urbanism will for good or ill transform not only the city but the world," and urged others to test and revise his theories through further analysis and empirical research.

Urbanism as Many Ways of Life

Taking up Wirth's challenge, other sociologists have begun to feel that Wirth's emphasis on size, diversity, and density applies particularly to the American industrial city, and especially to what we call the inner city. We cannot apply it to entire urban areas, much less to cities all over the world.

We must first distinguish among the main urban areas. The *inner city* refers to slums that typically surround the central business district of American industrial cities. The *outer city* includes stable residential areas of working-class and middle-class people. The *suburbs* are "the latest and most modern ring of the outer city, distinguished from it only by yet lower densities, and by the often irrelevant fact of the ring's location outside the city limits."[17]

In today's highly affluent, mobile society, says Herbert Gans, residential location has less impact on social life than do other factors such as social class and the stage of the life cycle in which the residents of a given area find themselves. Many city dwellers are protected against the negative consequences of size, diversity, and density by "social structures and cultural patterns which they either brought to the city, or developed by living in it."[18]

It is true, says Gans, that many people in the inner city fit Wirth's picture of isolated individuals torn from accustomed social moorings and unable to develop new ones, who are therefore prey to social anarchy. But many do not. "Economic condition, cultural characteristics, life-cycle stages, and residential instability explain ways of life more satisfactorily than number, density, or heterogeneity." Class, ethnicity, and stage in the life cycle are the main factors on which city dwellers construct communities that give them roots in an ever-changing and demanding environment. Gans says primary groups emerge within these communities, particularly among compatible neighbors. These are most apparent in the outer city and the suburbs, least so in the inner city.

Gans described five main types of people who live in the inner city:

1. *Cosmopolites* such as students, artists, writers, musicians, entertainers, and other intellectuals and professionals, who *choose* to live there because they want to be near "cultural" facilities

2. *Unmarried people and childless couples* who may move later, but meanwhile prefer to be near the heart of things

3. *Ethnic villagers* who live much as they did in the peasant villages of Europe, Asia, Mexico, or Puerto Rico, with strong kinship and other primary group ties, weak ties to formal organizations, and suspicion of everything and everyone outside their neighborhood. They live in the inner city partly by choice, partly from necessity.

4. *The deprived,* who live there because they have no choice. This includes the very poor, the emotionally disturbed or otherwise handicapped, broken families, and many nonwhites.

5. *The trapped and downwardly mobile* who cannot afford to move despite new neighbors they may be prejudiced against. Often these are old people on small pensions.

In spite of crowding, these groups are isolated from one another. Cosmopolites feel detached because of their subculture, the unmarried and childless because they plan to move on. Neither are particularly in-

---

[17] Herbert J. Gans, "Urbanism and Suburbanism as Ways of Life: A Re-evaluation of Definitions," in Arnold Rose, ed., *Human Behavior and Social Processes* (Boston: Houghton Mifflin, 1962), pp. 625–648.

[18] *Ibid.*

Drawing by W. Miller; © 1971
The New Yorker Magazine, Inc.

"Good morning, Cross Bronx Expressway."

terested in the welfare of the other residents of the inner city. The deprived and trapped clearly suffer the undesirable consequences of city living as Wirth saw them, but Gans believes they result from residential instability rather than sheer numbers, density, or heterogeneity. The neighborhoods of "ethnic villagers" are the most stable and most characterized by primary relationships.

Despite various myths about suburbia, Gans does not see very much difference between the outer city and the suburbs. In both, fairly homogeneous neighborhoods, made up largely of families in the child-raising years, develop. In the outer city people become segregated into distinct neighborhoods on the basis of "place and nature of

work, income, racial and ethnic characteristics, social status, custom, habit, taste, preference, and prejudice"[19]—a process Wirth believed applied to the city as a whole. Gans sees the outer city not as anonymous and impersonal but as "quasi-primary" by virtue of its separation into fairly homogeneous neighborhoods. An Italian or Polish working-class neighborhood, for example, is very much like a small town. It tends to break up, says a social anthropologist, when residents become upwardly mobile—a greater change than a simple transition from a rural setting to this type of urban neighborhood.[20]

Gans' studies of suburbia led him to question many popular images. It is often assumed that the move from city to suburb plunges one into a new way of life that changes behavior and personality, imposes conformity and other-direction, and "is socially, culturally, and emotionally destructive."[21] He lived as a participant observer in Levittown, New York, for the first two years of its existence, "to find out how a new community comes into being, how people change when they leave the city, and how they live and politic in suburbia."[22]

Like outer-city neighborhoods, suburban neighborhoods exhibit a quasi-primary way of life, but this is not due to peculiarly suburban pressures for conformity and sociability. The new suburbanites came, he found, to seek compatible neighbors, and they engage in more "neighboring" than formerly because they are similar and friendly. They need one another. The first criterion of a good neighbor is readiness to provide mutual aid. Residential location

[19] Wirth, "Urbanism as a Way of Life."
[20] Joel M. Halpern, *The Changing Village Community* (Englewood Cliffs, N.J.: Prentice-Hall, 1967), p. 39.
[21] Gans, *The Levittowners: Ways of Life and Politics in a New Suburban Community* (New York: Pantheon Books, 1967), p. 153.
[22] *Ibid.*, p. v.

300

In many suburbs primary relationships develop among families in the child-rearing years. *Mimi Forsyth/Monkmeyer Press Photo Service.*

does have consequences for roles and relationships, but people do not *live* in cities, small towns, or suburbs, but rather in small areas such as blocks. Some features of the quasi-primary way of life in both outer city and suburb, therefore, evolve from the fact that families in their child-rearing years happen to occupy adjacent dwellings.

Like Wirth, Gans suggests the need for further research based on the hypothesis that the greater the freedom of choice as to place of residence, the more important such characteristics as class and stage in the life cycle are in understanding behavior. After discovering these characteristics and holding them constant, then the sociologist can go on to find out which aspects of culture, social organization, and personality may be consequences of the settlement pattern itself.

Subcultural Theory: A New Approach

A third approach to urbanism has been proposed by Fischer.[23] His *subcultural theory*

attempts to synthesize the views of Wirth and Gans. Fischer agrees with Gans that urbanism has the effects it has "not because it destroys social worlds (as Wirth suggested) but more often because it creates them."[24]

Fischer does agree with Wirth that size is very important. A certain *critical mass* of people is necessary to support a viable subculture. There are, as Gans pointed out, ethnic subcultures and life-stage subcultures. Fischer also points out occupational subcultures (the police are a good example) and recreational subcultures (the Friends of the Opera), both of which arise out of the heterogeneity of the city and serve to restore people's lost sense of community.

Not all subcultures are supportive of the social order, however. The larger the population, the more likely it is to support deviant subcultures. Crime is a daily fact of life for city dwellers. As size and density increase so do victimless crimes and crimes against property. This is not true of violent crimes,

[23] "Toward a Subcultural Theory of Urbanism," *American Journal of Sociology,* 80 (May 1975), pp. 1319–1341.

[24] *The Urban Experience,* p. 37.

301

however. Murder, for example, is more frequent in both rural areas and large cities than it is in small towns. (See Figure 13-1)[25]

Fear of crime is thus very real to city dwellers and may further explain why they are unwilling to involve themselves in other people's problems. The Kitty Genovese case,

in which a woman in Queens, New York, was repeatedly stabbed while her neighbors did not interfere even to the extent of calling the police made it seem that city people are callous and uncaring. However, Fischer suggests that city dwellers have become so used to depending on agents of formal authority that they just didn't know what to do in an emergency situation. They lack initiative rather than heart.

[25] *Ibid.*, p. 91.

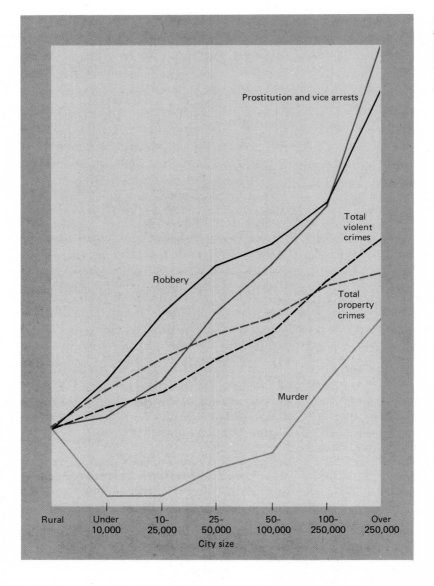

Figure 13-1 Crime rates by city size (1970). *From J. Edgar Hoover, Crime in the United States, 1970. Federal Bureau of Investigation. (Washington, D.C.: U.S. Government Printing Office, 1971.)*

Fischer agrees with Wirth that the majority of a city dweller's interpersonal contacts are secondary and instrumental. City dwellers may be seen as impersonal, not because they really are, but because the majority of their activities require them to be. Frequent contact with people from other urban subcultures may also contribute to the city dweller's apparent reserve and lack of openness.

According to Fischer, the emotional insulation that city dwellers must build up may have a positive side. City dwellers have been found to be much more unconventional in their beliefs and behavior than non–city dwellers (see Figure 13-2). Perhaps cultural innovations, which are born in our cities and diffuse to the rest of the country, are a result of the city dweller's "protective devices." [26] These protective devices, however, are rarely totally successful. City dwellers do experience relatively high levels of irritation, anxiety, and nervous strain.

The Ecology of American Cities

Ecology, as used in biology, refers to the way plants and animals are distributed over a given area and to their interdependence. **Human ecology** is concerned with the distribution of various functions, groups, and kinds of buildings within a given area and the processes involved in that distribution. Urban ecological processes—the steps by which a city grows and changes—are related to technological change, physical mobility, the degree of freedom of choice of various groups, competition for space and desirable locations, and economic advantage. Such values as traditional attachment to a certain place can also influence the growth of cities.

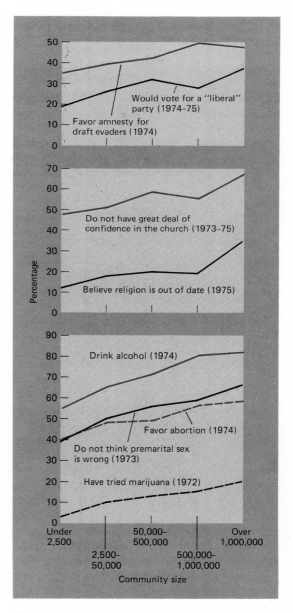

Figure 13-2 Percentage of the U.S. population endorsing or engaging in nontraditional behavior, by community size. *From various issues of Gallup Opinion Index (1972–1975).*

[26] *Ibid.,* p. 31.

Urban Ecological Processes

Concentration refers to the drawing of population into given areas of varying degrees of density. It is often highest at the center of a city and is affected by access to transportation and by variations in people's economic capacity to choose a place to live or do business. **Centralization** is the drawing together of institutions and activities, the assembling of people to work rather than to reside in a given area. Some highly centralized areas may show a low density in census statistics because these are based on dwelling rather than working place. The downtown or central business district is usually the area of greatest centralization. Executives and white-collar workers alike commute from the outer city and the suburbs.

Subcenters scattered through every metropolitan area, often at important intersections, result from the same process. This clustering of activities in outlying sections is also evidence of **decentralization,** for it indicates the spread of activities and dwelling places farther and farther out from the center of the city. Suburbanization, one aspect of decentralization, is made possible, like urbanization itself, by technological change. The automobile, delivery truck, telephone, freeway, and some surviving commuter trains, as well as the shorter work day and work week, make it possible for home and work-place to be many miles apart. (Still, four out of five commuters spend less than half an hour getting to work.) Regional shopping centers, which have mushroomed in the last two decades, make it unnecessary for suburbanites to "go downtown," and decentralized industries and businesses have brought more and more jobs to the suburbs.

Specialization refers to the clustering of particular types of institutions and activities in "bright lights" districts, wholesale areas, civic and "cultural" centers, financial districts, planned industrial areas, and professional or office buildings. **Routinization** is the regular movement of people from home

Modern transportation makes it possible for suburban residents to live in outlying areas and commute to work in the large cities. *Syd Greenberg / Design Photographers International, Inc.*

to work, and of goods from point of origin to point of use, in patterns that recur daily, weekly, seasonally, or even annually.[27]

Of special interest to sociologists are the processes by which "birds of a feather flock together"—segregation, invasion, and succession. **Segregation** is sometimes used synonymously with specialization to refer to functions of different areas. More often we think of it as the drawing together of similar types of people. Whether they want to because of similar background or are compelled to by discrimination and poverty, individuals tend to gravitate to areas where they can compete most effectively and where others of similar race, culture, economic status, and point of view dwell. The "ghetto" (once the Jewish immigrant neighborhood, now largely black in many cities), Littly Italy, Chinatown, "Nob Hill," the "Main Line," and the "wrong side of the tracks"—known by different names in different cities—are all results of segregation.

The clusters of similar people, institutions, and interests resulting from segregation and specialization are called *natural areas* because they seem to be the unplanned results of social and economic forces. Each natural area is somewhat of a unit, with a relatively homogeneous population, perhaps its own customs and standards of decency, and even a language of its own. Each large city has its "hobohemia" (Skid Row), its Greenwich Village or Latin Quarter, where the unconventional or eccentric concentrate; its cultural and racial colonies; its ultra-smart residential area; and its dingy world of furnished rooms.

But these areas are not static. Areas change through the process of invasion. **Invasion** is the penetration of a segregated area by an institutional function or population group different from the one already there. In a rapidly growing city, the commercial and industrial districts invade residential areas. One racial or cultural group may invade an area occupied by another, or an economically inferior but otherwise similar group may invade an upper-class area, as in the rooming-house districts that once were rows of dignified brick and brownstone residences. Invasion may be resisted, even to the extent of mob behavior. In other cases, invasion is successful and rapid. When an invasion is successful and the new type of institution or population is established in the area, we say **succession** has taken place. One section of Chicago, for example, was successively inhabited by Czechs, Jews, Italians, and blacks.

Models of Urban Growth

Using these general concepts, urban sociologists have developed several models of city growth (see Figure 13-3). All have at least one city that conforms to them, but none is generally applicable to all cities.

The first was developed by Ernest Burgess, using Chicago as an example.[28] Burgess described Chicago's growth pattern, which he felt was fairly typical, in terms of *concentric zones.* In this model, the main business, entertainment, and government facilities are located in the first zone, or nucleus. Next is a zone of transition—an old residential area taken over by stores and tenements that is being invaded in turn by small businesses and factories. Ghettos, Chinatowns, Little Italies, and the like are found here. The third zone is blue-collar homes, mainly multiple-family dwellings. The fourth zone is also residential but is the home

[27] Gerald Breese, *Urbanization in Newly Developing Countries* (Englewood Cliffs, N.J.: Prentice-Hall, 1966), p. 114. Breese points out that specialization is greatest in Western cities; elsewhere there is more mixing of various land uses.

[28] Robert E. Park, Ernest W. Burgess, and Roderick D. McKenzie, *The City* (Chicago: University of Chicago Press, 1925), Ch. 2.

of white-collar and upper-middle-class families who live in single-family houses or expensive apartments. Outside of the fourth zone are the suburbs and commuter areas.

A second model, the *sector model,* was developed by Homer Hoyt.[29] In analyzing city growth patterns, Hoyt concentrated on the development of transportation links between the various sectors. The central business district in the sector model is pretty much the same as in the concentric zone model. The residential districts in both models are also very similar to each other. In the sector model, however, manufacturing extends out from the center, but does not

end at the edge of the transition zone, as Burgess suggested. Instead, it extends out along the main transportation routes to the borders of the metropolitan area. Minneapolis and San Francisco conform fairly well to this model.

A third model was developed by Chauncy Harris and Edward Ullman.[30] Their *multiple-nuclei* model assumes that there are many minor commercial and residential centers, not just one, and that each will expand in any direction in which space is available. Expansion around these several nuclei may be concentric or sectional. Boston is a good example of a multiple-nuclei city.

The way buildings, people, and activities are sorted out into areas and patterns in our society is largely haphazard—the result of many uncoordinated decisions. One very important decision reflects the physical and political power of the automobile. The Interstate Highway System, the largest public

[29] *The Structure and Growth of Residential Neighborhoods in American Cities* (Washington, D.C.: Federal Housing Administration, 1939).

[30] "The Nature of Cities," *Annals of the American Academy of Political and Social Science,* 242 (November 1945): 7–71.

Figure 13-3 Three generalized models of the internal spatial structure of cities. *From Chauncy D. Harris and Edward L. Ullman, "The Nature of Cities," Annals of the American Academy of Political and Social Science: 242 (November, 1945). Courtesy of Chauncy D. Harris and Edward L. Ullman.*

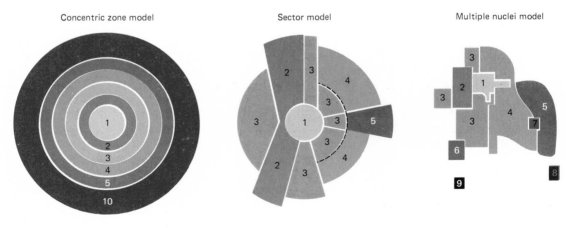

District:

1. Central business district
2. Wholesale, light manufacturing
3. Low-class residential
4. Medium-class residential
5. High-class residential
6. Heavy manufacturing
7. Outlying business district
8. Residential suburb
9. Industrial suburb
10. Commuters' zone

works project in modern history, was originally intended to serve interstate traffic and connect the most densely settled areas of the country. This project had several unforeseen consequences, some good and some bad.

As a result of the Interstate Highway System, significant numbers of people were able to move to the suburbs without having to give up their city jobs. New suburbs attracted industry, schools, and shopping, while similar inner-city institutions declined. In many cities, public transportation is inadequate and people must use their cars to get to work. Parking these cars is a major problem in most cities. The movement of people and industry to the suburbs has eroded the tax base of many cities, making them even more ill-equipped than before to deal with urban problems, many of which have been caused by the Interstate Highway System itself.[31]

While we cannot blame the decay of inner cities on the highway system alone, we can with some justification point to the lack of planning. Had highway advocates considered the long-range effect of their project on the economy and social structures of the cities they sought to connect, they might have proceeded differently—devoting some of their funds to mass transit and urban renewal.

The City in Newly Developing Countries

Thus far we have been concerned almost exclusively with American cities, with some side glances at the classic cities of Europe, where people have evolved a truly urbane way of life over the centuries. What of cities in newly developing countries? How is urbanization in these countries related to industrialization? What ecological patterns do their cities assume? What does empirical observation in such cities demonstrate about urbanism as a way of life?

The Growth of Cities

The acceleration of the urban trend in recent decades has been most startling in the Third World. While the *proportion* of the population living in cities is low in many underdeveloped countries, their populations are so enormous that they have millions of city-dwellers. Some are overurbanized. Because industrialization lags far behind urbanization, millions of migrants from rural areas are unemployed or underemployed, and the high urban birth rate swells the potential labor force.

In India and China, only about 8 percent of the population lives in cities of 100,000 or more. Yet because of their huge populations, about 35 percent of all the people in the world living in such large cities are Asians, and it is very likely that by 1975 Asians will constitute nearly half of such city-dwellers. Between 1900 and 1950, Asia experienced a gain of 444 percent in the proportion living in large cities; Africa, 629 percent. United Nations experts predict that by the end of the 1970s the poor countries of Asia, Africa, and Latin America will have 360 cities of at least half a million. Bombay and Calcutta may reach 20 or 30 million each. The late Secretary-General of the U.N., U Thant, called them "exploding cities in unexploding economies."

While the population of Latin America grows about 3 percent a year, its urban population grows between 5 and 7 percent a year. From 1955 to 1970, its urban population increased by 50 percent. Latin America is now about half urban. By 1980 it may be 60 to 65 percent urban. Mexico City adds

[31]Carl H. Madden, "The Cost of a Livable Environment," *AIA Journal* (May 1971): 26–30.

350,000 people a year. If this rate continues, the 1970 population of 8 million would double in 20 years. São Paolo, Brazil, had 800,000 people in 1940 and expects 13 million by 1990.[32]

Many of the large cities in developing countries, particularly in Latin America, are *primate cities,* overwhelmingly larger than the next largest cities, and overwhelmingly dominant. Most national functions are concentrated in these cities. They are the centers of political and economic power, of admin-

istration and commerce, the chief points of contact with the outside world. Such cities tend to be parasitic, exploiting a backward countryside rather than promoting development. Many are geared for import and export rather than for industry. They attract foreign political representatives, travelers, and tradesmen. They serve as diffusion points for social change and are magnets for rural migrants with or without marketable skills and talents.[33] These rural migrants often do not adopt urban ways but rather "peasantize" cities. Within the city, they

[32] James Nelson Goodsell, "Latin Americans Flock to Cities," *Christian Science Monitor* (Dec. 31, 1970).

[33] Irving Louis Horowitz, *Three Worlds of Development: The Theory and Practice of International Stratification* (New York: Oxford University Press, 1966), pp. 34–35; and Breese, *Urbanization in Newly Developing Countries,* pp. 40–43.

New high rises in Sao Paulo, Brazil, adjoin the old residential area, which is now a slum. *John Littlewood/Editorial Photocolo Archives, Inc.*

create communities that cushion the shock of change to urban living.

Urban Ecology in the Third World

The pattern of urban settlement in most newly developing countries is very different from that of an American industrial city. "Just as modern metropolitanism seems to represent *a social and economic community composed of many politically defined cities,* the form of urbanism on view in backward areas (and even in some Western cities) may consist of *politically defined cities composed of many social and economic communities.*"[34] And where many American metropolitan areas include a decaying central city, largely black, surrounded by more affluent, largely white suburbs, the picture of a burgeoning Latin American or Asian city is often that of an older established commercial-administrative city surrounded by a densely settled ring of shanty towns. There is also usually a "Western" area including suburbs, new central business district developments, and possibly new planned industrial districts.[35]

Because industrialization lags so far behind urbanization in many of these countries, the squatter areas on the city's fringe are miserably poor. Large families crowd into tiny shacks, often made of scraps of tin cans, old gasoline drums, tar paper, cartons, sheets of zinc, and palm or cane thatch. According to the Organization of American States, half of Latin America's city-dwellers live *below* subsistence level. Besides living in these shanty towns—the aptly

named *Villas Miseria* of Buenos Aires, the mud huts in which a third of Lima's people live, the "bustees" of Indian cities—squatters also occupy vacant spaces within the cities, even in swamps and sewers. They carry on many of their activities, often marginal economic services such as shoe shining or barbering, on the street. In Calcutta—one of the largest cities in the world—300,000 people have nowhere to *sleep* but the street.

Rural Life in an Urbanizing World

The urban revolution we have been describing began on the farm, and its brushfire speed is due in large part to the application of technology to agriculture.

To understand how food supply has changed from primitive times to the present is to recognize that when man depended upon hunting it required eight square miles to support one person. When he combined hunting with foraging, the area required to support one person was reduced from eight to one square mile. The development of the use of the hoe to cultivate land made it possible for one square mile to support three people, and the tremendous advance associated with the use of the plow made it possible for 750 people to be supported on one square mile of land surface. Modern agriculture, with its use of power, makes it possible, on the average, for one square mile to support 2000 people.[36]

This rural revolution is especially advanced in the United States. In 1920 nearly 32 million people, about 30 percent of the population, lived on 6.5 million farms averaging 147 acres. In 1950, 23 million people, 15.3 percent, lived on 5.6 million farms averaging 213 acres. The change in

[34] Leo F. Schnore and Eric E. Lampard, "Social Science and the City: A Survey of Research Needs," in Leo F. Schnore, ed., *Social Science and the City: A Survey of Urban Research* (New York, Frederick A. Praeger, 1968), p. 30.

[35] Breese, *Urbanization in Newly Developing Countries,* p. 116.

[36] J. A. Shellenberger, "The 'Green Revolution' Revisited," *Current* (Sept. 1969): 37–41.

Small family farms, like this one in Wisconsin, are vanishing from the American scene. *David Herman/Design Photographers International, Inc.*

the next two decades was even more dramatic, as cities burgeoned and agriculture became ever more commercialized. By 1970, only about 10 million people, or 5 percent of the population, lived on fewer than 3 million farms, averaging 387 acres. But not all those living on farms work in farming. The agricultural labor force, which includes unpaid family members who work at least 15 hours a week, numbered nearly 10 million in 1950. By 1970 only a little over 3.5 million, or 4.5 percent of the labor force, were farm workers.

The traditional American farm is still a one-family enterprise. Two out of three farms are "small, part-time, residential, or hobby farms." But the other 1 million farms produce nearly all of the farm products

marketed.[37] Dairy farms in the "milk sheds" of large cities, assembly-line chicken farms, huge specialized fruit and vegetable farms with acres upon acres of strawberries, or lettuce, or onions, or potatoes—these are "agri-businesses," factories without chimneys. Where the average farm worker fed twelve people in 1940, he now feeds fifty-one.[38] This means a huge investment in equipment, fertilizer, and other supplies. Similar trends occur in other heavily industrialized countries. As Japan's economy boomed in the 1960s, the proportion of agricultural workers declined from 31 to 16.3 percent of the labor force.

But modern agricultural technology has not reached much of the world, and about 60 percent of the world's workers are still in agriculture.[39] According to U.N. Community Development experts, there are from 3 to 5 million rural communities, ranging from nomadic tribes to densely settled agricultural villages of several thousand. About 80 percent of the populations of the less developed countries live in such communities. Productivity remains low. In Peru nearly a third of farm units are cultivated without even the aid of draft animals. In upland Guatemala, there is one animal-drawn plow per 1,000 farms. Few countries have achieved even a fifth of American productivity. In India, output per farm worker is *one-fiftieth* that of the United States.[40] Although two out of three Chinese work on farms, they produce less than a third of the national product.[41]

[37] John A. Schnittker, "The Farmer in the Till," *The Atlantic* (Aug. 1969).

[38] Earl L. Butz, "The Farmer as the Good Guy," *The New York Times* (April 15, 1972): L 31. The figure in 1951 was 16; in 1960, 28.

[39] *The New York Times* (Dec. 22, 1970).

[40] Yujiro Hayami and V. W. Ruttan, "Agricultural Productivity Differences among Countries," *The American Economic Review* (Dec. 1970).

[41] W. Klatt, "A Review of China's Economy in 1970," *The China Quarterly* (July–Sept. 1970): 115.

The Convergence of Urban and Rural Life Styles

As we have seen, the urban trend appears to be inexorable and irreversible. What does this mean for traditional rural life? "It is possible," says Joel Halpern, "to conceive of the export of trained technicians, skills, and products to the villages and the incorporation of rural people into town life as resulting in the similtaneous peasantization of the cities and the urbanization of villages. . . . In the process cities are modified but rural society is transformed."[42]

This modification and transformation mean, first of all, the elimination of great differences between rural and urban modes of life. It is during the height of the transition from rural to urban living that people are most conscious of these differences. In the late 1800s and early 1900s in the United States, for example, rural-urban political conflicts were intense, and people thought in terms of such stereotypes as "rubes" or "hayseeds" and "city slickers." Now the boundary between rural and urban is diffuse and unclear—socially, culturally, and geographically. Many people of many kinds live in urban fringes classified as rural areas. There are upper-class and working-class suburban fringes, magnificent estates next to shacks, country clubs near garbage dumps and farms.

Aside from this blurring of distinctions, farmers are increasingly like city dwellers. They listen to stock market reports before they sell their products. Their children see the same movies, watch the same TV shows, buy the same records, wear the same kind of clothes, read the same comics, magazines, and schoolbooks as their city cousins. Rural housewives use the same appliances and furnishings as do urban housewives and shop at the same kind of shopping centers.

[42] *The Changing Village Community*, pp. 2, 125.

Problems of the Agricultural Revolution

In many countries, however, urban-rural distinctions are still sharp, and strains created by the transition to modern agriculture are easily apparent. The older generation may cling to traditional ways, while the young look down on agriculture as a low-status occupation. In the Soviet Union, a wide gap between rural and urban ways of living persists. Recreation, schooling, communications, and consumer goods are all vastly inferior in rural areas. Some collective farms have tried to stem the exodus of youth to cities by establishing a ritual inducting youths into formal membership at age sixteen, and even having them swear an oath of allegiance, hoping that this will instill a sense of loyalty.[43] China is trying to integrate the cities and the countryside by emphasizing rural industrial development and urging city-based factories to engage in agriculture.[44]

The transition to commercial agriculture means that thousands, even millions, of "displaced persons" must somehow be taken care of. During the earliest stages of English modernization, between the thirteenth and sixteenth centuries, agriculture was transformed from subsistence to commercial farming. The Black Death (bubonic plague) contributed to this change by killing about a quarter of the population of Europe in the fourteenth century, including from 30 to 50 percent of the peasants in England. Prices of agricultural products fell because of the sudden drop in population. Because prices were low and labor scarce, landowners looked for new ways to use the land.

One of these uses was sheep farming. The weavers of Flanders needed wool; their old

[43] *The New York Times* (Jan. 15, 1969).
[44] *China: Inside the People's Republic*, by the Committee of Concerned Asian Scholars (New York: Bantam Books, 1972), p. 106.

sources on the continent of Europe were cut off by the ravages of long-drawn-out religious wars and the wolves that prowled the desolate countryside. English landowners therefore enclosed untilled land, waste land, and the commons on which the peasants had for centuries been allowed to graze their livestock. They stocked some of the enclosed land with sheep and, as they prospered, were able to experiment with new and improved agricultural techniques. The poorer peasants suffered from the enclosures, having no place to graze their livestock, and many of them fled to town. There they constituted a labor pool upon which the new factory-owners could draw.

The same process is occurring in underdeveloped lands, but its problems are aggravated by the population explosion. The "Green Revolution," which improves agricultural yields with better seeds, fertilizers, insecticides, and machinery, displaces subsistence farmers and many laborers. As Pakistani landowners buy tractors, they dismiss their tenant farmers, who farmed perhaps 10 acres with hoes and bullock-drawn plows. It has been estimated that mechanization reduces labor requirements from about eight persons per 100 acres to four. With each worker supporting a family of five, about 4 million Pakistanis will be displaced by 1985 if mechanization continues. And government policy aids those who buy tractors rather than those who are displaced by them. It supports wheat prices and keeps taxes low.[45] Like black farm workers displaced by cotton picking machines, like Brazilians who see more hope in the miserable *favelas* clinging to Rio's hillsides than on a plot of land in the country, they may find no jobs in the city. The cards may be stacked against them because they have less schooling, different customs, and perhaps are of a dif-

ferent racial background than the city dwellers. But their individual characteristics are not as crucial to their assimilation as the features of social organization that facilitate or impede their urbanization in the social sense. The city's "gatekeepers," official and unofficial—police and court officials, even storekeepers and bartenders—have decision-making and counseling power that either furthers or thwarts integration into the community.[46]

In most cases these migrants "can't go home again," physically or psychologically. The old homestead is disappearing in all highly mobile industrializing societies. The once autonomous rural village has lost much of its social and cultural integrity. Even for those who remain, "the local standards set by family, neighborhood, and community become less meaningful in terms of potential rewards, and they lack the coercive power they once had."[47] When farmers need tractors, gasoline, fertilizers, schools, and hospitals, they are tied to the larger society as peasants are not. The nation-state demands their loyalty if it is to bring them modern facilities.

Many of us, perhaps, tend to romanticize farming as a way of life, just as we mourn the mythical "noble savage." In many ways it was not at all idyllic. It was often very difficult and constricting, as reflected in the Spanish saying that "A small village is a great hell," where everyone knows everyone else's business. "But it was a way of life, and it was cherished by most of those who knew it. . . . It is striking to see how much public and private effort is put into the promotion of change and how little into constructive channeling of the sweeping effect of change. The disappearance of the rural way of life

[45]"Pakistani Landless and Jobless Increased by Green Revolution," *The New York Times* (Nov. 1, 1970).

[46]Lyle W. Shannon and Magdaline Shannon, "The Assimilation of Migrants to Cities: Anthropological and Sociological Contributions," in Schnore, *Social Science and the City,* pp. 49–75.

[47]Halpern, *The Changing Village Community,* p. 124.

was actually a painful expulsion of a part of society out the back door, not only because abandonment of farms was and is not the choice of most rural people but also because there are no (or few) programs to rectify economic hardship or to assist in occupational and social readjustment."[48]

The Future of Cities

Some people predict that the city as we know it will die because it is no longer necessary. Arthur Clarke, who wrote the science-fiction film *2001: A Space Odyssey,* says that in the near future, thanks to advances in electronic communications, executives will have in their homes a general-purpose communications console comprising a TV screen, a TV camera, a microphone, a computer keyboard and readout device. They will be able to get in touch with anyone who has a similar system. They will not have to travel on business. They will communicate rather than commute.

Clarke's idea is still science fiction, but it does point out one of the main reasons for the existence of cities in their present form. It is already very easy to decentralize industry, but the central business district is, under the present system, necessary for administrative offices. Peter Hall sees the growth of white-collar occupations of all kinds as the most important single explanation for the growth of world cities since 1850. If we grant this premise, new means of handling white-collar and executive work, such as Clarke's, will eliminate the need for the central business district.[49]

What new forms might we envision for cities, and how can we achieve them? Some planned cities actually exist. Others are still on paper. The Scandinavian countries exhibited unusual foresight, buying up large tracts of open land decades ago. Stockholm has extended its subway system to four or five satellite cities. Helsinki's suburb of Tapiola is half park and has a density of only twenty-eight people per acre. It was built by the Finnish Housing Foundation, a nonprofit organization founded by the Family Welfare League and five other associations. Its directors had to supervise construction engineers, who, like their counterparts elsewhere, would have found it easier to bulldoze trees than to work around them. Tapiola includes different kinds of dwellings at different prices, some industry, easy access to recreational and cultural facilities, and proximity to a freeway that takes residents to the capital in 20 minutes.

Columbia, Maryland, covers 22 square miles and includes eight villages with a wide price range in housing. Each village has four to six residential neighborhoods and a downtown area. Hundreds of acres of undeveloped land remain, to be kept open for relief from the city.

Not all cities need conform to the same pattern or fulfill the same functions. We might have cities that are primarily for ceremonial public celebrations and rituals, university cities, scientific cities for research and development, festival or arts cities such as Salzburg and Venice, recreational cities like Las Vegas, convention and conference cities, communications cities, museum cities such as Florence, Athens, and Williamsburg, and industrial and political and commercial cities such as now dominate our urban culture. We might even have cities that are strictly experimental, for trying out new life styles and patterns of social relationships.[50]

[48]Kenneth R. Schneider, *Destiny of Change: How Relevant Is Man in the Age of Development?* (New York: Holt, Rinehart & Winston, 1968), p. 31.

[49]*The World Cities,* p. 27.

[50]Athelstan Spilhaus, "The Experimental City," *Daedalus* (Fall 1967).

Meanwhile, how can we live with cities as they are now and as they seem destined to become in the foreseeable future? In the underdeveloped nations, the enormous problems of the population explosion and the need for economic development are inseparable from any successful solution to the problem of the millions of migrants living at or below subsistence level. In many European nations, long-range plans for "new towns" and reconstruction or preservation of existing ones are administered by the central government. In the United States, the "urban crisis" threatens to get much worse before it is resolved, for several reasons: the race problem, our transportation system and policy, the political fragmentation of metropolitan areas, and above all our negative attitudes toward planning and toward cities themselves.

We seem to have a cultural aversion to planning. "Urban renewal" has usually meant piecemeal renovation, adding a highway there or office building here, clearing slums here or lengthening subway systems there. Often elderly people on pensions and disadvantaged minorities are removed from their homes with no provision for new ones. One plan in San Francisco, for example, called for the destruction of 4,000 housing units and the construction of fewer than 300 in the same area. High-rise housing projects for low-income groups or welfare families are other examples of bad planning, with disastrous unforeseen consequences. When people live on streets in one- or two-family houses, they exercise social control, watching their neighbors and preventing some delinquent acts. But in a high-rise apartment building muggings, robberies, and other assaults go undetected. And without control of crime, the city may be truly doomed.

There is no one answer to the problems of the city. Attempts at systems analysis show how incredibly complex the interrelationships of variables are. Urban problems are ongoing or open-ended problems. If we hope to solve them in any degree, we are going to have to continue working at them indefinitely.

Perhaps Americans do not really care about cities. The myth of pastoral America persists even as the reality vanishes. Most Americans do not value sophistication, urbanity, and cosmopolitanism. Only 14 percent want to live in large cities or suburbs, and 22 percent in medium-sized cities or suburbs, while 30 percent would prefer a small town or city and 34 percent would like to live in open country.[51] "The American urban place is a noncity because Americans wish it to be just that."[52] Not caring for the crowded central city, they are abandoning it to the powerless who have no choice but to live there.

Summary

Attitudes toward cities differ almost as greatly as cities themselves. Urban sociologists have often reflected the conditions of their times and the biases of their cultures, particularly in studies of the relationship between demographic patterns of settlement and culture, social structure, and personality—the relationship between where people live and how they live.

[51] National Public Opinion Survey conducted in 1971 for the Commission on Population Growth and the American Future. *Population and the American Future,* p. 36.

[52] Elazar, "Are We a Nation of Cities?"

A city, in the demographic sense, is a relatively dense concentration of people settled in a relatively small geographic area. The social definition of a city includes several features: heterogeneity, specialization, interdependence, mobility, and an "urban way of life" that results from these factors and has certain consequences for the social relationships and personalities of city-dwellers. Demographic urbanization refers to the proportion living in urban areas, or an increase in that proportion. Social urbanization refers to the adoption of an urban way of life.

Although cities date back nearly 6,000 years, the great shift to urban living came with industrialization and has been especially marked since 1850. In 1970 more than a quarter of the people in the world lived in cities of 20,000 or more, and 10 percent in cities of half a million people or more. In general, the more highly industrialized a country, the more highly urbanized it is. But some preindustrial countries are overurbanized, with numerous migrants from rural areas living below subsistence levels in the slum areas of large cities.

Forty million Americans left farms for cities between 1920 and 1970. Metropolitan areas, especially their suburbs, have grown fastest of all. Suburbs now contain more people than rural areas, small towns, or central cities. Urban density drops as suburbanization proceeds. Urban regions, constellations of urban centers and their hinterlands, will probably contain five out of six Americans by the year 2000.

Louis Wirth believed that the size, diversity, and density of the city result in a distinctive urban way of life which includes features of social organization and certain personality traits. This way of life has serious consequences such as a higher rate of personal and social disorganization and delinquency than in rural areas. Herbert Gans finds that urbanism is many ways of life, and that these are more closely related to class and to stage in the life cycle than to place of residence. The suburb and the outer city are made up of family neighborhoods. The traits and problems Wirth discerned apply most closely to the inner city, and especially to those who have no choice but to live there or who are not established residents but recent rural migrants. Claude Fischer's subcultural theory synthesizes the views of Wirth and Gans.

Ecological processes, the steps by which a city grows and changes, include concentration of population, centralization of activities, decentralization of both people and activities, specialization, routinization, segregation, invasion, and succession. The resulting patterns of land use reflect transportation technology and policy, the competition of different groups for space and desirable locations, relative economic advantage and other factors that affect freedom of choice, and such values as sentimental attraction to a certain place or interest in certain kinds of activities.

In many cities in newly developing countries, migrants avoid culture shock by clustering with others from their former communities, and continuing their ways as much as possible. This results in "peasantization" of cities. The urban revolution is also a rural revolution. Cities began when a surplus of food became available, and they grow most swiftly and successfully where agriculture is most commercialized and mechanized. Agricultural workers constitute only about 4.5 percent of the labor force in the United States, about 16 percent in Japan. But in the world as a whole, six out of ten workers are still agricultural, and in many countries, productivity is very low. Nonetheless, the urban trend continues, and rural villages lose autonomy as the need for industrial products ties them to the larger society, and teachers and other social change agents help prepare their children for a different way of life.

Some predict cities will soon be made obsolete by new communication and transportation technology. Others see them as essential centers of civilization. A few planned cities serve as models for possible future "new towns." But in most of the Third World, the pressing problems of the population explosion and the urgency of achieving economic development make such plans seem visionary. In our own country, the cultural bias against both the city itself and planning in general may explain why we fail to come to grips with "the urban crisis."

Glossary

Centralization Concentration of institutions and activities in a given area.

City (demographic definition) A relatively dense concentration of people settled in a relatively small geographic area.

City (social definition) A city as demographically defined, plus a distinctive way of life.

Concentration The drawing together of population into given areas of varying degrees of density.

Decentralization The spread of activities and dwelling places farther and farther out from the center of a city.

Human ecology The study of the distribution of various functions, groups of people, and kinds of building within a given area, and of the processes involved in that distribution.

Invasion The penetration of a segregated area by an institutional function or population group different from the one already there.

Metropolitan area A social and economic community embracing a number of cities and urban fringe areas.

Routinization The regular movement of people and goods in time and space.

Segregation The drawing together of similar types of people, voluntarily or involuntarily.

Specialization The clustering of particular types of institutions and activities in different districts.

Suburbanization The movement of people out of central cities into surrounding urban areas.

Succession The replacement of a group or institution through invasion.

Urban regions Areas of a million or more people including a continuous zone of metropolitan areas and the counties between them, with the entire population near at least one city.

Urbanism The distinct way of life that characterizes cities.

Urbanization (demographic definition) The proportion of a total population concentrated in urban areas, or a rise in this proportion.

Urbanization (social definition) A change in the way of life of people attributable to demographic urbanization.

part

5

Social Institutions

chapter
14

The Family

Susan Gaines and Benjamin Barton are both 28 years old. She is a commercial artist and he is a freelance writer. They were married a year ago, after living together for a year. They take weekly turns shopping and cooking, as well as cleaning up the kitchen. They live in an apartment in an older section of San Francisco. For two hours one day a week they both clean house. "We both hate it, but it's not too bad when we do it together." The houseplants are divided into "his" and "hers." She is still known as Susan Gaines, although, she says, it makes her mother-in-law feel a little funny.

"Why did we get married? Because I felt insecure. He always had to prove his commitment to our relationship, and I didn't want to work on the relationship if it wasn't going to last. When we got married we could stop talking about it. It was nice to take it for granted. His mother likes me. She kept warning him to marry me quickly or I might get away.

"About having children, I really am up in the air. I'm not ready to bring anyone else into this relationship. We're having too much fun. My career is not at the point where I could take time off yet. And kids are very expensive. Besides, I don't know how my parents put up with me and my sister!

"I love being married, but I hate being introduced as a wife. When we get together with other couples, the wives are the boring ones. No one at a party asks me what I do. I'm just Benjamin's wife. I hate to go.

I know it's already a minus. The word 'wife' has a negative sound for me.

"Right after being married I was depressed and confused for a while. I had to overcome stereotypes about what it means to be married. I cleaned kitchen counters like mad. A friend told me she scrubbed floors compulsively for six months. But I got over that. I am so happy I can't believe I'm married. But I try very hard not to be 'just a wife'!"

Susan and Ben represent one of many forms of the pivotal social institution we call the family. Their relationship and attitudes are very different from those typical of their parents' generation. Even if there were a "typical" marriage today, theirs probably would not fit the pattern. But many aspects of their marriage reflect the impact of changing sex roles and other influences on the modern family.

No law says everyone must find a mate or live in a family, but nearly everyone does. In this chapter, after defining marriage and the family, we look at the various forms and functions of the family. We discuss the stages of the life cycle of the American family from its beginnings in mate selection and marriage, through childrearing, the empty nest, and the inevitable dissolution, whether it is voluntary or involuntary. We examine the changes in family structure that are occurring today and look at the future of the family, including alternative forms of family life.

320

What Is the Family?

The family is very familiar to us. Most of us regard it as so secret, private, and sacred that we tend to regard any deviations from our ideal as wrong. Many Americans believe that ideal is a father, mother, and children, living together in a single house, in affection, respect, and privacy. They don't ask why the Browns stay together year after year, but why the Adams got a divorce. Not why so many women accept an inferior status, but why so many are protesting. Not what are the dangers to children of being isolated with one woman all day long, but why some women trust their young children to others and take jobs outside the home. Arlene and Jerome Skolnick suggest that sociologists must recognize that they, too, are bound in large part by the mystique surrounding the family. But they must attempt to make the familiar seem strange, to question conventional assumptions about the small family unit, sex differences, and human nature.[1]

In that spirit even the definition of the family becomes an exercise in caution and precision. For almost every generalization we make about its structure and its functions, we find some exception in culture. The Kaingang, a nomadic tribe in Brazil, had a family structure that we would have difficulty fitting into a definition of the family as found in Western societies. Their shifting sexual interests determined the structure of their family groups. Man-and-woman relationships were informal, almost accidental. Children belonged to parents much as pets do in the United States. Another group, the Nayar caste of India, centered their family life around women because the men were away a lot. No general definition fits *all* the data; what we call

[1] *Family in Transition: Rethinking Marriage, Sexuality, Child Rearing and Family Organization* (Boston: Little, Brown, 1971), p. *vii*.

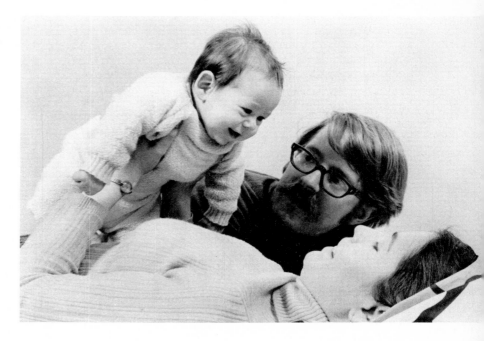

While the family has numerous forms, it is universal. *Raimondo Borea/Editorial Photocolor Archives.*

"universal" may be only nearly so. However, the concept of *family,* regardless of variations in form, is universal.

Let us begin with the obvious fact that babies are born and must be cared for. Each society has some durable kinship units that provide for infant care and childrearing. Each has some way of defining every person's relationship to many others. A set of norms outlines a kinship structure, with reciprocal statuses and roles, rights and obligations, according to age and sex, and biological and sexual relationships. **Kinship** includes the tie between progenitors and descendants (parents and children, grandchildren, etc.) and the tie of common descent (brothers and sisters, cousins, and so on). But in some societies the kinship structure is not entirely dependent on biological relationships. The Trobrianders, for example, do not understand the father's role in producing children, yet they view the father as kin. In other societies the biological father is not part of the kinship structure at all. *Social* definitions, then, rather than biology, determine who is kin. The kinship tie involves special rights of possession and is generally the closest bond in a society, closer than friendship.[2]

Within the kinship structure exists a family system defined by cultural norms regarding mate selection, number of spouses, and so on. We can also think of the family as a concrete group—but we cannot say "father, mother, and children," for there are other kinds of family groups. Lévi-Strauss defines the **family** as the married man and woman, who function semi-independently within the larger kin network.[3] Whether or not Susan and Benjamin ever have children, they are a family.

Marriage is the established procedure for founding a family and is usually symbolized by a ceremony. It "most characteristically functions in the sexual realm . . . to license parenthood and legitimize children."[4] It typically (though again not invariably) involves the expectation of common residence, economic cooperation, and reproduction.[5] The marriage contract differs from ordinary contracts in that, with marriage, each person takes on a new status and assumes broad obligations (rather than duties in some limited aspect of life). In the United States, the legal system "reflects the moral consensus of the society that fulfillment of marriage and kinship obligations is very important."[6]

The family institution of every society includes norms that prescribe whom people may or may not marry. Some have norms prescribing whom they *must* marry—a mother's brother's daughter, for example. **Endogamy** demands marriage *within* a certain group, which is usually determined by such criteria as residence, nationality, class, race, or religion. **Exogamy** means marriage must be *outside* a certain group. A mate must come from some other clan in the tribe, for example.

Incest avoidance (the incest taboo) is the most nearly universal social custom. In fact, some anthropologists consider it the basis of all social organization. With rare exceptions, sexual relationships and marriages are prohibited between brothers and sisters, parents and children. In many societies the taboo extends to numerous other relationships as well. As a consequence, families are mutually interdependent. They must ex-

[2] Ira L. Reiss, *The Family System in America* (New York: Holt, Rinehart and Winston, 1971), p. 19.
[3] Claude Levi-Strauss, "The Family," in Harry L. Shapiro, ed., *Man, Culture, and Society* (New York: Oxford University Press, 1966), pp. 266–267.

[4] David A. Schulz, *The Changing Family: Its Function and Future,* 2nd ed. (Englewood Cliffs, N.J.: Prentice-Hall, 1976), p. 64.
[5] Gerald R. Leslie, *The Family in Social Context* (New York: Oxford University Press, 1967), p. 27.
[6] Robin M. Williams, Jr., *American Society: A Sociological Interpretation,* 3rd ed. (New York: Alfred A. Knopf, 1970), p. 54.

change children to found new families. The incest taboo thus promotes social cohesion by creating a complex network of marital ties among different groups in a society. It also limits friction within the family by removing the element of sexual jealousy and competition. Another effect of prohibiting sexual relations between close family members has to do with genetics. Close inbreeding has a degenerating effect on the population. Although primitive people may not have understood how babies are made, they may have realized that inbreeding had negative consequences.

Cultural rules defining permissible forms of marriage vary. **Monogamy,** where one person is married to only one mate at a time, is the form we are most familiar with. Sexual exclusivity is assumed, but not necessarily required. A **polygamous** marriage is the marriage of a person to more than one spouse. A **polyandrous** marriage involves one woman and several men. A **polygynous** marriage, on the other hand, is formed by the union of several women with one man. Although the monogamous form is required by law in the United States, other societies allow more diversity (see Table 14-1).

Forms of the Family

Although we are most familiar with the family composed of a man, a woman, and their children, this is only one kind of family group. We can classify families according to whether they place more emphasis on the **consanguineal** relationship—that of "blood kin"—or on the **conjugal** one—that of marriage.

Nuclear Families

A **nuclear family** stresses conjugal ties. It consists of a husband-father, a wife-mother,

Table 14-1 Type of Marriage Preferred

Type	Number of Societies	Percentage of All Societies
Monogamy	137	16
Polygyny	712	83
Polyandry	4	0+
Unknown	9	1
Total	862	100

Source: adapted from George P. Murdock, *Ethnographic Atlas* (Pittsburgh: University of Pittsburgh Press, 1967).

and one or more offspring-siblings. It may be conceived of as including several dyads: husband-wife, mother-offspring, father-offspring, and perhaps sibling-sibling. The nuclear family is found almost everywhere because it is the simplest way of joining the sexual dyad and the maternal dyad, both of which are essential to conceiving and raising children. But this does not mean, insists Richard Adams, "that the nuclear family is an indispensable, basic, stable, family type, and that its absence must therefore represent a breakdown." Households based on the maternal dyad, if we accept this view, are neither abnormal nor disorganized but "alternative or secondary norms." [7]

The typical independent American nuclear family is a conjugal family. In a conjugal system, the man's primary duties are to his wife and children. He leaves his parents to care for his own nuclear family. Because conjugal families include only two generations, they are transitory. As parents die and children marry, the unit disintegrates and new ones are formed. In such a system, each person belongs first to a *family of orientation*,

[7] "An Inquiry into the Nature of the Family," in Gertrude R. Dole and Robert L. Carneiro, eds., *Essays in the Science of Culture* (New York: Crowell, 1960), pp. 35–49.

The nuclear family consists of a husband-father, wife-mother, and offspring. It is found almost everywhere. *Design Photographers International, Inc.*

into which he or she is born and socialized. Later a *family of procreation* is formed. Descent is reckoned *bilaterally* or *bilineally*. That is, the father's and mother's ancestors are regarded as equally important. Descent is rarely reckoned very far back, however, and ancestral ties are vague, as are ties with uncles, aunts, and cousins. Residence is *neolocal*. That is, the newly married couple leaves both sets of parents and establishes a new residence, perhaps at a great distance. In a conjugal system there is considerable latitude in the performance of family roles.

Extended Family

When other kin and other generations are included in the family system we speak of an **extended family.** The stress is on kinship rather than marriage, on consanguineal rather than conjugal ties. The simplest kind of extended family consists of three generations living together: husband and wife, children, and a grandmother, for example.

But traditional extended families typically consist of joint households in which the conjugal families are subordinate to the large group. There is close cooperation in work and economic dealings.

Consanguine systems stress the ties of parents and children, brothers and sisters, rather than husband and wife. In a consanguine extended family one spouse, usually the wife, is considered "an outsider whose wishes and needs must be subordinated to the continuity and welfare of the extended kin group."[8] Descent is traced either through the mother's line or the father's, but rarely through both. The continuity of the line from generation to generation is considered all-important. In *patrilineal* families (with paternal rules of descent), the wife usually moves into the husband's household. In *matrilineal* ones, residence may be either *patrilocal* or *matrilocal* (with the parents of husband or wife).

[8] Leslie, *The Family in Social Context,* p. 35.

324

Members of a consanguine family are expected to play their roles in the traditional manner. Individualism is discouraged. The family comes first. The extended family affords its members a great sense of security, even though it is also constricting. It is not dissolved by divorce, desertion, or even death. A child has many people besides his or her parents and siblings to turn to in crises.

Family Form and Social Complexity

According to Gerald Leslie about one-fourth of all societies, including some non-industrial ones such as Eskimo societies, have the nuclear conjugal family only. Another fourth have polygamous but not extended families. About one-half have some form of extended family. The extended family predominates in pastoral and agricultural economies (see Figure 14-1). "Most societies in the world today have unilineal descent systems, extended families, and male domination."[9] In the United States, the nuclear family (with children) is by far the preferred form (see Table 14-2). In most of these one spouse, usually the husband, is the sole breadwinner. This pattern is common in

[9] *Ibid.*, p. 69.

The extended family includes other generations and other kin. The stress is on kinship rather than marriage. *Nancy Hays/Monkmeyer Press Photo Service.*

modern industrial societies. Many of its functions are quite different from those of traditional extended families.

Figure 14-1 Relationship between extended families and complexity of society. *Adapted from Burton Pasternak, Introduction to Kinship and Social Organization (Englewood Cliffs, N.J.: Prentice Hall, 1976), p. 88.*

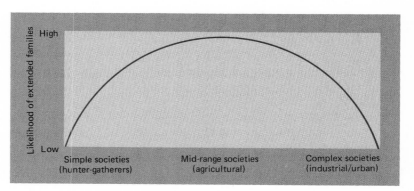

Table 14-2 Family Types in the United States

Family Type	Percentage Distribution
Nuclear family (with children)	
One partner working	30
Both working	14
Nuclear family (without children)	
One partner working	4
Both working	11
Single parent	13
Remarried	15
Other traditional	5
"Experimental" marriages & families	8

Source: adapted from Betty Cogswell and Marvin Sussman, "Changing Family and Marriage Forms: Implications for Human Service Systems," *The Family Coordinator* 21, 4 (October 1972), p. 507.

Functions of the Family

The family as an institution performs many functions. Some are universal—so basic they are found in the family groups of all societies, no matter what their form. Others are peculiar to certain types of societies such as folk or urban society.

Reproduction

Our biological nature has had a basic effect on the formation of the family. Other animals are sexually receptive only during certain periods called *estrus,* or heat. Humans, on the other hand, are sexually active at any time. Having a husband or wife provides a person with a socially acceptable outlet for sex. Most societies limit sexual expression to sex-in-marriage. Some do not object to or may even encourage premarital sex, while others actively discourage it. Most societies have rules about extramarital sex, but some enforce them less strictly than others. In any case, a marriage partner is the distinctly preferred sex partner.

A second factor that encourages the formation of stable families is the help and protection needed by women during and after pregnancy. In one way or another, society instills in its members the desire to have children, reinforcing the powerful sex drive with the injunction to "Be fruitful and multiply and replenish the earth." Even in societies with great freedom of sexual expression, conception is surrounded by norms and sanctions that legitimize reproduction and ensure that the newborn will be given a chance to survive.

Childrearing

In addition to ensuring the survival of its children, the family also gives them their initial status in the community. In some societies, this *ascribed status* is theirs for life. In other, less rigid societies, it is merely a starting place for a career based on personal achievement.

The family also functions as the chief agent of cultural transmission during the early years of life. The family teaches its children the language, folkways, mores, values, and beliefs of the culture as interpreted by the parents. In short, it socializes the children and prepares them, with varying degrees of success, for participation in the larger society.

Economic Functions of the Family

In folk societies, the family is nearly self-sufficient. The family can provide its own food, clothing, and shelter. It can find productive roles for all its members, even toddlers and old people. This is not the case with the modern urban family. The family is still the main unit of consumption, but production goes on largely outside the home. Generally only those members who have jobs can be considered independent. The rest of the family, to the Internal Revenue Service and to themselves, are dependents. Money is brought home to be used by the family for food, clothing, shelter, and so on. Thus, the modern family is highly dependent on the larger society for economic well-being. It is rarely if ever economically self-sufficient. Other functions once performed by the family have been taken over by other institutions—such as schools, churches, police, or homes for the aged.

Emotional Satisfaction

As society has become more complex, people increasingly find their work and personal contacts outside the family lacking in meaning and emotional satisfaction. In industrial societies, nuclear families have become relatively isolated from kin and other families. The nuclear family has become the chief source of emotional security, affection, and acceptance. Some observers have suggested that families do not appear to be up to the task, that the demands of family members have become excessive as extrafamilial sources of satisfaction have dried up. In our society, for example, the socialization practices of middle-class families have resulted in children with an "almost insatiable need for acceptance and security, expressed as a need to love and be loved." [10] This may be one reason why over 95 percent of Americans marry at least once in their lifetime.

The Nuclear Family in Industrial Society

Talcott Parsons believes the change to the isolated nuclear family charged with providing psychological security and response is ideally suited to the needs of modern societies. As a society industrializes, its institutions undergo differentiation. Units that formerly had several functions find they must concentrate on the one or two they perform best, because other, more specialized units have taken over some of their former functions and can perform them better. The loss of economic production in the home leaves the family free to concentrate on the socialization of children and on mutual affection and emotional support. And the occupational system is better off. The family is physically mobile, so it can go where jobs are available. The head of the family is not tied to the status ascribed by the extended family, so he is motivated to achieve for himself and his wife and children. When children grow up, they are free to leave home for the world of work. If a wife is a drag on his occupational advancement, a man is free to find a more satisfactory partner. Romantic love, too, is functional, for it motivates people to choose mates, marry, and thus contribute to society, even though the family can no longer exert pressure on them to marry for the sake of family continuity, much less choose mates for their children. Even the youth culture of today performs a valuable function. The family, which keeps children emotionally dependent in the early years, suddenly cuts back on emotional support at adolescence to impress on them that they must fend for themselves eventually. In their peer group they find emotional support.[11]

This optimistic functional view of the modern nuclear family has been questioned and qualified. First of all, a woman "liberated" from the extended family finds her domestic burdens greater rather than less. "If there is a peculiar fit between industrial work and the conjugal family, there is a peculiar lack of fit between domestic work and the conjugal family: any kind of eco-

---

[10] Schulz, *The Changing Family,* p. 154.

[11] Hyman Rodman, "Talcott Parsons' View of the Changing American Family," in *Marriage, Family, and Society: A Reader* (New York: Random House, 1965), pp. 262–283.

nomic analysis would suggest that such tasks as child care, meal preparation, and clothes washing make more sense as communal work than as the reduplicated tasks of isolated individuals."[12] Second, children are more vulnerable to the power of parents alone, and parents (especially mothers) often are more resentful because they are burdened with their constant care. Third, the high rate of divorce indicates that the nuclear family is a brittle institution. It carries perhaps too great a burden in being made the chief source of happiness, the chief refuge from the pressures of the world of work. Yet even those whose marriages collapse usually try again, indicating that there is strong faith in the power of marriage and the family to provide psychological satisfactions.

Another qualification of the thesis that modernization reduces the family to an isolated nuclear unit is that there are still extended families in many industrial societies, including our own.

Marvin Sussman and others have demonstrated that the American family is not so "isolated" as some studies have suggested. Sussman studied the relationships of 95 middle-class white Protestant couples and their 195 married children living away from home. This and other studies indicate that there exists a very active "network of mutual aid," which includes financial support or aid (direct or indirect), emotional support, visiting, babysitting, help with household tasks and repairs, and help during illness or after childbirth. One norm of this arrangement is an unspoken understanding that parents do not interfere or criticize. Grandma becomes adept at biting her tongue. This adjustment is easiest if the son-in-law or daughter-in-law is of similar background. Alienation from parents is far more frequent in interethnic marriages, for example.[13]

This "modified extended family" does not interfere with the demands of an industrial economy for social and physical mobility. It is actually easier to maintain such family ties now than it was a generation or two ago. Long-distance calls are cheaper and faster, planes more frequent and more reliable, highways and automobiles better. Children appear to value the sense of emotional support that an extended family affords, just as grandparents like to feel included in the affections of the younger generation. There are also cliques or networks of unrelated nuclear families, often living in the same neighborhood, who routinely extend mutual aid and feel they can depend on one another in times of crisis.

The Life Cycle of the Family

Just as individuals live through childhood, adolescence, adulthood, and old age, families can be seen as going through various stages. Sociologists differ on how many stages compose the family life cycle. Evelyn Duvall[14] proposed a model made up of eight stages that cover varying lengths of time (see Figure 14-2). Given the current life expectancy of 77 years for women and 68 for men, the cycle may cover half a century or more for couples who stay together.

Stage I: Couple without children
Stage II: Oldest child under 30 months old
Stage III: Oldest child age 2 1/2 to 6
Stage IV: Oldest child age 6 to 13

[13] Marvin B. Sussman, "The Help Pattern in the Middle-Class Family," *American Sociological Review,* 15 (Feb. 1953), pp. 22–23; "The Isolated Nuclear Family: Fact or Fiction," *Social Problems,* 6 (Spring 1959), pp. 333–340; "Family Continuity," *Marriage and Family Living,* 16 (May 1954), pp. 113–118.
[14] *Family Development,* 5th ed. (Philadelphia: Lippincott, 1969).

[12] Skolnick and Skolnick, *Family in Transition,* p. 19.

Stage V: Oldest child age 13 to 20
Stage VI: From when oldest child leaves
              to when youngest child leaves
Stage VII: Empty nest to retirement
Stage VIII: Retirement to death of one or
              both parents

An occupational cycle runs parallel to this family cycle and may be more important to the husband. If a couple chooses not to

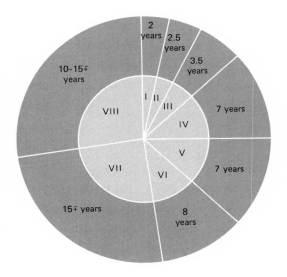

Figure 14-2 The length of each stage of the family life cycle in contemporary American society. *From Evelyn Duvall, Family Development, 4th. ed. (Philadelphia: Lippincott, 1971), p. 121.*

have children, it is likely that the occupational cycle has more relevance for both of them. However, the vast majority of married couples do have children. Therefore, keeping this model in mind, let us sketch the main stages of the family life cycle.

Mate Selection

Before the family life cycle can start, one needs to find a mate. This can be accom-

plished in a number of ways depending on the nature of the society. In traditional societies, where institutions are closely interwoven, marriage is rarely a private contract, and love, sexuality, and marriage are not regarded as inseparable parts of the culture complex of the family. Because marriage involves alliances between whole families besides the couple involved and has economic ramifications, such societies prefer not to leave the choice of a mate to chance or personal whim. Marriages are likely to be arranged by the parents, elders, or other family authorities, with or without the consent of the bride and groom-to-be. In fact, they may still be children at the time. Marriage for love in many developing nations, including Southern Europe, "is considered a luxury and a privilege of the rich." [15]

In our society, where the nuclear family is designed to be independent of such outside influence and where families no longer cooperate economically in the traditional way, such arrangements have largely gone out of fashion. Young people are theoretically free to select anyone who strikes their fancy. While traditional societies base marriage on practical considerations, in modern Western societies love and marriage supposedly go together like a horse and carriage.

Love can be a threat to a society's system of stratification. Love is blind to race, educational level, religious affiliation, and income. Parents, however, are not blind to these things. Therefore, although in the United States people are allowed to fall in love at will, the choice of a mate is subtly limited to "eligibles," those who meet certain criteria. Because most American young people resent overt parental interference in their intimate affairs, such teaching generally occurs early as part of the process of socialization. Later,

[15] Constantina Safilios-Rothschild, *Love, Sex, and Sex Roles* (Englewood Cliffs, N.J.: Prentice-Hall, 1977), p. 19.

parental pressures, framed in terms of disapproval, may be enough to recall those early lessons.

This is not to imply that such parents are simply being selfish or snobbish, though some may be. By seeking to limit their children's choice to someone of similar background, parents are trying to maximize the chances of marital success. In any case, regardless of how it is accomplished, most people do choose mates from the same socioeconomic background, educational level, age bracket, and so on. Similarity of background is a good indicator of marital stability.

Except in unusual circumstances, there are still quite a number of people to pick from. How is the final choice made? Dating provides a way to experiment without obligation. One can go out with various kinds of people and learn about one's needs without a great deal of involvement. Thus, dating can narrow the choices still further. But how do people pick those they actually marry?

One theory, proposed by Robert Winch, is based on the idea of complementary needs.[16] This theory says that while people's social backgrounds should be similar their psychological needs should not be. Thus, a person who needs a lot of affection would do well to find a person who enjoys emotional expression. Because it is rare to find any one person who can gratify all our needs, the selection of a mate may still be difficult and may not ensure marital stability.

Another theory has been suggested by Bernard Murstein.[17] Because we are exposed to so many people in the course of a day, something must be special about them if they

stand out from the crowd enough to attract our attention. This something is called the *stimulus.* In more confined situations, where contact is facilitated, such as offices, airplanes, and coffee shops, a stimulus may not be necessary. Then the relationship goes directly to the *value* stage.

During the value stage, couples see if they have similar attitudes about things. Here, like does attract like, although some people may take longer to discover this than others. That agreement on values is important is indirectly reflected in the fact that most people do marry people of similar social class and age (two crude but largely valid indications of value similarity).

Next is the *role* stage where the couple plays at being married. This may be during a formal engagement period or may involve living together. According to Murstein, complementarity of roles is more critical than complementarity of personal needs. He feels that the most reliable predictor of marital success is the couple's willingness to tolerate flexibility in role expectations and behavior. If personal needs actually were more important, such flexibility would be disruptive, not constructive.

Marriage

The family life cycle begins with marriage. Marriage involves many adjustments. Most American parents try not to do or talk about certain things "in front of the children." So, just as people may enter marriage with an inadequate sexual education, they may also enter it with unrealistic expectations acquired more from the movies than from real life. If the wife's parents hid their disagreements, she may be devastated by the first quarrel with her new husband. His mother may never have told him how overburdened she felt by her household duties. And he

[16] *Mate Selection* (New York: Harper, 1958).
[17] "Stimulus-Value Roles: A Theory of Marital Choice," *Journal of Marriage and the Family*, Vol. 32 (1970), pp. 465–481.

may be resentful if his wife asks him to help with the dishes or the laundry.

Along with minor problems such as getting used to living with another person who possibly has irritating habits, the couple must make some major decisions. One involves how the family will make its money and how that money will be spent. Increasingly, both the husband and wife work (see Figure 14-3). This can cause some strain because there may be work-related conflicts or limitations on the time one or both can devote to family life.

Sociologists have found considerable differences in husband-wife relationships in different social classes. Mirra Komarovsky in a study of blue-collar marriages found that working-class couples accept traditional stereotypes of masculine and feminine sex roles, are typically less satisfied with marriage than the better-educated middle-class couples, and do not include friendship and companionship between spouses in their conception of marriage. The wife's circle of friends is limited mostly to relatives and neighbors. The husband spends his spare time with "the boys."[18] College students of both sexes, in contrast, named companionship as the most important thing they sought in marriage.

American women are now marrying later than in the past. Most men and women marry between ages 20 and 24. In 1960, 28 percent of women in that age group were single. The proportion rose to 39 percent in 1974. It is too early to say whether young people are simply postponing marriage or planning to live single all their lives. But one indication that they are simply postponing it is found in the fact that while the percentage of single

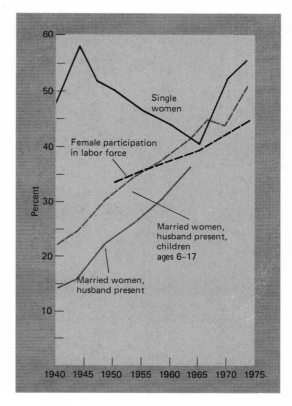

Figure 14-3 Trends and patterns of women in the labor force. *From Statistical Abstract of the United States, 1974, pp. 336, 341.*

women under 35 who remain single has risen sharply, the percentage of single women over 35 has declined. Part of this change may be due to the "marriage squeeze." Women generally marry men who are two or three years older. Women born during the postwar baby boom and looking for mates born before it had fewer to choose from. In the next five years or so, the drop in the birth rate that occurred in the 1960s means that men in turn will feel a marriage squeeze

---

[18] "Blue-Collar Marriages and Families," in Louise Kapp Howe, ed., *The White Majority* (New York: Random House, 1970), pp. 35–44.

Marriage involves many adjustments and requires working through both major and minor problems. Sociologists find considerable differences in husband-wife relationships in different social classes. *Mary Orovan/Design Photographers International, Inc.*

because there will be fewer women to choose from.[19]

Parenthood

The most important decision the couple faces is whether or not to have children. Many are content to let the decision be made for them. In spite of the fact that middle- and upper-class women are generally knowledgeable about birth control, only about one-third of all pregnancies are planned. This is not to say that all those babies are unwanted and remain unloved after birth. No doubt the majority are accepted willingly. But "children do not necessarily improve a marriage. They may create as many or more problems than they resolve. Nevertheless, romantic notions about parenthood

tend to prevent the newly married couple from examining why *they* should have children. They simply assume they ought to have them."[20]

Recent data appear to indicate that this attitude is changing. An increasing number of women are postponing childbearing within marriage and reducing the number of children they expect to have. Of women married between 1955 and 1960, 70 percent had their first baby within two years. The figure dropped to 60 percent for those married between 1965 and 1970. And in just three years the number of wives under thirty who planned to have no children increased by 23 percent. The 1974 birth rate was even lower than during the Depression years.[21]

Whether it was planned or not, the birth of the first child is always a crisis. Family

[19] Roxann A. Van Dusen and Eleanor Bernert Sheldon, "The Changing Status of American Women," *American Psychologist,* Vol. 31, No. 2 (February 1976), pp. 106–116.

[20] Schulz, *The Changing Family,* p. 118.
[21] Van Dusen and Sheldon, "The Changing Status of American Women," p. 109.

relationships become more complex as the twosome becomes a threesome. Work patterns and income distribution need to be reorganized. Space, time, and attention become more limited. The father may resent the fact that his work prevents him from being involved with his baby. The mother may resent the fact that her involvement with the baby prevents her from fulfilling other personal needs.

The presence of children may cause changes in the couple's sex life, which has already been considerably disrupted by pregnancy and postpartum abstinence. Couples may have to wait until late at night to minimize the risk that their children will invade their privacy. They may then be too tired to fully satisfy each other. Their discomfort about displaying erotic behavior in front of the children may cause them to mask any desire they may feel. This can have very negative effects on the couple's relationship. It may even be hard for the couple to have an intimate conversation to discuss mutual problems because children are present.

One of the primary responsibilities of the family is the socialization of children. A dramatic change in childrearing practices is the increasing reliance on expert advice. This has led in turn to several fads. For example, from 1930 to 1945, working-class parents were more permissive than middle-class parents. They were more likely to feed their babies on demand, more likely to wean them later, and more likely to delay toilet training. This trend was reversed after World War II, when middle-class mothers became more permissive.[22]

Class differences are also apparent in parents' selection of social values to teach their children. Middle-class parents are more likely to stress academic success, helping with household chores, and self-reliance. Lower-class parents are more likely to stress obedience and conformity. This may be because the careers available for each class stress those qualities. A doctor needs to be academically competent, while a machinist needs to be able to follow instructions.

There are class differences in discipline as well. Middle-class parents are likely to analyze their children's motives before administering punishment, while lower-class parents react to the behavior's consequences.[23] Lower-class parents are more likely to use physical punishment, while middle-class parents are more likely to attempt to appeal to reason or to threaten withdrawal of love. If the parents are warm and loving, use of these techniques can be the most effective way to encourage the child to internalize norms and values. The least effective strategy is employed by cold, distant parents who rely on assertion of power.[24] This description is most characteristic of upper-class parents. They typically exert more control over their children's lives. They have more power simply because upper-class children seemingly have more to lose if they defy their parents than lower-class children do. Another factor is the greater likelihood that upper-class families are a closely knit extended kin group. That's a lot of voices for one child to ignore, especially with so much at stake.

Styles in socialization are changing in all social classes, according to a 1977 survey

---

[22] *Ibid.*, p. 169.

[23] Victor Gecas and F. Ivan Nye, "Sex and Class Differences in Parent-Child Interaction: A Test of Kohn's Hypothesis," *Journal of Marriage and the Family,* Vol. 36, No. 4 (Nov. 1974), pp. 743–755.

[24] Boyd C. Rollins and Darwin L. Thomas, "A Theory of Parental Power and Child Compliance," in Ronald E. Cromwell and David H. Olson, eds., *Power in Families* (New York: John Wiley and Sons, 1975), pp. 38–60.

of 1,230 households with one or more children under age thirteen. The survey was conducted by pollster Daniel Yankelovich. He found that 43 percent belong to what he calls the "New Breed." They stress freedom and self-fulfillment rather than authority and material success. In effect, they say, "We have our own lives to lead so we will not sacrifice ourselves completely for you. But you don't owe us anything once you are grown." The 57 percent he calls "Traditionalists" are less permissive. They stress older American values. They believe they should sacrifice for their children, who in turn should feel a sense of obligation. Yet both groups feel the tug of the other's values. Despite their distrust of authority and material success, most of the New Breed parents stress hard work and respect for authority, along with attitudes toward sex, saving, and patriotism that they themselves have discarded.[25]

However the children are brought up, they ultimately come of age. And, like their parents before them, they leave the parental home—the family of orientation—and may eventually begin their own family life cycle.

The Empty Nest

The "empty nest" period preceding retirement has become longer in recent years because people are living longer and having fewer children. This stage may shorten to its former length, however, if the trend toward earlier retirement continues. In any case, it is a time of readjustment, particularly for the wife, on whom the major burden of child care has fallen. She finds herself alone again with her husband after a long time of sharing him with her children. It may be a relaxing time of rediscovery or a realization that one is living with a stranger.

The couple may have more free time but not know what to do with it. It may be difficult for the wife to resume her career. Finding a new role to play now that motherhood and housekeeping are secondary may be a major problem of adjustment. The husband may be having parallel readjustment difficulties. He may feel that he has done all he can occupationally and that his achievements have fallen short of his hopes. His own feelings of despondency may prevent him from being responsive to his wife's difficulties.

Along with these role changes, the couple must adjust to physiological changes. Menopause and the decline of male potency, plus the physical body changes that signal an end to youth, may result in psychological problems of readjustment.

Retirement

Three major problems arise during this last stage of the cycle. First, the chances are that, sometime during this stage, one member of the couple will die and leave the other widowed. The husband usually dies first since he usually is older and male life expectancy is lower. In 1973, 76.9 percent of the men in the United States over age 65 and 77 percent of the women were living alone. In 1968, the figures were only 69.8 percent and 72.2 percent, respectively.[26] Widowhood comes at a later age than formerly because people are living longer. But this makes

---

[25] Daniel Yankelovich, *The American Family Report: Raising Children in a Changing Society.*

[26] U.S. Bureau of the Census, *Statistical Abstract: 1974* (Washington, D.C.: U.S. Government Printing Office, 1974), p. 43.

Because of the emphasis on the nuclear family in our society, the elderly sometimes find themselves outsiders and may prefer to be with friends and neighbors rather than with their families. *J. Berndt/Stock, Boston.*

To be retired in a society that judges individuals by occupations can seriously lower self-esteem. Volunteer work, such as tutoring, can give senior citizens a stronger sense of worth. *Sybil Shelton/Monkmeyer Press Photo Service.*

adjusting to the single life even harder. The emphasis on the nuclear family in our society often makes it hard for children to help their elderly single parents or to find a comfortable place for them within the family circle. Parents sense their reluctance. One study found that elderly widows preferred to associate more with friends and neighbors than with their families.[27]

[27] Greg Arling, "The Elderly Widow and Her Family, Neighbors, and Friends," *Journal of Marriage and the Family,* Vol. 38, No. 3 (Nov. 1976), pp. 757–768.

335

Another problem facing the elderly couple is an inadequate income. The government's social security plan may be social because it has been arranged by the society. But it cannot be said to supply much security. Yet many couples are totally dependent on it and may have a meager income for many years. A third problem is that of self-esteem. In a society that judges people and ranks them on the basis of their occupation, to be retired is to be a nonperson. They may find themselves unprepared for retirement psychologically as well as financially.

Marital Satisfaction and the Life Cycle

Women apparently experience a decline in marital satisfaction during the first 10 years or until their children enter school.[28] While men seem to respond more to events outside the home, the presence or absence of children has the greatest effect on women. Thus, one could legitimately speak of two marriages—"his" and "hers." If both partners have worked throughout, "their" marriage might be more accurate.

According to Brent Miller, the number of things the couple does together is the best predictor of marital satisfaction.[29] Thus, children's effect on marital satisfaction may be indirect. Their presence may prevent the wife from spending as much time as she would like with her husband. Her satisfaction with her marriage is likely to be greatest before the children arrive and after they leave. In most cases, satisfaction does resume

after the children are on their own. However, most people surveyed were middle- and upper-class. The results might be different with lower-class couples because of economic strains and lack of preparation for retirement.

Marital Problems

Divorce

At any stage of the life cycle, a marriage can become so strained that one or both partners may decide to dissolve it. However, divorce is most likely to occur during the childrearing years. If the marriage makes it through the first 10 years, it has a good chance of going all the way. The first marriage generally lasts 7.6 years.[30]

It is well known that the divorce rate is going up in the United States. Many people are alarmed by this fact and think it means the institution of the family is breaking down. On the face of it, the statistics do appear to justify their fears. For example, in 1973, there were 2,277,000 marriages, and 913,000 divorces.[31] That would mean one in every 2.5 marriages ended in divorce. But these statistics can be interpreted another way. For example, most of those who divorce will remarry. So while more people go through divorces, the number of people at any time who are single is still relatively quite small. While marriage is becoming more voluntary, it is not dying out.

The main cause of divorce appears to be not following the "rules" for mate selection.

[28] Boyd C. Rollins and Harold Feldman, "Marital Satisfaction and the Family Life Cycle," *Journal of Marriage and the Family,* Vol. 32 (Feb. 1970), pp. 20–28.

[29] "A Multivariate Developmental Model of Marital Satisfaction," *Journal of Marriage and the Family,* Vol. 38, No. 3 (Nov. 1976), pp. 643–657.

[30] Paul Glick and Arthur Norton, "Frequency, Duration, and Probability of Marriage and Divorce," *Journal of Marriage and the Family,* No. 33 (May 1971), p. 311.

[31] *Statistical Abstract: 1974,* p. 66.

Differences in social class, religion, age, educational level, race, and so on, can intensify the adjustment difficulties faced by married couples. Highly likely prospects for divorce are those who are under 21 when they marry, blacks, and people with low incomes and less education. Another factor that may be related to the rising divorce rate involves the sorts of marriages formed by the children of divorced parents. One study found that such marriages were more unstable than those of people whose parents had not divorced. It is suggested that having only one parent may have led the daughters to select unsuitable mates due to lack of supervision and control. Sons, on the other hand, were limited economically rather than socially. It was more likely that higher education was no longer affordable. Thus, the son may have rushed into an unsuitable marriage or was simply not able to marry the kind of partner he desired.[32] As divorces increase, the number of children involved also increases. This fact alone may cause our divorce rate to rise for some time to come.

The high divorce rate doesn't mean that Americans approve of divorce. Although it no longer carries the stigma it once did, divorce is still seen as a social and personal tragedy in most societies. They employ various strategies to prevent divorce. The first is to encourage children to select marriage partners with similar backgrounds. Another social measure involves making judgments about which sources of marital strain are unimportant and thus inadequate as grounds for divorce. Although he may irritate her because he cannot balance a checkbook, and she may irritate him because she doesn't put her clothes away, these strains are considered trivial by the larger society. Another way is to lower children's expectations of what marriage will be like. If women learn as children not to expect intimate companionship from their husbands, they won't be disappointed when they don't get it. A fourth and extremely important way in which society attempts to limit divorces is through law. This does work. States that allow no-fault divorces have the highest divorce rates in the nation.

But in spite of society's attempts to prevent it, divorce continues to occur. The problems encountered when a couple divorces are more or less the same as when a marriage is ended by death. But they may be harder for the divorced couple to cope with because there is little guidance and support from society. People whose marriages are ended by death are supported by custom, ritual, and the moral obligation to comfort the survivors. "Dead spouses are good spouses."[33] Social pressures in our couple-oriented society and lack of support from an extended family encourage remarriage.

Violence in the Family

Ideally, the family is a sanctuary, a place of harmony amidst the discordances of everyday life. But the incidence of husband-wife violence appears to be increasing. Several factors may account for this increase. First, as others have noted, "violence is as American as apple pie." It is our most common response when we are angry or frustrated, and it takes many years of practice to learn to control our tempers. When

[32] Charles W. Mueller and Hallowel Pope, "Marital Instability: A Study of Its Transmission between Generations," *Journal of Marriage and the Family*, Vol. 39, No. 1 (Feb. 1977), pp. 83–92.

[33] William J. Goode, *The Family* (Englewood Cliffs, N.J.: Prentice-Hall, 1964), p. 99.

presented with violence, our tendency is to respond with violence. Animals have specific sounds and postures that indicate submission, that say, "I don't want to fight you, please don't hurt me." According to Schulz, "men and women will not either submit to violence or flee from it as a matter of instinct; their tendency is to try to stand up to it."[34] Thus, in violent families, violence tends to escalate rather than dissipate once it is expressed.

Another factor is the isolation of the nuclear family from the larger society. There is such a strong respect for the privacy of the family that authorities are reluctant to interfere until the situation becomes extreme.

The family may not be capable of fulfilling its members' intimate emotional needs while coping with the stresses of modern life. Goode suggests that a family is more prone to violence when one of its members feels cheated, when there is a gross inequality in giving and taking behaviors.[35] Frustration may come from outside the family as well. A man may physically abuse his family because he resents being responsible for them or because his life is unmanageable and they are captive targets.

Most abuse is directed at wives and children. Both the mother and father are equally likely to be child abusers, but for obvious reasons, wife abuse is vastly more common than husband abuse. Children have little choice. Though wretched and battered, unless they become wards of the state, they may have nowhere else to go. But wives are free to leave. In spite of this, many women refuse to press charges against their husbands nor will they readily obtain a divorce.

If the violence is not severe and only occurs occasionally, if the wife was beaten as a child, and if she is dependent on her husband's income, she may be unwilling to leave for personal reasons. Even if she is willing, social constraints make it difficult. Some abused wives have painted an idyllic picture of their marriages for public consumption, and many find the idea of revealing the truth to their neighbors highly unpleasant. But the major factor may be the lack of official response to their plight.

In one study, more than 75 percent of abused wives did try to get outside help, but found such help ineffective.[36] Police and the courts are generally indifferent to the problem. They may consider that a certain amount of violence is the husband's right, or that the wife deserves it, or that they shouldn't interfere in any action that occurs in the home between "consenting" adults. The California Penal Code states that before a wife can press charges against her husband, she must be more severely injured than is commonly defined as battery when committed by a stranger.[37] Both external indifference and and personal feelings may keep an abused wife from leaving her husband.

Child abuse is even harder to detect and help. It is generally a consistent pattern of behavior. If a child is abused once, it is very likely to go unreported. Either the husband or the wife is likely to commit the abuse, and one is likely to protect the other should

[34] *The Changing Family*, p. 195.

[35] William J. Goode, "Force and Violence in the Family," *Journal of Marriage and the Family*, Vol. 33 (Nov. 1971), p. 631.

[36] Richard J. Gelles, "Abused Wives: Why Do They Stay," *Journal of Marriage and the Family*, Vol. 38, No. 3 (Nov. 1976), pp. 659–668.

[37] Robert Calvert, "Criminal and Civil Liability in Husband-Wife Assaults," in Suzanne K. Steinmetz and Murray A. Straus, eds., *Violence in the Family* (New York: Harper & Row, 1974), p. 89.

a doctor or other professional become suspicious. Child abuse is very hard to prove. Many professionals were long reluctant to report suspected cases to the authorities because they were afraid of countersuits if the parent was not convicted. In 1967, however, a law was passed that protects professionals from such reprisals. Since then, reports of child abuse have become more frequent, though it is unclear whether this is due to increased incidence or the new law.

What kind of family is most likely to abuse a child? Usually it is larger than average and from the lower class. The vast majority of children are abused by their natural parents, not by stepparents. Physical punishment is rarely a help to the child, but it can be a release for the parent. Lower-class parents are more likely to resort to it and yet they exercise the least control over their children. The children are likely to respond to physical violence with more aggressive behavior, whether the parents are loving or not. Parents in turn are likely to respond to aggression with excessive violence, feeling that the child "had it coming." Such behavior may simply serve as a model to teach the child more effective ways of being aggressive. It has been suggested that exposure to aggressive models is more likely to result in aggression than is frustration caused by emotional deprivation.[38]

Some investigators have suggested that violence in the family could be reduced by increasing the amount of honest, brutally frank communication. The idea is that if people would restrict themselves to verbal violence, they would have an adequate outlet for their frustration without resorting to

physical abuse. One study, however, concluded that the opposite is the case. Expressing violence in words "may only be a modern psychological version of the old medical practice of bloodletting—harmless but useless in some cases and injurious or fatal in others."[39] It appears that learning to be verbally aggressive simply makes it easier to learn to be physically aggressive.

TV is apparently an effective substitute for family violence. Many television programs are violent and thus provide vicarious release of tension. But possibly more important, watching TV gives family members a chance to get away from each other. Many families with limited means live in rather cramped quarters with little privacy. Television provides needed relief from constant interaction. Lower-class people do watch more TV, possibly because family members are less likely to have places of their own to retreat to. Upper-class children who are subjected to rigid discipline, however, have been found to watch a lot of TV. It probably has a sedative effect for all classes. Because family tensions don't go away by themselves, however, television may simply delay the inevitable.[40]

The Changing Family

There is no one family type we can call the modern type, the natural type, the universal type, or even the ideal type. What can we

[38] A. Bandura and R. H. Walters, *Adolescent Aggression* (New York: Ronald Press, 1959).

[39] Murray A. Straus, "Leveling, Civility, and Violence in the Family," *Journal of Marriage and the Family,* Vol. 36 (Feb. 1974), p. 14.

[40] Paul C. Rosenblatt and Michael R. Cunningham, "Television Watching and Family Tensions," *Journal of Marriage and the Family,* Vol. 38, No. 1 (Feb. 1976), pp. 105–111.

Some studies show that watching TV gives family members the needed relief from constant interaction with each other. *Mini Forsyth/Monkmeyer Press Photo Service.*

say with any confidence, then, about the future of the family?

Effects of Demographic Change on the Family Life Cycle

The population explosion and effective contraception have changed the value of the reproductive function of the family. Parenthood is increasingly voluntary (see Figure 14-4). Loosening of taboos on sex relations outside of marriage and on the portrayal of sex in the mass media have also contributed to a change in the once close association of the sex act with the possibility and the hope or fear of pregnancy. A number of groups advocate free birth control, legalized abortion, and zero population growth. Some

want to define parenthood as a privilege—perhaps involving a license—rather than as a right or a natural happenstance.

The fact that women live longer and have fewer children than before has contributed to a fundamental redefinition both of their status and of husband-wife relationships. The "empty nest" period between the departure of the last child and the death of one spouse has increased to an average of 20 years. It is now nearly half of the average 45-year marriage. The average period from marriage to the birth of the last child has decreased from 11 years for women born in the late 1800s to about 8 years for those born in the 1950s.[41] With an average life expectancy of 77, a woman has many years to fill with other activities than child-rearing and housekeeping.

[41] U.S. Bureau of the Census, 1973.

340

One consequence is a great increase in the number of women employed outside the home. In 1974, more than 42 percent of the gainfully employed working population in the U.S. over age ten consisted of females. They earn, however, only about 60 percent of the male income. They are greatly underrepresented in professional, academic, and political positions. Laws, hiring and wage policies, and public opinion appear to be reducing these discriminatory practices. But the traditional definitions of division of labor in the home, and of proper patterns of interaction between husband and wife, are more resistant to change. The possession of a uterus seems to be regarded as a unique qualification for doing domestic chores. It has also long meant a much more rigid set of sexual mores than that applied to men. Women are increasingly rebelling against the notion that they need men for identity. Both sexes will be better able to fulfill their human potential when they are freed from the constrictions of traditional sex roles.

When life expectancy was shorter and the family was a unit of economic production needing children as helpers and inheritors, and when the extended family network provided emotional support and security regardless of the personal relationships of a married pair, 20-year-olds could take marriage vows "until death do us part" without reservations. Now the possibility of having to live in double harness for 50 years or more is less attractive. The fact that divorce has lost much of its stigma makes lifelong married happiness a romantic dream, an ideal that is often not fulfilled. Some social scientists and others concerned with family relationships advocate a sort of "two-step" marriage, in which the couple lives together for a specified period without having children, to be more sure of their mutual compatibility, and then possibly takes a far more

serious step, entering into a more permanent arrangement, probably with the idea of having children.

Alternative Forms of the Family

The nuclear conjugal family is often held to be the ideal agent for socializing children. But increasing recognition of the fact that not all parents are loving, nurturing parents, combined with the increasing number of

Figure 14-4 Comparison of legitimate and illegitimate birthrates. *From Current Population Reports (Washington, D.C.: U.S. Government Printing Office, 1970).*

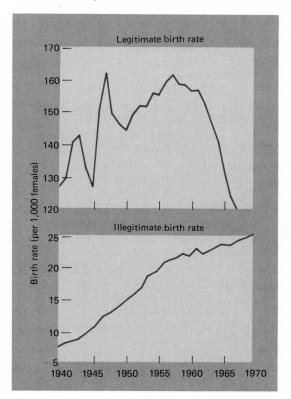

working mothers, has led to a reexamination of child-care patterns and to proposals for such innovations as day-care centers, communes, and part-time jobs for both husband and wife so that each can take a turn at child care and domestic chores.

"Maternal deprivation" has been held, especially by psychoanalytic childrearing specialists, to be uniformly threatening to children. Recent research, however, "has emphasized the need for environmental stimulation as well as loving care and has shown that even within the confines of an institution, infants' development can be normalized and even accelerated by providing them with interesting sights and playthings."[42] Day-care centers, supervised playgrounds, and similar institutions could relieve the strain for both parents and children, and enrich the cultural environment of many whose parents provide them with little stimulation.

Experiments in communal living sometimes include children who are regarded as belonging to the whole group and therefore are free of the concentrated emotion, whether "smother-love" or hostility, that may affect them in the nuclear family. But communal living is not the answer for everybody. Two other very common alternative forms of the family have come about as a result of our higher divorce rate: the single-parent family and serial monogamy.

Since 1960, the number of single-parent families in the U.S. grew seven times faster than two-parent families. In 1975, there were 4.9 million single-parent families, while in 1970, there were only 3.3 million. Of those 4.9 million families, 4.4 million were composed of a mother and her children. Fathers are increasingly requesting custody of their children after divorce. Increasingly, their requests are being granted, but still only 10 percent of single-parent families are headed by fathers. More than 11 million children—over one-sixth of the population under 18—live in single-parent families.[43]

The problems such families face—increased responsibilities for the single parent, adjustment difficulties for the children, and economic limitations—are compounded by society's negative attitudes. Instead of being seen as a legitimate family structure, single-parent families are referred to as "broken," or even worse, as "deteriorating."[44] Public policy makers do not recognize the validity of the single-parent family either. It is connected in their minds with welfare. But middle-class parents need day-care centers too, as well as other forms of assistance. Denying legitimacy to the single-parent family is rationalized by the idea that it is usually a transitory state. The majority of divorced people do indeed remarry. But at any given time, nearly 5 million families have only one parent. And many never have two. Thus, a significant number of people are being denied help because their family structure does not conform to the ideal conception of a family.

When a single-parent family that resulted from divorce is changed to a two-parent

[42] B. L. White, "An Experimental Approach to the Effect of Experience on Early Human Behavior," in J. P. Hill, ed., *Minnesota Symposium of Child Psychology*, Vol. 1 (Minneapolis: University of Minnesota Press, 1967), pp. 201–226.

[43] U.S. Bureau of the Census, "Household and Family Characteristics: March 1975," *Current Population Reports*, Series P-20, No. 291 (Feb. 1976), p. 7.

[44] This negative judgment has particular importance because it was contained in the Moynihan Report on the black family. If Americans had been less dogmatic about what constitutes a family, female-headed households would have been seen as legitimate families, not as breeders of ghetto pathology.

family, we call this phenomenon **serial monogamy.** That is, serial monogamy means that people increasingly regard marriage as voluntary but still monogamous. They may reject a particular mate but they respect the institution itself. Many people are disturbed by this trend. They believe that marriage should be a permanent union. "It is the transformation of marriage into a short-lived, fair-weather friendship that people see as a threat to family life and that they feel rising divorce rates are pointing toward."[45] But alarmists might take comfort from the fact that very few people marry more than twice. Many believe it is better to pull out of a bad marriage than to live with a mistake "till death do you part." With our longer life expectancy, we may need to redefine both love and marriage. We must face the fact that neither may last forever, but both

may take place several times in a life span. This means relaxing our expectations rather than diminishing our commitment to the marital relationship. Conceivably such a redefinition "might help us enjoy a marriage as long as it lasts and not necessarily view it or ourselves as failures when it ends."[46]

Communes, group marriages, and other experimental forms of family life have met with mixed success thus far. But it is the quality of our relationships that is much more important then its forms or structures. What matters, says sociologist Constantina Safilios-Rothschild, is that all family members should be free "to develop their potential and individual personalities and to find the most satisfactory arrangements and combinations for their needs, rather than to achieve an 'ideal' standardized family life model."[47]

Summary

The family is a pivotal and universal social institution. It appears in all societies, although its forms and functions differ.

Marriage is generally the basis of family life. Choice of mate is limited by social rules such as endogamy, exogamy, and the incest taboo. Forms of marriage include monogamy, polygamy, polyandry, and polygyny.

A nuclear family consists of husband, wife, and their children. It is also a conjugal family. The rights and needs of the husband and wife take precedence over other kin obligations. In an extended family, other

relatives are included. In consanguinal extended families, blood ties come before marriage obligations.

The family, regardless of its form, performs many functions. One universal function is the control of reproduction and support of the woman during and after pregnancy. The family gives children their initial status in the community and is responsible for childrearing. It is the primary agency of socialization. In modern society,

[45] Mary Jo Bane, *Here to Stay: American Families in the Twentieth Century* (New York: Basic Books, 1976).

[46] Safilios-Rothschild, *Love, Sex, and Sex Roles*, p. 21.

[47] Constantina Safilios-Rothschild, *Women and Social Policy* (Englewood Cliffs, N.J.: Prentice-Hall, 1973), p. 105.

the nuclear family becomes increasingly responsible for satisfying its members' intimate emotional needs. It is highly dependent on the larger society for economic well-being. Other functions such as formal education and protection have been taken over by the state in complex societies.

The family can be seen as having a life cycle composed of various stages: mate selection, marriage, parenthood, the empty nest, and retirement. Most people choose mates from similar age groups, social class, and educational level—often for reasons other than love. Married couples need to make decisions involving work and the distribution of the income from work. They also need to decide whether or not to have children. Whether planned or not, the first child's arrival forces the couple to reorganize their work patterns, income, space, time, and attention to accommodate the new baby. The empty nest stage, when the children have grown and left home, represents a period of psychological readjustment to changing roles and body images. During the last stage in the family life cycle, retirement, married people must adjust to retirement and less adequate incomes and to the death of one of the couple.

Marital satisfaction usually declines when there are children present and rises when they leave. The number of shared activities a couple engages in is the best predictor of marital satisfaction.

The increasing divorce rate is one of several marital difficulties. Most divorced people do remarry. Marriage is not dying out but is becoming increasingly voluntary. Violence in the family is another major marital problem. Common targets are wives and children.

The family is undergoing much change. The population explosion and contraceptive devices have contributed to redefinitions of the reproductive role and parenthood. The fact that women live longer and have fewer children has contributed to an ongoing redefinition of their status and of husband-wife relationships. Alternative family forms have developed that do not conform to the ideal of the middle-class American family. The two most common forms are the single-parent family and serial monogamy. Over one-sixth of the population under 18 lives in single-parent families. The problems of such families are compounded by society's failure to recognize them as a valid form.

Serial monogamy results when people remarry following divorce. Many people are alarmed by this trend, but few people marry more than twice. Thus, marriage itself still appears to be a healthy institution, and sociologists believe that flexibility in its form makes for happier relationships.

Glossary

Conjugal relationships Those of married couples.

Consaguineal relationships Those of "blood kin."

Endogamy Marriage within a certain group.

Exogamy Marriage outside of a certain group.

Extended family One stressing kinship ties.

Family A married man and woman and their children, if any, who function semi-independently within the larger kin network.

Incest avoidance (Incest Taboo) The prohibiting of sexual relationships between parents and children and brothers and sisters.

Kinship The tie between progenitors and descendents (parents and children, etc.) and the tie of common descent (brothers, sisters, cousins, etc.).

Marriage A society established procedure for founding a family.

Monogamy Marriage involving one person married to only one mate.

Nuclear family One stressing conjugal ties.

Polyandry One woman married to several men at one time.

Polygamy Marriage of a person to more than one spouse.

Polygyny One man married to several women at one time.

Serial monogamy The formation of a new conjugal relationship following divorce.

chapter

15

Religion and Education

Every society has priests and teachers. In small folk societies they may be the same person, even the father or patriarch of each family. In modern societies they have special statuses in formal institutions—the church and the school. Both play important roles in socialization and social control. Religion concentrates on values and beliefs; education on skills and knowledge. Both are concerned with norms.

The unrest and change in the relationships of the sexes and of generations—in the institution of the family— are also found in religion and in all that concerns teaching and learning. In this chapter we define religion and education. We see how each institution varies in form and function, not only in different societies, but also in different classes and ethnic groups within a society. We examine the consequences of modernization, the new directions each institution is taking, and its prospects for the future.

What Is Religion?

In a very general sense, **religion** is the social institution—the complex of norms—that deals with *sacred* things, things that lie beyond our knowledge and control. Sacredness exists in the mind of the believer and can be ascribed to almost any object or idea. It is *transcendental*. That is, it transcends or goes beyond the empirical-technical realm of action, the world of observable everyday reality. Like all of culture, says Peter Berger, religion is "an enterprise of world building." But it occupies a distinctive place in the general culture, for it is the "attempt to conceive of the entire universe as humanly significant [and] locates the individual's life in an all-embracing fabric of meanings that, by its very nature, transcends that life." It protects us from anomie or normlessness, constructing a shelter that makes the terror of death less overwhelming, suffering less painful, injustice more tolerable.[1]

Religion includes patterns of thought, action, and feelings. Like other institutions, it may be embodied in a "seamless web," a total fabric of life (as in some folk and premodern societies). Or it may be "institutionalized," that is, normalized and stabilized as an accepted and recognized way of meeting some recurrent need. Like other institutions, it has certain consequences and fulfills certain functions for society and the individual.

Religion must be distinguished from another nearly universal phenomenon, *magic*. Like religion, magic involves the idea of a "beyond"—of something that transcends empirical reality—and the idea that we can establish some kind of contact with transcendental or supra-empirical forces. But in addition, magic offers ways of *manipulating*

[1] *The Sacred Canopy: Elements of a Sociological Theory of Religion* (Garden City, N.Y.: Doubleday, 1967), pp. 28, 54–55, 100.

these forces through ritual, in order to bring about changes in empirical reality. Such manipulation is commonly found where an enterprise involves danger or uncertainty. Bronislaw Malinowski noted that the Trobriand Islanders used no magical rituals when fishing in the lagoon, where conditions were safe and results quite predictable. But they employed such rituals in deep-sea fishing, which was risky. They performed magical rites to prevent death in childbirth and religious rites to celebrate the birth.[2]

In studying religion, sociologists are not concerned with the truth or falsity of religious beliefs. Beliefs about ultimate reality are always matters of faith and are the realm of theological dispute. Sociologists *are* concerned with the relationships between religion and other aspects of culture and social organization. They are also concerned with the social processes through which beliefs and practices arise, develop, and perhaps become institutionalized in an organization.

Inevitably they involve trust, which is the basis of social order and therefore must be defined by moral obligations. We need some system of meanings to evaluate actions. This ethical system is nearly always bound up with and supported by religion.

We cannot be certain about tomorrow. When Costa Ricans mention a plan or hope, even something as ordinary as "I'll see you tonight," they almost always add, *"si Dios quiere"* (God willing). People are also powerless to affect and control all the conditions of life.

The myth system of a society, and especially its religion or religions, provides human life with a sense of meaning—of aim, purpose, and design. It provides a view of the world and of our role in that world. It answers the questions to which Omar Khayyám believed no answer existed:

Into this Universe, and Why not knowing,
Nor Whence, like Water willy-nilly flowing,
And out of it, as Wind along the Waste,
We know not Whither, willy-nilly blowing.

The Origins of Religion

Speculation about the origins of religion is a fascinating exercise. But it must remain largely that—speculation, based on empathy, introspection, and some anthropological and historical data. Most such speculation centers on "the human condition"—features built into the nature and quality of life.

Life is full of puzzles—dreams, accidents, birth, death, plagues, earthquakes, eclipses, famines. We cannot stand meaninglessness. We seek some explanation of the pattern of bane and blessing. Neither can we stand loneliness. But our relationships with others involve power and coercion, love and loss.

Variations in Form, Content, and Expression

Because they are rooted in the human condition, religions around the world have much in common. But religion is limited only by the capacity to imagine, both within and beyond the bounds of culture. The range of religious beliefs, practices, and experiences is enormous.

Religious Beliefs

Beliefs are the intellectual aspect of religion, expressed in the dramatic assertions of myths; the poetry, proverbs, preaching, and prophecies of scriptures; and the distilled theology of dogmas, doctrines, and creeds.

[2] Bronislaw Malinowski, *Magic, Science, and Religion* (Garden City, N.Y.: Doubleday, Anchor Books, 1948), pp. 28–38.

The range of religious beliefs and practice is quite wide. But the religions of the world also have much in common. *Elizabeth H. Burpee/Design Photographers International, Inc.*

They provide the answers to empirically unanswerable questions. Is there a God? Where is He, or She? Where are They? In Heaven, all around us, in ourselves, on Mount Olympus? We tend to conceive of our gods as very much like us—perhaps physically, perhaps only in personality traits. This is, we *anthropomorphize* them. The Greeks attributed jealousy, lust, vengefulness, and other human failings, as well as wisdom, courage, and chastity, to their gods. The traits of a deity reflect the values of a culture. The Eskimos, who live from hunting and fishing, worship a sea goddess who usually appears as a seal. The militaristic Aztecs, Romans, and Norsemen had gods of war. Agrarian cultures have gods of fertility.

The belief system also defines the relationship of deities to mankind. Gods may be vindictive and punishing, loving and nurturing, capricious and demanding. The power and will of God or the gods impart blessings and sorrow. Why did my child die? It was the will of God. What God does is well done. I displeased the gods. Why did we have a good harvest? God is good. We pleased the gods. It seems that without such explanations many people cannot live happily or even sanely.

Religions define the meaning of human life in various ways. *Eschatological* religions (such as Christianity) are concerned with "last things" such as death, judgment, and a future life in eternal glory or damnation. Some religions are also concerned with death and judgment, but lack the idea of heaven or hell. Still others have no conception of a judgment in after life.

A special aspect of belief systems is what Max Weber called *theodicy,* the doctrine that justifies our present status and reconciles our image of what *ought to be* with what *is.* Why does one man work hard and get nowhere? Why did my child die and his survive? Theodicy answers such questions and thus gives meaning to inequality, suffering, and injustice. Weber saw the theodicy of *dominance* as appropriate to an elite (e.g., the Brahmin caste's justification of their status through the Hindu religion). A theodicy of *mobility* fits the middle classes in transitional and modern societies. They are bent on economic gain and see rationality as a break with the past and a means to personal advancement. (Weber elaborated on this theodicy in *The Protestant Ethic and the Spirit of Capitalism.*) Finally, a theodicy of *escape* is appropriate to the poor and oppressed and outcast. Religion may promise escape through action in this world, bringing about radical social change (as in secular doctrines such as Marxism). More often escape to a better world after death is promised to those who keep the faith. Theodicy, then, may be correlated with social class status and political ideology. The religion of the oppressed may be revolutionary. The religion of the elite may serve to preserve and justify the status quo. The Church of England, for example, has been dubbed "the Conservative Party at Prayer."

Religious Practice

Religious beliefs are overtly expressed in a variety of practices, including private or family devotions and prayers. In Western civilization we usually think in terms of *collective* religious practices centering around churches and temples. The main element of collective worship is ritual, the dramatization of our relationships with the sacred in speech, gesture, song, sacramental meals, and sacrifice. Rituals serve to mark life crises, to celebrate and sanctify birth, puberty, and marriage. They reassert religious identity and reiterate the group's definition of death. The myths and mysteries of a faith are reenacted in the dramas of the mass, Passover, the crucifixion.

Although religious belief and its consequences for behavior in everyday life are not necessarily reflected in church membership and attendance, these do serve as rough indicators.[3] Americans are particularly concerned with religious identity. "Indeed, . . . an American cannot be simply an atheist; he must be a Catholic atheist, a Protestant atheist, or a Jewish atheist."[4]

Church membership, like membership in voluntary associations in general, is roughly correlated with social class, although "one cannot help wondering whether high-status church membership is frequently a matter of form rather than substance."[5] Nearly

one-fourth of Christian Scientists, Episcopalians, and Congregationalists are upper class; fewer than half are lower class. At the other end, fewer than one-tenth of Roman Catholics, Baptists, and Mormons are from the upper class. Roughly two-thirds are from the lower class. But these relative rankings are not absolute categorizations. "Baptists may be *relatively* lower class, but they claim their Rockefellers as well."[6] Furthermore, lower-class Episcopalians may be more religiously involved and committed than upper-class members. And upper-class Baptists may control their predominantly lower-class churches.

Perhaps a more revealing study of the relationship between religious affiliation and social class is a comparison along the lines of formalism vs. emotionalism. Studying 40 black churches in Chicago, V. E. Daniel used five criteria—emotional demonstration, thought content of sermons, prayers, hymns, and the use of liturgy—to identify four basic religious types. He then showed the relationship between class status and preference for these types. Ecstatic sects or cults, in which worship often took the form

[3] See N. J. Demerath, III, and Phillip E. Hammond, *Religion in Social Context: Tradition and Transition* (New York: Random House, 1969), chap. 4, "Assessing Individual Religiosity"; and N. J. Demerath, III, *Social Class in American Protestantism* (Chicago: Rand McNally, 1965), pp. 1–25, for discussions of the pitfalls of these indicators.

[4] Demerath and Hammond, *Religion in Social Context,* p. 131.

[5] *Ibid.,* p. 121.

[6] Demerath, *Social Class in American Protestantism.*

Jehovah's Witnesses baptize several hundred members at a district convention. This sect is an example of radical adventists who predict drastic change in the world. *Wide World Photos.*

of a dancing crowd, were almost solidly lower class. Semi-demonstrative groups, in which the congregation assented to the preacher's points with spontaneous "Amens," were lower-middle class. The upper-middle class preferred deliberative or sermon-centered rituals. The upper class preferred liturgical denominations, with a very formal, traditional ritual.[7]

Religious Experience

Besides culturally patterned beliefs and practices, religion has a third dimension—individual subjective experience or emotion. This experience can range from a mild feeling of goodness and rightness for having attended church to an ecstatic sense of mystical communion with the divine. Obviously this dimension is extremely difficult to analyze and measure.

Charles Glock calls the "experiential" dimension of religion "all those feelings, perceptions, and sensations which are experienced by an actor or defined by a religious group or a society as involving some connection, however slight, with a divine essence, i.e., with God, with ultimate reality, with transcendental authority. It is, in effect, spirituality—emotional experience defined as religious which in its extreme forms would be represented by conversion, the visitation of the Holy Spirit, mysticism."[8] Even the most intense mystical experiences are culturally conditioned. One cannot see a vision for which the culture has not prepared him. Indian youths fasted and prayed in isolation until they saw some animal that became their totem. Bernadette saw the Virgin because she was raised a Catholic. Asians experience yogic trances.

What is a genuinely religious experience? Joachim Wach says it must meet four criteria. It is a response not to any single phenomenon but to ultimate reality, something that conditions our entire world of experience. It involves our total being, not only our mind, will, or emotions. It is, at least potentially, the most intense experience possible, for it can win out over all other loyalties. Finally, it involves a commitment impelling a person to action (thus distinguishing it from an intense esthetic experience and joining it to the moral sphere).[9]

Gerhard Lenski defines four ways of expressing religious commitment. Two are behavioral and thus lend themselves to measurement: associational involvement (attendance at church) and communal involvement (whether one's spouse and close friends are members of one's socio-religious group). The other two are more strictly mental: doctrinal orthodoxy or assent to the traditional beliefs of one's church, and devotionalism, the frequency of private prayer and scripture reading.[10]

The Institutionalization of Religion

Like all cultural norms, religious ones are more or less institutionalized—that is, formalized, stabilized, and socially recognized as the right and proper way to do something. In small folk societies so much of the culture is imbued with sacredness that we find religious ritual in the family and work group. Food may be holy, the head of every household a priest.

[7] "Ritual and Stratification in Chicago Negro Churches," *American Sociological Review* 7 (June 1942): 352–61.

[8] *Religion and the Face of America* (Berkeley: University of California Press, 1958), pp. 25–42.

[9] *Types of Religious Experience, Christian and Non-Christian* (Chicago: University of Chicago Press, 1951), pp. 32–33.

[10] *The Religious Factor* (Garden City, N.Y.: Doubleday, 1961).

Many Eastern religions are not as institutionalized as Western religions. Almost every Thai man is a Buddhist priest at one time or another. These Buddhists' vows forbid gambling of any kind, but there is nothing sinful in their perusing the numbers of lottery tickets. *Wide World Photos.*

Specialization, Organization, and Bureaucratization

As societies grow, religious roles become more specialized. A hierarchy and a bureaucracy develop. First, a shaman who is thought to have special knowledge of and connections with the sacred performs religious rituals. As the society grows the need for shamen increases. Gradually a priest class emerges, and with it a **church,** a large established religious organization with political and economic realities. Historically the established churches of the West have struggled for power with the political rulers. It took centuries of bloody wars and persecutions to establish the separation of church and state, a process still not complete in some societies. In many Asian religions, in particular, institutionalization has not gone to the lengths it has in Western society. Almost every Thai man is a Buddhist priest at one time or another, for example, and worship is less structured than in Western churches.

Church and Sect

A process that has fascinated a number of scholars is the interplay between church and **sect,** the dissident groups that find the compromise with "worldly realities" morally repugnant and break off to form a "purer" group of their own. Christianity itself provides many classic instances of this process from its very beginnings. Jesus, the charismatic leader, gathered a band of disciples to protest corruption in the temples. He drew to him the poor and outcast and dispossessed, and they formed a dissident sect, persecuted as such sects are likely to be.

Once Christianity became the established, powerful religion of Europe and the Americas, it in turn gave rise to sects. An otherworldly religion, Christianity doesn't fit political and economic realities. In compromising with the world, the church accepted the domination of middle- and upper-class values and interests. It played down its other-

354

worldliness and its message of equality and social justice. Members of the lower classes felt ignored or neglected. Often they gathered around an inspiring personality who promised salvation and escape through a return to the purity of true Christian principles. Some sects have seceded from the church entirely. Others have reformed it and been absorbed. Still others have been incorporated as quasi-autonomous bodies, such as orders of monks.

Where a church has a hierarchy of authority, a sect is a band of brothers, with a nonbureaucratic organizational structure. Where a church has a ritualized worship service, a sect engages in spontaneous worship with group participation. Where a church has a flexible doctrine that evolves as it is reinterpreted and argued, a sect insists on doctrinal purity (not necessarily conservative or fundamentalist). Where a church tends to prescribe a system of relative ethics that recognizes possible conflicts and allows

compromise, a sect has a total ideology of life and ethics that allows no compromise. Where a church accommodates to the secular society and seeks to work within it, a sect is either aloof from society or antagonistic toward it. Where the church draws its clergy from seminaries and divinity schools, the sect has a ministry of laymen with no professional pedigree.

Secessionist sects may dissolve when the charismatic founder dies. But if they have already built up a strong body of belief and practice they may survive and develop in one of several directions. (1) They may grow into a church, as did Christianity, with a professional priesthood, a more evangelistic recruitment procedure, a higher social class membership, a hierarchical structure, and a formal ritual. "Conversionist" sects, orient-

The Amish are a socially isolated sect, neither compromising with the world nor seeking to change it. *Mark Chester/Monkmeyer Press Photo Service.*

ed to individual salvation, are most likely to become full-fledged churches, such as the Pentecostals and the Salvation Army, for example. "Gnostic" sects, which accept the prevailing goals of the society but seek new means to reach them, are also likely to grow into churches. Christian Science, which is unusual in that its membership comes largely from the middle class, is one example. (2) But those which allow no compromise with society and urge severe changes in it become not churches but institutionalized sects. Examples are "radical adventists" such as Jehovah's Witnesses (who predict and prepare for a sudden and drastic change in the world) and "introversionist" groups such as the Quakers (who reject societal goals and posit new ones that call upon different inner resources from individuals).[11] (3) Some sects, like the Amish and Hutterites, remain geographically and socially isolated, neither compromising with nor seeking to change the world. (4) The Mormons are a special instance of a sect that became a distinct subsociety. They are "a specifically religious organization as the institutional core of a more diffuse social entity with its own history, its own traditions, its conviction of peculiarity, and even its native territory or homeland"—plus a sense of mission.[12]

Like sectariansim, **mysticism** is a protest against the formality of an institutionalized church. It emphasizes purely personal and inward experience. Both sects and mystics, like social protest movements, contribute to the vitality of institutions by forcing reexamination of their values and premises, their patterns of behavior and social relationships. Sects challenge abuses within a church that they see as violating its original values. Mys-

tics remind us of the essentially private nature of the religious experience.

Religion and Modernization

Diffuse, pervasive tribal religions, the established state religions of premodern societies, and churches in modern and post-industrial societies all experience the consequences of modernizing processes. First, as a society becomes larger in scope, competing beliefs are incorporated into the same socio-cultural order with varying degrees of success. That is, religious pluralism appears, resulting sometimes in cooperation and compromise, other times in hostility and conflict. Second, secularization affects religious belief and practice. Third, there is some tendency, especially apparent in American society, toward the homogenization of religious belief and practice under an overarching "civil religion." Fourth, like other institutions, religion becomes less diffuse and more specific in organization and function—more compartmentalized.

Religious Pluralism

A common religion is an effective source of social cohesion, providing as it does a strong set of common values. The Reformation and the rise of nation-states led finally—after bloody wars—to acceptance of the idea that various religions can coexist within a society. But in a pluralistic society, says Berger, the classical task of religion can no longer be fulfilled: "that of constructing a common world within which all of social life receives ultimate meaning binding on everybody."[13] Instead, we have subworlds, fragmented universes of meaning perhaps no

[11] Based on a summary of voluminous literature on the church-sect scheme in Demerath and Hammond, *Religion in Social Context,* pp. 69–77, 157–63.

[12] Thomas F. O'Dea, *The Sociology of Religion* (Englewood Cliffs, N.J.: Prentice-Hall, 1966), pp. 66–71.

[13] Berger, *The Sacred Canopy,* p. 132.

larger than the nuclear family, perhaps as large as a church.

Conflict and animosity are likely in a pluralist society where missionary orientations predominate in the various churches, as in Christianity and Islam. In Asian society, in contrast, numerous religions coexist. In fact a person may follow more than one with no conflict. But as a result of the other trends—secularization, compartmentalization, and homogenization—religious pluralism may take on the character of a competitive market in which people are asked to name a "religious preference." While essentially private even if it involves church membership, that preference can be changed (especially from one Protestant denomination to another) with little soul-searching.

Some see this kind of pluralism and competition as contributing to the vitality of religion as an institution. In countries where several faiths compete, religion becomes a way of defining one's identity, and religious interest remains high. Holland, Ireland, Switzerland, Canada, and the United States are examples.

What accounts for this interest besides the cultural demand for a religious identity? It has been suggested that the voluntary nature of religious affiliation, the separation of church and state since the founding of our nation, means that each church needs enthusiastically committed laypeople in order to survive. When people are free to choose, their loyalty is more enduring. But this also means that to "keep the customers coming," the churches have to accommodate their teachings and practices to the demands of their members. Thus a certain degree of theological laxity exists.

Secularization

In the process of secularization, the realm of the sacred shrinks, the realm of the profane or ordinary grows. "Mysteries are replaced by problems."[14] The term referred originally to the removal of territory and other property from the control of church authorities. In a broader sense, **secularization** is "the process by which sectors of society and culture are removed from the domination of religious institutions and symbols."[15] Science has been perhaps the foremost secularizing agent, dispelling much of the mystery and hence the sacredness of the natural world. But the Protestant Reformation, says Berger, opened the world to secularization. It removed mystery, miracle, and magic from religion itself.[16]

With secularization, reverence for traditional beliefs and values is replaced by a rational–utilitarian attitude that permits them to be discarded or changed with relative ease. Some consider this paganization; others, liberation. In any case, secularization must be recognized as an empirical phenomenon of tremendous importance. Economic institutions have been almost entirely divorced from the realm of the sacred, as have political institutions. Yet we still find sacredness associated with the state. Wars and new administrations are begun with prayers. The family is also largely sacred. Art, literature, and philosophy, once imbued with religious content, are increasingly secular. All over the world, the secular-rational attitude is increasing.

What happens when people become aware of the lack of fit between the traditional religious values of revelation and other-worldly salvation and the modern secular values of rationality and material success? Most fundamentalist sects withdraw, emphasizing the difference in values. Others, especially theologians, may seek radical changes in dogma. A third possible reaction is to secularize the doctrine itself

[14] O'Dea, *The Sociology of Religion*, p. 86.
[15] Berger, *The Sacred Canopy*, p. 107.
[16] *Ibid.*, pp. 11–12.

in order to attract more people. A fourth alternative, however, seems to be more common in American churches—"to leave traditional doctrine understated and, wherever possible, unmentioned."[17] Theological discussion is considered impolite and embarrassing. In our society one can have the appearance of religiosity without the emotional commitment. "Religion-in-general" is regarded as a good thing.

American churches allied themselves with democratic principles from the start. Thus the government could ally itself with religion in general. As a result, we have developed a "civil religion" consisting of vaguely defined ideas such as belief in God. We are "one nation under God." Almost all the institutions of the society celebrate this civil religion, which promotes unity amid our diversity and allows the churches themselves to persist in their theological differences without endangering social cohesion.

Functions and Consequences of Religion

People may or may not find meaning and identity in religion. Nevertheless, their involvement in religion has consequences for themselves and their society—as both manifest (intended) and latent (unintended) consequences.

Religion increases respect for the norms of the society by relating them to the sacred. . . . Religious rites renew the respect for the norms, and solidify the coherence of the group. Thus religion has a positive function with respect to social solidarity and social control. But this function is obviously not the intention or purpose of those who believe in the religion and practice the rites. Their manifest purpose is concerned with an

answer to the problem of meaning and with acting out in the rites a relationship to ultimacy—to God, the gods, or however the particular religion conceives the sacred object.[18]

Some sociologists believe ethics and religion are inseparable, that the notion of group welfare is not enough to make people obey any form of the Golden Rule. Supernatural rewards and punishments, they say, are necessary sanctions. "The tendency in most civilizations has been to have the ethical system supervised by religion, and in the last analysis enforced by it. When the neighbors and the police have failed, there is still the all-seeing eye and the threat of eternal torment."[19]

One exception is found in Japanese culture. Their religion is subtle and vague although pervasive. Japanese can adhere to both the Buddhist religion and the peculiarly Japanese Shinto religion. They do not belong to a congregation nor must they attend regular services. But on some national holidays the Japanese go to shrines and temples to pay their respects to the spirits of their ancestors "on the yonder shore," assuring them that they are remembered and cherished. They light candles and offer prayers, and tend the graves. But they are gay and festive, for the ancestors are still part of the family. Japanese notions of right and wrong, however, come from Confucian social ethics for right conduct in this world. They are guided not by fear of supernatural sanctions but by fear of shame if their neighbors or relatives think they have failed in some duty or obligation.

Many American Protestant churches have been charged with being mere social centers, with more emphasis on activities and clubs than worship. Taking the functionalist view, Talcott Parsons assesses the role of such churches in American society:

---

[17] Demerath and Hammond, *Religion in Social Context*, p. 172.

[18] O'Dea, *The Sociology of Religion*, p. 73.
[19] Hertzler, *Social Institutions*, p. 429.

While the Japanese go to temples on some national holidays, they generally do not belong to a congregation nor necessarily attend regular services. *Vivienne/Design Photographers International, Inc.*

It is not uncommon to suggest . . . that modern churchgoers are "not really" religious at all, but are only interested in sociability. In my opinion this is a misinterpretation. This associational aspect of the modern denominational parish is a predictable feature of the development of modern society when the fact is taken into account that family and church have such intimate intrinsic relations with each other. Each, in its own specialized way, involves "the whole person."[20]

By sanctifying norms and legitimating social institutions, religion obviously serves as a guardian of the status quo. But it can also be innovative, even revolutionary. In its "prophetic role," religion provides a standard of values against which institutionalized norms and values may be measured—and often found wanting. The Biblical prophets, like the charismatic leaders of dissident sects, thundered against corruption and compromise with the world. Many of today's religious leaders seek to promote social change, especially in the realm of social justice. Once guardians of the feudal order, now many Latin American priests have aligned themselves with revolutionary groups. Some priests have been defrocked, others censured, and still others have left the priesthood of their own volition. But the trend appears significant.[21]

The "prophetic" role in American religion is rarely played at the parish level. Here

[20] From "Mental Illness and 'Spiritual Malaise': The Role of the Psychiatrist and the Minister of Religion," *Social Structure and Personality* (New York: Association Press, 1964), pp. 305–13.

[21] James Nelson Goodsell, "Church in Latin America: A Rising Tide of Challenges and Questions," *Christian Science Monitor* (Dec. 26, 1970).

homogeneity is valued, and many parishioners object to having their priests or ministers march in civil rights demonstrations or preach school integration. Pronouncements and action along these lines come typically from those who are not bound by local congregations—from campus clergy, denominational conventions, and ecumenical meetings.

Transcendental religions and democratic societies stand in a special relationship to one another, as demonstrated in our own society. As summarized by Thomas O'Dea:

Democratic societies require certain values, among which the worth of the individual, an ethic of social justice, and the priority of the general welfare over individual and sub-group interests are strategic. These values in the West owe much to prophetic and evangelical religion . . . and to secularized social movements whose values have been remotely derived from such religious sources. . . .

However, if religion compromises with the general society . . . [it] becomes but one more institution adjusted to the prevailing winds of dominant opinion. . . . If religions of transcendence are to remain genuinely so, and if they are to continue to contribute positively to democratic society, then a degree of "healthy unadjustment" between religion and society must remain, despite the fact that this unadjustment itself will be the source of some conflict and will have some dysfunctional consequences. . . . The strain between religion and society . . . may prove in the long run to have important functional consequences of a positive character in preserving the very values which are requisite to a democratic society.[22]

Religious Groupings

Religious differences once led to bitter hatreds and conflicts. In early New England, those who had fled the Old World to seek religious freedom were the first to deny it to others. The Constitution guaranteed religious freedom, but prejudice and discrimination die slowly. Although neither has completely disappeared, Jews have occupied high offices and won high honors, and Catholicism is no longer a barrier to the presidency. Accommodation, acculturation, and even cooperation are the themes of interreligious relations today.

What generalizations do sociologists make about the role of religious differences in modern America? Among the chief ones are these.

Most Americans accept the three major religious divisions as part of the right and natural order of things. In a famous book-length essay called *Protestant-Catholic-Jew,* theologian Will Herberg observes, "The only separateness or diversity that America recognizes as permanent, and yet also involving no status of inferiority, is the diversity or separateness of religious community."[23]

Not only is religious pluralism considered part of the American heritage, religion itself is regarded as "a good thing." That is, it is good to have belief or faith *as such,* without regard to the particular dogma or doctrine. All the major religions are felt to affirm the spiritual ideals and moral values of a greater whole called "The American Way of Life."

And indeed the churches of different faiths tend to reflect our culture, just as the different nationality groupings do. Observers have often commented that the religions of America are much more like one another than they are like their European counterparts. The structures, rituals, and social activities of both Catholic and Jewish congregations have become more and more "Americanized." In conservative and reform Judaism, for example, English is used in part

---

[22] O'Dea, *The Sociology of Religion,* p. 106.

[23] *Protestant-Catholic-Jew,* rev. ed. (Garden City, N.Y.: Doubleday, 1960), p. 38.

of the service and in the business affairs of the synagogue; sermons are preached, the sexes worship together, and age- and sex-graded recreational and educational programs have been introduced—all of these being substantial breaks with orthodoxy in the direction of American middle-class norms.

Almost all Americans regard religious identity as extremely important, regardless of whether or not they actually attend churches or temples. As national origins retreat farther and farther into the past, and as mobility and the mass media minimize the importance of regions, religious identity has come to be regarded as not only legitimate but necessary. A person's religious "brand name" gives identity and social location. The army and the hospital, as well as the neighbors, want to know.

The social necessity of "belonging" is reflected in a spectacular rise in church membership. In 1970, about 63 percent of Americans were formally affiliated with a church, as compared with 36 percent in 1900.[24] Furthermore, 70 to 75 percent of Americans *regard* themselves as church members even if not all are formally on the rolls. Even more indicative of the feeling that one must have a religion is that 95 percent of Americans identify themselves as either Protestant (68 percent), Catholic (23 percent), or Jewish (4 percent).[25]

This stress on religious identity is part of what Gordon calls the "structural pluralism" of our society. Most primary relationships take place within the boundaries of the three main religious divisions. Intermarriage among nationality groups is largely confined to each major religion. Recent data on intermarriage are lacking, largely because the Census Bureau yielded to pressure and did not ask questions about religion in the 1960 and 1970 censuses. The last year for

which adequate data exist, 1957, revealed that 7 percent of marriages involving at least one Jewish person were mixed, 9 percent of Protestant, and 22 percent of Catholic. But the data do not reveal trends, for they included all marriages, with an average age in the early or mid-forties. Furthermore, a careful study would distinguish between spouses brought up in different religions and those brought up in the same religion.[26]

A study of interfaith marriage in Canada indicates that it is increasing. Between 1927 and 1957 mixed marriages involving Protestants rose from 5 percent to 11.6 percent; Catholics, 7.2 percent to 11.5 percent; and Jews, 3 percent to 6.8 percent. The smaller the percentage of a religious group in a community, the greater the tendency to marry someone of another faith.[27] Adolescent friendships also tend to be confined to the same religious society. Many parents try to guard their children against the possibility of marrying outside their religion. A study of close friendships by Gerhard Lenski showed that 77 percent of the Jews in his Detroit sample said that all or nearly all their closest friends were of the same religion. Forty-four percent of the Catholics and 38 percent of the Protestants reported similar in-group ties.[28] The rate of in-group friendship is highest—80 percent—among Catholics who attend parochial schools.[29]

---

[24] *American Almanac for 1971*, p. 4.

[25] Herberg, *Protestant-Catholic-Jew*, pp. 46–49.

[26] Because of conversion after marriage, the same group could show 85% of marriages of the same faith if present status only were used, and 68% if religion as children were used. [See Ira L. Reiss, *The Family System in America* (New York: Holt, Rinehart and Winston, 1971), chap. 19, "Deviance and the Family: Intermarriage."]

[27] David M. Heer, "The Trend of Interfaith Marriages in Canada, 1927–1957," *American Sociological Review* 27 (April 1962): 245–50.

[28] *The Religious Factor* (Garden City, N.Y.: Doubleday, 1961).

[29] Joseph H. Fichter, S. J., *Parochial School: A Sociological Study* (South Bend, Ind.: University of Notre Dame Press, 1958).

Studies show that children who attend Catholic schools share the same attitudes as the dominant majority. *David Strickler/Monkmeyer Press Photo Service.*

Even Catholics who attend parochial schools, however, have been found to accept almost exactly the same values as the dominant majority. It is probably true of almost every American that "the social, cultural, and economic state he finds himself in is a better index to his thinking and behavior than his religion."[30] Only over a few issues that involve the relation of church and state—birth control, abortion, divorce, and public aid to parochial schools, for example—do Americans divide along religious lines.

Some studies, however, conclude that religious prejudices are still forces to be reckoned with, and that religious beliefs may be associated with other types of intergroup prejudice as well. Although theologians and clergyman are prominent in interfaith projects and try to promote interracial peace, many laypeople—70 percent in one survey—believe their priests and ministers should confine themselves to the private religious lives of their congregations.[31] Christian churches have officially denounced the notion that Jews continue to bear guilt for the crucifixion of Christ. Yet half the American Christians polled and many clergymen continue to subscribe to that notion. From one-half to two-thirds of American Christians would deny civil liberties to people who do not believe in God, bar them from holding public office, and remove them from a teaching position in the schools, though most do not act upon this attitude.[32]

Rodney Stark and Charles Y. Glock conclude from their studies that the image of man as having completely free will results in a tendency to blame the disadvantaged for their own plight. This is also true of the disadvantaged themselves. "The more committed a black was to Christian beliefs and institutions, the more ready he was to see the lowly condition of blacks as self-inflicted," and to trust that God will correct it in His own good time. People, in short, get what they deserve in this life and the next. But church members more strongly

[30] John Leo, "The American Catholic Is Changing," in Milton L. Barron, ed., *Minorities in a Changing World* (New York: Alfred A. Knopf, 1967), pp. 305–18.

[31] Jeffrey K. Hadden, *The Gathering Storm in the Churches* (Garden City, N.Y.: Doubleday, 1969).

[32] Rodney Stark and Charles Y. Glock, "Prejudice and the Churches," in Charles Y. Glock and Ellen Siegelman, eds., *Prejudice U.S.A.* (New York: Frederick A. Praeger, 1969), pp. 70–95.

committed to New Testament ethics than to these ideas display less prejudice and more social concern.[33]

The Future of Religion

It would be rash to assert that religion has not declined in influence in many spheres of life. By many empirical indices traditional orthodoxy has indeed declined. But that religion itself is at the lowest ebb ever is debatable. Christianity has gained millions of new adherents in the Third World. In the West, there is "the rather ironic situation

[33] *Ibid.*

Owen Franken/Stock Boston.

of a spiritual revolution that has virtually nothing to do with churches."[34] Even the debate during the 1960s over the "death of God" was essentially a redefinition of meanings.

According to the Gallup poll, more and more Americans each year think religion is losing influence in American life. In 1947 14 percent thought so; in 1962, 31 percent; in 1967, 57 percent; in 1969, 70 percent; in 1970, 75 percent. This may be interpreted in several ways. Is there a decline in the influence of traditional beliefs and sentiments? The answer is very likely yes. Have clergymen been active in influencing their congregations to apply the principles of individual worth and social justice in their daily lives? The answer appears to be no. As we saw above, parish clergy might find themselves preaching to empty pews if they were as daring there as those in the higher echelons of church bureaucracy can be in speaking out for racial integration, for example.

The church's emphasis is overwhelmingly on man's relationship to God. The implications of the faith for man's relation to man are left largely to the individual to work out for himself, with God's help but without the help of the churches. . . . *How the majority of Americans behave, and what they value, is not informed by religious faith but by the norms and values of the larger society.* . . . Looking at American society as a whole [rather than particular minority religious movements] organized religion at present is neither a prominent witness to its own value system nor a major focal point around which ultimate commitments to norms, values, and beliefs are formed.[35]

Beginning among Protestants in the 1800s and joined by Catholics in recent decades,

[34] Edward Fiske, "Religion: More of the New, Less of the Old," in Lester Markel, ed., *World in Review* (New York: *The New York Times*/Rand McNally, 1972), pp. 130–31.
[35] Charles Glock and Rodney Stark, *Religion and Society in Tension* (Chicago: Rand McNally, 1965), pp. 182–84. [Emphasis added]

the ecumenical movement is aimed at achieving universal Christian accord, and to some extent action, on matters of mutual concern through international, interdenominational organizations. Ecumenism is fostered by the fact that churches are large and bureaucratized, and their administrators have similar problems, many of which can best be solved through merger or cooperation. Many communities now have interdenominational churches. In small towns, in particular, rules are worked out so no one church dominates in civic affairs. Surveys are made of new suburban developments to see which church should be established there.

Unrest, innovation, and experiment characterize the Catholic Church today, especially in countries where religious interest and involvement are high. Between 1963 and early 1971, 25,000 of the world's 540,000 ordained Catholic priests left the priesthood. The Pope implied that the main reason was their objection to the rule of mandatory celibacy. Encouraged by the Vatican II Decree on the Appropriate Renewal of the Religious Life, many orders of nuns have examined their constitutions, experimented with innovations, and followed the Council's recommendation that they become less isolated and more involved in the world. Those who stay within the orders often accept innovations such as more modern dress and more community service. Many have left the convent.

A new phenomenon is a search for the sacred, or "neo-sacred," in directions that are often occult and bizarre. There are covens of witches and warlocks. Semi-monastic cults stress vegetarianism, meditation, and asceticism. Mutual-help communities organize loosely. Groups experiment with extrasensory perception and other parapsychological phenomena. Many see Eastern religions as an escape from the pressures of modern society (the Krishna people). Astrology is very much in vogue, as are Tarot cards and the I Ching as systems of divination that are supposed to help a person make decisions. Others find the sacred closer to home, in the Christian gospel. The "Jesus People" try to live by the simplest precepts of early Christianity.

This "return to the sacred" is seen by some as part of a general disillusionment with science and technology. Andrew Greeley believes "that what is going on is authentically, if perhaps transiently and bizarrely, religious. Personal meaning, community, encounter with the ecstatic and the transcendental, and the refusal to believe that mere reason can explain either life or personhood—all of these have traditionally been considered religious postures. [The religious cultists are] looking for an explanation for life and for themselves."[36] They are, in short, seeking what religion has universally provided: "definition beyond the extent of our knowledge, and security beyond the guarantees of human relationships."[37]

What Is Education?

In its broadest sense, education is synonymous with socialization and includes any process whereby one individual or group passes elements of culture to another. Recognizing that effective socialization is basic to the continuation of society, every society also practices **education** in a narrower sense. It deliberately transmits selected knowledge, skills, and values to prepare individuals for effective membership in the society.

[36] Andrew M. Greeley, "There's a New-Time Religion on Campus," *The New York Times Magazine* (June 1, 1969): 14–15 *et passim*.

[37] O'Dea, *The Sociology of Religion*, p. 9.

From the standpoint of the individual, education is not synonymous with the mere acquisition of information. That may be stored in and retrieved from libraries, computers, and many other sources. Nor is it synonymous with schooling, with acquiring skills and knowledge (such as the 3 R's or history). Even learning, or deep and intensive scholarship, is not truly education. A Shakespearean scholar may know every detail of folios and quartos but fail to grasp the feeling and meaning of the plays. True education results in an ability to grasp relationships between facts and ideas.

Just as in the family and religion, there is great unrest, ferment, and innovation in the area of education. What should be taught? How? To whom? These are all controversial questions today. There isn't even agreement on the nature of the raw material. Is the child a blank page to be written on? A noble savage born good, who will learn if left alone? A barbarian who needs to be tamed and broken and fitted into a proper place? A pre-programmed system whose unfolding we must grasp so we can suit the content and method of teaching to the proper stage of development?

Unlike the family and religion, education is a public institution whose main directions are worked out through political processes. In modern society it is much more formal and organized than either family or religion. And in most modern societies it is compulsory. There is no other recognized path by which the average child may be socialized and awarded an achieved status.

The sociologist may see an educational system, first of all, as part of a total social system that both reflects and influences the social and cultural order of which it is a part. The class system, cultural values, the power structure, the balance of individual freedom and social control, the homogeneity or heterogeneity of race, religion, and na-

tionality, the degree of urbanization and industrialization—all these factors exert a strong and inevitable influence on the school system of any community or society.

A sociologist may also look at it—and at each school within it—as a subsystem with a subculture and social organization of its own. It has a system of statuses and roles, a body of values, skills, and traditions, its own rituals, and its own special language. Each school and each classroom within the school forms an interacting social group. Social psychologists are especially interested in the relationship between the structure of the group and the behavior changes that result from its interaction.

In spite of its essentially conservative nature, education cannot escape the effects of changes in the form and function of the family and in the size, distribution, and composition of the population; of technological changes and economic trends; and of changes in political philosophy and political power.

Goals, Functions, and Consequences of Education

To unravel the "functions" of education, we must distinguish between the intentions of individuals and of policy-makers, and the consequences, whether intended or not, of structures and processes. What, other than force, motivates children to go to school and keep going? What do parents expect? What do school boards have in mind when they allocate resources?

Somewhat arbitrarily, let us divide the "functions" of education according to its contribution to social goals and to individual goals.

Society and Education

Education plays an important role in both social stability and social change. It transmits the culture. It teaches the beliefs, values, knowledge, and skills that all members of the society presumably should share. It also trains people to do certain jobs. It screens them, places them according to ability and achievement, rejects the failures. In short, it allocates individuals to various statuses. (As we have seen in several contexts, this function is complemented by ascription according to family status by class and ethnic background.) In modern society the schools are also custodial institutions, "baby-sitters" for the younger generation. Another latent function of modern schools—and one parents have more or less consciously in mind when they choose neighborhoods and schools for their children—is that of providing a "pool" of possible acceptable mates.

A system of education is also a source of innovation and change. A governor of the colony of Virginia said in the seventeenth century: "Thank God there are no free schools or printing; . . . for learning has brought disobedience and heresy into the world, and printing has divulged them. . . . God keep us from both." The university in particular encourages research and innovation in both the humanities and the sciences. It grants prizes and awards and funds for novelists, poets, and painters as well as for physicists, social scientists, chemists, and biologists.

The Individual and Education

Individuals may see education as an end in itself or as an instrumental means to ends. It is *the* path to success in modern society, the only way to get the skills and knowledge and credentials for a good job. Lifetime earnings in the United States are directly correlated with the amount of formal schooling. The Carnegie Commission on Higher Education reported in 1971 that median income in 1968 for heads of households with five grades of schooling or less was $2920; 6 to 8 grades, $5170; 9 to 11 grades, $7260; a high school diploma, $8940; a bachelor's degree, $11,240; and an advanced or professional degree, $13,120.

The same study also tried to relate amount of schooling to happiness. In reply to a questionnaire on marital happiness, 38 percent of those with a grade school education, 46 percent of those with a high school education, and 60 percent of those with a college education said they were "very happy." The more schooling people had, the more introspective they were about behavior and the more likely to report problems and feelings of inadequacy. They were also more sensitive to the parental role, but there was no reported difference in the recognition of parent-child problems. Schooling was also correlated with job satisfaction. 70 percent of those with 11 years or less, 78 percent of those with high school diplomas, and 89 percent of college graduates said they enjoyed their work. Furthermore, the Commission found that the more schooling people had, the more liberal and tolerant they were likely to be, the less subject to unemployment; the more thoughtful in spending, and the more likely to vote.[38]

Modernization and Education

A shortage of educated people is usually identified as the chief obstacle to modernization. Developing nations typically are divided

[38] *The New York Times* (Oct. 6, 1971).

into an educated elite and the illiterate masses. Both understand the value of education. Pakistani villagers, for example, disagree about almost everything, but will contribute funds toward a school. The People's Republic of China is deeply committed to education and exercises strong central control over it. The two leading industrial nations, the United States and the Soviet Union, are also those with the most open and widespread systems of free public education.

Industrializing nations need a system of popular education to train people for industrial and commercial occupations, for political leadership and bureaucratic positions, for simply getting around a city with its numerous secondary contacts. They also need it to weld many different subcultural groups into a nation-state. And any system of popular voting demands at least a minimum of literacy.

A system of education based on such societal requirements tends to stress verbal skills and rationality rather than emotions. The pay-off may seem much too far removed from what goes on in the classroom. And as modernization advances and knowledge explodes, education takes up more and more years of the life span. As a result, there are dropouts and failures all along the line, most of whom find there is no alternative road to success in the mainstream. In the Third World, half of those who enter elementary school fail to finish fourth grade. In 1971, UNESCO estimated that there are 810 million illiterates in the world, 34 percent of all those over age 15. In thirty-seven African countries south of the Sahara 60 percent of those entering school leave before really learning to read and write.

The crisis of education in modernizing countries is twofold. On the one side, there is not enough space for the number of students who want in. On the other side of the coin, there aren't enough jobs for those who do complete their education. The unevenness of education adds to unrest. Semiliterate youth flock to cities with no marketable skills, their familial and tribal bridges burned behind them. This cultural lag can be traced to a sharp increase in aspirations, the scarcity of resources to support mass education, and the inertia of societies themselves.

Public policy encouraging economic expansion and the population explosion, as well as higher aspirations, has created a tremendous demand for education since World War II, in industrial as well as in developing nations. Between 1950 and 1963 world-wide primary school enrollment increased over 50 percent, secondary and high school enrollment over 100 percent. Yet British universities have to turn away over one-quarter of the qualified applicants. In West Germany 6,500 qualified candidates applied for 2,800 places in medical school.[39]

The American system early established a policy of casting the net wide, of giving as many as possible from the lower classes and deprived minorities an opportunity. Statistics indicate the extent of success. In 1900 only 6 percent of American youngsters went through high school, 0.25 percent through college. By 1940, 38 percent of young adults had high school diplomas and 6 percent had college degrees. By 1970, 75 percent had graduated from high school and 16 percent from college. At the same time, achievement as measured by standard tests had risen.[40]

[39] Philip H. Coombs, *The World Educational Crisis: A Systems Analysis* (New York: Oxford University Press, 1968), pp. 4, 17–35.

[40] Morris Janowitz, "Institution Building in Urban Education," in David Street, ed., *Innovation in Mass Education* (New York: John Wiley, 1969).

Cultural Variations in Educational Systems

Although modernization leads to a certain degree of uniformity in systems of education as well as other aspects of culture, many forces make for variation from one society to another. The pattern of control may be centralized or decentralized. The relation of school and community may be distant or close. Content may be varied or uniform. Methods may be authoritarian or democratic, based on rote learning or problem-solving. The system of recruitment may be open or selective. A high value may be placed on education or a low one (reflected in resources committed to it rather than mere lip service). These variations may go together in unexpected ways. For example, control in the United States is extremely decentra-

lized, with tens of thousands of local school boards taking the responsibility of hiring teachers and allocating resources. Yet content displays a great degree of uniformity all over the nation. The system of teacher training, the nation-wide textbook industry, standardized testing and college entrance requirements all lead toward uniformity.

Education in China today reflects a total commitment to education and a total central control. It is guided by a pervasive ideology and a driving goal. China's educational endeavor "in its totality may be said to be the most extensive and ambitious attempt thus far at human engineering."[41] One indicator of the level of commitment is the rise in literacy from 20 percent in 1949, the year of Communist victory, to 80 percent two decades later. Every aspect of schooling

[41] C. T. Hu, *Aspects of Chinese Education* (New York: Columbia University, Teachers College Press, 1969), p. 1.

The People's Republic of China displays a strong commitment to education under central control. *Design Photographers International, Inc.*

serves the end of indoctrination. A typical arithmetic problem shows how a greedy landlord of the pre-revolutionary era loaned 5 tou (a tou being about 40 lbs.) of rice to a tenant in a famine year at 50 percent interest, compounded. He could not finish paying for 3 years, and had to pay nearly 17 tou. A map in a geography lesson shows China menaced by an eagle (the United States), a bear (Russia), and a lion (the British imperialism of the past century). Five-year-olds sing about unity with the peoples of Asia, Africa, and Latin America in the struggle against the imperialists. "Political power comes from the barrel of a rifle," they recite, and then drill with wooden guns.

The two goals of education are to make everyone both "red" (ideologically sound) and "expert" (trained in some field that contributes to economic development). To ensure that expertness does not produce a separate class of intelligentsia, Mao engineered the Cultural Revolution of 1966–1967. Students were turned loose to purge the "bourgeois intellectuals" and revitalize the revolutionary spirit. Their rampages were finally subdued under army control and a new pattern of education was instituted. School terms were shortened to 5 years of primary and 5 years of secondary schooling. At age fifteen or sixteen everyone must go to work in factories or fields for a couple of years. Then they may apply for a training course of 2 or 3 years at a university. The academic content of courses has been reduced and the political content increased. The "bitter remembrances" of the society are vividly portrayed. Almost every course is taught through Mao's maxims and philosophy. School and work are amalgamated as much as possible. Schools establish factories and farms. Factories, communes, and cooperatives establish schools. Students work as responsible employees. In one school, for example, they spend part of each day making

diodes for transistors; in another, steps for buses. Model citizens are held up for imitation. All groups are trained to practice "thought reform" through criticism and self-criticism. The old education, it is said, made people think of their own fame and fortune rather than the good of the society. The Cultural Revolution was therefore anti-individualistic as well as anti-intellectual.[42]

Subcultural Variations in Education

The value placed on education, the level of aspiration, access to education, the degree of adjustment and profit from schooling— all these vary with social class and ethnic background. For example, the Jews, long urbanites with a cultural-religious respect for learning, place an extremely high value on education, both as a means to an end and an end in itself. The aspect of subcultural variation that has received the most attention, however, is the relationship between social class status and education.

August Hollingshead's "Elmtown's Youth" tested the hypothesis that the behavior of adolescents in and about school was significantly related to the positions their families occupied in the social class structure of the community. The hypothesis was con-

[42] Joan Robinson, *The Cultural Revolution in China* (Baltimore: Penguin, 1969). See also *Report From Red China, The New York Times* (New York: Avon, 1971), chap. 5, "The Children of Chairman Mao: Education and Child-Rearing," by Tillman F. Durdin; Committee of Concerned Asian Scholars, *China! Inside the People's Republic* (New York: Bantam, 1972), chap. 7, "Education"; and Harriet C. Mills, "Thought Reform: Ideological Remolding in China," in Patricia Cayo Sexton, ed., *Readings on the School in Society* (Englewood Cliffs, N.J.: Prentice-Hall, 1968), pp. 164–74.

firmed: School-board policy, adolescent attitudes, participation in extracurricular activities, membership in cliques, progress in school, and recognition by teachers were all determined in large part by class background.[43]

Theoretically, the American system is open as compared to the traditional class-oriented selective system in European schools. Until recently European children were sorted into various kinds of schools at age ten or eleven. Thereafter they were destined either for trades, commercial and clerical work, or the university with its opportunities for professional standing. But some American high schools operate on a track system, which has the same effect.

Under the track system, those from culturally deprived homes are automatically passed through the grades regardless of performance, until legal school-leaving age is reached. At that time they are dumped out on the streets, where they will spend the rest of their lives grubbing for existence through the offal of our cities. The second track is for those with low, but passable, achievement records. They are placed in the manual-arts, nonacademic track and are destined for the menial, semiskilled trades. The highest, of course, are put into the liberal-arts, college-preparatory programs, and they inevitably will end up with college degrees and Establishment jobs. The point is that the track system reinforces—and even magnifies—the initial condition with which students begin life. Before the average child is ten years old the school system has already determined, beyond the child's ability to influence it, his entire lifetime career.[44]

Ideally, at least, the "comprehensive" high school, offering different curricula but mingling the students as much as possible and offering a maximum freedom of choice, is the type least likely to perpetuate class distinctions. But most teachers have middle-class backgrounds and unconsciously tend to discriminate against lower-class children. One aspect of this discrimination is the "self-fulfilling prophecy." They expect less of children from deprived homes, and therefore the children achieve less. The best-known study of this phenomenon—the "Rosenthal effect"—was carried out in Oak School, a public elementary school in a lower-class community of a medium-size city. About one-sixth of the pupils were Mexican-Americans. Each of the six grades was divided into one fast, one medium, and one slow classroom, primarily on the basis of reading ability. Mexican-Americans were heavily over-represented in the slow track. To test the proposition that favorable expectations by teachers could lead to an increase in intellectual competence, all the children were given a standard nonverbal test of intelligence at the very beginning of the school year. Each of the eighteen teachers was given the names of those children in her classroom who had done well on the test. This list included about 20 percent of the children and was allegedly based on the tests. But actually it had been chosen according to a table of random numbers. "The difference between the special children and the ordinary children, then, was only in the mind of the teacher."[45]

Retesting showed that 19 percent of the control-group children of the first and second grades gained 20 or more points in IQ, while 47 percent of the experimental group made such a gain. Children in the medium

---

[43] August B. Hollingshead, *Elmtown's Youth* (New York: John Wiley, 1949), chap. 8, "The High School in Action."

[44] Harvey Wheeler, "A Moral Equivalent for Riots," *Saturday Review* (May 11, 1968): 19–22 *et passim.*

[45] Robert Rosenthal and Lenore Jacobson, *Pygmalion in the Classroom: Teacher Expectation and Pupils' Intellectual Development* (New York: Holt, Rinehart and Winston, 1968).

While American education is theoretically open, in reality the system tends to perpetuate class differences. *Michael Dobo/Stock, Boston.*

track made the greatest improvement. The boys who looked most Mexican—and therefore probably surprised their teachers most by showing up on a list of probable "bloomers"—benefited most from their teachers' positive prophecies. And those of the lower track who had *not* been chosen as probable intellectual bloomers, but did make spectacular gains, were viewed very negatively by their teachers. Expectations, then, did affect performance. But it was not made clear just how the process works. "The phenomenon of subtle interpersonal influence guiding progress in the classroom is as complex as it is fascinating."[46]

The impact of class status on educational opportunity and achievement is much greater in European countries than in the United States. In France the chances of getting a professional education are 58.5 percent for the children of professionals, and less than 2 percent for the children of agricultural and other workers.[47] Despite many educational reforms in Great Britain, more than a third leave school at age fifteen. The system has never succeeded in absorbing the working class. In the United States over 94 percent of those age fourteen to seventeen, nearly 48 percent of those age eighteen to nineteen, and 21.5 percent of those age twenty to twenty-four are in school.[48] Over 8 million

[46] Peter and Carol Gumpert, "The Teacher as Pygmalion: Comments on the Psychology of Expectation," *The Urban Review* 3, No. 1 (Sept. 1968): 21–25.

[47] Coombs, *The World Crisis in Education*, pp. 32–33.
[48] *Information Please Almanac* (1972), p. 658.

371

young people were in college in 1972. It is estimated that by 1985 there will be nearly 12 million. And many of these come from hitherto deprived groups. In the country as a whole, over 9 percent of freshman were blacks in 1972, as compared to 5.8 percent four years earlier. Many of these attended urban community colleges; 55–65 percent were not in black colleges, which enrolled most blacks until the mid-1960s.[49]

Ferment and Experiment in Education

In America especially, people are seriously questioning all aspects of the educational system: social organization, the content and methods of teaching, the goals of schooling—even the very existence of a formal school system. Inside and outside the system, there is much experimentation and innovation. One anthropologist sees the ferment in American education as a symptom of cultural transformation—"a transformation that produces serious conflict. . . . The core of the change can best be conceived as a radical shift in values." Basing his generalizations on the responses of several hundred students to a series of twenty-four open-ended statements, such as "The individual is—," "All men are born—," George Spindler outlined a shift from traditional to emergent values. Puritan morality vs. moral relativism; the work-success ethic and achievement orientation vs. sociability and hedonism; future-time orientation vs. present-time orientation; individualism vs. consideration for others and conformity—these are the main

outlines of traditional and emergent values. Most likely to champion traditional values are school boards, with the general public and parents close to them in conservatism. Some students also cling to traditional values and are more conservative than school administrators. Younger teachers are more likely to hold emergent values than older ones. And emergent values are strongest of all among students from families oriented toward such values.[50]

Social Organization

School systems are charged with being vast, rigid bureaucracies isolated from the community and unresponsive to students. Two of the many changes suggested involve closer ties with the community and a change in student status and role.

Schools should prepare children not for some ideal pattern of suburban middle-class life but for their communities as they are. Teachers should be aware of the problems a ghetto child faces outside the school and talk about them. An absolute moral rule like "It is wrong to fight" does a slum kid little good. More useful would be a talk on the theme "It is wrong to allow others to manipulate you into a fight." One sign that members of the community themselves want closer communication with their children's schools is the movement toward decentralization of urban systems. Neighborhood school boards oversee some aspects of schooling.

Students themselves are demanding greater power and participation, more control over what they are taught and how they

[49] William Stief, "Blacks in College: The Most Exciting Thing Around," *The Progressive* (Sept. 1971): 32–34.

[50] "Education in a Transforming American Culture," in George D. Spindler, ed., *Education and Culture: Anthropological Approaches* (New York: Holt, Rinehart and Winston, 1963).

are evaluated. Not only slum schools with their largely custodial function, but *most* schools are authoritarian. Not only do students feel they lack a meaningful function in the general socio-cultural order, they also feel powerless in their own schools. A Carnegie study found the three most damaging features of United States high schools were encouragement of docility and conformity, overregulation of students' lives, and a pallid uniform curriculum. Various reform movements and experiments are designed to make the system more open, personal, and flexible.

Another problem is that schooling now begins earlier in life and extends later and later. Most people age two to twenty are in school, and there are numerous programs for adults. As Hutchins put it, this trend is commendable if it is not an attempt to answer the question "How can we get everybody in schools and keep them there as long as possible?" but rather, "How can we give everybody a chance to learn all his life?"[51]

Content of Education

In a rapidly changing society, what shall we teach the young? If we give them narrowly specific skills, the advance of science and technology soon makes those skills obsolete. Some educators suggest that children must learn to learn. They must learn to think not of details but of big concepts. They must learn to see problems (other than how to con the teacher or pass the course or get a good grade). They should be encouraged to guess and brainstorm, rather than being spoon-fed information they are to learn by rote and spit back on command. They must not be coddled and taught some ideal world

that does not exist—though ideals and values must of course be part of the content. But if the conflict and tension students see all around them are ignored in school, how will they learn to cope and understand? Classroom materials tend to be innocuous, partly because of the conflicting cross-pressures of different interest groups. This is apparent even in some universities, where the public, exerting power through legislatures, clamps down on expressions of unorthodox views and dissent.

A student who does not see the relevance of content to his or her own life will not be motivated to learn. The curriculum in most American schools has some relevance for the economic future of the advantaged, very little for the "disadvantaged." Neil Postman and Charles Weingartner suggest that children should be taught to ask and pursue questions they perceive as important to their own lives. They should go find the answers wherever they can be found, whether or not that is in the school. They repeat "a sad little joke about a fifth-grade teacher in a ghetto school who asked a grim Negro boy, during the course of a 'science' lesson, 'How many legs does a grasshopper have?' 'Oh, man,' he replied, 'I sure wish I had *your* problems!' "[52]

Goals and Methods

Closely interwined with the content of education are its goals and methods. Do schools emphasize the lives and growth of the students, or getting through a prescribed curriculum? Do educators and administrators think about what they are doing, and why?

---

[51] Robert M. Hutchins, "Toward a Learning Society."

[52] *Teaching as a Subversive Activity* (New York: Dell, 1970), p. 93. See chap. 11, "Two Alternatives," for fascinating examples of curricula centered around questions and reality.

"Free" schools, both within the system and outside it, are experimenting with goals and methods. One approach is exemplified by Summerhill, whose headmaster, A. S. Neill, believed that if children are free of fear, they will learn.[53] While Summerhill has aroused much controversy, it has served as a catalyst, prompting much debate and experimentation. In America, for example, free schools have developed outside the formal system—"street academies," such as George Dennison's short-lived First Street School,[54] and free high schools and universities based on the principle of self-regulation. Europeans have experimented with freer schools within the system—for example, the British primary schools, which adopted many innovations. Children are taught to work independently in an environment thoughtfully planned to permit choices from an array of materials. They help one another, move about freely, work at their individual pace. The teacher moves among them asking and answering questions as they do many different things. He or she is the organizer, catalyst, and consultant, who listens, diagnoses, advises, and introduces new ideas, words, and materials.

A lot of things have happened in recent decades. How can schools incorporate the new means of communication and information processing without further dehumanizing the process of education? Those who dismiss television and computers as "hardware" and "gadgets" have failed to come to terms with the fact that by the time average American children reach school they are already packed with information picked up

from 3,000 to 4,000 hours of watching TV. The success of "Sesame Street" with youngsters from three to five suggests the possibilities. Yet the danger of dehumanization remains. There must be a live teacher in the room, a responsive human being who *uses* the TV or the teaching machine. The latter may be better for some students than a disapproving teacher, for it is impersonal, does not condemn, gives another chance.

The evaluation of students' potential and achievement is vital to their self-conceptions. In a school with a strict system of grading, competition rather than cooperation guides interaction. The system of evaluating the individual student, it has been argued, is a major flaw in public education. Intelligence tests are of doubtful validity. Achievement tests are either unfair or self-defeating for those from deprived backgrounds. A more constructive approach would be to evaluate not students but teachers, principals, school districts, and educational systems. This would lead to such questions as, How can we protect the teacher from social and administrative pressures? In spite of centralization and bureaucratization, each school is a unit in itself. Teachers are isolated from one another, principals from teachers. Yet both are vulnerable to community power and hence fearful of innovation.[55]

Education in the Post-Industrial Society

With the emergence of a post-industrial society, skills and techniques quickly become obsolete. Reeducation is necessary in all fields of expertise and professionalism. Leisure time increases greatly.

[53] A. S. Neill, *Summerhill: A Radical Approach to Child Rearing* (New York: Hart Publishing Company, 1960); and *Summerhill: For and Against.*

[54] George Dennison, *The Lives of Children: The Story of the First Street School* (New York: Random House, 1969).

[55] Janowitz, "Institution Building in Urban Education."

As these trends accelerate, manpower becomes less important, the achievement of full human potential more so. The post-industrial society does not need people trained to give a routine response—its machines do that. It needs imaginative, resourceful, flexible human beings. Human brains can do research and apply their findings; machines can do routine activities. Humans alone can respond richly to other humans, as teachers, parents, helpers, physicians, and friends.

The university has always played a crucial role in storing, transmitting, and changing the culture. "It is in the universities that lies, still, the best potential for learning to come to terms with our age. They will realize that potential fully when they succeed in bridging the current dichotomy between 'schooling' and 'adult education' with a con-cept of continuing education that is alive and sensitive to what will from now on in certainly be a world that will stand still no longer."[56] Despite charges that the universities have "sold out" (because they accept grants for research that may be turned to the ends of the military-industrial complex, for example), they occupy a very special place in free societies.

In rearing "unknown children for an unknown future," insists Margaret Mead, we must find ways of teaching and learning that keep the future open. We must recognize that "for the first time human beings throughout the world, in their information about one another and responses to one another, have become a community that is united by shared knowledge and danger."[57]

Summary

Religion is an attempt to give meaning to the things that lie beyond knowledge and control. Leaving the truth or falsity of specific beliefs to theologians and to the faithful or the doubters, sociologists study religion objectively, as a system of meaning and purpose with great consequences for society and the individual.

Religion may spring from the universal elements of the human condition—uncertainty, the need for trust in social relationships, powerlessness over death, catastrophe and misfortune, and inequality and injustice.

Explanations for these conditions are ex-pressed in systems of belief in the sacred, in the relationship of the sacred to mankind, in the meaning of human life. Some religions are eschatological, concerned with "last things" such as death and judgment and the after-life. Judgment is tied into morality in this life. A special aspect of a religious

[56] Emmanuel G. Mesthene, "The University, Adult Education, and the Age of Technology," *Adult Leadership* 15, No. 4 (Oct. 1966): 113–45 *et passim.*
[57] Margaret Mead, *Culture and Commitment* (Garden City, N.Y.: Doubleday, 1970), p. 54.

belief system is its theodicy, which reconciles what is with what ought to be.

Religious practices are typically collective, whether in the family or in a formal congregation. Church attendance, affiliation, and patterns of worship show some correlation with social class status.

Religious experience ranges from mild to ecstatic and is difficult to measure empirically. Even the most mystical experience appears to be culturally conditioned to some extent.

The relationship between church and sect is a cycle of institutionalization and compromise with worldly values. Sects break off, usually under a charismatic leader, and frequently evolve into an institutionalized church that in turn compromises with the world.

Modernization results in religious pluralism. Secularization replaces mysteries with problems to be solved scientifically and rationally.

The purposes for which people engage in religious practices and seek religious explanations may have no clear connection with the consequences of their religion for society. These consequences include social cohesion and social control through reinforcement of ethical norms. Religion can be either conservative or innovative. It can be a comfort and a guide to behavior for individuals.

Although the influence of orthodox religious beliefs appears to be declining, there is evidence of continuing interest in religion.

Education differs from religion in being both public and compulsory. Education is both conservative (a means of transmitting the culture) and innovative (an institu-

tionalized system for advancing knowledge). It is the main avenue to participation and success in modern society.

Industrializing nations typically give high priority to education, but their manpower requirements and the social demand for education are not always well adjusted. Education in modern society tends to stress the verbal and rational at the expense of the expressive and creative aspects of behavior.

The relationship between social class status and educational aspirations and achievements has been demonstrated by numerous empirical studies. Track systems of sorting students tend to rigidify a class system. Experiments suggest that the expectations of teachers can affect individual achievement (the "Rosenthal" effect). There are indications that the American class system, always comparatively open, is becoming more so, especially in higher education.

Unrest, experiment, and innovation are occurring in education at all levels, possibly as a result of the shift from traditional to emergent and conflicting values. Greater student participation, greater exposure to the community, and greater community control are among demands related to social organization. Experiments with "free schools" can be seen both within and outside formal systems of education.

As we enter a post-industrial stage, rote learning and technical skills are of less value in an automated system of production and a rapidly changing society. Emphasis must be put on imagination, resourcefulness, and flexibility. The universities in particular play a crucial role in shaping the emerging society.

Glossary

Church A large established religious organization that compromises with political and economic realities.

Education Informal or deliberate transmission of selected knowledge, skills, and values to prepare individuals for effective membership in a society.

Mysticism Emphasis on purely personal religious experience rather than collective formal organization.

Religion The social institution that deals with sacred things, which lie beyond human knowledge and control.

Sect A dissident group that tries to preserve the purity of a faith and avoid compromise with "worldly realities."

Secularization The trend toward removal of sectors of society and culture from domination by religious institutions and symbols.

chapter

16

Politics and the Economy

As people grow older, they may not have families, may not participate in a formal religion, and may no longer be involved in education. But everyone—from birth to death—is part of some political order and some sort of economic system.

One of our Founding Fathers, James Madison, said, "If men were angels there would be no need for government." But people are not angels. They fight, compete, covet, and deviate from social norms. They live in groups that need direction, coordination, and planning. Thus, government is one of the pivotal social institutions. It is universal. It is found in even the simplest cultures, where, like economic arrangements, it is often meshed with other institutions. In modern society, it more commonly stands above other institutions and guides and supports them through legal controls of family life, education, and the like. Government, more than any other institution, determines the balance of freedom and control in a society and ensures its survival and cohesion.

In this chapter, after examining such basic concepts as power, authority, legitimacy, the state, government, and politics, we discuss variations in forms of government. Then we look at some ways in which political change occurs and consider some recent trends in political institutions. In the second part of this chapter, we look at economic institutions, which also have an important effect on people's lives. Indeed, one's share in the economy may determine the part one plays in its politics. We look at what an economy is and what it does, at the basic economic institutions, and how the major economic "isms" developed.

The Bases of Political Institutions

Political institutions are based on three important concepts: power, authority, and legitimacy. Their interrelationship may be put in a nutshell: *authority is legitimate power.* That is, authority is power rightfully held and exercised.

Power

Power is a relationship between people in which one person or group is able to influence the behavior of other people or groups in an intended direction. It is exerted in three main ways—through force, domination, or manipulation.[1]

Force includes any kind of physical manipulation, imprisonment, or execution. The state alone claims the authority—the legitimate power—to regulate the use of force. *Domination* is power exerted by means of commands or requests. Like the use of force, it also involves a relationship of authority, such as that of employer and em-

[1] Herbert Goldhamer and Edward A. Shils, "Types of Power and Status," *The American Journal of Sociology,* 45 (1939), pp. 171–182.

ployee or parent and child. But its use is not limited to government. It is characteristic of any hierarchy.

Manipulation can be exercised regardless of status, authority, or physical size, for that matter. A child can exert power over a parent, and a wife can "handle" a husband. An advertiser can convince consumers of the worth of a product, and a propagandist can convince the masses that "Black is white, Night is day," as in George Orwell's novel, *1984.* In all these cases the influenced people may be unaware that they are being manipulated. No commands, requests, or threats of force are involved, but the manipulators are nonetheless exerting power to achieve behavior they desire. Some forms of interaction—for example, collective bargaining—combine elements of all three power relationships.

Power can be distributed in a society in several ways. In many nation-states, there is a distinct *power elite* that appears to have control of all the resources of the society—land ownership, military power, religion, the media of communication, and political power. These states are considered to be polarized. There is a deep gulf between the elite and the masses, between the "haves" and the "have nots."

In other nation-states, power is *pluralistic.* It is fragmented and diffused rather than concentrated and polarized. Many people have the right to vote. Some people may have more of one resource, some have more of another, but no one group has all the wealth, education, political appeal to voters, and so on. There are many centers of power and many different groups with different interests. In such a state, political roles are highly differentiated. Besides the rulers—the executives, lawmakers, judges, and bureaucrats—participants in the political process include voters, citizens, politicians, members of many different pressure groups, and political parties.

The ideology of a pluralistic society includes the beliefs that the functions of government should be limited and that dispersing the right to social action among as many other agencies of power and achievement as possible will help realize the values of freedom, variety, spontaneity, and autonomy. By means of free periodic elections, such a society keeps the rulers responsible to the ruled.

In contrast with the pluralistic society, and also to be differentiated from the polarized society with a power elite, is the *monistic* state. Such a state is based on the ideology that the state is the supreme good, that only the state realizes the prime values of order, harmony, and singleness of purpose. Under this system, the scope of government functions is all-embracing. The modern version of monism is *totalitarianism,* in which education, propaganda, and economic, military, and police power are all concentrated in the hands of the state, and in which all activities, public and private, are judged in terms of their contribution to the good of the state. The vote is an empty privilege, for the voters have no real choice of personnel or policies. Therefore, the rulers cannot be held responsible by the ruled.

Authority

Much of the power of government is exercised by means of commands or requests, but always behind them is the ultimate threat of force. The policeman directing traffic merely uses hand signals, but he has power over people's behavior for two reasons. They have been trained or socialized to respect the authority symbolized by the uniform. And they know, whether they think of it consciously or not, that disobedience can mean fines and loss of the privilege of driving.

Authority, then, is power that is recognized and accepted by those who are subjected to it as being validly held by those who exercise it. Like power in general, authority is not limited to government. It is associated with status in any sphere—the family, religion, art, education, science.

The authority of government, to be lasting, must be founded on a broad *consensus* in the society—a general agreement on important goals and values and on proper procedures for attaining and preserving them. Such a consensus has its roots in the central myth of the society, the set of fundamental beliefs, values, and goals that gives a unity of purpose to the society. It has a sacred character, as does, for example, "The American Way of Life." Such central myths hold sway over the minds of rulers and ruled alike. They are the ultimate basis for social cohesion.

The two opposing views concerning the source of authority are the democratic and authoritarian views. According to the *democratic* view, authority resides in the governed, who confer it voluntarily upon the rulers. The rulers act as the agents of the governed and are accountable for their actions to the governed, who can supervise the use of power and can revoke authority if it is abused. The procedures according to which authority may be used are outlined in a constitution, a collection of written documents and unwritten customs. Not all governments that have formal written constitutions are democratic, however, nor do all democratic governments have written constitutions. A truly constitutional government is *limited* in purpose and method by the constitution, which serves to guarantee freedom as well as order and predictability.

Most governments throughout history— and most governments today, despite lip service to democratic forms and ideals— have been *authoritarian*. According to this view of the relationship between the rulers and the governed, authority is exercised *over* the governed. It is the governed rather than

Handelsman in The Saturday Review

"A limited monarchy—what an interesting idea! Why didn't I think of that?"

the rulers who are held responsible and accountable for their actions and who must obey. Authority is based on some criterion of legitimacy other than the consent of the governed. Among these external criteria have been "God, grandparents, and guns," in Leslie Lipson's catchy phrase, that is, divine right, ancestry, and force.[2] Another source of legitimacy claimed by authoritarians is some quality, acquired or inherent, that marks one as a member of the elite and hence best fitted to govern. Plato thought the ideal state should be ruled by "philosopher kings." The wisest, the richest, and the oldest have at different times and in different societies assumed authority on

[2] Leslie Lipson, *The Great Issues of Politics,* 6th ed. (Englewood Cliffs, N.J.: Prentice-Hall, 1976).

the basis of belief in their superior capacities.[3]

Legitimacy

Our acceptance of the central myth gives our government an extremely high degree of **legitimacy.** Almost all Americans accept our form of government as right and proper and believe that government officials hold their power legitimately. Consensus on basic, general principles is high. Attacks on government are usually made in terms of specific persons or policies and are not directed at the system itself.

But what are the particular bases of the legitimacy of any ruler or any set of rules and of the particular people who occupy the statuses of the institution of government at any one time? Max Weber distinguished three bases for claims to legitimacy: rational-legal, traditional, and charismatic.[4] These are pure types useful for purposes of analysis. Although each type is more likely to appear in one kind of social order than another, in any given case elements of all three may be present.

In the case of *rational-legal authority,* a body of generalized rules applies equally and impersonally to the rulers and the ruled. Authority goes with the particular offices or statuses and does not belong to the particular people who may occupy those offices. Bureaucratic administration typically accompanies this type of authority.

Traditional authority, in contrast, bases claim to legitimacy on the belief that the particular social order has always existed. Rules are not enacted, but are considered a natural part of the social order. The statuses of authority are inseparable from the people who exercise them. Thus loyalty is due to the person rather than the office. The ruler's claim to legitimacy lies in the sacred traditions by virtue of which he or she exercises authority. The divine right of kings and the power of a tribal chieftain who has inherited the status or won it by ritual means are examples of legitimacy based on tradition.

Whereas rational-legal and traditional authority are characteristic of established social orders, *charismatic leaders* exercise a claim to authority that is in conflict with the bases of legitimacy in such settled societies. Weber saw religious proselytizing and the use of force as the charismatic leader's typical fields of action. Such leaders have a sense of sacred mission, claim moral authority, and exact conformity as a duty. Such leaders are granted authority because of their forceful and magnetic personalities. If the mission succeeds, the movement becomes the new pattern of the social order. Then authority becomes institutionalized in a traditional or rational-legal direction. All social orders do attempt, however, to paint their established leaders with a charismatic halo.

Government and the State

However authority is legitimated, it is manifested primarily as an attribute of the nation-state and the government. Government stands in the same relationship to the state as the driver to a vehicle.

The Nation-State

The **nation-state** is the comprehensive political organization of a society. The distinction between the state and its government is clear in constitutional monarchies such as England. In England, the Queen is the chief of state, but the prime minister is the head

---

[3] *Ibid.,* pp. 220–229.

[4] Max Weber, *The Theory of Social and Economic Organization,* A. M. Henderson and Talcott Parsons, trans. (New York: The Free Press, 1947), pp. 56–77.

In England, the Queen is the head of state, but the Prime Minister is the head of the government. *Wide World Photos.*

of the government. In the United States, on the other hand, the president plays both roles. Regardless of its form of government, the nation-state is a specific territory that has sovereignty and a monopoly of the use of force within its borders.

A nation-state is always identified with a definite *territory,* whether large or small. Both postage-stamp-size Luxembourg and the giant Soviet Union are nation-states. The boundaries of the nation-state are usually jealously guarded, because they mark off the ingroup from the outgroup and contribute to a sense of solidarity. The population of a nation-state consists mainly of citizens, and there are clear ways of defining who is a citizen and who is an alien, and how the status of citizenship is acquired or forfeited. Most citizens acquire their status at birth. Immigrants may acquire it by marriage or by naturalization, which usually requires renunciation of citizenship in any other nation-state and a pledge of allegiance to the new nation-state.

The concept of *sovereignty* means that regardless of its area, population, or any other considerations, the nation-state is on an equal footing with other sovereign nation-states in the world, as in the United Nations, where each nation-state has one vote. The nation-state may enter into treaties and confederations with other states and make concessions to aliens traveling or residing within its borders, but it does so voluntarily and on a basis of formal legal and political equality with all other states. (Its actual *capability*—the power at its command—is another story.)

The outstanding feature of sovereign authority is the *monopoly over the use of force* that a nation-state claims within its borders. Other groups—gangsters, mobs, criminals—may use force, but they do so illegally and the state reserves the right to punish them. Parents may spank their children, but if they become brutal, the state claims the right to step in and protect children from their own parents.

The nation-state not only regulates the use of force, but also claims the exclusive right to the power of imprisonment and execution. Let us imagine that a number of men take another man into an isolated room in a quiet building one midnight and kill him. Is this a violation of the mores and laws, a crime? Not if the room is a gas chamber, the building is a state penitentiary, and the man has been convicted of murder and condemned to death. Regardless of how we may feel about capital punishment, we must grant that the action was legitimate—that the group of men, as representatives of the government, had authority to put the man to death.

Government

To a member of American society, government appears as a highly visible and explicit institution. It has clearly defined procedures, sanctions, and personnel, all of which are used in enforcing written rules and regulations. It functions in the name of clearly defined units of area and population—townships, precincts, wards, cities, districts, counties, states, and the nation.

But **government** may mean three different things. In the general sense of a *function,* government is the process of governing, of keeping order and enforcing norms. With reference to a particular society, government may be seen in two other ways: as an institution and as an association. The *institution* of government is the enduring complex of norms or procedures and the structure of statuses or offices through which the process of governing is carried on in a society. Thus we would say that American government includes the norms set down in the Constitution and the laws, and the structure of legislative, executive, and judiciary branches including the statuses of president, Supreme Court justice, senator, congressman, sheriff, customs inspector, and many more elected and appointed offices. In the sense of an *association,* the government is the particular set of elected and appointed officials who occupy the statuses and perform the functions of government at any given time—President Carter, Justice Marshall, Senator Goldwater, Congressman Rodino, Sheriff Jones, Customs Inspector Smith.

The Role of Law in Modern Society

The basic function of modern government is to maintain the social order and promote social welfare. It does this by exerting formal control through existing laws and by drafting new laws that readjust the order itself when changing conditions demand it.

Modern societies can exist only with coherent systems of formal laws. **Laws** are deliberately formulated, clearly stated norms enforced by highly visible and specialized agencies—government officials. Laws state what must be done, may be done, and must not be done, and they prescribe punishments for their violation.

Because a modern society is a changing society, the power to make the laws is a crucially important one. A legitimate lawmaking body is a great social invention for readjusting the social order in a peaceful and orderly fashion. When problems arise for which no law exists, the legislature (or its counterpart in a society where laws are made by other officials) must think of new laws to handle them. The success of the lawmaking body in doing this is often vital to the survival of the society as a going concern in a changing world. Governments that are rigid, that lack adequate means for meeting new problems and making fundamental changes in legal arrangements, are prone to lose effectiveness and thus to collapse in revolution and chaos.[5] Different kinds of law help keep a society functioning. Five functions of law are particularly important.

First, laws, like other social norms, *give predictability* to many situations. The folkways do this by setting predictable ways of eating, speaking, and greeting. The mores

[5] Karl N. Llewellyn, "Law and Civilization," in Lyman Jay Gould and E. Williams Steele, eds., *People, Power, and Politics* (New York: Random House, 1961), p. 328.

do this by setting patterns for basic relationships such as husband and wife, parent and child. Common law—law not enacted by any specific lawmaking body but based on custom and court decisions—also does this by providing mutual understandings concerning rights and responsibilities, such as those of a common-law husband or wife. And formally enacted laws add predictability to many situations not adequately covered by custom—traffic regulation, radio and television broadcasting, garbage collection, and the like. They also give predictable minimum security against the hazards of unemployment, illness, and old age.

Second, laws are part of the *dispute-adjusting machinery* of government. Conflicts and disputes can arise over property, contracts, rights of various kinds. Laws provide a precedent and a mechanism for settling them. The legendary case of Solomon and

the two women who claimed the same child illustrates this function of government. So does the search for ways of preventing a strike in a crucial industry such as the railroads.

Third, laws *define crimes* that threaten the life, peace, and property of members of the society or the existence of the society itself—murder, assault, arson, theft, fraud, extortion, and treason—and provide sanctions for them. But criminal law, dramatic as it is, forms only a tiny part of the great body of law that maintains and readjusts the social order.

Fourth, law *provides channels* for the members of the society to accomplish various things they want done that involve neither patterned interaction (as in traffic), conflict, nor crime. These laws provide for ways of making wills, taking mortgages, investing in securities, dividing estates, adopting children, and similar actions. "The civil law is full of these devices to make it easier for

The power to make laws is very important in modern societies. *Wide World Photos.*

people to accomplish what they want in their relations with other people; to make it easier for people to deal at long range, or over long time periods, and still have some moderate guaranty that the arrangements made will stand."[6] Similarly, laws may enable a government itself to plan economic development, build dams, support schools, aid foreign countries, conserve resources, and try to reach the moon.

Fifth, laws also *implement social reforms* that are designed to bring real patterns closer to ideal ones. Governments are entrusted with the task of preserving the dominant cultural values. When no other agency seems adequate to the task, the government must eventually step in. Thus, the American national government has become the chief defender of civil rights.

Politics

Politics is the process by which any organized group finds its leaders and decides its policies. According to this broad definition, politics is present in any collection of human beings with conflicting goals and interests: in an office, a college department, a church hierarchy, even a church congregation.

In this chapter, however, we use **politics** in a narrower sense, as *the struggle for power to name the personnel and decide the policies of the government.* Various means are used: influencing the nomination, election, or the appointment of government personnel; influencing public opinion through propaganda of various kinds, and influencing lawmakers through pressure groups. This description of politics is especially true where the form of government is based on the ideal of "a government of laws and not of men." Its meaning changes where participation in

the processes of politics and government is limited to a small portion of the citizenry, as it is in the Soviet Union.

Changing Political Institutions

We may look at changes in political institutions either as changes in a particular system, or as more general changes in the nature of government. Here we look at general trends in the forms and functions of government and of relationships among governments in the world as a whole.

Trends in the Form and Function of Government

We have already mentioned in several contexts a number of changes in the nature of government in the modern world. Let us list them more explicitly here.

First, the rapid shift to large-scale, urban, industrial society has meant a corresponding change in the *scale* of government. As problems have crossed the borders of local communities, the national government has become ever larger and more important in the life of each society. Mass communications media have drawn the remotest members of modern societies into the orbit of influence of the state and invited them either to play a role in the formation of public opinion or to accept the policies of their rulers.

Second, the scope of the *functions* of government has increased correspondingly. The central government is now held responsible for the economic and political security of all citizens. No one is supposed to remain at an unfair disadvantage in life chances. The increasing division of labor and the divisions into various nationality groups, religions, races, and classes within a society

[6] Llewellyn, "Law and Civilization," p. 326.

The state must work to minimize inequalities. If one group feels it gets less than its share of power over government, the resulting alienation can breed antisocial violent behavior, as was seen during the 1977 blackout in New York City. *Wide World Photos.*

have created multigroup societies, and the differences and conflicts among these groups must somehow be resolved. If any one group feels discriminated against either in its life chances or in its share of power over government (in states where the rulers are responsible to the ruled), their resulting alienation is a breeding ground for antisocial, violent behavior. To fulfill its primary function of preserving the cohesion of society, the state must work to minimize inequalities and settle conflicts.

Third, in all societies there tends to be a shift from traditional to rational-legal authority. Technical experts are consulted on questions of government policy. Bureaucrats are entrusted with administration.

These changes in the scale and functions of government and the nature of authority are apparent in the two main alternative systems of government in the modern world, which have been described by Robert Mac-Iver as "evolutionary socio-capitalist democracy" and "the authoritarian system of communist dictatorship" (which becomes more or less totalitarian as conditions change).[7] Differences persist between them. Democracies guarantee civil rights, are pluralistic, and separate the concepts of state and society. Dictatorships, on the other hand, deny civil liberties. They are monistic and identify state and society as one. In spite of these differences, cooperation and peaceful competition rather than deadly conflict are possible between such different types of government. The Soviet Union gives many signs of becoming more moderate, as does the People's Republic of China. The United States also appears more aware of the advantages of peaceful co-existence.

World Trends in Government and International Relations

The most significant trends in government and international relations in the past three decades include: the rise of many new nations, often through revolution; the bipolarization of power and then a reversal of

[7] R. M. MacIver, *The Web of Government*, rev. ed. (New York: Macmillan, 1965), p. 131.

388

this trend; and the emergence of a curiously mixed role for the sentiment of nationalism.

THE RISE OF NEW NATIONS Never in history have so many new nations been formed and claimed sovereignty as during the years since World War II. A century ago more than half the world's territory was ruled by European colonial powers. Today most of these territories are new and independent nations. Many had their beginnings in revolutionary movements.

Colonial powers unwittingly prepared the ground for revolution and nurtured the spirit of nationalism. They disrupted traditional societies by introducing some industry and commerce (thus drawing people to the cities, plantations, and mines from their close-knit tribal communities) and by weakening or destroying the authority of native leaders. They distributed Western goods and Western ideas, which awakened desires for material progress, freedom, and sovereignty. They educated a number of the natives, but then blocked their progress beyond a certain point. Thus they created a class of frustrated and resentful intellectuals, who longed for reforms but saw no hope for achieving them unless the colonial masters and their allies in the native elite were ousted. Such fervent, idealistic, and charismatic leaders as Gandhi preached nationalism and anticolonialism, rejected alien ways, and idealized the native culture. In many cases they tried nonviolent measures, then lost faith in them and eventually turned to conspiracy, terror, and violent revolution. Some colonial masters, like Great Britain, bowed out with as much grace as they could before things reached this point. Others, like the French and Portuguese, stayed and fought, overestimating the power of military force against a native populace convinced of the rightness of its cause.

Much of the foreign policy of the Soviet Union and of the United States has been aimed at capturing the allegiance of these new nations and persuading them to follow one model or the other for governing their societies. But many leaders have refused allegiance and rejected both models. Some have adopted democratic forms and guaranteed a measure of civil liberties, but the new nations do not provide fertile soil for democratic institutions.

Democracy demands rather special conditions, of which perhaps the most important is a long cultural tradition resulting in a strong consensus on certain norms and values. In most of the new nations there are deep cleavages of tribe, race, religion, and urban-rural residence, and a deep gulf between the generations. There are also shortages of trained personnel. Finally, the sense of urgency in the face of pressing problems of disease, poverty, and ignorance makes the leaders impatient with the slower processes of democracy. As a result they have typically instituted an authoritarian system dominated by one party and have emphasized central planning and government control. But they have generally rejected the police-state methods of Stalinism and have tried to preserve the values of pluralism.

BIPOLARIZATION OF POWER AND ITS REVERSAL World War II was followed by a period when the two superpowers, the United States and the Soviet Union, were engaged in a cold war fought with every technique short of full-scale military aggression. Most nation-states clustered around the two great powers as satellites, allies, or spheres of influence. An uneasy peace was based on mutual fear of nuclear annihilation. The Soviet Union, by exploiting and encouraging nationalist and anticolonial movements, aligned itself on the side of revolution and liberation. The United States felt forced to take the other tack and thereby appeared to support the colonial status quo. Massive programs of foreign aid were often heavily in favor of military support for the existing, generally oppressive, regimes. But there were also programs of aid to economic development, which the Soviet Union eventually copied.

In recent years there has been a shift away from a bipolar balance of power. Many new nations refuse alignments. Soviet satellites demand (with varying success) a greater degree of autonomy. The Chinese refuse to identify themselves with the Soviet Union, and, through foreign aid, have developed satellites of their own. One nation after another joins the "atomic club." Even Western allies do not unhesitatingly accept American policy. Whether this multipolarity is preferable to the separation of the world into two giant power blocs is a difficult question to answer, especially in an age when one careless mistake or one rash moment on the part of someone empowered to push "the" button can bring on World War III.

THE SENTIMENT OF NATIONALISM Even while many new nations are emerging, the nation-state may be becoming out-of-date. In an atomic age, no nation can protect its citizens. Only a world government can do so. At the same time, the sentiment of nationalism fosters a sense of identity and purpose among the uprooted citizens of the new nations who are undergoing the wrenching changes of industrialization and urbanization.

The concept of national sovereignty, however, means that each nation recognizes no superior. Therefore the only basis on which international relations can proceed is one of complete legal and status equality with all other nations. This equality of status is recognized in the Charter of the United Nations, for example, and is expressed in the symbolism and protocol of formal international intercourse. Sovereignty is regarded by citizens of nation-states as something to be jealously protected from infringement, something sacred that demands

respect and honor from other nations. However, this myth ignores the realities of actual power, and it blocks the acceptance of supranational controls.

No legal authority exists that can make binding rules and enforce them on all states. There is no true world community. There is no consensus on goals and values, no common loyalty, and no reliable set of mutual expectations and understandings. There is no code of behavior based on universally accepted mores and enforced by universal sanctions. As a result, conflicts among nations continue, and some explode into war.

Basic Economic Functions

We do not live by bread alone, but we live by bread first of all. Our biological nature demands food and drink, and, in almost every environment, clothing and shelter. Of course, our wants do not end with these basic physiological needs. Our culture determines the kinds of food, clothing, and shelter we will want, within the limitations of our physical environment. Culture also determines our wants for the "embroideries of existence" such as tom-toms, guitars, books, cars, candles, diamonds, gold nose-rings, water skis, or throwing spears.

In some cultures wants appear to be so well adjusted to the existing resources and the existing level of technology that most people are seldom conscious of an unsatisfied want and unreflectingly make their choices according to cultural norms. In an industrial society, however, people's wants appear to be boundless.

Because time, energy, and natural resources—unlike wants—are limited, every society, like every family, must *economize*. That is, it must decide (whether deliberately or not) how much time, energy, and resources will go toward meeting this or that need and satisfying this or that want, at the expense of which other needs and wants. These decisions are made within the framework of the economy. An **economy** is a complex of equipment, techniques, statuses, roles, norms, and beliefs. Its function is to use available resources to produce and distribute the goods and services that will go toward satisfying the needs and wants of the society's members. It has three main aspects: technology, social structure, and beliefs.

Technology includes the instruments and techniques of production and distribution—the equipment and know-how. These instruments and techniques multiply the effectiveness of the time and energy spent in work.

The *social structure* of an economy is the pattern of statuses and roles that allots various economic functions, powers, responsibilities, and rewards to different individuals and groups in the society. It includes the relative statuses and roles of workers in different occupations, of employers and managers, of consumers, of the state and its bureaucracy.

The *belief system* underlying an economy incorporates cultural values and serves to explain and justify the social organization of the economy and to motivate its members to perform their economic roles. Beliefs and values are deeply interwoven with the structure and functioning of an economy.

Decisions of Production

A society's goals and values decide three fundamental questions of production. *Which* of a number of alternative goods and services will be produced? *How much* of those goods and services will be produced? And, *how* shall these goods be produced? That is, with what combination of the society's resources?

Economists usually distinguish four main resources, which they call the **factors of production.** These are land, labor, capital, and management. *Land* includes the soil itself plus all the natural resources, such as minerals, forests, waters, climate, harbors, and rainfall. *Labor* is the use of people's time, energy, and abilities for production and distribution of goods and services. The quality and availability of labor depend on the size and age-composition of the population, its health and education, and its motivation to work.

Capital, the third factor, can be produced only by saving. That is, present consumption must be sacrificed in the hope of enjoying greater consumption in the future. The primitive man who ignored his hunger while he chipped away at a stone arrowhead instead of gathering berries to eat at once hoped to eat better in the long run if he made a tool for hunting. He was saving—postponing consumption—to produce capital. *Capital* includes all tools and equipment used in further production, whether the productive tool is a stone ax or a steel plant.

Today, people defer consumption by putting aside money (whether in a private savings account, a corporation's reinvestment fund, or a nation's tax revenue) to invest in tools of production. Money under a mattress is not invested; it is merely hoarded. The word *investment* always implies a hope of greater future return, whether an individual is investing by buying stock in a corporation or the corporation is investing in a new, automated factory. Both American and Soviet corporations invest part of their profits in more productive equipment. Capital is not limited to capitalist societies.

The fourth factor of production has traditionally been called "management," but it might more accurately be called *decision making.* In the early stages of industrialization, the decision to combine the factors of production rests with the *entrepreneur*—the person who initiates an enterprise. That person may see an opportunity to introduce a new product or a better machine, or may see the economic potential of a new invention. It is this person's particular role to launch a productive organization by bringing together money (generally someone else's), management, labor, and materials. As the enterprise becomes established, another kind of decision making—management, or administration of the functioning of the organization from day to day—becomes more important. The entrepreneur sees opportunities and seizes them. The manager implements the entrepreneur's vision by skill at organization and administration.

Decisions of Distribution

No society above subsistence level distributes the products of its economy and services with strict equality. As soon as there is division of labor in a society, there is a differential evaluation of functions and different amounts of goods, services, power, privilege, and prestige as rewards. No matter how important a job may be (garbage collecting, for example), if it is easy to fill (does not require much education or training), it is not highly rewarded.

In modern society, the demand for various kinds of skills makes itself felt in the labor market. When there are too many farmers, the submarginal and inefficient ones find themselves so poorly rewarded that they may go to the city in search of jobs. When there is a shortage of electronics engineers, high salaries attract more young people to the field.

Basic Economic Institutions

The basic economic institutions of property, contract, and occupation permit an economy to function by regulating the ownership of goods and services and the terms under which they may be exchanged. These three institutions interact in the market in the process of exchange. They are present, if only implicitly, in even the simplest economy and permit it to function according to shared expectations and understandings. The more complex the economy, the more elaborate, precise, and explicit the rules.

Property

Property is the institution by which a community or society defines rights and obligations with respect to things that are scarce, valued, and transferable. These things may be tangible, like a coat or a farm, or they may be intangible, like a brand name or the words of a song or book. They may be public property, owned by the community as a whole, or private property, owned by an individual or small group.

Three kinds of property rights may be distinguished: the right to *use* (a factory, a plot of land, a poem); the right to *control* (to decide whether the factory should produce vacuum cleaners or sewing machines, or the land grow corn or cotton); and the right of *disposal* (by destruction or transfer through sale or gift). A society puts limits on all these rights. Americans are not allowed to use their private land to grow marijuana, nor does the right of disposal allow us to burn down our own houses. Copyrights protect all three kinds of rights with respect to things like the words of a song or book.

Contract

The institution of contract permits property to change hands. **Contract** is used in a general sense to refer to a set of shared values and norms (that is, an institution) that serves as the common ground for bargaining and sets limits to the pursuit of self-interest. Within the framework of these shared values and norms, any specific agreement on terms

(left) Land and labor are two primary resources or factors of production. *Danny Lyon/Magnum Photos, Inc.* (right) Capital is a third, main factor of production. *Daniel S. Brody/Editorial Photocolor Archives.*

of exchange can occur. **A contract** in the specific sense is an agreement between two or more parties—individuals or groups—that each will or will not do a certain legitimate thing in return for some legitimate act by the other party. In the economic sense, a contract is an exchange of promises. For example, a promise of a certain kind and amount of labor is exchanged for a certain kind and amount of pay. Property may be exchanged for money or for a promise to pay at some future date (as in a charge account or an installment plan).

The contract may be written or unwritten. The fulfillment of the second half of the contract (the pay) may occur immediately or may be deferred for hours, months, or even years. The agreement may be as simple as the unspoken understanding by which the storekeeper hands you a loaf of bread expecting that you will pay for it in a moment. It may be as complicated as an actor's contract, with pages and pages of fine print, and as long-drawn-out as a 99-year lease.

A contract is enforceable by the society, which defines the legitimacy of contracts both in terms of what may be agreed upon and how it may be arrived at. Child labor, slavery, sexual services, and criminal deeds cannot be legitimately contracted for in most modern societies. If the agreement is arrived at by the use of force or fraud by one of the parties, it is not enforceable by the state. In the United States, for example, most states provide that a marriage in which one of the parties was forced or tricked into marrying may be annulled.

If a society did not stand behind the institution of contract, economic life would come to a standstill. Buying and selling, borrowing and lending, hiring and working for hire would cease. The role of the state is to stand ready to enforce the promises, in case either party tries to wriggle out of the contract.

393

The institution of contract, then, lends stability to the social order by guaranteeing the fulfillment of a promise where self-interest might tempt one party to default. However, the web of expectations is so strong that sanctions rarely need to be used.

Occupation

The institution of **occupation** defines people's economic roles, separating them from other social roles. It defines what people may expect from others in each occupation. For example, employers, customers, or clients may have expectations of people in the roles of secretary, sales clerk, or lawyer. Second, occupation also defines the obligations of the secretary, sales clerk, or lawyer with respect to skill, responsibility, and role performance. By taking a job, hanging out a shingle, or opening a store a person is, in effect, promising to fulfill those expectations and meet those obligations. A baby sitter promises to keep the children safe and perhaps fed, clean, and happy. A doctor promises to use good judgment in trying to restore the patient to health as fully as possible. A secretary promises to take dictation, type letters, answer the telephone, and keep an appointment schedule.

In the simplest societies, division of labor may be limited to men's work and women's work, as culturally defined. What is done by men in one tribe—weaving or pottery making, for example—may be done by women in another. But even in simple societies, specialization usually extends further. One man may devote all his time to fashioning spears, another to fishing, a third to hunting, while most of the rest cultivate crops.

The more complex an economy, the more specialized are occupations and the more closely are occupational roles defined. In a modern industrial society, where different skills must mesh in efficient production, "job descriptions" clearly outline expectations and obligations. Some occupations, however, are ambiguously defined. Their members must strive to keep their economic roles clear and limited and to prevent those who employ their skills from interfering with their non-economic roles. Consider the protests of teachers over janitorial duties and having to supervise lunchrooms. And both in and out of the classroom, there has been the frequent demand that they behave far more puritanically than the parents of their pupils.

Exchange

Regardless of the degree of specialization, members of each occupation need or want the products of those in other occupations. They must, therefore, arrive at some shared understandings about how to exchange them. Property defines the terms of ownership of the products, contract defines the terms of exchange, and different occupations produce the different products that make exchange necessary and possible.

Exchange is a social process through which each party acquires something he or she wants but cannot easily get otherwise. The transaction is carried on under the terms of a contract which is sanctioned implicitly or explicitly by the society.

Exchange may be carried on in a variety of ways, depending on cultural norms. Many preliterate tribes practice forms of *indirect exchange,* such as gift exchange. One person makes a gift of goods or services to the other with no spoken agreement about a return of equivalent value. In the long run, however, these goods or services are paid for with other gifts.

Redistribution is a form of indirect exchange in which products are brought together and parceled out again with no apparent regard for individual contributions. Taxation is one form of redistribution, in which the involuntary contributions of a society's taxable members are redistributed in the form of goods and services that benefit the whole society or some of its disadvantaged members (or, in many societies, some of its more powerful members).

Direct exchange may be carried on through barter or through purchase with money. Barter is most common in simple societies where only comparatively few products are exchanged. The value of the goods and services is arrived at by bargaining or haggling, making a series of offers and counteroffers until a compromise agreement is arrived at. This method of exchange is time-consuming, though often enjoyable for both parties. But it is impractical where there is a huge volume of business, where goods are standardized, and where a regular market price prevails.

Exchanges for money are far more convenient and faster than barter. Money serves as a *medium of exchange.* It makes it unnecessary to offer one's own goods and services directly for those one wants to buy. It also serves as a *standard of value.* Almost all exchange values can be expressed in terms of money, and the comparative values of goods and services can be established without resort to the long process of haggling typical of barter. It is easy enough for a farmer to exchange eggs for groceries when both have set prices.

Two other functions of money are essential to modern industrial society. It serves as a *store of value,* for it is usable at any time, present or future. Society is very much concerned with keeping this value from fluctuating greatly. Its leaders try to prevent inflation (a decrease in the buying power of each unit of money), which can be disastrous for those who have small, fixed incomes. It is also necessary to avoid deflation (an increase in the buying power of each unit) to protect property holders and encourage confidence in the economy and continued investment. Finally, money also

serves as a *standard of deferred payments* in such things as mortgages or bank loans, in which one gets present money and agrees to pay back future money.

In order to perform all these functions, money must be universally accepted. Money may be an intrinsically valuable good with a well-established value, such as cigarettes, cattle, gold, rice, or salt. Most money, however, has little or no intrinsic value, but consists of very convenient and portable paper bills and metal coins that have a uniform value set by public authority and issued by the government in various denominations. Even more convenience and flexibility is lent the system of exchange by such substitutes for currency as checks and credit cards.

The Market

The **market** is an institution that coordinates occupation, property, and contract in such a way that exchange can be readily carried on. It allows the suppliers of goods or services to meet those who are seeking them. It may be as regular, concrete, and simple as the weekly market in a Guatemalan town, where Indians sit in the central square waiting for buyers for their products. Or it may be as diffuse as the many-sided market of a capitalist society, in which we speak of markets for labor, capital, and professional services, as well as the more easily identifiable markets for consumer goods. In the absence of interfering factors, the price arrived at depends on the relationship of the supply and demand at any given time. If the demand increases, the price tends to rise. If the demand falls, the price tends to fall. The reverse is true if the supply increases or decreases.

One basic question any system must decide is to what extent "pure" market factors and this "law of supply and demand" will have free play. To what extent should their

A market may be as simple as the weekly market in a South American town. *Peter Menzel/Stock, Boston.*

operations be regulated or nullified by law, custom, government regulation, agreement among industrial, commercial, or labor organizations, and so on? This question is at the heart of the various economic "isms" such as capitalism, socialism, and communism.

The Development of Economic Systems

In traditional society, economic arrangements are embedded in the whole fabric of life. But as alternative ways of constituting the social structure of an economic system appear, traditional arrangements are defended and explained or attacked and condemned in competing philosophies or "isms." Some of these "isms" have such heavy emotional weight that they persist even when the structures themselves have changed so much that theory and reality are far apart. This is the case with both capitalism and Marxism in the modern world.

Laissez Faire and the Capitalist System

During the long period of transition from feudalism to industrialism, the early nation-states—England, France, and Spain, for example—arose, grew in power, and claimed colonies. Trade and commerce became respectable. *Mercantilism* glorified the wealth and power of the state and justified central control and planning. But the imperial nations' regulation of industry and commerce and their attempts to keep a stranglehold on their colonies were not workable when industrialization got under way. Merchants and producers grew ever more impatient with their restraints and resorted to such evasions as smuggling. "Let us manufacture, let us trade," said a French finance minister in despair. "*Laissez faire*" ("let us do" or "let us make") became the name of the new philosophy.

Laissez faire was very much in tune with the times—the "enlightenment" period of the American and French revolutions. Adam Smith, a Scottish professor of moral philosophy, was its main advocate. Smith published his *Wealth of Nations* in 1776. In it, he attacked government control of industry and commerce. He outlined a neat, self-adjusting market system in which individuals motivated by self-interest work for the common good without realizing it, as if guided by an "invisible hand."

An economic system, said Smith, exists

396

to *produce* wealth and provide a higher standard of living for the people in general. Only through increased division of labor can people produce more and thus be able to exchange and consume more. They need as wide a market as possible in order to exchange what they produce most efficiently for the products someone else produces. This principle of *comparative advantage* applies to nations as well as individuals, and thus there should be international freedom of trade.

Government, Smith insisted, should do only two things: maintain a social climate and institutional sanctions (freedom of contract, private property, and so on) that will encourage business and industry in general without favoring or restricting anyone in particular, and supply those services that people need but cannot supply so well for themselves, such as education, public works, protection of the helpless, and national defense.

What, then, would take the place of government regulation? Smith described the "obvious and simple system of natural liberty" as having its own built-in controls that would work neatly and automatically if only governments and monopolists would not interfere. This system is based on the premises that people are rational, that they seek their own goals, and that all the factors of production are free and mobile. From these premises, Smith concluded that free competition in the open market guarantees efficient production, and that the economic operations of self-seeking, rational people work for the common good. The law of supply and demand makes the system self-adjusting and self-regulating, with no need of planning or outside controls.

Marxism and the Soviet Economy

Millions of Americans who never heard of Adam Smith believe in free enterprise, competition, and the law of supply and demand. Communist nations have an even more explicit ideology that they believe applies to all aspects of life. Yet in both the Soviet Union and the United States, theory and practice are far apart at many points. The demands of the industrial system create striking similarities in the two societies, even though core cultural values and political systems are very different.

Like Smith's theory, Marxism reflected the times. Marx's picture of the miserable and exploited factory worker was a true one when he wrote. But his prophecies have, on the whole, been far off the mark even in the Soviet Union.

Marx expected the revolution that would spell the downfall of capitalism to occur in a highly industrialized country, probably in Western Europe, as a result of a proletarian uprising. No such revolution ever took place. The first revolution based on Marxist philosophy occurred in Russia, a backward agricultural country populated mostly by illiterate peasants. And it was carried out, not by the proletariat, but by a band of intellectual conspirators who in the moment of seizing power found that all their long years of debate over the meaning of Marxism had done little to guide them in practice.

Central control and planning characterize the Soviet economy. The government owns "all land and natural resources; owns and operates all industry, communications media, transport, banks and financial institutions, and municipal utilities; owns and operates most urban retail and wholesale distribution facilities and most housing; and directly operates a small but important portion of all farms."[8] Socialist property also includes three types of government-controlled cooperatives: collective farms, indus-

[8] Thomas Fitzsimmons, Peter Malof, and John C. Fiske, *USSR, Its People, Its Society, Its Culture* (New Haven, Conn.: HRAF Press, 1960), p. 195.

trial cooperatives (that produce some consumer goods and supply such services as shoe repairing and restaurant operations), and consumer cooperatives (for retail and wholesale distribution in rural areas). Private property permitted in the Soviet Union includes such personal possessions as clothing, books, household furnishings, and restricted bank accounts. Members of collective farms are permitted to own houses (but not the land on which they stand), work garden plots, keep some livestock, and sell their products on the open market. Although these private plots make up only 3 percent of the country's cultivated land, they contribute more than half the output of eggs and potatoes and nearly half the meat and vegetables consumed in the country.[9]

[9]Raymond H. Anderson, "Broad Controls over Land Use Foreshadowed in Soviet Union," *The New York Times,* June 25, 1968.

The agencies that control and plan production and distribution are organized into a hierarchy. The central economic agency is subject to the directives of the political leaders. Various balances of local autonomy and central control are tried from time to time in an effort to correct weaknesses in the system.

Where the American corporation uses retained earnings to make up the bulk of its investment capital, the Soviet system enforces involuntary saving by means of a "turnover tax" that is a substitute for low wages, income taxes, and high prices. It is a sales tax (about 44 percent in a typical year) on food and other consumer goods, levied not when they are sold to the consumer but as they leave the producers' hands and enter the distribution network. A very large proportion of these involuntary savings has long been invested in capital goods industries. But the current trend is to reduce

While collective farms make up all but three percent of the Soviet Union's cultivated land, the private plots contribute nearly half of the eggs, meat, and vegetables consumed in the country. *Wide World Photos.*

the proportion in favor of more consumer goods. The level of production of such goods has risen so much that advertising of various brands has now appeared.

Thus it would seem that, in the relation of theory and practice, the Soviet economy, like our own, is a mixed one. The American and Soviet systems represent two general approaches to organizing industrial society, based on two different philosophies, but they have certain basic similarities. Both are industrial societies. They tend toward the values, social structure, and technology common to all industrial societies. They emphasize science, rationality, and work. Their class systems are based on achievement rather than ascription. Both continually support the search for technological innovation. Both have experienced a trend toward concentration and collectivization of industry into huge corporations. In both societies, production is carried on by a distinct class of professional managers and technicians who do not own the means of production. Both societies get their work done by unequal distribution of rewards, which appeals to the desire for material gain. In both societies, the leaders have selected and emphasized those portions of the economic philosophy that suited their purposes. Yet they have been limited in such selective distortion by the fact that the creed is also believed in by large numbers of less powerful people.

Changes in the American Economy

The two most obvious changes in our economy are the emergence of a highly sophisticated technology and the rise of giant corporations (which have their counterparts in the giant producing collectives of the Soviet system). In addition, market forces have lost some of their significance as planning has become more important. The government has assumed a greatly changed role in the economy. Property relationships and decision-making power have shifted. The demand for highly educated specialists has increased enormously.

We may think of the American economy, suggests John Kenneth Galbraith, as consisting of two completely different sectors. The world of the giant corporations, which he calls the "industrial system," consists of 500 or 600 firms that provide "nearly all communications, nearly all production and distribution of electric power, much transportation, most manufacturing and mining, a substantial share of retail trade, and a considerable amount of entertainment." [10] Outside of this industrial system fall most agricultural enterprises, some mining and trucking, professional and artistic pursuits, some retail trade, and most personal and domestic services.

The classical economic laws of the market—supply and demand, and so on—still apply to some degree. But today the industrial sector is characterized far more by planning and certainty than by the free play of market forces. It appears that it could scarcely be otherwise. In large corporations with advanced technological systems and complex organizations of highly trained specialists, plans for producing any one item are made well in advance. Such plans, once made, are hard to change. Because long-term planning demands certainty, market forces are avoided by various means. For example, the corporation may achieve "vertical integration" by buying companies that supply raw materials at one end of the process and distribution outlets at the other. Corporations may agree on "just prices" for things they buy and sell. They may enter mutually advantageous long-term contracts with suppliers and customers. Moreover, in their quest for certainty they generally have the support of the state.

[10] John Kenneth Galbraith, *The New Industrial State* (Boston: Houghton Mifflin, 1967), p. 9.

The relationship between government and the national economy has changed markedly over the last four decades. It has changed so much that our system is more accurately called a "mixed economy." It is a mixture of planning and the market. Among the main shifts in the role of government is the increasing size of the public sector—the share of the Gross National Product spent by federal, state, and local governments. In addition, the government attempts to eliminate many uncertainties by regulating wages and prices and by adjusting demand by manipulating the interest rate and the tax rate. It also supports the most advanced research and experimentation, which would be too risky for even a huge corporation.[11]

The rise of the giant corporation with an advanced technology and a complex organization has meant a shift in power and

[11] *Ibid.*, p. 3.

Automation transfers the work of people to machines. As the shift to automation continues, the line between manual and nonmanual labor becomes more blurred. *Gary Wolinsky/Stock, Boston.*

a change in the pattern of property rights. No one person can own a huge enterprise. The right of disposal is diffused among many shareholders. The rights of use and control are in the hands of the managers. Workers does not own the tools they use. Ownership and management are increasingly separated. Usually a small minority of stockholders has voting control and tends to perpetuate the same management year after year.

The managers have come to hold the greatest power in the industrial sector. Their power over the decisions of the industrial sector appears to be channeled not by sheer desire for profits but rather by a combination of three factors: their close identification with the corporation so that its success is their success ("Who are you with?" is a typical opening line when two businessmen meet), emphasis on conformity and cooperation rather than individualistic competition for status, and stress on long-range performance and a good public image for the corporation.

Just as industrialism and the accompanying concentration and mass production have changed the nature of management, they have also changed the nature of labor. Social

psychologists see work as giving people status and integrating them into society. To place a man we no longer ask where he comes from nor who his ancestors were. We ask, "What does he do?" A person's occupation is closely linked with socioeconomic status, style of life, satisfactions, experiences, and attitudes. The unemployed worker, consequently, feels disoriented and unworthy for more reasons than the mere loss of a paycheck.

Workers in Western democracies are increasingly property owners, voters, and members of the society whose status as a citizen is respected. They have won relative security against the hazards of illness, accident, unemployment, and old age. This change results from a general increase in productivity, a rise in the standard of living, improved education, and the power of labor unions. Further changes are coming about as automation is increasingly adopted.

The term *automation* is used in several ways. In the broadest sense, it refers to all technological changes that transfer the work of people to machines. More precisely, it refers to a change in technology that promises to be as dramatic as the shift from handicraft work to the assembly line, and to have as great an impact on industrial society. In this sense automation consists of processes that eliminate direct human labor, whether of hands or brains, and regulate the flow of work through mechanical and electronic devices.

Automation makes it possible for fewer men working shorter hours to produce more goods than previously. On the other hand, automated jobs require incessant attention and concentration and thus may create more nervous strain than do nonautomated jobs. Automation tends to eliminate not only the repetitive tasks of the assembly line but also the repetitive paper shuffling of the clerk and bookkeeper. The line between manual and nonmanual labor will blur as automation continues.

The greatest fear aroused by automation is that it will throw people out of work. It seems probable that, like many other technological innovations, automation will in the short run eliminate many jobs. Most innovations have in the long run created new jobs. The automobile has created jobs not only in production lines but in highway construction, petroleum refining, and gas stations. Automation displaces mostly the unskilled. But a more effective program of technical training will help these same people fill jobs that now go begging for lack of trained personnel. Just to build and service the new machines will require great skill.

Like other advances, automation cuts down on the hours of work necessary for production. It therefore creates a new problem for society—that of giving more meaning to leisure time. It creates new opportunities for service industries and for creative arts, for recreation and entertainment. But neither absorption of the displaced worker nor new jobs and products nor more constructive use of leisure time will happen without new social inventions and effective public and private planning.

Summary

Political and economic institutions are two pivotal institutions that affect all human beings.

Political institutions are based on the concepts of power, authority, and legitimacy. Power is the capacity to influence the behavior of other people or groups in an intended direction. Power is exerted through force, domination, or manipulation.

Power may be distributed in various ways. In some states, there is a power elite that has control of all the resources of society. In other states, power is pluralistic and is split among many groups in the society. The monistic state is based on the ideology that the state is supreme. The modern version of monism is totalitarianism, in which all power is concentrated in the state and all activities are judged in terms of their contribution to the state.

Authority is power that is recognized as legitimate by those who are subjected to it. The source of authority can be democratic or authoritarian. In a democracy the government acts for and is accountable to the governed. Most governments, however, are authoritarian. In these, authority is exercised over the governed who are held to be accountable to the government.

Max Weber distinguished three bases for legitimacy. In rational-legal authority the same rules apply to the rulers and the ruled. Traditional authority, on the other hand, bases its claim to legitimacy on the nature of the social order, which is seen as having always existed. A third type of authority is given to a leader who attracts followers who are impressed by his charismatic personality.

The nation-state is the dominant political organization of a society. A state is always identified with a definite territory and a population of citizens. It is a sovereign entity having equal formal status with all other states and total control of the exercise of authority within its borders.

Government, more than any other institution, determines the balance of freedom and control in a society and ensures its survival and cohesion. Government is the process of keeping social order by enforcing social norms and adjusting them to new demands. The government is the institution

or association that exercises the legitimate power of the state.

Laws are deliberately formulated, clearly stated norms enforced by government officials. Laws give predictability to situations, adjust disputes, and define crimes. Civil laws allow people to do a number of necessary things, such as transfer property. Laws also implement social reform.

Politics is the process by which any organized group finds its leaders and decides its policies. It is the struggle for power to name the personnel and decide the policies of the government.

The trend to large-scale, urban, industrial society has led to an increase in the scale of government. The scope of the government's functions has increased correspondingly. All societies are shifting gradually away from traditional to rational-legal authority as the basis for legitimate power.

The most significant trends in international relations among governments include the rise of many new nations, the bipolarization of power, and a mixed role for nationalistic sentiment.

Economic institutions also have a pervasive effect in people's lives. Biology, geography, and culture combine to determine our wants and needs. How these are satisfied is the business of our economic institutions. Because time, energy, and natural resources are limited, every society must decide how much of each will go toward meeting the needs and wants of the people.

An economy is the institutional complex that uses available resources to produce and distribute the goods and services that will satisfy the needs and wants of the society's members. It has three main aspects: technology, social structure, and beliefs. The four factors of production are land, labor, capital, and management, or decision making.

The basic economic institutions of property, contract, and occupation permit an economy to function by regulating the ownership of goods and services and the terms under which they may be exchanged. Property defines the ownership of goods and services, contract defines the terms under which they may be exchanged, and the different occupations produce the different products that make exchange necessary.

Exchange is a social process. Indirect exchange involves giving someone a gift without previously agreeing about something of equal value being returned to the giver. Taxation is a form of indirect exchange through which goods and services are redistributed.

Markets are institutions that coordinate occupation, property, and contract in such a way that exchange can be readily carried on. Suppliers can meet purchasers in the market, and goods and services are exchanged according to the law of supply and demand.

Various economic philosophies or "isms" gradually developed as societies became more complex. Laissez faire economics was outlined by Adam Smith in response to the strict central control exercised by early nation-states. Smith believed that a free market would result in a rational, self-adjusting economy. In capitalistic societies, private individuals own the means of production. Motivated by the desire for profit and the demands of consumers, they make the decisions about the allocation of productive resources.

Communism, on the other hand, has its roots in Marxism and reflects the totalitarian ideology. Most economic control—of production and distribution—rests with the state. Central control and planning characterize communist economies.

Two major changes in the American economy are the emergence of a highly sophisticated technology and the rise of giant corporations. Other changes include the increased importance of planning over free market forces, the greater role of the state in the economy, shifts in property relationships and decision-making power, and increased demand for highly educated specialists.

Glossary

Authority Power that is recognized and accepted by those subject to it as validly held by those who exercise it.

Contract The institution that allows for the transfer of property; in the specific sense, a contract is an agreement or exchange of promises enforceable by the society.

The economy The institution that allocates time, energy and resources to produce and distribute goods and services the members of a society need and want.

Exchange The social process through which each party to a contract acquires something he or she wants but cannot easily get otherwise.

Factors of production The four main resources of a society—land, labor, capital, and decision-making (including entrepreneurship and management).

Government The process of keeping order and enforcing norms; the institution that carries out that process; or the specific set of officials who govern at any one time.

Laws Deliberately formulated and clearly stated norms that are enforced by government officials.

Legitimacy The degree to which a form of government is considered right and proper and its officials rightfully in authority.

Market An institution that coordinates occupation, property, and contract in such a way that exchange can be readily carried on.

Nation-State The comprehensive political organization of a society, including territorial bounds, sovereignty, and a monopoly of the use of force within its borders.

Occupation The institution that defines the rights and obligations of various economic roles.

Politics The process by which any organized group finds its leaders and decides its policies; specifically, the struggle for power to name the personnel and decide the policies of the government.

Power The capacity to influence the behavior of other people or groups in an intended direction; control over the decisions that affect the way people live and over the allocation of scarce and valuable resources.

Property The institution by which a society defines rights and obligations with respect to things that are scarce, valuable, and transferable.

part

6

Social Change

BETTER·ACTIVE·TODAY·THAN·RADIOACTIVE·Tomorrow

chapter

17

Collective Behavior and Social Movements

Welfare mothers sit in for day-care centers. A Peruvian crowd flees a soccer stadium in panic, crushing dozens of people to death. Small groups of women meet regularly to raise their "consciousness of oppression." Parents go to court to have their daughters admitted to the Little League. Ghetto mobs smash windows, burn buildings, loot stores. Thousands march on the White House to protest the Vietnam War. Millions learn of these and other events from the papers and the news on TV, discuss them, form opinions, and debate.

What do all these phenomena have in common? They are not part of the established culture and social structure. They are not normal, routine occurrences. They are instances of **collective behavior,** "large group activity that comes into being and develops along lines that are not laid out by preestablished social definitions [and arises to meet] undefined and unstructured situations."[1]

We can conceive of human behavior as a continuum from unrelated behavior of individuals at one extreme to organized group behavior regulated by traditions and rules at the other. Collective behavior falls between the two. At the end nearer individ-

ual behavior we might place panic behavior. Near the other extreme, and often merging into it, are social movements. Unlike other forms of collective behavior, **social movements** are comparatively stable, organized, and lasting. They are collective actions directed toward the achievement or obstruction of change in some aspect or aspects of the sociocultural order. Collective behavior comprises, then, both brief and sudden behavior, as well as long-lasting, organized behavior.

In this chapter we examine, first, the elementary forms of collective behavior apparent in the action of such groups as crowds. Besides discussing the nature of crowds, we inquire into the mass and the public. How are such groupings related to social change and social movements? What kinds of collective actions for social change and protest can we identify? How do social movements arise, gain momentum, and acquire leaders, followers, and ideologies? What tactics and strategies do they use? What functions and consequences do they have for society and personality?

*Elementary
Collective Behavior*

As we saw in our discussion of symbolic interaction, we do not ordinarily respond directly to other people. We first interpret one another's actions or remarks and then

---

[1] Herbert Blumer, "Collective Behavior," in J. G. Gittler, ed., *Review of Sociology* (New York: John Wiley & Sons, 1957), p. 130. Blumer is recognized as having constructed the landmark outline of the field of collective behavior. The section on Elementary Collective Groupings follows his conceptual scheme closely.

408

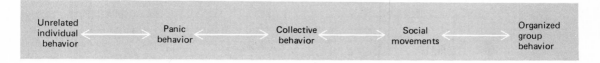

| Unrelated individual behavior | ⟷ | Panic behavior | ⟷ | Collective behavior | ⟷ | Social movements | ⟷ | Organized group behavior |

Figure 17-1 All these forms of behavior are related. But, moving from left to right on the continuum, people's behavior becomes increasingly interrelated and organized.

act on the basis of our interpretation. Herbert Blumer distinguishes this interpretative interaction from *circular reaction,* in which persons reflect (rather than interpret) one another's feelings and in so doing intensify this feeling. It is this kind of interaction that builds up restlessness, fear, and excitement in a herd of cattle and results in a stampede.

When many individuals are restless—that is, discontented, frustrated, and perhaps alienated and lonely—and engage in circular reaction, we may speak of *social unrest.* It typically arises when there are significant changes in the lives of many people who have something in common and become sensitized to that fact—women, workers, blacks, students. Social unrest may be confined to a small area, or may spread through a large population. It may be vague and mild, or intense and acute. It involves a strong urge to act, but has no specific goals. It results in random, aimless, excited behavior, mingled with apprehension and a readiness to accept rumors uncritically and to follow suggestions readily.

This aimless, random behavior, or *milling,* is the circular reaction of people in physical proximity. During the process they become more sensitized and responsive to one another. They focus on one another, ignoring outside stimuli, and become ready to respond to one another "quickly, directly, and unwittingly."[2] A more intense form of milling is *collective excitement,* which compels attention and becomes contagious. It arouses

people emotionally and releases them from many controls by establishing norms. When collective excitement is intense and widespread, social contagion is very likely to occur. **Social contagion** has been defined as "the relatively rapid, unwitting, and nonrational dissemination of a mood, impulse, or form of conduct." It is especially apparent in panics, war hysteria, crazes, and fads.[3] This social contagion attracts and infects many who may have begun as mere observers. Some sociologists do not agree that people involved in elementary collective behavior necessarily behave unwittingly and irrationally. Recent researchers believe that people in such situations are more aware and rational than had previously been supposed.[4]

Blumer distinguishes four kinds of elementary collective groupings. He calls them elementary because—in the ideal case—they arise and act outside of set cultural patterns. They are the acting crowd, the expressive crowd, the mass, and the public. Each emerges under a special set of conditions.

The Acting Crowd

A **crowd** is a temporary grouping of a large number of people who are conscious of one another's physical presence or nearness. They may engage in relatively controlled

[2] Blumer, "Collective Behavior," in Alfred McClung Lee, ed., *Principles of Sociology,* 2nd ed. (New York: Barnes and Noble, 1951).

[3] *Ibid.*
[4] Richard Berk, *Collective Behavior* (Dubuque, Iowa: William C. Brown, 1975).

The crowd at a football game have a common focus of attention and behave in regularized ways, but they do not engage in truly collective behavior. *Ellis Herwig/Stock, Boston.*

interaction and lack an organized structure. The casual grouping of people watching a construction project is potentially a crowd, but it is not likely to engage in any interaction beyond the exchange of amused comments and glances. It is a simple aggregate, not a collectivity. Some crowds are so conventionalized that they do not engage in truly collective behavior. For example, the stadium full of people watching the Rose Bowl game have a common focus of attention, and they behave in established and regularized ways.

Most studies of crowd behavior are concerned with *acting* crowds. Such crowds are aggressively directed toward a specific aim: to beseige a police station to protest alleged police brutality, to occupy the Dean's office. Verbal milling—rumor—may have caused them to gather. Their action may also have been planned to some extent. In any case, they gather (or begin to engage in collective behavior) when an exciting event or goal catches their attention. They start milling physically. They move around and talk to one another, conveying their excitement and creating rapport. In the process they arrive at a common focus of attention. It may or may not be the original stimulus, but it gives them an objective. Being suggestible to others in the crowd (but ignoring authorities who may try to break them up), they readily respond to leaders who urge action.

This action may be strange, shocking, and frightening, because the crowd as an emergent social system has no culture and hence no morals. It acts on impulse, for its members do not pause to interpret stimuli as they do in ordinary interaction.

Dissenting from this model of the acting crowd, Carl J. Couch insists that the crowd is a distinctive social system, to be sure, but no more pathological and bizarre than many others. It is often less destructive than the social agents that try to control it. It is not really irrational if other means of achieving its goal have failed and crowd action promises to be effective. It is no more emotional

410

than those it acts against. Its members are less subject to control, not because they are mentally disturbed but because they are lost in the anonymity of the crowd where sanctions are less effective.[5] Crowd behavior is not entirely different from conventional behavior. Typically, participants justify their behavior in terms of some existing social norm or value, perhaps one they feel has not been observed by the authorities.[6]

The Expressive Crowd

While an acting crowd focuses outward on one objective (often political) and acts to reach it, an *expressive crowd* has no such goal. Each member engages in expressive actions—uninhibited physical movements, laughing, shouting, weeping, dancing—and experiences a release of tensions. This behavior often assumes a rhythm. Thus the expressive crowd is often a "dancing crowd." Cults, sects, and primitive religions may originate in expressive crowd behavior. Because the experience brings emotional catharsis and joy, and because the people feel the support of others with whom they are in rapport, it may seem to them that they are mysteriously possessed by some outside power. The crowd may project this feeling onto a person or object that they invest with sacredness—a snake, a song, a prophet— and strive to repeat the experience through religious ritual.

The Mass

A **mass** is a large number of people who react to a common stimulus but seek individual goals and make individual choices and

decisions. They may be physically close, as in a gold rush, but every person is out for himself or herself. More typical of modern society is the dispersed, anonymous *mass audience* or *mass market*. The mass media of modern society—books, newspapers, magazines, radio, television, and movies—reach huge audiences whose members are not in communication with one another and who do not interact. But, by conveying a common body of images and understandings, the media help create a readiness to interact in other forms of collective behavior. The mass as consumers are persuaded to buy standardized and mass-produced products advertised in these media.

Although the people who make up a mass belong to many diverse groups and are physically separate, they have a common focus of interest. Each responds, however, with detached anonymity. Each of us seeks to answer our own needs. We accept or reject a new toothpaste, a political party platform or candidate, a fashion, a philosophy, or a creed. When many such decisions converge, the mass can make or break a politician or manufacturer.

The Public and Public Opinion

The type of collectivity known as a public is especially important in modern democratic societies. A **public** is a vaguely defined number of people who for a time confront an issue, disagree on how to resolve it, and discuss it. (It is not to be confused with a *following*, made up of the fans of some hero such as a political leader, singer, or movie star.)

A public is not fixed and permanent. It emerges with an issue and dissolves when the issue fades from the scene. It is not a group. It has no norms or rules to dictate the answer to the issue, no fixed set of social relationships, and no feeling of common identity. Unlike the mass, it interacts. Unlike

---

[5] "Collective Behavior: An Examination of Some Stereotypes," *Social Problems* 15 (1968): 310–322.

[6] Ralph H. Turner, "Collective Behavior," in Robert E. L. Faris, *Handbook of Modern Sociology* (Chicago: Rand McNally, 1964), pp. 382–425.

Demonstrations combine elements of acting and expressive crowds. *Wide World Photos.*

the crowd, it engages in *interpretative* interaction. Its members, in contrast to those in a crowd, are self-conscious and critical. There is some emphasis on fact and reason, even though the propaganda of interest groups can exert pressures toward irrationality.

The public, through discussion and argument, strives to arrive at **public opinion**—a collective opinion or decision on the issue around which the public has formed. Although it is not unanimous or even necessarily the will of the majority, public opinion is nonetheless a collective product. "A given public opinion is likely to be anywhere between a highly emotional and prejudiced point of view and a highly intelligent and thoughtful opinion. . . . Perhaps it would be accurate to say that public opinion is rational, but need not be intelligent."[7]

A true public depends on freedom of association, of speech, and of the press. If these freedoms are missing, what might have

been a public becomes an audience. The Soviet leaders, for example, give their citizens a feeling that they are members of publics by arranging numerous small local discussion groups. The right solutions to the problems to be discussed are, however, specified in advance. Strong pressure is exerted against any incorrect thinking. And communication and participation at this level have little effect on what goes on at the top level. True public opinion, in contrast, can affect policies. It is communicated to the decision-makers and influences their decisions.

Besides these four basic general groupings, Blumer identifies others. Some combine elements of acting and expressive crowds and may in some cases have been influenced indirectly by the mass media and public opinion. They may also be reacting to a natural disaster such as an earthquake or to a rumor of a brutal crime. These collective groupings include panics, strikes, riots, mutinies, and "popular justice" or vigilante groups.

[7] Blumer, "Collective Behavior," p. 83.

412

Riots

Riots have been worldwide and very much in the news in recent years. They show us how social unrest leads to elementary collective behavior in one kind of acting crowd.

A **riot** is an outwardly hostile, illegitimate, and aggressive action by an acting crowd. It is relatively spontaneous and temporary. Unlike rebellion and insurrection, it usually does not aim to overthrow the government. The "riots" of vacationing college students on ocean beaches are more expressive than aggressive. Although they may include senseless violence and destruction, participants are not protesting anything much but boredom. The riots that concern us here are, as Martin Luther King, Jr., said, "the language of those to whom no one listens."

Like all collective behavior, riots are unpredictable. But a few generalizations have been established. The precipitating incident may be an arrest or fury over some event such as an assassination. First there is a small active core of participants with a relatively passive audience. The forming crowd engages in milling, clustering around several impromptu leaders who help define the situation and make various suggestions

The larger a riot gets and the longer deviant acts go unpunished, the easier it becomes to participate. The Watts riots in Los Angeles in 1965 and subsequent urban riots were violent and greatly destructive. *Wide World Photos.*

for action. The focus of action shifts according to how the police respond. The situation may get out of control swiftly. As members of the crowd perceive that deviant acts go unpunished, they begin to act on the complaints and grievances that circulated during the milling period. New norms emerge, such as "Burn out the white businessmen who exploit us, but spare 'soul brothers.'"

There is a sense of group solidarity, but little organization. People join out of different motives and engage in somewhat different kinds of action. Some want to act out their grievances. Some come out of sheer curiosity. Still others use it for their own ends, perhaps by picking up a TV set to take home. The larger the riot gets, the easier it seems to participate, as most deviant acts go unpunished. Violence sometimes reaches a deadly peak. Reports and rumors of sniping add to the terror. Finally, rioting ends, sometimes having lasted as long as 4 or 5 days.

What do riots accomplish, if anything? Death and destruction, which hit the ghetto-dwellers themselves hardest, are measurable enough. What about social change?

Riots in general may invite brutal repression. Or they may be tolerated because they can serve to spend the energies of angry people. They may also bring about change, directly or indirectly. Student riots in the 1960s helped topple several governments (in Indonesia, for example). But such direct consequences are unusual. Most contributions to social change are indirect. Riots are, in essence, a bargaining device used by powerless groups—a way of saying "Listen to me!"

We have little evidence that recent American rioters were able to achieve positive goals. They were indeed saying "Listen to me," and they were heard. But they were answered with an even louder "No!" In fact, the most apparent consequences of the riots in recent years have been polarization and

heightened conflict. Attempts at control by uniformed authorities confirm the ghetto's estimate of white justice. Ghetto violence in turn confirms many whites in their prejudices. Extremists on both sides may see arming in "self-defense" as the only possible measure in anticipation of further violence. Some fear that the ghetto riots of the 1960s may give way to two armed camps engaged in terror and counterterror.[8]

Collective Behavior and Social Change

We may seek the sources of collective behavior in the modernization process itself, demographic changes, the loss of firm identity and a feeling of belonging, and such technological innovations as the mass media and swift transportation. To these must be added a growing awareness of social problems and a loss of faith in the power and determination of established authorities to solve these problems.

Modernization and Unrest

Modernization can create unrest by bringing together in cities and industries many people of differing interests and values, and by breaking up old traditions. Centralizing governments and industrializing economies

[8]Richard P. Sherman, ed., *The Negro and the City* (Englewood Cliffs, N.J.: Prentice-Hall, 1970), chap. 6, "Urban Violence"; Joseph Boskin, *Urban Racial Violence in the Twentieth Century* (Beverly Hills: Glencoe Press, 1969); J. Paul Mitchell, ed., *Race Riots in Black and White* (Englewood Cliffs, N.J.: Prentice-Hall, 1970); Gary T. Marx, "Riot," *Encyclopaedia Britannica;* Leonard Gordon, *A City in Racial Crisis: The Case of Detroit Pre- and Post- the 1967 Riot* (Wm. C. Brown, 1971); Bob Clark, "Nightmare Journey," *Ebony* (Oct. 1967): 121–130; and Sol Stern, "The Call of the Black Panthers," *The New York Times* (Aug. 6, 1967).

erase the old boundaries of traditional communities and the power of local authorities.

Modern technology itself can be a source of collective behavior. Mass communication and swift transportation contribute to unrest, to unity in groups that find common ground, and to polarization. At the same time, the more flamboyant and extremist elements of each movement, being the most newsworthy, get the major share of attention. This tends to create a reaction. Women's Lib advocates may all be labeled "bra-burners." Blacks may all be identified with armed militants. Students are stereotyped as disrespectful and obscene.

The unevenness of the modernization process can also create unrest. Uprooted peasants and farmers may have nowhere to go except city slums, because there are no jobs ready for them in industry. Education may create too many professionals and not enough technicians. Universal suffrage may be granted before a populace knows what to do with it. Jobs become obsolete and people feel useless and unwanted. Small wonder, then, that "a spectacular abundance of social movements marks the society whose traditions have been shaken by industrial urbanism and whose structure is scarred by cleavages between diverse groups."[9]

Demographic Changes

Changes in the composition and distribution of population may also contribute to unrest. The recent upsurge of Women's Liberation may be accounted for in part by demographic changes such as longer life expectancy and smaller families. These changes leave a woman with many years to fill after her children, if indeed she has any, are old enough to fend for themselves. The world-wide wave of student protests may also be

accounted for in part by demographic changes. There is not a larger proportion of young people in modern societies. Traditional societies, with their low life expectancies and high birth rates, have comparatively more young people. But the sheer numbers of young people, the prolongation of youth, and their concentration in college communities all contribute to unrest and collective behavior. United Nations sociologists say that in 1969 there were 750 million persons in the 12–25 age group. They predict there will be 1 billion by 1980.

In the United States, colleges are used as "warehouses for the temporary storage of a population [our postindustrial society] knows not what else to do with."[10] There is no place for youth in the mainstream of full social participation. Some must stay on campus for years because of the rigid requirements of their professional and technical specialties. Being concentrated in a community of their peers, with easy communication, they tend to develop solidarity of sentiments and their own subcultural style of life.

Another example of the influence of population composition and distribution is the massive migration of rural Southern blacks to the slums of Northern cities during the 1950s and 1960s, which contributed to social unrest.

Alienation: Loss of Identity and Community

Modernization creates urban societies of mobile persons who often feel dehumanized because they are treated as things rather than as unique people. They lose their sense of belonging, of rootedness in a certain

---

[9]C. Wendell King, *Social Movements in the United States* (New York: Random House, 1956), p. 13.

[10]Bennett M. Berger, "The New Stage of American Man—Almost Endless Adolescence," *The New York Times Magazine* (Nov. 2, 1969).

Colleges can be seen as warehouses for the temporary storage of a part of the population not yet in the mainstream of full social participation. *Owen Franken/Stock, Boston.*

group, a certain community, a certain place. Modernization changes place into space.

While the mobile and uprooted are more free in many ways than the stable members of traditional societies, they may suffer problems of identity. As they move from one community, job, class, and even family, to another, they have to make rapid adjustments. Is this a road to richer identity and more freedom, "or merely a wallet full of membership cards that don't mean anything? A crucial point seems to be reached when people enter statuses at a faster rate than they can grow the loyalties, self images, character, habits, and life styles that go with them."[11]

Another identity problem is felt by those attracted to the Women's Liberation movement. They feel they never have been allowed to have an identity of their own. Their maiden names are their fathers'; their married names are their husbands'.

[11] Orrin Klapp, *Collective Search for Identity* (New York: Holt, Rinehart and Winston, 1968), p. 17.

A feeling of powerlessness is conspicuous in alienated people such as ghetto-dwellers. They typically have low levels of social participation, not only in voluntary associations but in informal friendships. Others feel powerless for lack of opportunity, finding their efforts blocked at every turn. They wonder if anything they do matters, if they really count. And Orrin Klapp insists there is a lack of *meaning* in modern life, that it is boring, empty, and emotionally impoverished.[12]

Awareness of Social Problems and the Crisis of Authority

The word "unrest" suggests irrationality, vagueness, and maladjustment of personality. But social unrest may result from rational recognition of social conditions that call for change. In a democracy, dissent may be recognized to some extent as a way of evaluating and revitalizing the social order. When awareness is combined with a loss of faith in the power and willingness of those in

[12] *Ibid.*

416

authority to cope with problems (war, pollution, starvation), the stage is set for collective behavior and social movements. When those in power are perceived as arbitrary, inept, and ineffective—or even lacking in self-confidence—there is a crisis of authority. Under these circumstances, protest often becomes loud, desperate, and even violent.

Progress by dissent then is characteristic of human societies. It has been responsible for the growth and success of democracy in the last four hundred years, and the decline and failure of absolute forms of government. For the crucial feature of democracy is not simply that the majority rules, but that the minority is free to persuade people to come over to its side and make a new majority. Of course, the minority is abused at first—Socrates was, and so was Charles Darwin. But the strength of democracy is that the dissident minority is not silenced. On the contrary, it is the business of the minority to convert the majority. This is how a democratic society invigorates and renews itself in change as no totalitarian society can.[13]

The Study of Social Movements

A **social movement** is "a collectivity acting with some continuity to promote a change or resist a change in the society or group of which it is a part."[14] Unlike a riot, it is not an outburst, but a continuing effort. Its members agree on what is wrong with the social order, what should replace it, and how the change might be brought about. A social movement usually transcends local boundaries. Whether or not they formally join an organization, pay dues, and carry

[13] J. B. Bronowski, "Protest—Past and Present," *The American Scholar* (Autumn, 1969).

[14] Ralph H. Turner and Lewis M. Killian, *Collective Behavior,* 2nd ed. (Englewood Cliffs, N.J.: Prentice-Hall, 1972), p. 246.

cards, members feel a sense of belonging and participation.

Kinds of Social Movements

There are many possible approaches to the study of social movements. Psychologists are especially interested in the personalities of leaders and followers of various kinds of movements. Political scientists study them as a source of reform, a check on power, or the first stage of new political parties. Anthropologists see them in relation to cultural conflicts, often produced by contact between modern and traditional societies.

Sociologists are especially interested in the relationship of social movements to social change (both as cause and effect), to demographic and ecological variables, and to social institutions. They study the various kinds of movements, their careers, their strategies and tactics.

Although all social movements are "collective actions to establish a new order of life," in Blumer's comprehensive defintion, they exhibit great variety. Some are oriented toward action, others toward expressiveness. Some have broad, sweeping goals, others narrow and specific ones. Some have immediate goals, others long-range ones. Some are diffuse and uncoordinated. Others are clear-cut and well organized. Some are pluralistic, made up of a number of groups with the same general goal but differing ideas of specific ends and means. Others are monolithic, consisting of one strong organization.

Relation to the Status Quo

Perhaps the most common way of classifying social movements is according to their orientation to the status quo. *Reactionary* social movements reject the status quo (in whole or in part) because old values and goals have been abandoned. They speak of the good old days and seek to restore a presumably superior way of life. To the John Birch Society, for example, it is "the American Way of Life" as they define it. To the Ku Klux Klan, it is the restoration of white supremacy. *Conservative* movements aim to keep things as they are, to maintain the status quo. Their goals have for some time been those of the society in general, and they resist changes that threaten those goals.

Reform or *revisionary* movements work for partial change within the system—changes in specific norms, beliefs, values, or relationships. They seek to promote or defeat laws about abortion or homosexuality or school segregation. Or they may seek to clean up a city's government or to meet the needs of retarded children. They do not threaten the existing structure. *Revolutionary* movements, in contrast, reject the total social order as inadequate or evil and aim to replace it with something different. ("Liberals" are usually reformers; "radicals" may be either reactionaries or revolutionaries.) Such movements, including the political revolutions of the American colonies, France, Russia, Cuba, and China, have been frequent.[15] *Separatist* or withdrawal movements consider the status quo hopeless and seek only to escape it by setting up their own social order. Many sects and secret societies build alternative societies. Finally, *expressive* movements, such as some dancing sects, provide emotional release from the tensions and pressures generated by the status quo as it affects different groups.

[15] The concept of revolution assumes many forms. It is generally distinguished from insurrection or revolt that merely seeks to replace one ruling elite with another. Often it is limited to sudden and violent changes in the political structure. As we use it here, a revolution is a fundamental change in many aspects of a sociocultural order—culture, social structure, and the distribution of wealth, power, and prestige. But it does not always come about through a concerted social movement with a definite goal; industrialization, for example, did not.

The modern era has been characterized by several mass movements that seek revolutionary change. Communism, like Nazism, promises total social change and demands total allegiance. Mass movements arise out of serious social disorganization, such as that in Germany after World War I and China after years of foreign domination, civil strife, and war with Japan. The leaders of such movements are convinced that they hold the key to the future.

When a revolutionary movement gains control of the society, it typically uses totalitarian methods to maintain control. Often it directs the attention of the people toward external expansion, war, and internal enemies or scapegoats to heighten the feeling of unity and of the urgency of building a new order. This was true of the Stalin era in the Soviet Union as well as of Hitler's Germany and Castro's Cuba. Only now is the People's Republic of China showing signs of relaxing this stance. Its leaders are aware that coercion and fear have limits in motivating people, and they have come to depend largely on persuasion.

General and Specific Movements

The Back-to-Africa Movement of Marcus Garvey had a definite goal and a definite leader. It was thus a specific organization. Today's black protest movement embraces many groups and styles. It includes ghetto riots, marches on Washington, organizations that seek legal reforms for civil rights, black militant organizations, and separatist movements. Similarly, the Women's Liberation movement has no monolithic organization but is a coalition of many groups. Some are as small as those meeting weekly in someone's living room and as large as National Organization for Women. It also includes many different points of view on goals and tactics. The student protest movement, too, is a general one. It is held together not by organization but by similar beliefs about war, racism, poverty, and the role of the university, and by a new life style.

Rebellion and Protest vs. Education

Some social movements consist mostly of protest in its various forms. They seem to lack a program. They have "no place to go." Klapp thinks the contagious ghetto violence of the 1960s, New Left activism, radical right extremism, the countercultural rebellion, and the drug-oriented dropout movement have this in common. They all are characterized by protest against the status quo (the "Establishment" to those on the left, an ideologically corrupt welfare state to those on the right). And they protest against "progress" (which is seen as leading to all-powerful bureaucracies or to socialism). "All, frustrated, seem to turn to irrational directions, and seem more concerned with style, slogans, and emotional outlets than with practical progress."[16]

There are some useful distinctions to be made between protest and educational movements. Protest movements generally occur when society is ready for a change, yet, for various reasons, does not make it. Educational movements, on the other hand, are designed to encourage the society to make a change it may not yet be ready for. The two sorts of movements have different techniques. Compare, for instance, the violent, illegitimate aggression of the Watts riots with the legitimate, dignified work of the NAACP.[17]

Millennial Movements

Millennial movements believe the end of the world—at least as we know it—is at hand. They are based on a "future-oriented religious ideology." They reject the present as "totally evil and abysmally corrupt" and look forward to a time when "the world will be inhabited by a humanity liberated from all the limitations of human existence, redeemed from pain and transience, from fallibility and sin, thus becoming at once perfectly happy. The world will be utterly, completely, and irrevocably changed. Radical millenarian movements regard the millennium as imminent and live in tense expectation and preparation for it."[18] Adherents of some such movements expect the millennium to arrive suddenly and miraculously. Others believe it will be born out of "unprecedented cataclysms, disastrous upheavals, and bloody calamities." Members gather, watch for signs, and purify themselves with rituals. In some movements, the follower must be active and responsible. "Every minute and every deed count and everything must be sacrificed to the cause." Most such movements are also *messianic*. That is, they believe "redemption is brought about by a messiah who mediates between the divine and the human." Fundamentalist Christians who await the second coming of Jesus are examples.

Millenarianism is essentially a religion of the deprived, of oppressed peasants or desperately poor city-dwellers. It appears after wars, plagues, and famines when despair is coupled with political helplessness. Being revolutionary, it is a very potent agent of change. It may be the forerunner of political action. If a millenarian sect is frequently proven wrong in its prediction of the end of the world, its disillusioned members may turn to political action.

[16]*Collective Search for Identity*, p. 57.

[17]"Reflections on Protest," *Social Education* 30, No. 1 (Jan. 1966): 28–29, 33.

[18]Yonina Talmon, "The Millennial Dream," *The European Journal of Sociology* 2 (1962): 130–144. Quotations in this paragraph and the next are from this source.

The "cargo cult" of Melanesia is a crude and extreme form of millenarian movement. It emerged after contact with white people, whose array of goods or "cargo" seemed beyond the reach of dark-skinned islanders. Not understanding the Western economic system, they ascribed this affluence to magical rituals that white people selfishly kept secret. Trying to discover those secrets, they experimented with contraptions of tin cans and string that resembled radios and telephones. They made "refrigerators" of packing boxes to be ready for the magical appearance of canned foods and beer. They cleared spaces in the jungle for fleets of airplanes loaded with goods. One group abandoned all its usual rice-growing and pig-raising activities to make a landing field on a mountaintop for Boeing 707s. Another raised money to bring Lyndon Johnson to rule them in place of the Australians. Many believe that the arrival of the cargo will usher in the millennium of peace and happiness, free them from bondage, and banish all human ills.[19]

Crusading Movements

A crusade is a type of movement that rises above ordinary life because it requires one to leave business-as-usual and commit himself earnestly to something he believes in deeply. [It] carries both a cross and a sword. The sword signifies attack on wrong, defense of right, and cutting the bonds of ordinary concern. The cross signifies commitment to higher ideals, mystiques—indeed, every crusade has a cultic aspect, whatever its practical goals, because it needs and uses ritual and achieves redemption of identity along with its practical work.[20]

[19] See Robert Trumbull, "No One Had to Walk More Than Two Days to Reach a Polling Place," *The New York Times Magazine* (May 7, 1972): 32 ff., for an account of the consequences of self-government in Papua, New Guinea.

[20] Klapp, *Collective Search for Identity*, p. 257.

A *crusade* differs from ordinary movements in its militance, its righteousness, its image of evil, and its sense of uphill struggle. Any member can be a hero. Carrie Nation's hatchet and Don Quixote's lance are crusading symbols. The commitment of members ranges from zeal to fanaticism. Because a crusade rejects compromise, it may be a threat to democracy. Absolute morality may lead to authoritarianism.

A John Birch Society meeting is like a church service for the faithful. Members "come away confirmed and uplifted, feeling that life has more significance." The crusader role confers a feeling of "rightness" and power. It gives one a new self. Civil rights crusaders who went to Mississippi in the dangerous summer of 1964 had to break with the routines and obligations of normal

Carrie Nation was part of a crusade—the temperance movement—that succeeded for a while in banning (though not eliminating) alcoholic consumption. *Wide World Photos.*

life and start a new life, with a sense of courage and purpose.[21]

The Career of Social Movements

Not all protest is channeled into social movements, and not all social movements become highly organized and focused. "A movement has to be constructed and has to carve out a career in what is practically always an opposed, resistant, or at least indifferent world."[22] Values and norms emerge, are formulated, revised, and reformulated. Goals are defined and narrowed, tactics decided upon and changed as the situation or new leadership may determine. Different types of leaders are prominent at different stages and in different kinds of movements. Followers have varying motives for joining and varying degrees of commitment. Some movements finally become institutionalized as an accepted part of the sociocultural order.

Emergence

Some movements emerge from crowds, others from publics. A crowd tends to develop a uniform course of action and to impose it on its members. A public considers different positions before determining a course of action. A crowd gives birth to a social movement if it develops an enduring sense of group identity and adopts a plan of action that can be carried out only through sustained activity. Crowd activity may continue to be an aspect of the movement. A social movement emerges from a public if its members not only interact and discover common ground, but also decide to organize

in order to promote their views more effectively.

Movements may also emerge from other movements. Many of the early activists in Women's Liberation were involved in the civil rights and antiwar movements (just as suffragettes were first abolitionists). When they found they were treated not as equals in those movements, but as envelope-stuffers and coffee-fetchers, they began to communicate their resentment to one another. Similarly, the student protest movement of the mid-1960s emerged out of the Civil Rights movement. Some of the leaders of the Free Speech movement at Berkeley in 1964 had spent the summer trying to register black voters in Mississippi. Increasingly, social movements (Common Cause, for example) may be organized by a small number of professionals, who know how to raise money and mobilize the media and other resources toward the realization of their goals.[23]

First, a vague sense of oppression must be defined, the oppressors identified, the resentment justified, and the means for overcoming it outlined. Several books that appeared during the sixties and early seventies performed these functions for Women's Liberation. The first was Betty Friedan's *The Feminine Mystique,* followed by Kate Millett's *Sexual Politics,* and Robin Morgan's anthology, *Sisterhood Is Powerful.*[24] Among various definitions of the situation is the Redstockings Manifesto:

Women are an oppressed class. Our oppression is total, affecting every facet of our lives. We are exploited as sex objects, breeders, domestic

---

[21] *Ibid.,* chap. 8, "Crusades."
[22] Blumer, "Collective Behavior."

[23] John McCarthy and Mayer Zald, *The Trends of Social Movements in America: Professionalization and Resource Mobilization* (Morristown, N.J.: General Learning Press, 1973).
[24] *The Feminine Mystique* (New York: Dell, 1963); *Sexual Politics* (New York: New American Library, 1969); *Sisterhood Is Powerful; An Anthology of Writings from the Women's Liberation Movement* (New York: Random House, Vintage Books, 1970).

servants, and cheap labor. We are considered inferior beings, whose only purpose is to enhance men's lives. Our humanity is denied. . . .

We identify the agents of our oppression as men. Male supremacy is the oldest, most basic form of oppression.[25]

Other less sweeping definitions of the situation deal with job discrimination, the lack of choice and opportunity in careers, the constricting nature of conventional sex roles—male as well as female—and the waste of energy and talent involved.

During the initial phase, a movement may be formless and confused. Despite unrest and enthusiasm, tactics may be crude or unformulated, aims undefined or very general. There is danger that the movement will fail because of disagreements, lack of experience, and scant resources. The success of a social movement in getting off the ground often depends on its leadership.

Stages of Organization and Kinds of Leaders

An emerging social movement often has a *charismatic leader,* whose power is based on the force of personality rather than on traditional right or legal sanction. A charismatic leader is typically bold, impulsive, and dramatic—a symbol of the values of the new movement. Charisma is an aura, difficult to define, shared by saints and demagogues. Jesus and John Kennedy had charisma; so did Hitler. Charismatic leaders are agitators and prophets. They inspire confidence and loyalty and build morale by communicating the conviction that the purposes of the movement are absolutely right. They have faith that its goals will ultimately be attained and believe that the movement is charged with a sacred mission. Such leaders may seem impractical, idealistic, or even fanatical to

outsiders, but to their followers they are heroes. Martyrdom, the ultimate heroism, makes abandonment of the movement a betrayal.[26]

A charismatic leader has a band of faithful lieutenants who try to gain followers by conversion, agitation, and promises. Some are fanatical "true believers." Their sense of mission is strong. Such people are also hard-core activists as compared to the rank-and-file members and the sympathizers on the fringes of the movement.

One task of leaders is to build unity and continuity into a movement. "Many movements are composed of diverse segments, each with its own structure, loosely united only by their allegiance to the central explicit values and by the tendency of outsiders to view them as parts of a single whole. Yet there is a strain toward centralization in any movement, and lack of a unified structure can be a source of weakness."[27] Different segments compete for members and dispute goals and tactics.

Whether it is one large organization or a loose coalition, an organized movement is headed by a *legal-administrative leader* (who may also be the founder or charismatic leader). This kind of leader is more tolerant of compromise than the inspiring, single-minded charismatic leader. Such leaders must be practical to oversee the details of organization, recruitment, strategy, financing, and discipline. An organized social movement has a division of labor and a structure of authority—a name, a headquarters, perhaps local units, and a constitution. Examples are Planned Parenthood, Project Hope, and the NAACP.

A third kind of leader is the *intellectual leader* who formulates the movement's *ideology.* The intellectual leader develops a set

---

[25] Morgan, *Sisterhood Is Powerful,* pp. 533–534.

[26] Killian, "Social Movements," in Faris, *Handbook of Modern Sociology.*

[27] Killian, "Social Movements."

of ideas about how things came to be as bad as they are, how they can be changed, and why it is right to work for change through the particular movement.

Social movements, once organized, tend to become ends in themselves. Their administrative leaders, in particular, come to have a vested interest in them. The March of Dimes, established to combat infantile paralysis, did not dissolve when this goal was reached. Instead, it redefined its purpose to include the battle against birth defects.

Strategies and Tactics of Social Movements

A **strategy** is the general program for reaching the goals of a movement. **Tactics** are the specific techniques and activities used to gain new members or attain goals. The NAACP, for example, adopted a legalistic strategy, using the tactics of negotiation, voting, educational training, and bringing test cases of civil rights violations into the courts. Strategies and tactics vary with the nature of the movement's goals, its diffuseness or centralization, and its orientation to the status quo. They also depend on the nature of its leadership and the stage of its career. In the earliest stages, the strategies may be oriented more toward creating unrest among potential followers than toward attacking wrongs.

Strategies and tactics may be legal or illegal, violent or nonviolent. Some movements may resort to military revolt or economic boycott. They may use legislative, judicial, or executive authority in support of unpopular rights. Others (for example, proselytizing religious movements and reform movements requiring popular support)[28] depend primarily on widespread

conversion of individuals to the beliefs and practices of the movement.

In democracies with free speech and tolerance of dissent, reform movements find political strategies effective. They try to influence public opinion, put pressure on legislators, and are willing to compromise. Ralph Nader exemplifies the crusading re former. He unearths evidence of wrongs, publicizes them, and influences public opinion and legislation. But when goals are not clear, strategies may shift between constructive activism and senseless violence. A leader of the New Left, challenged to define its goals, once responded, "First we'll make the revolution—then we'll find out what for."

ORDERLY AND DISORDERLY PROTESTS The President's Commission on Campus Unrest distinguished between orderly and disorderly protest. It defined *orderly protest* as "peaceful manifestation of dissent, such as holding meetings, picketing, vigils, demonstrations, and marches—all of which are protected by the First Amendment." *Disorderly protest* includes disruptive tactics, violence, and terrorism. Disruptive tactics interfere with normal activity. Violence involves physical injury to people and the willful destruction of property. Terrorism involves the careful planning and systematic use of violence to create an atmosphere of fear.

Women's Liberationists have used expressive symbolism spiced with humor. Posters calling for a strike used the slogan "Don't Iron While the Strike is Hot." Women journalists in New Orleans ran pictures of the groom in wedding announcements. Women in the Netherlands placed pink ribbons across the doors of men's public urinals, protesting the lack of such conveniences for women.

NONVIOLENCE AND CIVIL DISOBEDIENCE Such tactics as sit-ins are sometimes defined as disorderly protest because they disrupt nor-

[28] *Ibid.*, pp. 426–455.

mal routine. They have, however, been highly effective in dramatizing injustice and changing public policy. Nonviolence, or passive resistance, is associated with the concept of **civil disobedience,** the deliberate breaking of some law or ordinance on moral gounds. Civil disobedience does not reject an entire system. Rather it denies the legitimacy of certain laws, policies, or specific practices. This denial is based on a conviction that core cultural values are being violated. Often its adherents declare themselves more deeply committed to the ideals of the system (American democracy, for example) than those who conform passively and obey without question.

Those who engage in civil disobedience ideally adhere to nonviolence. They are ready to accept legal punishment and keep as close a connection as possible between the action and the object of protest. Like its leading proponents, Mahandis Gandhi and Martin Luther King, Jr., they refuse to use violence themselves and are willing to give themselves to the violence of their opponents (perhaps the formal agents of social control) in order to display a superior moral force. Gandhi simply sat down, crossed his legs, and refused to move. Civil rights and antiwar protesters stood their ground and, when arrested, went limp and had to be dragged away.

DISRUPTION AND VIOLENCE Quasi-violent or disruptive tactics may dramatize a movement, but they may also provoke a strong backlash, especially when they have no obvious connection with the object of protest. In England in 1912–1914 women suffragists used disruptive methods as well as passive resistance and violence. One day in London women produced hammers, sticks, and stones from their bags, and for 15 or 20 minutes broke store windows on main streets. They slashed upholstery in railroad cars, poured jam down mailboxes, cut phone wires, planted homemade bombs, turned in false fire alarms, and set fires. They taunted and spat on policemen.

A small minority in the student and black protest movements is attracted to violence and terrorism, quoting with approval Mao's dictum that "political power grows out of the barrel of a gun," and citing Franz Fanon's

Civil disobedience ideally involves nonviolence, and protesters accept legal punishment. One standard tactic is for demonstrators to go limp when arrested, forcing the police or other agents of social control to drag them away. *Wide World Photos.*

argument in *The Wretched of the Earth* that violence is useful, therapeutic, and indispensable. They condemn any compromise, any work within the system (which they consider totally corrupt).

Americans generally subscribe to a myth that all our progress has come about peacefully, through reform and wise legislation. Yet there have been violent urban, agrarian, and racial-religious-ethnic disorders.[29] Furthermore, Americans tend to put a great deal of faith in the use of force to solve problems. If force fails, our tendency is to use more force.[30]

Timely reform and peaceful protest drain away the urge toward violence. Repression controls it only temporarily. "In any social system, whether a nation, a conquered country, a gang, a prison, or a family," says William J. Goode, "violence breeds violence. If you use violence to control people, they will hate you and use it themselves when they get the chance. . . . All social order and obedience to authority rests basically on people's belief that the system is fundamentally decent, fair, honorable, and protective to its members."[31]

Institutionalization

A movement to promote social change may fade away for various reasons. It may have its teeth pulled when its goals become official policy, as happened to the Townsend movement of the 1930s, when social security legislation provided its goal of old-age pensions. Or it may become part of "the Establishment" itself, as the organized labor movement has done. Unions have long been the recognized agents for bargaining with management over wages, benefits, and conditions of work. Dissident sects may grow into organized, respectable churches. A revolutionary movement may topple the government and take over the seats of power. Then it becomes institutionalized, as have the Communist revolutions in Russia and China.

Institutions, as we have seen in previous chapters, do not stay the same forever, or even for very long. One way they change is through collective behavior and social movements which arise out of social unrest.

Summary

Collective behavior is large-group activity that is not defined by established norms and occurs in unstructured situations. Social movements are collective actions directed toward achieving or obstructing some change in the sociocultural order.

Circular reaction is an elementary form of collective behavior, distinguished from interpretative interaction by the fact that people do not pause to interpret stimuli and delay reaction, but reflect one another's state of feeling and intensify it. When many restless individuals engage in circular reaction, a state of social unrest exists, involving a strong urge to act, but no specific goals. It results in milling, either physical or verbal

---

[29] Richard Maxwell Brown, *American Violence* (Englewood Cliffs, N.J.: Prentice-Hall, 1970).

[30] Stringfellow Barr, "Violence and the Home of the Brave," in Irving Louis Horowitz, ed., *The Troubled Conscience: American Social Issues* (Santa Barbara: Center for the Study of Democratic Institutions, 1971), p. 6.

[31] *The New York Times* (Sept. 20, 1971), commenting on the Attica prison riot.

(rumor), which leads to collective excitement. If sufficiently intense and widespread, this in turn produces social contagion, the rapid and nonrational spread of a mood, impulse, or form of conduct.

These mechanisms are especially evident in crowd behavior. Acting crowds are aggressively directed toward a specific aim. Expressive crowds engage in tension-releasing behavior and may lead to the formation of religious organizations. A riot is a relatively spontaneous and temporary outburst of hostile, illegitimate, and aggressive action by an acting crowd with some expressive tendencies.

A mass is a large number of people who react to a common stimulus as separate, anonymous individuals and make choices and decisions for individual reasons. The mass media create a set of common images and understandings that help create a readiness to interact in other forms of collective behavior.

A public forms around an issue and debates it, arriving at public opinion, which is based to some extent on fact and reason. True publics can form only where there is freedom of speech, of the press, and of association.

Much collective behavior may be attributed to the dislocations inherent in the process of modernization, which uproots people from traditional communities and cultures and brings many diverse groups together. Changes in the composition and distribution of population, alienation due to loss of identity and community, the ease of communication and transportation, awareness of social problems, and a crisis of authority—all of these contribute to the frequency of collective behavior episodes and the number of social movements.

Social movements exhibit great variety in goals, means, and organization. In relation to the status quo, they may be reactionary, conservative, reformist, revolutionary, separatist, or expressive. They may have specific goals and clear-cut organizations, or be general and diffuse, embracing many groups and different beliefs and tactics. Protest movements are designed to push a society toward a change for which it is ready, educational ones to make it more willing to accept change.

Millennial movements look forward to a cataclysmic end of the world and a new and perfect world that will replace it, often heralded by the appearance of a messiah. Crusading movements are militant and righteous and require deep commitment, allowing no compromise.

Social movements may or may not complete a career from emergence out of social unrest, through clear-cut organization, to institutionalization within the social order. A movement may be founded by a charismatic leader who symbolizes its values and goals and attracts loyal disciples and followers. Intellectual leaders formulate an ideology that defines the situation and explains and justifies the new goals and values. As a movement grows, a division of labor and a structure of authority are necessary, and an administrative leader takes charge of practical details.

The strategies or general programs of social movements may be oriented toward societal manipulation regardless of popular support, or to personal conversion (an attempt to win support). Tactics include political pressure, expressive symbolism, protest demonstrations and marches, constructive activism, education, passive resistance, disruption, violence, and terrorism. Nonviolent passive resistance is the technique of many who advocate civil disobedience as a last resort. Violence invites violent repression and provokes a backlash. Finally a movement may be institutionalized—accepted as the right and proper institution for performing some legitimate function.

Glossary

Civil disobedience The deliberate breaking of some law or ordinance on moral grounds.

Collective behavior Large group activity that arises and develops outside of established social definitions to meet undefined and unstructured situations.

Crowd A temporary grouping of a large number of people who are conscious of one another's physical nearness; it may be primarily active or expressive.

Mass A large number of people who react to a common stimulus but seek individual goals and make individual choices and decisions, whether or not they are in physical proximity.

Public A vaguely defined number of people who for a time confront an issue, disagree on how to resolve it, and discuss it.

Public opinion A collective opinion or decision on the issue around which a public has formed.

Riot An outwardly hostile, illegitimate, and aggressive action by an acting crowd.

Social contagion The relatively rapid, unwitting, and nonrational dissemination of a mood, impulse, or form of conduct.

Social movements Comparatively stable, organized, and lasting collective actions directed toward the achievement or obstruction of change in some aspect of the sociocultural order.

Strategy The general program for reaching the goals of a movement.

Tactics The specific techniques and activities used to gain new members for a movement and achieve its goals.

chapter

18

Social and Cultural Change

Anyone who tries to keep up with the news must sometimes feel depressed by the prophets of doom. We may feel helpless in the face of runaway technology and our inability to adapt to social change fast enough to avoid serious problems. Each of us must sometimes feel tempted to forget the whole thing and bury our heads in the sand.

But a sociologist cannot give in to this temptation. Even the most pessimistic social scientists keep on trying to make sense of the confusion of the current scene. Others are optimists who see glimmers of hope and believe a better social order is in the making. In any case, we keep trying to understand and explain, hoping that those goals of scientific endeavor—prediction and control—may also be served by our efforts.

In this chapter, we look at social change in general and at the process of modernization in particular. Then we look at social planning, the way societies can work to harness the forces of social change in constructive ways.

Social change includes significant alterations in social structure, in cultural definitions, and in the material products of sociocultural action. Social structure may change in size, in the degrees of formality and informality, in the types of social relationships, and in the system of statuses and roles. Cultural change is reflected in changing knowledge, beliefs, values, and norms. Material products will change as a result of advances in science and technology.

Theories of Social Change

Students of social change have various theories about where we are headed. Are we progressing toward something better, or going downhill after a golden age? Does the career of every society follow the same general pattern? Let us look at some of the most influential theories.

Evolutionary Theories

A century ago Darwin's theory of biological evolution inspired anthropologists to theorize that social arrangements and cultural forms are tested in a process similar to natural selection. If the elements of culture and society prove adaptive and useful, they survive. According to this theory, human history is a movement toward ever higher forms, from savagery through barbarism to civilization. A reverse kind of evolutionary theory, called primitivism, says that we are sliding from an original state of natural goodness into evil. Some evolutionists see history as a steady, straight path. Others think progress occurs in spurts. Still others describe history in terms of stages, either regular stairsteps upward or with some regressions. Contemporary cultural evolutionists like Leslie White argue that culture is an independent force. They say it evolves toward ever greater use of physical

430

power sources and ever greater control of the environment.

Ralph Linton saw some valid elements in evolutionary theory. In general, he said, changes in culture have been directed toward "a better adjustment of the social organism to its environment." But there are exceptions. Some changes reach the point where they endanger the society as a whole. Just as the Irish elk evolved enormous antlers that endangered its survival, modern warfare indicates that "man is an ape with a brain too active for his own good."[1] Nonetheless, human history as a whole displays certain common sequences. Hunting and gathering appears to have preceded food raising everywhere, just as agriculture and settled village life preceded cities. Stone tools generally preceded metal tools. Metals that could be worked cold preceded those that had to be smelted and forged.

Cyclical Theories

Cyclical theorists of social change insist that there is no long-term trend toward the perfection of humanity and society. Rather, civilizations rise and fall, swing from one extreme to another, or experience shorter-range ups and downs. Pitirim Sorokin, for example, argued that societies are oriented toward either "sensate" or "ideational" values. He felt that a certain amount of development in either direction is bound to be followed by its opposite. As the pendulum swings, there are periods when an "idealistic" mixture prevails. He detected this pattern in painting, literature, law, war, and revolution. Medieval Catholic art, for example, was thoroughly ideational or spiritual. During the Renaissance, there was a glorious mix-

ture of the ideational and the sensate, and modern art typifies the sensate to excess.[2]

"Rise and fall" theories of change compare societies to living organisms, which pass through a sort of life cycle. They are born, grow, decay, and die. A leading proponent of this view was Oswald Spengler. He analyzed Western societies and found them to be nearing late middle age.[3] According to Spengler, it is not possible for societies to rejuvenate themselves. Change leads to extinction, not perfection. Those who share Spengler's view like to compare modern American society with that of ancient Rome. The Roman empire passed through an extremely decadent period before its fall.

Seeing ups and downs or pendulum swings in our social history prevents us from thinking of contemporary events as unique and from expecting current trends to continue indefinitely. Perhaps this viewpoint can save us from feeling that we are all "going to hell in a hand-basket." Political sociologist Seymour Martin Lipset lends perspective to the turmoil of the 1960s and 1970s, for example. He outlines several periods in American history since 1918, each of which was marked by right-wing trends that some observers thought would go on for much longer than they did. But all these trends declined. Then the '30s saw a great shift toward liberal attitudes, particularly in economics, as a result of the Depression. In the 1950s, dissent and personal deviance were so lacking that social critics worried about the blandness and conformity of college students. A decade and more of activism followed. And now there are indications of a swing back to an emphasis on individual success and enjoyment rather than social action.

---

[1] *The Tree of Culture* (New York: Alfred A. Knopf, 1955), pp. 50–51.

[2] *Social and Cultural Dynamics* (New York: American Book, 1937), vol. 1. chap. 4.

[3] *Decline of the West* (New York: Modern Library, 1965; originally published in 1918).

Systems Theory

Some theorists hold that the functioning of every social system has equilibrium as its goal. Changes in one part of the system produce adaptations in other parts, restoring the balance of the social machine, the health of the social organism. Those who subscribe to the systems model of society see change as a positive element, contributing to the dynamics of systems in a way that keeps them from deteriorating.

Robert Merton has used the example of the urban political machine headed by a "boss" to illustrate the idea of the *manifest* or intended consequences and the *latent* or unintended consequences of a social structure. Because a sociocultural order is a complex, interdependent, even fragile system, you can never "do just one thing." Many planned changes have unexpected and unintended consequences, which may or may not be desirable.

In our decentralized system of government, certain needs went unfulfilled until the boss set up an organization that met them. The manifest function of his machine was to serve as a highly efficient go-between for public and private business. But the machine also had latent consequences, many of them desirable. It served as a channel of social mobility for many men of low social and economic status. Perhaps sons of immigrants who could not rise through the conventional channels of schooling and work could gain wealth and power as faithful precinct captains for the boss.

The most important latent function of the machine, perhaps, was to humanize assistance to the poor, many of whom could not speak English. The precinct captain was always available in time of need to help a widow with a basket of food or coal, to find someone a job, or to settle minor violations of the law. This network of personal relations paid off in votes. The grateful voter preferred such help to that of the impersonal welfare worker. The precinct captain did not pry or demand proof of eligibility. And he had connections in city hall and elsewhere that the welfare worker lacked. Reformers who saw only the manifest function of the machine—a way for the boss to gain power

The late Richard J. Daley, who was mayor of Chicago from 1955–1977, was one of the last of the big city bosses. The political machine has both manifest and latent consequences—some positive, some negative. *Wide World Photos.*

and wealth by handing over votes to political leaders—failed to break the power of the machine by simply attacking it as corrupt. They did not provide alternatives for its latent functions, either by eliminating the needs or by meeting them in other ways.

Deterministic vs. Voluntaristic Theories

What role do people themselves play in social and cultural change? None at all, say advocates of determinist theories. According to determinists, change proceeds according to blind forces over which we have no control. Such theories typically center around one aspect of culture and social structure such as technology, the economic system, or the class structure.

Voluntaristic theories, in contrast, give people credit or blame for what happens in society. Universal aspects of human nature, in one version of voluntaristic theory, are universal sources of change. People, says Wilbert E. Moore, are problem-solving animals who see the poor adjustments between their culture and social structure as challenges. They work to invent new ways and to get them adopted: new gadgets, new techniques, new laws, new values, new patterns of social relationships.[4]

There is always a margin of individuality and nonconformity in personality. Some theorists attribute change to unique individuals or groups rather than to the nature of the species as a whole. The course of history, they say, is determined by the chance appearance of such people as Napoleon and Lenin, Isaac Newton and Madame Curie, Jesus and Pope John XXIII, Peter the Great and Mao Tse-Tung, Gandhi and Martin Luther King, Jr., Beethoven and the Beatles. Others see more ordinary people as agents

[4]See *Social Change* (Englewood Cliffs, N.J.: Prentice-Hall, 1963).

of change. A Peace Corps worker can help a village establish a pure water supply. A congressman can push for reform of welfare legislation. A teacher can encourage (or fail to encourage) development of human potential. A parent can teach (or fail to teach) norms and values. A planner can initiate change. A sociologist can point out possible alternatives and their probable consequences.

Conflict Theory

Conflict is inevitable in any society. Some see conflict as necessarily destructive. Others see it as a creative source of change. In fact, to some, conflict is the only possible means of renewing a society. A political system that works well has institutionalized various means of resolving conflicts without violence.

Marxism is a theory that has elements of evolution, conflict, voluntarism, and determinism. Marx was an evolutionist in the sense that he believed that society proceeds inevitably toward the utopia of perfect communism. He was a conflict theorist in that he saw the class struggle as the means by which each stage in the evolution of society toward communism is brought about. He was a voluntarist in the sense that he believed that people must unite and work to bring about the downfall of their oppressors. And he was a determinist in the sense that these actions, voluntary though they may seem, occur only because each person is a member of a certain class and cannot help behaving accordingly. Marx, then, felt that change is built into the nature of a social structure because of the tension and conflict between classes, and that such change is directed toward a vague, wonderful, and presumably unchanging utopia.

World events in our century show how such beliefs can effect social change. Although Marx would hardly recognize many of the twists his ideas have been given to fit different circumstances, the Russian, Chinese, and Cuban revolutions reflect his influence, as do revolts and insurrections in many other settings.[5]

Factors Influencing Social Change

Some cultures are more responsive to change than others. The level of technology; the knowledge, beliefs, and values of the culture; its level of complexity; and the degree of contact it has with other cultures all promote or retard social change.

The Role of Technology

Technological determinists argue that changes in technology are the source of all other cultural and social change. For example, William F. Ogburn traced direct connections between such phenomena as the invention of the automobile self-starter and the emancipation of women. When it became easy for women to drive cars, they entered the business world. This in turn changed their role and the nature of family relationships. Technological changes call for adaptive changes in nonmaterial culture, which is inherently more conservative. These are often so slow in coming that a social problem or maladjustment Ogburn called "cultural lag" occurs.[6]

Technology is often cast as the villain of the modern melodrama. It is obvious that its growth has been rapid and to a large extent uncontrolled. Many of its effects have been unanticipated. Such social problems as pollution, unemployment, and the threat of nuclear war appear to be largely consequences of technological change. But to condemn technology altogether is to forget that it also saves lives, makes deserts bloom, and lets us hear music in our living rooms.

Technological and economic factors cannot be accepted as prime causes in social change, says Robin Williams. But they are important in any theory of change in modern societies. Technology doesn't cause sociocultural change directly, but it does made change possible. The automobile and telephone, for example, made suburbs possible. And whether or not we blame many of our social problems on technology, we can hardly solve them without employing science and technology.

Knowledge, Beliefs, and Values

If human decisions rather than blind forces provide the essential dynamics of change, then we must emphasize the role of knowledge, beliefs, and values in bringing about—or retarding—change. Kenneth Boulding sees learning as the primary source of the great transition from agricultural to industrial-urban and now to postindustrial civilization.[7] The value judgment that change—in a desired direction, of course—is progress has given great momentum to Western societies. The idea that "God helps those who help themselves" also gives impetus to change. Traditionalism and fatalism, in contrast, retard it. In the face of other pressures for change, values "stand as focal points of system identity and heavily defended strongholds against change. A social structure may withstand extensive change in its other components—people and artifacts, for example—so long as its values hold

---

[5] For an example of neo-Marxist interpretation in the United States, see Roderick Aya and Norman Miller, eds., *The New American Revolution* (New York: The Free Press, 1971).

[6] William F. Ogburn, *Social Change* (New York: Huebsch, 1922).

[7] *The Meaning of the Twentieth Century: The Great Transition* (New York: Harper & Row, 1964), p. 27.

firm. When values go, . . . the total social edifice tends to crumble."[8]

NONCONFORMIST RELIGION AND THE RISE OF CAPITALISM The most famous argument for the theory that cultural beliefs and values can be instrumental in bringing about fundamental change was made by Max Weber. He asked, "Why did industrial capitalism arise in England and the Netherlands?" He theorized that in order to build a factory system, people had to be motivated to save and invest rather than spend—"a form of insanity." Nonconformist Protestantism, especially Calvinism, provided this motivation. Many English and Dutch Protestants chose production as their calling. To prove that they were predestined to be saved rather than damned, they lived hard-working, thrifty, ascetic lives. They put their profits back into industry rather than spending them for enjoyment and display. Thus the Protestant ethic, a set of cultural beliefs and values, provided much impetus for economic development.

MORAL CRISIS Some theorists see a gap between society's ideals or core values and its real patterns as an important source of social change. When this strain appears especially disruptive, many members of the society feel a sense of moral crisis—of guilt and self-accusation. They identify the strain as a social problem and seek to bring the real patterns into correspondence with the ideal. They may do so through dissent, protest, legislation, planning, reform, or revolution. For example, many see the extent of poverty in the United States as a violation of our core values. But awareness of a problem is not enough to produce change. It has been said that the *real* cultural lag in a society

is that between knowledge of a problem and its solution.

ANOMIE AND ALIENATION Mutual trust and agreement on core values hold a society together. Anomie and alienation indicate mutual distrust and estrangement among members of groups and among groups within a society. This climate fosters social change, especially through various forms of collective behavior. Alienated persons are more likely than others to be aware of problems that call for change. Anomie in society is comparable to anarchy in government. It is not necessarily a "bad" state of affairs. It may lead to a better social order. It does, however, tend to disrupt the workings of a society and to spread through the system. If this loss of trust pervades a society, people lose faith and withdraw the energy and motivation that keep things going. The whole sociocultural system may collapse.[9]

Invention and the Complexity of the Culture Base

The more varied, complex, specialized, and differentiated a sociocultural system, the more likely it is to change and to change rapidly. This principle is most obvious in connection with technological innovation. All innovators, except for some who make purely accidental discoveries, have only the existing storehouse of knowledge with which to work. Thomas Edison could not have invented the electric light or the phonograph if the steps that laid the groundwork for these inventions had not already been taken. Leonardo da Vinci, for all his fascination with the idea of flight and the amazing draftsmanship of his models for flying ma-

---

[8] Joseph A. Monane, *A Sociology of Human Systems* (New York: Appleton-Century-Crofts, 1967), p. 161.

[9] Robin M. Williams, Jr., *American Society: A Sociological Interpretation*, 3rd ed. (New York: Alfred A. Knopf, 1970), p. 587.

chines, could never have succeeded in inventing the airplane. Such necessary preliminary inventions as the gasoline engine were still far in the future. Recognizing his debt to his predecessors, Isaac Newton said: "If I saw farther, 'twas because I stood on giant shoulders."

Because it rests on existing culture elements, change occurs much more rapidly in a complex culture than in a simple one. If there are ten thousand elements in a culture and they yield one invention, a culture with ten times that number will yield not ten, but far more. Culture does not, of course, multiply quite that rapidly and predictably. It would be overwhelmingly complex if it did. As we shall see, there are barriers that block acceptance of innovations and slow the rate of change. But the fact remains that a complex culture has a greater potential for change than does a simple one.

Culture Contact and Diffusion

Culture in general could not grow without inventors and discoverers. But the great bulk of any rich and complex culture comes not from innovations within the society but from diffusion. **Diffusion** is the process by which culture traits and patterns spread from one society to another or from one group to another within a society. It occurs through contact, whether face-to-face or not, between the members of different societies and groups. Marco Polo's Chinese cook introduced spaghetti to Italy, and centuries later Italian immigrants brought it to America. All over the world, missionaries have introduced new moral codes, new religious beliefs, and new customs in dress, hygiene, and schooling. Commerce diffuses movies, soft drinks, chewing gum, clothes, utensils, and gadgets of all kinds to all the corners of the earth. Conquerors impose their own ways and sometimes adopt some patterns

Culture patterns spread from one society to another through the process of diffusion. *Owen Franken/Stock, Boston.*

of the subordinate culture. The ancient Romans adopted much of Greek culture, for example. Members of the Peace Corps and foreign aid organizations engage in planned diffusion of knowledge, skills, values, and norms.

Millions and millions of radios and TV sets reach people all around the world. The increasing use of communications satellites may turn the world into what Marshall McLuhan calls "a global village" in which everyone knows the news almost as soon as it happens. Along with movies, these have created in the poor a desire for change, not only in our own society but all over the world. People are not only creative and imitative. They are envious as well.

Factors Limiting Social Change

We have touched on some factors that lead people to accept or even seek change. Intelligence, curiosity, restlessness, imitativeness, envy, and desire for novelty lead people everywhere to seek change. And the succession of generations makes acceptance easier. Anomie, alienation, conflict, a sense of moral crisis, and a definition of change as progress all create a climate receptive to change. Some societies, especially modern secular ones, value innovation in general. But, regardless of the social climate, every society is only *selectively* accumulative for several reasons.

First, in varying degrees, all people value consistency and tend to accept only those innovations that are compatible with established norms, values, and beliefs. Moslem women, for example, will not adopt health practices that include examination by a male doctor. Second, the attitude toward the lending culture or the innovators in their own culture influences acceptance or rejection. Many Africans despise Afro hairdos because they define them as symbols of Americanism and imperialism. Others like them because they come from America, "the

home of exciting and popular soul music."[10] Third, an innovation may or may not fill a gap in another culture. The cultivation of maize spread from the New World to Africa and Europe because there was a need for such a grain. But Orientals and Central Americans show little interest in potatoes because they already have a starchy food, rice.

Fourth, the rationality and desirability of a change may be obvious, but the sheer inconvenience and irritation of the shift block change. Only now is the United States beginning the gradual process of changing from medieval weights and measures (pounds, gallons, acres, feet) to the simple and sensible metric system used in science and in most societies. Although the change may cost $11 billion, it is said it will save a fourth of the time school children now spend in learning arithmetic and will cut perhaps $705 million a year from the cost of schooling.[11] Our spelling is far from phonetic. We struggle along with a calendar devised by ancient Egyptians, formalized in 45 B.C., and last altered in 1582. But which generation will take upon itself the burden of changing them to more rational systems?

In addition, only very simple elements can be adopted without some alteration to fit the culture. Often only the *form* of a culture element is adopted, and it is given a different meaning. The colorful masked dances of the Pueblo Indians are associated with fertility, rain, and good crops. The Navajo borrowed them and reinterpreted them as useful in healing disease. An old cultural element and a new one may be merged in a creative synthesis. Pagan religions often revolved around one great goddess who was the mother and guardian of life. With the diffusion of the Christian

---

[10] Stanley Meisler, "Afro Haircut 'Out' in Africa," *Detroit News* (Oct. 8, 1970).
[11] *The New York Times* (Dec. 13, 1970).

religion, her identity became merged with that of the Virgin Mary. The local goddess became the local Madonna, still credited with many of the powers and traits of the original pagan goddess.

Modernization

Modernization is the transition from traditional folk society to urban industrial society. This transition (which does not always—or even often—take place smoothly and evenly) affects every institution, every community, and every life. Modernization is a comprehensive term, embracing many changes that tend to occur together. Its central feature is industrialization. With this, in spirals of cause and effect, go changes in government, the family, education, religion, and social organization. There is a shift from rural to urban living. And there are changes in knowledge, beliefs, values, self-conceptions, and ways of life.

Changes in Cultural Systems

During the modernization process, ways of thinking, doing, believing, and evaluating change a lot. The general tendency is toward uniformity of culture. Beliefs, values, and tastes come to be widely shared by people of different groups and categories. Mass education, mass literacy, travel, mobility, mass production, mass markets, the growth of centralized government, and mass communication all lead toward uniformity. Patterns of consumption and use of leisure time become increasingly standardized.[12]

SCIENCE AND KNOWLEDGE One student of the future calls the growth of knowledge "the most basic and influential of all general social trends. . . . It does not depend upon any other social trend, though other trends may accelerate the growth of knowledge."[13] Beginning with the revival of Greek science in the twelfth century, the growth of knowledge has now reached explosive proportions. Modern societies actively seek more knowledge, employing professionals in research, institutionalizing the process, and investing huge sums. Of about $25 billion spent on research and development in the United States in 1970, the federal government invested over $15 billion. About 30 percent was related to defense and about 13 percent to space exploration.[14] Computers allow us to organize and store this vast outpouring of data and to process and retrieve it with incredible speed.

TECHNOLOGY Technological advances in agricultural and industrial production, transportation, and communication—the continuing Industrial Revolution—are the most conspicuous features of modernization. One basis for this acceleration of productivity is the harnessing of ever more efficient and powerful sources of energy. A full-grown adult produces only 1/20 of 1 horsepower in a working day of 8 to 12 hours. An entire primitive society can produce a total of perhaps 4 horsepower per day. For most of recorded history, 99 percent of all productivity came from human labor. The remaining 1 percent was generated by wind, water, and work animals. The steam engine, the generation of electricity, and the invention of the internal combustion engine were milestones in the "energy revolution." It was

---

[12] Harold L. Wilensky, "Mass Society and Mass Culture," in Gerald D. Bell, ed., *Organizations and Human Behavior* (Englewood Cliffs, N.J.: Prentice-Hall, 1967), pp. 41–60.

[13] Burnham P. Beckwith, *The Next 500 Years* (Exposition-University Book, published by the World Future Society, 1968).

[14] *The American Almanac* (1971), p. 519. Estimates.

estimated that in 1960 only about 1/200 of 1 percent of all energy expended in production of goods and services in the United States came from human muscle. A decade later, the total horsepower of all mechanical engines and turbines was close to 19 billion, or about 94 horsepower per capita. Most of this energy comes from fossil fuels, such as coal, oil, and gas.[15] As a result, more goods have been produced during the past 100 years than in all previous human history.[16] Solar and nuclear sources may eventually replace fossil fuels. Already the ability to split the atom has created a revolution in weaponry.

The application of science, knowledge, and power to means of communication and transportation is an integral part of the Industrial Revolution. The communications revolution has produced great changes. Millions of poor people in remote corners of the world become aware of new possibilities as they read (if they are literate) and as they see movies, listen to radio, and, increasingly, watch TV. And nothing is more revolutionary than a road, which opens up isolated communities, allowing their members to travel to work or market and to see and buy new things. Roads also bring officials, businessmen, vote seekers, and perhaps doctors and tourists into the community. As people become physically mobile, their image of the world changes. They see a different possible future for themselves and their children. The automobile and bus, the jet plane, and the space capsule shake them from their traditional moorings, mentally as well as physically.

[15] *Ibid.*, Table 773, p. 505. This was over six times the amount generated in 1940, and in per capita figures about five times as much. About 94 percent of this power is used in automotive vehicles.

[16] Cyril Edwin Black, "Change as a Condition of Modern Life," in Myron Weiner, ed., *Modernization: The Dynamics of Growth* (New York: Basic Books, 1966), p. 18.

NORMS AND VALUES Everyone has always wanted the things modernization promises—health, long life, and material well-being. What is new in societies aspiring to modernity is the hope of achieving these goals largely by one's own efforts, and quickly. Extensive changes in values "are the most fundamental condition for economic transformation."[17] The most important of these are secularization and individualization.

Secularization, a shift from sacred to worldly values, implies that doctrines, dogmas, and traditions are opened to skeptical questioning. The attitude of reverence for traditional procedures, norms, beliefs, and associations is replaced by a rational-utilitarian attitude that permits them to be discarded or changed with relative ease.

In a traditional or sacred society, many statuses are compounded (adult-male-hunter-warrior, for example), and their accompanying roles are diffuse, applying to many situations. Decisions are not made by considering alternatives. They are made ritualistically: "That is how it has always been done." The natural environment is seen as a mystery to be feared or as an illusion to be ignored. Almost everything has sacred meaning. Corn or bread is holy.

In modern, secular society, while some norms are highly specific and prescriptive (occupational norms in particular), many others such as sex roles are blurred and conflicting. They are subject to a wide latitude of interpretation and redefinition in interaction. The natural environment is seen as an orderly universe governed by laws that can be understood and forces that can be tamed. All industrial societies, no matter how they are organized, value rationality and technical knowledge, efficiency, progress, education, mobility, work, and high productivity.

[17] Wilbert E. Moore, *Social Change* (Englewood Cliffs, N.J.: Prentice-Hall, 1963), p. 93.

In modern society, the demand for people to work in primary production decreases. The need for specialized jobs, both skilled and semiskilled, increases. *Ellis Herwig/Stock, Boston.*

Changes in Social Systems

As societies modernize, political and economic units generally become larger. People and institutions become more specialized. Social contacts are more numerous and the proportion of formal and impersonal relationships greater. The class system becomes more fluid, open, and ambiguous. In short, the system as a whole grows more complex and its parts more interdependent.

CHANGE OF SCALE Traditional societies are organized on a small scale and in a rural setting. They are typified by the nonliterate tribe, the medieval manor, and the peasant village. The ability to communicate at a distance and to cover ground swiftly makes it possible for modern societies to include larger territories. During the transition, folk communities often crumble, and the nation-state becomes the focus of loyalty and source of identity.

Our world grows even as it shrinks. Jet planes, radio, TV, movies, and newspapers make people more and more aware of all the other millions of human beings in the world. And in spite of all its divisions, the world is increasingly a single system. It has increasingly common value orientations and a common pool of knowledge and techniques. There are so many interrelationships that events in one society often affect many others.

SPECIALIZATION, COMPLEXITY, AND INTERDEPENDENCE In a traditional society, economic roles are relatively undifferentiated. Communities are largely self-sufficient, producing their own food, clothing, and shelter. In a modern society the roles of producer and distributor are distinct from that of consumer. They are broken down into infinite specialties and narrowly defined. Fewer and fewer people work in primary production (farming, fishing, and forestry) as modernization proceeds. More and more take on specialized jobs in industry. The proportion in service occupations and professions keeps growing. The demand for unskilled and semiskilled workers, which is high in the early stages of industrialization, falls during later stages. In highly industrialized societies there is a rising demand for scientists and technicians, as well as for those in service occupations such as finance, insurance, wholesale and retail distribution, and transportation.

Various institutional functions are embedded in the fabric of traditional society.

440

It is hard to label one activity as wholly economic and another as wholly religious or political. Family life, religion, government, education, and the tasks of getting food, clothing, and shelter are all woven together and have sacred meanings. In modern society, life is more segmented. Its various aspects are put into separate compartments, so to speak. The economic aspect is quite distinct from others. Leisure and play are altogether distinct from work, which is set apart from the rest of life by the tyranny of the clock. A number of agencies and associations with quite specific functions arise within the system. Some take over functions that once were performed by the family (such as education of children and care of the aged). Others connect and coordinate the various specialized parts of the complex system (government and market agencies, for example). Most production is handled by huge corporations with nationwide or world-wide markets.

SOCIAL STRATIFICATION Status in small folk communities rests primarily on ascribed statuses: sex, age, and kinship. There may be little differentiation in wealth, power, and prestige. A modern society, in contrast, has a relatively open and mobile class structure in which status depends largely on achievement, on individual efforts to gain the education and skills an industrial society demands and rewards. The labor force of necessity is hierarchically organized, for industry needs both the manager and the managed. Various skills are differentially valued and unequally rewarded. But advancement within this hierarchy is far more likely to reflect achievement than ascribed qualities.

SOCIAL RELATIONSHIPS As the scale of social organization grows larger, the importance

Where the extended family is strong, social change tends to be slower. *Bohdan Hrynewych/Stock, Boston.*

of family and community declines, and social relationships become increasingly impersonal, functional, and secondary.

The extended family is the cornerstone of a traditional society. Its members share the family income regardless of their contribution to it. Productive workers provide for old, ill, disabled, and even lazy family members. Economists see this tradition as diluting the workers' incentive to work hard, save, and invest. In modern societies, the nuclear family of parents and children constitutes the extent of the breadwinner's responsibilities. The incentives to work, save, and invest are therefore supposedly stronger. Where the extended family is strong, change tends to be slower. The grandparent generation is closely woven into the fabric of family life and teaches children the traditional ways. In modern society, the discontinuity of family life—the generation gap—is both cause and effect of rapid change.

Modernization typically brings about "an eclipse of community." As many functions once performed by family and local community are turned over to large formal organizations, individuals become more dependent on authorities and impersonal agencies. Loyalties to community, neighborhood, and relatives outside the immediate family fade.[18] People lose the middle range of human association "between the complete intimacy and protection of the family and the awesome anonymity and performance-governed behavior of the cosmopolitan society."[19] This means a loss of many primary contacts, of a sense of roots, and of informal social controls.

Yet, the need for intimate personal relationships is so strong that many kinds of groups emerge within the anonymity and formality of the larger society to fill this need. Work groups, office cliques, army buddies, fraternal societies, and voluntary associations of many kinds emerge or are organized. Some intimate relationships, such as care of the aged are commercialized. Prostitution is an another example.

Changes in Personality

Living in sociocultural orders as different as traditional and modern societies, members of *Homo sapiens* exhibit such varied personalities that we may speak of different types of people. Between the traditional type and the modern type is the transitional type. This type lives the modernization process and feels peculiar mixtures of freedom and loss that occur with this wrenching social change.

We can draw a profile of the traditional type from what we have said about the traditional sociocultural order. Traditional people follow a well-worn path marked out by their elders and feel shame if they fail to conform. They feel merged with family and village. They are fatalists, accepting things as they are. They cannot conceive of changing their status. They suffer "from a poverty of wants as well as from a poverty of ideas for satisfying them."[20] They tend to be authoritarian: There is only one right way. They cannot conceive of being someone else or living somewhere else.

A member of modern society, on the other hand, is likely to be urban, literate, educated for a specialized occupation, mobile, and politically active. But "it is only when man has undergone a change in spirit—has acquired new ways of thinking, feeling, and

[18] Maurice R. Stein, *The Eclipse of Community: An Interpretation of American Studies* (New York: Harper & Row, 1960), p. 329.

[19] Kenneth R. Schneider, *Destiny of Change: How Relevant Is Man in the Age of Development?* (New York: Holt, Rinehart and Winston, 1968), pp. 106–107.

[20] Irving Louis Horowitz, *Three Worlds of Development: The Theory and Practice of International Stratification* (New York: Oxford University Press, 1966), p. 300.

acting—that we come to consider him truly modern."[21]

Modern people are flexible, adaptable, ready to accept new ideas and try new methods. They live with change, choice, and decisions. They are oriented to the present and the future rather than to the past. They are rational and orderly, and believe in planning and organizing. Their self-conceptions are based not on kinship and community, but on experience and achievement. They feel that people should be rewarded according to their contribution, not their connections or the whims of those in power. They can imagine themselves in other statuses, situations, and places.

Modern people have faith in science and technology. They believe they can learn to dominate their environment, to control floods, for example, or prevent storms. They admire professional competence, craftsmanship, technical skill.[22] They do not believe that everything is determined either by fate or by the peculiar qualities of particular people. It follows that they are activists and believe that they can change things. Modern people, then, are participants—in the market, the political forum, and other aspects of social life.

The Transition from Traditional to Modern Society

In most of Asia, Africa, and Latin America, the need for modernization—especially for economic development—becomes ever more urgent because of the grim race be-tween exploding populations and the ability to feed them. In contrast to Westerners, who worry about "runaway technology," people in the less developed countries struggle for sheer survival and the beginnings of industrialization.

The Beginnings of Modernization

Where does modernization begin? Healthy human beings in sufficient but not overwhelming numbers, along with abundant natural resources, contribute to the speed of modernization and the ease with which it is achieved. But the impulse to modernize comes from the awareness, discontent, and aspirations of many people. Modernization depends on effective leadership, risk taking, and the society's institutional structure.

The first sign that a community or society will modernize is the appearance of people with new discontents and new desires. They are pried loose from their rocklike attachment to kin and birthplace, perhaps physically as well as psychologically. They are aware that things could be better.

A transitional person, then, "is miserable and, most importantly, is newly aware of his misery. To a greater or lesser degree, men of all nations have accepted the originally Western convictions that there is progress and that all men should share in it."[23] Traditional society is passing because relatively few people still want to live by its rules. And the transitional person "blames his shortcomings, his failings, and his condition on society rather than on himself as in former times."[24]

The expectations of transitional people are for the most part realistic and specific. They do not have utopian visions. Their

[21]Alex Inkeles, "The Modernization of Man," in Weiner, *Modernization.*

[22]Kenneth Keniston, "Does Human Nature Change in a Technological Revolution?" *The New York Times* (Jan. 6, 1969), citing studies of astronauts.

[23]William McCord, "Portrait of Transitional Man," in Irving Louis Horowitz, ed., *The New Sociology* (New York: Oxford University Press, 1965), p. 441.

[24]Horowitz, *Three Worlds of Development,* p. 291.

"revolution of rising expectations" consists mainly of "a hope that their immediate, limited economic needs can be satisfied, and a desire that their children may escape the compulsions of poverty."[25] Yet they do not believe they can realize even these hopes without a fundamental change in the social order.

Besides a large pool of people ready to modernize, a society must have entrepreneurs and leaders. As we saw earlier, Max Weber associated the beginnings of industrial capitalism with the ways in which nonconformist religion contributed to a spirit of enterprise.[26] Others believe that in the early stages of industrialization, most entrepreneurs come from among people who have experienced some loss of status in the traditional society. The elite are encouraged to follow military, professional, and literary careers. They look down on business, especially manufacturing. Only commerce and industry are open to the group that has lost status or been denied respect. Some of its members take the risk of starting new enterprises.[27] At the village level, the first to adopt new ways—such as birth control and vaccination—are the more aggressive individuals, often regarded as deviants by their fellow villagers.

[25] McCord, "Portrait of Transitional Man." He cites surveys in three Indian cities, which showed that people regarded the rise in food prices and unemployment as the most serious problems requiring government attention, and a study in Africa in which 98% mentioned poverty and hunger as their greatest fears and 60% expressed a fear that their children might have to steal or commit other crimes in order to live.

[26] See *The Protestant Ethic and the Spirit of Capitalism.* This thesis has been questioned by some social scientists, who suggest that some other factor may have been responsible for both nonconformity in religion and the spirit of enterprise.

[27] Everett E. Hagen, *On the Theory of Social Change: How Economic Growth Begins* (Homewood, Ill.: Dorsey, 1962). Hagen traces the loss of status back several generations from the entrepreneurs and sees its effects in personality changes over the generations.

Institutions and Modernization

The general shape of the institutional structure is extremely important in modernization. To modernize successfuly, a society must be both stable and adaptable. It must be capable of internal transformation and accept the need for continual change. These conditions are most likely to be fulfilled where a centralized, large-scale institutional framework already exists. Within this framework the different institutional systems need to be relatively autonomous. China, for example, was extremely stable but not adaptable. Great upheavals were necessary before modernization could proceed. In India, in contrast, the cultural and political orders were more or less separate. Such autonomy of the various cultural, social, and political institutions means that change can begin in one sphere without threatening the others.

EDUCATION   A system of formal education is important for modernization.[28] Universities train managers, technicians, administrators, and other modernizing agents. They are connected with the universities of developed countries to provide a channel for the stimulation and guidance of change. The decade of the 1960s saw the establishment of numerous universities. In 1950 Africa between the Sahara and South Africa had no university. By 1965 three dozen had been founded. In Indian universities there is a shift away from classical studies toward science, engineering, and agriculture.[29]

ECONOMIC TAKE-OFF   Two essential economic changes are basic to industrialization. There must be a shift from subsistence to commercial agriculture. And there must be a great increase in savings and investment. Some

[28] Inkeles, "The Modernization of Man."
[29] Schneider, *Destiny of Change,* pp. 19–20.

farmers must convert to mechanized modern farming, feeding more people per man-hour of work. Others must leave the land to work in factories. This process of displacement is often stressful and creates huge social problems. Cities all over the underdeveloped world are ringed with the slums of dispossessed migrants from rural areas.

Only by sacrificing present consumption (saving) at a sufficient rate—perhaps 10–20 percent of the national income—and investing in more productive equipment and tools (capital) does a society achieve "take-off" into sustained economic growth. This is extremely difficult in nations where most people live at the barest minimum of subsistence. It demands great sacrifice, voluntary or involuntary. In England and other countries that industrialized early, this saving was forced upon the workers through long hours and miserable wages for men, women, and children. They were denied immediate consumption of the fruits of their labors. Entrepreneurs also denied themselves. Rather than indulging in conspicuous consumption (as did later industrialists), they reinvested their profits. This allowed economic growth to proceed rapidly. In the Soviet Union, repression and terror were used to push rapid industrialization. Production of consumer goods was minimal as compared to heavy industry. Even today, a hidden "turnover tax" of about 44 percent of the price of consumer goods goes back to the Soviet government. The effect is to drain off the purchasing power of wages in a less conspicuous way than through low wages and high income taxes.

POLITICAL INSTITUTIONS In their patterns of historical development, stage of industrialization, and forms of government, the nations of the earth are generally divided into three categories.

The *West* includes the nations that evolved from feudalism into some form of capitalism, not through invasion or conquest but in a haphazard, unplanned, "natural," way.

The *Eastern* nations include the Soviet Union and its bloc, in which a radical, abrupt shift from feudalism to socialism occurred. Russian society was the first to engage in serious debate over the relationship between economic backwardness and political modernization. The rigid ideology that guided Soviet modernization resulted in an emphasis on heavy industry rather than consumer goods. It put an emphasis on size rather than quality and on central planning from above with little feedback from below. Today, however, there is a great deal of experimentation within the Soviet Union itself as well as in other communist nations.

The *Third World* is "a social universe in limbo and outside the power dyad of East and West." Much of it was colonized until World War II. The Third World today is "thoroughly dedicated to becoming industrialized (and is) a self-defined and self-conscious association of nation-states." China has recently emerged as a marginal member of the Third World bloc. It resembles that sector in its organizational and economic problems, but its ideological stance is very different. Neither the West nor the East has captured the imagination of the Third World. "The 'mix' in the Third World is ostensibly between *degrees of* (rather than *choices between*) capitalism and socialism at the economic level, and libertarianism and totalitarianism politically."[30] Yet they are not truly independent. They receive aid from the advanced nations, which have the power to set market prices paid for Third World raw materials as well as prices of goods imported by these nations. And while their formal systems of government are nearly always parliamentary and democratic, their real systems are almost without exception authoritarian.

[30] Horowitz, *Three Worlds of Development*, p. 3.

The Unevenness of Modernization

Quite aside from the tremendous and growing gap between the industrial, exporting, affluent nations and the underdeveloped nations of the world, modernization is an uneven process. Social change "moves ahead by a complicated leapfrog process, creating recurrent crises of adjustment. The first paradox of development, then, is that a developing society must change in all ways at once, but cannot conceivably plan such

Modernization is an uneven process having different rates of change in various aspects of the sociocultural order. *Gary Wolinsky/Stock, Boston.*

a regular, coordinated pattern of growth. A certain amount of social unrest is invariably created."[31]

The unevenness of modernization is apparent in the different rates of change in various aspects of the sociocultural order and in interruptions of various kinds. Neither continents nor nations develop as wholes, but geographic areas within them develop at different rates. Northern Italy around Milan, for example, is highly industrial. Southern Italy is backward, and many of its people migrate north and experience all the problems of immigrants. Almost invariably, agricultural productivity lags behind industrial productivity, and the peasants suffer most from the transition. This is especially apparent in the highly industrialized Soviet Union, with its backward agriculture. In 1960, there were 160 farm laborers to 100 factory workers.[32]

Post-Industrial Society

The concept of polar types may seem to imply that there is a point at which the members of a developing society may stop and say, "There! We did it! Now we are a modern society!" But continual change is even more characteristic of advanced industrial societies than of underdeveloped societies. Many observers say the United States is the first society to enter a post-industrial stage. How does it differ from the model of urban industrial society?

Where traditional society relied on muscle power and industrial society on mechanical power, post-industrial society relies on brain power multiplied by electronic means, such as computers. Capital and business enterprise are rapidly being replaced by scientific knowledge as the chief generator of wealth.

[31] Neil J. Smelser, "The Modernization of Social Relations," in Weiner, *Modernization*, pp. 110–121.
[32] Horowitz, *Three Worlds of Development*, p. 145.

This is especially apparent in the largest American ventures—aerospace, communications, and military development. The university "becomes an intensely involved think-tank, the source of much sustained political planning and social innovation and no longer a withdrawn ivory tower."[33]

Just as in the early phases of industrialization, many roles become obsolete in post-industrial societies. There is less demand for unskilled labor and even for specialized technicians. Knowledge changes so fast that even experienced workers may find themselves behind newer employees. Lower-level white-collar employees and middle management may be unable to compete with the speed, accuracy, and dependability of computers. There may ultimately be a three-class occupational structure of professionals, technicians, and service workers.[34]

Bureaucracy as we know it may disappear. When necessary, executives will call upon the diverse professional skills of relative strangers who will work on a specific problem. Children will not be taught the skills of simple recall demanded of clerks but will be educated for an unknown future. They must learn how to think, how to find out, and how to create new knowledge. Already there are organizations, such as consultant and research firms, that produce, process, and apply knowledge. Their rapid rise is seen as part of the promise that a society can guide its own future course.

Social Planning

Social change and social problems are closely related. Each can be seen as both cause and effect of the other. Social problems arise when social changes make different groups aware of conflicting values and interests. And many social changes result from attempts to resolve social problems, whether through peaceful or violent means, through established channels or collective behavior.

Very simply, a condition is considered to be a **social problem** when it has direct or indirect negative effects on a significant proportion of the population. Implicit in the definition of a social problem is the notion that there is a solution to the problem, that the conditions can be changed. There are several types of problems. One is deviant behavior perceived by significant numbers of people as a violation of cultural norms and values (drug addiction, for example). Another is the blockage or frustration of the personal goals of specific social categories of people within a social system (such as race discrimination). Threats to the continued organization and stability of the system itself (such as violent protest or the population explosion) are another type of social problem.

The perception of a social problem varies. For example, some define abortion as a social problem, while others see it as a solution of a personal problem and believe that anti-abortion laws constitute the real problem.[35] Some blame social problems on "evil" people, others on a "sick" or "evil" society. Still others attribute them to a number of factors that make for maladjustment among members of a group or among groups within a larger system. Fatalists believe nothing can be done about them. Activists believe something can and should be done.

---

[33] *The New York Times* (Jan. 6, 1969).

[34] Robert Perrucci and Marc Pilisuk, eds., *The Triple Revolution: Social Problems in Depth* (Boston: Little, Brown, 1968), p. 173.

[35] Robert K. Merton and Robert Nisbet list fifteen social problems in their text, *Contemporary Social Problems*, 3rd ed. (New York: Harcourt Brace Jovanovich, 1971): drug use, mental disorders, delinquency, organized crime, alcohol abuse, suicide, sexual deviance, population increase, race relations, family disorganization, work and automation, urban conflict, poverty, violence, and the youth revolution.

Sociologists take both theoretical and practical approaches to social problems. They see problems as laboratories for developing and testing theories about social structure and social psychology. Durkheim, in his study of suicide, and Thomas and Znaniecki, in their study of Polish immigrants to the United States, related social problems to the larger social changes of industrialism, secularism, urbanism, and individualism.[36] In a more directly practical vein, sociologists try to make clear what the costs and consequences of various problems are. They also look at the costs and consequences of alternative policies for dealing with these problems. They may recognize latent problems that might have serious consequences long before they become recognized as problems by significant numbers of people.

Planning Social Change

Most societies still play a passive role in change, struggling to adapt to changes. But the idea of planning is gaining ground. *Planning* is "the more or less efficient and foresightful devising of means to reach specified goals."[37] It involves choices of goals, predictions of likely or possible future states of affairs, and decisions on means.

Although private corporations plan many years ahead, only recently—and then only in piecemeal efforts—have Americans adopted planning in the public sector of national life. We have usually associated planning with rigid, totalitarian "Five-year Plans." We have believed instead in the goodness of spontaneous change as an essential part of the American Dream. At the opposite extreme is the policy of authoritarian intervention followed by Soviet central planners. Such planning involves little concern for the second-order consequences of means used to reach a goal. In the early years of Soviet modernization, for example, master plans were imposed from above with no effort to build consensus or to profit from feedback from the people. Such plans required large applications of power through coercion and control and invited massive resistance and alienation. The consequences were enormous waste of human, physical, and social resources and great oppression and suffering.[38]

Somewhere in the middle are the British, who have long been known for handling problems by "muddling through." This does not mean they disdain planning. Rather, they are keenly aware of the possible consequences of any course of action and of the impossibility of precise prediction. They prefer to proceed with great sensitivity to feedback and are disposed to change tactics when necessary.[39]

Most planning so far, says Alvin Toffler, has several shortcomings. It focuses on economic growth with technology as its primary tool. It is short-range (even 5 years is a very short time for real planning, and Americans tend to regard 1- and 2-year forecasts as "long-range" planning). It is controlled by bureaucrats and hence is undemocratic. Furthermore, it is essentially deterministic. It assumes that the framework is given, and plans must be made within it. Then as things get more and more out of control, people turn more and more to mysticism and nos-

[36] Emile Durkheim, *Suicide* (1897), J. A. Spaulding and G. Simpson, trans. (New York: The Free Press, 1951); and William I. Thomas and Florian Znaniecki, *The Polish Peasant in Europe and America* (Boston: Badger, 1920).

[37] Bob Ross, "Is Planning a Revolution?" in Steven E. Deutsch and John Howard, eds., *Where It's At: Radical Perspectives in Sociology* (New York: Harper & Row, 1970), p. 218.

[38] Warren Breed, *The Self-Guiding Society* (New York: The Free Press, 1971), p. 176.

[39] Raymond A. Bauer, ed., *Social Indicators* (Cambridge, Mass.: The M.I.T. Press, 1966), p. 7.

Planned communities, such as Columbia, Maryland, just outside of Washington, D.C., may represent more competent management and anticipation of change. *Wide World Photos.*

talgia in their disillusionment.[40] This inept, undemocratic, antihuman planning, Toffler argues, is not really planning at all. What we need is a new strategy, "social futurism," through which we can arrive at greater competence in managing change.

If we subscribe to the notion that we can to some extent "invent the future," we must be guided by some ideas about that future. *Prediction* identifies the most probable future state of affairs. *Anticipation* takes into account a broad range of possible outcomes in order to keep open more options than does prediction alone. Prediction and anticipation combined with imagination and social philosophy—ideas of what the future *should* or *should not* be like—play a role in guiding planning.

PREDICTION AND ANTICIPATION OF SOCIAL CHANGE   There are two main procedures for predicting the future (aside from crystal gazing, horoscope reading, and studying the entrails of chickens). One is *projection* of current trends into the future, assuming that they will go on indefinitely. Many such projections concentrate almost entirely on technology, depicting marvels of transportation and communication, housekeeping, and even baby producing. But the prediction of social trends is trickier in some ways. Population projections, for example, have often proven wrong. Trends do not necessarily continue. In the evolution of social systems, as in the evolution of plant and animal life, there are surprises.

[40]"The Strategy of Social Futurism," in Alvin Toffler, ed., *The Futurists* (New York: Random House, 1972), pp. 96–130.

449

The other important method of prediction is based on identifying *key patterns* of culture and social structure. De Tocqueville, for example, listed what he thought were the central features of American society in the early 1800s. He especially noted the trends toward economic and social equality and constructed a fairly accurate pattern of the future. Similarly, contemporary social scientists may identify key features of a future society and predict a number of other features that are likely to accompany them.

Simple prediction of the most probable state of affairs is not enough. We must also *anticipate* a broad range of possible outcomes so that we will be better able to deal with them in the event that they do occur.[41] Daniel Bell says we seek pre-vision "as much to 'halt' a future as to help it come into being. The function of prediction is not, as often stated, to aid social control, but to widen the spheres of moral choice. Without that normative commitment, the social sciences become a mere technology rather than humanistic discipline."[42]

CHOICE OF GOALS   One criterion of farsighted planning is to keep as many options open for the next generation as possible. This means that long-range plans cannot be too specific and detailed. It also means that they must be made with a keen sense of priorities and of consequences.

The members of society, especially those in charge of planning, must weigh priorities in determining their goals. They must also consider possible consequences of the means chosen for reaching those goals. We are forced to think, for example, about "the central issue of the politics of this generation"—the conflict between our wishes as private consumers and our concern with getting the best out of what we use collectively. We also see how the means we choose to fulfill some desire may actually frustrate us in achieving it, just as people fleeing the city have turned the countryside into urban sprawl.[43]

Who should decide on the goals? Not systems engineers and professional planners or political decision makers. They may have the "know-how" but not the "know-what," in Norbert Wiener's phrase.[44] They must be joined by humanists, artists, architects, and social scientists, who may form (and are forming, in various institutes) "unique coalitions of resources to serve man and society."

Approaches to Social Planning

INFORMATION   The essence of planning is the exchange of information through communication with continuous feedback about the success or failure of goal-directed efforts. Adaptive systems (amoebas, persons, groups, societies) continually process information from inside and outside the system in an attempt to adapt. In planning social changes, how can such information be made relevant and useful? How do we know if things are getting better or worse?

Assessment of actual and proposed changes and their perceived or predicted consequences can be made through a system of social accounting based on sets of social indicators, which serve as feedback. These indicators let the society know how well or badly it is doing in attaining its social goals. A **social indicator** is defined as a statistic that helps observers directly measure the

---

[41] Bauer, *Social Indicators*, pp. 17–18.

[42] Daniel Bell, "Twelve Modes of Prediction—A Preliminary Sorting of Approaches in the Social Sciences," in Warren G. Bennis, Kenneth D. Benne, and Robert Chin, eds., *The Planning of Change*, 2nd ed. (New York: Holt, Rinehart and Winston, 1969), pp. 532–552.

[43] Andrew Shonfield, "Thinking about the Future," *Encounter* (Feb. 1969).

[44] *The Human Use of Human Beings: Cybernetics and Society* (New York: Avon, 1967), p. 254.

welfare of the society and make judgments about conditions. Statistics on the number of doctors or policemen would not be social indicators, whereas figures on health or crime rates could be.[45] Social indicators, then, could allow comparisons of the state of affairs in different areas of concern, both over time and across societies and groups within a society. Let us take infant mortality as an example of how a social indicator might be used. Statistical information must be broken down by geographic regions and by racial and ethnic patterns before it can be analyzed. The analysis should then determine the factors needed to decrease the rate of infant mortality. These factors might include, for example, establishing more health facilities and increasing the number of trained medical personnel.

Many people suggest that a "Social Report" comparable to the Annual Economic Report be instituted. It might use such indicators of change as infant mortality, average weekly hours of work, labor force participation of women age 35–64, percentage of population illiterate, income of lowest fifth of population, or percentage of Gross National Product spent on health, education, and welfare. A Social Report would not be used for social control by government, any more than the Annual Economic Report is used to control industry and commerce. But it would inform the public, highlight issues, and suggest courses of action. It will take time, though, to work out the system of social accounting we need, especially to measure the qualitative aspects of life.[46]

USE OF THE COMPUTER Computer-happy systems engineers, says one observer, are not oriented to human beings in their construction of large-scale industrial, military, and space systems. In fact, they keep trying to lessen human responsibility. They set their goals and means more according to what their equipment is capable of doing than according to "the full moral, intellectual, and even physical requirements of mankind."[47]

Computers need not, however, be limited to such narrow use. Just as computers guide astronauts to the moon, they can be employed in guiding society toward its goals. The use of computers for public planning is only beginning to be explored. The Rand Institute, for example, is using computer-aided techniques to help New York City's government with some of its day-to-day problems.

The philosophy behind all efforts to plan and guide social change can be summed up in this way:

Harnessing societal energy is the societal equivalent of the physicists' harnessing of nuclear energy. Unleashed in an explosion, it becomes the most destructive force ever known. Released gradually and employed in men's service, it can change human life.[48]

Summary

Social change includes significant alterations in social organization, cultural definitions, and material products of sociocultural action.

There are various theories concerning the direction and pattern of change. Evolutionary theorists see people becoming ever better

[45] U.S. Department of Health, Education, and Welfare, *Toward a Social Report,* with Introductory Commentary by Wilbur J. Cohen (Ann Arbor: University of Michigan Press, 1970), p. 97.

[46] *Ibid.,* p. x.
[47] Robert Boguslaw, *The New Utopians: A Study of System Design and Social Change* (Englewood Cliffs, N.J.: Prentice-Hall, 1965), p. 6.
[48] Breed, *The Self-Guiding Society,* p. 7.

adjusted to the environment and gaining more control of sources of energy. Cyclical theories are stated in terms of pendulum swings between extremes, the rise and fall of societies, and the short-term ups and downs of self-exhausting trends. Modern systems theory sees social systems as adapting to change in an effort to restore equilibrium. Conflict theories see conflict, internal or external, as inevitable within systems. Some regard conflict as a creative source of change, others as the only possible means of change.

Several factors influence social change. Technological determinism holds that changes in material culture are the source of all other cultural and social changes, and that cultural lag occurs when adaptive changes in nonmaterial culture come too slowly. Knowledge, beliefs, and values powerfully influence the direction, rate, and consequences of change. The more complex the culture base, the more likely change is to occur through invention and to proceed rapidly. Most elements in any complex culture, however, have been introduced by the process of diffusion.

Modernization, the transition from traditional folk society to modern urban society, includes many changes that tend to occur together, the chief of which is industrialization. Modernization includes secularization of values, with an emphasis on science, rationality, skill, work, progress, and education.

Social organization changes. Political and economic units grow larger. Roles become more specialized, and complexity and interdependence increase. The class system becomes relatively open and mobile. The extended family declines in importance. The feeling of identity with the local community diminishes.

Traditional people are typically identified with family and community. They are fatal-istic, authoritarian, and lacking in empathy and imagination. Modern people are urban, literate, educated for a specialized occupation, and dependent on formal agencies for many services. They are activist, adaptable, rational, and organized. They have faith in science and technology. Their self-conceptions are based more on achievement and experience than on ascribed status.

The gap between affluent developed societies and underdeveloped ones is growing. This inequality may be the most serious challenge to the human race. Underdeveloped nations are full of "transitional people," newly aware of their poverty and inclined to blame the social order rather than themselves for their difficulties.

The nations of the earth are often thought of as divided into three general categories according to their patterns of historical development, their stage of industrialization, and their forms of government. The West includes advanced industrialized nations. The East is also advanced industrially, but tends to be authoritarian. The Third World has gone from colonialism to nationhood largely since World War II. The process of modernization is uneven not only among nations but also within nations.

Social change may create problems, which in turn may create a demand for further change.

Planning for guided change involves the choice of goals and means, as well as prediction and anticipation. Those who accept the need for planning assume that peaceful change is preferable to violent change. They understand that social systems are complex and interdependent and that error is inherent in the action of systems. They believe that things do not usually improve spontaneously.

Those planners who think of a society as a complex adaptive system see informa-

79379 HOCHSTEDLER KEVIN P

GLOBE 5081

PRINTED IN U.S.A.

tion, in the form of social indicators, as essential. Computer analysis holds promise of handling the numerous variables involved in projecting trends into the future and predicting the consequences of alternative choices and decisions. Such planning may be seen as "harnessing societal energy."

Glossary

Diffusion The process by which culture traits and patterns spread from one society or group to another.

Modernization The transition from traditional folk society to urban industrial society.

Secularization A shift from sacred to worldly values.

Social change Significant alterations in social structure, in cultural definitions, and in the material products of sociocultural action.

Social indicator A statistic that helps observers directly measure the welfare of a society and make judgments about conditions.

Social problem A condition that has negative effects on a significant portion of a population and is regarded as demanding a solution.

Bibliography

chapter 1
The Study of Society

BOULDING, KENNETH, *The Meaning of the Twentieth Century: The Great Transition* (New York: Harper & Row, Publishers, 1964). Especially chap 2, "Science as the Basis of the Great Transition."

GOULDNER, ALVIN W., *The Coming Crisis of Western Sociology* (New York: Avon Books, 1970). For those who want to go more deeply into the history of sociological theory and the trends and prospects of the discipline.

Knowledge into Action: Improving the Nation's Use of the Social Sciences. Report of the Special Commission on the Social Sciences of the National Science Board, National Science Foundation (Washington, D.C.: U.S. Government Printing Office, 1969). Recommendations for practical applications of social science.

LYND, ROBERT, *Knowledge for What? The Place of Social Science in American Culture* (Princeton, N.J.: Princeton University Press, 1948). One of the most eloquent arguments against the idea that social science can be value-free.

MILLS, C. WRIGHT, *The Sociological Imagination* (New York: Grove Press, 1959). Provocative.

REDFIELD, ROBERT, *The Social Uses of Social Science: The Papers of Robert Redfield*, ed. Margaret Park Redfield (Chicago: University of Chicago Press, 1963). "Social science justifies itself to the extent to which it makes life comprehensible and significant."

STEIN, MAURICE, and VIDICH, ARTHUR, eds., *Sociology on Trial* (Englewood Cliffs, N.J.: Prentice-Hall, Inc., 1963). "A sociology of sociology by sociologists," arguing for the importance of the role of social critic.

chapter 2
The Conduct of Social Inquiry

BATTEN, THELMA F., *Reasoning and Research: A Guide for Social Science Methods* (Boston: Little, Brown and Company, 1971). Text and exercises designed to help a student evaluate evidence.

BLUMER, HERBERT, *Symbolic Interactionism: Perspective and Method* (Englewood Cliffs, N.J.: Prentice-Hall, Inc., 1969). A lucid exposition of the value of a humanist, qualitative approach to sociological research.

BRUYN, SEVERYN T., *The Human Perspective in Sociology: The Methodology of Participant Observation* (Englewood Cliffs, N.J.: Prentice-Hall, Inc., 1966). Since an empirical science must respect the nature of its subject matter, sociology must study human behavior by appropriate methods rather than by trying to emulate the physical sciences slavishly.

CAMERON, WILLIAM BRUCE, *Informal Sociology: A Casual Introduction to Sociological Thinking* (New York: Random House, Inc., 1963). Especially five informal essays on "Theory and Methods," pp. 3–66.

FILSTEAD, WILLIAM J., ed., *Qualitative Methodology: Firsthand Involvement with the Social World* (Chicago: Markham Publishing Co., 1970). The author intends "to provoke those who measure everything and understand nothing."

HAMMOND, PHILLIP E., ed., *Sociologists at Work: Essays on the Craft of Social Research* (Garden City, N.Y.: Doubleday & Company, Inc., Anchor Books, 1967). Sociologists tell how actual research projects were conducted. Anecdotal and fascinating as a supplement to a study of methods.

SMITH, HERMAN, *Strategies of Social Research* (Englewood Cliffs, N.J.: Prentice-Hall, Inc., 1976). A standard text surveying social research methods.

chapter 3
Culture

BOWEN, ELENORE SMITH (pseud.), *Return to Laughter* (Garden City, N.Y.: Doubleday, 1964). An engrossing not-so-fictional account of the experiences of the author, whose real name is Laura Bohannon, in a Nigerian tribe.

CARROLL, JOHN B., ed., *Language, Thought, and Reality: Selected Writings of Benjamin Lee Whorf* (Cambridge, Mass.: M.I.T. Press, 1956). Essays by a recognized authority on language.

HAYS, H. R., *From Ape to Angel: An Informal History of Social Anthropology* (New York: Alfred A. Knopf, 1965). A breezy account of various social anthropologists and schools of thought.

HOWELLS, WILLIAM, *Mankind in the Making*, rev. ed. (Garden City, N.Y.: Doubleday, 1967). Subtitled *The Story of Human Evolution*, this book is well written and witty.

KLAPP, ORRIN E., *Collective Search for Identity* (New York: Holt, Rinehart & Winston, 1969). Especially chap. 4, "The Language of Ritual."

KLUCKHOHN, CLYDE, *Mirror for Man* (New York: Fawcett World Library, 1964). A highly readable and reliable introduction to anthropology, written for the layman and specialist.

KLUCKHOHN, FLORENCE ROCKWOOD, "Dominant and Variant Value Orientations," in James Fadiman, ed., *The Proper Study of Man* (New York: Macmillan, 1971).

LERNER, MAX, *America as a Civilization* (New York: Simon and Schuster, 1957). Especially chap. 9, "Character and Society."

LINTON, RALPH, *The Study of Man* (New York: Appleton-Century-Crofts, 1936). A classic of anthropology. Paperback edition, 1964.

MEANS, RICHARD L., *The Ethical Imperative: The Crisis in American Values* (Garden City, N.Y.: Doubleday, 1970). An effort to develop an objective theory of values in relation to social problems.

PFEIFFER, JOHN, E., *The Emergence of Man* (New York: Harper & Row, 1969). Well written, well illustrated, comprehensive.

POWDERMAKER, HORTENSE, *Stranger and Friend: The Way of an Anthropologist* (New York: W. W. Norton, 1966). A fascinating account of how the author came to be an anthropologist, and of her fieldwork experiences in Lesu, Mississippi, Hollywood, and Rhodesia.

REICH, CHARLES A., *The Greening of America* (New York: Random House, 1970). A popular book predicting that changes in values will bring about a social revolution.

ROSZAK, THEODORE, *The Making of a Counter Culture* (Garden City, N.Y.: Doubleday, Anchor, 1969). Shows how some thinkers have called into question the conventional scientific world view—"the myth of objective consciousness"—and undermined the foundations of technology-dominated society.

VOGT, EVON Z., and ALBERT, ETHEL M., eds., *People of Rimrock: A Study of Values in Five Cultures* (Cambridge: Harvard University Press, 1966). A report on five neighboring communities in western New Mexico: Navaho and Zuñi Indians, Mormons, Texan homesteaders, and Spanish-Americans.

WILLIAMS, ROBIN M., JR., *American Society: A Sociological Interpretation*, 3rd ed. (New York: Alfred A. Knopf, 1970). Chap. 11, "Values in American Society," is an excellent discussion at far greater length than the one in this chapter, which is based in part on Williams' analysis.

chapter 4
The Importance of Culture

FOSTER, GEORGE M., *Traditional Cultures and the Impact of Technological Change* (New York: Harper & Row, 1962). This fascinating account of induced change vividly points up the importance of understanding culture.

FRIED, MORTON H., *Readings in Anthropology, Vol. II: Cultural Anthropology*, 2nd ed. (New York: Thomas Y. Crowell, 1968). Especially the first four selections and the section on culture and personality.

GOODMAN, MARY ELLEN, *The Individual and Culture* (Homewood, Illinois: The Dorsey Press, 1967). Comparisons of cultural attitudes toward the individual, and of the effects of various cultures on personality.

HALL, EDWARD, *The Hidden Dimension* (Garden City, N.Y.: Doubleday, Anchor, 1969). Brief but fascinating account of cultural differences stressing such nonverbal aspects as the uses of space.

HALL, EDWARD T., *The Silent Language* (Greenwich, Conn.: Fawcett, 1959). Written in readable and amusing style, this book describes nonverbal patterns of behavior as barriers to cross-cultural understanding.

HERSKOVITS, MELVILLE, JR., *Man and His Works* (New York: Alfred A. Knopf, 1948). See chap. 5, "The Problem of Cultural Relativism."

JENNINGS, JESSE D., and HOEBEL, E. ADAMSON, *Readings in Anthropology,* 2nd ed. (New York: McGraw-Hill, 1956). Part 10, "Applied Anthropology," contains several interesting readings. Reading No. 40 is Horace Miner's delightful "Body Ritual Among the Nacirema."

KLUCKHOHN, CLYDE, *Mirror for Man* (New York: Fawcett World Library, 1964). Especially valuable in counteracting ethnocentrism are chaps. 1, 2, 9, and 10.

LEE, DOROTHY, ed., *Freedom and Culture* (Englewood Cliffs, N.J.: Prentice-Hall, 1959). Unusually provocative essays, including several on the relationship of language to ways of life and thought.

LINTON, RALPH, *The Cultural Background of Personality* (New York: Appleton-Century, 1945). A small classic by a towering figure in anthropology.

WESTIN, ALAN F., FRANKLIN, JULIAN H., SWEARER, HOWARD R., and SIGMUND, PAUL E. eds., *Views of America* (New York: Harcourt Brace Jovanovich, Inc., 1966). Views from Western Europe, the Communist world, and the developing nations.

chapter 5
Socialization

BECKER, HOWARD S., GEER, BLANCHE, HUGHES, EVERETT C., and STRAUSS, ANSELM *Boys in White: Student Culture in Medical School* (Chicago: University of Chicago Press, 1961). A study of occupational socialization.

BENEDICT, RUTH, *Patterns of Culture* (New York: Penguin Books, 1946). A classic comparison of the modal personality types of several cultures.

BLUMER, HERBERT, *Symbolic Interactionism: Perspective and Method* (Englewood Cliffs, N.J.: Prentice-Hall, Inc., 1969). Essays on symbolic interactionist theory by one of its outstanding proponents.

BRONFENBRENNER, URIE, *Two Worlds of Childhood: U.S. and U.S.S.R.* (New York: Russell Sage Foundation, 1970), with the assistance of John C. Condry, Jr. A challenging comparison of two systems of socialization.

CLAUSEN, JOHN, *Socialization and Society* (Boston: Little Brown, 1969). Especially chapters 1–4.

ERIKSON, ERIK H., *Childhood and Society* (New York: W. W. Norton, 1950). A neo-Freudian view of socialization.

——, *Identity: Youth and Crisis* (New York: W. W. Norton, 1968). The life cycle theory, with special emphasis on the identity crisis of adolescence.

GORDON, CHAD, and GERGEN, KENNETH H., eds., *The Self in Social Interaction* (New York: John Wiley & Sons, 1968). Vol. 1, *Classic and Contemporary Perspectives,* includes readings from many of the theorists mentioned in this chapter.

KESSEN, WILLIAM, *Childhood in China* (New Haven: Yale University Press, 1975). Based on only a brief period of observation but very well done.

LEVINE, ROBERT, *Culture, Behavior, and Personality* (Chicago: Aldine, 1973). An excellent overview of the general literature on socialization.

LINTON, RALPH, *The Cultural Background of Personality* (New York: Appleton-Century-Crofts, 1945). An excellent assessment of the relationship of culture, society, and personality.

MAY, ROLLO, *Man's Search for Himself* (New York: W. W. Norton & Company, Inc., 1953). A humanist psychologist's richly suggestive discussion of the experience of becoming a person.

MEAD, GEORGE HERBERT, *Mind, Self, and Society,* Charles W. Morris, ed. (Chicago: University of Chicago Press, 1934). The landmark presentation of symbolic interactionist theory.

MEAD, MARGARET, *Sex and Temperament in Three Primitive Societies* (New York: New American Library, 1950). Demonstrates the importance of cultural definitions of male and female roles in shaping personality.

ROSOW, IRVING, *Socialization to Old Age* (Berkeley: University of California Press, 1975). Analysis of change in self-image in the later years of life.

SPITZER, STEPHAN P., ed., *The Sociology of Personality: An Enduring Problem in Psychology* (New York: Van Nostrand Reinhold, 1969). Especially readings 4, 5, 12, and 13.

chapter 6
Deviance and Social Control

BECKER, HOWARD, ed., *The Other Side: Perspectives on Deviance* (New York: The Free Press of Glencoe, 1964). Provocative readings, including some that argue that deviance plays a positive role in society.

COHEN, ALBERT, *Deviance and Control* (Englewood Cliffs, N.J.: Prentice-Hall, Inc., 1966). Succinct discussion of deviance; especially useful on the functions of deviance.

CRESSEY, DONALD R., and WARD, DAVID A., *Delinquency, Crime, and Social Process* (New York: Harper & Row, 1969). The statistical distribution of criminal and delinquent behavior in time and space; and the process by which individuals come to engage in such behavior.

DINITZ, SIMON, DYNES, RUSSELL R., and CLARKE, ALFRED C., *Deviance: Studies in the Process of Stigmatization and Societal Reaction* (New York: Oxford University Press, 1969). Selected articles on every major aspect of deviance, illustrating recent critical issues.

DOUGLAS, JACK D., ed., *Observations of Deviance* (New York: Random House, 1970). Insights into deviant styles and ways of life.

DRAPKIN, ISRAEL, and VIANO, EMILIO, *Victimology* (Lexington, Mass.: Heath, 1974). Discusses the effects of deviance on victims and the contributions of victims to their victimization.

KIESLER, CHARLES A., and KIESLER, SARA B., *Conformity* (Reading, Mass.: Addison-Wesley Publishing Company, 1969). A small book on conformity—what it means and when it happens, distinguishing between compliance and private acceptance.

LEMERT, EDWIN M., *Human Deviance, Social Problems, and Social Control* (Englewood Cliffs, N.J.: Prentice-Hall, Inc., 1967). Describes the process of becoming "a deviant."

MASLOW, ABRAHAM H., *Toward a Psychology of Being,* 2nd ed. (New York: Van Nostrand Reinhold, 1968). "This book is unmistakably a normative social psychology. That is, it accepts the search for values as one of the essential and feasible tasks of a science of society."

MATZA, DAVID, *Becoming Deviant* (Englewood Cliffs, N.J.: Prentice-Hall, Inc., 1969). A short book discussing the process of becoming deviant and the importance of labeling.

QUINNEY, RICHARD, *The Social Reality of Crime* (Boston: Little, Brown, 1970). Develops the conflict perspective on deviance.

RUBINGTON, EARL, and WEINBERG, MARTIN S., *Deviance: The Interactionist Perspective* (New York: Macmillan, 1968). A collection of readings that "makes sense of deviance as somehow being both product and process of social interaction," and discusses the conditions under which deviance emerges, develops, and changes over time. Stresses the importance of social perceptions and definitions of deviance.

SCHEFF, THOMAS J., ed., *Mental Illness and Social Processes* (New York: Harper & Row, 1967). Stresses the social reaction to mental illness—that is, the recurring patterns of behavior among individuals and organizations attempting to cope with persons who are defined as mentally ill.

SCHUR, EDWIN, *Labeling Deviant Behavior* (New York: Harper, 1971). Concise presentation of the labeling perspective.

SCHUR, EDWIN M., *Our Criminal Society: The Social and Legal Sources of Crime in America* (Englewood Cliffs, N.J.: Prentice-Hall, Inc., 1969). Concerned with issues of public policy; also provides a systematic review of key findings and theories about crime.

SHERIF, MUZAFER, *The Psychology of Social Norms* (New York: Harper Torchbooks, 1964). A full discussion of the classic experiment discussed in this chapter, the theory behind it, and its implications.

SHORT, JAMES F., JR., ed., *Gang Delinquency and Delinquent Subcultures* (New York: Harper & Row, 1968). Emphasizes empirical research and its vital and creative interplay with theory.

chapter 7
Social Interaction and Social Structure

BANTON, MICHAEL, *Roles: An Introduction to the Study of Social Relations* (New York: Basic Books, 1965). A highly readable book, with a somewhat different definition of status and role from ours.

BUCKLEY, WALTER, *Sociology and Modern Systems Theory* (Englewood Cliffs, N.J.: Prentice-Hall, Inc., 1967). "An exploratory sketch of a revolutionary scientific perspective and conceptual framework as it might be applied to the socio-cultural system."

COSER, LEWIS A., *Continuities in the Study of Social Conflict* (New York: The Free Press, 1967). The functions and dysfunctions of conflict; theories of conflict and their applications to current politics.

GOFFMAN, ERVING, *Interaction Ritual: Essays in Face-to-Face Behavior* (Chicago: Aldine, 1967). The study of face-to-face interaction in natural settings, using a "drama" analogy.

GREER, SCOTT A., *Social Organization* (Garden City, N.Y.: Doubleday, 1955). A small classic.

LINTON, RALPH, *The Study of Man* (New York: Appleton-Century-Crofts, 1936). Chapter VIII, "Status and Role," is a classic statement on the subject. Reprinted in Schuler *et al.*, *Readings in Sociology*, 4th ed., selection 22.

LYMAN, STANFORD M., and MARVIN B. SCOTT, *A Sociology of the Absurd* (New York: Appleton-Century-Crofts, 1970). Based on the idea that the individual, trying to make sense of a meaningless world, should be the central concern of sociology.

MEAD, MARGARET, ed., *Cooperation and Competition Among Primitive Peoples*, rev. ed. (Boston: Beacon Press, 1961). A comparison of thirteen cultures, with emphasis on social structure and personality.

chapter 8
Social Groups

BELL, GERALD D., ed., *Organizations and Human Behavior: A Book of Readings* (Englewood Cliffs, N.J.: Prentice-Hall, Inc., 1967). Readings 4, 7–13, 16, and 17.

CARTWRIGHT, DORWIN, and ZANDER, ALVIN, *Group Dynamics: Research and Theory, 3rd ed.* (New York: Harper & Row, 1968). A collection of 42 readings.

ETZIONI, AMITAI, *Modern Organizations* (Englewood Cliffs, N.J.: Prentice-Hall, Inc., 1964). Special emphasis on structure of organizations.

GREER, SCOTT A., *Social Organization* (Garden City, N.Y.: Doubleday, 1955). Also useful for this chapter.

HARE, A. PAUL, BORGATTA, EDGAR F., and BALES, ROBERT F., eds., *Small Groups: Studies in Social Interaction*, rev. ed. (New York: Alfred A. Knopf, 1966). Collection of readings.

HOMANS, GEORGE CASPAR, *Social Behavior: Its Ele-mentary Forms* (New York: Harcourt, Brace & World, 1961). Defines elementary social behavior as "the face-to-face contact between individuals, in which the reward each gets from the behavior of the others is relatively direct and immediate."

MILLS, THEODORE M., *The Sociology of Small Groups* (Englewood Cliffs, N.J.: Prentice-Hall, Inc., 1967). Emphasizes ways of thinking about groups rather than current research findings.

OLMSTED, MICHAEL S., *The Small Group* (New York: Random House, 1959). Good descriptions of various classic studies of small groups, and some theoretical observations.

chapter 9
Social Stratification

BENDIX, REINHARD, and LIPSET, SEYMOUR MARTIN, eds., *Class, Status, and Power: Social Stratification in Comparative Perspective*, 2nd ed. (New York: The Free Press, 1966). A huge and important book of readings.

BLAU, PETER, and DUNCAN, OTIS DUDLEY, *The American Occupational Structure* (New York: Wiley, 1967). Classic work which transformed the study of social mobility into a study of the factors affecting status attainment.

COLEMAN, RICHARD P., and NEUGARTEN, BERNICE L., *Social Status in the City* (San Francisco: Jossey-Bass, 1971). A study of Kansas City using both evaluated participation techniques and more objective indices.

DOMHOFF, G. WILLIAM, *Who Rules America?* (Englewood Cliffs, N.J.: Prentice-Hall, Inc., 1967). Concludes that even though America is a democracy, it does have a governing class.

FERMAN, LOUIS A., KORNBLUH, JOYCE L., and HABER, ALAN, *Poverty in America*, rev. ed. (Ann Arbor: The University of Michigan Press, 1968). A comprehensive anthology with an introduction by Michael Harrington.

FICKER, VICTOR B., and GRAVES, HERBERT S., *Deprivation in America* (Beverly Hills, Calif.: Glencoe Press, 1971). This slim volume portrays vividly the housing, health, education, hunger, and hopelessness of the poor.

HARRINGTON, MICHAEL, *The Other America: Poverty in the United States* (Baltimore: Penguin Books, 1963). The angry book that helped spark the "war on poverty."

HOWE, LOUISE KAPP, ed., *The White Majority: Be-*

tween Poverty and Affluence (New York: Random House, Vintage Books, 1970). Readings about "average Americans" of the white lower-middle and working classes, based on the belief that they are stereotyped and misunderstood by the higher classes.

LEWIS, OSCAR, *A Death in the Sánchez Family* (New York: Random House, 1969); *La Vida: A Puerto Rican Family in the Culture of Poverty—San Juan and New York* (New York: Random House, 1965); and *The Children of Sánchez* (New York: Random House, 1961). Horowitz says Lewis fuses "the art of biography, the insight of history, and the facts of society."

MATRAS, JUDAH, *Social Inequality, Stratification, and Mobility* (Englewood Cliffs, N.J.: Prentice-Hall, Inc., 1976). Excellent overview of both theory and empirical work in stratification and mobility.

MILLER, HERMAN P., *Rich Man, Poor Man*, 2nd ed. (New York: Thomas Y. Crowell, 1971). An authoritative survey of economic distribution in the United States by a Census Bureau expert.

ROACH, JACK L., GROSS, LLEWELLYN, and GURSSLIN, ORVILLE R., *Social Stratification in the United States* (Englewood Cliffs, N.J.: Prentice-Hall, Inc., 1969). Survey and critique of sociological writing on stratification in the United States, especially since 1950. Theory, methodology, and empirical reports.

TUMIN, MELVIN M., *Social Stratification: The Forms and Functions of Inequality* (Englewood Cliffs, N.J.: Prentice-Hall, Inc., 1967). An excellent text, plus social commentary.

chapter 10
Minorities and Intergroup Relations

ANDERSON, CHARLES, *White Protestant Americans: From National Origins to Religious Groups* (Englewood Cliffs, N.J.: Prentice-Hall, Inc., 1970). One of the excellent books in the "Ethnic Groups in American Life" series edited by Milton Gordon. Others are listed below.

BLAUNER, ROBERT, *Racial Oppression in America* (New York: Harper & Row, 1972). Develops the concept of internal colonialism.

FRANKLIN, JOHN HOPE, *From Slavery to Freedom: A History of Negro Americans*, 3rd ed. (New York: Alfred A. Knopf, 1967). By a leading black historian.

GLOCK, CHARLES Y., and SIEGELMAN, ELLEN, eds., *Prejudice U.S.A.* (New York: Frederick A. Praeger, 1969). Based on the premise that the greatest promise for reducing prejudice and discrimination lies with schools, churches, mass media, industry and labor, and governmental agencies.

GORDON, MILTON, *Assimilation in American Life: The Role of Race, Religion, and National Origins* (New York: Oxford University Press, 1964). Advances the theory of structural pluralism as a basic element of our social structure.

GREELEY, ANDREW, *Ethnicity in the United States* (New York: Wiley, 1974). Very useful for basic concepts and historical background.

KILLIAN, LEWIS, *The Impossible Revolution* (New York: Random House, 1968). Traces the development (and subsequent decline) of black protest.

KITANO, HARRY H. L., *Japanese Americans: The Evolution of a Subculture* (Englewood Cliffs, N.J.: Prentice-Hall, Inc., 1969). The author calls this book a success story with all the elements of melodrama.

KNOWLES, LOUIS L., and PREWITT, KENNETH, eds., *Institutional Racism in America* (Englewood Cliffs, N.J.: Prentice-Hall, Inc., 1969). Pursues the theme of the Kerner Report that white racism is at the root of interracial conflict.

MOORE, JOAN, *Mexican Americans*, Second edition (Englewood Cliffs, N.J.: Prentice-Hall, Inc., 1976). Excellent overview and sociological analysis of a minority group.

NEWMAN, WILLIAM, *American Pluralism* (New York: Harper & Row, 1973). Focuses on social exchange, including direct conflict, between ethnic groups and its consequences for society.

OSOFSKY, GILBERT, *The Burden of Race: A Documentary History of Negro-White Relations in America* (New York: Harper & Row, 1967). Documents with interpretation.

PINKNEY, ALPHONSO, *Black Americans* (Englewood Cliffs, N.J.: Prentice-Hall, Inc., 1969). Can a society that prefers piecemeal reform avoid increased racial conflict? The author's prognosis is not favorable.

ROSE, PETER I., ed., *The Ghetto and Beyond: Essays on Jewish Life in America* (New York: Random House, 1969). A stimulating collection of readings.

WILLIAMS, ROBIN M., JR., *Strangers Next Door: Ethnic Relations in American Communities* (Englewood Cliffs, N.J.: Prentice-Hall, Inc., 1964). In collaboration with John P. Dean and Edward A. Suchman. Demonstrates that tension and conflict grow out of established social structures and practices—not from irrational individual attitudes alone.

WOODWARD, C. VANN, *The Strange Career of Jim Crow,* rev. ed. (London: Oxford University Press, 1966). Focuses on the history of physical segregation and does not attempt to treat all types of racial discrimination and injustice.

chapter 11
Sex Roles

CHAFETZ, JANET SALTZMAN, *Masculine/Feminine or Human?* (Itasca, Ill., F. E. Peacock, 1974). Brief overview on the sociology of sex roles.

CHESLER, PHYLLIS, *Women and Madness* (Garden City, N.Y.: Doubleday, 1972). Analysis on women and mental illness.

FARRELL, WARREN, *The Liberated Man* (New York: Random House, 1974) Discusses sexism with men as the point of reference, analyzing the problems that arise from men internalizing the masculine stereotype.

HUTT, CORINNE, *Males & Females* (Baltimore: Penguin Books, 1972). Concise summary of the biological bases of sex differences.

MACCOBY, ELEANOR and JACKLIN, CAROL *Psychology of Sex Differences* (Stanford, Calif: Stanford University Press, 1974). Thorough coverage of empirical findings on individual differences between males and females. Excellent bibliography.

PLECK, JOSEPH and SAWYER, JACK eds., *Men and Masculinity* (Englewood Cliffs, N.J., 1974). A social psychology of the male role, which is seen as overly restrictive.

ROSSI, ALICE ed., *The Feminist Papers* (New York, Columbia University Press, 1973). Useful background on the American's women's movement in the last century.

SAFILIOS-ROTHSCHILD, CONSTANTINA, *Love, Sex, and Sex Roles* (Englewood Cliffs, N.J., Prentice-Hall, Inc., 1977). Excellent discussion of changing sex roles.

chapter 12
Population and Ecology

CAMPBELL, REX R., and WADE, JERRY L., eds., *Society and Environment: The Coming Collision* (Boston: Allyn and Bacon, 1972). Fifty-four classic articles on ecology.

COMMONER, BARRY, *Science and Survival* (New York: Viking, 1966). By one of the first to sound the alarm.

DE BELL, GARRETT, ed., *The Environmental Handbook* (New York: Ballantine/Friends of the Earth, 1970). Prepared for the first environmental teach-in.

DISCH, ROBERT, ed., *The Ecological Conscience: Values for Survival* (Englewood Cliffs, N.J.: Prentice-Hall, Inc., 1970). Argues that the environmental crisis is potentially lethal because it can only be met through levels of international cooperation unknown to world history.

EHRLICH, PAUL R. and ANNE H., *Population, Resources, Environment: Issues in Human Ecology* (San Francisco: W. H. Freeman, 1970). A hard-hitting book about "the damage being done by overpopulation and overdevelopment to the only life-supporting planet we know." Intended not merely to frighten or discourage, but to inform and convince readers about the elements and dimensions of the crisis.

HARTLEY, SHIRLEY FOSTER, *Population: Quantity vs. Quality* (Englewood Cliffs, N.J.: Prentice-Hall, Inc., 1972). A well-written "sociological examination of the causes and consequences of the population explosion."

HAUSER, PHILIP M., ed., *The Population Dilemma,* 2nd ed. (Englewood Cliffs, N.J.: Prentice-Hall, Inc., 1969). For the American Assembly of Columbia University. Sets forth "the key population facts, the major problems being generated by accelerating growth, the basic policy issues, and the more important policy and action alternatives."

HEER, DAVID M., *Society and Population,* 2nd ed. (Englewood Cliffs, N.J.: Prentice-Hall, Inc., 1975). "This book is intended to reveal some of the ways in which an understanding of population is important to a proper study of sociology, and to help explain the causes and effects of the current population explosion."

Population and the American Future (New York: New American Library, 1972). Report of the President's Commission on Population Growth and the American Future, emphasizing that unbridled growth multiplies problems of all kinds and impairs the quality of life.

REVELLE, ROGER, and LANDSBERG, HANS H., eds., *America's Changing Environment* (Boston: Beacon, 1970). A book about decision-making on environmental problems; sees ecology as an ethical science concerned with politics.

SHEPARD, PAUL, and McKINLEY, DANIEL, eds. *The Subversive Science: Essays Toward an Ecology of Man* (Boston: Houghton Mifflin, 1969). An excellent anthology.

SWATEK, PAUL, *The User's Guide to the Protection of the Environment* (New York: Ballantine/ Friends of the Earth, 1971). The subtitle, "the indispensable guide to making every purchase count," indicates how life styles may be changed to harmonize with the ecological conscience.

U.S. BUREAU OF THE CENSUS, *Statistical Abstract of the United States, 1976* (Washington, D.C.: U.S. Government Printing Office, 1976). Issued yearly. Highly useful reference.

chapter 13
Urban Life

ABRAHAMSON, MARK, *Urban Sociology* (Englewood Cliffs, N.J.: Prentice-Hall, Inc., 1976). Fairly concise but comprehensive survey of urban sociology.

BREESE, GERALD, ed., *The City in Newly Developing Countries: Readings on Urbanism and Urbanization* (Englewood Cliffs, N.J.: Prentice-Hall, Inc., 1969). Readings to accompany the editor's introductory book, below.

———, *Urbanization in Newly Developing Countries* (Englewood Cliffs, N.J.: Prentice-Hall, Inc., 1966). A vividly written exploratory discussion of the subject.

ELIAS, C. E., JR., GILLIES, JAMES, and RIEMER, SVEND, eds., *Metropolis: Values in Conflict* (Belmont, Calif.: Wadsworth, 1964). Provocative readings, some representing opposed viewpoints.

FAVA, SYLVIA FLEIS, ed., *Urbanism in World Perspective: A Reader* (New York: Thomas Y. Crowell, 1968). An excellent selection of readings on urban theory, housing, ecology, social organization, and the social psychology of urban life, in cross-cultural perspective.

FISCHER, CLAUDE, *The Urban Experience* (New York: Harcourt, Brace, Jovanovich, 1976). Excellent analysis of the contemporary urban situation.

GANS, HERBERT J., *The Levittowners* (New York: Random House, 1967). Report on two years of participant observation in a new suburb.

GREEN, CONSTANCE McLAUGHLIN, *The Rise of Urban America* (New York: Harper & Row, 1965). Urban development in the United States from colonial days to the 1960s; concise, sprightly, and clear.

GREER, SCOTT, *Governing the Metropolis* (New York: John Wiley, 1962). Lucidly written. Part I, "The Creation of a Metropolitan World," is especially pertinent to this chapter.

HALPERN, JOEL M., *The Changing Village Community* (Englewood Cliffs, N.J.: Prentice-Hall, Inc., 1967). General ideas about contemporary change in rural areas, with concrete examples of changes in village communities throughout the world.

JACOBS, PAUL, *Prelude to Riot: A View of Urban America from the Bottom* (New York: Random House, Vintage Books, 1967). About the relationships between the government and the minority poor in Los Angeles.

MUMFORD, LEWIS, *The Culture of Cities* (New York: Harcourt Brace Jovanovich, Inc., 1938). A classic.

TAYLOR, LEE, and JONES, JR., ARTHUR R., *Rural Life and Urbanized Society* (New York: Oxford University Press, 1964). The theme: that in the United States both rural and urban residents live in relation to the same pattern of social organization.

chapter 14
The Family

ADAMS, BERT N., *The American Family: A Sociological Interpretation* (Chicago: Markham, 1971). A theoretical monograph as well as an introductory text and a series of essays on the family, focusing on the American family.

BILLINGSLEY, ANDREW, *Black Families in White America* (Englewood Cliffs, N.J.: Prentice-Hall, Inc., 1968). The central theme is that the black family can best be understood as a varied and complex institution in the black community and white society.

CUBER, JOHN and HARROFF, PEGGY, *Sex and the Significant Americans* (Baltimore: Penguin Books, 1965). Discusses family patterns and dynamics in the upper-middle-class.

GEIGER, H. KENT, ed., *Comparative Perspectives on Marriage and the Family* (Boston: Little, Brown, 1968). A valuable little book drawing on Israel, Japan, China, and other societies for a comparative view of many issues in the sociology of the family.

GOODE, WILLIAM J., *The Family* (Englewood Cliffs, N.J.: Prentice-Hall, Inc., 1964). A short introduction showing "the fruitfulness of sociological theory when applied to family relations."

————, *World Revolution and Family Patterns* (New York: The Free Press of Glencoe, 1963). Modernization and the family. Demonstrates how the family changes in response to changes in other institutions *and* how other institutions are influenced by changes in the family.

KEPHARDT, WILLIAM, *Extraordinary Groups* (New York: St. Martins, 1976). Good discussion of alternative forms, including communes.

KOMAROVSKY, MIRRA, *Dilemmas of Masculinity* (New York: W. W. Norton, 1976). On the changing roles of men and women.

————, *Blue-Collar Marriage* (New York: Random House, 1964). Working-class contrasted with middle-class marriages.

LESLIE, GERALD R., *The Family in Social Context* (New York: Oxford University Press, 1967). A well-written introductory text.

LOPATA, HELENA, *Occupation Housewife,* (London, Oxford University Press, 1971). Excellent discussion of family roles in the 1950s and 1960s.

REISS, IRA L., *The Family System in America* (New York: Holt, Rinehart & Winston, 1976). Carefully documented generalizations.

SCANZONI, JOHN, *Sexual Bargaining* (Englewood Cliffs, N.J., Prentice-Hall, Inc., 1972). Analyzes male-female reward-seeking, reciprocity and conflict as a key to understanding the dynamics of marriage.

SCHULZ, DAVID A., *The Changing Family: Its Function and Future* 2nd ed. (Englewood Cliffs, N.J.: Prentice-Hall, Inc., 1976). Emphasizes how the family has changed and, with the aid of a cross-cultural perspective, how it might change further.

SKOLNICK, ARLENE S. and JEROME H., *Family in Transition: Rethinking Marriage, Sexuality, Child Rearing, and Family Organization* (Boston: Little, Brown, 1971). A stimulating book of readings, challenging conventional views, both popular and professional, about marriage and the family.

TURNER, RALPH H., *Family Interaction* (New York: Wiley, 1970). Stresses the internal processes of individual families.

chapter 15
Religion and Education

Religion

BERGER, PETER L., *The Sacred Canopy: Elements of a Sociological Theory of Religion* (Garden City, N.Y.: Doubleday, 1967). Religion as man's attempt to locate his life in an ultimately meaningful order.

BIRNBAUM, NORMAN, and LENZER, GERTRUD, eds., *Sociology and Religion; A Book of Readings* (Englewood Cliffs, N.J.: Prentice-Hall, Inc., 1969). Stresses the role of religion in human history.

DEMERATH, N. J., III, and HAMMOND, PHILLIP E., *Religion in Social Context: Tradition and Transition* (New York: Random House, 1969). A short text focusing critically on pivotal literature and ideas in the sociology of religion.

GLOCK, CHARLES, and STARK, RODNEY, *Religion and Society in Tension* (Chicago: Rand McNally, 1965). The dilemmas of organized religion in modern society.

HERBERG, WILL, *Protestant-Catholic-Jew,* rev. ed. (New York: Doubleday, 1960). A fascinating analysis of the status, history, and interrelationships of the three major religious groupings in America.

O'DEA, THOMAS F., *The Sociology of Religion* (Englewood Cliffs, N.J.: Prentice-Hall, Inc., 1966). A small book using empirical generalizations to present theory.

ROBERTSON, ROLAND, ed., *Sociology of Religion* (Baltimore: Penguin, 1969). Readings center on religion as a provider—and historically the major provider—of meaning in human societies.

SMART, NINIAN, *The Religious Experience of Mankind* (New York: Scribner's, 1969). The major world religions, the nature of religion, and contemporary manifestations.

WILLIAMS, ROBIN M., JR., *American Society: A Sociological Interpretation,* 3rd ed. (New York: Alfred A. Knopf, 1970). Section 9, "Religion in America."

Education

CARNOY, MARTIN and LEVIN, HENRY, *The Limits of School Reform* (New York: David McKay, 1976). Assesses what has happened to the school reform efforts of the 1960s and early 1970s.

COOMBS, PHILIP H., *The World Educational Crisis: A Systems Analysis* (New York: Oxford University Press, 1968). The crisis is seen as the failure of educational systems to meet the needs of a rapidly developing and changing world.

HANSON, JOHN W., and BREMBECK, COLE S., eds., *Education and the Development of Nations* (New York: Holt, Rinehart & Winston, 1966). Deals with the capacity of education to assist in the development of nations and to bring about desirable social change.

JENCKS, CHRISTOPHER *et al., Inequality: A Reassessment of the Effect of Family and Schooling in America* (New York, Basic Books, 1972). A strong attack on the notion that more and better education will solve America's social problems.

NEILL, A. S., *Summerhill: A Radical Approach to Child Rearing* (New York: Hart, 1960). The stimulating and controversial account of a free private school in England. See also *Summerhill: For and Against* (New York: Hart, 1970). Articles expressing, usually in lively prose, widely varying reactions to the school and its philosophy.

POSTMAN, NEIL, and WEINGARTNER, CHARLES, *Teaching as a Subversive Activity* (New York: Dell, 1970). A hard-hitting book arguing for worthwhile goals, effective methods, and relevant content.

SEXTON, PATRICIA CAYO, *The American School: A Sociological Analysis* (Englewood Cliffs, N.J.: Prentice-Hall, Inc., 1967). Stresses the importance of power and the economic system, values and ideology, and urbanization; and the inefficiency and obsolescence of the school system in this context.

SILBERMAN, CHARLES E., *Crisis in the Classroom: The Remaking of American Education* (New York: Random House, 1970). Analyzes the successes and failures of American education, and suggests innovations, including "free schools" along the British model.

WILLIAMS, ROBIN M., JR., *American Society: A Sociological Interpretation,* 3rd ed. (New York: Alfred A. Knopf, 1970). Section 8, "American Education."

chapter 16

Politics and the Economy

Politics

BARGHOORN, FREDERICK C., *Politics in the USSR* (Boston: Little, Brown and Company, 1966). A functional analysis of Soviet politics, including political culture and socialization, the form and content of interest group activity, and the policy-making process.

BELL, DANIEL, ed., *The Radical Right* (New York: Doubleday & Company, Inc., 1964). Ultraconservative movements.

BRINTON, CRANE, *The Anatomy of Revolution* (New York: Random House, Inc., 1959). A preliminary analysis based on four major revolutions.

BROGAN, D. W., *Politics in America* (New York: Doubleday & Company, Inc., 1960). An excellent discussion by a British observer.

DAHL, ROBERT A., *Who Governs?* (New Haven, Conn.: Yale University Press, 1961). Stresses the pluralistic nature of the power structure.

DEUTSCH, KARL W., *The Analysis of International Relations* (Englewood Cliffs, N.J.: Prentice-Hall, Inc., 1968). Stresses the interdependence of peoples, all of whom are minorities in a world of "foreigners."

EBENSTEIN, WILLIAM, *Today's Isms: Communism, Fascism, Capitalism, Socialism* (Englewood Cliffs, N.J.: Prentice-Hall, Inc., 1970). Sees totalitarianism and democracy as two ways of life dividing the modern world.

HOFFER, ERIC, *The True Believer* (New York: The New American Library, Inc., 1958). On the fanatics who lead and join mass movements.

LIPSET, SEYMOUR MARTIN, *Political Man: The Social Bases of Politics* (New York: Doubleday & Company, Inc., 1960). A comparison of the workings of democracy in various countries based on studies of attitudes and participation.

MACIVER, R. M., *The Web of Government* (rev. ed) (New York: The Macmillan Company, 1965). An authoritative, comprehensive, and seemingly timeless analysis.

MEADOWS, DONELLA H., MEADOWS, DENNIS L., RANDERS, JORGEN, and BERHENS, WILLIAM F., III, *The Limits to Growth: A Report for the Club of Rome's Project on the Predicament of Mankind* (New York: Universe Books, 1972). Presents a systems approach to the problems of exponential growth in a finite earth, and suggests approaches to global equilibrium.

MEANS, RICHARD L., *The Ethical Imperative: The Crisis in American Values* (Garden City, N.Y.: Doubleday, 1970). An attempt to overcome the dualism in American thought between individual and collective values.

The Economy

BELSHAW, CYRIL S., *Traditional Exchange and Modern Markets* (Englewood Cliffs, N.J.: Prentice-Hall, Inc., 1965). Sees the institutions of exchange and the market as keys to understanding economic development.

BLAUNER, ROBERT, *Alienation and Freedom: The Factory Worker and His Industry* (Chicago: University of Chicago Press, 1964). This book is about factory workers in different kinds of industrial settings, the objective features and the subjective meanings of their work.

BURKE, JOHN G., ed., *The New Technology and Human Values* (Belmont, Calif.: Wadsworth Publishing Co., Inc., 1966). See especially the readings on education and automation.

FAUNCE, WILLIAM A., *Problems of an Industrial Society* (New York: McGraw-Hill Book Company, 1968). "The basic theme of this book is that the causes of alienation, ambivalence, and ambiguity in social goals and behavior are inherent in the structure of industrial society."

GALBRAITH, JOHN KENNETH, *The New Industrial State* (Boston: Houghton Mifflin Company, 1967). Current trends in the continuing industrial revolution.

HEILBRONER, ROBERT, *The Economic Problem,* 3rd ed., (Englewood Cliffs, N.J.: Prentice-Hall, Inc., 1972). Especially chaps. 1, 2, 32, 34, 35, and 36. Extremely well written.

————, *The Worldly Philosophers* (rev. ed.) (New York: Simon and Schuster, Inc., 1961). Ideas of leading economists. Good historical perspective, well written.

MAYO, ELTON, *The Human Problems of an Industrial Civilization* (New York: The Viking Press, 1960). New edition, with an introduction relating the 1933 report to contemporary society. The famous Hawthorne Experiment is detailed here.

SMELSER, NEIL J., *The Sociology of Economic Life,* (Englewood Cliffs, N.J.: Prentice-Hall, Inc., 1976). Another volume in the Foundations of Modern Sociology series, this book concerns the relations between the economic and social aspects of life—how they overlap and how they influence one another.

TOFFLER, ALVIN, ed., *The Futurists* (New York: Random House, 1972). See especially Kenneth Boulding, "The Economics of the Coming Spaceship Earth," comparing our obsolete "cowboy" economy with the "spaceman" economy we must develop.

WATERS, MAURICE, *The United Nations: International Organization and Administration* (New York: Macmillan, 1967). The role of the United Nations in a world of sovereign nation-states.

chapter 17
Collective Behavior and Social Movements

BERK, RICHARD, *Collective Behavior* (Dubuque, Iowa: Wm. C. Brown, 1974). Excellent small overview of the field.

BOSKIN, JOSEPH, *Urban Racial Violence in the Twentieth Century* (Beverly Hills: Glencoe Press, 1969). Deals with conflict as expressed in two forms of violence: the urban racial riot and the racial protest riot.

CAMERON, WILLIAM BRUCE, *Modern Social Movements: A Sociological Outline* (New York: Random House, 1966). General principles with interesting examples, and a good bibliography.

EPSTEIN, CYNTHIS FUCHS, and GOODE, WILLIAM J., eds., *The Other Half: Roads to Women's Equality* (Englewood Cliffs, N.J.: Prentice-Hall, Inc., 1971). Brings together analyses of current issues, sociological studies of women's position in society, and historical perspectives on the present movement.

EVANS, ROBERT R., ed., *Readings in Collective Behavior* (Chicago: Rand McNally, 1969). Theoretical, descriptive, and anlaytical studies of collective behavior (not including social movements).

GUSFIELD, JOSEPH R., ed., *Protest, Reform, and Revolt: A Reader in Social Movements* (New York: John Wiley, 1970). Perspectives for understanding human activity and conflict in relation to social change.

HOROWITZ, IRVING LOUIS, ed., *The Troubled Conscience: American Social Issues* (Santa Barbara: Center for the Study of Democratic Institutions, 1971). Essays about four major social issues: the relationships of revolutionaries to reformists, the young to the old, blacks to whites, and people to their environment.

KLAPP, ORRIN E., *Collective Search for Identity* (New York: Holt, Rinehart & Winston, 1969). Deals with identity-seeking movements of mass society: fashions, fads, poses, ritual, cultic movements, recreation, heroes and celebrities, and crusades.

MITCHELL, J. PAUL, ed. *Race Riots in Black and White* (Englewood Cliffs, N.J.: Prentice-Hall, Inc., 1970). The historical context.

SAFILIOS-ROTHSCHILD, CONSTANTINA, ed., *Toward a Sociology of Women* (Lexington, Mass.: Xerox College Publishing, 1972).

THOMPSON, MARY LOU, ed., *Voices of the New Feminism* (Boston: Beacon, 1970). An excellent collection of essays on Women's Liberation; background, ideology, goals.

TURNER, RALPH H., and KILLIAN, LEWIS M., *Collective Behavior*, 2nd ed. (Englewood Cliffs, N.J.: Prentice-Hall, Inc., 1972). An excellent text by two authorities in the field.

WEAVER, GARY R. and JAMES H., eds., *The University and Revolution* (Englewood Cliffs, N.J.: Prentice-Hall, Inc., 1969). "The approaches and backgrounds of contributions to this anthology are as diverse and spontaneous as is the student movement itself."

chapter 18

Social and Cultural Change

APPLEBAUM, RICHARD B., *Theories of Social change* (Chicago: Markham, 1970). A somewhat technical review.

ARON, RAYMOND, *The Industrial Society: Three Essays on Ideology and Development* (New York: Simon and Schuster, 1967). By a leading French sociologist.

BAUER, RAYMOND A., ed., *Social Indicators* (Cambridge: M.I.T. Press, 1966). Discussions of social systems accounting, social indicators, and social planning.

BENNIS, WARREN G., BENNE, KENNETH D., and CHIN, ROBERT, eds., *The Planning of Change*, 2nd ed. (New York: Holt, Rinehart, & Winston, 1969). Seeks to "contribute to the unfinished task of merging and reconciling the arts of social practice and the sciences of human behavior."

BREED, WARREN, *The Self-Guiding Society* (New York: The Free Press, 1971). A shorter version of Amitai Etzioni, *The Active Society* (New York: The Free Press, 1968). The central thesis is that "the post-modern society has the option to change its course."

BUCKLEY, WALTER, *Sociology and Modern Systems Theory* (Englewood Cliffs, N.J.: Prentice-Hall, Inc., 1967). Depicts the socio-cultural order as a complex adaptive system.

EISENSTADT, S. N., *Modernization: Protest and Change* (Englewood Cliffs, N.J.: Prentice-Hall, Inc., 1966). Analyzes the major characteristics and problems of modern and modernizing societies, especially the ability of the institutional framework to absorb the social changes inherent in the modernization process.

FOSTER, GEORGE, *Traditional Cultures and the Impact of Technological Change* (New York: Harper & Row, 1962). An interesting account of attempts to introduce change.

GROSS, BERTRAM, ed., *Social Intelligence for America's Future: Explorations in Societal Problems* (Boston: Allyn and Bacon, 1969). "Suggests an agenda for improving the quality of our social information and for creating social agencies more responsive to the needs of a developing American society."

HAVELOCK, RONALD G., et al., *Planning for Innovation Through Dissemination and Utilization of Knowledge* (Ann Arbor: Institute for Social Research, The University of Michigan, 1971). A voluminous report that "provides a framework for understanding the processes of innovation, dissemination, and knowledge utilization, and reviews the relevant literature in education and other fields of practice within this framework."

HOROWITZ, IRVING LOUIS, *Three Worlds of Development: The Theory and Practice of International Stratification* (New York: Oxford University Press, 1966). A qualitative study of the interaction of the three main sources of economic, political, and social power.

LERNER, DANIEL, *The Passing of Traditional Society: Modernizing the Middle East* (New York: Macmillan, 1958). Fascinating account of changes in a Turkish village, and in other societies.

MOORE, WILBERT E., *Order and Change: Essays in Comparative Sociology* (New York: John Wiley, 1967). By an expert on the subject of social change.

MOORE, WILBERT E., *Social Change*, 2nd ed. (Englewood Cliffs, N.J.: Prentice-Hall, Inc., 1975). Especially chap. 5, "Modernization."

MYRDAL, GUNNAR, *The Challenge of World Poverty: A World Anti-Poverty Program in Outline* (New York: Pantheon, 1970). Stresses the urgency of institutional reform.

SCHNEIDER, KENNETH R., *Destiny of Change: How Relevant is Man in the Age of Development?* (New York: Holt, Rinehart & Winston, 1968). A readable, thought-provoking book about modern society and the individual's place within it.

SILVERT, KALMAN H., *Man's Power: A Biased Guide to Political Thought and Action* (New York:

Viking, 1970). Emphasizes the role of human decisions in social change.

TOFFLER, ALVIN, *Future Shock* (New York: Random House, 1970). This bestseller is based on many studies and predictions, including sociological ones.

———, ed., *The Futurists* (New York: Random House, 1972). "The purpose of this collection is to make accessible a few of the works of the best-known and . . . most influential futurists."

U.S. DEPARTMENT OF HEALTH, EDUCATION, AND WELFARE, *Toward a Social Report,* with an introductory commentary by Wilbur J. Cohen (Ann Arbor: The University of Michigan Press, 1970). Deals with indicators of social change useful in periodic reporting on the state of the nation and progress toward social goals.

WIENER, NORBERT, *The Human Use of Human Beings: Cybernetics and Society* (New York: Avon, 1967). The relation between computer technology and the social sciences.

Glossary

Absolute poverty Extreme inadequacy of food, clothing and shelter. (*p. 185*)

Accommodation The reduction of conflict and the restoration of peaceful interaction. (*p. 141*)

Achieved status A status attained by one's own efforts or a stroke of good fortune. (*p. 147*)

Alienation A feeling that one is a stranger to one's environment, to others, and even to oneself. (*p. 112*)

Anomie A condition of normlessness; results when there is a scarcity of institutionalized means to satisfy people's legitimate needs. (*p. 112*)

Anthropology The study of biological and behavioral similarities and differences among the various peoples of the world. (*p. 5*)

Ascribed status A status into which a person is born or one which is automatically assigned with the passage of time. (*p. 147*)

Assimilation The social process whereby individuals and groups come to share the same sentiments, values, and goals. (*p. 141*)

Authority Power that is recognized and accepted by those subject to it as validly held by those who exercise it. (*p. 381*)

Behaviorism The theory that personality is entirely learned and that behavior is the result of conditioning. (*p. 79*)

Beliefs Answers to the mysteries of human existence, based on faith and emotion rather than reason and science. (*p. 43*)

Biological determinism The theory that human nature is simply an expression or unfolding of inborn drives or tendencies. (*p. 78*)

Birth rate The number of live births per 1,000 population. (*p. 270*)

Bureaucracy A hierarchical social structure for administering large scale organizations rationally, efficiently, and impersonally. (*p. 167*)

Case study An in-depth examination of a person, group, or society. (*p. 26*)

Caste system A system of stratification into hereditary, endogamous, and permanent strata called castes. (*p. 177*)

Centralization Concentration of institutions and activities in a given area. (*p. 304*)

Ceremony A formal, dignified procedure that impresses participants and observers with the importance of an occasion. (*p. 51*)

Church A large established religious organization that compromises with political and economic realities. (*p. 354*)

City (demographic definition) A relatively dense concentration of people settled in a relatively small geographic area. (*p. 290*)

City (social definition) A city as demographically defined, plus a distinctive way of life. (*p. 290*)

Civil disobedience The deliberate breaking of some law or ordinance on moral grounds. (*p. 424*)

Collective behavior Large group activity that arises and develops outside of established social definitions to meet undefined and unstructured situations. (*p. 408*)

Commitment The willingness of members to remain with and contribute to a group. (*p. 170*)

Competition The striving of two or more social actors for the same limited goal. (*p. 139*)

Complex A system of interrelated culture traits that functions together as a unit (*p. 47*)

Concentration The drawing together of population into given areas of varying degrees of density. (*p. 304*)

Concept A word or phrase that represents a class of phenomena. (*p. 19*)

Conflict Interaction in which one social actor tries to deprive, control, injure, or eliminate another against the other's will. (*p. 139*)

Conjugal relationships Those of married couples. (*p. 323*)

Consaguineal relationships Those of "blood kin." (*p. 323*)

Consensus Agreement within a social group on norms, values, and goals. (*p. 169*)

Contract The institution that allows for the transfer of property; in the specific sense, a contract is an agreement or exchange of promises enforceable by the society. (*p. 392*)

Control Power over the behavior of group members employed through positive and negative sanctions or through coercion. (*p. 169*)

Conventional signs or symbols Those signs that derive meaning from usage and mutual agreement and are not naturally linked to the things they stand for (e.g. words and gestures). (*p. 36*)

Cooperation The combined effort of two or more social actors to reach a shared goal. (*p. 138*)

Coordination The systematic meshing of roles by leaders so that group goals may be achieved. (*p. 169*)

Crimes Deviant acts prohibited by law and punishable by law enforcement agencies. (*p. 107*)

Crowd A temporary grouping of a large number of people who are conscious of one another's physical nearness; it may be primarily active or expressive. (*p. 409*)

Cultural determinism The theory that human nature and personality depend on the society into which a baby happens to be born and individuals have no control over its culture. (*p. 79*)

Cultural integration The sharing of common norms, understandings, social structures, and material traits; a matter of scope and degree of sharing. (*p. 48*)

Cultural relativity An attitude of respect for cultural differences. (*p. 71*)

Culture The learned portion of human behavior. (*p. 34*)

A culture The distinctive way of life of a society. (*p. 34*)

Culture shock The difficulty felt in adapting to the ways of a strange society or subcultural group. (*p. 70*)

Data (singular *datum*) Empirically verified descriptions of phenomena; facts or findings. (*p. 18*)

Decentralization The spread of activities and dwelling places farther and farther out from the center of a city. (*p. 304*)

Demographic transition The shift from high birth and death rates through a period of high population growth to a new balance of low birth and death rates. (*p. 272*)

Demography The science concerned with human populations. (*p. 268*)

Dependency ratio The number of people under 15 and over 65 as compared to those considered productive, ages 15–64. (*p. 268*)

Deviance Behavior contrary to the norms of a social group, exceeding its limits of tolerance for nonconformist behavior and subject to punishment if discovered. (*p. 106*)

Differential association Exposure to deviants as an essential part of learning some kinds of deviant behavior. (*p. 115*)

Diffusion The process by which culture traits and patterns spread from one society or group to another. (*p. 67; 436*)

Discrimination Unfavorable behavior based on prejudice against an ascribed status group. (*p. 209*)

Ecology The study of all forms of life and their natural settings, and of their interdependence. (*p. 278*)

Economics The study of people's activities as they use their environment to produce goods and services, and as they distribute and consume them. (*p. 5*)

The economy The institution that allocates time, energy and resources to produce and distribute goods and services the members of a society need and want. (*p. 391*)

Ecosystem The sum total of living and non-living elements that support a chain of life within a given area. (*p. 279*)

Education Informal or deliberate transmission of selected knowledge, skills, and values to prepare individuals for effective membership in a society. (*p. 364*)

Empiricism The systematic collection and analysis of social facts. (*p. 8*)

Endogamy Marriage within a certain group. (*p. 322*)

Estate system A system of stratification in which strata are defined by law and are relatively rigid and permanent, with some mobility. (*p. 177*)

Ethnic groups All social groups based on the categories of race, religion, or nationality, forming subsocieties with subcultures. (*p. 216*)

Ethnocentrism The tendency to judge other groups and cultures by the norms of one's own and to regard them as inherently inferior. (*p. 68*)

Evaluation research Applied research used to measure the results of specific social programs. (*p. 28*)

Exchange The social process through which each party to a contract acquires something he or she wants but cannot easily get otherwise. (*p. 394*)

Exogamy Marriage outside of a certain group. (*p. 322*)

Experiment Intervention in, or creation of, a situation in order to control or manipulate a variable and observe or measure the result. (*p. 26*)

Extended family One stressing kinship ties. (*p. 324*)

Factors of production The four main resources of a society—land, labor, capital, and decision-making (including entrepreneurship and management). (*p. 391*)

Fads Fashions that come and go very quickly. (*p. 42*)

Family A married man and woman and their children, if any, who function semi-independently within the larger kin network. (*p. 322*)

Fashions Shortlived folkways with status value that motivates wide-spread conformity. (*p. 41*)

Fertility rate The number of births per 1,000 women of reproductive age (usually 15–45). (*p. 270*)

Festivals Times of joyous feasting and celebration. (*p. 52*)

Folk society A small traditional society; an ideal type contrasted to a modern society. (*p. 151*)

Folkways Norms of proper behavior that govern most of our daily routine and ordinary contacts with others and are informally enforced. (*p. 39*)

Formal control —Institutionalized means for preventing or punishing deviant behavior; involves laws, police, courts, and corrections. (*p. 125*)

Formal organization A clearly outlined social structure deliberately created for a specific purpose and not dependent on specific group members; characteristic mainly of large groups. (*p. 165*)

Geographic determinism The fallacious idea that habitat, or geographic setting, determines culture. (*p. 66*)

Government The process of keeping order and enforcing norms; the institution that carries out that process; or the specific set of officials who govern at any one time. (*p. 385*)

Group cohesion The unity that enables groups to endure as identifiable units. (*p. 169*)

History The study of the human past. (*p. 6*)

Human ecology The study of the distribution of various functions, groups of people, and kinds of building within a given area, and of the processes involved in that distribution. (*p. 303*)

Human society A complex system of relationships among individuals and groups, based on culture. (*p. 137*)

Humanism The approach stressing empathy, role-taking and understanding the meaning, value, and purpose of human behavior. (*p. 17*)

Humanistic psychology The school of thought that stresses subjective experience and the search for meaning and value in existence. (*p. 82*)

Hypothesis A statement of a probable relationship between two or more variables. (*p. 24*)

Identity A sense of personal sameness continuing through time, a concept central to neo-Freudian theory. (*p. 81*)

Incest avoidance (Incest Taboo) The prohibiting of sexual relationships between parents and children and brothers and sisters. (*p. 322*)

Informal control Social control through socialization and peer group pressure. (*p. 123*)

Informal organization Non-institutionalized social structure that emerges in the course of social interaction in a small group. (*p. 165*)

Institutional discrimination Impersonal discriminatory policies and practices woven into the social structure through such institutions as the economy, government, and education. (*p. 214*)

Institutions Clusters of norms organized and established for the pursuit of some need or activity of a social group. (*p. 46*)

Intergroup prejudice An attitude of hostility or rejection based on stereotypes. (*p. 209*)

Invasion The penetration of a segregated area by an institutional function or population group different from the one already there. (*p. 305*)

Kinship The tie between progenitors and descendents (parents and children, etc.) and the tie of common descent (brothers, sisters, cousins, etc.). (*p. 322*)

Knowledge Lore or science that involves intellectual awareness and technical control of matter, time, space, and events as well as unconscious assumptions underlying behavior. (*p. 43*)

Labeling The process of reinforcing deviant behavior by attaching a label to the person who commits it. (*p. 115*)

Language A system of symbols that are voluntarily produced in speech and possibly in writing and have specific and arbitrary meanings in a given society. (*p. 36*)

Large group A group consisting of more than twenty people; it may be as large as a nation-state; generally has smaller sub-groups. (*p. 160*)

Laws Deliberately formulated and clearly stated norms that are enforced by authorities (p. 42; 385); also propositions that refer to unvarying associations universally agreed upon within a science. (*p. 20*)

Legitimacy The degree to which a form of government is considered right and proper and its officials rightfully in authority. (*p. 383*)

Macrosociology The study of large-scale social phenomena such as total societies or worldwide trends. (*p. 16*)

Market An institution that coordinates oc-cupation, property, and contract in such a way that exchange can be readily carried on. (*p. 395*)

Marriage A society's established procedure for founding a family. (*p.322*)

Mass A large number of people who react to a common stimulus but seek individual goals and make individual choices and decisions, whether or not they are in physical proximity. (*p. 411*)

Material culture Man-made things (artifacts) and man-made alterations in the environment. (*p. 44*)

Metropolitan area A social and economic community embracing a number of cities and urban fringe areas. (*p. 295*)

Microsociology The study of small-scale social phenomena such as social roles and relationships among individuals. (*p. 17*)

Minority A category of people who are subordinate in power to the majority, though they may outnumber the latter. (*p. 209*)

Model An analogy that serves as the skeleton of a theory. (*p. 21*)

Modern society A large urbanized society based on advanced technology and a highly developed store of knowledge; an ideal type contrasted to a folk society. (*p. 153*)

Modernization The transition from traditional folk society to urban industrial society. (*p. 438*)

Monogamy Marriage involving one person married to only one mate. (*p. 323*)

Mores Norms of obligatory behavior considered vital to the welfare of the group, including taboos on prohibited behavior; heavily charged with emotional meaning. (*p. 40*)

Mysticism Emphasis on purely personal religious experience rather than collective formal organization. (*p. 356*)

Myth The embodiment of a society's values, hopes and fears in stories and legends; in conceptions of the origins and place of human beings in the universe and of the events of each life and society; and the underlying taken-for-granted assumptions central to a culture. (*p. 51*)

Nation-State The comprehensive political organization of a society, including territorial bounds, sovereignty, and a monopoly of the use of force within its borders. (*p. 383*)

Natural signs Those signs that derive their meaning from concrete situations, e.g. the red glow of burning wood. (*p. 36*)

Nonparticipant observation Observation of a situation without personal involvement in it. (*p. 26*)

Norms Rules or patterns for behavior. (*p. 38*)

Nuclear family One stressing conjugal ties. (*p. 323*)

Occupation The institution that defines the rights and obligations of various economic roles. (*p. 394*)

Open-class system A system of stratification in which, although one's initial status is that of one's parents, there is opportunity to rise or fall according to merit. (*p. 177*)

Participant observation The method by which the researcher both participates in and observes a situation. (*p. 26*)

Pattern A specific and enduring system of trait complexes. (*p. 47*)

Personality The organized ways of behaving and feeling that characterize given individuals. (*p. 78*)

Pluralism The pattern of intergroup relations in which various ethnic groups are considered as different but equal, or as different and ranked in a loose hierarchy in which ethnic background is one criterion of social class status. (*p. 216*)

Political Science The study of political life and government and of the distribution of power in a society. (*p. 5*)

Politics The process by which any organized group finds its leaders and decides its policies; specifically, the struggle for power to name the personnel and decide the policies of the government. (*p. 387*)

Polyandry One woman married to several men at one time. (*p. 323*)

Polygamy Marriage of a person to more than one spouse. (*p. 323*)

Polygyny One man married to several women at one time. (*p. 323*)

Positivism The approach stressing use of objective information, experiments, and measurable data. (*p. 17*)

Power The capacity to influence the behavior of other people or groups in an intended direction; control over the decisions that affect the way people live and over the allocation of scarce and valuable resources. (*p. 186; 380*)

Prejudice A negative prejudgment of a person or group on the basis of ascribed status. (*p. 209*)

Primary relationships Personal, spontaneous, sentimental, and inclusive social relationships characterized by expressive interaction. (*p. 162*)

Property The institution by which a society defines rights and obligations with respect to things that are scarce, valuable, and transferable. (*p. 392*)

Proposition A statement of a relationship between two or more facts or concepts. (*p. 19*)

Psychoanalytic theory The Freudian theory that culture is merely a reflection of individual psychology and is based on the effort to handle the problems of sex and aggression, especially in childhood. (*p. 81*)

Psychology The study of individual behavior (*p. 6*)

Public A vaguely defined number of people who for a time confront an issue, disagree on how to resolve it, and discuss it. (*p. 411*)

Public opinion A collective opinion or decision on the issue around which a public has formed. (*p. 412*)

Racial determinism The fallacious idea that each group inherits its culture as part of its biological heritage from the race to which it belongs. (*p. 65*)

Racism The doctrine that behavior is based on stable traits which characterize separate racial groups as superior and inferior. (*p. 211*)

Rate of natural increase The difference between the number of births and the number of deaths per 1,000 population (*p. 270*)

Recidivism Return to criminal acts after arrest and imprisonment. (*p. 125*)

Relative poverty Comparative inadequacy of resources when measured against the advantages of others. (*p. 185*)

Religion The social institution that deals with sacred things, which lie beyond human knowledge and control. (*p. 348*)

Riot An outwardly hostile, illegitimate, and aggressive action by an acting crowd. (*p. 413*)

Ritual A formal, rhythmic series of symbolic acts repeated on ceremonial occasions. (*p. 51*)

Role A bundle of norms that defines the rights, obligations, and privileges of a person who occupies a particular status. (*p. 145*)

Role performance The way a specific person plays the role corresponding to a status. (*p. 148*)

Routinization The regular movement of people and goods in time and space. (*p. 304*)

Sample survey A mass interview of a sample drawn from a certain population, measuring large numbers of people on a few characteristics. (*p. 25*)

Sanctions Rewards for observing the norms and punishments for violating them. (*p. 38*)

Secondary relationships Impersonal, superficial, transitory and segmental relationships characterized by instrumental interaction. (*p. 163*)

Sect A dissident group that tries to preserve the purity of a faith and avoid compromise with "worldly realities." (*p. 354*)

Secularization The trend toward removal of sectors of society and culture from domination by religious institutions and symbols; a shift from sacred to worldly values. (*p. 357; 439*)

Segregation Isolation, voluntarily or involuntarily, of one group from another; a form of discrimination. (*p. 210; 305*)

Self the core of personality, accounting for its unity and structure. (*p. 82*)

Self-conception Our image of ourselves, including a sense of identity, self-esteem, and an ideal self. (*p. 88*)

Serial monogamy The formation of a new conjugal relationship following divorce. (*p. 343*)

Sex ratio The number of males compared to the number of females in a given group or category. (*p. 268*)

Situation drift Nondeliberate commission of deviant acts attributable to circumstances. (*p. 114*)

Small group From two to twenty people who repeatedly interact face to face. (*p. 158*)

Social change Significant alterations in social structure, in cultural definitions, and in the material products of sociocultural action. (*p. 430*)

Social contagion The relatively rapid, unwitting, and nonrational dissemination of a mood, impulse, or form of conduct. (*p. 409*)

Social group Two or more people who interact, feel a sense of identity that sets them off from others, and have social relationships consisting of interrelated and reciprocal statuses. (*p. 143*)

Social indicator A statistic that helps observers directly measure the welfare of a society and make judgements about conditions. (*p. 450*)

Social interaction The reciprocal influencing of behavior through symbolic communication between people (*p. 137*)

Social mobility The movement of persons up or down the ranking order of a system of social stratification. (*p. 198*)

Social movements Comparatively stable, organized, and lasting collective actions directed toward the achievement or obstruction of change in some aspect of the sociocultural order. (*p. 408; 417*)

Social problem A condition that has negative effects on a significant portion of a population and is regarded as demanding a solution. (*p. 447*)

Social relationships Patterns of more or less recurrent, regular and expected interaction between two or more social actors, which may be persons or groups. (*p. 142*)

Social stratification An institutionalized system of social inequality that ranks individuals and groups according to their share of scarce and desirable resources such as wealth, prestige, and power. (*p. 174*)

Social stratum A category of people with similar amounts of wealth, prestige, and power, and similar life chances and ways of life. (*p. 175*)

Social structure The web of organized relationships among individuals and groups that defines their mutual rights and responsibilities; the network of interrelated statuses in a group; its persisting pattern of relationships. (*p. 46; 137*)

Socialization The process of becoming a functioning member of the human race and part of a social group. (*p. 78*)

Society An association of living creatures functioning in organized relationships of mutual dependence. (*p. 136*)

A society A group that is organized into a more or less permanent division of labor, lives in a certain territory, and shares common goals. (*p. 48; 136*)

Sociology The systematic study of human relationships. (*p. 4; 6*)

Specialization The clustering of particular types of institutions and activities in different districts. (*p. 304*)

Stereotypes Faulty and inflexible generalizations about a group or category of people. (*p. 209*)

Strategy The general program for reaching the goals of a movement. (*p. 423*)

Stratification The system that ranks individuals and groups in various levels according to prestige, power, and privilege. (*p. 46*)

Status A position in a social structure. (*p. 143*)

Subculture The way of life of a subsociety. (*p. 48*)

Subsociety A distinctive cultural group

within a society. (*p. 48*)

Suburbanization The movement of people out of central cities into surrounding urban areas. (*p. 296*)

Succession The replacement of a group or institution through invasion. (*p. 305*)

Symbolic interactionism The theory of the emergence of the self as the process by which a newborn baby becomes a human being. (*p. 82*)

Tactics The specific techniques and activities used to gain new members for a movement and achieve its goals. (*p. 423*)

Technicways The skills or habits associated with material utilitarian objects. (*p. 41*)

Technology The body of skills and knowledge, and tools and machines, involved in producing goods and services. (*p. 46*)

Theory A set of systematically related propositions aimed at explaining phenomena. (*p. 20*)

Trait The smallest unit of culture—one item of behavior, one idea, or one object. (*p. 47*)

Typology A way of grouping or classifying data and ideas. (*p. 21*)

Urban regions Areas of a million or more people including a continuous zone of metropolitan areas and the counties between them, with the entire population near at least one city. (*p. 297*)

Urbanism The distinct way of life that characterizes cities. (*p. 298*)

Urbanization (demographic definition) The proportion of a total population concentrated in urban areas, or a rise in this proportion. (*p. 291*)

Urbanization (social definition) A change in the way of life of people attributable to demographic urbanization. (*p. 291*)

Values The underlying standards or principles by which social and personal goals are chosen and the criteria by which means and ends are judged. (*p. 43*)

Variable An action or attribute that can be measured or categorized. (*p. 24*)

Voluntary associations Groups organized by individuals who share some common interest or activity. (*p. 166*)

Zero population growth (ZPG) A balance of births and deaths that allows only for population replacement. (*p. 272*)

Index